About the Author

Dušan Petkovic is a professor in the Department of Computer Science at the Polytechnic in Rosenheim, Germany. He is the author of *SQL Server 7: A Beginner's Guide* and *SQL Server 2000: A Beginner's Guide*, and is a frequent contributor to *SQL Server Magazine*.

Microsoft SQL Server™ 2005: A Beginner's Guide

Dušan Petkovic

McGraw-Hill/Osborne

New York   Chicago   San Francisco
Lisbon   London   Madrid   Mexico City   Milan
New Delhi   San Juan   Seoul   Singapore   Sydney   Toronto

The McGraw·Hill Companies

McGraw-Hill/Osborne
2100 Powell Street, 10th Floor
Emeryville, California 94608
U.S.A.

To arrange bulk purchase discounts for sales promotions, premiums, or fund-raisers, please contact **McGraw-Hill**/Osborne at the above address.

Microsoft SQL Server™ 2005: A Beginner's Guide

34567890 FGR FGR 019876

ISBN 0-07-226093-9

Acquisitions Editor	Wendy Rinaldi
Project Editor	Jody L. McKenzie
Acquisitions Coordinator	Alexander McDonald
Technical Editor	Todd Meister
Copy Editor	Judy Wilson
Proofreader	Susie Elkind
Indexer	Jack Lewis
Composition	International Typesetting and Composition
Illustration	International Typesetting and Composition
Cover Series Design	Pattie Lee

This book was composed with Adobe® InDesign®.

Contents

Part III   SQL Server: System Administration

Acknowledgments

I would like to thank my wife Sibille for her support in the last 20 years of working with database systems. Her patience with me during this time allowed me to concentrate on my job and on writing books.

I would also like to thank Wendy Rinaldi and Alex McDonald, as well as project editor Jody McKenzie, for their extraordinary support during the work on this book.

Introduction

Relational database systems (RDBMS) are the most important database systems used in the software industry today. One of the most outstanding systems is MS SQL Server. There are a couple of reasons why SQL Server is the best choice for a broad spectrum of end-users and database programmers building business applications. SQL Server is certainly the best database system for Windows operating systems, because it is tightly integrated with them. The number of installed Windows systems is increasing rapidly, and due to the best integration (and low pricing) SQL Server is certainly a big database system!

Second, SQL Server is the easiest database system to use: in addition to the well-known user interface, Microsoft offers several different tools to help you create database objects, tune your database applications, and manage system administration's tasks.

Third, bundling at least four products in one—Relational Database Engine, Analysis Services, Reporting Services, and Integration Services—also brings the overall system to the winning position. A possibility to use one system for operational tasks as well as for business intelligence is what users want and need.

Goals of the Book

SQL Server 2005: A Beginner's Guide follows two existing books: *SQL Server 7: A Beginner's Guide* and *SQL Server 2000: A Beginner's Guide*.

Generally, all *new* SQL Server users who want to get a good understanding of this database system and to work successfully with it will find this book very helpful. A special group of users, which this book addresses, are MS Access users who want to use another (and more powerful) database system than Access, but also want to stay with the known operating system and Windows user interface. The book also addresses *all* users of the SQL Server system. For this reason it is divided into several parts: *end users* will find the first two parts of the book the most interesting for them, while the third part provides know-how for *database* and *system administrators*. The second part of the book is dedicated to *database application programmers*, while several chapters address the special task facing them: tuning database applications. The second to the last part of the book provides insight for users who want to use business intelligence components of the system.

NOTE

If you are the person who has to install the SQL Server system, please start reading from Part III, beginning with Chapter 16, because that part handles administering and installing the system.

For all these reasons, the book gives you the overall introduction to the complete SQL Server system. In contrast to SQL Server books online (BOL), which are very voluminous and hence often not easy to use, the book teaches you all topics of this database system and especially provides explanations for connections between different topics.

Working with the Sample Database

An introductory book like this requires a sample database that can be easily understood by each reader. For this reason, I used a very simple concept for the sample database: it has only four tables with several rows each. On the other hand, its logic is complex enough to demonstrate the hundreds of examples included in the text of the book. The sample database that you will use in this book represents a company with departments and employees. Each employee belongs to exactly one department, which itself has one or more employees. Jobs of employees center around projects: each employee works at the same time for one or more projects, and each project engages one or more employees.

The tables of the sample database are shown here:

The table **department**

dept_no	dept_name	location
d1	Research	Dallas
d2	Accounting	Seattle
d3	Marketing	Dallas

The table **employee**

emp_no	emp_fname	Emp_lname	dept_no
25348	Matthew	Smith	d3
10102	Ann	Jones	d3
18316	John	Barrimore	d1
29346	James	James	d2

9031	Elisa	Bertoni	d2
2581	Elke	Hansel	d2
28559	Sybill	Moser	d1

The table **project**

project_no	project_name	Budget
p1	Apollo	120000
p2	Gemini	95000
p3	Mercury	185600

The table **works_on**

emp_no	project_no	Job	enter_date
10102	p1	Analyst	1997.10.1
10102	p3	Manager	1999.1.1
25348	p2	Clerk	1998.2.15
18316	p2	NULL	1998.6.1
29346	p2	NULL	1997.12.15
2581	p3	Analyst	1998.10.15
9031	p1	Manager	1998.4.15
28559	p1	NULL	1998.8.1
28559	p2	Clerk	1999.2.1
9031	p3	Clerk	1997.11.15
29346	p1	Clerk	1998.1.4

You can download the sample database from McGraw-Hill/Osborne's web site (www.osborne.com) or my own home page (www.fh-rosenheim.de/~petkovic). Also, all of the examples that are in the book can be downloaded from my home page.

Organization of the Book

The book has 30 chapters and is divided into five different parts. The first part of the book (Chapters 1 and 2) describes the notion of database systems in general and SQL Server in particular; the second part (Chapters 3 through 15) is intended for end users and application programmers, while the third part (Chapters 16 through 24) describes all objectives of SQL Server system administration.

The fourth part of the book (Chapter 25 through 28) is dedicated to the Microsoft Analysis Services. MS Analysis Services allow users to analyze and query data in data warehouses and data marts. Finally, the last part of the book (Chapters 29 and 30) describes how solutions can be built using XML.

Chapter 1 discusses databases in general and SQL Server in particular. The notion of normal forms and the sample database are presented here. The chapter also introduces the syntax conventions that are used in the rest of the book.

Chapter 2 describes the component called SQL Server Management Studio. The goal of this presentation at the beginning of the book is to give you the possibility to create database objects and to query data without knowledge of the SQL database language.

Chapter 3 begins a new part of the book and describes one of most important parts of an RDBMS: a database language. For all RDBMS, there is only one language that counts: SQL. In this chapter, all components of SQL Server's own database language, called Transact-SQL, are described. You can also find the basic concepts and existing data types of SQL in this chapter. Finally, SQL Server system functions and operators are described.

Chapter 4 describes all data definition language (DDL) statements of Transact-SQL. At the beginning of the chapter, all DDL statements are separated in three groups. The first group contains all forms of the CREATE statement that are used to create database objects. A modification of a structure of some database objects is executed using different forms of the ALTER statement from the second group. Finally, the third group contains all forms of the DROP statement, which is used to remove different database objects.

Chapters 5 and 6 discuss the most important Transact-SQL statement: SELECT. These chapters introduce you to how data in a database can be retrieved and describe the use of simple and complex queries. Each clause concerning SELECT is separately defined and explained with reference to the sample database.

In Chapter 7, we discuss the four Transact-SQL statements used for updating data: INSERT, UPDATE, DELETE, and TRUNCATE TABLE. Each of these statements is explained by numerous examples.

Transact-SQL is a complete computational language. This means, all procedural extensions are the inseparable part of the language. Chapter 8 describes these extensions that can be used to create powerful programs called stored procedures and user-defined functions (UDFs), programs that are stored on the server and can be reused. Some stored procedures are written by users; others are provided by Microsoft and are referred to as system stored procedures. The creation and execution of so called CLR stored procedures and UDFs is also discussed in this chapter.

Every user (especially database applications programmers) can tune their applications to get better system response and therefore better performance. The first and most powerful method is the use of indices. The first part of Chapter 9 describes the creation of indices, while the second part discusses the overall possibilities to achieve better performance.

In Chapter 10 introduces the notion of a view. This chapter explains all Transact-SQL statements concerning views using numerous examples. A special form of views called indexed views is also explained. At the end of the chapter, you will find the discussion of the existing restrictions concerning update of views.

One of most important parts of an RDBMS is a system catalog. The system catalog contains all of the information concerning database objects and their relationships. The most important system tables belonging to the SQL Server system catalog are described in Chapter 11 and examples concerning querying those tables are given. The system supports system procedures and information schema, which allow the alternate way to query the system catalog. SQL Server 2005 introduces catalog views, which present another layer to system tables and which should be used to query system information.

In Chapter 12 you will find the answer to two primary questions concerning the protection of data in the database against unauthorized access. These questions concern authorization (which user has been granted legitimate access to the database system) and authentication (which access privileges are valid for a particular user). There are three Transact-SQL statements discussed in this chapter—GRANT, DENY, and REVOKE—that provide the access privileges of database objects against unauthorized access. The use of views for the same purpose is also explained.

There are two ways of keeping SQL Server databases in a consistent state with respect to the constructs specified in the database: procedural and declarative. After the definition of declarative integrity constraints in Chapter 4, Chapter 13 describes the implementation of procedural integrity constraints using triggers. Each example in this chapter concerns an integrity problem that you may face in your everyday life as a database application programmer.

Chapter 14 describes the concept of a transaction and the Transact-SQL statements that control a transaction. Locking as a method to solve concurrency control problems is discussed further. At the end of the chapter, you will learn what isolation levels and deadlocks are.

In Chapter 15, some internal and external issues concerning the relational database server are discussed. System databases and system architecture are two different internal facilities of the SQL Server system. First, there is a detailed description of the disk storage elements, system databases, and utilities. After that, we describe Unicode, which allows the use of different languages within the SQL Server system and supports their specific properties.

The third part of the book describes system administration issues and starts with Chapter 16, which is an introduction to the system administrator's tools and tasks. This short chapter lists all existing components, which will be explained in detail in the following chapters.

The first system administration task is the installation of the entire system. Although the system installation is a straightforward task, there are certain steps that need explanation. We handle all of these steps in Chapter 17.

Chapter 18 deals with storage management responsibilities of the system administrator. This includes how to create databases and their transaction logs using SQL Server Management Studio, how to expand the size of databases and logs, and how to drop databases.

Chapter 19 addresses the issues concerning system and database access. It covers the discussion and the implementation of system security modes (Windows mode and Mixed mode). This chapter also discusses creating and managing the different types of user accounts, including SQL Server logins and roles.

Chapter 20 provides an overview of the fault tolerance methods used to implement a backup strategy using either SQL Server Management Studio or corresponding Transact-SQL statements. The first part of the chapter specifies the different methods used to implement a backup strategy. The second part of the chapter discusses the restoration of databases. We describe methods for recovery of user-defined databases and transaction logs, as well as recovery of system databases.

SQL Server is one of a few RDBMS that includes the facilities to automate certain system administration jobs, such as backing up data and using the scheduling and alert features to notify operators. A SQL Server component called SQL Server Agent schedules and automates such problems. This component, together with the SQL Server Services, is described in Chapter 21.

Chapter 22 discusses performance issues and the tools for tuning SQL Server that are relevant to daily administration of the system. After introductory notes concerning the measurements of performance, the factors that affect performance are described and the tools for monitoring are presented.

SQL Server supports data partitioning since SQL Server 7. The main drawback of the solutions for data partitioning in the previous versions is that they are not transparent to the application. Chapter 23 explains range partitioning of data and indices, which is entirely transparent to the application.

Chapter 24 provides an introduction to data replication including notions such as the publisher and subscriber. The different models of replication are shown, as well as the installation of publishers and subscribers using SQL Server Management Studio.

The fourth part of the book is dedicated to Microsoft Analysis Services. Chapter 25 introduces to you the notion of data warehousing. The first part of the chapter explains the differences between the online transaction processing on one side and the data warehousing on the other side. The data store for a data warehousing process can be either a data warehouse or a data mart. Both types of data stores are discussed and their differences are listed in the second part of the chapter. The data warehouse design is explained at the end of the chapter.

In contrast to Chapter 25, which describes general properties of business intelligence systems, Chapter 26 discusses specific properties of MS Analysis Services. At the beginning of the chapter the architecture of Analysis Services is described. The second part of the chapter discusses the main component of Analysis Services called Business Intelligence Development Studio.

Chapter 27 explains how you can use Transact-SQL to solve business intelligence problems. This chapter discusses all SQL extensions, such as CUBE and ROLLUP operators, rank functions, TOP **n** clause, and the PIVOT relational operator.

Chapter 28 describes a Microsoft enterprise reporting solution called Reporting Services. This new component is used to design and deploy reports. We discuss the development environment that is used to design and create reports. Also, we show you different ways to deliver a designed and deployed report.

The last part of the book is dedicated to one of the most important topics in SQL Server: XML. Chapter 29 gives you an overview of the language, while the last chapter of the book discusses the use of XML in the SQL Server database system.

Almost all chapters include at their end numerous exercises, which you can use to improve your knowledge concerning the chapter's content. All solutions to the given exercises can be found either at McGraw-Hill/Osborne's web site (www.osborne.com) or my own home page (www.fh-rosenheim.de/~petkovic).

Outline of Changes

SQL Server 2005 is the first main release of the Microsoft enterprise database system since the year 2000. Therefore, there are a lot of new features, which are described in this book. Each chapter of the previous book (*SQL Server 2000: A Beginner's Guide*) was updated according to the corresponding modifications in SQL Server 2005. In this section we will list chapters of this book in which you will find significant changes from the previous edition.

Chapter 2	The most important front-end components of SQL Server 2000 are Enterprise Manager and Query Analyzer. The SQL Server 2005 administrator's primary tool for interacting with the system is SQL Server Management Studio. For this reason, Chapter 2 has been totally rewritten and describes this new integrated environment.
Chapter 6	This chapter contains one of the most important extensions of the Transact-SQL language: common table expressions (CTE). The use of CTEs to implement nonrecursive as well as recursive queries is shown at the end of the chapter.
Chapter 8	The previous versions of SQL Server allow you to implement stored procedures and user-defined functions (UDFs) using Transact-SQL. In SQL Server 2005, you can additionally use common language runtime (CLR) to implement both. Chapter 8 has two new sections, "Stored Procedures and CLR" and "User-Defined Functions and CLR," which describe how you can use the language C# to implement CLR programs. Another new topic, exception handling, is also described in a section of this chapter called "Handling Events with TRY and CATCH Statements."
Chapter 11	SQL Server 2005 introduces a new way to query system information: catalog views. The set of most important views, which belongs to this new interface, is described in a section called "Catalog Views."
Chapter 12	The security model of SQL Server 2005 is significantly different from the security models of the previous versions of this database system. For this reason, Chapter 12 was totally rewritten and describes numerous new topics, such as new encryption policy and user-schema separation.
Chapter 13	In this chapter, there is a new section concerning implementation of CLR triggers (also see changes in Chapter 8). DDL triggers are also described in this chapter.
Chapter 14	There is a new section called "Snapshot Isolation Level," which describes a new isolation level that SQL Server 2005 supports.
Chapter 15	Minor changes concerning the new **sqlcmd** utility have been made.
Chapter 16	Minor changes concerning the new SQL Computer Manager component have been made.
Chapter 17	This chapter has been rewritten, because the installation of the database system differs significantly from the installation of the previous version.
Chapter 20	A new section called "High Availability," which contains a description of log shipping and failover clustering, has been added.
Chapter 22	A description of the new tool called Database Tuning Advisor has been added.
Chapter 23	This is an entirely new chapter, which discusses data partitioning.
Chapter 26	A description of the new integrated environment called BI Development Studio has been added.
Chapter 27	This is almost an entirely new chapter, which describes SQL-OLAP. (The corresponding chapter in the previous book, Chapter 28, contains other material as well as small parts of the new one.)
Chapter 28	This is an entirely new chapter describing Microsoft Reporting Services.
Chapter 29	In the previous book, XML was described in one chapter (Chapter 29). This new book has two chapters concerning XML. This chapter is an introduction to the topic.
Chapter 30	This is an entirely new chapter describing SQL Server 2005 as a "native XML database system."

Conventions Used in this Book

The following conventions are used in this book:

- ► UPPERCASE indicates Transact-SQL keywords.

- ► **Boldface** indicates the names of database objects (the database itself, tables, and columns) in the text.

- ► *Italics* indicates new terms or items of emphasis. (All syntax conventions are described in detail at the end of Chapter 1.)

For the SQL Server 2005 component called Relational Database Engine, we use several different names. Usually the name is specified using the phrase "relational database server" or "database server." (The phrases "SQL Server system" or just "SQL Server" are also used to describe this component.)

SQL Server: Basic Concepts

CHAPTER 1

Database Systems and SQL Server

IN THIS CHAPTER:

Database Systems: An Overview

Relational Database Systems

SQL: A Relational Database Language

Database Design

Overview of Microsoft SQL Server

MS SQL Server is a database management system (DBMS) developed and marketed by Microsoft. This system is the most important part of Microsoft .NET technology. (MS .NET is the latest generation of Microsoft connecting technology. It includes a wide variety of tools and services that allow developers to build powerful systems through Web Services.) MS SQL Server runs exclusively under Microsoft operating systems Windows 2000, Windows Server 2003, and Windows XP. Microsoft's decision to concentrate on their own operating systems has a lot of benefits and one disadvantage. The most important benefits are as follows:

▶ MS SQL Server works as a natural extension of Windows 2000, Windows Server 2003, and Windows XP, because it is so closely integrated with this operating system. As such, the user does not have to learn another user interface to work with this database system.

▶ MS SQL Server has the same easy setup and maintenance of Windows operating systems. This unity is accomplished through easy installation of the system, elimination of many complicated tasks concerning database administration, and, generally, using a graphical computing environment for every system administration task.

▶ MS SQL Server uses the services of Windows operating systems to offer new or extended database capabilities, such as sending and receiving messages and managing login security.

On the other hand, by focusing only upon Microsoft operating systems, SQL Server cannot benefit from the advanced properties of an operating system such as UNIX, which, in some areas like enhanced parallel architectures or enterprise computing, still has advantages over Windows operating systems.

The most important aspects of SQL Server are as follows:

▶ SQL Server is easy to use.

▶ SQL Server scales from a mobile laptop to symmetric multiprocessor (SMP) systems.

▶ SQL Server provides business intelligence features that until now have only been available in Oracle and other more expensive DBMSs.

Almost all relational DBMSs originated under the UNIX operating system. The consequence is that existing user interfaces provided by these systems are rather difficult to use. Microsoft's goal is to make SQL Server the easiest database system for implementing and managing database applications. One way SQL Server helps to achieve this goal is by providing wizards for almost all administrative tasks.

Scalability means that the same DBMS runs on mobile laptop computers, single-processing systems, and multiprocessing hardware systems. One of the goals of such a DBMS is to scale from the single-processing computer to an SMP if the DBMS becomes CPU-bound because of CPU-intensive database applications.

Microsoft bundled the Analysis Services with SQL Server to create a comprehensive approach to the process of data warehousing. The goal of Analysis Services is to make it easier to build data warehouse and data mart solutions using Microsoft's new OLAP technology as well as the existing technology of other data warehouse software companies. Part IV will provide additional detailed information on the data warehousing features of MS SQL Server.

NOTE

The SQL Server database system was originally developed and implemented by Sybase Inc. Microsoft licensed this DBMS in 1988 for the OS/2 operating system and began implementing it for Windows operating systems in the early 1990s. At almost the same time, the further development of SQL Server for OS/2 was canceled. In April 1994, Microsoft ended their cooperative agreement with Sybase Inc.

SQL Server was, from the beginning, designed as a client/server DBMS. The client/server architecture has been developed to manage a large number of different computers (PCs, workstations, and SMP machines), which are connected using a network. The functionality of SQL Server is divided between clients and server(s). A client provides one or more different user interfaces that are used to formulate a user request to a DBMS. The server (i.e., DBMS) processes this request and sends the result back to the client.

NOTE

The client/server architecture does not necessarily include a DBMS. It is also possible to have other exclusively specialized servers, such as a print server and computing server, in such an environment. However, a DBMS is almost always a part of client/server architecture.

Database Systems: An Overview

A database system is an overall collection of different database software components and databases containing the following parts:

- ▶ Database application programs
- ▶ Front-end (i.e., client) components
- ▶ Database management system(s)
- ▶ Databases

A database application program is special-purpose software that is designed and implemented by users or implemented by third-party software companies. In contrast, front-end components are general-purpose database software designed and implemented by a database company or delivered as third-party software. By using database application programs and front-end components, users can manage and query data within the database.

The task of a database management system is to manage data stored in a database. In general, a database can be viewed from at least two perspectives: the user's and a DBMS's. Users view a database as a collection of data that logically belongs together. For a DBMS, a database is simply a series of bytes, usually stored on a disk.

Although these two views of a database are totally different, they do have something in common. The database system not only needs to provide interfaces that enable users to create databases and retrieve or modify data, but it also needs to provide system components to manage the stored data. A database system must provide the following features:

- ▶ Variety of user interfaces
- ▶ Physical data independence
- ▶ Logical data independence
- ▶ Query optimization
- ▶ Data integrity
- ▶ Concurrency control
- ▶ Backup and recovery
- ▶ Security and authorization

The following sections briefly describe these features.

Variety of User Interfaces

Most databases are designed and implemented for use by many different types of users with varied levels of knowledge. For this reason, a database system should offer many distinct user interfaces. These interfaces include query by example, natural language, and forms for end users, as well as interactive query language for experienced users.

Physical Data Independence

Physical data independence means that the database application programs do not depend on the physical structure of the stored data in a database. This important feature makes it possible to make changes in the stored data without having to make any changes in database application programs. For example, if the stored data is previously ordered using one criterion, and if this later should be changed using another, the modification of the physical data should not affect the existing database applications or the existing database *schema* (a description of a database generated by the data definition language of the DBMS).

Logical Data Independence

In file processing (using traditional programming languages), the declaration of a file is done in application programs, so any changes to the structure of that file usually require the modification of all programs using it. Database systems provide logical data independence—in other words, it is possible to make changes in the logical structure of the database separately from the database application programs. For example, if the structure of an object named PERSON exists in the DBMS and we want to add an attribute to PERSON (say the address), only the logical structure of the database has to be modified, and none of the existing application programs requires changing.

Query Optimization

Every database system contains a subcomponent called an *optimizer* that considers a variety of possible execution strategies for querying the data and then selects the most efficient one. The selected strategy is called the *execution plan* of the query. The optimizer makes its decisions using considerations such as how big the tables are that are involved in the query, what indices exist, and what Boolean operator

(AND, OR, or NOT) is used in the WHERE clause. (Indices and query optimization are discussed in detail in Chapter 9.)

Data Integrity

One of the tasks of a DBMS is to identify logically inconsistent data and reject their storage in a database. (The date February 30 and the time 5:77:00 P.M. are two examples of such data.) Additionally, most real-life problems that are implemented using database systems have *integrity constraints* that must hold true for the data. (One example of an integrity constraint might be the company's employee number, which must be a five-digit integer.) The task of maintaining integrity can be handled by the user in application programs or by the DBMS. As much as possible, this task should be handled by the DBMS. (Data integrity is discussed in two chapters of this book: declarative integrity in Chapter 4 and procedural integrity in Chapter 13.)

Concurrency Control

A DBMS is a multiuser software system, meaning that many user applications access a database at the same time. Therefore, each DBMS must have some kind of control mechanism to ensure that several applications, trying to update the same data, do so in some controlled way. The following is an example of a problem that can arise if a DBMS does not contain such control mechanisms:

1. The owners of bank account 4711 at bank X have an account balance of $2,000.

2. The two joint owners of this bank account, Mrs. A and Mr. B, go to two different bank tellers, and each withdraws $1,000 *at the same time*.

3. After these transactions, the amount of money in bank account 4711 should be $0 and not $1,000.

All DBMSs have the necessary mechanisms to handle cases like this example. Concurrency control is discussed in detail in Chapter 14.

Backup and Recovery

A DBMS must have a subsystem that is responsible for recovery from hardware or software errors. For example, if a failure occurs while a database application updates a hundred rows of a table, the recovery subsystem must roll back all previously executed updates to ensure that the corresponding data is consistent after the error occurs. (See Chapter 20 for further discussion on backup and recovery.)

Security and Authorization

Security means that the data stored in a database is protected against any kind of unauthorized user or against a misuse. For example, access to the data item **salary** containing employee salaries of a company should be allowed only to authorized persons. Additionally, some users may have only read access to the data, whereas others may have read and write access to the same data.

Each DBMS provides some kind of authorization control by means of *user accounts* that grant and revoke privileges to the users of the system. Chapter 12 discusses this topic in detail.

Relational Database Systems

MS SQL Server is a relational DBMS. The notion of relational database systems was first introduced by E. F. Codd in his article "A Relational Model of Data for Large Shared Data Banks" in 1970. In contrast to earlier database systems (network and hierarchical), *relational database systems* are based upon the relational data model, which has a strong mathematical background.

NOTE

A data model is a collection of concepts, their relationships, and their constraints that are used to represent data of a real-world problem.

The central concept of the relational data model is a relation—that is, a table. Therefore, from the user's point of view, a relational database contains tables and nothing but tables. In a table, there are one or more columns and zero or more rows. At every row and column position in a table there is always exactly one data value.

Working with the Book's Sample Database

The sample database that we will use in this book represents a company with departments and employees. Each employee belongs to exactly one department, which itself has one or more employees. Jobs of employees center around projects: each employee works at the same time for one or more projects, and each project engages one or more employees.

The data of the sample database can be represented using four tables:

► department
► employee
► project
► works_on

Tables 1-1 through 1-4 show all the tables of the sample database.

dept_no	dept_name	location
d1	Research	Dallas
d2	Accounting	Seattle
d3	Marketing	Dallas

Table 1-1 *The Table **department***

emp_no	emp_fname	emp_lname	dept_no
25348	Matthew	Smith	d3
10102	Ann	Jones	d3
18316	John	Barrimore	d1
29346	James	James	d2
9031	Elke	Hansel	d2
2581	Elsa	Bertoni	d2
28559	Sybill	Moser	d1

Table 1-2 *The Table **employee***

project_no	project_name	budget
p1	Apollo	120000
p2	Gemini	95000
p3	Mercury	185600

Table 1-3 *The Table **project***

emp_no	project_no	Job	enter_date
10102	p1	Analyst	1997.10.1 00:00:00
10102	p3	Manager	1999.1.1 00:00:00
25348	p2	Clerk	1998.2.15 00:00:00
18316	p2	NULL	1998.6.1 00:00:00
29346	p2	NULL	1997.12.15 00:00:00
2581	p3	Analyst	1998.10.15 00:00:00
9031	p1	Manager	1998.4.15 00:00:00
28559	p1	NULL	1998.8.1. 00:00:00
28559	p2	Clerk	1999.2.1 00:00:00
9031	p3	Clerk	1997.11.15 00:00:00
29346	p1	Clerk	1998.1.4 00:00:00

Table 1-4   *The Table* **works_on**

The table **department** represents all departments of the company. Each department has the following attributes:

> department (dept_no, dept_name, location)

dept_no represents the unique number of each department. **dept_name** is its name, and **location** is the location of the corresponding department.

The table **employee** represents all employees working for a company. Each employee has the following attributes:

> employee (emp_no, emp_fname, emp_lname, dept_no)

emp_no represents the unique number of each employee. **emp_fname** and **emp_lname** are the first and last name of each employee, respectively. Finally, **dept_no** is the number of the department to which the employee belongs.

Each project of a company is represented in the table **project**. This table has the following columns:

> project (project_no, project_name, budget)

project_no represents the unique number of each project. **project_name** and **budget** specify the name and the budget of each project, respectively.

The table **works_on** specifies the relationship between employees and projects. It has the following columns:

works_on (emp_no, project_no, job, enter_date)

emp_no specifies the employee number and **project_no** the number of the project on which the employee works. The combination of data values belonging to these two columns is always unique. **job** and **enter_date** specify the task and the starting date of an employee in the corresponding project, respectively.

Using the sample database, it is possible to describe some important properties of relational database systems:

▶ Rows in a table do not have any particular order.

▶ Columns in a table do not have any particular order.

▶ Every column must have a unique name within a table. On the other hand, columns from different tables may have the same name. (For example, the sample database has a column **dept_no** in the table **department** and a column with the same name in the table **employee**.)

▶ Every single data item in the table must be single valued. This means that in every row and column position of a table there is never a set of multiple data values.

▶ For every table, there is at least one identifier (i.e., a combination of columns with the property that no two rows have the same combination of data values for these columns). In the relational data model, such an identifier is called a *candidate key*. If there is more than one candidate key within a table, the database designer designates one of them as the *primary key* of the table. For example, the column **dept_no** is the primary key of the table **department**; the columns **emp_no** and **project_no** are the primary keys of the tables **employee** and **project**, respectively. Finally, the primary key for the table **works_on** is the combination of the columns (**emp_no**, **project_no**).

▶ In a table, there are never two identical rows. (This property is only theoretical; SQL Server and all other relational database systems generally allow the existence of identical rows within a table.)

SQL: A Relational Database Language

The SQL Server relational language is called Transact-SQL. It is a dialect of the most important database language today: SQL, an abbreviation for Structured Query Language. The origin of SQL is closely connected with the project called

System R, which was designed and implemented by IBM in the early 1980s. This project showed that it is possible, using the theoretical foundations of E. F. Codd, to build a relational database system. SQL was built in the project's first phase, the goal of which was to implement a prototype with only limited functionality.

After the success of System R, a lot of new companies built their own relational database systems using SQL as the language of choice. All these implementations were expanded dialects of the language, as every company implemented its own extensions. For this reason, the American National Standards Institute (ANSI) and the International Standards Organization (ISO) founded a committee in 1982 with the goal of designing a standard version of SQL. The first standard of SQL, which was based primarily on the IBM dialect of this language, was released in 1986. After the release of an intermediate standard in 1989, a much more voluminous standard called SQL92 was developed and finally released in December 1992. After that, both standards organizations developed a new standard, SQL:1999, that encompasses several new database concepts, including triggers, stored procedures, and numerous object-oriented concepts. The main parts of the SQL:1999 standard were released in September 1999. Recently, the ANSI committee released the SQL standard called SQL:2003.

In contrast to traditional languages like C, C++, and Java, SQL is a set-oriented language. (The former are also called record-oriented languages) This means that SQL can query many rows from one or more tables using just one statement. This feature is one of the most important advantages of SQL, allowing the use of this language at a logically higher level than procedural languages.

Another important property of SQL is its nonprocedurality. Every program written in a procedural language (C, C++, Java) describes *how* a task is accomplished, step by step. In contrast to this, SQL, as any other nonprocedural language, describes *what* it is that the user wants. Thus, the system is responsible for finding the appropriate way to solve users' requests.

SQL, like all database languages, contains two sublanguages: a data definition language (DDL) and a data manipulation language (DML). DDL statements are used to describe the structure of database tables. The DDL contains three generic SQL statements: CREATE object, ALTER object, and DROP object. These generate, alter, and remove database objects, such as databases, tables, columns, and indexes. These statements are discussed in detail in Chapter 4. In contrast, the DML encompasses all operations that manipulate the data. There are always four generic operations for manipulating the database: retrieval, insertion, deletion, and modification. The retrieval statement SELECT is described in Chapters 5 and 6, while the INSERT, DELETE, and UPDATE statements are discussed in detail in Chapter 7.

Convention	Indication
Italics	New terms or items of emphasis.
UPPERCASE	Transact-SQL keywords—for example, CREATE TABLE. Additional information about Transact-SQL keywords can be found in Chapter 2.
lowercase	Variables in Transact-SQL statements—for example, CREATE TABLE tablename. (The user must replace "tablename" with the actual name of the table.)
var1 | var2	Alternative use of the items **var1**, **var2**. (You may choose only one of the items separated by vertical bar.)
{ }	Alternative use of more items. Example: { expression | USER | NULL }
[ ]	Optional item(s) are written in brackets. Example: [FOR LOAD]
{ }...	Item(s) in braces can be repeated any number of times. Example: {, @param1 typ1} ...
bold	Name of database object (database itself, tables, columns) in the text.
<u>Default</u>	The default value is always underlined. Example: <u>ALL</u> | DISTINCT

Table 1-5 *Syntax Conventions*

Syntax Conventions

In this book, we will use the conventions shown in Table 1-5 for the syntax of the Transact-SQL statements and for the indication of the text.

NOTE

In contrast to brackets and braces, which belong to syntax conventions, parentheses, "(" and ")", belong to the syntax of a statement and must always be typed!

Database Design

Designing a database is a very important phase in the database life cycle, which precedes all other phases except the requirements collection and the analysis. If the database design is created merely intuitively and without any plan, the resulting database will most likely not meet the user requirements concerning performance. Another consequence of a bad database design is superfluous data redundancy, which in itself has two disadvantages: the existence of data anomalies and the use of an unnecessary amount of disk space.

Normalization of data is a process during which the existing tables of a database are tested to find certain dependencies between the columns of a table. If such dependencies exist, the table is restructured into multiple (usually two) tables, which eliminates any column dependencies. If one of these generated tables still contains data dependencies, the process of normalization must be repeated until all dependencies are resolved.

The process of eliminating data redundancy in a table is based upon the theory of functional dependencies. A *functional dependency* means that by using the known value of one column, the corresponding value of another column can always be uniquely determined. (The same is true for column groups.) The functional dependencies between columns A and B is denoted by $A \rightarrow B$, specifying that a value of column A can always be used to determine the corresponding value of column B. ("B is functionally dependent on A.")

The following example shows the functional dependency between two attributes of the table **employee** in the sample database.

EXAMPLE 1.1

$$emp\_no \rightarrow emp\_lname$$

By having a unique value for the employee number, the corresponding last name of employee (and all other corresponding attributes) can be determined. (This kind of functional dependency, where a column is dependent upon the key of a table, is called *trivial* functional dependency.)

Another kind of functional dependency is called *multivalued dependency*. In contrast to the functional dependency just described, the multivalued dependency is specified for multivalued attributes. This means that by using the known value of one attribute (column), the corresponding *set of values* of another multivalued attribute can be uniquely determined. The multivalued dependency is denoted by $\rightarrow\rightarrow$.

The next example shows the multivalued dependency that holds for two attributes of the object BOOK.

EXAMPLE 1.2

$$ISBN \rightarrow\rightarrow Authors$$

The ISBN of a book always determines all of its authors. Therefore, the attribute **Authors** is multivalued dependent on the attribute **isbn**.

Normal Forms

Normal forms are used for the process of normalization of data and therefore for the database design. In theory, there are at least five different normal forms, of which the first three are the most important for practical use. The third normal form for a table can be achieved by testing the first and second normal forms at the intermediate states, and as such, the goal of good database design can usually be fulfilled if all tables of a database are in the third normal form.

NOTE

The multivalued dependency is used to test the fourth normal form of a table. Therefore, this kind of dependency will not be used further in this book.

First Normal Form

First normal form (1NF) means that a table has no multivalued attributes or composite attributes. (A composite attribute contains other attributes and can therefore be divided into smaller parts.) All relational tables are by definition in 1NF, because the value of any column in a row must be *atomic*—that is, single valued.

We will demonstrate the first normal form using part of the **works_on** table from the sample database (Table 1-6). The rows of the table **works_on** could be grouped together, using the employee number. The resulting Table 1-7 is not in 1NF because the column **project_no** contains a set of values (p1, p3).

emp_no	project_no	·················
10102	p1	··············
10102	p3	··············
·············	·············	··············

Table 1-6   *Part of the Table **works_on***

emp_no	project_no	·················
10102	(p1, p3)	··············
·············	·············	··············

Table 1-7   *This "Table" Is Not in 1NF*

Second Normal Form

A table is in second normal form (2NF) if it is in 1NF and there is no nonkey column dependent on a partial key of that table. This means if (A,B) is a combination of two table columns building the key, then there is no column of the table depending either on only A or only B.

For example, let us take a look at the **works_on1** table in Table 1-8, which is identical to the table **works_on**, except for the additional column **dept_no**. The primary key of this table is the combination of columns (**emp_no**, **project_no**). The column **dept_no** is dependent on the partial key **emp_no** (and is independent of **project_no**), so this table is not in 2NF. (The original table **works_on** is in 2NF.)

NOTE

Every table with a one-column primary key is always in 2NF.

Third Normal Form

A table is in third normal form (3NF) if it is in 2NF and there are no functional dependencies between nonkey columns. For example, the **employee1** table in Table 1-9, which is identical to the table **employee**, except for the additional column **dept_name**, is not in 3NF, because for every known value of the column **dept_no** the corresponding value of the column **dept_name** can be uniquely determined. (The original table **employee**, and all other tables of the sample database, are in 3NF.)

emp_no	project_no	job	enter_date	dept_no
10102	p1	Analyst	1997.10.1 00:00:00	d3
10102	p3	Manager	1999.1.1 00:00:00	d3
25348	p2	Clerk	1998.2.15 00:00:00	d3
18316	p2	NULL	1998.6.1 00:00:00	d1
....	....	....		....

Table 1-8   *The Table **works_on1***

emp_no	emp_fname	emp_lname	dept_no	dept_name
25348	Matthew	Smith	d3	Marketing
10102	Ann	Jones	d3	Marketing
18316	John	Barrimore	d1	Research
29346	James	James	d2	Accounting
....	....	....	....	....

Table 1-9   *The Table **employee1***

Entity-Relationship (ER) Model

The data in a database could easily be designed using only one table that contains all data. The main disadvantage of such a database design is its high redundancy of data. For example, if your database contains data concerning employees and their projects (assuming each employee works at the same time for one or more projects, and each project engages one or more employees), the data stored in a single table contains a lot of columns and many rows. The main disadvantage of such a table is that data is difficult to keep consistent because of its redundancy.

The ER model is used to design relational databases by removing all existing redundancy in the data. The basic object of the ER model is an *entity*, that is, a real-world object. Each entity has several *attributes* that are properties of the entity and therefore describe it. Based on its type, an attribute can be

- ▶ Atomic (or single valued)
- ▶ Multivalued
- ▶ Composite

An attribute is called atomic if it is always represented by a single value for a particular entity. For example, a person's marital status is always an atomic attribute. Most attributes are atomic attributes. A multivalued attribute may have one or more values for a particular entity. For example, **Location** as the attribute of an entity called ENTERPRISE is multivalued, because each enterprise can have one or more locations. Composite attributes are not atomic because they are assembled using some other atomic attributes. A typical example of a composite attribute is a person's address, which is composed of atomic attributes, such as **City**, **Zip**, and **Street**. The entity PERSON in Example 1.3 has several atomic attributes, one composite attribute, **Address,** and a multivalued attribute, **College_degree**.

EXAMPLE 1.3

PERSON (Personal_nr, F_name, L_name, Address(City,Zip,Street), {College_degree})

Each entity has one or more key attributes that are attributes (or a combination of two or more attributes) whose values are unique for each particular entity. In Example 1.3, the attribute **Personal_nr** is the key attribute of the entity PERSON.

Besides entity and attribute, *relationship* is another basic concept of the ER model. A relationship exists when an entity refers to one (or more) other entities. The number of participating entities defines the degree of a relationship. For example, the relationship **works_on** between entities EMPLOYEE and PROJECT has degree two.

Every existing relationship between two entities must be one of the following three types: 1:1, 1:N, and M:N. (This property of a relationship is also called cardinality ratio.) For example, the relationship between the entities DEPARTMENT and EMPLOYEE is 1:N because each employee belongs to exactly one department, which itself has one or more employees. Also, the relationship between the entities PROJECT and EMPLOYEE is M:N, because each project engages one or more employees and each employee works at the same time for one or more projects. A relationship can also have its own attributes (see Figure 1-1). Figure 1-1 shows an example of an ER diagram. (The ER diagram is the graphical notation used to

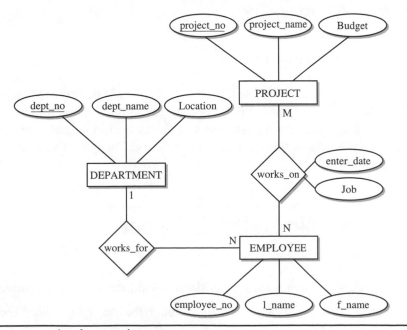

Figure 1-1   *Example of an ER diagram*

describe the ER model.) Using this notation, entities are modeled using rectangular boxes, with the entity name written inside the box. Attributes are shown in ovals, and each attribute is attached to a particular entity (or relationship) using a straight line. Finally, relationships are modeled using diamonds, and entities participating in the relationship are attached to it using straight lines. The cardinality ratio of each entity is written on the corresponding line.

Conclusion

SQL Server is a relational database management system for distributed client/server computing. Like all other database management systems, it provides the following features:

- ► Variety of user interfaces
- ► Physical data independence
- ► Logical data independence
- ► Query optimization
- ► Data integrity
- ► Concurrency control
- ► Backup and recovery
- ► Security and authorization

The next chapter introduces the new general tool called SQL Server Management Studio. SQL Server Management Studio is a system administration tool for managing almost every task concerning database systems as well as an end-user tool for executing and analyzing ad hoc queries. Chapter 1 and Chapter 2 form the introductory part of this book.

Overview of Microsoft SQL Server

The most important benefits of Microsoft SQL Server are as follows:

- ► SQL Server works as a natural extension of Windows *operating systems*.
- ► SQL Server is relatively easy to manage through the use of a graphical computing environment for almost every task of system and database administration.

▶ SQL Server uses services of Windows operating systems to offer new or extended database capabilities, such as sending and receiving messages and managing login security.

▶ SQL Server is easy to use.

▶ SQL Server scales from a mobile laptop to symmetric multiprocessor systems.

▶ SQL Server provides data warehousing features that up until now have only been available in Oracle and other more expensive DBMSs.

Exercises

E.1.1
What does "data independence" mean and which two forms of data independence exist?

E.1.2
Which is the main concept of the relational model?

E.1.3
What does the table **employee** represent in the real world? And what does the row in this table with the data for Ann Jones represent?

E.1.4
What does the table **works_on** represent in the real world (and in relation to the other tables of the sample database)?

E.1.5
Let **book** be a table with two columns: **isbn** and **title**. Assuming that **isbn** is unique and there are no identical titles, answer the following questions:
   A. Is **title** a key of the table?
   B. Does **isbn** functionally depend on **title**?
   C. Is the table **book** in 3NF?

E.1.6
Let **order** be a table with the following columns: **order_no**, **customer_no**, **discount**. If the column **customer_no** is functionally dependent on **order_no** and the column

discount is functionally dependent on **customer_no**, answer the following questions and explain in detail your answers:

    A. Is **order_no** a key of the table?

    B. Is **customer_no** a key of the table?

E.1.7

Let **company** be a table with the following columns: **company_no, location**. Each company has one or more locations. In which normal form is the table **company**?

E.1.8

Let **supplier** be a table with the following columns: **supplier_no, article, city**. The key of the table is the combination of the first two columns. Each supplier delivers several articles and each article is delivered by several suppliers. There is only one supplier in each city. Answer the following questions:

    A. In which normal form is the table **supplier**?

    B. How can you resolve the existing functional dependencies?

E.1.9

Let $R(\underline{A}, \underline{B}, C)$ be a relation with the functional dependency: B -> C. (The attributes A and B build the composite key and the attribute C is functionally dependent on B.) In which normal form is the relation R?

E.1.10

Let $R(\underline{A}, \underline{B}, C)$ be a relation with the functional dependency: C -> B. (The attributes A and B build the composite key and the attribute B is functionally dependent on C.) In which normal form is the relation R?

SQL Server Management Studio

IN THIS CHAPTER

The SQL Server Program Group and Books Online

Introduction to SQL Server Management Studio

S QL Server provides a number of tools that serve different purposes, such as installation, database query, and replication. All these tools have user-friendly graphical interfaces. This chapter examines first the **Start** menu and discusses briefly Books Online, the online reference source with all necessary information concerning SQL Server. After that, the most important SQL Server front-end component, SQL Server Management Studio, will be introduced. By the end of this chapter, you should be able to create and manage database objects using this tool. You will also learn all the functions necessary for creating and executing any Transact-SQL statements.

NOTE

This chapter is dedicated to the activities of the end user. Therefore, only the functionality of SQL Server Management Studio with respect to the creation of database objects is described in detail. All administrative tasks and all tasks related to Analysis Services and other components, which this tool also supports, will be discussed later, beginning with Chapter 17.

The SQL Server Program Group and Books Online

To see the SQL Server program group, you have to click **Start** | **Programs** and, finally, **Microsoft SQL Server 2005**. The SQL Server program group comprises all applications you will use during your work with SQL Server. In this chapter we will look only at particular applications, starting with SQL Server Books Online (BOL).

Books Online is the online documentation that is delivered and installed with all other SQL Server software components.

The toolbar of the **Books Online** has, among others, buttons for four different features:

- ► Contents
- ► Index
- ► Search
- ► Favorites

If you click the **Contents** button, you will see the content of the whole online documentation divided into different books. Each specific topic (such as MS SQL Server 2005 Mobile Edition, for instance) is divided into subtopics, which can be opened by clicking the corresponding plus (+) symbol of the tree. You can view the content of each subfolder in the same way—that is, by clicking the + symbols of the corresponding book and all superfolders of that folder.

The **Index** window shows an alphabetically sorted sequence of each keyword that appears in the online documentation. There are two ways to select one of the keywords: by double-clicking the keyword in the list or by typing the starting letters of it. In the latter case, the system selects (and highlights) the alphabetically first keyword in the list that has the typed letters at its beginning.

The **Search** button is the most used button. It allows you to type a phrase (or a single word) that is then used in the search process to display all topics where they appear. (SQL Server uses its own Full Text Search component to support this process.) Besides Books Online, SQL Server 2005 searches the phrase also in MSDN Online and Codezone Community. (The Codezone Community is a site for third-party tips, code samples, advice, and news from independent experts on the Microsoft .NET Framework and Microsoft Visual Studio.)

The results of the search process are displayed in the middle of the default pane. After clicking the **Search** button, the corresponding results appear in the pane. Each result includes the title of the document and a short description of the topic. The total number of search results appears also in the upper-right corner of the pane.

The **Favorites** tab allows you to store selected keywords (and phrases). To select again one of the stored topics, double-click the entry in the list of your favorites.

Introduction to SQL Server Management Studio

The SQL Server administrator's primary tool for interacting with the system is SQL Server Management Studio. Both administrators and end users can use this tool to administer multiple servers, develop databases, and replicate data, among other things. To open this tool, click the **Start** menu, **Programs**, **Microsoft SQL Server 2005**, and then **SQL Server Management Studio** in the SQL Server program group. Every user with access to SQL Server can also use SQL Server Management Studio. Figure 2-1 shows the **Connect to Server** dialog box, which appears right after choosing SQL Server Management Studio. In the dialog box, you have to choose the server type (Database Engine, in this case) and select or type the name of the server that you want to use. Also, you have to choose between two existing authentication types.

If you select **Windows Authentication**, you will be connected to SQL Server using your Windows account. If you select the other option (**SQL Server Authentication**), SQL Server uses its own authentication. The former option is much simpler, while the latter enhances SQL server security with an additional security level. (For more information concerning SQL Server security, see Chapter 12.)

After connecting to a database server, the default window settings appear (see Figure 2-2). The default appearance is similar to Visual Studio, so users can

Figure 2-1   *The Connect to Server dialog box*

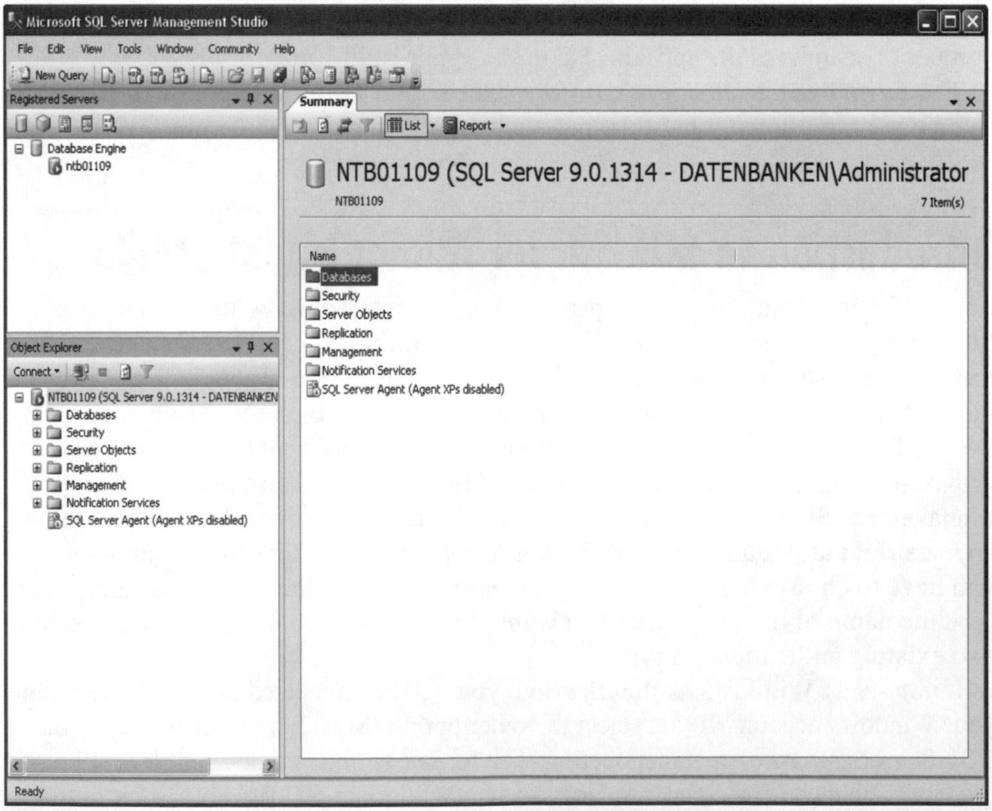

Figure 2-2   *SQL Server Management Studio: default windows settings*

leverage their experience of developing in Visual Studio to use this SQL Server component more easily.

NOTE

SQL Server Management Studio is a completely new application that gives you unique interface to manage servers and create queries across all SQL Server components. This means that SQL Server Management Studio offers one interface for Database Engine, Analysis Services, SQL Server Mobile (former SQL Server CE), Integration Services, and Reporting Services . As such, SQL Server Management Studio replaces Enterprise Manager and Query Analyzer.

SQL Server Management Studio opens by default with several component windows: the **Registered Servers** window, the **Object Explorer** window, and the **Document** window. (If any of these windows do not appear, select the **View** menu and choose the omitted window.)

The **Registered Servers** window lists servers that you manage. The list can be either enhanced with new servers or one or more existing servers can be removed from the list.

The **Object Explorer** window contains a tree view of all the database objects in a server. This includes Database Engine databases, objects of Analysis Services, Integration Services, and Report Services, as well as objects of and SQL Server Mobile.

The **Document** window contains query editors and browser windows. When you first start up Management Studio, the **Summary** window is displayed, containing the information of the default instance of SQL Server on the current computer. All windows of Management Studio can be grouped into two groups: The central, non-movable area with the **Document** window and the peripheral, movable areas with all component windows.

Each of the component windows can be docked or hidden. By right-clicking the bar over the top of the corresponding window, you can choose between the following presentation possibilities: **Floating**, **Dockable**, **Tabbed Document**, **Hide**, and **Auto Hide**.

To hide a window, right-click the bar at the top of the window and choose **Hide**. (The alternative way is to click the **x** in the upper-right corner of the window.) The corresponding window closes. A removed window can be retrieved by selecting the window name from the **View** menu.

To minimize a window, right-click the bar and choose **Auto Hide**. SQL Server Management Studio minimizes the window and stores it on the left side of the screen. (The alternative way is to click the **Auto Hide** button in the upper-right corner of the window.) To reopen such a window, move your mouse over the tabs on the left side of the screen. Click the pushpin to pin the window in the open position. (The difference between the **Hide** and **Auto Hide** options is that the former option removes the window from SQL Server Management Studio, while the latter collapses the window to the side panel.)

If you use the **Dockable** option, you can also move components of SQL Server Management Studio and dock them in different positions. To move a component, click and drag the title bar of the component into the middle of the document window. The component undocks and will remain floating until you drop it.

To restore the default configuration, click the **Window** menu and select **Reset Window Layout**.

NOTE

You will find that there will often be several ways of accomplishing the same task within SQL Server Management Studio. This chapter will indicate more than one way to do things; later, only a single method will be given. Different people prefer different methods (some like to double-click, some like to click the +/– signs, some like to right-click, others like to use the pull-down menus, and others like to use the keyboard as much as possible). Experiment with the different ways to navigate, and use the methods that feel most natural to you.

A subobject appears only if you click the plus (+) sign of its direct predecessor. A right-click on an object and the selection of the **Properties** function displays the properties of that object. The minus (–) sign indicates that an object is currently expanded (for example, server). To compress all subobjects of an object, click its minus sign. (Another possibility would be to double-click the folder, or press the LEFT-ARROW key while the folder is selected.)

Using Management Studio with the SQL Server Database Engine

SQL Server Management Studio has two main purposes:

► Administration of the database servers
► Management of database objects

The administration tasks, which can be started using SQL Server Management Studio, are, among others:

► Registration of servers
► Addition of new server groups
► Management of several servers on one computer

▶ Starting and stopping SQL Server

▶ Database management

The first two administration tasks can be done using the **Registered Servers** component; for the other tasks, you use Object Explorer.

The following tasks concerning database objects can be performed:

▶ Creation and modification of database objects without using the Transact-SQL language

▶ Management of database objects and their usage

▶ Generation and execution of SQL statements

NOTE

With SQL Server Management Studio, you can manage objects of Database Engine, Analysis Services, Reporting Services, and Integration Services. In this chapter we will demonstrate the use of Management Studio concerning only Database Engine.

Registering Servers

SQL Server Management Studio separates the activities of registering servers and exploring server objects. Every server (local or remote) must be registered before use. A server can be registered during the first execution of SQL Server Management Studio or later. To register a database server in the **Registered Servers** window, right-click the **Database Engine** folder and select **New** and **Server Registration**. Figure 2-3 shows the registration of the server named NTB01109 in the **New Server Registration** window. You can export a registered server's registration information to an XML file and then import it into the same or another server by right-clicking the registered server and choosing **Export**. (The same is true for server groups.)

SQL Server Management Studio also separates the registering of a server and connecting to a server. This means that registering a server does not automatically connect you to the server. To connect to a server from the **Registered Servers** window, right-click the server, choose **Connect**, and then **New Query**. You can also connect to a server from the **Object Explorer** window if you right-click the server name and choose **Connect**.

Creating a New Server Group

There are two ways to create server groups. In the **Registered Servers** window, right-click **Database Engine**, choose **New**, and select **Server Registration**. In the

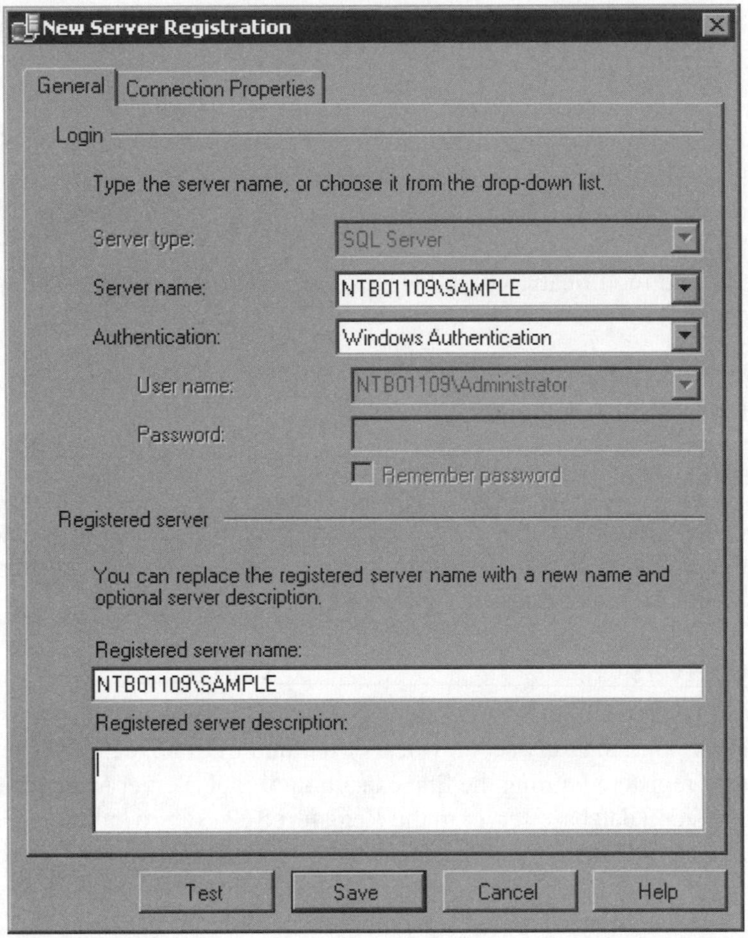

Figure 2-3 *The New Server Registration window*

New Server Group dialog box, enter a (unique) name and select an existing location for the group.

You can also create a server group after connecting to a server. In this case, right-click a server in the **Registered Servers** window, select **New**, and click **Server Group**.

Managing Servers

SQL Server Management Studio allows you to administer multiple database engines (called instances) on one computer using the Object Explorer component of SQL Server Management Studio. Each instance of SQL Server has its own set of database objects (system and user databases) that are not shared between different instances.

The installation and management of SQL Server instances will be discussed in detail in Chapters 16 and 17.

To manage a server and its configuration, right-click the server name in Object Explorer and choose **Properties** (see Figure 2-4). The **Server Properties** dialog box contains several different options, like **Permissions** and **Security**. The **Permissions** dialog box shows all logins and roles that can access the server. The lower part of the dialog box shows all permissions that can be granted to the logins and roles. The **Security** dialog box contains the information concerning the authentication mode of the server and the login auditing mode.

You can replace the existing server name with a new name. Right-click the server in the **Object Explorer** window and choose **Register**. Now you can rename the server in the **Register Server** dialog box.

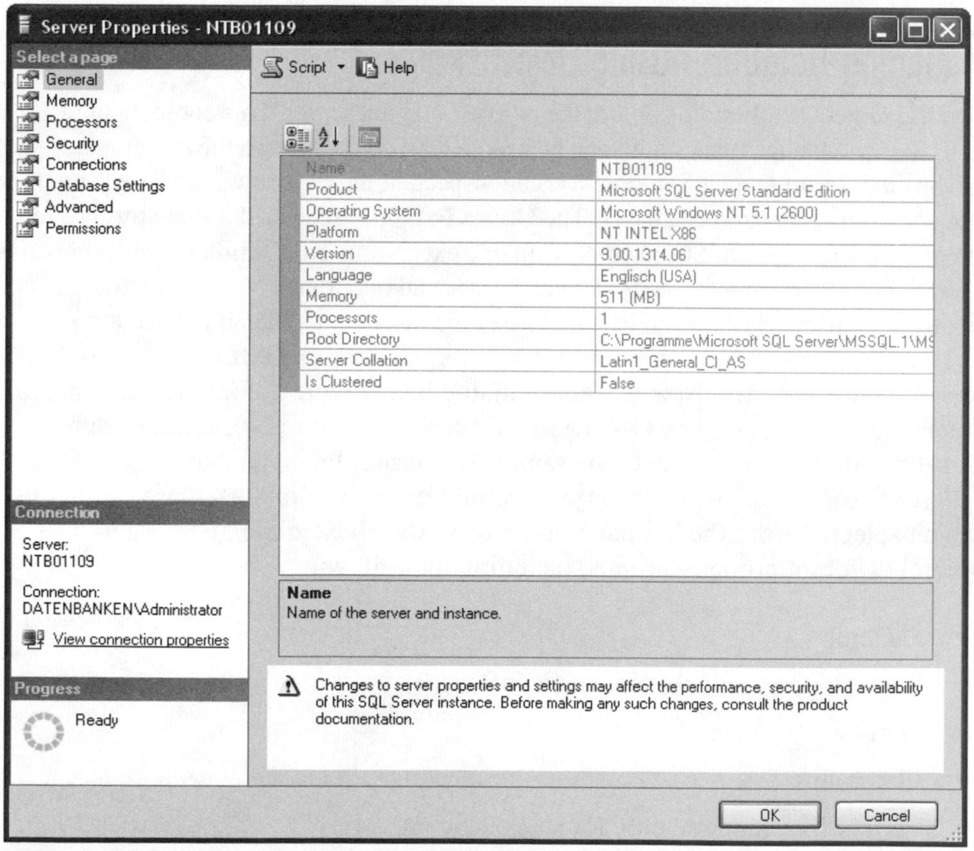

Figure 2-4   *The Server Properties dialog box*

Starting and Stopping SQL Server

SQL Server can be started automatically each time the Windows operating system starts or by using SQL Server Management Studio. In the **Object Explorer** window, right-click the selected server and click **Start** in the pull-down menu. The pull-down menu also contains the corresponding **Stop** function that stops the activated server. The additional **Pause** function pauses the whole system, which means that new users are not allowed to log into the system.

Managing Databases

You can create a new database using SQL Server Management Studio and its component Object Explorer or Transact-SQL. (The next section discusses database creation and modification using Object Explorer. Database creation using the Transact-SQL language will be discussed in Chapter 4.)

Managing Databases Using Object Explorer

You use Object Explorer to explore the objects within a server. This component of SQL Server Management Studio can be used after a connection to the server is established. From Object Explorer you can inspect all the objects within a server and manage your server and databases. The Object Explorer tree has the same form as in the previous versions of SQL Server, with one exception: The **Database** folder contains several subfolders, one for the system databases and one for each new database that is created by a user. (System and user databases are discussed in detail in Chapter 3.)

To create a database using Object Explorer, right-click **Databases** and select **New Database**. In **the New Database** dialog box (Figure 2-5), type the name of the new database and click **OK**. (As you can see in Figure 2-5, we use the **New Database** dialog box to create the sample database.) Each database has several different properties, such as file type, initial size, and so on. Database properties can be selected from the left pane of the **New Database** dialog box. There are several different property groups, including the following:

- ▶ General
- ▶ Files (appears only for an existing database)
- ▶ Options
- ▶ Filegroups
- ▶ Permissions (appears only for an existing database)
- ▶ Mirroring (appears only for an existing database)
- ▶ Extended Properties

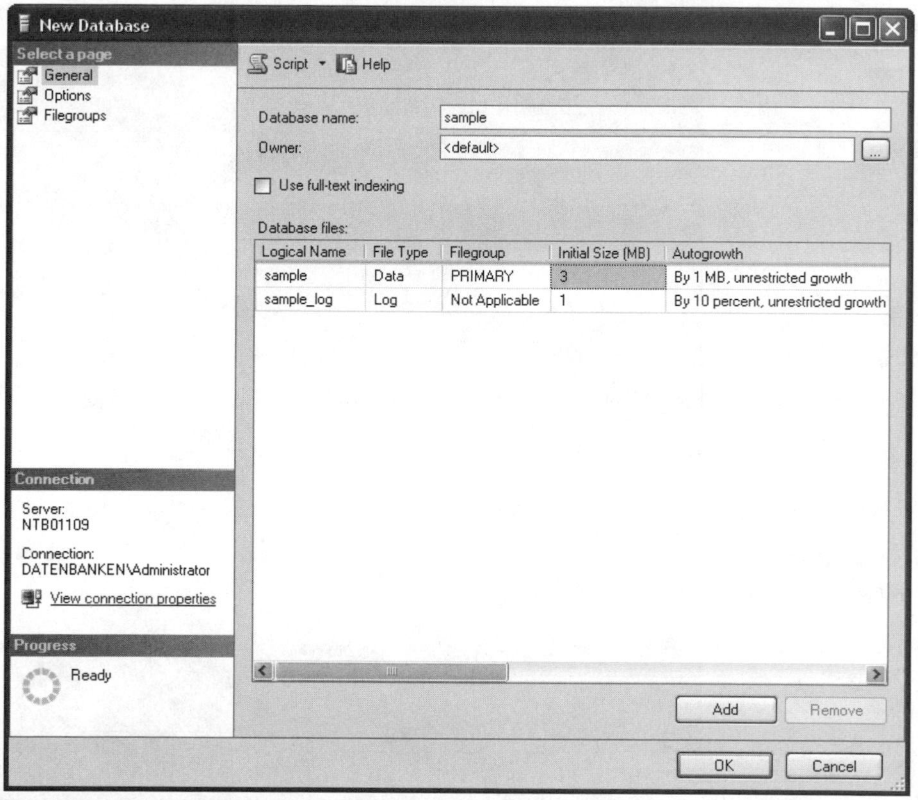

Figure 2-5 *The New Database dialog box*

General properties of the database (Figure 2-6) include, among others, the database name, the owner of the database, its collation, and size. The properties of the data files that belong to a particular database comprise the name and initial size of the file, where the database will be stored, and the type of the file (PRIMARY, for instance). A database can be stored in multiple files.

NOTE

*SQL Server has dynamic disk space management. This means databases can be set up to automatically expand and shrink as needed. If you want to change the **Autogrowth** property of the **Files** option, click . . . in the **Autogrowth** column and make your changes in the **Change Autogrowth** dialog box. The **Enable Autogrowth** check box should be checked to allow the database to autogrow. Each time there is insufficient space within the file when data is added to the database, the server will request the additional space from the operating system. The amount (in megabytes) of the additional space is set by the number in the **File Growth** frame of the same dialog box. You can also decide whether the file can grow without any restrictions (the default value) or not. If you restrict the file growth, you have to specify the maximum file size (in MB).*

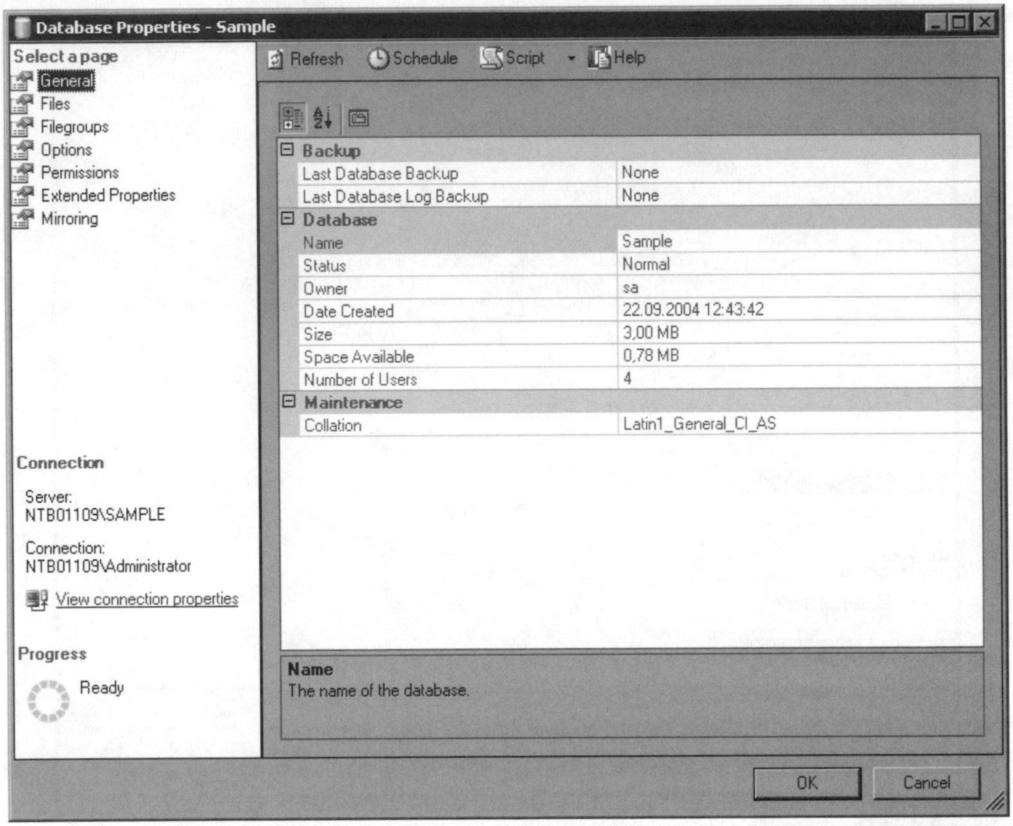

Figure 2-6 *The Database Properties dialog box: the General page*

The **Filegroups** properties of a database contain name(s) of the filegroup(s) to which the database file belongs, the art of the filegroup (default or nondefault), and the allowed operation on the filegroup (read/write or read only).

All database-level options can be displayed and modified by choosing the **Options** properties. There are several groups of options: **Automatic**, **Cursor**, **Miscellaneous**, **Recovery**, and **State**. Three options concern the state of a database:

▶ **Database Read-Only**   Allows read-only access to the database. This prohibits users from modifying any data. (The default value is **False**.)

▶ **Database State**   Describes the state of the database. (The default value is **Normal**.)

▶ **Restrict Access**   Restricts the use of the database to one user at a time. (The default value is **Multiple**.)

If you choose the **Permissions** properties, SQL Server will display the corresponding dialog box with all users and roles along with their permissions. (For the discussion of permissions, see Chapter 12.)

Object Explorer can also be used to modify an existing database. Using Object Explorer, you can modify files and filegroups that belong to the database. To add new data files, right-click the database name, choose **Properties**, and select **Files**. In the **Database Properties** dialog box, click **Add** and type the name of the new file. (In this dialog box, you can also change the autogrowth properties and the location of each existing file.) You can also add a (secondary) filegroup for the database by selecting **Filegroups** and clicking **Add**. (A list of all properties that can be modified is given with the definition of the CREATE DATABASE statement in Chapter 4.)

> ### NOTE
> *Only the system administrator or the database owner can modify the database properties mentioned above.*

To delete a database using Object Explorer, right-click the database name and choose **Delete**.

Managing Tables Using Object Explorer

The next task after the creation of a database is the creation of all tables belonging to it. Again, you can create tables by using either Object Explorer or Transact-SQL.

To create a table using Object Explorer, right-click the subfolder **Tables** of the database, and then click **New Table**. The creation of a table and all other database objects using the Transact-SQL language will be discussed in detail in Chapter 4.

To demonstrate the creation of a table using Object Explorer, the **department** table of the sample database will be used as an example. Enter the names of all columns with their properties in the **New Table** dialog box. Column names, their data types, as well as the NULL property of the column, must be entered in the two-dimensional matrix, as shown in Figure 2-7.

All data types supported by SQL Server can be displayed (and one of them selected) by clicking the arrow sign in the **Data Type** column (the arrow appears after the cell has been selected). Subsequently, you can type entries in the **Length**, **Precision**, and **Scale** rows for the chosen data type in the **Column Properties** window (see Figure 2-7). Some data types, such as CHARACTER, require a value for the **Length** row, and some, such as DECIMAL, require a value in the **Precision** and **Scale** rows. On the other hand, data types such as INTEGER do not need any of these entries to be specified. (The valid entries for a specified data type are highlighted in the list of all possible column properties.)

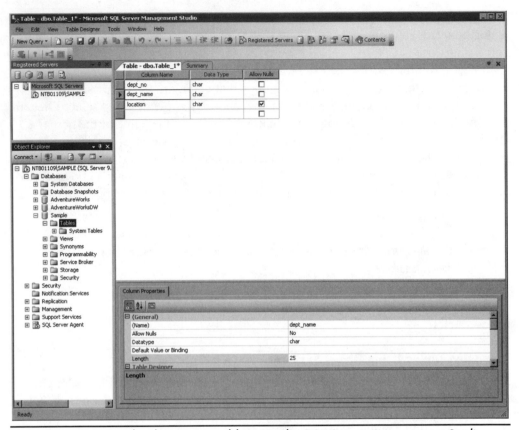

Figure 2-7 *Creating the department table using the SQL Server Management Studio*

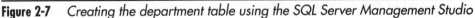

The **Allow Nulls** column must be checked if you want a table column to permit null values to be inserted into that column. Similarly, if there is a default value, it should be entered in the **Default Value or Binding** row of the **Column Properties** window. (A default value is a value that will be inserted in a table column when there is no explicit value entered for it.)

The column **dept_no** is the primary key of the **department** table. (For the discussion of primary keys of the sample database, see Chapter 1.) To specify a column as the primary key of a table, you must first right-click the column and then choose **Set Primary Key**. Finally, close the component window with the information concerning the new table. After that, the system will display the **Choose Name** dialog box, where you can type the table name.

To view the properties of an existing table, first double-click the folder of the database to which the table belongs. Subsequently, double-click **Tables**, and then right-click the name of the table and choose **Properties**. Figure 2-8 shows the **Table Properties** dialog box for the **department** table.

To rename a table, double-click the Tables folder and choose **Rename**. Also, to remove a table, double-click the **Tables** folder in the database to which the table belongs and select **Delete**.

If you create all four tables of the sample database (**employee**, **department**, **project**, and **works_on**), you can use another existing feature of SQL Server Management Studio to display the corresponding E/R- diagram of the sample database. (The process of converting the existing tables of a database in the corresponding E/R- diagram is called *reverse engineering*.)

To create the E/R- model of the sample database, right-click the **Database Diagrams** subfolder of the sample database folder and then select **New Database Diagram**. The first (and only) step is to select tables that will be added to the diagram.

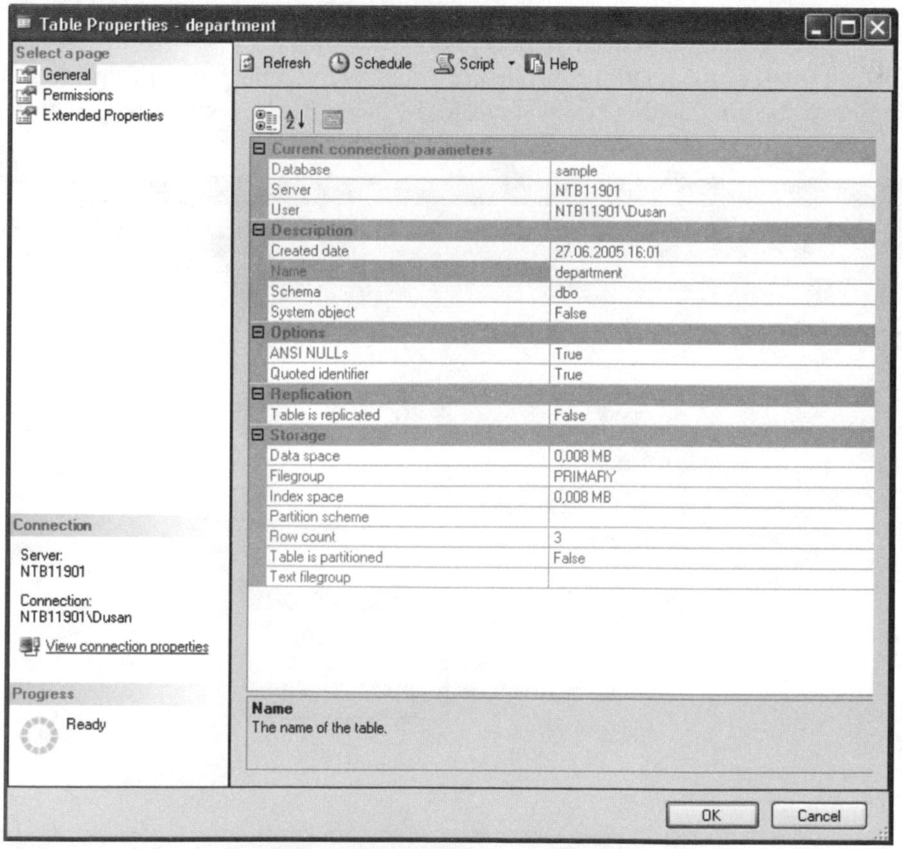

Figure 2-8 *The Table Properties dialog box for the department table*

After adding all four tables of the sample database, the wizard completes the work and creates the diagram (see Figure 2-9).

The diagram in Figure 2-9 is not the final diagram of the sample database, because it shows all four tables with their columns (and the corresponding primary keys), but it does not show any relationship between the tables. A relationship between two tables is based on the primary key of one table and the (possible) corresponding column(s) of the other. (For a detailed discussion of these relationships and referential integrity, see Chapter 4.)

There are exactly three relationships between the existing tables of the sample database: First, the tables **department** and **employee** have a 1:N relationship, because for each value in the primary key column of the **department** table (**dept_no**), there is one or more corresponding values in the column **dept_no** of the **employee** table **employee**. Analogously, there is a relationship between the tables **employee** and **works_on**, because only those values that exist in the primary key of the **employee** table (**emp_no**) appear also in the column **emp_no** of the **works_on** table. (The third relationship is between the tables **project** and **works_on**.)

To create each of the relationships described above, you have to redesign the diagram with the column that corresponds to the primary key column of the other

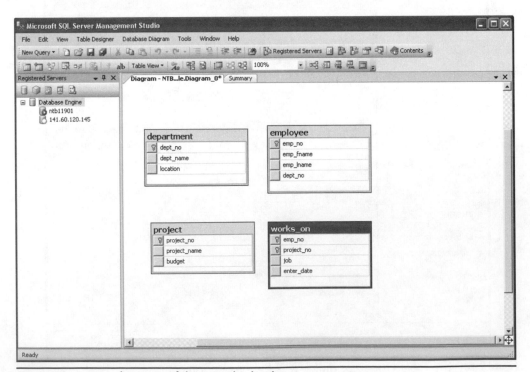

Figure 2-9 *First diagram of the sample database*

table. (Such a column is called a *foreign key*.) To show this, you can use the **employee** table and define its column **dept_no** as the foreign key of the **department** table.

Click the created diagram (it is called **sample_diagram** in our example), right-click the graphical form of the **employee** table in the detail pane, and select **Relationships**. In the **Foreign Key Relationships** dialog box, select **Add**.

Expand **Tables and Columns Specification** and click…. In the **Tables and Columns** dialog box, select the table with the corresponding primary key (the **department** table). Choose the **dept_name** column of this table as the primary key and the column with the same name in the **employee** table as the foreign key and click **OK**.

Figure 2-10 shows the modified **sample_diagram** diagram after all three relationships in the **sample** database have been created.

Authoring Activities Using SQL Server Management Studio

In the previous section we described the capabilities of SQL Server Management Studio, which concern management tasks. Beside these, SQL Server Management Studio gives you a complete authoring environment for all types of queries in SQL Server. You can create, save, load, and edit queries that execute SQL Server and other queries.

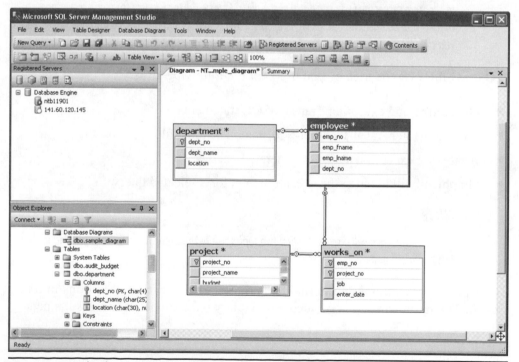

Figure 2-10   *The final diagram of the sample database*

SQL Server Management Studio allows you to work on queries without being connected to a particular SQL Server instance. This tool also gives you the option of developing your queries in a particular environment, where you can associate your queries with projects.

The authoring capability in SQL Server is associated with the **Query Editor** window of SQL Server Management Studio.

Query Editor

If you want to launch the **Query Editor** window, click the **New Query** button in the toolbar of SQL Server Management Studio. The **Query Editor** window appears.

Once you open the **Query Editor** window, the status bar at the bottom of the window will tell you whether your query is in a connected or disconnected state. If you are not connected automatically to the server, the **Connect to SQL Server** dialog box appears, where you can type the name of the database server to which you want to connect and select the authentication mode.

NOTE

*Disconnected editing has more flexibility than connected editing. You can edit queries without having to choose a server, and you can disconnect a given **Query Editor** window from one server and connect it to another, without having to open another window. (You can use the disconnected editing if you click the **Cancel** button in the **Connect to SQL Server** dialog box.)*

Query Editor can be used by end users for the following tasks:

▶ Generating and executing Transact-SQL statements

▶ Storing the generated Transact-SQL statements in a file

▶ Analyzing execution plans for generated queries

▶ Graphically illustrating the execution plan for a selected query

NOTE

In this chapter we will discuss the first two topics, while the other two will be explained in detail in Chapters 9 and 22.

Query Editor contains an internal text editor and a selection of buttons in its toolbar. The main window is divided into a query pane (upper) and a results pane (lower). (See Figure 2-11.) Users enter the Transact-SQL statements (queries) that they want to execute into the query pane, and after SQL Server has processed the queries, the output is displayed in the results pane.

The following example will show you how queries are entered and processed by SQL Server. If you type the two Transact-SQL statements shown in Figure 2-11, click the **Query** button in the Query Editor's toolbar and select **Execute** or click F5. The results of these statements will be shown in the results pane of Query Editor.

NOTE

*You can open several different windows—that is, several different connections to one or more SQL Server instances. You create new connections by clicking the **New Query** button in the toolbar.*

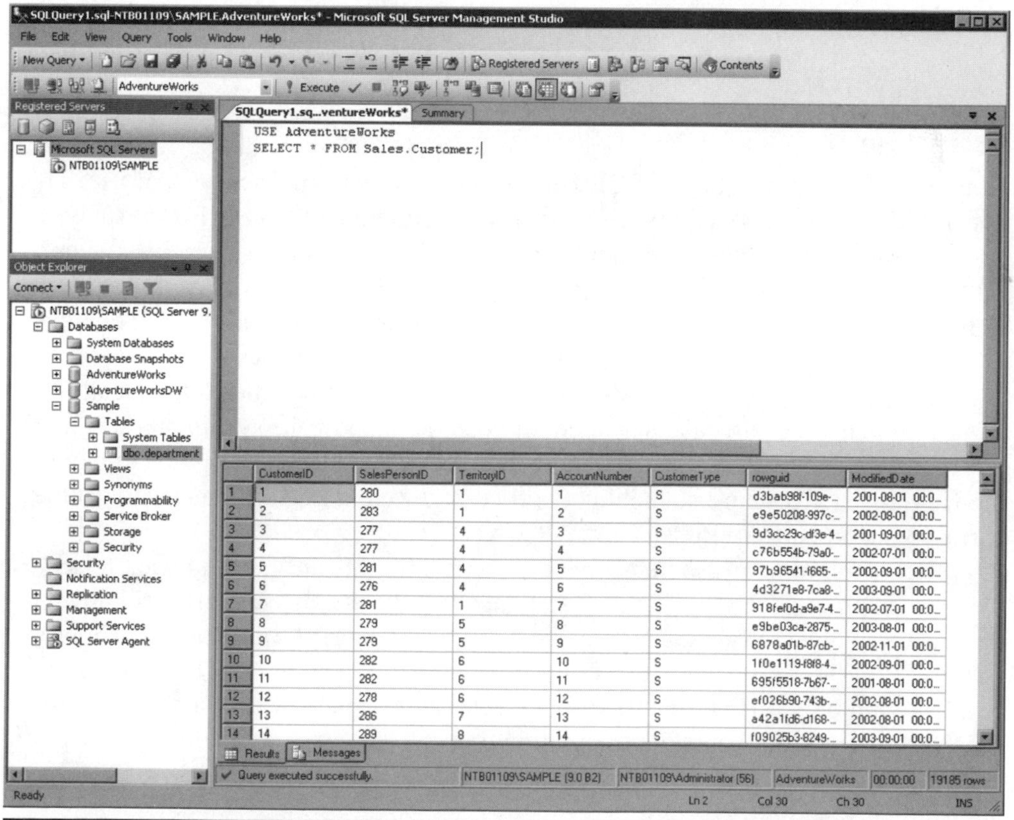

![Screenshot of Microsoft SQL Server Management Studio Query Editor showing the query "USE AdventureWorks / SELECT * FROM Sales.Customer;" in the query pane and a results grid below with columns CustomerID, SalesPersonID, TerritoryID, AccountNumber, CustomerType, rowguid, and ModifiedDate.]

Figure 2-11 *Query Editor with a query and its results*

NOTE

*The first statement in Figure 2-11, USE, specifies the **AdventureWorks** database as the current database. The second statement, SELECT, displays all the rows of the **Customer** table, which belongs to this database.*

SQL Server contains the additional information that is displayed in the status bar of the **Query Editor** window. The following information is displayed:

▶ The status of the current operation (in the left corner of the window)

▶ Database server name

▶ Current user name and server process ID

▶ Current database name

▶ Elapsed time for the execution of the last query

▶ The number of retrieved rows

Query Pane

One of the main properties of SQL Server Management Studio is ease of use. This general idea is also applied to the **Query Editor** component. Query Editor supports a lot of features that make coding of Transact-SQL statements easier. First, Query Editor uses syntax highlighting to improve the readability of Transact-SQL statements. It displays all reserved words in blue, all variables in black, strings in red, and comments in green. (For a discussion of reserved words, see the next chapter.)

There is also the context-sensitive help function called **Dynamic Help** that allows you to get help on a particular statement. If you do not know the syntax of a statement, just highlight that statement in the editor and select the **Dynamic Help** function on the **Help** menu. You can also highlight options of different SQL statements to get the corresponding text from Books Online.

Object Explorer can also help you edit queries. For instance, if you want to see the corresponding CREATE TABLE statement for the **employee** table, drill down to this database object, right-click the table name, select **Script Table as**, and choose **CREATE to New Query Editor Window**. Figure 2-12 shows the **Query Editor** window with the CREATE TABLE statement. (This capability extends also to other objects, such as stored procedures and functions.)

Solution-Based Query Editing

Query editing in SQL Server Management Studio is solution-based. If you start a blank query using the **New Query** button, it will still be based on a blank solution. You can see this by choosing Solution Explorer from the **View** menu, right after opening your blank query.

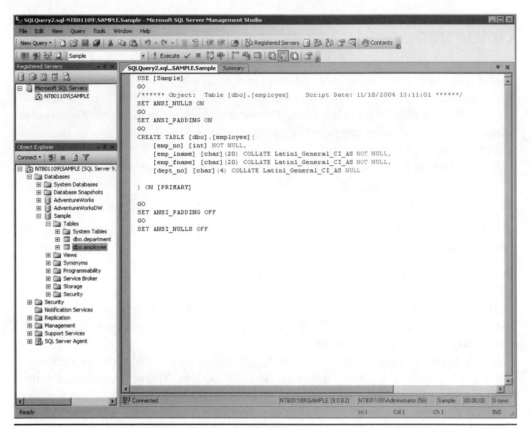

Figure 2-12   *The Query Editor windows with the CREATE TABLE statement*

A solution can have zero, one, or more projects associated with it. If you want to associate a project with the solution, close your blank solution, Solution Explorer, and the **Query Editor** window, and start a new project by clicking on the **File** Menu and selecting **New** and then **Project**. The project is a method of organizing files in a selected location. You can choose a name for the project and select its location on disk. When you create a new project, by default you will start a new solution. You can add a project to an existing solution using the **Solution Explorer** component.

Once the new project and solution are created, Solution Explorer will show nodes in each project for **Connections**, **Queries**, and **Miscellaneous files**.

SQL Server Management Studio supports version control using the integration with MS Visual Source Safe. As we already stated, Solution Explorer allows you to organize and store related scripts as parts of a project. These script files can be checked in and out of the version control system directly from Solution Explorer.

Conclusion

This chapter covers the new SQL Server component called SQL Server Management Studio. This tool is very useful for end users as well as administrators. First, it allows many administrative functions to be performed. These are touched on here but are covered in more detail later in the book. The most important functions of SQL Server Management Studio concerning end users—database and table creation—are discussed in more detail in this chapter.

SQL Server Management Studio contains several component windows:

▶ Registered Servers

▶ Object Explorer

▶ Query Editor

▶ Solution Explorer

The **Registered Servers** component window allows you to register SQL Server instances and connect to them. The Object Explorer window contains a tree view of all the database objects in a server.

Query Editor is a subcomponent of SQL Server Management Studio that allows end users to generate, execute, and store Transact-SQL statements. Additionally, it provides the ability to analyze queries by displaying the execution plan, and it also provides the ability to create suggestions with respect to index creation.

The Solution Explorer component allows you to create solutions. A solution can have zero or more projects associated with it.

The next chapter introduces the Transact-SQL language and describes its main components. After introducing the basic concepts and existing data types, the chapter also describes system functions that Transact-SQL supports.

Exercises

E.2.1

Using SQL Server Management Studio, create a database called **test**. The database is stored in the file named **testdate_a** of the directory C:\tmp and the space allocated is 10MB. The file in which the database is located should grow with portions of 2MB and should not be larger than 20MB.

E.2.2

Using SQL Server Management Studio, change the transaction log for the **test** database. The initial size of the file is 3MB, with growth of 20 percent. Allow the file for the transaction log to autogrow.

E.2.3

Using SQL Server Management Studio, allow the use of the **test** database only to the database owner and system administrator. Is it possible that several users could use the database at the same time?

E.2.4

Using SQL Server Management Studio, create all four tables of the sample database (see Chapter 1) with all their columns.

E.2.5

Using SQL Server Management Studio, view which tables the **AdventureWorks** database contains. After that, choose the **person.address** table and view its properties.

E.2.6

Using Query Editor, type the following Transact-SQL statement:

CREATE DATABASE test

Explain the error message shown in the result pane.

E.2.7

Store the Transact-SQL statement (E.2.6) in the file C:\tmp\createdb.sql.

E.2.8

Using Query Editor, how can you make the **test** database the current database?

E.2.9

Using Query Editor, make the **AdventureWorks** database the current database and execute the following Transact-SQL statement: SELECT * FROM Sales.Customer
Stop the execution of that statement. How can you do it?

Transact-SQL Language

CHAPTER
3

SQL Components

This chapter introduces the elementary objects and basic operators supported by SQL Server. First, the basic language elements, including constants, identifiers, and delimiters, are described. Every elementary object has a corresponding data type, and the subsequent section discusses data types in detail. Additionally, all existing operators and functions of SQL Server are explained. At the end of the chapter, NULL values are introduced.

SQL's Basic Objects

The language of SQL Server, Transact-SQL, has the same basic features as other common programming languages:

- Constants or literal values
- Delimiters
- Identifiers
- Reserved keywords

A *literal* value is an alphanumerical, hexadecimal, or numeric constant. A string constant contains one or more characters of the SQL Server character set enclosed in two single straight quotation marks or double straight quotation marks (single quotation marks are preferred due to the multiple uses of double quotation marks, as discussed in a moment). If you want to include the single quotation mark within a string delimited by single quotation marks, use two consecutive single quotation marks within the string. Hexadecimal constants are used to represent nonprintable characters (and other binary data). Each hexadecimal constant begins with the characters "0x" followed by an even number of characters or numbers. Examples 3.1 and 3.2 illustrate some valid and invalid string constants and hexadecimal constants.

EXAMPLE 3.1

Some valid string constants and hexadecimal constants:

> 'Philadelphia'
> "Berkeley, CA 94710"
> '9876'
> 'Apostrophe is displayed like this: can''t ' (note the two consecutive single
>   quotation marks)
> 0x53514C0D

EXAMPLE 3.2

The following are *not* string constants:

'AB'C' (odd number of single quotes)
'New York" (same type of quotation mark—single or double—must be used
at each end of the string)

Beginning with SQL Server Version 6.0, double quotation marks have had two meanings. In addition to enclosing strings, quotation marks can also be used as delimiters for so-called *delimited identifiers*. Delimited identifiers are a special kind of identifier usually used to allow the use of reserved keywords as identifiers and also to allow spaces in the names of database objects.

NOTE

Differentiation between single quotes and quotation marks was first introduced in the SQL92 standard. In the case of identifiers, this standard differentiates between regular and delimited identifiers. Two key differences are that delimited identifiers are enclosed in quotation marks (Transact-SQL also supports the use of square brackets: [identifier]) and are case sensitive. Single quotes are only used for delimiting strings. Generally, delimited identifiers were introduced to allow the specification of identifiers, which are otherwise identical to reserved keywords. Specifically, delimited identifiers protect you from using names (identifiers, variable names) that could be introduced as reserved keywords in one of the future SQL standards. Additionally, delimited identifiers can contain characters that are normally illegal within identifier names, such as blanks.

In SQL Server, the use of quotation marks is defined using the QUOTED_IDENTIFIER option of the SET statement. If this option is set to ON, an identifier in quotation marks will be defined as a delimited identifier. In this case, quotation marks cannot be used for delimiting strings. By default, quotation marks can be used in the same way as single quotes for delimiting strings. However, to avoid ambiguity, the use of single quotes for string constants is preferred.

The numeric constants include all integer, fixed-point, and floating-point values with and without signs (see Example 3.3).

EXAMPLE 3.3

The following are numeric constants:

130
−130.00
−0.357E5 (scientific notation—nEm means n multiplied by 10^m)
22.3E-3

A constant always has a data type and a length, and both depend on the format of the constant. Additionally, every numeric constant has a precision and a scale factor. (The data types of the different kinds of literal values are explained later in this chapter.)

Comments

There are different ways to specify a comment in a Transact-SQL statement. The pairs of characters /* and */ mark the enclosed text as a comment. In this case, the comment may extend over several lines. Furthermore, the characters -- (two hyphens) indicate that the remainder of the current line is a comment (see Examples 13.1 and 13.2 for the use of comments). (The two characters -- comply with the ANSI SQL standard, while /* and */ are the extensions of the Transact-SQL language.)

Identifiers

In Transact-SQL, identifiers are used to identify database objects such as tables and indices. They are represented by character strings that may include up to 128 characters and can contain letters, numerals, or the following characters: _ , @, #, and $. Each name must begin with a letter or one of the following characters: _ , #, or @. The character # at the beginning of a table or stored procedure name denotes a temporary object, while @ at the beginning of a name denotes a variable. As indicated earlier, these rules don't apply to delimited identifiers (also known as quoted identifiers), which can contain, or begin with, any character (other than the delimiters themselves).

Reserved Keywords

Each programming language has a set of names with reserved meanings, which must be written and used in the defined format. Names of this kind are called *reserved keywords*. Transact-SQL uses a variety of such names, which, as in many other programming languages, cannot be used as object names (unless the objects are specified as delimited, or quoted, identifiers, but the use of reserved words as object names is not recommended).

NOTE

In Transact-SQL, the names of all data types and system functions, such as CHARACTER and INTEGER, are not reserved keywords. They can therefore be used for denoting objects. (Do not use reserved words as object names! Such a use makes Transact-SQL statements difficult to read and understand.)

Data Types

All the data values of a column must be of the same data type. Transact-SQL uses different data types, which can be categorized in the following way:

▶ Numeric data types

▶ String data types

▶ Data types for date and/or time

▶ Derived data types

▶ Miscellaneous data types

▶ User-defined data types

Numeric Data Types

Numeric data types are used to represent numbers. Transact-SQL uses the following numeric data types:

Data Type	Explanation
INT	Represents integer values, which can be stored in 4 bytes. INT is the short form for INTEGER.
SMALLINT	Represents integer values, which can be stored in 2 bytes. (The range of values of the SMALLINT data type is therefore between -32768 and 32767.)
TINYINT	Represents non-negative integer values, which can be stored in 1 byte. (The range of values of the TINYINT data type is between 0 and 255.)
BIGINT	Represents integer values, which can be stored in 8 bytes. The range of values of the BIGINT data type is therefore between -2^{63} and $2^{63}-1$.
DECIMAL(p,[s])	Describes fixed-point values. The argument **p** (precision) specifies the total number of digits with assumed decimal point **s** (scale) digits from the right. (DECIMAL values are stored, depending on the value of **p**, in 5 to 17 bytes. DEC is the short form for DECIMAL.)
NUMERIC(p,[s])	Synonym for DECIMAL.
REAL	Used for floating-point values. The range of positive values is approximately from $2.23E-308$ through $1.79E+308$, and the range of negative values is approximately from $-1.18E-38$ through $-1.18E+38$ (the value zero can also be stored).
FLOAT[(p)]	Represents floating-point values, like REAL. **p** defines the precision with $\mathbf{p}<25$ as single precision (4 byte) and $\mathbf{p}>=25$ as double precision (8 byte).
MONEY	Used for representing monetary values. MONEY values correspond to 8-byte DECIMAL values and are rounded to four digits after the decimal point.
SMALLMONEY	Corresponds to the data type MONEY but is stored in 4 bytes.

String Data Types

There are three types of string data types: character strings, binary strings, and bit strings. The following character string data types are used:

Data Type	Explanation
CHAR[(n)]	Represents a string, where **n** is the number of characters inside the string. The maximum value of **n** is 8000. CHARACTER(n) is an additional equivalent form for CHAR(n). If **n** is omitted, the length of the string is assumed to be 1.
VARCHAR[(n)]	Describes a string with varying length ($0 < n \leq 8000$). In contrast to the CHAR data type, the values for the VARCHAR data type are stored in their actual length. This data type has two synonyms: CHAR VARYING and CHARACTER VARYING.
NCHAR[(n)]	The NCHAR data type stores fixed-length Unicode character data. (Unicode will be discussed in detail in Chapter 15.) The main difference between the CHAR and NCHAR data types is that each NCHAR character is stored in 2 bytes, while each CHAR character uses 1 byte of storage space. The maximum number of characters in a column of NCHAR data type is 4000 because each character is stored in two bytes.
NVARCHAR[(n)]	The NVARCHAR data type stores Unicode characters of varying lengths. The main difference between the VARCHAR and the NVARCHAR data types is that each NVARCHAR character is stored in 2 bytes, while each VARCHAR character uses 1 byte of storage space. The maximum number of characters in a column of NVARCHAR data type is 4000.
TEXT[(n)]	Defines a fixed-length string up to 2GB. (This data type is described later in the chapter, as is the data type IMAGE.)
NTEXT[(n)]	The NTEXT data type stores large character data of varying length. The maximum number of bytes in a column of NTEXT data type is $2^{30} - 1$. This data can be a sequence of single-byte or multibyte characters. The main difference between the TEXT and the NTEXT data types is that each NTEXT character is stored in 2 bytes, while each TEXT character uses 1 byte of storage space.

NOTE

*VARCHAR denotes a string of variable length, which can contain printable and nonprintable characters as well as null values. The data type VARCHAR is identical to the data type CHAR except for one difference: if the content of a CHAR(n) string is shorter than **n** characters, the rest of the string is padded with blanks. (A value of the VARCHAR data type is always stored in its actual length.)*

Binary data types describe data objects being represented in the internal format of the system. The binary string data types are described here:

Data Type	Explanation
BINARY[(n)]	Specifies a bit string of fixed length with exactly **n** bytes (0 < **n** ≤ 8000).
VARBINARY[(n)]	Specifies a bit string of variable length with up to **n** bytes (0 < **n** ≤ 8000).
IMAGE[(n)]	Specifies a bit string of fixed length with nearly unlimited values. (The limit lies at $2^{31} - 1$ bytes.)
BIT	Used for specifying the Boolean data type with three possible values: false, true, and NULL. Each value of this data type is stored in 1 bit. Columns of type BIT cannot be indexed.

NOTE

The previously mentioned string data type TEXT, together with the data type IMAGE, constitutes the text/image data type. Data objects of the type IMAGE can contain any kind of data (load modules, audio/video), while data objects of the data type TEXT can contain any text data (i.e., printable data). These data types are marked as deprecated features and can be replaced by VARCHAR(MAX) and VARBINARY(MAX) data types (see the following section).

Text/image data are stored separately from all other values of a database using a b-tree structure that points to the fragments of text/image data. (b-tree is a treelike data structure in which all of the bottom nodes are the same number of levels away from the root of the tree.) For each table that contains more than one column with text/image data, all values of the columns are stored together.

Using VARCHAR(MAX) and VARBINARY(MAX)

SQL Server 2005 introduces three new data types concerning LOBs (large objects):

- ► VARCHAR(MAX)
- ► NVARCHAR(MAX)
- ► VARBINARY(MAX)

The MAX option expands the storage capabilities of of the VARCHAR, NVAR-CHAR, and VARBINARY data types. (VARCHAR(MAX), NVARCHAR(MAX), and VARBINARY(MAX) are called Large Value data types.) The Large Value data types allow you to store up to $2^{31} - 1$ bytes of data. These data types are similar in behavior to VARCHAR, NVARCHAR, and VARBINARY data types, and this similarity allows SQL Server to store and retrieve large character, Unicode, and binary data more efficiently.

The Large Value data types can replace the text/image data already described in this section. On the other hand, they allow you to work with SQL Server in a way that was not possible using the TEXT, NTEXT and IMAGE data types from previous versions of SQL Server. For example, in SQL Server, you can now define variables that can store large amounts of data (2**31 bytes of character and binary data, and 2**30 bytes of Unicode data).

NOTE

With these new data types, SQL Server eliminates the difference between small and large values to provide you with a comprehensive programming model.

Specifying Date and Time

SQL Server supports the following date and time data types:

Data Type	Explanation
DATETIME	Specifies a date and time, with each value being stored as an integer value in 4 bytes.
SMALLDATETIME	Specifies a date and time, with each value being stored as an integer value in 2 bytes.

The data types DATETIME and SMALLDATETIME are stored as numeric values. The date value is stored in the first 4- or 2-byte field as the number of days starting from January 1, 1753 (DATETIME) or January 1, 1900 (SMALLDATETIME) and ranging through December 31, 9999 (DATETIME) or June 6, 2079 (SMALL-DATETIME). The time value is stored in the second 4- or 2-byte field as the number of three-hundredths of a second (DATETIME) or minutes (SMALLDATETIME) having passed since midnight.

The date value in the Transact-SQL language is by default specified as a string in a format like "mm dd yyyy" (e.g., 'Jan 10 1993') inside two single quotes or double quotation marks. (Note that the relative order of month, day, and year can be controlled by the SET DATEFORMAT statement; additionally, SQL Server recognizes numeric month values with delimiters of / or -). Similarly, the time value is specified in the format 'hh:mm AM' or 'hh:mm PM' (e.g., '11:31 PM'). See Examples 3.4 and 3.5 for possible date and time entries.

NOTE

SQL Server supports a variety of input formats for date and time values. Both objects are identified separately; thus, date and time values can be specified in any order or alone. If one of the values is omitted, SQL Server uses the default values. (The default value for time is 12:00 AM, and the default date is January 1, 1900.)

EXAMPLE 3.4

The following date descriptions can be entered:

>   '28/5/1959' (with SET DATEFORMAT dmy)
>   'May 28, 1959'
>   '1959 MAY 28'

EXAMPLE 3.5

The following time expressions can be used:

>   '8:45 AM'
>   '4 pm'

Derived Data Types

SQL Server supports two data types that can be derived from simple data types: TIMESTAMP and SYSNAME.

Data Type	Explanation
TIMESTAMP	Specifies a column being defined as VARBINARY(8) (or BINARY(8), depending on nullability of the column). The system maintains a current value (not a date or time) for each database (accessible via the global variable @@dbts), which it increments whenever any row with a timestamp column is inserted or updated (and sets the timestamp column to that value). Thus, timestamp columns can be used to determine the relative time when rows were last changed.
SYSNAME	Specifies the name of database objects in the system catalog (defined as NVARCHAR(128)).

Miscellaneous Data Types

SQL Server supports several data types that do not belong to any of the data type groups described previously. They are as follows:

- ► CURSOR
- ► UNIQUEIDENTIFIER
- ► SQL_VARIANT
- ► TABLE
- ► XML

The data type CURSOR allows the creation of a cursor variable in a stored procedure. (Cursors allow processing of data one row at a time. The description of cursors is beyond the scope of this book.) This data type cannot be used as the data type for a column in a table.

As its name implies, UNIQUEIDENTIFIER is a unique identification number stored as a 16-byte binary string. This data type is closely related to the GUID (globally unique identifier), which is used for data replication (see Chapter 25). The initialization of a column or a variable of type UNIQUEIDENTIFIER can be provided using the function NEWID or with a string constant written in a special form using hexadecimal digits and hyphens.

The SQL_VARIANT data type can be used to store values of various data types at the same time, such as numeric values, strings, and date values. (The only types of values that cannot be stored are text/image and TIMESTAMP.) Each value of an SQL_VARIANT column has two parts: the data value and the information that describes the value. (This information contains all properties of the actual data type of the value, such as length, scale, and precision.) SQL Server supports the SQL_VARIANT_PROPERTY function, which displays the attached information for each value of a SQL_VARIANT column. For the use of the SQL_VARIANT data type, see Example 4.11.

NOTE

Declare a column of a table using the SQL_VARIANT data type only if it is really necessary. A column should have this data type if its values may be of different types or if it is not possible to determine the type of a column during the database design process.

The TABLE data type specifies what its name says: the data type that can store rows with several and different values. Such a data type can be used in many useful cases. However, SQL Server restricts its use to two areas:

▶ As a local variable

▶ As a return value of a user-defined function. (Local variables, as well as user-defined functions, are defined in Chapter 8.)

The use of the TABLE data type is shown in Example 8.10.

SQL Server 2005 introduces an Extensible Markup Language (XML) data type that allows you to store an XML fragment or document in SQL Server databases. Instances of an XML data type can be columns in different database objects, such as table, function or stored procedure arguments, or variables in a function or stored procedure. The XML data type is described in detail in Chapter 30.

User-Defined Data Types

SQL Server 2005 introduces the new user-defined data type (UDT), which can be used to create your own data types. Procedural objects, including user-defined functions, procedures, and triggers, can be written in languages such as C# and Visual Basic 2005. UDTs can be created using these languages, too.

The description of UDTs is outside the scope of this book.

Predicates

A *predicate* defines a logical condition being applied to rows in a table. The common logical conditions with two values (true, false) are extended in the SQL language by a third value (unknown or not applicable).

The Transact-SQL language supports the following predicates, which are described in detail in Chapter 5:

▶ All relational operators

▶ BETWEEN operator

▶ IN operator

▶ LIKE operator

▶ NULL operator

▶ ALL and ANY operators

▶ EXISTS function

Aggregate Functions

Aggregate functions are applied to a group of data values (in other words, from multiple rows) from a column. Aggregate functions always return a single value. The Transact-SQL language supports six aggregate functions:

- ▶ AVG
- ▶ MAX
- ▶ MIN
- ▶ SUM
- ▶ COUNT
- ▶ COUNT_BIG

AVG (short for *average*) calculates the arithmetic mean of the data values contained within a column. The column must contain numeric values. MAX calculates the maximum, and MIN the minimum, data value of the column. The column can contain numeric, string, and date/time values.

SUM calculates the total of all data values in a column. The column must contain numeric values. COUNT calculates the number of (non-null) data values in a column. The only aggregate function not being applied to columns is COUNT(*). This function returns the number of rows (whether or not particular columns have null values). COUNT_BIG function is analogous to the COUNT function. The only difference is that COUNT_BIG returns a value of the BIGINT data type. Aggregate functions, together with statistical aggregates and superaggregates, are described in detail in Chapter 5.

NOTE

Since SQL Server 2005, it is possible to write user-defined aggregates using .NET languages, such as C# and Visual Basic 2005.

Scalar Functions

In addition to aggregate functions, SQL Server provides several scalar functions that are used in the construction of scalar expressions. (A scalar function operates on a single value or list of values, as opposed to aggregate functions, which operate on the data from multiple rows.) Scalar functions can be categorized as follows:

- ▶ Numeric functions
- ▶ Date functions
- ▶ String functions
- ▶ Text/image functions
- ▶ System functions

Numeric Functions

Numeric functions within the Transact-SQL language are mathematical functions for modifying numeric values. The following numeric functions are available:

Function	Explanation
ABS(n)	Returns the absolute value (i.e., negative values are returned as positive) of the numeric expression **n**. Example: SELECT ABS(−5.767) = 5.767, SELECT ABS(6.384) = 6.384
ACOS(n)	Calculates arc cosine of **n. n**, as well as the resulting value, belongs to the FLOAT data type.
ASIN(n)	Calculates the arc sine of **n. n**, as well as the resulting value, belongs to the FLOAT data type.
ATAN(n)	Calculates the arc tangent of **n. n**, as well as the resulting value, belongs to the FLOAT data type.
ATN2(n,m)	Calculates the arc tangent of **n/m. n, m**, as well as the resulting value, belongs to the FLOAT data type.
CEILING(n)	Returns the smallest integer value greater or equal to the specified value **n**. Examples: SELECT CEILING(4.88) = 5, SELECT CEILING(−4.88) = −4
COS(n)	Calculates the cosine of **n. n**, as well as the resulting value, belongs to the FLOAT data type.
COT(n)	Calculates the cotangent of **n. n**, as well as the resulting value, belongs to the FLOAT data type.
DEGREES(n)	Converts radians to degrees. Examples: SELECT DEGREES(PI()/2) = 90.0, SELECT DEGREES(0.75) = 42.97
EXP(n)	Calculates the value $e^{**}n$. Examples: SELECT EXP(0.75= 2.12, SELECT EXP(1) = 2.7183
FLOOR(n)	Calculates the largest integer value less than or equal to the specified values **n**. Example: SELECT FLOOR(4.88) = 4
LOG(n)	Calculates the natural (i.e., base e) logarithm of **n**. Examples: SELECT LOG(4.67) = 1.54, SELECT LOG(0.12) = −2.12

Function	Explanation
LOG10(n)	Calculates the logarithm (base 10) for **n**. Examples: SELECT $LOG_{10}(4.67) = 0.67$, SELECT $LOG_{10}(0.12) = -0.92$
PI()	Returns the value of the number pi (3.14).
POWER(x,y)	Calculates the value **x**y**. Examples: SELECT POWER(3.12,5) = 295.65, SELECT POWER(81,0.5) = 9
RADIANS(n)	Converts degrees to radians. Examples: SELECT RADIANS(90.0) = 1.57, SELECT RADIANS(42.97) = 0.75
RAND	Returns a random number between 0 and 1 with a FLOAT data type.
ROUND(n,p,t)	Rounds the values of the number **n** by using the precision **p**. Use positive values of **p** for rounding right of the decimal point and negative values to round on the left side. An optional parameter t causes **n** to be truncated. Examples: SELECT ROUND(5.4567,3) = 5.4570, SELECT ROUND(345.4567,−1) = 350.0000, SELECT ROUND(345.4567,−1,1) = 340.0000
ROWCOUNT_BIG	Returns the number of rows that have been affected by the last Transact-SQL statement executed by the system. The return value of this function has the BIGINT data type. (See also the global variable @@ROWCOUNT.)
SIGN(n)	Returns the sign of the value **n** as a number (+1 for positive, −1 for negative value, and 0 for zero). Example: SELECT SIGN(0.88) = 1
SIN(n)	Calculates the sine of **n**. **n**, as well as the resulting value, belongs to the FLOAT data type.
SQRT(n)	Calculates the square root of **n**. Example: SELECT SQRT(9) = 3
SQUARE(n)	Returns the square of the given expression. **n** belongs to the FLOAT data type.
TAN(n)	Calculates the tangent of **n**. **n**, as well as the resulting value, belongs to the FLOAT data type.

Date Functions

Date functions calculate the respective date or time portion of an expression or return the value from a time interval. All date functions use the following date or time units:

- ► yy (year)
- ► qq (quarter)
- ► mm (month)
- ► dy (day of year) for a single day within the year $(0 < n < 367)$
- ► dd (day) for a day
- ► dw (day of week) for a weekday

- ► wk (week)
- ► hh (hour)
- ► mi (minute)
- ► ss (second)
- ► ms (millisecond)

SQL Server supports the following date functions:

Function	Explanation
GETDATE()	Returns the current system date and time. Example: SELECT GETDATE() = 2005-01-01 13:03:31.390
DATEPART(item,date)	Returns the specified part **item** of a date **date** as an integer. Examples: SELECT DATEPART(month, '01.01.2005') = 1, SELECT DATEPART(weekday, '01.01.2005') = 7
DATENAME(item, date)	Returns the specified part **item** of the date **date** as a character string (Mon,Tue,...). Example: SELECT DATENAME(weekday,'01.01.2005') = Saturday
DATEDIFF(item,dat1,dat2)	Calculates the difference between the two date parts **dat1** and **dat2** and returns the result as an integer in units specified by the value **item**. Example: SELECT DATEDIFF(YEAR, BirthDate, GETDATE()) AS Age FROM employees = returns the age of each employee
DATEADD(item,number,date)	Adds the number **number** of units specified by the value **item** to the given date **date**. Example: SELECT DATEADD(DAY,3,HireDate) AS Age FROM employees = adds 3 days to the enterdate of every employee

String Functions

String functions are used for manipulating data values in a column, usually of a string data type. SQL Server supports the following string functions:

Function	Explanation
ASCII(character)	Converts the specified character to the equivalent integer (ASCII-) Code. Returns an integer. Example: SELECT ASCII('A') = 65
CAST(a AS type [(length)])	Converts an expression **a** into the specified data type **type** (if possible). **a** could be any valid SQL Server expression. Example: SELECT CAST(3000000000 AS BIGINT) = 3000000000
CHAR(integer)	Converts the ASCII-Code to the equivalent character. Example: SELECT CHAR(65) = 'A'
CONVERT(type[(length)],a)	Equivalent to CAST, but the arguments are specified differently. CONVERT can be used with any data type.

Function	Explanation
CHARINDEX(z1,z2)	Returns the starting position where the partial string z1 first occus in the string **z2**. Returns 0 if **z1** does not occur in **z2**. Example: SELECT CHARINDEX ('bl','table') $= 3$
DIFFERENCE(z1,z2)	Returns the difference of SOUNDEX values of two strings **z1** and **z2**. (SOUNDEX returns a number, which specifies the sound of a string. With this method, strings with similar sounds can be determined.) Example: SELECT DIFFERENCE('spelling', 'telling') $= 2$ (sounds a little bit similar, 0 $=$ doesn't sound similar)
LOWER(z1)	Converts all uppercase letters of the string **z1** to lowercase letters. Lowercase letters and numbers, and other characters, do not change. Example: SELECT LOWER ("BiG") $=$ "big"
LTRIM(z)	Removes leading blanks in the string **z**. Example: SELECT LTRIM(' String') $=$ 'String'
NEWID()	Creates a unique ID number that consists of a 16-byte binary string intended to store the UNIQUEIDENTIFIER data type. Example: SELECT NEWID() $=$ e.g., D9792566-ABDD-11D3-9FC6-0050041D4A60
REPLICATE(z,i)	Repeats string **z, i** times. Example: SELECT REPLICATE('a',10) $=$ aaaaaaaaaa
REVERSE(z)	Displays the string **z** in the reverse order. Example: SELECT REVERSE ('calculate') $=$ etaluclac
RIGHT(z,length)	Returns the last **length** characters from the string **z**. Example: SELECT RIGHT-('Notebook',4) $=$ book
RTRIM(z)	Removes trailing blanks of the string **z**. Example: SELECT RTRIM('Notebook ') $=$ 'Notebook'
SOUNDEX(a)	Returns a four-character SOUNDEX code to determine the similarity between two strings. Example: SELECT SOUNDEX('spelling') $=$ S145
SPACE(length)	Returns a string with spaces of length specified by **length**. Example: SELECT SPACE(5) $=$ " "
STR(f,[len [,d]])	Converts the specified float expression **f** into a string. **len** is the length of the string including decimal point, sign, digits, and spaces (10 by default), and **d** is the number of digits to the right of the decimal point to be returned. Example: SELECT STR(3.45678,4,2) $=$ '3.46'
STUFF(z1,a,length,z2)	Replaces the partial string **z1** with the partial string **z2** starting at position **a**, replacing **length** characters of **z1**. Examples: SELECT STUFF ('Notebook',5,0,' in a ') $=$ 'Note in a book', SELECT STUFF('Notebook',1,4, 'Hand') $=$ 'Handbook'
SUBSTRING(z,a,length)	Creates a partial string from string **z** starting at the position **a** with a length of **length**. Example: SELECT SUBSTRING('wardrobe',1,4) $=$ 'ward'
UPPER(z)	Converts all lowercase letters of string **z** to uppercase letters. Uppercase letters and numbers do not change. Example: SELECT UPPER('loWer') $=$ 'LOWER'

Text/Image Functions

Text/image functions are designed for use with columns of the text/image data types. SQL Server supports the following text/image functions:

Function	Explanation
PATINDEX(%pattern%, expr)	Returns an integer value specifying the position of the string **pattern** in the expression **expr**. If the value 0 is returned, the string was not found. Example: SELECT PATINDEX('%gs%','longstring') = 4, SELECT RIGHT(ContactName, LEN(ContactName)-PATINDEX('% %',ContactName)) AS 'First Name' FROM Customers = returns all First Names from the column customers
TEXTPTR(column)	Returns a pointer pointing to the first page in which the TEXT or IMAGE column **column** is stored. The result can be used with the UPDATETEXT, WRITETEXT, or READTEXT statements (see Chapter 8). Avoid using this feature, because it will be removed in a future version of SQL Server.
TEXTVALID("table.column",pointer)	Returns 1 if the pointer **pointer** is valid for the TEXT or IMAGE column **column**. Avoid using this feature, because it will be removed in a future version of SQL Server.

In addition to these functions, the TEXTSIZE option in the SET statement defines the maximum number of bytes that can be returned with a SELECT statement from a **text/image** column. The current value is stored in the global variable @@**textsize** (see Chapter 8 for additional information).

System Functions

SQL Server system functions provide extensive information about database objects. Most system functions use an internal numeric identifier (ID), which is assigned to each database object by SQL Server at its creation. Using this identifier, the SQL Server system can uniquely identify each object. System functions can be grouped into functions with and without parameters. The SQL Server system functions with parameters are described here:

Function	Explanation
COALESCE(a1,a2,...)	Returns for a given list of expressions a_1, a_2,... the value of the first expression that is not NULL.
COL_LENGTH(obj, col)	Returns the length of the column **col** belonging to a database object (table or view) **obj**. Example: SELECT COL_LENGTH('customers','CustomerID') = 10
COL_NAME(o_id,s_id)	Returns the name of the column belonging to the object **o_id** with the identifier **s_id**. Example: SELECT COL_NAME(OBJECT_ID('products') ,4) = 'CategoryID'

Function	Explanation
DATABASEPROPERTYEX (database, property)	Returns the current setting of the specified database option or property for the specified database. (This system function is described in detail in Chapter 18.)
DATALENGTH(z)	Calculates the length (in bytes) of the result of the expression **z**. Example: SELECT DATALENGTH(ProductName) FROM Products returns the length of each field
DB_ID([db_name])	Returns the identifier of the database **db_name**. If no name is specified, the identifier of the current database is returned. Example: SELECT DB_ID('AdventureWorks') = 6
DB_NAME([db_id])	Returns the name of the database with the identifier **db_id**. If no identifier is specified, the name of the current database is displayed. Example: SELECT DB_NAME(6) = 'AdventureWorks'
GETANSINULL('dbnam')	Returns 1 if the use of null values in the **database** dbnam complies with the ANSI SQL standard. (See also the explanation of null values at the end of this chapter.) Example: SELECT GETANSINULL('AdventureWorks') = 1
HOST_ID()	Returns the identifier of the host system. If no name is specified, the identifier of the current database is returned. Example: SELECT HOST_ID() = 106
HOST_NAME()	Returns the name of the host. If no identifier is specified, the name of the current database is returned. Example: SELECT HOST_NAME() = ORACLENIX
INDEX_COL(table, i, no)	Returns the name of the indexed column in the table **table**, defined by the index identifier i and the position **no** of the column in the index.
ISNULL(expr, value)	Returns the value of **expr** if that value is not null; otherwise, it returns **value** (see Example 5.22).
NULLIF($expr_1$,$expr_2$)	Returns the null value if the expressions $expr_1$ and $expr_2$ are equal. Example: SELECT NULLIF(project_no, 'p1') FROM projects. (Returns NULL for the project with the project_no = 'p1')
OBJECT_ID(obj_name)	Returns the identifier of the database object **obj_name**. Example: SELECT OBJECT_ID('products') = 453576654
OBJECT_NAME(obj_id)	Returns the name of the database object with the identifier **obj_id**. Example: SELECT OBJECT_NAME (453576654) = 'products'
SUSER_SID([name])	Returns the user's security identification number (SID) from the login name **name**. If no name is specified, the identifier of the current user is retrieved. Example: SELECT SUSER_SID('sa') = 0x01
SUSER_SNAME([sid])	Returns the user's login name from the user's security identification number **sid**. If no identifier is specified, the name of the current user is retrieved. Example: SELECT SUSER_SNAME(0x01) = 'sa'
USER_ID([user_name])	Returns the identifier of the user **user_name**. If no name is specified, the identifier of the current user is retrieved. Example: SELECT USER_ID('guest') = 2
USER_NAME([id])	Returns the name of the user with the identifier **id**. If no name is specified, the name of the current user is retrieved. Example: SELECT USER_NAME(2) = 'guest'

The following system functions of SQL Server do not use parameters:

Function	Explanation
CURRENT_TIMESTAMP	Returns the current date and time. Example: SELECT CURRENT_TIMESTAMP = "2000-01-11 17:22:55.670"
CURRENT_USER	Returns the name of the current user. Example: SELECT CURRENT_USER = "dbo"
SYSTEM_USER	Returns the login ID of the current user. Example: SELECT SYSTEM_USER = "sa"
USER	Same as CURRENT_USER.

All string functions can be nested in any order; for example, REVERSE(CURRENT_USER).

Scalar Operators

Scalar operators are used for operations with scalar values. SQL Server supports numeric and Boolean operators as well as concatenation.

There are unary and binary arithmetic operators. Unary operators are + and − (as signs). Binary arithmetic operators are +, −, *, /, and %. (The first four binary operators have their respective mathematical meanings, whereas % is the modulo operator.)

Boolean operators have two different notations in SQL Server depending on whether they are applied to bit strings or to other data types. The operators NOT, AND, and OR are applied to all data types (except BIT). They are described in detail in Chapter 5.

The bitwise operators for manipulating bit strings are listed here, and Example 3.6 shows how they are used:

     ~ (complement, i.e., NOT)
     & (conjunction of bit strings, i.e., AND)
     | (disjunction of bit strings, i.e., OR)
     ^ (exclusive disjunction, i.e., XOR or Exclusive OR)

EXAMPLE 3.6

     ~(1001001) = (0110110)
     (11001001) | (10101101) = (11101101)
     (11001001) & (10101101) = (10001001)
     (11001001) ^ (10101101) = (01100100)

The concatenation operator + can be used to concatenate two character strings or bit strings.

Global Variables

Global variables are special system variables that can be used as if they were scalar constants. SQL Server supports the following global variables, which have to be preceded by the prefix @@:

Variable	Explanation
@@CONNECTIONS	Returns the number of login attempts since starting SQL Server.
@@CPU_BUSY	Returns the total CPU time (in units of milliseconds) used since starting SQL Server.
@@DBTS	Returns the current value of the TIMESTAMP column for the current database.
@@ERROR	Returns the information about the return value of the last executed Transact-SQL statement (see Example 14.1).
@@IDENTITY	Returns the last inserted value for the column with the IDENTITY property.
@@IDLE	Returns the time (in units of milliseconds) that SQL Server has been idle since it was first started.
@@IO_BUSY	Returns the used I/O time (in units of milliseconds) since starting SQL Server.
@@LANGID	Returns the identifier of the language that is currently used by SQL Server.
@@LANGUAGE	Returns the name of the language that is currently used by SQL Server.
@@MAX_CONNECTIONS	Returns the maximum number of actual connections to SQL Server.
@@VERSION	Returns the current version of the SQL Server software.
@@NESTLEVEL	Returns the current nesting level of the stored procedure being executed.
@@PROCID	Returns the identifier for the stored procedure currently being executed.
@@ROWCOUNT	Returns the number of rows that have been affected by the last Transact-SQL statement executed by the system.
@@SERVERNAME	Retrieves the information concerning the local database server. This information contains, among other things, the name of the server and the name of the instance.
@@SPID	Returns the identifier of the server process.
@@TEXTSIZE	Retrieves the current maximum number of bytes for text/image objects, which can be returned as the result of a SELECT statement.
@@TOTAL_READ	Returns the total number of read operations since SQL Server was first started.
@@TOTAL_WRITE	Returns the total number of write operations since SQL Server was first started.

Null Values

A null value is a special value that may be assigned to a column. This value is normally used when information in a column is missing, unknown, or not applicable. For example, in the case of an unknown home telephone number for a company's employee, it is recommended that the null value be assigned to the column **home_ telephon_no**.

Any arithmetic expression results in a NULL if any operand of that expression is itself a null value. Therefore, in unary arithmetic expressions (if A is an expression with a null value), both +A and −A return NULL. In binary expressions, if one (or both) of the operands A or B has the null value, A + B, A − B, A * B, A/B, and A%B also result in a NULL. (A and B have to be numerical expressions.)

If an expression contains a relational operation and one (or both) of the operands has (have) the null value, the result of this operation will be NULL. Hence, each of the expressions A = B, A <> B, A < B, and A > B also returns NULL.

In the Boolean AND, OR, and NOT, the behavior of the null values is specified by the following truth tables, where T stands for true, U for unknown (NULL), and F for false. In these tables, follow the row and column represented by the values of the Boolean expressions that the operator works on, and the value where they intersect represents the resulting value.

AND	T	U	F	OR	T	U	F	NOT	
T	T	U	F	T	T	T	T	T	F
U	U	U	F	U	T	U	U	U	U
F	F	F	F	F	T	U	F	F	T

Any null value in the argument of aggregate functions AVG, SUM, MAX, MIN, and COUNT is eliminated before the respective function is calculated (except for the function COUNT(*)). If a column contains only null values, the function returns NULL. The aggregate function COUNT(*) handles all null values the same as non-null values. If the column contains only null values, the result of the function COUNT(DISTINCT column_ name) is 0.

A null value has to be different from all other values. For numeric data types, there is a distinction between the value zero and NULL. The same is true for the empty string and NULL for string data types.

A column of a table allows null values if its definition (see Chapter 4) explicitly contains NULL. On the other hand, null values are not permitted if the definition of a column explicitly contains NOT NULL. If the user does not specify NULL or NOT NULL for a column with a data type (except TIMESTAMP), the following values are assigned:

▶ NULL: If the ANSI_NULL_DFLT_ON option of the SET statement is set to ON or the option 'ANSI null default' of the system procedure **sp_dboption** has the value TRUE.

▶ NOT NULL: If the ANSI_NULL_DFLT_OFF option of the SET statement is set to ON or the option 'ANSI null default' of the system procedure **sp_dboption** is set to FALSE.

If the SET statement and the system procedure **sp_dboption** are not both activated, a column will contain the value NOT NULL by default. (The columns of TIMESTAMP data type can only be declared as NOT NULL columns.)

EXAMPLE 3.7

```
sp_dboption projects, 'ANSI null default', TRUE
```

After the execution of the system procedure **sp_dboption** in Example 3.7, all columns of the database **projects** will have NULL as a nullability setting (unless NOT NULL is specified when the column is created).

There is also another option of the SET statement—CONCAT_NULL_YIELDS_ NULL. This database option influences the concatenation operation with a null value so that anything you concatenate to a null value will yield NULL again. For instance, 'San Francisco' + NULL = NULL.

Conclusion

The basic features of SQL Server consist of Transact-SQL data types, predicates, and functions. Data types supported by SQL Server comply with data types of the ANSI SQL92 standard. SQL Server supports a variety of useful system functions.

The next chapter will introduce you to Transact-SQL statements. The data definition language portion of Transact-SQL comprises all of the statements needed for creating, altering, and removing database objects.

Exercises

E.3.1

What is a difference between the numeric data types INT, SMALLINT, and TINYINT?

E.3.2

What is a difference between the data types CHAR and VARCHAR? When should you use the latter (instead of the former) and vice versa?

E.3.3

How can you set the format of a column with the DATETIME data type so that its values can be entered in the form "yyyy/mm/dd"?

In the following two exercises, use the SELECT statement in the Query Editor component window of SQL Server Management Studio to display the result of all system functions and global variables. (For instance, SELECT host_id() displays the ID number of the current host.)

E.3.4

Using SQL Server system functions, find the ID number of the **AdventureWorks** database (Exercise 2.1).

E.3.5

Using the system variables, display the current version of the SQL Server software and the language that is used by this software.

E.3.6

Using the bitwise operators **&**, |, and ^, calculate the following operations with the bit strings:

    (11100101) & (01010111)
    (10011011) | (11001001)
    (10110111) ^ (10110001)

E.3.7

What is the result of the following expressions?

> A + NULL
> NULL = NULL
> B OR NULL
> B AND NULL
> A is a numerical and B a logical expression.

E.3.8

When can you use both single quotes and quotation marks to define string and DATETIME constants?

E.3.9

What is a delimited identifier and when do you need it?

CHAPTER
4

Data Definition Language

IN THIS CHAPTER

Creating Database Objects

Modifying Database Objects

Removing Database Objects

This chapter describes all of the Transact-SQL statements concerning data definition language (DDL). At the beginning of the chapter, all DDL statements are divided into three groups. The first group includes statements that create objects, the second group includes statements that modify objects, and the third group includes statements that remove objects.

Creating Database Objects

The organization of a database involves many different objects. All objects of a database can be physical or logical. The physical objects are related to the organization of the data on the physical device (disk). SQL Server's physical objects are files and filegroups. Logical objects represent a user's view of a database. Databases, tables, columns, and views (virtual tables) are examples of logical objects.

The first database object that has to be created is a database itself. SQL Server supports both system and user databases. An authorized user can create user databases, while system databases are generated during the installation of SQL Server. The SQL Server system databases are

- ▶ **master**
- ▶ **tempdb**
- ▶ **model**
- ▶ **msdb**

This chapter describes the creation, alteration, and removal of user databases, while all system databases will be covered in detail in Chapter 15.

Creation of a Database

Two basic methods are used to create a SQL Server database. The first method involves using SQL Server Management Studio (see Chapter 2). The second method involves using the Transact-SQL statement CREATE DATABASE. This statement has the general form:

```
CREATE DATABASE db_name
    [ON [PRIMARY] file_spec1 {, file_spec2} ...]
    [LOG ON file_spec3 {, file_spec4} ...]
```

[COLLATE *collation_name*]
[FOR {ATTACH | ATTACH_REBUILD_LOG }]

NOTE

For the syntax of the Transact-SQL statements, we use conventions described in the section "Syntax Conventions" in Chapter 1. According to the conventions, optional item(s) are written in brackets and braces followed by the "..." indicating that item(s) can be repeated any number of times.

db_name is the name of the database. The maximum size of a database name is 128 characters. (The rules for identifiers described in Chapter 3 apply to database names.) The maximum number of databases managed by a single SQL Server system is 32,767.

All databases in SQL Server are stored in files. These files can be explicitly specified by the system administrator or implicitly provided by the system. If the ON option exists in the CREATE DATABASE statement, all files containing the data of a database are explicitly specified.

NOTE

SQL Server uses disk files to store data. Each disk file contains data of a single database. Files themselves can be organized into filegroups. Filegroups provide the ability to distribute data over different disk drives and to back up and restore subsets of the database (useful for very large databases).

file_spec1, **file_spec2**,... represent file specifications, which include further options such as the logical name of the file, the physical name, and the size (see Example 4.2). The PRIMARY option specifies the first (and most important) file that contains system tables and other important internal information concerning the database. If the PRIMARY option is omitted, the first file listed in the specification is used as the primary file.

The system administrator uses the LOG ON option to define one or more files as the physical destination of the transaction log of the database. If the LOG ON option is not specified, the transaction log of the database will still be created because every database must have at least one transaction log file. (SQL Server keeps a record of each change it makes to the database. SQL Server keeps all those records, in particular before and after values, in one or more files called the transaction log. Each database of the system has its own transaction log.)

With the COLLATE option, you can specify the default collation for the database. If the COLLATE option is not specified, the database is assigned the default collation of the **model** database, which is the same as the default collation of the SQL Server instance. (For more information on collation, see Chapter 15.)

The FOR ATTACH option specifies that the database is created by attaching an existing set of operating system files. If this option is used, you have to explicitly specify the first primary file. The FOR ATTACH_REBUILD_LOG option specifies that the database is created by attaching an existing set of operating system files. If one or more transaction log files are missing, the log file is rebuilt.

During the creation of a new database, SQL Server uses the **model** database as a template. The properties of a **model** database can be changed to suit the personal conception of the system administrator.

Ideally, only a limited number of users should have the authorization to create a database. After the installation of the system, only the system administrator has this privilege. The system administrator can subsequently grant this privilege to other users via the GRANT CREATE DATABASE statement. The creator of the database is called the database owner and has special privileges concerning the database and its objects. (Granting and revoking database privileges is discussed in detail in Chapter 12.)

Example 4.1 creates a simple database without any further specifications. To execute this statement, type it in the **Query Editor** window of SQL Server Management Studio and press F5.

EXAMPLE 4.1

```
USE master
CREATE DATABASE sample
```

Example 4.1 creates a database named **sample** with default specifications. SQL Server creates by default two files. The logical name of the data file is **sample**, and its original size is 2 MB. Similarly, the logical name of the transaction log is **sample_log**, and its original size is 1 MB.

Example 4.2 creates a database with explicit specifications for database and transaction log files. (The directory C:\DATA must exist before you execute the CREATE DATABASE statement in Example 4.2.)

EXAMPLE 4.2

```
CREATE DATABASE projects
  ON (NAME=projects_dat,
     FILENAME = 'C:\DATA\projects.mdf',
     SIZE = 10,
```

```
        MAXSIZE = 100,
        FILEGROWTH = 5)
LOG ON
  (NAME=projects_log,
        FILENAME = 'C:\DATA\projects.ldf',
        SIZE = 40,
        MAXSIZE = 100,
        FILEGROWTH = 10)
```

Example 4.2 creates a database called **projects**. Because the PRIMARY option is omitted, the first file is assumed as the primary file. This file has the logical name **projects_dat** and is stored in the file **projects.mdf**. The original size of this file is 10MB. Additional portions of 5MB of disk storage are allocated by the system, if needed. (The KB, TB, and MB suffixes can be used to specify kilobytes, terabytes, or megabytes, respectively—the default is MB.) If the MAXSIZE option is not specified or is set to UNLIMITED, the file will grow until the disk is full.

There is also a single transaction log file with the logical name **projects_log** and the physical name **projects.ldf**. All options of the file specification for the transaction log have the same name and meaning as the corresponding options of the file specification for the data file.

Using the Transact-SQL language, a user can select the current database with the USE statement. (The alternative way is to select the database name in the **Database** pull-down menu in the toolbar of SQL Server Mangement Studio.)

The system administrator can assign a default database to a user by using the system procedure **sp_defaultdb** (see Chapter 12). In this case, the users do not need to execute the USE statement if they want to use their default database.

Creation of a Snapshot Database

The CREATE DATABASE statement can also be used to create a database snapshot of an existing database (source database). A database snapshot is transactionally consistent with the source database as it existed at the time of the snapshot's creation. You can have multiple snapshots for an existing database.

The syntax for the creation of a snapshot is

```
CREATE DATABASE database_snapshot_name
    ON   file_spec1 {, file_spec2} ...]
AS SNAPSHOT OF source_database_name
```

As you can see from the syntax, if you want to create a database snapshot, you have to add the AS SNAPSHOT OF clause in the CREATE DATABASE statement.

CREATE TABLE: A Basic Form

The CREATE TABLE statement creates a new base table with all corresponding columns and their data types. The basic form of the CREATE TABLE statement is

```
CREATE TABLE table_name
    (col_name1 type1 [NOT NULL| NULL]
    [{, col_name2 type2 [NOT NULL| NULL]} ...])
```

NOTE

The notion of the base table specifies the named table, which exists in its own right. Besides base tables, there are also some special kinds of tables such as temporary tables and views (see Chapters 5 and 10, respectively).

table_name is the name of the created base table. The maximum number of tables per database is limited by the number of objects in the database (there can be more than 2 billion objects in a database, including tables, views, stored procedures, triggers, rules, defaults, and constraints). **col_name1**, **col_name2**,... are the names of the table columns. The maximum number of columns per base table is 1,024. **type1**, **type2**,... are data types of corresponding columns (see Chapter 3).

NOTE

The name of a database object can generally contain four parts in the form:
[server_name.[db_name.[schema_name.]]]object_name
***object_name** is the name of the database object. **schema_name** is the name of the schema, to which the object belongs. (You can find the description of schema later in this chapter.) **server_name** and **db_name** are names of the server and database to which the database object belongs. Table names, combined with the schema name, must be unique within the database. Similarly, column names must be unique in the table.*

The first column-level constraint that will be discussed in this book is the existence and nonexistence of null values within a column. If the NOT NULL is specified, the assignment of null values for the column is not allowed. (In that case, the column may not contain nulls, and if there is a null value to be inserted, SQL Server returns an error message.)

The privilege to create a table in a database, immediately after the creation of the database, is implicitly granted to the system administrator and the database owner. After that, the system administrator and the database owner can grant the table privilege to other users by using the GRANT CREATE TABLE statement. (Granting and revoking table privileges is discussed in detail in Chapter 12.)

The creator of a table must not be its owner. This means that if the table is created in the form **schema_name.table_name** and the owner name of that schema is not identical to the current user, the table owner will be the owner of the schema. Similarly, a table created with the CREATE TABLE statement must not belong to the current database, if some other (existing) database name is specified as the prefix of the table name.

Temporary tables are a special kind of base table. They are stored in the **tempdb** database and are automatically dropped at the end of the session. The properties of temporary tables and examples concerning them are given at the end of Chapter 5.

Example 4.3 shows the creation of all tables of the sample database.

EXAMPLE 4.3

```
USE sample
CREATE TABLE employee  (emp_no INTEGER NOT NULL,
            emp_fname CHAR(20) NOT NULL,
            emp_lname CHAR(20) NOT NULL,
            dept_no CHAR(4) NULL)
CREATE TABLE department(dept_no CHAR(4) NOT NULL,
            dept_name CHAR(25) NOT NULL,
            location CHAR(30) NULL)
CREATE TABLE project   (project_no CHAR(4) NOT NULL,
            project_name CHAR(15) NOT NULL,
            budget FLOAT NULL)
CREATE TABLE works_on  (emp_no INTEGER NOT NULL,
            project_no CHAR(4) NOT NULL,
            job CHAR (15) NULL,
            enter_date DATETIME NULL)
```

CREATE TABLE: The Enhanced Form

The enhanced form of the CREATE TABLE statement has the following syntax:

```
CREATE TABLE table_name
  (col_name1 <column_description>
  {[col_name2 <column_description>]} ...
  {table_constraint} ...
  [ON{ partition_schema_name ( column_name [,...n ] )| filegroup |
"DEFAULT " } ]

<column_description> ::= data_type [DEFAULT {expression1  | NULL }
      [ IDENTITY [(init_value, incr)]] [NOT NULL | NULL] [column-
constraint]
  [COLLATE <collation_name>]
```

The ON clause with the definition of the partition schema specifies optionally the partition schema of the table. (See Chapter 23 for the definition of the table partitions.)

The DEFAULT clause in the column definition specifies the default value of the column—that is, whenever a new row is inserted into the table, the default value for the particular column will be used if there is no value specified for it. A constant value, such as the system functions USER, CURRENT_USER, SESSION_USER, SYSTEM_USER, CURRENT_TIMESTAMP, and NULL, among others, can be used as the default values (see Example 4.4).

A column with the IDENTITY property allows only integer values, which are usually implicitly assigned by the system (see Example 5.55). Each value, which should be inserted in the column, is calculated by incrementing the last inserted value of the column. Therefore, the definition of a column with the IDENTITY property contains (implicitly or explicitly) an initial value and an increment. (The default values for the initial value and the increment are both 1.)

NOTE

Because SQL Server generates the values with the IDENTITY property, these values are always different, even when multiple users are adding rows at the same time. This feature is very useful in a multiuser environment, where it is quite difficult for an ordinary program to generate unique numeric values (see Example 5.55).

The following restrictions apply to the IDENTITY property:

▶ The column must be numeric—that is, of type INTEGER, SMALLINT, TINYINT, NUMERIC, or DECIMAL. (If the column is of the type NUMERIC or DECIMAL, the number of digits to the right of the decimal point must be 0.)

▶ There can be at most one column in the table with the IDENTITY property.

▶ The column with this property does not allow null values.

The IDENTITY property can be used with the CREATE TABLE, the ALTER TABLE, and the SELECT statements. The use of this property with the SELECT statement will be discussed in the next chapter.

CREATE TABLE and Declarative Integrity Constraints

One of the most important features that a DBMS must provide is a way of maintaining the integrity of data. The constraints, which are used to check the modification or insertion of data, are called *integrity constraints*. The task of maintaining integrity constraints can be handled by the user in application programs or by the DBMS. The most important benefits of handling integrity constraints by the DBMS are the following:

▶ Increased reliability of data

▶ Reduced programming time

▶ Simple maintenance

Using the DBMS to define integrity constraints increases the reliability of data because there is no possibility that the integrity constraints can be forgotten by a programmer. (If an integrity constraint is handled by application programs, *all* programs concerning the constraint must include the corresponding code. If the code is omitted in one application program, the consistency of data is compromised.)

An integrity constraint not handled by the DBMS must be defined in every application program that uses the data involved in the constraint. In contrast, the same integrity constraint must be defined only once if it is to be handled by the DBMS. Additionally, application-enforced constraints are usually more complex to code than are database-enforced constraints.

If an integrity constraint is handled by the DBMS, the modification of the structure of the constraint must be handled only once, in the DBMS. The modification of a structure in application programs requires the modification of every program that involves the corresponding code.

There are two groups of integrity constraints handled by a DBMS:

▶ Declarative integrity constraints

▶ Procedural integrity constraints that are handled by triggers (for the definition of triggers, see Chapter 13)

The declarative constraints are defined using the DDL statements CREATE TABLE and ALTER TABLE. They can be column-level constraints or table-level constraints. Column-level constraints, together with the data type and other column properties, are placed within the declaration of the column, while table-level constraints are always defined at the end of the CREATE TABLE or ALTER TABLE statement, after the definition of all columns (see Examples 4.5 and 4.6).

NOTE

There is only one difference between column-level constraints and table-level constraints: a column-level constraint can be applied only upon one column, while a table-level constraint can cover more than one column of a table (see Example 4.7).

Each declarative constraint has a name. The name of the constraint can be explicitly assigned using the CONSTRAINT option in the CREATE TABLE statement or the ALTER TABLE statement. If the CONSTRAINT option is omitted, SQL Server assigns an implicit name for the constraint.

NOTE

Using explicit constraint names is strongly recommended, although they are optional. The search for a name of a specific integrity constraint can be greatly enhanced if an explicit name for that constraint is used.

All declarative constraints can be categorized into five groups:

▶ Default values

▶ Uniqueness

▶ Definition of the primary keys

▶ Definition of the foreign keys and the referential constraints

▶ CHECK clause

The definition of the default value using the DEFAULT option has been shown earlier in this chapter (also see the next example). All other constraints are described in detail in the following sections.

The UNIQUE Clause

Sometimes more than one column or group of columns of the table have unique values and therefore can be used as the primary key. All columns or groups of columns that qualify to be primary keys are called *candidate keys*. Each candidate key is defined using the UNIQUE clause in the CREATE TABLE or the ALTER TABLE statement.

The UNIQUE clause has the following form:

```
[CONSTRAINT c_name]
    UNIQUE [CLUSTERED | NONCLUSTERED] (col_name1 [{, col_
name2} ...])
```

The CONSTRAINT option in the UNIQUE clause assigns an explicit name to the candidate key. The option CLUSTERED or NONCLUSTERED relates to the fact that SQL Server always generates an index for each candidate key of a table. The index can be clustered—that is, the physical order of rows is specified using the indexed order of the column values. If the order is not specified, the index is nonclustered (see also Chapter 9). The default value is NONCLUSTERED. **col_name1**, **col_name2**,... are column names that build the candidate key. (The maximum number of columns per candidate key is 16.)

Example 4.4 shows the use of the UNIQUE clause and the DEFAULT option.

EXAMPLE 4.4

```
USE sample
CREATE TABLE projects  (project_no CHAR(4)  DEFAULT 'p1',
            project_name CHAR(15) NOT NULL,
            budget FLOAT NULL
        CONSTRAINT unique_no UNIQUE (project_no))
```

Each value of the column **project_no** of the table **projects** is unique, including the null value. (Just as with any other value with a UNIQUE constraint, if null values are allowed on a column with a UNIQUE constraint, there can be at most one row with the null value.) If an existing value should be inserted into the column **project_no**, SQL Server rejects it. The explicit name of the constraint that is defined in Example 4.4 is **unique_no**. The DEFAULT option in Example 4.4 is used to specify the value p1 as the default value for the **project_no** column.

The PRIMARY KEY Clause

The *primary key* of a table is a column or group of columns whose values are different in every row. Each primary key is defined using the PRIMARY KEY clause in the CREATE TABLE or the ALTER TABLE statement.

The PRIMARY KEY clause has the following form:

```
[CONSTRAINT c_name]
PRIMARY KEY [CLUSTERED | NONCLUSTERED] (col_name1 [{,col_name2} ...])
```

All options of the PRIMARY KEY clause have the same meaning as the corresponding options with the same name in the UNIQUE clause. In contrast to UNIQUE, the PRIMARY KEY column must be NOT NULL, and its default value is CLUSTERED. In Examples 4.5 through 4.8 you will re-create all tables from the sample database once or several times. For this reason, before you execute one of these examples, delete the corresponding table(s) using the DROP TABLE statement. (For a description of this statement, see the section "Removing Database Objects" toward the end of this chapter.)

EXAMPLE 4.5

```
USE sample
CREATE TABLE employee  (emp_no INTEGER NOT NULL,
            emp_fname CHAR(20) NOT NULL,
            emp_lname CHAR(20) NOT NULL,
            dept_no CHAR(4) NULL,
            CONSTRAINT prim_empl PRIMARY KEY (emp_no))
```

The **employee** table is re-created and its primary key defined in Example 4.5. The primary key of the table is specified using the declarative integrity constraint named **prim_empl**. This integrity constraint is a table-level constraint and is specified after the definition of all columns of the table **employee**.

Example 4.6 is equivalent to Example 4.5 except for the specification of the primary key of the **employee** table as a column-level constraint.

EXAMPLE 4.6

```
USE sample
CREATE TABLE employee
    (emp_no INTEGER NOT NULL CONSTRAINT prim_empl PRIMARY KEY,
    emp_fname CHAR(20) NOT NULL,
    emp_lname CHAR(20) NOT NULL,
    dept_no CHAR(4) NULL)
```

The FOREIGN KEY Clause

A *foreign key* is a column or group of columns in one table that contain(s) values that match the PRIMARY KEY values in the same or another table. Each foreign key is defined using the FOREIGN KEY clause combined with the REFERENCES clause.

The FOREIGN KEY clause has the following form:

```
[CONSTRAINT c_name]
      [[FOREIGN KEY] (col_name1 [{, col_name2} ...]])
      REFERENCES table_name (col_name3 [{, col_name4} ...])
          [ON DELETE {NO ACTION|CASCADE |SET NULL |SET DEFAULT}]
          [ON UPDATE {NO ACTION |CASCADE |SET NULL |SET DEFAULT}]
```

The FOREIGN KEY clause defines all columns explicitly that belong to the foreign key. The REFERENCES clause specifies the table name with all columns that build the corresponding PRIMARY KEY. The number and the data types of the columns in the FOREIGN KEY clause must match the number and the corresponding data types of columns in the REFERENCES clause (and, of course, both of these must match the number and data types of the columns in the PRIMARY KEY of the referenced table).

The table that contains the foreign key is called the *referencing table*, and the table that contains the corresponding primary key is called the *parent table* or *referenced table*.

EXAMPLE 4.7

```
USE sample
CREATE TABLE works_on  (emp_no INTEGER NOT NULL,
        project_no CHAR(4) NOT NULL,
          job CHAR (15) NULL,
          enter_date DATETIME NULL,
          CONSTRAINT prim_works PRIMARY KEY(emp_no, project_no),
          CONSTRAINT foreign_works FOREIGN KEY(emp_no)
            REFERENCES employee (emp_no))
```

The **works_on** table in Example 4.7 is specified with two declarative integrity constraints: **prim_works** and **foreign_works**. Both constraints are table-level constraints, where the former specifies the primary key and the latter the foreign key of the **works_on** table. Further, the constraint **foreign_works** specifies the **employee** table as the parent table and its **emp_no** column as the corresponding primary key of the column with the same name in the referencing **works_on** table.

The FOREIGN KEY clause can be omitted if the foreign key is defined as a column-level constraint, because the column being constrained is the implicit column "list" of the

FOREIGN KEY, and the keyword REFERENCES is sufficient to indicate what kind of constraint this is. The maximum number of FOREIGN KEY constraints in a table is 63.

A definition of the foreign keys in tables of a database imposes the specification of another important integrity constraint: the referential constraint, described next.

Referential Constraints

A *referential constraint* enforces update rules for the tables with the foreign key and the corresponding primary key constraint. Examples 4.6 and 4.7 specify two such constraints: **prim_empl** and **foreign_works**. The REFERENCES clause in Example 4.7 determines the **employee** table as the parent table.

There are four cases in which the modification of the values in the foreign key or in the primary key can cause problems. All of these cases will be shown using the sample database. The first two cases affect modifications of the referencing table, while the last two concern modifications of the parent table.

Case 1

Insert a new row into the **works_on** table with the employee number 11111.

The insertion of the new row in the referencing table **works_on** introduces a new employee number for which there is no matching employee in the parent table **employee**. If the referential constraint for both tables is specified as is done in Examples 4.6 and 4.7, SQL Server rejects the insertion of a new row. For readers who are familiar with the SQL language, the corresponding Transact-SQL statement is

```
USE sample
INSERT INTO works_on (emp_no, ...)
    VALUES (11111, ...)
```

Case 2

Modify the employee number 10102 in all rows of the **works_on** table. The new number is 11111.

In Case 2, the existing value of the foreign key in the **works_on** table should be replaced using the new value, for which there is no matching value in the parent table **employee**. If the referential constraint for both tables is specified as is done in Examples 4.6 and 4.7, SQL Server rejects the modification of the rows in the **works_on** table. The corresponding Transact-SQL statement is

```
USE sample
UPDATE works_on
    SET emp_no = 11111 WHERE emp_no = 10102
```

Case 3

Modify the employee number 10102 in the corresponding row of the **employee** table. The new number is 22222.

In Case 3, the existing value of the primary key in the parent table and the foreign key of the referencing table is modified only in the parent table. The values in the referencing table are unchanged. Therefore, SQL Server rejects the modification of the row with the employee number 10102 in the **employee** table. Referential integrity requires that no rows in the referencing table (the one with the FOREIGN KEY clause) can exist unless a corresponding row in the parent table (the one with the PRIMARY KEY clause) also exists. Otherwise, the rows in the parent table would be "orphaned." If the modification described above were permitted, then rows in the **works_on** table having the employee number 10102 would be orphaned; therefore, SQL Server would reject it. The corresponding Transact-SQL statement is

```
USE sample
UPDATE employee
   SET emp_no = 22222 WHERE emp_no = 10102
```

Case 4

Delete the row of the **employee** table with the employee number 10102.

Case 4 is similar to Case 3. The deletion would remove the employee for which matching rows exist in the referencing table.

Example 4.8 shows the definition of tables of the sample database with all existing primary key and foreign key constraints.

EXAMPLE 4.8

```
USE sample
CREATE TABLE department(dept_no CHAR(4) NOT NULL,
            dept_name CHAR(25) NOT NULL,
            location CHAR(30) NULL,
            CONSTRAINT prim_dept PRIMARY KEY (dept_no))
CREATE TABLE employee  (emp_no INTEGER NOT NULL,
         emp_fname CHAR(20) NOT NULL,
         emp_lname CHAR(20) NOT NULL,
      dept_no CHAR(4) NULL,
      CONSTRAINT prim_emp PRIMARY KEY (emp_no),
      CONSTRAINT foreign_emp FOREIGN KEY(dept_no) REFERENCES
department(dept_no))
```

```
CREATE TABLE project  (project_no CHAR(4) NOT NULL,
        project_name CHAR(15) NOT NULL,
         budget FLOAT NULL,
         CONSTRAINT prim_proj PRIMARY KEY (project_no))
CREATE TABLE works_on  (emp_no INTEGER NOT NULL,
  project_no CHAR(4) NOT NULL,
  job CHAR (15) NULL,
  enter_date DATETIME NULL,
  CONSTRAINT prim_works PRIMARY KEY(emp_no, project_no),
  CONSTRAINT foreign1_works FOREIGN KEY(emp_no) REFERENCES
employee(emp_no),
  CONSTRAINT foreign2_works FOREIGN KEY(project_no) REFERENCES
project(project_no))
```

The ON DELETE and ON UPDATE Options

SQL Server can react differently if the values of the primary key of a table should be modified or deleted. If you try to update values of a foreign key, and these modifications result in inconsistencies in the corresponding primary key (see Case 1 and Case 2 in the previous section), the database system will always reject the modification and will display a message similar to the following:

Server: Msg 547, Level 16, State 1, Line 1
UPDATE statement conflicted with COLUMN FOREIGN KEY constraint 'FKemployee'. The conflict occurred in database 'sample', table 'employee', column 'dept_no'. The statement has been terminated.

But if you try to modify the values of a primary key, and these modifications result in inconsistencies in the corresponding foreign key (see Case 3 and Case 4 in the previous section), a database system could react very flexibly. Generally, there are four options regarding how a database system can react:

► NO ACTION

► CASCADE

► SET NULL

► SET DEFAULT

The NO ACTION option allows you to modify (i.e., update or delete) only those values of the parent table that do not have any corresponding values in the foreign key of the referencing table. The CASCADE option allows you to modify (i.e., update or delete) all values of the parent table. If this option is specified, a row is updated (i.e., deleted) from the referencing table if the corresponding value in the primary key has been updated or the whole row with that value has been deleted from the parent table.

The SET NULL option allows you again to update or delete all values of the parent table. If you want to update a value of the parent table and this modification would lead to data inconsistencies in the referencing table, the database system sets all corresponding values in the foreign key of the referencing table to NULL. Similarly, if you want to delete the row in the parent table and the deletion of the value in the primary key would lead to data inconsistencies, the database system sets all corresponding values in the foreign key to NULL. That way, all data inconsistencies are omitted. The SET DEFAULT option is analogous to the SET NULL option, with one exception: All corresponding values in the foreign key are set to a default value. (Obviously, the default value must still exist in the primary key of the parent table after modification.)

NOTE

SQL Server 2005 supports all four alternatives.

Example 4.9 shows the use of the ON DELETE and ON UPDATE options.

EXAMPLE 4.9

```
USE sample
CREATE TABLE works_on1
(emp_no INTEGER NOT NULL,
  project_no CHAR(4) NOT NULL,
  job CHAR (15) NULL,
  enter_date DATETIME NULL,
  CONSTRAINT prim_works1 PRIMARY KEY(emp_no, project_no),
  CONSTRAINT foreign1_works1 FOREIGN KEY(emp_no)
      REFERENCES employee(emp_no) ON DELETE CASCADE,
  CONSTRAINT foreign2_works1 FOREIGN KEY(project_no)
      REFERENCES project(project_no) ON UPDATE CASCADE)
```

Example 4.9 shows the creation of the **works_on1** table that uses the ON DELETE CASCADE and ON UPDATE CASCADE options. If you load the **works_on1** table with the content shown in Table 1-4, each deletion of a row in the **employee** table will cause the deletion of all rows in the **works_on1** table that have the corresponding value in the **emp_no** column. Similarly, each update of a value in the **project_no** column of the **project** table will cause the same modification on all corresponding values in the **project_no** column of the **works_on1** table.

The CHECK Clause

The *check constraint* specifies conditions for the data inserted into a column. Each row inserted into a table or each value updating the value of the column must meet these conditions. The CHECK clause is used to specify check constraints. This clause can be defined in the CREATE TABLE or the ALTER TABLE statement. The syntax of the CHECK clause is

```
[CONSTRAINT c_name]
    CHECK [NOT FOR REPLICATION] expression
```

expression must evaluate to a Boolean value (TRUE or FALSE) and can reference any columns in the current table (or just the current column if specified as a column-level constraint), but no other tables. The CHECK clause is not enforced during a replication of the data if the option NOT FOR REPLICATION exists. (A database, or a part of it, is said to be replicated if it is stored at more than one site. Replication can be used to enhance the availability of data. Chapter 24 describes data replication.)

EXAMPLE 4.10

```
USE sample
CREATE TABLE customer
    (cust_no INTEGER NOT NULL,
    cust_group CHAR(3) NULL,
    CHECK (cust_group IN ('c1', 'c2', 'c10')))
```

The **customer** table that is created in Example 4.10 contains the **cust_group** column with the corresponding check constraint. SQL Server returns an error if the **cust_group** column, after a modification of its existing values or after the insertion of a new row, would contain a value different from the values in the set ('c1', 'c2', 'c10').

The following example shows the creation of the table, with a column of the SQL_VARIANT type.

EXAMPLE 4.11

```
USE sample
CREATE TABLE Item_Attributes  (
     item_id INT NOT NULL,
     attribute NVARCHAR(30) NOT NULL,
     value SQL_VARIANT NOT NULL,
     PRIMARY KEY (item_id, attribute) )
```

In Example 4.11 there is the **value** column, which is of type SQL_VARIANT. The SQL_VARIANT data type can be used to store values of various data types at the same time, such as numeric values, strings, and date values. Note that the SQL_VARIANT data type is used in Example 4.11 because different attribute values may be of different data types. For example, the size attribute stores an integer attribute value, and a name attribute stores a character string attribute value.

Creating Other Database Objects

The CREATE DEFAULT statement creates a default value. The created default is then assigned (or "bound") to a column, and if during the insertion of new rows no value is explicitly specified for the column, the column will be assigned the default value rather than NULL. Establishing (or binding) the default value for a particular column must be done using the system procedure **sp_bindefault**. The preferred method of establishing default values for columns is to specify them in the DEFAULT clause of the CREATE TABLE statement, as discussed previously.

A *rule* is a condition that is defined for the values of a column or for an alias data type. Rules are created using the CREATE RULE statement. After its creation, the rule must be bound to a column or an alias data type using the system procedure **sp_bindrule**. Both of the statements CREATE DEFAULT and CREATE RULE will be discussed in detail later in this chapter.

The database contains not only base tables that exist in their own right but also *views*, which are virtual tables. The data of a base table exists physically—that is, it is stored on a disk—while a view is derived from one or more base tables. The CREATE VIEW statement creates a new view from one or more existing tables (or views) using a SELECT statement, which is an inseparable part of the CREATE VIEW statement. Since the creation of a view always contains a query, the CREATE VIEW statement belongs to the data manipulation language (DML) rather than to the data definition language (DDL). For this reason, the creation and removal of views is discussed in Chapter 10, after the presentation of all Transact-SQL statements for data modification.

The CREATE INDEX statement creates a new *index* on a specified table. The indices are primarily used to allow efficient access to the data stored on a disk. The existence of an index can greatly improve the access to data. Indices, together with the CREATE INDEX statement, are discussed in detail in Chapter 9.

A *stored procedure* is an additional database object that can be created using the corresponding CREATE PROCEDURE statement. (A stored procedure is a special kind of sequence of statements written in Transact-SQL, using the SQL language and SQL extensions. Chapter 8 describes stored procedures in detail.)

A *trigger* is a database object that specifies an action as a result of an operation. This means that when a particular data-modifying action (modification, insertion, or deletion) occurs on a particular table, SQL Server automatically invokes one or more additional action(s). The CREATE TRIGGER statement creates a new trigger. Triggers are described in detail in Chapter 13.

A *schema* is a database object that includes statements for creation of tables, views, and user privileges. (You can think of a schema as a construct that collects together several tables, corresponding views, and user privileges.) The next example shows the use of the CREATE SCHEMA statement.

EXAMPLE 4.12

```
USE sample
CREATE SCHEMA AUTHORIZATION pete
CREATE TABLE salesman
   (no INT NOT NULL UNIQUE,
    fname CHAR(20) NOT NULL,
    lname CHAR(20) NOT NULL,
    product_no CHAR(10))
CREATE TABLE product
     (product_no CHAR(10) NOT NULL UNIQUE,
      product_name CHAR(20) NULL,
      price MONEY NULL)
CREATE VIEW product_info
    AS SELECT product_no, product_name
       FROM product
```

Example 4.12 creates a schema that contains two tables, **salesman** and **product,** and one view, **product_info**. The schema is owned by the user **pete**. (For more information concerning schemas, see Chapter 12.)

> **NOTE**
> _____
>
> *SQL Server 2005 treats the notion of schema the same way as it is treated in the ANSI SQL standard. In the ANSI SQL-92 standard, a schema is defined as a collection of database objects that are owned by a single principal and form a single namespace. A namespace is a set of objects that cannot have duplicate names. For example, two tables can have the same name only if they are in separate schemas. In SQL Server 2000, database users and schemas are implicitly connected; i.e., every database user is the owner of a schema that has the same name as the user. SQL Server 2000 did have a CREATE SCHEMA statement, but it did not actually create a schema. CREATE SCHEMA provided a way to create objects and grant permissions in a single statement that also helped administrators avoid missing dependencies. (Schema is a very important concept in SQL Server 2005 security model. For this reason, you can find the detailed description of schema in Chapter 12.)*

Integrity Constraints and Domains

A *domain* is the set of all possible legitimate values that columns of a table may contain. Almost all DBMSs use data types to define the set of possible values for a column. This method of enforcing "domain integrity" is incomplete, as can be seen from the following example.

The **person** table has a column, **zip**, that specifies the ZIP code of the city in which the person lives. This column can be defined using SMALLINT or CHAR(5) data types. The definition with the SMALLINT data type is inaccurate, because the SMALLINT data type contains all positive and negative values between $-2^{15}-1$ and 2^{15}. The definition of a ZIP code using the CHAR(5) is even more inaccurate, because all characters and special signs can also be used in such a case. Therefore, for an accurate definition of ZIP codes, we need to define an interval of positive integers between 00601 and 99950 and assign it to the column **zip**.

CHECK constraints (defined in the CREATE TABLE or ALTER TABLE statement) can enforce more precise domain integrity because their expressions are flexible, and they are always enforced when the column is inserted or modified.

SQL Server provides support for domains with three different mechanisms:

► Creation of an alias data type using either the CREATE TYPE statement or the **sp_addtype** system procedure

► Creation of default values

► Defining Rules

Alias Data Types

An alias data type is a special kind of data type that is defined by users using the existing base data types. The system procedure **sp_addtype** is used to create a new alias data type. After the execution of the **sp_addtype** procedure, SQL Server inserts a new row into the system table **systypes**.

The system procedure **sp_addtype** has the following syntax:

sp_addtype type_name data_type [,null_type]

type_name is the name of the new alias data type that must be unique in the current database. **data_type** is a Transact-SQL base data type on which the alias data type is based. **length** must be specified for all character-based data types. **null_type** specifies how the new alias data type handles null values (NULL or NOT NULL).

Example 4.13 shows the first step in the creation of the new data type **zip**.

EXAMPLE 4.13

    USE sample
    sp_addtype zip, INTEGER, NULL

An existing alias data type can be used with the CREATE TABLE statement to define one or more columns in a database. The use of the system procedure **sp_addtype** is only the first step in the creation of a domain. Using the Transact-SQL statements CREATE DEFAULT and CREATE RULE and the system procedures **sp_bindefault** and **sp_ bindrule**, it is possible to further define properties for an existing alias data type. All these statements and system procedures are described in the following two sections.

The system procedure **sp_droptype** removes an existing alias data type.

NOTE

*The use of the **sp_addtype** system procedure to create alias data types is a deprecated feature in SQL Server 2005. Therefore, avoid using **sp_addtype**, and use CREATE TYPE instead.*

The better way to create an alias data type is to use the CREATE TYPE statement, because the **sp_addtype** system procedure will be removed in one of the future versions of the SQL Server system. The syntax of the CREATE TYPE statement is as follows:

```
CREATE TYPE [ type_schema_name. ] type_name
{ [ FROM base_type [ ( precision [ , scale ] ) ] [ NULL | NOT NULL ] ]
  | [ EXTERNAL NAME assembly_name [ .class_name ] ]}
```

An alias data type created using the CREATE TYPE statement corresponds to the data type created by the **sp_addtype** system procedure. The following example shows the creation of an alias data type using the CREATE TYPE statement. (To execute Example 4.14 without errors, you must first drop the existing type **zip** using the **sp_droptype** system procedure.)

EXAMPLE 4.14

```
USE sample
CREATE TYPE zip
   FROM CHAR(5) NOT NULL
```

The previous example creates an alias type **zip** based on the CHAR data type.
The CREATE TYPE statement can also be used to create a user-defined data type, which is a complex data type created by a user. The implementation of a user-defined data type in SQL Server is defined in a class of an assembly in the .NET common language runtime (CLR). This means that you can use one of the .NET languages like C# or Visual Basic 2005 to implement the new data type. Further description of the user-defined types is outside the scope of this book.

Creation of Default Values

SQL Server provides two methods for declaring default values for a column of a table. The first method uses the DEFAULT clause in the CREATE TABLE or ALTER TABLE statement and is described at the beginning of this chapter. The second method uses the CREATE DEFAULT statement and the **sp_bindefault** system procedure.

The Transact-SQL statement declares a general default value, which subsequently can be bound to a column of a table in a current database. The syntax of this statement is

```
CREATE DEFAULT default_name
   AS expression
```

The system procedure **sp_bindefault** is used to bind the defined default value to specific columns.

NOTE

After the creation of a database, only the system administrator and the database owner have the privilege of creating defaults. They can then grant this privilege to other users using the GRANT CREATE DEFAULT statement. (Granting and revoking of privileges is discussed in detail in Chapter 12.)

EXAMPLE 4.15

```
USE sample
CREATE DEFAULT zip_default AS 94710
GO
sp_bindefault 'zip_default', 'zip'
```

The CREATE DEFAULT statement in Example 4.15 first declares the default value (94710) for a default named **zip_default**. After that, the system procedure **sp_bindefault** is used to bind this default value to the alias data type **zip** (which was created in Example 4.13). (**sp_bindefault** also contains the option FUTUREONLY, which leaves existing columns with this alias data type unchanged.)

NOTE

The CREATE DEFAULT statement is a SQL Server extension to the SQL standard. The SQL standard as well as SQL Server support another integrity constraint clause called DEFAULT, which can also be used to define the default value of a column. You should use the standardized DEFAULT clause instead of the CREATE RULE statement. (The DEFAULT clause is described earlier in this chapter.)

The system procedure **sp_unbindefault** removes the connection between the default and the data type of the corresponding column.

Define Rules

In the previous two sections, we described two necessary steps to define a new domain and to bind it to one or more columns of the current database. But if we use only those two steps, the new domain will have exactly the same set of possible data values as the underlying base data type (in this case, INTEGER).

Often it is necessary to restrict the values of an alias data type to a specific set of values. (For example, ZIP codes in the United States can be between 00601 and 99950.) This can be done using rules. The Transact-SQL statement

CREATE RULE rule AS condition

creates a rule that can be bound to a column or an alias data type to restrict their values. **condition** can be any expression that is valid in a WHERE clause of a SELECT statement (SELECT statements will be covered in depth in Chapters 5 and 6). Additionally, **condition** contains a variable, which has a prefix @. The variable corresponds to the value that is inserted in the column using the INSERT or the UPDATE statement.

 NOTE

The CREATE RULE statement is a SQL Server extension to the SQL standard. The SQL standard as well as SQL Server support another integrity constraint clause called CHECK, which can also be used to define rules. You should use the CHECK clause instead of the CREATE RULE statement, because first, it is standardized and second, SQL Server can use this clause during the optimization of corresponding queries. (The CHECK clause is explained earlier in this chapter.)

After the creation of a database, only the system administrator and the database owner have the privilege of creating rules. They can then grant this privilege to other users using the GRANT CREATE RULE statement.

EXAMPLE 4.16

```
USE sample
CREATE RULE zip_rule
    AS @number > 600 and @number < 99951
```

After its definition, the rule has to be bound to a column or to an alias data type. The system procedure **sp_bindrule** provides this binding.

EXAMPLE 4.17

```
USE sample
sp_bindrule zip_rule, 'zip'
```

The system procedure **sp_bindrule** in Example 4.17 binds the rule **zip_rule** (Example 4.15) to the alias data type **zip** (Example 4.13). Hence, the domain of the data type **zip** is restricted with this step to the range between 00601 and 99950. (The system procedure **sp_bindrule** also contains the option FUTUREONLY, which leaves existing bindings between a column and the rule unchanged.)

The system procedure **sp_unbindrule** unbinds an existing rule from a column or an alias data type in the current database.

The alias data type can now be used for the definition of one or more columns in the current database; in Example 4.18, it is used in the CREATE TABLE statement.

EXAMPLE 4.18

```
USE sample
CREATE TABLE address
  (city CHAR(25) NOT NULL,
   zip_code ZIP,
   street CHAR(30) NULL)
```

If you try now to insert a row with a string value or any integer value outside the interval between 600 and 99950, you will get an error.

Modifying Database Objects

SQL Server supports changing the structure of the following database objects, among others:

- ▶ Database
- ▶ Table
- ▶ Schema
- ▶ Stored procedure
- ▶ View
- ▶ Trigger

Changing the structure of a database, table, and schema is described in this chapter, while the modification of the structure of the last three database objects is described in Chapters 8, 10, and 13, respectively.

Altering a Database

The ALTER DATABASE statement changes the physical structure of a database. This statement has the following form:

```
ALTER DATABASE db_name
    ADD FILE file_spec1 [TO FILEGROUP group_name1]
    | ADD LOG FILE file_spec2
    | REMOVE FILE 'file_name'
    | MODIFY FILE (NAME = old_name, NEWNAME = new_name ...)
    | CREATE FILEGROUP group_name2 | DROP FILEGROUP filegroup_name3
    | SET option_specifications   [ WITH terminations]
```

This statement allows the creation and the modification of database files, transaction log files, and/or filegroups. The three clauses ADD FILE, MODIFY FILE, and REMOVE FILE specify the creation of a new file, the modification of an existing file, and the deletion of an existing file, respectively. Additionally, a new file can be assigned to an existing filegroup using the TO FILEGROUP option.

The CREATE FILEGROUP clause creates a new filegroup, while DELETE FILEGROUP removes an existing filegroup from the system. There is also a clause concerning transaction logs. The ADD LOG FILE clause creates a new transaction log and adds it to the existing transaction logs of the database.

file_spec1, **file_spec2**,... represent file specifications, which include further options such as the logical name and the physical name of the file (see Example 4.19).

EXAMPLE 4.19

```
USE master
GO
ALTER DATABASE projects
ADD FILE (NAME=projects_dat1,
    FILENAME = 'C:\DATA\projects1.mdf',
    SIZE = 10,
    MAXSIZE = 100,
    FILEGROWTH = 5)
```

The ALTER DATABASE statement in Example 4.19 adds a new file to store the data of the **projects** database.

SQL Server supports the SET clause in the ALTER DATABASE statement. Using this clause, you can set several different options. All options that you can set are divided into five groups:

▶ State options

▶ Cursor options

▶ Auto options

▶ SQL options

▶ Recovery options

The state options control:

▶ User access to the database (SINGLE_USER, RESTRICTED_USER, or MULTI_USER)

▶ The status of the database (ONLINE, OFFLINE, or EMERGENCY)

▶ The read/write modus (READ_ONLY or READ_WRITE)

The cursor options control the way cursors are used. (Cursors allow processing data one row at a time and are used with stored procedures. For more information on stored procedures, see Chapter 8.) The auto options control, among other things, the art of the database shutdown (the option AUTO_CLOSE) and how index statistics are built (the options AUTO_CREATE_STATISTICS and AUTO_UPDATE_STATISTICS). Index statistics are described in detail in Chapter 9.

The SQL options control the ANSI compliance of the database and its objects. All SQL options can be edited using the DATABASEPROPERTYEX() function and modified using the **sp_dboption** system procedure. The function and the system procedure are described in detail in Chapter 18. The recovery options FULL, BULK-LOGGED, and SIMPLE influence the art of database recovery. (For more information on this topic, see Chapter 20.)

The system procedure **sp_renamedb** modifies the name of an existing database (and any other existing database object).

Altering a Table: A Basic Form

The ALTER TABLE statement modifies the schema of a table. SQL Server allows addition, removal, and modification of one or more columns from an existing table. The ALTER TABLE statement has the following basic form:

```
ALTER TABLE table_name
    ADD col_name type [NULL | IDENTITY]
```

[{, col_name type [NULL | IDENTITY]} ...]
DROP COLUMN col_name [{, col_name} ...]
ALTER COLUMN col_name type {NULL | IDENTITY}
[{, col_name type NULL | IDENTITY} ...]

The owner of a table, the system administrator, and the database owner have the privilege of modifying the schema of the table.

EXAMPLE 4.20

```
USE sample
ALTER TABLE employee
    ADD telephone_no CHAR(12) NULL
```

The ALTER TABLE statement in Example 4.20 adds the column **telephone_no** to the **employee** table. Note that new columns must either be nullable or must have a default constraint (this becomes obvious when you think about how this new column for existing rows can be populated).

The DROP COLUMN clause provides the ability to drop an existing column of the table.

EXAMPLE 4.21

```
USE sample
ALTER TABLE employee
    DROP COLUMN telephone_no
```

The ALTER TABLE statement in Example 4.21 removes the **telephone_no** column, which was added to the **employee** table in Example 4.20.

SQL Server also supports an ALTER COLUMN clause. This clause allows for modification of properties of an existing column.

EXAMPLE 4.22

```
USE sample
ALTER TABLE department
    ALTER COLUMN location CHAR(25) NOT NULL
```

The ALTER TABLE statement in Example 4.22 changes the previous properties of the **location** column (CHAR(30), nullable) to (CHAR(25), not nullable) of the **department** table.

Altering a Table: Enhanced Form

The enhanced form of the ALTER TABLE statement specifies the creation or modification of integrity constraints. Its syntax is as follows:

```
ALTER TABLE table_name
    [WITH CHECK | NOCHECK]
    ADD col_name type [{NULL | IDENTITY}]
    [{, col_name type NULL | IDENTITY} ...]
    DROP COLUMN col_name [{, col_name} ...]
    ALTER COLUMN col_name type {NULL | IDENTITY}
    [{, col_name type NULL | IDENTITY} ...]
    ADD table_constraint
    DROP table_constraint
```

In relation to the basic form of the ALTER TABLE statement, the enhanced form contains three new features:

► Adding a new integrity constraint

► Dropping an existing integrity constraint

► The CHECK or NOCHECK option

EXAMPLE 4.23

```
USE sample
CREATE TABLE sales
    (order_no INTEGER NOT NULL PRIMARY KEY,
    order_date DATETIME NOT NULL,
    ship_date DATETIME NOT NULL)
ALTER TABLE sales
    ADD CONSTRAINT order_check CHECK(order_date <= ship_date)
```

The first Transact-SQL statement in Example 4.23 creates the **sales** table with two columns of the data type DATETIME: **order_date** and **ship_date**. The subsequent ALTER TABLE statement defines an integrity constraint named **order_check**, which compares both of the values and displays an error message if the shipping date is earlier than the order date.

Example 4.24 shows the use of the ALTER TABLE statement to define the primary key and the foreign key of a table.

EXAMPLE 4.24

```
USE sample
ALTER TABLE product
    ADD CONSTRAINT prim_prod PRIMARY KEY(product_no)
ALTER TABLE salesman
    ADD CONSTRAINT prim_sales PRIMARY KEY (no),
    CONSTRAINT foreign_sales FOREIGN KEY(product_no)
    REFERENCES product
```

The first ALTER TABLE statement in Example 4.24 declares the primary key for the **product** table (Example 4.12). The second statement defines the primary and foreign keys of the **salesman** table.

Each declarative integrity constraint can be removed using the DROP clause of the ALTER TABLE statement (see the following example).

EXAMPLE 4.25

```
USE sample
ALTER TABLE sales
DROP CONSTRAINT order_check
```

The ALTER TABLE statement in Example 4.25 drops the CHECK constraint **order_check**, defined in Example 4.23.

As previously stated, an integrity constraint always has a name that can be explicitly declared using the CONSTRAINT option or implicitly declared by the system. The name of all the declared constraints for a table can be viewed using the system procedure **sp_helpconstraint**.

Example 4.26 shows the use of the system procedure **sp_helpconstraint**.

EXAMPLE 4.26

```
USE sample
sp_helpconstraint employee
```

The result (part of it) is

Object Name	constraint_ type	constraint_ name	delete_ action	update_ action	constraint_ keys
employee	PRIMARY KEY (clustered)	prim_empl	(N/A)	(N/A)	emp_no

Table is referenced by

projects.dbo.works_on:
foreign_works

A constraint that is created with the WITH CHECK option is enforced during future insert and update operations. Additionally, the existing values in the column(s) are checked against the constraint. Otherwise, a constraint that is created with the WITH NOCHECK constraint is disabled in both cases. Both options can be applied only with the CHECK and the FOREIGN KEY constraints.

The system procedure **sp_rename** modifies the name of an existing table (and any other existing database object). Examples 4.27 and 4.28 show the use of this system procedure.

EXAMPLE 4.27

```
USE sample
sp_rename department, subdivision
```

The result is

The object 'department' was renamed to 'subdivision'.

EXAMPLE 4.28

```
USE sample
sp_rename 'sales.order_no' , ordernumber
```

The result is

The column was renamed to 'ordernumber'.

Example 4.28 renames the **order_no** column in the **sales** table (Example 4.23). If the object to be renamed is a column in a table, the specification must be in the form **table_name.column_name**.

Removing Database Objects

All Transact-SQL statements to remove a database object have the general form:

DROP object object_name

Each CREATE object statement has the corresponding DROP object statement.
The statement

DROP DATABASE database1 {, database2 ...}

removes one or more databases. This means the database is dropped from system
tables in the **master** database, and all of the operating system files that make up
the database are deleted. Only the database owner or the system administrator can
remove a database.

One or more tables can be removed from a database with the following statement:

DROP TABLE table_name1 {, table_name2 ...}

All data, indices, and triggers belonging to the removed table are also dropped.
(In contrast, all views that are defined using the dropped table are not removed.)
Only the table owner (or the database owner) can remove a table.

In addition to DATABASE and TABLE, **objects** in the DROP statement can be,
among others:

► DEFAULT

► RULE

► TYPE

► PROCEDURE

► INDEX

► VIEW

► TRIGGER

► SCHEMA

► STATISTICS

The statement DROP DEFAULT removes an existing default. Similarly, the statements DROP RULE and DROP TYPE drop a rule, i.e., a type. The rest of the statements are described in different chapters: the DROP PROCEDURE statement in Chapter 8, the DROP VIEW statement in Chapter 10, the DROP INDEX statement in Chapter 9, and the DROP TRIGGER statement in Chapter 13. Finally, DROP STATISTICS corresponds to the UPDATE STATISTICS statement, which is described in Chapter 9.

Conclusion

SQL Server supports many data definition statements that create, alter, and remove database objects. The following database objects, among others, can be created and removed using the CREATE object and the DROP object statement, respectively:

- ▶ Database
- ▶ Table
- ▶ Schema
- ▶ View
- ▶ Trigger
- ▶ Stored procedure
- ▶ Index
- ▶ Rule
- ▶ Default

A structure of the first five database objects in the above list can be altered using the ALTER **object** statement.

The Transact-SQL language provides four data manipulation statements: SELECT, INSERT, UPDATE, and DELETE. The next chapter is concerned with the simple form of the SELECT statement.

Exercises

E.4.1

Using the CREATE DATABASE statement, create a new database named **test_db** with explicit specifications for database and transaction log files. The database file with the logical name **test_db_dat** is stored in the file C:\tmp\test_db.mdf, the initial size is 5MB, the maximum size is unlimited, and the file growth is 8 percent. The log file called **test_db_log** is stored in the file C:\tmp\test_db_log.ldf, the initial size is 2MB, the maximum size is 10MB, and the file growth is 500KB.

E.4.2

Using the ALTER DATABASE statement, add a new log file to the **test_db** database. The log is stored in the file C:\tmp\emp_log.ldf and the initial size of the file is 2MB, with growth of 2MB and an unlimited maximum size.

E.4.3

Using the ALTER DATABASE statement, change the file size of the **test_db** database to 10MB.

E.4.4

In Example 4.3, there are some columns of the four created tables defined with the NOT NULL specification. For which column is this specification required and for which is it not required?

E.4.5

Why are the columns **dept_no** and **project_no** in Example 4.3 defined as CHAR-values (and not as numerical values)?

E.4.6

Create the tables **customers** and **orders** with the following columns. (Do not declare the corresponding primary and foreign keys.)

Table Customers	Table Orders
customerid char(5) not null,	orderid integer not null,
companyName varchar(40) not null,	customerid char(5) not null,
contactName char(30) null,	orderdate datetime null,
address varchar(60) null,	shippeddate datetime null,
city char(15) null,	freight money null,
phone char(24) null,	shipname varchar(40) null,
fax char(24) null	shipaddress varchar(60) null,
	quantity integer null

E.4.7

Using the ALTER TABLE statement, add a new column named **shipregion** to the **orders** table. The fields should be nullable and contain integers.

E.4.8

Using the ALTER TABLE statement, change the data type of the column **shipregion** from INTEGER to CHARACTER with length 8. The fields may contain null values.

E.4.9

Delete the formerly created column **shipregion**.

E.4.10

Describe exactly what happens if a table is deleted with the DROP TABLE statement.

E.4.11

Re-create the tables **customers** and **orders**, enhancing their definition with all primary and foreign keys constraints.

E.4.12

Using SQL Server Management Studio, try to insert a new row into the **orders** table with the following values:

(10, 'ord01', getdate(), getdate(), 100.0, 'Windstar', 'Ocean', 1).

Why is it not possible?

E.4.13

Using the ALTER TABLE statement, add the current system date and time as the default value to the **orderdate** column of the **orders** table.

E.4.14

Using the ALTER TABLE statement, create an integrity constraint that limits the possible values of the **quantity** column in the **orders** table to values between 1 and 30.

E.4.15

With the help of the corresponding system procedures and the Transact-SQL statements CREATE DEFAULT and CREATE RULE, create the alias data type

"Western Countries". The possible values for the new data type are CA (for California), WA (for Washington), OR (for Oregon), and NM (for New Mexico). The default value is CA. Finally, create a table called **regions** with the columns **city** and **country**, using the new data type for the latter.

E.4.16

Display all integrity constraints for the **orders** table.

E.4.17

Delete the primary key of the **customers** table. Why isn't that working?

E.4.18

Delete the integrity constraint defined in Exercise 4.6.

E.4.19

Rename the **city** column of the **customers** table. The new name is **town**.

CHAPTER
5

Simple Queries

This chapter and the next describe the most important Transact-SQL statement—SELECT. In this chapter you will learn how to use the SELECT statement to perform simple queries. Every clause in this statement is described, and numerous examples using our sample database are given to demonstrate the practical use of each clause. The second part of this chapter introduces aggregate functions and the UNION operator.

SELECT Statement: A Basic Form

The Transact-SQL language has one basic statement for retrieving information from a database: the SELECT statement. With this statement, it is possible to query information from one or more tables of a database (or even from multiple databases). The result of a SELECT statement is another table, which is also known as a *result set*.

The simplest form of the SELECT statement contains both a SELECT and a FROM clause. This form of the SELECT statement has the following syntax:

```
SELECT [ ALL |DISTINCT] column_list
    FROM tab_1 [tab_alias1] [{,tab_2 [tab_alias2]}...]
```

tab_1, **tab_2**,… are names of tables from which information is retrieved. **tab_alias1**, **tab_alias2**,… provide aliases for the corresponding tables. An alias is another name for the corresponding table that can be used as a shorthand way of referring to the table or as a way to refer to two logical instances of the same physical table. Don't worry; this will become clearer as examples are presented.

NOTE

This chapter demonstrates the retrieval of information from a single table in a database. The next chapter describes the use of a join operation, and therefore the query of more than one table in a database.

column_list contains one or more of the following specifications:

▶ The asterisk symbol (*), which specifies all columns of the named tables in the FROM clause (or from a single table when qualified, as in: tab_2.*)

▶ The explicit specification of column names to be retrieved

▶ The specification **column_name** [as] **column_heading**, which is a way to replace the name of a column or to assign a new name to an expression

▶ An expression

▶ A system or an aggregate function

NOTE

In addition to the specifications listed above, there are other options that will be partly presented later in this chapter and in the next chapter.

A SELECT statement can retrieve either certain columns or rows from a table. The first operation is called *projection* (or *SELECT list*), and the second one is called *selection* (or *select operation*). The combination of both operations is also possible in a SELECT statement.

NOTE

Before you start to execute queries in this chapter, please re-create the entire sample database.

EXAMPLE 5.1

Get full details of all departments.

```
USE sample
SELECT * from department
```

The result is

dept_no	dept_name	location
d1	Research	Dallas
d2	Accounting	Seattle
d3	Marketing	Dallas

The SELECT statement in Example 5.1 retrieves all rows and all columns from the **department** table. The symbol * is shorthand for a list of all column names in the table named in the FROM clause, in the order in which those columns are defined in the CREATE TABLE statement for that table. The column names serve as column headings of the resulting output.

EXAMPLE 5.2

Get full details of all departments.

```
USE sample
SELECT dept_no, dept_name, location
    FROM department
```

The result is

dept_no	dept_name	location
d1	Research	Dallas
d2	Accounting	Seattle
d3	Marketing	Dallas

The SELECT statement in Example 5.2 is equivalent to the SELECT statement in Example 5.1. Generally, the FROM clause contains several options concerning locks. All these options, together with the notion of the transaction, will be explained in detail in Chapter 14.

WHERE Clause

The simplest form of the SELECT statement, described in the previous section, is not very useful for queries. In practice, there are always several more clauses in a SELECT statement than in the statements shown in Examples 5.1 and 5.2. The following is the syntax of the SELECT statement with (almost) all possible clauses:

```
SELECT select_list
[INTO new_table_]
FROM table
[WHERE search_condition]
[GROUP BY group_by_expression]
[HAVING search_condition]
[ORDER BY order_expression [ASC | DESC] ]
```

NOTE

The clauses in the SELECT statement must be written in syntactical order — for example, the GROUP BY clause must come after the WHERE clause and before the HAVING clause.

In this section we will start with the definition of the first clause (after the FROM clause): WHERE. Often, it is necessary to define one or more conditions that limit the selected rows. The WHERE clause specifies a Boolean expression (an expression that returns a value of TRUE or FALSE) that is tested for each row to be returned (potentially). If the expression is true, then the row is returned; if it is false, it is discarded (see Example 5.3).

EXAMPLE 5.3

Get the names and numbers of all departments located in Dallas.

```
USE sample
SELECT dept_name, dept_no
   FROM department
   WHERE location = 'Dallas'
```

The result is

dept_name	dept_no
Research	d1
Marketing	d3

In addition to the equal sign, the WHERE clause can contain other comparison operators, including the following:

<> (or !=)	not equal
<	less than
>	greater than
>=	greater than or equal
<=	less than or equal
!>	not greater than
!<	not less than

Example 5.4 shows the use of a comparison operator in the WHERE clause.

EXAMPLE 5.4

Get the last and first names for all employees with employee numbers ≥ 15000.

```
USE sample
SELECT emp_lname, emp_fname
   FROM employee
   WHERE emp_no >= 15000
```

The result is

emp_lname	emp_fname
Smith	Matthew
Barrimore	John
James	James
Moser	Sybill

An expression can also be a part of the condition in the WHERE clause. Example 5.5 shows this.

EXAMPLE 5.5

Get the project names for all projects with budgets > 60000 £. The current rate of exchange is 0.51 £ per $1.

```
USE sample
SELECT project_name
   FROM project
   WHERE budget*0.51 > 60000
```

The result is

project_name
Apollo
Mercury

Comparisons of strings (that is, values of data types CHAR, VARCHAR, NCHAR, NVARCHAR, TEXT, or NTEXT) are executed in accordance with the collating sequence in effect (this is the "sort order" specified when SQL Server was installed). If two strings are compared using ASCII code (or any other code), each of the corresponding (first, second, third, and so on) characters will be compared. One character is smaller than the other if it appears in the code table before the other one. Two strings of different lengths will be compared, after the shorter one is padded at the right with blanks, so the length of both strings will be equal. Numbers compare algebraically. Values of data type DATETIME compare in chronological order.

NOTE

Columns with TEXT and IMAGE data types cannot be used in the WHERE clause. (The only exceptions are with the LIKE and IS NULL operators.)

Boolean Operators

WHERE clause conditions can either be simple or contain multiple conditions. Multiple conditions can be built using the Boolean operators AND, OR, and NOT (see Example 5.6). The behavior of these operators has been described in Chapter 3 using truth tables.

EXAMPLE 5.6

Get employee and project numbers of all clerks that work on project p2.

```
USE sample
SELECT emp_no, project_no
  FROM works_on
  WHERE project_no = 'p2'
  AND job = 'Clerk'
```

The result is

emp_no	project_no
25348	p2
28559	p2

If two conditions are connected by the AND operator, rows are retrieved for which both conditions are true.

EXAMPLE 5.7

Get employee numbers for all employees that work either for project p1 or project p2 (or both).

```
USE sample
SELECT project_no, emp_no
  FROM works_on
  WHERE project_no = 'p1'
  OR project_no = 'p2'
```

The result is

project_no	emp_no
p1	10102
p2	25348
p2	18316
p2	29346
p1	9031
p1	28559
p2	28559
p1	29346

If two conditions are connected by the OR operator, all rows of a table are retrieved in which either the first or the second condition (or both) are true.

The result of Example 5.7 contains some duplicate values of column **emp_no**. If this redundant information is to be eliminated, the DISTINCT option should be used, as shown here:

```
USE sample
SELECT DISTINCT emp_no
  FROM works_on
  WHERE project_no = 'p1'
  OR project_no = 'p2'
```

In this case, the result is

emp_no
9031
10102
18316
25348
28559
29346

NOTE

Columns with TEXT and IMAGE data types cannot be retrieved with the DISTINCT option.

Note that the DISTINCT clause can be used only once in a SELECT list, and it must precede all column names in that list. Therefore, Example 5.8 is *wrong*.

EXAMPLE 5.8 (EXAMPLE OF AN ILLEGAL STATEMENT)

```
USE sample
SELECT emp_fname, DISTINCT emp_no
    FROM works_on
    WHERE project_no = 'p1'
    OR project_no = 'p2'
```

The result is

```
Server: Msg 156, Level 15, State 1, Line 1
Incorrect syntax near the keyword 'DISTINCT'.
```

NOTE

When there is more than one column in the SELECT list, the DISTINCT clause displays all rows where the combination of columns is distinct.

The WHERE clause may include any number of the same or different Boolean operations. You should be aware that the three Boolean operations have different priorities for evaluation: the NOT operation has the highest priority, AND is evaluated next, and the

OR operation has the lowest priority. If you do not pay attention to these different priorities for Boolean operations, you will get unexpected results, as Example 5.9 shows.

EXAMPLE 5.9

```
USE sample
SELECT *
  FROM employee
  WHERE emp_no = 25348 AND emp_lname = 'Smith'
  OR emp_fname = 'Matthew' AND dept_no = 'd1'

SELECT *
  FROM employee
  WHERE ((emp_no = 25348 AND emp_lname = 'Smith')
  OR emp_fname ='Matthew') AND dept_no = 'd1'
```

The result is

emp_no	emp_fname	emp_lname	dept_no
25348	Matthew	Smith	d3

emp_no	emp_fname	emp_lname	dept_no

As the results of Example 5.9 show, the two SELECT statements display two different results. In the first SELECT statement, the system evaluates both AND operators first (from the left to the right), and then the OR operator is evaluated. In the second SELECT statement, the use of parentheses changes the operation execution, with all expressions within parentheses being executed first, in sequence from left to right. As you can see, the first statement returned one row, while the second one returned zero rows.

The existence of several Boolean operations in a WHERE clause complicates the corresponding SELECT statement and makes it error prone. In such cases, the use of parentheses is highly recommended, even if they are not necessary. The readability of such SELECT statements will be greatly improved, and possible errors can be avoided.

Here is the first SELECT statement from Example 5.9 (modified using the recommended form):

```
USE sample
SELECT *
   FROM employee
   WHERE (emp_no = 25348 AND emp_lname = 'Smith')
   OR (emp_fname = 'Matthew' AND dept_no = 'd1')
```

The third Boolean operator, NOT, changes the logical value of the corresponding condition. The truth table for NOT in Chapter 3 shows that the negation of the true value is false and vice versa; the negation of the NULL value is also NULL.

EXAMPLE 5.10

Get employee numbers and first names of all employees who do not belong to the department d2.

```
USE sample
SELECT emp_no, emp_lname
   FROM employee
   WHERE NOT dept_no = 'd2'
```

The result is

emp_no	emp_lname
25348	Smith
10102	Jones
18316	Barrimore
28559	Moser

In this case, the NOT operator can be replaced by the comparison operator <> (not equal). Example 5.11 is thus equivalent to Example 5.10.

 NOTE

In this book we use the operator **< >** *(instead of* **! =** *) to remain consistent with the SQL standard.*

EXAMPLE 5.11

```
USE sample
SELECT emp_no, emp_lname
   FROM employee
   WHERE dept_no <> 'd2'
```

IN and BETWEEN Operators

An IN operator allows the specification of two or more expressions to be used for a query search. The result of the condition returns true if the value of the corresponding column equals one of the expressions specified by the IN predicate.

EXAMPLE 5.12

Get all the columns for employees whose employee numbers equal either 29346 or 28559 or 25348.

```
USE sample
SELECT *
   FROM employee
   WHERE emp_no IN (29346, 28559, 25348)
```

The result is

emp_no	emp_fname	emp_lname	dept_no
25348	Matthew	Smith	d3
29346	James	James	d2
28559	Sybill	Moser	d1

An IN operator is equivalent to a series of conditions, connected with one or more OR operators. (The number of OR operators is equal to the number of expressions following the IN operator minus one.) Example 5.13 is equivalent to Example 5.12.

EXAMPLE 5.13

```
USE sample
SELECT *
   FROM employee
```

```
        WHERE emp_no = 29346
        OR emp_no = 28559
        OR emp_no = 25348
```

The IN operator can be used together with the Boolean operator NOT (see Example 5.14). In this case, the query retrieves rows that do not include any of the listed values in the corresponding columns.

EXAMPLE 5.14

Get all columns for employees whose employee numbers are neither 10102 nor 9031.

```
        USE sample
        SELECT *
          FROM employee
          WHERE emp_no NOT IN (10102, 9031)
```

The result is

emp_no	emp_fname	emp_lname	dept_no
25348	Matthew	Smith	d3
18316	John	Barrimore	d1
29346	James	James	d2
2581	Elke	Hansel	d2
28559	Sybill	Moser	d1

In contrast to the IN operator, which specifies each individual value, the BETWEEN operator specifies a range, which determines the lower and upper bounds of qualifying values.

EXAMPLE 5.15

Get the names and budgets for all projects whose budgets are between $95,000 and $120,000 inclusive.

```
        USE sample
        SELECT project_name, budget
          FROM project
          WHERE budget BETWEEN 95000 AND 120000
```

The result is

project_name	budget
Apollo	120000.0
Gemini	95000.0

The BETWEEN operator searches for all values in the range inclusively; that is, qualifying values can be between *or equal to* the lower and upper boundary values.

The BETWEEN operator is logically equal to two individual comparisons, which are connected with the Boolean operator AND. Example 5.16 is equivalent to Example 5.15.

EXAMPLE 5.16

```
USE sample
SELECT project_name, budget
   FROM project
   WHERE budget >= 95000 AND budget <= 120000
```

Like the BETWEEN operator, the NOT BETWEEN operator can be used to search for column values that do not fall within the specified range. The BETWEEN operator can also be applied to columns with character and date values (see Example 5.17).

EXAMPLE 5.17

Get employee numbers of all analysts who did not enter their project in 1998.

```
USE sample
SELECT emp_no
   FROM works_on
   WHERE job = 'Analyst'
   AND enter_date NOT BETWEEN '01.01.1998' AND '12.31.1998'
```

The result is

emp_no
10102
2581

Examples 5.18 and 5.19 show another query that can be written using two different but equivalent ways.

EXAMPLE 5.18

Get the names of all projects with budgets that are less than $100,000 and greater than $150,000.

```
USE sample
SELECT project_name
  FROM project
    WHERE budget NOT BETWEEN 100000 AND 150000
```

The result is

project_name
Gemini
Mercury

Using comparison operators, the solution will look different than in Example 5.18.

EXAMPLE 5.19

Get the names of all projects with budgets that are less than $100,000 and greater than $150,000.

```
USE sample
SELECT project_name
  FROM project
    WHERE budget < 100000 OR budget > 150000
```

NOTE

Although the English phrasing suggests the use of the AND operator (see the text in Example 5.19), the logical meaning of the query demands the use of the OR operator, because if you use AND instead of OR, you will get no results at all. (The reason is that there cannot be a budget that is at the same time less than $100,000 and greater than $150,000.) Therefore, Example 5.19 shows a possible problem that can appear between English phrasing of an exercise and its logical meaning.

Queries Involving Null Values

A NULL in the CREATE TABLE or ALTER TABLE statement specifies that a special value called NULL (which usually represents unknown values) is allowed in the column. These values differ from all other values in a database. In the SELECT statement, the

WHERE clause generally returns rows for which the comparison evaluates to true. Our concern regarding queries is, how will comparisons involving NULL values be evaluated in the WHERE clause?

All comparisons with NULL values will return false (even when preceded by NOT). To retrieve the rows with NULL values in the column, Transact-SQL includes the operator feature IS [NOT] NULL. This specification in a WHERE clause of a SELECT statement has the following general form:

column IS [NOT] NULL

Example 5.20 shows the use of the operator IS NULL.

EXAMPLE 5.20

Get employee numbers and corresponding project numbers for employees with unknown jobs who work on project p2.

```
USE sample
SELECT emp_no, project_no
  FROM works_on
  WHERE project_no = 'p2'
  AND job IS NULL
```

The result is

emp_no	project_no
18316	p2
29346	p2

Example 5.21 shows syntactically correct, but logically incorrect, usage of NULL.

EXAMPLE 5.21

```
USE sample
SELECT project_no, job
  FROM works_on
  WHERE  job <> NULL
```

The result is

project_no	job

The condition

    column IS NOT NULL

is equivalent to the condition

    NOT (column IS NULL)

The system function ISNULL allows a display of the specified value as substitution for NULL (see Example 5.22).

EXAMPLE 5.22

```
USE sample
SELECT emp_no, ISNULL(job, 'Job unknown') task
   FROM works_on
   WHERE project_no = 'p1'
```

The result is

emp_no	task
10102	Analyst
9031	Manager
28559	Job unknown
29346	Clerk

In Example 5.22, we use a column heading **task** for the **job** column.

LIKE Operator

LIKE is an operator that compares column values with a specified pattern. The data type of the column can be any character or the DATETIME data type. The general form of the LIKE operator is

    column [NOT] LIKE 'pattern'

pattern may be a string or date constant or expression (including columns of tables) and must be compatible with the data type of the corresponding column. For the specified column, the comparison between the value in a row and the pattern evaluates to true if the column value matches the pattern expression.

Certain characters within the pattern—called wildcard characters—have a specific interpretation. Two of them are

% (percent sign)
_ (underscore)

The percent sign specifies any sequence of zero or more characters. The underscore specifies any single character. Example 5.23 shows the use of the percent sign.

EXAMPLE 5.23

Get the names and numbers of all employees whose last names begin with the letter *J*.

```
USE sample
SELECT emp_fname, emp_lname, emp_no
  FROM employee
  WHERE emp_lname LIKE 'J%'
```

The result is

emp_fname	emp_lname	emp_no
Ann	Jones	10102
James	James	29346

Example 5.24 shows the use of the wildcard characters % and _.

EXAMPLE 5.24

Get the names and numbers of all employees whose first names contain the letter *a* as the second character.

```
USE sample
SELECT emp_fname, emp_lname, emp_no
  FROM employee
  WHERE emp_fname LIKE '_a%'
```

The result is

emp_fname	emp_lname	emp_no
Matthew	Smith	25348
James	James	29346

In addition to the percent sign and the underscore, Transact-SQL supports other characters that have a special meaning when used with the LIKE operator. These characters ([,], and ^) are best explained in the next two examples.

EXAMPLE 5.25

Get full details of all departments whose locations begin with a character in the range *C* through *F*.

```
USE sample
SELECT *
  FROM department
  WHERE location LIKE '[C-F]%'
```

The result is

dept_no	dept_name	location
d1	Research	Dallas
d3	Marketing	Dallas

As shown in Example 5.25, the square brackets, [and], delimit a range or list of characters. The order in which characters appear in a range is defined by the collating sequence, which is determined when SQL Server is installed or later.

The character ^ specifies the negation of a range or a list of characters. This character has this meaning only within a pair of square brackets (see Example 5.26).

EXAMPLE 5.26

Get the numbers and names of all employees whose last names do not begin with the letters *J*, *K*, *L*, *M*, *N*, or *O* and whose first names do not begin with the letters *E* or *Z*.

```
USE sample
SELECT emp_no, emp_fname, emp_lname
  FROM employee
  WHERE emp_lname LIKE '[^J-O]%'
  AND emp_fname LIKE '[^EZ]%'
```

The result is

emp_no	emp_fname	emp_lname
25348	Matthew	Smith
18316	John	Barrimore

The condition

　　　column NOT LIKE 'pattern'

is equivalent to the condition

　　　NOT (column LIKE 'pattern')

Example 5.27 shows the use of the LIKE operator (together with NOT).

EXAMPLE 5.27

Get full details of all employees whose first names do not end with the character *n*.

```
USE sample
SELECT *
  FROM employee
  WHERE emp_fname NOT LIKE '%n'
```

The result is:

emp_no	emp_fname	emp_lname	dept_no
25348	Matthew	Smith	d3
29346	James	James	d2
2581	Elke	Hansel	d2
9031	Elsa	Bertoni	d2
28559	Sybill	Moser	d1

Any of the wildcard characters (%, _, [,], or ^) enclosed in square brackets stand for themselves. An equivalent feature is available through the ESCAPE option. Therefore, both SELECT statements in Example 5.28 have the same meaning.

EXAMPLE 5.28

```
USE sample
SELECT project_no, project_name
  FROM project
  WHERE project_name LIKE '%[_]%'
```

```
SELECT project_no, project_name
    FROM project
    WHERE project_name LIKE '%!_%' ESCAPE '!'
```

The result is

project_no	project_name

project_no	project_name

Both SELECT statements search for the underscore as an actual character in the column **project_name**. In the first SELECT statement, this search is established by enclosing the sign _ in square brackets. The second SELECT statement uses a character (in the example, it is the character !) as an escape character. The escape character overrides the meaning of the underscore as the wildcard character and leaves it to be interpreted as an ordinary character. (Our result contains no rows because there are no project names including the underscore character.)

NOTE

The SQL standard only supports the use of %, _, and the ESCAPE operator. For this reason, we recommend using the ESCAPE operator instead of a pair of square brackets if any wildcard character must stand for itself.

Simple Subqueries

All previous examples in this chapter contain comparisons of column values with an expression or constant. Additionally, the Transact-SQL language offers the ability to compare column values with the result of another SELECT statement. Such SELECT statements, which are nested in the WHERE clause of another SELECT statement, are called subqueries. The first SELECT statement in a subquery is often called the *outer query*—in contrast to the *inner query*, which denotes the second SELECT statement. The inner query will always be evaluated first, and the outer query receives the values of the inner query.

NOTE

A subquery can also be nested in an INSERT, UPDATE, or a DELETE statement, which will be discussed in Chapter 7.

There are two types of subqueries:

► Simple
► Correlated

In a simple subquery, the inner query is evaluated exactly once. A correlated subquery differs from a simple one in that its value depends upon a variable from the outer query. Therefore, the inner query of a correlated subquery is evaluated each time the system retrieves a new row from the outer query. The correlated subquery will be discussed in Chapter 6.

A simple subquery can be used with the following operators:

► Comparison operators
► IN operator
► ANY or ALL operator
► EXISTS function

Subqueries and Comparison Operators

Example 5.29 shows the simple subquery that is used with the operator =.

EXAMPLE 5.29

Get the first and last names of employees who work in the research department.

```
USE sample
SELECT emp_fname, emp_lname
  FROM employee
  WHERE dept_no =
  (SELECT dept_no
    FROM department
    WHERE dept_name = 'Research')
```

The result is

emp_fname	emp_lname
John	Barrimore
Sybill	Moser

SQL Server first evaluates the inner query. That query returns the number of the research department (d1). Thus, after the evaluation of the inner query, the subquery in Example 5.29 can be represented with the following equivalent query:

```
USE sample
SELECT emp_fname, emp_lname
  FROM employee
  WHERE dept_no = 'd1'
```

A subquery can be used with other comparison operators, too. Example 5.30 shows the use of the operator <.

EXAMPLE 5.30

Get all project numbers of employees whose employee numbers are smaller than the number of the employee named Moser.

```
USE sample
SELECT DISTINCT project_no
  FROM works_on
  WHERE emp_no <
  (SELECT emp_no
    FROM employee
    WHERE emp_lname = 'Moser')
```

The result is

project_no
p1
p2
p3

Any comparison operator can be used, provided the inner query returns exactly one row. This is obvious, because the comparison between particular column values of the outer query and a set of values (as a result of the inner query) is not possible.

Subqueries and IN Operator

The IN operator allows the specification of a set of expressions (or constants) that are subsequently used for the query search. This operator can be applied to a subquery for the same reason—that is, when the result of an inner query contains a set of values.

Example 5.31 shows the use of the IN operator.

EXAMPLE 5.31

Get full details of all employees whose departments are located in Dallas.

```
USE sample
SELECT *
  FROM employee
  WHERE dept_no IN
  (SELECT dept_no
     FROM department
     WHERE location = 'Dallas')
```

The result is

emp_no	emp_fname	emp_lname	dept_no
25348	Matthew	Smith	d3
10102	Ann	Jones	d3
18316	John	Barrimore	d1
28559	Sybill	Moser	d1

Each inner query may contain further queries. This type of subquery is called a subquery with multiple levels of nesting. The maximum number of inner queries in a subquery depends on the amount of memory SQL Server has for each SELECT statement. In the case of subqueries with multiple levels of nesting, the system first evaluates the innermost query and returns the result to the query on the next nesting level, and so on. Finally, the outermost query evaluates the final outcome.

EXAMPLE 5.32

Get the last names of all employees who work on the project Apollo.

```
USE sample
SELECT emp_lname
  FROM employee
  WHERE emp_no IN
  (SELECT emp_no
```

```
FROM works_on
WHERE project_no IN
(SELECT project_no
    FROM project
    WHERE project_name = 'Apollo'))
```

The result is

emp_lname
Jones
James
Bertoni
Moser

The innermost query in Example 5.32 evaluates to the **project_no** value p1. The middle inner query compares this value with all values of the **project_no** column in the **works_on** table. The result of this intermediate query is the set of employee numbers: (10102, 29346, 9031, 28559). Finally, the outermost query displays the corresponding last names for the selected employee numbers.

ANY and ALL Operators

The operators ANY and ALL are always used in combination with one of the comparison operators. The general syntax of both operators is

column operator [ANY | ALL] query

where **operator** stands for a comparison operator.

NOTE

Do not use ANY and ALL operators! Every query using ANY or ALL can be better formulated with the EXISTS function (see Chapter 6). Additionally, the semantic meaning of the ANY operator can be easily confused with the semantic meaning of the ALL operator and vice versa.

The ANY operator evaluates to true if the result of an inner query contains at least one row that satisfies the comparison. Example 5.33 shows the use of the ANY operator.

EXAMPLE 5.33

Get the employee numbers, project numbers, and job names for employees who have not spent the most time on one of the projects.

```
USE sample
SELECT DISTINCT emp_no, project_no, job
  FROM works_on
  WHERE enter_date > ANY
  (SELECT  enter_date
    FROM works_on)
```

The result is

emp_no	project_no	job
2581	p3	Analyst
9031	p1	Manager
9031	p3	Clerk
10102	p3	Manager
18316	p2	NULL
25348	p2	Clerk
28559	p1	NULL
28559	p2	Clerk
29346	p1	Clerk
29346	p2	NULL

Each value of the **enter_date** column in Example 5.33 is compared with all values of this column. For all dates of this column, except the oldest one, the comparison is evaluated to true at least once. The row with the oldest date does not belong to the result because the comparison does not evaluate to true in any case. In other words, the expression "enter_date > ANY (SELECT enter_date FROM works_on)" is true if there are *any* (one or more) rows in the **works_on** table with a value of the **enter_date** column less than the value of **enter_date** for the current row. This will be true for all but the minimum (or earliest) value of **enter_date** in the table.

The keyword SOME is the synonym for ANY.

Example 5.34 shows the use of the ANY operator.

EXAMPLE 5.34

Get the first and last names for all employees who work on project p1.

```
USE sample
SELECT emp_fname, emp_lname
  FROM employee
  WHERE emp_no = ANY
  (SELECT emp_no
    FROM works_on
    WHERE project_no = 'p1')
```

The result is

emp_fname	emp_lname
Ann	Jones
James	James
Elsa	Bertoni
Sybill	Moser

The ALL operator evaluates to true if the evaluation of the table column in the inner query returns all values of that column. Example 5.35 shows the use of the ALL operator.

EXAMPLE 5.35

Get jobs of the employee with the smallest employee number.

```
USE sample
SELECT job
  FROM works_on
  WHERE emp_no <= ALL
  (SELECT emp_no
    FROM employee)
```

The result is

Job
Analyst

EXISTS Function

The EXISTS function checks the inner query of a subquery and evaluates to true if its result contains at least one row. The syntax of the EXISTS function is

> [NOT] EXISTS (query)

Chapter 6 contains all examples regarding the EXISTS function.

Queries in the FROM Clause

The previous versions of SQL Server only allowed you to place a query in the WHERE clause of the SELECT statement, as shown in earlier examples. Generally, it should be possible to write a query any place in a SELECT statement where a table can appear. (The result of a query is always a table or, in a special case, an expression.) SQL Server now allows you to write a query as part of the FROM clause. Example 5.36 shows the use of a query inside the FROM clause.

EXAMPLE 5.36

Get the names of all employees with employee numbers greater than or equal to 10000.

```
USE sample
SELECT emp_fname, emp_lname
  FROM (SELECT *
          FROM employee
          WHERE emp_no >= 10000 ) AS empno_10000
```

The result is

emp_fname	emp_lname
Matthew	Smith
Ann	Jones
John	Barrimore
James	James
Sybill	Moser

The name **empno_10000** is an alias table name for the result of the SELECT statement in the FROM clause. (The alias for a table must be specified if a query is placed in the FROM clause of a SELECT statement.)

GROUP BY Clause

The GROUP BY clause defines one or more columns as a group such that all rows within any group have the same values for those columns. Example 5.37 shows the use of the GROUP BY clause.

EXAMPLE 5.37

Get all jobs of employees.

        USE sample
        SELECT job
          FROM works_on
          GROUP BY job

The result is

Job
NULL
Analyst
Clerk
Manager

In Example 5.37, the GROUP BY clause builds different groups for all possible values (NULL, too!) appearing in the **job** column.

NOTE

There is a restriction regarding the use of columns in the GROUP BY clause. Each column appearing in the SELECT list of the query must also appear in the GROUP BY clause. This does not hold for constants and for columns that are part of an aggregate function (see Example 5.45). This makes sense, because only columns in the GROUP BY clause are guaranteed to have a single value (for each group).

A table can be grouped by any combination of its columns. Example 5.38 shows the grouping of rows of the **works_on** table using two columns.

EXAMPLE 5.38

Group all employees using their project numbers and jobs.

```
USE sample
SELECT project_no, job
   FROM works_on
   GROUP BY project_no, job
```

The result is

project_no	job
p1	Analyst
p1	Clerk
p1	Manager
p1	NULL
p2	NULL
p2	Clerk
p3	Analyst
p3	Clerk
p3	Manager

The result of Example 5.38 shows that there are nine groups with different combinations of project numbers and jobs. The only two groups that contain more than one row are

p2	Clerk	25348, 28559
p2	NULL	18316, 29346

The sequence of the column names in the GROUP BY clause need not correspond to the sequence of the names in the SELECT list.

NOTE

Columns of data types TEXT and IMAGE cannot be used in the GROUP BY clause.

Aggregate Functions

Aggregates are functions that are used to get summary values. All aggregate functions can be divided into three groups:

▶ Convenient aggregate functions

▶ Statistical aggregate functions

▶ Superaggregates

The following sections describe these groups.

Convenient Aggregates

The Transact-SQL language supports six aggregate functions (an aggregate function is one that acts upon a set of values rather than a single one):

▶ MIN

▶ MAX

▶ SUM

▶ AVG

▶ COUNT

▶ COUNT_BIG

NOTE

There are several other aggregate functions, such as GROUPING, which will be described in detail in Chapter 27.

All aggregate functions operate on a single argument that can be a column or an expression. (The only exception is the second form of the COUNT and COUNT_BIG function: COUNT(*) and COUNT_BIG(*).) The result of each aggregate function is a constant value, which is displayed in a separate column of the result.

The aggregate functions appear in the SELECT list, which can include a GROUP BY clause. If there is no GROUP BY clause in the SELECT statement, and the SELECT list includes at least one aggregate function, then no simple columns can be included in the SELECT list (other than as arguments of an aggregate function). Therefore, Example 5.39 is *wrong*.

EXAMPLE 5.39 (EXAMPLE OF AN ILLEGAL STATEMENT)

```
USE sample
SELECT emp_lname, MIN (emp_no)
    FROM employee
```

The **emp_lname** column of the **employee** table must not appear in the SELECT list of Example 5.39, because it is not the argument of an aggregate function. On the other hand, all column names that are not arguments of an aggregate function may appear in the SELECT list if they are used for grouping.

The argument of an aggregate function can be preceded by one of two keywords:

► ALL

► DISTINCT

ALL indicates that all values of a column are to be considered. DISTINCT eliminates duplicate values of a column before the aggregate function is applied. (ALL is the default value.)

NOTE

Aggregate functions cannot be used in the WHERE clause of the SELECT statement.

Aggregate Functions MIN and MAX

The aggregate functions MIN and MAX compute the smallest and the largest values in the column, respectively. If there is a WHERE clause, the MIN and MAX functions return the smallest or largest of values from selected rows. Example 5.40 shows the use of the aggregate function MIN.

EXAMPLE 5.40

Get the smallest employee number.

```
USE sample
SELECT MIN(emp_no) min_employee_number
    FROM employee
```

The result is

min_employee_number
2581

Example 5.40 shows that column headings can also be applied to aggregate functions to enhance the readability of the result.

The result of Example 5.40 is not user friendly. For instance, the name of the employee with the smallest number is not known. As already shown in Example 5.39, the explicit specification of the **emp_name** column in the SELECT list is not allowed. To retrieve the name of the employee with the smallest employee number, we use a subquery in Example 5.41, where the inner query contains the SELECT statement of Example 5.40.

EXAMPLE 5.41

Get the number and the last name of the employee with the smallest employee number.

```
USE sample
SELECT emp_no, emp_lname
  FROM employee
  WHERE emp_no =
  (SELECT MIN(emp_no)
    FROM employee)
```

The result is

emp_no	emp_lname
2581	Hansel

Example 5.42 shows the use of the aggregate function MAX.

EXAMPLE 5.42

Get the employee number of the manager who was entered last in the **works_on** table.

```
USE sample
SELECT emp_no
  FROM works_on
  WHERE enter_date =
  (SELECT MAX(enter_date)
    FROM works_on
    WHERE job = 'Manager')
```

The result is

emp_no
10102

The argument of the functions MIN and MAX can also be a string value or a date. If the argument has a string value, the comparison between all values will be provided using the actual collating sequence. For all arguments of data type DATETIME, the earliest date specifies the smallest and the latest date the largest value in the column.

The DISTINCT option cannot be used with the aggregate functions MIN and MAX. All null values in the column that are the argument of the aggregate function MIN or MAX are always eliminated before MIN or MAX is applied.

Aggregate Function SUM

The aggregate function SUM calculates the sum of the values in the column. The argument of the function SUM must be numeric. Example 5.43 shows the use of the aggregate function SUM.

EXAMPLE 5.43

Calculate the sum of all budgets of projects.

```
USE sample
SELECT SUM (budget) sum_of_budgets
  FROM project
```

The result is

sum_of_budgets
401500.0

The use of the DISTINCT option eliminates all duplicate values in the column before the function SUM is applied. Similarly, all null values are always eliminated before SUM is applied.

Aggregate Function AVG

The aggregate function AVG calculates the average of the values in the column. The argument of the function AVG must be numeric (see Example 5.44).

EXAMPLE 5.44

Calculate the average of all budgets with a money amount greater than $100,000.

```
USE sample
SELECT AVG(budget) avg_budget
  FROM project
  WHERE budget > 100000
```

The result is

avg_budget

153250.0

All null values are eliminated before the function AVG is applied.

Aggregate Functions COUNT and COUNT_BIG

The aggregate function COUNT has two different forms. The syntax of the first form is

COUNT ([DISTINCT] col_name)

This form of the function COUNT calculates the number of values in the **col_name** column. When the DISTINCT keyword is used, all duplicate values are eliminated before the function COUNT is applied. This form of COUNT does not count rows with null values for the column.

Example 5.45 shows the use of the first form of the aggregate function COUNT.

EXAMPLE 5.45

Count all different jobs in each project.

```
USE sample
SELECT project_no, COUNT(DISTINCT job) job_count
   FROM works_on
   GROUP BY project_no
```

The result is

project_no	job_count
p1	4
p2	1
p3	3

As can be seen from the result of Example 5.45, all null values are eliminated before the function COUNT(DISTINCT col_name) or COUNT(col_name) is applied. (The sum of all values in the **job_count** column is 8 instead of 11.)

The second form of the function COUNT has the form COUNT(*). This aggregate function counts the number of rows in the table. Or if there is a WHERE clause in the SELECT statement, it returns the number of rows for which the WHERE condition is true. Example 5.46 shows the use of the second form of the aggregate function COUNT.

EXAMPLE 5.46

How many employees work on each project?

```
USE sample
SELECT project_no, COUNT(*) emp_count
  FROM works_on
  GROUP BY project_no
```

The result is

project_no	emp_count
p1	4
p2	4
p3	3

In contrast to the first form of the function COUNT, the second form does not eliminate null values (see Example 5.47).

EXAMPLE 5.47

Get the number of each job in all projects.

```
USE sample
SELECT job, COUNT(*) job_count
  FROM works_on
  GROUP BY job
```

The result is

Job	job_count
NULL	3
Analyst	2
Clerk	4
Manager	2

The COUNT_BIG function is analogous to the COUNT function. The only difference between them is their return values: COUNT_BIG always returns a value of the BIGINT data type, while the COUNT function always returns a value of the INTEGER data type.

Statistical Aggregates

The following aggregate functions belong to the group of statistical aggregates:

▶ VAR

▶ VARP

▶ STDEV

▶ STDEVP

Aggregate Functions VAR and VARP

The aggregate function VAR computes the variance of all the values listed in a column or expression. Example 5.48 shows the use of the VAR aggregate function.

EXAMPLE 5.48

```
USE sample
SELECT VAR(budget) variance_of_budgets
    FROM project
```

The result is

variance_of_budgets
2236583333.3333321

The aggregate function VARP computes the variance for the population of all the values listed in a column or expression.

Aggregate Functions STDEV and STDEVP

The aggregate function STDEV computes the standard deviation of all the values listed in a column of expression. (The standard deviation is computed as the square root of the corresponding variance.) Example 5.49 shows the use of the STDEV function.

EXAMPLE 5.49

```
USE sample
SELECT STDEV(budget) std_dev_of_budgets
    FROM project
```

The result is

std_dev_of_budgets
47292.529360706983

The aggregate function STDEVP computes the standard deviation for the population of all the values listed in a column or expression.

Superaggregates (Operators CUBE and ROLLUP)

The result of an aggregate function is always one-dimensional—that is, a constant. The Transact-SQL language supports some other functions that yield multidimensional results:

- ► CUBE
- ► ROLLUP

The application area of these two functions is a data warehouse. Therefore, they are described in detail in Chapter 27, which discusses data warehousing.

User-Defined Aggregate Functions

SQL Server 2005 supports the implementation of user-defined aggregate functions using the CREATE AGGREGATE statement. Using these functions you can implement and deploy aggregate functions that do not belong to aggregate functions supported by the SQL Server system. These functions are a special case of user-defined functions, which will be described in detail in Chapter 8 (see also Example 8.19).

HAVING Clause

The HAVING clause defines the condition that is then applied to groups of rows. The HAVING clause has the same meaning to groups of rows that the WHERE clause has to each individual row. The syntax of the HAVING clause is

        HAVING condition

where **condition** contains aggregate functions or constants.

   Example 5.50 shows the use of the HAVING clause with the aggregate function COUNT(*).

EXAMPLE 5.50

Get project numbers for all projects employing less than four persons.

```
USE sample
SELECT project_no
  FROM works_on
  GROUP BY project_no
  HAVING COUNT(*) < 4
```

   The result is

project_no

p3

   In Example 5.50, the system uses the GROUP BY clause to group all rows according to existing values in the **project_no** column. After that, it counts the number of rows in each group and selects those groups with three or fewer rows.

   The HAVING clause can also be used without aggregates. Example 5.51 shows this.

EXAMPLE 5.51

Group rows of the **works_on** table by jobs and eliminate those jobs that do not begin with the letter *M*.

```
USE sample
SELECT job
  FROM works_on
  GROUP BY job
    HAVING job LIKE 'M%'
```

The result is

job
Manager

The HAVING clause can also be used without the GROUP BY clause, although it is uncommon in practice. In such a case, all rows of the entire table belong to a single group.

NOTE

Columns with TEXT or IMAGE data types cannot be used with the HAVING clause.

ORDER BY Clause

The ORDER BY clause defines the particular order of the rows in the result of a query. This clause has the following syntax:

ORDER BY {[col_name | col_number [ASC | DESC]]} , ...

The **col_name** column defines the order. **col_number** is an alternative specification, which identifies the column by its ordinal position in the sequence of all columns in the SELECT list (1 for the first column, 2 for the second one, and so on). ASC indicates ascending and DESC indicates descending order, with ASC as the default value.

Example 5.52 shows the use of the ORDER BY clause.

EXAMPLE 5.52

Get employee names and employee numbers, in ascending order of employee numbers.

```
USE sample
SELECT emp_no, emp_fname, emp_lname
  FROM employee
  ORDER BY emp_no
```

The result is

emp_no	emp_fname	emp_lname
2581	Elke	Hansel
9031	Elsa	Bertoni
10102	Ann	Jones

18316	John	Barrimore
25348	Matthew	Smith
28559	Sybill	Moser
29346	James	James

NOTE

The columns in the ORDER BY clause need not appear in the SELECT list. However, the ORDER BY columns must appear in the SELECT list if SELECT DISTINCT is specified. Also, this clause may not reference columns from tables that are not listed in the FROM clause.

As the syntax of the ORDER BY clause shows, the order criterion may contain more than one column (see Example 5.53).

EXAMPLE 5.53

Get department numbers and employee names for employees with employee numbers < 20000, in ascending order of last and first names.

```
USE sample
SELECT emp_fname, emp_lname, dept_no
  FROM employee
  WHERE emp_no < 20000
  ORDER BY emp_lname, emp_fname
```

The result is

emp_fname	emp_lname	dept_no
John	Barrimore	d1
Elsa	Bertoni	d2
Elke	Hansel	d2
Ann	Jones	d3

It is also possible to identify the columns in the ORDER BY clause by the ordinal position of the column in the SELECT list. Hence, the ORDER BY clause in Example 5.53 could be written in the following form:

```
ORDER BY 2, 1
```

The use of column numbers instead of column names is an alternative solution, if the order criterion contains any aggregate function. (The other way is to use column headings, which then appear in the ORDER BY clause.) However, using column names rather than numbers in the ORDER BY clause is recommended to reduce the difficulty of maintaining the query if any columns need to be added or deleted from the SELECT list. Example 5.54 shows the use of column numbers.

EXAMPLE 5.54

For each project number, get the project number and the number of all employees, in descending order of the employee number.

```
USE sample
SELECT project_no, COUNT(*) emp_quantity
  FROM works_on
  GROUP BY project_no
  ORDER BY 2 DESC
```

The result is

project_no	emp_quantity
p1	4
p2	4
p3	3

The Transact-SQL language orders null values at the beginning of all values if the order is ascending, and at the end of all values if the order is descending.

NOTE

Columns with TEXT or IMAGE data types cannot be used in the ORDER BY clause.

SELECT Statement and IDENTITY Property

As already stated in Chapter 4, columns with numeric data types can have the IDENTITY property. SQL Server generates values of such columns sequentially, starting with an initial value.

Some system functions and global variables are related to the IDENTITY property. The IDENTITYCOL variable can be used instead of the name of the column with the IDENTITY property. Example 5.55 shows the use of the IDENTITY property and the IDENTITYCOL variable.

EXAMPLE 5.55

```
USE sample
CREATE TABLE product
   (product_no INTEGER IDENTITY(10000,1) NOT NULL,
     product_name CHAR(30) NOT NULL,
     price MONEY)

SELECT IDENTITYCOL
      FROM product
      WHERE product_name = 'Soap'
```

The result could be

product_no
10005

The **product** table is created first in Example 5.55. This table has the column **product_no** with the IDENTITY property. The values of the **product_no** column are automatically generated by the system, beginning with 10000 and incrementing by 1 for every subsequent value: 10000, 10001, 10002, and so on.

The system variable IDENTITYCOL in the SELECT statement corresponds to the name of the column with the IDENTITY property—that is, with the column **product_no**.

The system functions

► IDENT_SEED

► IDENT_INCR

► IDENT_CURRENT

can be used to find out the beginning value, the increment of the column, and the last identity value of the column with the IDENTITY property, respectively.

Normally, the system sets identity values; they are not supplied by the user. If, however, you want to supply your own values for particular rows, then before inserting the explicit value, the IDENTITY_INSERT option must be set to ON using the SET statement:

SET IDENTITY_INSERT table_name ON

Set Operators

In addition to the operators described in the previous sections, there are three set operators that connect two or more queries:

- ▶ UNION
- ▶ INTERSECTION
- ▶ DIFFERENCE

NOTE

Since SQL Server 2005, the Transact-SQL language supports all three operators.

The result of the union of two sets is the set of all elements appearing in either or both of the sets. Accordingly, the union of two tables is a new table consisting of all rows appearing in either or both of the tables.

The general form of the UNION operator is
select_1 UNION [ALL] select_2 {[UNION [ALL] select_3]}...

select_1, **select_2**,... are SELECT statements that build the union. If the ALL option is used, all resulting rows, including duplicates, are to be displayed. The ALL option has the same meaning with the UNION operator as in the SELECT list. There is only one difference: the option ALL is the default in the SELECT list, but it must be specified with the UNION operator to display all resulting rows, including duplicates.

The sample database in its original form is not suitable for a demonstration of the UNION operator. For this reason, we introduce a new table, **employee_enh**, which is identical to the existing **employee** table, up to the additional **domicile** column. The **domicile** column contains the place of residence of every employee.

The new **employee_enh** table has the following form:

emp_no	emp_fname	emp_lname	dept_no	domicile
25348	Matthew	Smith	d3	San Antonio
10102	Ann	Jones	d3	Houston
18316	John	Barrimore	d1	San Antonio
29346	James	James	d2	Seattle
9031	Elke	Bertoli	d2	Portland
2581	Elisa	Kim	d2	Tacoma
28559	Sybill	Moser	d1	Houston

Creation of the **employee_enh** table provides an opportunity to show the use of the INTO clause of the SELECT statement. SELECT INTO has two different parts: first, it creates the new table with the columns corresponding to the columns listed in the SELECT list. Second, the existing rows of the original table will be inserted in the new table. (The name of the new table appears with the INTO clause, and the name of the original table appears in the FROM clause of the SELECT statement.)

Example 5.56 shows the creation of the **employee_enh** table.

EXAMPLE 5.56

```
USE sample
SELECT *
  INTO employee_enh
  FROM employee
ALTER TABLE employee_enh
    ADD domicile CHAR(25) NULL
```

The SELECT INTO statement generates the **employee_enh** table and inserts all rows from the initial table into the new one (assuming there was no WHERE clause used with the SELECT INTO statement). Finally, the ALTER TABLE statement appends the **domicile** column to the **employee_enh** table.

After the execution of Example 5.56, the **domicile** column contains no values. The values can be added using the following UPDATE statements:

```
UPDATE employee_enh set domicile = 'San Antonio'
   WHERE emp_no = 25348
UPDATE employee_enh set domicile = 'Houston'
   WHERE emp_no = 10102
```

```
UPDATE employee_enh set domicile = 'San Antonio'
   WHERE emp_no = 18316
UPDATE employee_enh set domicile = 'Seattle'
   WHERE emp_no = 29346
UPDATE employee_enh set domicile = 'Portland'
   WHERE emp_no = 9031
UPDATE employee_enh set domicile = 'Tacoma'
   WHERE emp_no = 2581
UPDATE employee_enh set domicile = 'Houston'
   WHERE emp_no = 28559
```

Example 5.57 shows the union of the tables **employee_enh** and **department**.

EXAMPLE 5.57

```
USE sample
SELECT domicile
   FROM employee_enh
UNION
SELECT location
   FROM department
```

The result is

Domicile
San Antonio
Houston
Portland
Tacoma
Seattle
Dallas

Two tables can be connected with the UNION operator if they are compatible with each other. This means they have the same number of columns, and the corresponding columns have the compatible data types. (For example, INT and SMALLINT are compatible data types.)

The ordering of the result of the union can be done only if the ORDER BY clause is used with the last SELECT statement (see Example 5.58). The same is valid for the COMPUTE clause, which is described later in this chapter. The GROUP BY and the HAVING clauses can be used with the particular SELECT statements, but not with the union itself.

EXAMPLE 5.58

Get the employee number for employees who either belong to department d1 or entered their project before 1/1/1998, in ascending order of employee number.

```
USE sample
SELECT emp_no
  FROM employee
  WHERE dept_no = 'd1'
UNION
SELECT emp_no
  FROM works_on
  WHERE enter_date < '01.01.1998'
ORDER BY 1
```

The result is

emp_no
9031
10102
18316
28559
29346

The OR and UNION operators are similar. Sometimes, the OR operator can be used instead of the UNION operator, as the two equivalent examples, Examples 5.59 and 5.60, show. In this case, the set of the SELECT statement is replaced through one SELECT statement with the set of OR operators.

EXAMPLE 5.59

Get employee numbers and names for employees who belong to either department d1 or d2.

```
USE sample
SELECT emp_no, emp_fname, emp_lname
  FROM employee
  WHERE dept_no = 'd1'
UNION
SELECT emp_no, emp_fname, emp_lname
  FROM employee
  WHERE dept_no = 'd2'
```

The result is

emp_no	emp_fname	emp_lname
2581	Elke	Hansel
9031	Elsa	Bertoni
29346	James	James
18316	John	Barrimore
28559	Sybill	Moser

EXAMPLE 5.60

```
USE sample
SELECT emp_no, emp_fname, emp_lname
   FROM employee
   WHERE dept_no ='d1' OR dept_no = 'd2'
```

The UNION operator can be replaced with the OR operator only if the same table is used in all SELECT statements connected by the UNION operator.

Besides UNION, there are two other set operators: INTERSECTION and EXCEPT. The intersection of two tables is the set of rows belonging to both tables. The difference of two tables is the set of all rows, where the resulting rows belong to the first table but not to the second one.

The Transact-SQL language supports these two operators directly. The following two examples show the use of both operators. In addition, the INTERSECTION operator can be simulated using the EXISTS function (see Example 6.21) and the EXCEPT operator using the NOT EXISTS function (see Example 6.22).

EXAMPLE 5.61

```
USE sample
SELECT emp_no
   FROM employee
   WHERE dept_no = 'd1'
INTERSECT
SELECT emp_no
   FROM works_on
   WHERE enter_date < '01.01.1999'
```

The result is

emp_no
28559
18316

In Example 5.61 the INTERSECT operator is used to find all employee numbers that belong to the result set of the first query as well as of the second query.

EXAMPLE 5.62

Get all names of the cities where employees live that are not the locations of any departments.

```
USE sample
SELECT DISTINCT domicile
FROM employee_enh
EXCEPT
SELECT location
FROM department
```

The result is

domicile
Houston
Portland
San Antonio
Tacoma

CASE Expressions

In database application programming, it is sometimes necessary to modify the representation of data. For instance, a person's gender can be coded using the values 1, 2, and 3 (for female, male, and child, respectively). Such a programming technique can reduce the time for the implementation of a program. The CASE expression in the Transact-SQL language makes this type of encoding easy to implement.

NOTE

CASE does not represent a statement (as in most programming languages) but an expression. Therefore, the CASE expression can be used (almost) everywhere where the Transact-SQL language allows the use of an expression.

The CASE expression has two different forms:

▶ Simple CASE expression

▶ Searched CASE expression

The syntax of the simple CASE expression is

```
CASE expression_1
  {WHEN expression_2 THEN result_1} ...
  [ELSE result_n]
END
```

A Transact-SQL statement with the simple CASE expression looks for the first expression in the list of all WHEN clauses that match **expression_1** and evaluates the corresponding THEN clause. If there is no match, the ELSE clause is evaluated.

The syntax of the searched CASE expression is

```
CASE
  {WHEN condition_1 THEN result_1} ...
    [ELSE result_n]
END
```

A Transact-SQL statement with the searched CASE expression looks for the first expression that evaluates to true. If none of the WHEN conditions evaluates to true, the value of the ELSE expression is returned. Example 5.63 shows the use of the searched CASE expression.

EXAMPLE 5.63

The following example shows the use of the searched CASE expression.

```
USE sample
SELECT project_name,
  CASE
    WHEN budget > 0 AND budget < 100000  THEN 1
    WHEN budget >= 100000 AND budget < 200000  THEN 2
```

```
        WHEN budget >= 200000 AND budget < 300000  THEN 3
        ELSE 4
      END budget_weight
   FROM project
```

The result is

project_name	budget_weight
Apollo	2
Gemini	1
Mercury	2

Budgets of all projects are weighted in Example 5.63, and the calculated weights (together with the name of the corresponding project) are displayed.

COMPUTE Clause

The COMPUTE clause uses aggregate functions (MIN, MAX, SUM, AVG, and COUNT) to calculate summary values that appear as additional rows in the result of a query. The aggregate functions used with the COMPUTE clause are referred to as row aggregate functions.

The aggregate functions are usually applied to rows of a table to calculate a scalar value, which then appears in the result query as an additional row (see Example 5.64). The query using this form of aggregate functions has, again, a row as a result.

The result of a COMPUTE clause is not a table: it is a report. Hence, the COMPUTE clause, in contrast to all other described operators and clauses, does not belong to the relational model, which is a basis for SQL Server and all other relational database systems.

The COMPUTE clause has an optional BY portion. BY defines the grouping form of the result. If BY is omitted, the row aggregate function is applied to all rows of a result query. The option BY **column_name** specifies that the values of the **column_name** column are used to build groups. The ORDER BY clause is required if the COMPUTE clause with BY is used.

NOTE

COMPUTE and COMPUTE BY clauses are marked for deprecation in future versions of SQL Server, because they generate multiple result sets, which are hard to handle. Simply stated, these two clauses do not belong to the relational model. You should use the ROLLUP statement instead (see Chapter 27).

Examples 5.64 and 5.65 show the use of the COMPUTE clause, with and without the BY portion.

EXAMPLE 5.64

```
USE sample
SELECT emp_no, project_no, enter_date
  FROM works_on
  WHERE project_no = 'p1' OR project_no = 'p2'
COMPUTE MIN(enter_date)
```

The result is

emp_no	project_no	enter_date
10102	p1	1997-10-01 00:00:00.000
25348	p2	1998-02-15 00:00:00.000
18316	p2	1998-06-01 00:00:00.000
29346	p2	1997-12-15 00:00:00.000
9031	p1	1998-04-15 00:00:00.000
28559	p1	1998-08-01 00:00:00.000
28559	p2	1999-02-01 00:00:00.000
29346	p1	1998-01-04 00:00:00.000

```
min
1997-10-01 00:00:00.000
```

EXAMPLE 5.65

```
USE sample
SELECT emp_no, project_no, enter_date
  FROM works_on
  WHERE project_no = 'p1' OR project_no = 'p2'
  ORDER BY project_no
COMPUTE MIN(enter_date) BY project_no
```

The result is

emp_no	project_no	enter_date
10102	p1	1997-10-01 00:00:00.000
9031	p1	1998-04-15 00:00:00.000
28559	p1	1998-08-01 00:00:00.000
29346	p1	1998-01-04 00:00:00.000

min
1997-10-01 00:00:00.000

emp_no	project_no	enter_date
25348	p2	1998-02-15 00:00:00.000
18316	p2	1998-06-01 00:00:00.000
29346	p2	1997-12-15 00:00:00.000
28559	p2	1999-02-01 00:00:00.000

min
1997-12-15 00:00:00.000

A COMPUTE clause can have multiple uses in a SELECT statement. Hence, Example 5.65 can be written using one SELECT statement and the following COMPUTE statements:

COMPUTE MIN(enter_date) BY project_no

COMPUTE MIN(enter_date)

Example 5.66 shows the use of multiple aggregate functions in a COMPUTE clause.

EXAMPLE 5.66

```
USE sample
SELECT project_no, budget
  FROM project
   WHERE budget < 150000
COMPUTE SUM(budget), AVG(budget)
```

The result is

project_no	budget
p1	120000.0
p2	95000.0

sum	avg
215000.0	107500.0

There are some restrictions concerning the COMPUTE clause:

▶ SELECT INTO is not allowed (because the result of the COMPUTE clause is *not* a table).

▶ All columns in the COMPUTE clause must appear in a SELECT list.

▶ The name of each column in the COMPUTE BY clause must appear in the ORDER BY clause.

▶ The order of the columns in the COMPUTE BY and the ORDER BY clauses must be identical.

Temporary Tables

A temporary table is a special kind of a table that differs in two ways from base tables:

▶ Each temporary table is implicitly dropped by the system.

▶ Each temporary table is stored in the **tempdb** system database.

Temporary tables can be local or global. Local temporary tables are removed at the end of the current session. They are specified with the prefix #—for example, **#table_name**. Global temporary tables, which are specified with the prefix ##, are dropped at the end of the session that created this table.

Examples 5.67 and 5.68 show the creation of the local temporary tables **project_temp** and **project_temp1**, respectively.

EXAMPLE 5.67

```
USE sample
CREATE TABLE #project_temp
   (project_no CHAR(4) NOT NULL,
    project_name CHAR(25) NOT NULL)
```

EXAMPLE 5.68

```
USE sample
SELECT project_no, project_name
  INTO #project_temp1
  FROM project
```

Examples 5.67 and 5.68 are almost equivalent. They use two different Transact-SQL statements to create the local temporary tables **project_temp** and **project_temp1**. However, Example 5.68 actually populates the temporary table with the data from the **project** table, while Example 5.67 does not.

Computed Columns

Computed columns are (by default) virtual columns not physically stored in the table. Their values are recalculated each time they are referenced in a query. The following is an example to demonstrate the use of computed columns.

EXAMPLE 5.69

```
USE sample
CREATE TABLE orders
    (orderid INT NOT NULL,
     price MONEY NOT NULL,
     quantity INT NOT NULL,
     orderdate DATETIME NOT NULL,
     total AS price * quantity PERSISTED,
     shippeddate AS DATEADD (DAY, 7, orderdate))
```

The **orders** table in Example 5.69 has two computed columns: **total** and **shippeddate**. The column **total** is computed using two other columns—**price** and **quantity**—while the other column—**shippeddate**—is computed using the date function DATEADD and the column **orderdate**.

With SQL Server 2005 you can use the PERSISTED keyword in the CREATE TABLE and ALTER TABLE statements to physically store computed columns in the table. The values of persisted computed columns are always updated when you modify a column on which the computed column depends. Also, you can create an index for a persisted computed column. (The column **total** in Example 5.69 specifies a persisted computed column, while **shippeddate** is a virtual computed column.)

There are several restrictions concerning computed columns:

► Column(s) that build the computed column must belong to the same table.

► The DEFAULT constraint cannot be attached to a computed column.

► The computed column cannot contain a subquery.

Since SQL Server 2000, you can define indices on a computed column if the following conditions are satisfied:

► The computed column must be deterministic. (Expressions are deterministic if they always return the same result for a given set of inputs.)

► The QUOTED_IDENTIFIER and ANSI_NULL options must be set ON when the CREATE TABLE statement with the computed column is executed.

► The result value of the computed column cannot evaluate to the VARCHAR(MAX), VARBINARY(MAX), or text/image data types.

Conclusion

We have now covered all of the features of the SELECT statement regarding data retrieval from only one table. Every SELECT statement that retrieves data from a table must contain at least the SELECT and the FROM clauses. The FROM clause specifies the table(s) from which the data is retrieved. The most important optional clause is the WHERE clause, containing one or more conditions that can be combined using the Boolean operators AND, OR, and NOT. Hence, the conditions in the WHERE clause place the restriction on the selected row.

The next chapter completes the handling of the SELECT statement, introducing the different kinds of join operations that allow the retrieval of data from more than one table.

Exercises

E.5.1

Get all rows of the **works_on** table.

E.5.2

Get the employee numbers for all clerks.

E.5.3

Get the employee numbers for employees working in project p2, and having employee numbers smaller than 10000. Solve this problem with two different but equivalent SELECT statements.

E.5.4

Get the employee numbers for employees who didn't enter their project in 1998.

E.5.5

Get the employee numbers for all employees who have a leading job (i.e., Analyst or Manager) in project p1.

E.5.6

Get the enter dates for all employees in project p2 whose jobs have not been determined yet.

E.5.7

Get the employee numbers and last names of all employees whose first names contain two letter *t*'s.

E.5.8

Get the employee numbers and first names of all employees whose last names have a letter *o* or *a* as the second character and end with the letters *es*.

E.5.9

Find the employee numbers of all employees whose departments are located in Seattle.

E.5.10

Find the last and first names of all employees who entered their projects on 04.01.1998.

E.5.11

Group all departments using their locations.

E.5.12

What is a difference between the DISTINCT and GROUP BY clauses?

E.5.13

How does the GROUP BY clause manage the NULL values? Does it correspond to the general treatment of these values?

E.5.14

What is the difference between COUNT(*) and COUNT(column)?

E.5.15

Find the biggest employee number.

E.5.16

Get the jobs that are done by more than two employees.

E.5.17

Find the employee numbers of all employees who are clerks or work for department d3.

E.5.18

Why is the following statement wrong?

```
SELECT project_name
  FROM project
  WHERE project_no =
     (SELECT project_no FROM works_on WHERE Job = 'Clerk')
```

Write the correct syntax form for the statement.

E.5.19

What is a practical use of temporary tables?

E.5.20

What is a difference between global and local temporary tables?

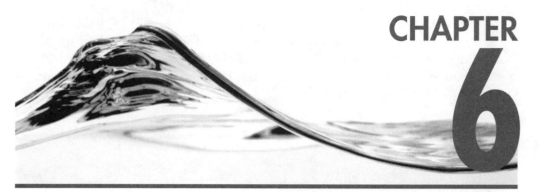

Complex Queries

Thihis chapter covers the more complex features of the SELECT statement. Queries that use more than one table to retrieve the result will be the focus here. In addition to looking at all forms of the join operator, which is the most important operator for relational DBMSs, the chapter discusses correlated subqueries and the EXISTS function.

Join Operator

The previous chapter demonstrated the use of the SELECT statement to query rows from one table of a database. If the Transact-SQL language only supports such simple SELECT statements, the attachment of two or more tables to retrieve data would not be possible. Consequently, all data of a database would have to be stored in one table. Although the storage of all the data of a database inside one table is possible, it has one main disadvantage—the stored data are highly redundant.

Transact-SQL provides the join operator, which allows retrieval of data from more than one table. This operator is probably the most important operator for relational database systems, because it allows data to be spread over many tables and thus achieves a vital property of database systems—nonredundant data.

NOTE

Chapter 5 introduced the UNION operator, which also attaches two or more tables. However, the UNION operator always attaches two or more SELECT statements, while the join operator "joins" two or more tables using just one SELECT. Further, the UNION operator attaches rows of tables, while, as you will see later, the join operator "joins" columns of tables.

The JOIN operator is applied to base tables and views. In this chapter, joins between base tables are discussed, while joins concerning views will be discussed in Chapter 10.

Two tables can be joined together in (at least) five different ways:

▶ Using equijoin

▶ Using Cartesian product (i.e., a cross join)

▶ Using a natural join

▶ Using a thetajoin

▶ Using an outer join

Two Syntax Forms to Implement Joins

To join two or more tables you can use two different syntax forms:

► ANSI join syntax

► SQL Server join syntax

The ANSI join syntax is introduced in the SQL92 standard and defines the join operation explicitly—that is, using the corresponding name for each type of join operation. This syntax enhances the readability of queries; therefore, its use is recommended. Rather than indicating the join relationships implicitly via the WHERE clause, the new join keywords specify them explicitly in the FROM clause. The keywords concerning the explicit definition of join are

► CROSS JOIN

► [INNER] JOIN

► LEFT [OUTER] JOIN

► RIGHT [OUTER] JOIN

► FULL [OUTER] JOIN

CROSS JOIN specifies the Cartesian product of two tables. INNER JOIN defines the natural join of two tables, while LEFT OUTER JOIN and RIGHT OUTER JOIN characterize the join operations of the same names, respectively. Finally, FULL OUTER JOIN specifies the union of the right and left outer joins. (All these different join operations will be explained in the following sections of this chapter.)

The SQL Server join syntax is "old-style" syntax, where each join operation is defined implicitly, using the so-called join columns. Each example in this chapter concerning the join operation is solved using both syntax forms: You will find the solution with the ANSI join syntax first; after that you will find the equivalent solution with the SQL Server join syntax.

Equijoin

Equijoin is best explained through the use of an example.

EXAMPLE 6.1

Get full details of each employee; that is, besides the employee's number, first and last names, and the corresponding department number, also get the name of his or her department and its location, with duplicate columns displayed.

ANSI join syntax:

```
USE sample
SELECT employee.*, department.*
    FROM employee INNER JOIN department
    ON employee.dept_no = department.dept_no
```

SQL Server join syntax:

```
USE sample
SELECT employee.*, department.*
  FROM employee, department
  WHERE employee.dept_no = department.dept_no
```

The result is

emp_no	emp_fname	emp_lname	dept_no	dept_no	dept_name	location
25348	Matthew	Smith	d3	d3	Marketing	Dallas
10102	Ann	Jones	d3	d3	Marketing	Dallas
18316	John	Barrimore	d1	d1	Research	Dallas
29346	James	James	d2	d2	Accounting	Seattle
9031	Elsa	Bertoni	d2	d2	Accounting	Seattle
2581	Elke	Hansel	d2	d2	Accounting	Seattle
28559	Sybill	Moser	d1	d1	Research	Dallas

The SELECT list in Example 6.1 includes all columns of the tables **employee** and **department**. This is a characteristic of an equijoin. Hence, the result of an equijoin always contains one or more pairs of columns that have identical values in every row.

The FROM clause in the SELECT statement specifies the tables, which are joined. The connection between these tables is specified in the WHERE clause using one or more pairs of corresponding columns in both tables. The condition employee.dept_no = department.dept_no in Example 6.1 specifies a *join condition*, and both columns are said to be *join columns*.

Example 6.1 can be used to show how a join operation works. Note that this is one illustration of how you can think about the join process; SQL Server actually has several strategies from which it chooses to implement the join operator. Imagine each row of the **employee** table combined with each row of the **department** table. The result of this combination is a table with 7 columns (4 from the table **employee** and 3 from the table **department**) and 21 rows (see Table 6-1).

emp_no	emp_fname	emp_lname	dept_no	dept_no	dept_name	location
*25348	Matthew	Smith	d3	d1	Research	Dallas
*10102	Ann	Jones	d3	d1	Research	Dallas
18316	John	Barrimore	d1	d1	Research	Dallas
*29346	James	James	d2	d1	Research	Dallas
*9031	Elsa	Bertoni	d2	d1	Research	Dallas
*2581	Elke	Hansel	d2	d1	Research	Dallas
28559	Sybill	Moser	d1	d1	Research	Dallas
*25348	Matthew	Smith	d3	d2	Accounting	Seattle
*10102	Ann	Jones	d3	d2	Accounting	Seattle
*18316	John	Barrimore	d1	d2	Accounting	Seattle
29346	James	James	d2	d2	Accounting	Seattle
9031	Elsa	Bertoni	d2	d2	Accounting	Seattle
2581	Elke	Hansel	d2	d2	Accounting	Seattle
*28559	Sybill	Moser	d1	d2	Accounting	Seattle
25348	Matthew	Smith	d3	d3	Marketing	Dallas
10102	Ann	Jones	d3	d3	Marketing	Dallas
*18316	John	Barrimore	d1	d3	Marketing	Dallas
*29346	James	James	d2	d3	Marketing	Dallas
*9031	Elsa	Bertoni	d2	d3	Marketing	Dallas
*2581	Elke	Hansel	d2	d3	Marketing	Dallas
*28559	Sybill	Moser	d1	d3	Marketing	Dallas

Table 6-1 *Result of the Cartesian Product Between the Tables **employee** and **department***

In the second step, all rows from Table 6-1 that do not satisfy the join condition employee.dept_no = department.dept_no are removed. These rows are prefixed in Table 6-1 with the * sign. The rest of the rows represent the result of Example 6.1.

The semantics of the corresponding join columns must be identical. This means that both columns must have the same logical meaning. It is not required that the corresponding join columns have the same name (or even an identical type), although this will often be the case.

NOTE

It is not possible for a database system to check the logical meaning of a column. (For instance, project number and employee number have nothing in common, although both columns are defined as integers.) Therefore, database systems can only check the data type and the length of string data types. SQL Server requires that the corresponding join columns have compatible data types, such as INT and SMALLINT. (The best way to declare corresponding join columns is by using alias data types.)

The sample database contains three pairs of columns in which each column of the pair has the same logical meaning (and, as is natural, they have the same names as well). The tables **employee** and **department** can be joined using the columns **employee.dept_no** and **department.dept_no**. The join columns of the tables **employee** and **works_on** are the columns **employee.emp_no** and **works_on.emp_no**. Finally, the tables **project** and **works_on** can be joined using the join columns **project.project_no** and **works_on.project_no**.

The names of columns in a SELECT statement can be qualified. "Qualifying" a column name means that, to avoid any possible ambiguity about which table the column belongs to, the column name is preceded by its table name (or the alias of the table), separated by a period: **table_name.column_name**.

In most SELECT statements a column name does not need any qualification, although the use of qualified names is generally recommended for readability. If column names within a SELECT statement are ambiguous (like the columns **employee.dept_no** and **department.dept_no** in Example 6.1), the qualified names for the columns *must* be used.

In a SELECT statement with a join, the WHERE clause can include other conditions in addition to the join condition (see Example 6.2).

EXAMPLE 6.2

Get full details of all employees who work on the project Gemini.
  ANSI join syntax:

```
USE sample
SELECT *
  FROM works_on JOIN project
  ON project.project_no = works_on.project_no
  WHERE project_name = 'Gemini'
```

SQL Server join syntax:

```
USE sample
SELECT project.*, works_on.*
  FROM works_on, project
  WHERE project.project_no = works_on.project_no
  AND project_name = 'Gemini'
```

The result is

emp_no	project_no	job	enter_date	project_no	project_name	budget
25348	P2	Clerk	1998-02-15	p2	Gemini	95000.0
18316	P2	NULL	1998-06-01	p2	Gemini	95000.0
29346	P2	NULL	1997-12-15	p2	Gemini	95000.0
28559	P2	Clerk	1999-02-01	p2	Gemini	95000.0

NOTE

*The qualification of the column **project_name** in Example 6.2 is not necessary, because there is no ambiguity regarding this name.*

Cartesian Product

The previous section illustrated a possible method of producing an equijoin. In the first step of this process, each row of the **employee** table is combined with each row of the **department** table. This intermediate result was made by the operation called Cartesian product.

EXAMPLE 6.3

ANSI join syntax:

```
USE sample
SELECT *
  FROM employee CROSS JOIN department
```

SQL Server join syntax:

```
USE sample
SELECT *
  FROM employee, department
```

The result of Example 6.3 is shown in Table 6-1. A Cartesian product combines each row of the first table with each row of the second one. In general, the Cartesian product of two tables such that the first table has *n* rows and the second table has *m* rows will produce a result with *n* times *m* rows (or *n*m*). Thus, the resulting set in Example 6.3 is 7*3 = 21 rows.

NOTE

The notation SELECT * FROM table1, table 2 is equivalent to the notation SELECT table1.*, table2.* FROM table1, table2. The * in this case means all columns from all tables in the FROM clause.

If the WHERE clause in a SELECT statement contains something other than the join condition, the result of the SELECT is still a Cartesian product of both tables, reduced to the rows that evaluate to true for the condition (see Example 6.4).

EXAMPLE 6.4

ANSI join syntax:

```
USE sample
SELECT *
  FROM works_on CROSS JOIN project
  WHERE works_on.project_no = 'p3'
```

SQL Server syntax:

```
USE sample
SELECT *
  FROM works_on, project
  WHERE works_on.project_no = 'p3'
```

The result is

emp_no	project_no	job	enter_date	project_no	project_name	budget
10102	P3	Manager	1999-01-01	p1	Apollo	120000.0
2581	P3	Analyst	1998-10-15	p1	Apollo	120000.0
9031	P3	Clerk	1997-11-15	p1	Apollo	120000.0
10102	P3	Manager	1999-01-01	p2	Gemini	95000.0
2581	P3	Analyst	1998-10-15	p2	Gemini	95000.0
9031	P3	Clerk	1997-11-15	p2	Gemini	95000.0
10102	P3	Manager	1999-01-01	p3	Mercury	186500.0
2581	P3	Analyst	1998-10-15	p3	Mercury	186500.0
9031	P3	Clerk	1997-11-15	p3	Mercury	186500.0

In practice, the use of a Cartesian product is highly unusual. Sometimes users generate the Cartesian product of two tables when they forget to include the join condition in the WHERE clause of the SELECT statement. In this case, the output does not correspond to the expected result because it contains too many rows. (The existence of many and unexpected rows in the result is a hint that a Cartesian product of two tables, rather than the intended join, has been produced.)

Natural Join

In the equijoin operation, there is always one or more pairs of columns that have identical values in every row. Eliminating one of these join columns from the SELECT list gives a user a simpler and more reasonable result. The operation that eliminates such columns from the equijoin is called a natural join.

Example 6.5 is equivalent to Example 6.1, displays the values of the dept_no column only once.

EXAMPLE 6.5

ANSI join syntax:

```
USE sample
SELECT employee.*, dept_name, location
    FROM employee JOIN department
    ON employee. dept_no = department.dept_no
```

SQL Server join syntax:

```
USE sample
SELECT employee.*, dept_name, location
   FROM employee, department
      WHERE employee. dept_no = department.dept_no
```

The result is

emp_no	emp_fname	emp_lname	dept_no	dept_name	location
25348	Matthew	Smith	D3	Marketing	Dallas
10102	Ann	Jones	D3	Marketing	Dallas
18316	John	Barrimore	D1	Research	Dallas
29346	James	James	D2	Accounting	Seattle
9031	Elsa	Bertoni	D2	Accounting	Seattle
2581	Elke	Hansel	D2	Accounting	Seattle
28559	Sybill	Moser	D1	Research	Dallas

The SELECT list in Example 6.5 contains all columns from the tables **employee** and **department** except for the **dept_no** column from the second table, which is a part of the join condition and therefore superfluous in the result.

NOTE

Natural join is the most useful form of all join operations. Therefore, unless otherwise specified, the term join always refers to the natural join operation.

The SELECT list of a natural join need not contain all nonidentical columns from both tables (it simply doesn't include the redundant join column). Example 6.6 shows this.

EXAMPLE 6.6

Get the department number for all employees who entered their projects on October 15, 1998.
   ANSI join syntax:

```
USE sample
SELECT dept_no
   FROM employee JOIN works_on
```

```
        ON employee.emp_no = works_on.emp_no
        WHERE enter_date = '10.15.1998'
```

SQL Server join syntax:

```
    USE sample
    SELECT dept_no
      FROM employee, works_on
      WHERE employee.emp_no = works_on.emp_no
      AND enter_date = '10.15.1998'
```

The result is

dept_no
d2

Thetajoin

Join columns need not be compared using the equality sign. A join operation using a general join condition—that is, using a comparison operator other than equality—is called a thetajoin. In Example 6.7, the **employee_enh** table is used.

EXAMPLE 6.7

Get all the combinations of employee information and department information where the domicile of an employee alphabetically precedes the location of a department.
ANSI join syntax:

```
    USE sample
    SELECT employee_enh.*, department.*
      FROM employee_enh JOIN department
      ON domicile < location
```

SQL Server syntax:

```
    USE sample
    SELECT employee_enh.*, department.*
      FROM employee_enh, department
      WHERE domicile < location
```

The result is

emp_no	emp_fname	emp_lname	dept_no	domicile	dept_no	dept_name	location
25348	Matthew	Smith	d3	San Antonio	d2	Accounting	Seattle
10102	Ann	Jones	d3	Houston	d2	Accounting	Seattle
18316	John	Barrimore	d1	San Antonio	d2	Accounting	Seattle
9031	Elsa	Bertoni	d2	Portland	d2	Accounting	Seattle
28559	Sybill	Moser	d1	Houston	d2	Accounting	Seattle

In Example 6.7, the corresponding values of columns **domicile** and **location** are compared. In every resulting row, the value of the **domicile** column is ordered alphabetically before the corresponding value of the **location** column.

Joining More Than Two Tables

Theoretically, there is no upper limit on the number of tables that can be joined using a SELECT statement. (One join condition always combines two tables!) However, SQL Server has an implementation restriction: the maximum number of tables that can be joined in a SELECT statement is 64.

NOTE

Usually, a maximum of 8–10 tables are joined in a SELECT statement. If you need to join more than 10 tables in a SELECT statement, your database design is probably not optimal.

The following example displays the first and last names of all analysts whose departments are located in Seattle.

EXAMPLE 6.8

ANSI join syntax:

```
USE sample
SELECT emp_fname, emp_lname
    FROM works_on
    JOIN employee ON works_on.emp_no=employee.emp_no
            JOIN department ON employee.dept_no=department.dept_no
    AND location = 'Seattle'
    AND job = 'analyst'
```

SQL Server join syntax:

```
USE sample
SELECT emp_fname, emp_lname
   FROM works_on, employee, department
   WHERE works_on.emp_no = employee.emp_no
   AND employee.dept_no = department.dept_no
   AND job = 'analyst'
   AND location = 'Seattle'
```

The result is

emp_fname	emp_lname
Elke	Hansel

The result in Example 6.8 can be obtained only if you join at least three tables: **works_on**, **employee**, and **department**. These tables can be joined using two pairs of join columns:

```
(works_on.emp_no, employee.emp_no)
(employee.dept_no,department.dept_no)
```

Example 6.9 uses all four tables from the sample database.

EXAMPLE 6.9

Get the project names (with redundant duplicates eliminated) being worked on by employees in the Accounting department.
ANSI join syntax:

```
USE sample
SELECT DISTINCT project_name
   FROM project JOIN works_on
   ON project.project_no = works_on.project_no
       JOIN employee ON works_on.emp_no = employee.emp_no
       JOIN department ON employee.dept_no = department.dept_no
   WHERE dept_name = 'Accounting'
```

SQL Server join syntax:

```
USE sample
SELECT DISTINCT project_name
  FROM project, works_on, employee, department
  WHERE project.project_no = works_on.project_no
  AND works_on.emp_no = employee.emp_no
  AND employee.dept_no = department.dept_no
  AND dept_name = 'Accounting'
```

The result is

project_name
Apollo
Gemini
Mercury

Notice that when joining three tables, you use two join conditions (linking two tables each) to achieve a natural join. When you join four tables, you use three such join conditions. In general, if you join *n* tables, you will need *n-1* join conditions to avoid a Cartesian product. Of course, more than *n-1* join conditions, as well as other conditions, are certainly permissible to further reduce the result set.

Joining a Table with Itself

In addition to joining two or more different tables, a join operation can also be applied to a single table. In this case, the table is joined with itself, whereby a single column of the table is compared with itself. The comparison of a column with itself means that the table name appears twice in the FROM clause of a SELECT statement. Therefore, you need to be able to reference the name of the same table twice. This can be accomplished using aliases. The same is true for the column names in the join condition of a SELECT statement. In order to distinguish both column names, you use the qualified names. Example 6.10 joins the **department** table with itself.

EXAMPLE 6.10

Get full details of all departments located at the same location as at least one other department.

ANSI join syntax:

```
USE sample
SELECT t1.dept_no, t1.dept_name, t1.location
    FROM department t1 JOIN department t2
        ON  t1. location = t2.location
    WHERE t1.dept_no <> t2.dept_no
```

SQL Server join syntax:

```
USE sample
SELECT DISTINCT t1.dept_no, t1.dept_name, t1.location
    FROM department t1, department t2
    WHERE t1. location = t2.location
    AND t1.dept_no <> t2.dept_no
```

The result is

dept_no	dept_name	location
d3	Marketing	Dallas
d1	Research	Dallas

The FROM clause in Example 6.10 contains two aliases for the **department** table: **t1** and **t2**. The first condition in the WHERE clause specifies the join columns, while the second condition eliminates unnecessary duplicates by making certain that each department is compared with *different* departments.

In Example 6.11, the **employee_enh** table is used.

EXAMPLE 6.11

Get the employee number, last name, and domicile of each employee who works for the same department and lives in the same city as at least one other employee.

ANSI join syntax:

```
USE sample
SELECT t1.emp_no, t1.emp_lname, t1.domicile
    FROM employee_enh t1 JOIN  employee_enh t2
        ON t1.domicile = t2.domicile
    WHERE t1.dept_no = t2.dept_no
    AND t1.emp_no <> t2.emp_no
```

SQL Server join syntax:

```
USE sample
SELECT DISTINCT t1.emp_no, t1.emp_lname, t1.domicile
  FROM employee_enh t1, employee_enh t2
  WHERE t1.domicile = t2.domicile
  AND t1.dept_no = t2.dept_no
  AND t1.emp_no <> t2.emp_no
```

The result is

emp_no	emp_lname	domicile

In Example 6.11, the join condition includes two pairs of identical columns: **domicile** and **dept_no**. The last condition, **t1.emp_no <> t2.emp_no**, prevents comparisons of employees with themselves. (In the sample database, there are no employees working for the same department and living in the same city as any other employees.)

Outer Join

In the previous examples of equijoin, thetajoin, and natural join, the resulting set included only rows from one table that have corresponding rows in the other table. Sometimes it is necessary to retrieve, in addition to the matching rows, the unmatched rows from one or both of the tables. Such an operation is called an *outer join*.

Examples 6.12 and 6.13 show the difference between natural join and the corresponding outer join. (All examples in this section use the **employee_enh** table.)

EXAMPLE 6.12

Get full details of all employees plus locations of their departments such that the living place and the working place of an employee are located in the same city.

ANSI join syntax:

```
USE sample
SELECT employee_enh.*, department.location
  FROM employee_enh JOIN department
       ON domicile = location
```

SQL Server join syntax:

```
USE sample
SELECT employee_enh.*, department.location
   FROM employee_enh, department
   WHERE domicile = location
```

The result is

emp_no	emp_fname	emp_lname	dept_no	domicile	location
29346	James	James	D2	Seattle	Seattle

Example 6.12 uses an equijoin to display the resulting set of rows. If you would also like to know all other existing living places of employees, you have to use the left outer join. SQL Server uses the operator LEFT OUTER JOIN to specify the left outer join. This is called a *left* outer join because all rows from the table on the *left* side of the operator are returned, whether or not they have a matching row in the table on the right. A *right* outer join is similar, but as you have probably guessed, it returns all rows of the table on the *right* of the symbol (and the operator is replaced by RIGHT OUTER JOIN).

EXAMPLE 6.13

Get full details for all employees plus locations of their departments, for all cities that are either the living places, or both living and working places, of employees.
ANSI join syntax:

```
USE sample
SELECT employee_enh.*, department.location
   FROM employee_enh LEFT OUTER JOIN department
      ON domicile = location
```

SQL Server join syntax:

```
USE sample
SELECT employee_enh.*, department.location
   FROM employee_enh, department
   WHERE domicile *= location
```

The result is

emp_no	emp_fname	emp_lname	dept_no	domicile	location
25348	Matthew	Smith	D3	San Antonio	NULL
10102	Ann	Jones	D3	Houston	NULL
18316	John	Barrimore	D1	San Antonio	NULL
29346	James	James	D2	Seattle	Seattle
9031	Elsa	Bertoni	D2	Portland	NULL
2581	Elke	Hansel	D2	Tacoma	NULL
28559	Sybill	Moser	D1	Houston	NULL

As you can see, when there is no corresponding row in the other table (**department**, in this case), its columns are populated by null values. Example 6.14 shows the use of the right outer join.

NOTE

The use of the operator "*=" for the left outer join is a deprecated feature in SQL Server 2005. The same is true for the operator "=*". For this reason, if you want to implement any kind of outer join, use the ANSI join syntax.

EXAMPLE 6.14

Get full details of all departments, plus living places of their employees, for all cities that are either the locations of departments or the living and working places of an employee.

ANSI join syntax:

```
USE sample
SELECT employee_enh.domicile, department.*
    FROM employee_enh RIGHT OUTER JOIN department
        ON domicile =location
```

The result is

domicile	dept_no	dept_name	location
Seattle	d2	Accounting	Seattle
NULL	d1	Research	Dallas
NULL	d3	Marketing	Dallas

In addition to the left and right outer joins, there is also the full outer join, which is defined as the union of the left and right outer joins. In other words, all rows from both tables are represented in the result set. If there is no corresponding row in one of the tables, its columns are returned with null values. This operation is specified using the FULL OUTER JOIN operator.

Every outer join operation can be simulated using the UNION operator plus the EXISTS function. Example 6.15 is equivalent to Example 6.13.

EXAMPLE 6.15

Get full details for all employees, plus locations of their departments, for all cities that are either the living places, or both living and working places, of employees.

```
USE sample
SELECT employee_enh.*, department.location
  FROM employee_enh JOIN department
  ON domicile = location
UNION
SELECT employee_enh.*, 'NULL'
  FROM employee_enh
  WHERE NOT EXISTS
  (SELECT *
    FROM department
    WHERE location = domicile)
```

The first SELECT statement in the union specifies the natural join of the tables **employee_enh** and **department** with the join columns **domicile** and **location**. This SELECT statement retrieves all cities that are at the same time the living places and working places of each employee. The second SELECT statement in the union retrieves, additionally, all rows from the **employee_enh** table that do not match the condition in the natural join.

Correlated Subqueries

A subquery is said to be a *correlated subquery* if the inner query depends on the outer query for any of its values. Examples 6.16 and 6.17 show how the same query can be formulated using a simple subquery and a correlated subquery.

EXAMPLE 6.16

Get the last names of all employees who work on the project p3.

```
USE sample
SELECT emp_lname
  FROM employee
  WHERE emp_no IN
  (SELECT emp_no
    FROM works_on
    WHERE project_no = 'p3')
```

The result is

emp_lname
Jones
Bertoni
Hansel

In the simple subquery of Example 6.16, the inner query is evaluated once, and the result set is passed to the outer query. The outer subquery then evaluates the final result.

EXAMPLE 6.17

Get the last names of all employees who work on project p3.

```
USE sample
SELECT emp_lname
  FROM employee
  WHERE 'p3' IN
  (SELECT project_no
    FROM works_on
    WHERE works_on.emp_no = employee.emp_no)
```

The inner query in Example 6.17 must be evaluated many times because it contains the **emp_no** column, which belongs to the **employee** table in the outer query, and the value of the **emp_no** column changes every time SQL Server examines a different row of the **employee** table in the outer query.

Let's walk through how SQL Server might process the query in Example 6.17. First, the system retrieves the first row of the **employee** table (for the outer query)

and compares the employee number of that column (25348) with values of the
works_on.emp_no column in the inner query. Since the only **project_no** for this
employee is p2, the inner query returns the value p2. The single value in the set is
not equal to the constant value p3 in the outer query, so the outer query's condition
(WHERE 'p3' IN …) is not met and no rows are returned by the outer query for this
employee. Then, the system retrieves the next row of the **employee** table and repeats
the comparison of employee numbers in both tables. The second employee has two
rows in the **works_on** table with **project_no** values of p1 and p3, so the result set
of the inner query is (p1,p3). One of the elements in the resulting set is equal to the
constant value p3, so the condition is evaluated to true and the corresponding value
of the **emp_lname** column in the second row (Jones) is displayed. The same process
will be applied to all rows of the **employee** table, and the final resulting set with
three rows is retrieved.

Example 6.18 shows the correlated subquery using the **department** table in both
inner and outer queries. This example is equivalent to Example 6.10.

EXAMPLE 6.18

Get full details of all departments at the same location.

```
USE sample
SELECT t1.*
  FROM department t1
  WHERE t1.location IN
  (SELECT t2.location
    FROM department t2
    WHERE t1.dept_no <> t2.dept_no)
```

The result is

dept_no	dept_name	location
d1	Research	Dallas
d3	Marketing	Dallas

More examples of correlated subqueries are shown in the next section.

EXISTS Function and Subqueries

The EXISTS function takes a subquery as an argument and returns true if the subquery
returns one or more rows, and it returns false if the subquery returns zero rows. This
function will be explained using examples.

EXAMPLE 6.19

Get the last names of all employees who work on project p1.

```
USE sample
SELECT emp_lname
  FROM employee
  WHERE EXISTS
  (SELECT *
    FROM works_on
    WHERE employee.emp_no = works_on.emp_no
  AND project_no = 'p1')
```

The result is

emp_lname
Jones
James
Bertoni
Moser

The subquery of the EXISTS function almost always depends on a variable from an outer query. Therefore, the EXISTS function usually specifies a correlated subquery.

Let's walk through how SQL Server might process the query in Example 6.19. First, the outer query considers the first row of the **employee** table (Smith). Next, the EXISTS subquery is evaluated to determine whether there are any rows in the **works_on** table whose employee number matches the one from the current row in the outer query, and whose **project_no** is p1. Because Mr. Smith does not work on the project p1, the result of the inner query is an empty set and the EXISTS function is evaluated to false. Therefore, the employee named Smith does not belong to the final resulting set. Using this process, all rows of the **employee** table are tested, and the resulting set is displayed.

Example 6.20 shows the use of the NOT EXISTS function.

EXAMPLE 6.20

Get the last names of all employees who work for departments not located in Seattle.

```
USE sample
SELECT emp_lname
```

```
FROM employee
WHERE NOT EXISTS
(SELECT *
  FROM department
  WHERE employee.dept_no = department.dept_no
  AND location = 'Seattle')
```

The result is

emp_lname
Smith
Jones
Barrimore
Moser

The SELECT list of an outer query involving the EXISTS function is not required to be of the form "SELECT *," as in the previous examples. The form "SELECT column_list," where **column_list** is one or more columns of the table, is an alternate form. Both forms are equivalent, because the EXISTS function tests only the existence (i.e., nonexistence) of rows in the resulting set. The first form (SELECT *) is recommended.

As already stated in Chapter 5, the EXISTS function can be used to represent both set operations: the intersection and the difference. Examples 6.21 and 6.22 use the EXISTS function and the NOT EXISTS function to represent the intersection and the difference of two tables, respectively.

EXAMPLE 6.21

Get names of all cities that are locations of departments as well as living places of employees.

```
USE sample
SELECT DISTINCT domicile
  FROM employee_enh
  WHERE EXISTS
  (SELECT *
    FROM department
    WHERE domicile = location)
```

The result is

domicile
Seattle

EXAMPLE 6.22

Get all names of the living places of employees that are not the locations of any departments.

```
USE sample
SELECT DISTINCT domicile
  FROM employee_enh
  WHERE NOT EXISTS
  (SELECT *
    FROM department
    WHERE domicile=location)
```

The result is

domicile
Houston
Portland
San Antonio
Tacoma

The EXISTS function can also be used to represent the ANY and ALL operators. Example 6.23 uses EXISTS to represent the ANY operator.

EXAMPLE 6.23

Get the first and last names of all employees who work on project p1.

```
USE sample
SELECT emp_fname, emp_lname
  FROM employee
  WHERE EXISTS
  (SELECT *
    FROM works_on
    WHERE project_no = 'p1'
    AND employee.emp_no = works_on.emp_no)
```

The result is

emp_fname	emp_lname
Ann	Jones
James	James
Elsa	Bertoni
Sybill	Moser

Example 6.24 uses NOT EXISTS to represent the ALL operator.

EXAMPLE 6.24

Get the job title of the employee with the smallest employee number.

```
USE sample
SELECT DISTINCT job
  FROM works_on
  WHERE NOT EXISTS
  (SELECT *
    FROM employee
    WHERE  works_on.emp_no > employee.emp_no)
```

The result is

job
Analyst

Should You Use Join or Subqueries?

Almost all SELECT statements that join tables and use the JOIN operator can be rewritten as subqueries and vice versa. Writing the SELECT in the form of a JOIN is often easier for SQL programmers to read and understand and can also help SQL Server find a more efficient strategy for retrieving the appropriate data. However, there are a few problems that can be solved more easily using subqueries, and there are others that can be solved more easily using joins.

Subquery Advantages

Subqueries are advantageous over joins when you have to calculate an aggregate value on the fly and use it in the outer query for comparison. Example 6.25 shows this.

EXAMPLE 6.25

Get the employee numbers and enter dates of all employees with enter dates equal to the earliest date.

```
USE sample
SELECT emp_no, enter_date
   FROM works_on
   WHERE enter_date = (SELECT min(enter_date)
                              FROM works_on)
```

This problem cannot be solved with a join, because you would have to write the aggregate function in the WHERE clause and it is not allowed. (You can solve the problem using two separate queries in relation to the **works_on** table.)

Join Advantages

Joins are advantageous over subqueries if the SELECT list in a query contains columns from more than one table. Example 6.26 shows this.

EXAMPLE 6.26

Get the employee numbers, last names, and jobs for all employees that entered their projects on October 15, 1998.

```
USE sample
SELECT employee.emp_no, emp_lname, job
   FROM employee, works_on
   WHERE employee.emp_no = works_on.emp_no
   AND enter_date = '10.15.1998'
```

The SELECT list of the query in Example 6.26 contains columns **emp_no** and **emp_lname** from the **employee** table and the **job** column from the **works_on** table. For this reason, the following (and equivalent) solution in Example 6.27 with the subquery displays an error, because subqueries can display information only from the outer table.

EXAMPLE 6.27 (DISPLAYS AN ERROR!!)

```
USE sample
SELECT emp_no, emp_lname, job
```

```
FROM employee
WHERE emp_no = (SELECT emp_no FROM works_on
                        WHERE enter_date = '10.15.1998')
```

Common Table Expressions

Common Table Expressions (CTE) is a named table expression that is supported by SQL Server 2005. There are two CTE types:

► Nonrecursive

► Recursive

The following sections describe both CTE forms.

CTE and Nonrecursive Queries

The nonrecursive form of a common table expression can be used as an alternative to derived tables and views. (A derived table is a table expression defined in the FROM clause of a SELECT statement that exists for the duration of the query.)

The following example shows the use of CTEs in nonrecursive queries.

EXAMPLE 6.28

```
USE sample
create table freights
  (orderid INT NOT NULL,
   orderdate DATETIME,
   shippeddate DATETIME,
   freight MONEY,
   price MONEY)
INSERT INTO freights
  VALUES (1111, '1.10.2005','1.20.2005', 30.45, 200.25)
INSERT INTO freights
  VALUES (2222, '2.11.2005', '2.21.2005', 89.25, 543.00)
INSERT INTO freights
  VALUES (3333, '3.12.2005','3.22.2005', 19.35, 120.25)
INSERT INTO freights
  VALUES (4444, '4.13.2005', '4.23.2005', 9.99,  154.35)
```

Example 6.28 creates the table **freights**, which will be used to show how CTEs can be applied for nonrecursive queries. Suppose that the **freights** table contains four rows, which are shown in Table 6-2. (The INSERT statements in Example 6.28 insert these rows in the **freights** table.)

EXAMPLE 6.29

```
USE sample
select orderid
  from freights
   where price > (SELECT AVG(price)
            from freights
            WHERE YEAR(orderdate) = '2005')
      AND freight > (SELECT AVG(price)
            from freights
            WHERE YEAR(orderdate) = '2005' )/10
```

The result is

orderid
22222

We use the query in Example 6.29 to find orders whose prices are greater than the average of all prices as well as whose freights are greater than 1/10 of the average of all prices.

The main property of this query is that it is space-consuming, because there is a same subquery that we have to write twice. One way to shorten the syntax of the query is to create a view containing the query that is contained in the repeated subquery, but that is rather complicated. In that case, we have to create the view and drop it when we are done with the query.

11111	2005-01-10 00:00:00.000	2005-01-20 00:00:00.000	30.45	200.25
22222	2005-02-11 00:00:00.000	2005-02-21 00:00:00.000	89.25	543.00
33333	2004-10-01 00:00:00.000	2005-10-10 00:00:00.000	19.35	120.25
44444	2004-11-01 00:00:00.000	2005-11-20 00:00:00.000	9.99	154.35

Table 6-2   *The Content of the **freights** Table*

A better way is to write a common table expression using the WITH clause. The following example shows the use of the WITH clause to shorten the definition of the query in Example 6.29.

EXAMPLE 6.30

```
USE sample;
WITH price_calc (year_2005) AS
  (SELECT AVG(price)
          from freights
          WHERE YEAR(orderdate) = '2005')
SELECT orderid
  FROM freights
  WHERE pricc > (SELECT year_2005
          FROM price_calc)
  AND freight > (SELECT year_2005
          FROM price_calc)/10
```

The syntax for the WITH clause in nonrecursive queries looks like this:

```
WITH cte_name (column_list) AS
    ( inner_query)
outer_query
```

cte_name is the name of the CTE that specifies a resulting table. The list of columns that belong to the table expression is written in brackets. (CTE in Example 6.30 is called **price_calc** and this table expression has one column: **year_2005**.) **inner_query** in the CTE syntax defines the SELECT statement, which specifies the result set of the corresponding table expression. After that, you can use the defined table expression in an outer query. (The outer query in Example 6.30 uses the CTE called **price_calc** and its column **year_2005** to simplify the subquery, which appears twice.)

Common Table Expressions and Recursive Queries

NOTE

The material in this section is complex. Therefore, we recommend skipping it on the first reading of the book.

You can use CTEs to implement recursion, because CTEs can contain references to themselves.

The basic syntax for a CTE for recursive queries is

```
WITH cte_name (column_list) AS
  (anchor_member
   UNION ALL
   recursive_member)
outer_query
```

cte_name and **column_list** has the same meaning as in CTEs for nonrecursive queries. The body of the WITH clause comprises two queries that are connected with the UNION ALL operator. The first query will be invoked only once, and it starts to accumulate the result of the recursion. If you look at this query, you will see that it does not reference the CTE (see Example 6.31). This query is called anchor query or seed.

The second query contains a reference to the CTE and represents the recursive portion of it. For this reason it is called the recursive part or recursive member. In the first invocation of the recursive part, the reference to CTE represents the result of the anchor query. The recursive part uses the query result of the first invocation. After that, the system repeatedly invokes the recursive part. The invocation of the recursive part ends when the result of the previous invocation is an empty set.

The UNION operator joins the rows accumulated so far, as well as the additional rows that are added in the current invocation. (The UNION ALL means that no duplicate rows will be eliminated from the result.)

Finally, **outer query** defines a query specification that uses the CTE to retrieve all invocations of the union of both members.

We will use the table definition in Example 6.31 to demonstrate the recursive form of CTEs.

EXAMPLE 6.31

```
USE sample
CREATE TABLE airplane
  (containing_assembly VARCHAR(10),
   contained_assembly VARCHAR(10),
   quantity_contained INT,
   unit_cost DECIMAL (6,2))
insert into airplane values ( 'Airplane', 'Fuselage', 1, 10)
insert into airplane values ( 'Airplane', 'Wings', 1, 11)
insert into airplane values ( 'Airplane', 'Tail', 1, 12)
```

insert into airplane values ('Fuselage', 'Cockpit', 1, 13)
insert into airplane values ('Fuselage', 'Cabin', 1, 14)
insert into airplane values ('Fuselage', 'Nose',1, 15)
insert into airplane values ('Cockpit', NULL, 1, 13)
insert into airplane values ('Cabin', NULL, 1, 14)
insert into airplane values ('Nose', NULL, 1, 15)
insert into airplane values ('Wings', NULL, 2, 11)
insert into airplane values ('Tail', NULL, 1, 12)

The table **airplane** contains four columns. The column **containing_assembly** specifies an assembly, while **contained_assembly** comprises the parts (one by one) that build the corresponding assembly. The third column, **quantity_contained**, specifies the number of a particular part, while the **unit_cost** column indicates the cost of each part. (Figure 6-1 shows graphically how an airplane with its parts could look.)

Suppose that the **airplane** table contains 11 rows, which are shown in Table 6-3. (The INSERT statements in Example 6.31 insert these rows in the **airplane** table.)

The following example shows the use of the WITH clause to define a query that calculates the total costs of each assembly.

EXAMPLE 6.32

```
USE sample
WITH list_of_parts(assembly, quantity, cost) AS
  (SELECT containing_assembly, quantity_contained, unit_cost
    FROM airplane
    WHERE contained_assembly IS NULL
  UNION ALL
  SELECT a.containing_assembly, a.quantity_contained,
      CAST(l.quantity*l.cost AS DECIMAL(6,2))
      FROM list_of_parts l,airplane a
      WHERE l.assembly = a.contained_assembly )
SELECT * FROM list_of_parts
```

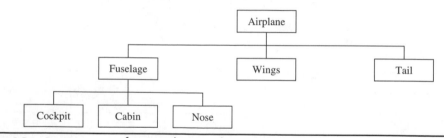

Figure 6-1   *Presentation of an airplane and its parts*

Airplane	Fuselage	1	10
Airplane	Wings	1	11
Airplane	Tail	1	12
Fuselage	Cockpit	1	13
Fuselage	Cabin	1	14
Fuselage	Nose	1	15
Cockpit	NULL	1	13
Cabin	NULL	1	14
Nose	NULL	1	15
Wings	NULL	2	11
Tail	NULL	1	12

Table 6-3   *The Content of the **airplane** Table*

The WITH clause defines the CTE called **list_of_parts**, which contains three columns: **assembly**, **quantity**, and **cost**. The first SELECT statement in Example 6.32 will be invoked only once, to accumulate the results of the first step in the recursion process.

If we use the following query

SELECT * FROM list_of_parts

to display the intermediate result of the CTE, we will get the following result:

Assembly	Quantity	Costs
Cockpit	1	13.00
Cabin	1	14.00
Nose	1	15.00
Wings	2	11.00
Tail	1	12.00
Airplane	1	12.00
Airplane	1	22.00
Fuselage	1	15.00
Airplane	1	15.00

Fuselage	1	14.00
Airplane	1	14.00
Fuselage	1	13.00
Airplane	1	13.00

The first five rows in the output above show the result set of the first invocation of the anchor part of the query in Example 6.32. All other rows are the result of the recursive part (second part) of the query in the same example. The recursive part of the query will be invoked twice: the first time for the fuselage assembly and the second time for the airplane itself.

We will use the query in Example 6.33 to get the costs for each assembly with all its subparts.

EXAMPLE 6.33

```
USE sample;
WITH list_of_parts(assembly, quantity, cost) AS
  (SELECT containing_assembly, quantity_contained ,unit_cost
    FROM airplane
    WHERE contained_assembly IS NULL
  UNION ALL
  SELECT a.containing_assembly, a.quantity_contained,
      CAST(l.quantity*l.cost AS DECIMAL(6,2))
       FROM list_of_parts l,airplane a
      WHERE l.assembly = a.contained_assembly )
SELECT assembly, SUM(quantity) parts, SUM(cost) sum_cost
    FROM  list_of_parts
    GROUP BY assembly
```

The output of the query in Example 6.33 is as follows:

Assembly	Parts	Sum_cost
Airplane	5	76.00
Cabin	1	14.00
Cockpit	1	13.00
Fuselage	3	42.00
Nose	1	15.00
Tail	1	12.00
Wings	2	11.00

NOTE

Example 6.33 has the same WITH clause as Example 6.32, but a different outer query.

There are several restrictions for a CTE in a recursive query:

▶ The CTE definition must contain at least two SELECT statements (an anchor member and one recursive member) combined by a UNION ALL set operator.

▶ The number of columns in the anchor and recursive members must be the same. (This is the direct consequence in relation to the UNION ALL operator.)

▶ The data type of a column in the recursive member must be the same as the data type of the corresponding column in the anchor member.

▶ The FROM clause of the recursive member must refer only once to the name of the CTE (see Example 6.32).

▶ The following options are not allowed in the definition part of a recursive member: SELECT DISTINCT, GROUP BY, HAVING, aggregation functions, TOP, and subqueries. (Also, the only join operation that is allowed in the query definition is an inner join.)

The APPLY Operator

The APPLY operator is similar to the recursive queries, because it uses CTE too. This operator allows you to invoke a table-valued function (see Chapter 8) for each row returned by an outer table expression of a query. The table-valued function acts as the right input, and the outer table expression acts as the left input. The right input is evaluated for each row from the left input, and the rows produced are combined for the final output. The list of columns produced by the APPLY operator is the set of columns in the left input followed by the list of columns returned by the right input.

A detailed description of the APPLY operator is outside the scope of this book.

Conclusion

This chapter and Chapter 5 have shown the use of the SELECT statement. Three other important DML statements—INSERT, DELETE, and UPDATE—will be described in the next chapter.

Exercises

Write all solutions concerning the exercises that use a join operation with the ANSI join syntax style as well as with the conventional (SQL Server) style.

E.6.1

Create:

    A. Equijoin

    B. Natural join

    C. Cartesian product

for the **project** and **works_on** tables.

E.6.2

If you intend to join several tables in a query (say **N**), how many join conditions are needed?

E.6.3

Get the employee numbers and job titles of all employees working on project Gemini.

E.6.4

Get the first and last names of all employees that work for departments Research or Accounting.

E.6.5

Get the enter dates of all clerks that belong to the department d1.

E.6.6

Get the names of projects on which two or more clerks are working.

E.6.7

Get the first and last names of the employees that are managers and that work on project Mercury.

E.6.8

Get the first and last names of all employees who entered the project at the same time as at least one other employee.

E.6.9

Get the employee numbers of the employees living in the same location and belonging to the same department as one another. (Hint: Use the extended sample database.)

E.6.10

Get the employee numbers of all employees belonging to the Marketing department. Find two equivalent solutions using:

   A. The JOIN operator

   B. The correlated subquery

Modification of a Table's Contents

In addition to the SELECT statement, which was introduced in Chapters 5 and 6, there are three other DML statements: INSERT, UPDATE, and DELETE. Like the SELECT statement, these three modification statements operate either on tables or on views. This chapter discusses these statements and gives examples of their use.

INSERT Statement

The INSERT statement inserts rows (or parts of them) into a table. It has two different forms:

1. INSERT [INTO] tab_name | view_name [(column_list)]
    { DEFAULT VALUES | VALUES ({DEFAULT | expression_1}...) }
2. INSERT INTO tab_name | view_name [(column_list)]
    {select_statement | execute_statement}

Using the first form, exactly one row (or parts of it) is inserted into the **tab_name** table or into the underlying table of the **view_name** view. The second form of the INSERT statement inserts the resulting set of rows from the SELECT statement or from the stored procedure, which is executed using the EXECUTE statement. (The stored procedure must return data, which is then inserted into the table. The SELECT statement can select values from a different table or the same table as the target of the INSERT statement, as long as the types of the columns are compatible.)

With both forms, every inserted value must have the compatible data type as the corresponding column of the table. To do so, all character-based values and date/time data must be enclosed in apostrophes (or quotation marks), while all numeric values need no such enclosing.

Inserting a Single Row

In the first and second forms of the INSERT statement, the explicit specification of the column list is optional. This means that omitting the list of columns is equivalent to specifying a list of all columns in the table.

The option DEFAULT VALUES inserts default values for all the columns. If a column is of the data type TIMESTAMP or has the IDENTITY property, the value, which is automatically incremented by the system, will be inserted. For other data types, the column is set to the appropriate non-null default value, if a default exists, or NULL if it doesn't. If the column is not nullable, and has no DEFAULT value, then the INSERT statement fails and an error will be indicated.

Examples 7.1 through 7.4 insert rows into the four tables of the sample database. This action shows the use of the INSERT statement to load a small amount of data into a database.

EXAMPLE 7.1

Load data into the **employee** table.

```
USE sample
INSERT INTO employee VALUES (25348, 'Matthew', 'Smith','d3')
INSERT INTO employee VALUES (10102, 'Ann', 'Jones','d3')
INSERT INTO employee VALUES (18316, 'John', 'Barrimore', 'd1')
INSERT INTO employee VALUES (29346, 'James', 'James', 'd2')
INSERT INTO employee VALUES (9031, 'Elsa', 'Bertoni', 'd2')
INSERT INTO employee VALUES (2581, 'Elke', 'Hansel', 'd2')
INSERT INTO employee VALUES (28559, 'Sybill', 'Moser', 'd1')
```

EXAMPLE 7.2

Load data into the **department** table.

```
USE sample
INSERT INTO department VALUES ('d1', 'Research', 'Dallas')
INSERT INTO department VALUES ('d2', 'Accounting', 'Seattle')
INSERT INTO department VALUES ('d3', 'Marketing', 'Dallas')
```

EXAMPLE 7.3

Load data into the **project** table.

```
USE sample
INSERT INTO project VALUES ('p1', 'Apollo', 120000.00)
INSERT INTO project VALUES ('p2', 'Gemini', 95000.00)
INSERT INTO project VALUES ('p3', 'Mercury', 186500.00)
```

EXAMPLE 7.4

Load data into the **works_on** table.

```
USE sample
INSERT INTO works_on VALUES (10102,'p1', 'Analyst', '1997.10.1')
INSERT INTO works_on VALUES (10102, 'p3', 'Manager', '1999.1.1')
INSERT INTO works_on VALUES (25348, 'p2', 'Clerk', '1998.2.15')
```

INSERT INTO works_on VALUES (18316, 'p2', NULL, '1998.6.1')
INSERT INTO works_on VALUES (29346, 'p2', NULL, '1997.12.15')
INSERT INTO works_on VALUES (2581, 'p3', 'Analyst', '1998.10.15')
INSERT INTO works_on VALUES (9031, 'p1', 'Manager', '1998.4.15')
INSERT INTO works_on VALUES (28559, 'p1', 'NULL', '1998.8.1')
INSERT INTO works_on VALUES (28559, 'p2', 'Clerk', '1999.2.1')
INSERT INTO works_on VALUES (9031, 'p3', 'Clerk', '1997.11.15')
INSERT INTO works_on VALUES (29346, 'p1','Clerk', '1998.1.4')

There are a few different ways to insert values into a new row. Examples 7.5 through 7.7 show these possibilities.

EXAMPLE 7.5

USE sample
INSERT INTO employee VALUES (15201, 'Dave', 'Davis', NULL)

The INSERT statement in Example 7.5 corresponds to the INSERT statements in Example 7.1. The explicit use of the keyword NULL inserts the null value into the corresponding column.

The insertion of values into some (but not all) of a table's columns usually requires the explicit specification of the corresponding columns. The omitted columns must be either nullable or have a DEFAULT value.

EXAMPLE 7.6

USE sample
INSERT INTO employee (emp_no, emp_fname, emp_lname)
        VALUES (15201, 'Dave', 'Davis')

Examples 7.5 and 7.6 are equivalent. The **department_nr** column is the only nullable column in the **employee** table because we declared all other columns in the **employee** table with the NOT NULL clause in the CREATE TABLE statement.

The order of column names in the VALUE clause of the INSERT statement can be different from the original order of those columns, which is determined in the CREATE TABLE statement. In this case, it is absolutely necessary to list the columns in the new order.

EXAMPLE 7.7

> USE sample
> INSERT INTO employee (emp_lname, emp_fname, dept_no, emp_no)
>   VALUES ('Davis', 'Dave', 'd1', 15201)

Inserting Multiple Rows

The second form of the INSERT statement inserts one or more rows selected with
a subquery.

EXAMPLE 7.8

Get all the numbers and names for departments located in Dallas, and load the selected
data into a new table.

> USE sample
> CREATE TABLE dallas_dept
>   (dept_no CHAR(4) NOT NULL,
>   dept_name CHAR(20) NOT NULL)
>
> INSERT INTO dallas_dept (dept_no, dept_name)
>   SELECT dept_no, dept_name
>   FROM department
>   WHERE location = 'Dallas'

The new table, **dallas_dept**, created in Example 7.8, has the same columns as the
department table except for the **location** column. The subquery in the INSERT statement selects all rows with the value 'Dallas' in the **location** column. The selected rows
will be subsequently inserted in the new table.

The content of the **dallas_dept** table can be selected with the following SELECT
statement:

> SELECT * FROM dallas_dept

The result is

dept_no	dept_name
d1	Research
d3	Marketing

EXAMPLE 7.9

Get all employee numbers, project numbers, and project enter dates for all clerks who work in project p2, and load the selected data into a new table.

```
USE sample
CREATE TABLE clerk_t
    (emp_no INT NOT NULL,
     project_no CHAR(4),
     enter_date DATETIME)

INSERT INTO clerk_t (emp_no, project_no, enter_date)
    SELECT emp_no, project_no, enter_date
      FROM works_on
      WHERE job = 'Clerk'
      AND project_no = 'p2'
```

The new table, **clerk_t**, contains the following rows:

emp_no	project_no	enter_date
25348	p2	1998-02-15 00:00:00.000
28559	p2	1999-02-01 00:00:00.000

The tables **dallas_dept** and **clerk_t** (Examples 7.8 and 7.9) were empty before the INSERT statement inserted the rows. If, however, the table already exists and there are rows in it, the new rows will be appended.

Inserting rows within a view has certain limitations. The INSERT statement and views will be discussed in detail in Chapter 9.

UPDATE Statement

The UPDATE statement modifies values of table rows. This statement has the general form:

```
UPDATE tab_name | view_name
    SET column_1 = expression [{column_2 = expression}...]
    [FROM tab_name1 | view_name1 [{tab_name2 |view_name2} ...]]
    [WHERE condition]
```

Rows in the **tab_name** table (or rows in the table that are associated with the **view_name** view) are modified in accordance with the WHERE clause. For each row to be modified, the UPDATE statement changes the values of the columns in the SET clause, assigning a constant (or generally an expression) to the associated column. If the WHERE clause is omitted, the UPDATE statement modifies all rows of the table. (The FROM clause will be discussed in relation to Example 7.13 later in this chapter.)

NOTE

An UPDATE statement can only modify data of a single table.

There are certain limitations to modifying rows using a view. The UPDATE statement and views will be discussed in detail in Chapter 9.

EXAMPLE 7.10

Set the task of employee number 18316, who works on project p2, to be 'Manager'.

```
USE sample
UPDATE works_on
   SET job = 'Manager'
   WHERE emp_no = 18316
   AND project_no = 'p2'
```

The UPDATE statement in Example 7.10 modifies exactly one row of the **works_on** table, because the combination of the columns **emp_no** and **project_no** builds the primary key of that table (and is therefore unique). This example modifies the task of the employee, which was previously unknown or set to NULL.

Example 7.11 modifies rows of a table with an expression.

EXAMPLE 7.11

Change the budgets of all projects to be represented in English pounds. The current rate of exchange is 0.56£ for $1.

```
USE sample
UPDATE project
   SET budget = budget*0.56
```

In the example, all rows of the **project** table will be modified because of the omitted WHERE clause. The modified rows of the **project** table can be displayed with the following Transact-SQL statement:

```
SELECT * FROM project
```

The result is

project_no	project_name	budget
p1	Apollo	67200
p2	Gemini	53200
p3	Mercury	104440

EXAMPLE 7.12

Due to her illness, set all tasks on all projects for Mrs. Jones to NULL.

```
USE sample
UPDATE works_on
    SET job = NULL
    WHERE emp_no IN
    (SELECT emp_no
      FROM employee
      WHERE emp_lname = 'Jones')
```

Example 7.12 uses a subquery in the WHERE clause of the UPDATE statement. Because of the use of the IN operator, more than one row can result from the subquery.

Example 7.12 can also be solved using the FROM clause of the UPDATE statement. The FROM clause contains the names of tables that are involved in the UPDATE statement. All these tables must be subsequently joined. Example 7.13 shows the use of the FROM clause. This example is identical to the previous one.

NOTE

The FROM clause is a Transact-SQL extension to the ANSI SQL standard.

EXAMPLE 7.13

```
USE sample
UPDATE works_on
  SET job = NULL
  FROM works_on, employee
  WHERE emp_lname = 'Jones'
  AND works_on.emp_no = employee.emp_no
```

Example 7.14 illustrates the use of CASE in the UPDATE statement. (For a detailed discussion of this expression, refer to Chapter 5.) The budget of each project will be increased by a percentage (20, 10, or 5) depending on its previous amount of money. Those projects with a lower budget will be increased by the higher percentages.

EXAMPLE 7.14

```
USE sample
UPDATE project
  SET budget = CASE
        WHEN budget > 0 and budget < 100000  THEN budget*1.2
        WHEN budget > = 100000 and budget < 200000  THEN budget*1.1
        ELSE budget*1.05
        END
```

DELETE Statement

The DELETE statement deletes rows from a table. This statement has two different forms:

1. DELETE table_name | view_name
    [FROM table_name1 | view_name1 [{,table_name2 | view_name2}...]]
    [WHERE predicate]
2. DELETE table_name | view_name
        [WHERE condition]

All rows that satisfy the condition in the WHERE clause will be deleted. Explicitly naming columns within the DELETE statement is not necessary (or allowed), because all columns of the appropriate rows will be deleted (see Example 7.15).

EXAMPLE 7.15

Delete all managers in the **works_on** table.

```
USE sample
DELETE FROM works_on
   WHERE job = 'Manager'
```

The WHERE clause in the DELETE statement can contain a subquery.

EXAMPLE 7.16

Mrs. Moser is on leave. Delete all rows in the database concerning her.

```
USE sample
DELETE FROM works_on
   WHERE emp_no IN
   (SELECT emp_no
      FROM employee
      WHERE emp_lname = 'Moser')

DELETE FROM employee
   WHERE emp_lname = 'Moser'
```

Example 7.16 can also be performed using the FROM clause. This clause has the same semantics as the FROM clause in the UPDATE statement. Example 7.17 is identical to the previous one.

EXAMPLE 7.17

```
USE sample
DELETE works_on
   FROM works_on, employee
   WHERE works_on.emp_no = employee.emp_no
   AND emp_lname = 'Moser'

DELETE FROM employee
   WHERE emp_lname = 'Moser'
```

The use of the WHERE clause in the DELETE statement is optional. If the WHERE clause is omitted, all rows of a table will be deleted (see Example 7.18).

EXAMPLE 7.18

```
USE sample
DELETE FROM works_on
```

There are certain limitations to deleting rows using a view. The DELETE statement and views will be discussed in detail in Chapter 10.

NOTE

There is a significant difference between the DELETE and the DROP TABLE statements. The DELETE statement deletes (partially or totally) the contents of a table. On the other hand, the DROP TABLE statement deletes both the contents and the schema of a table. Thus, after a DELETE statement, the table still exists in the database (although possibly with zero rows), but after a DROP TABLE statement, the table no longer exists.

SQL Server 2005 supports the OUTPUT clause, which concerns INSERT, UPDATE, and DELETE statements. This clause is discussed in Chapter 13.

Transact-SQL language also supports the TRUNCATE TABLE statement. This statement normally provides a "faster executing" version of the DELETE statement without the WHERE clause. The TRUNCATE TABLE statement deletes all rows from a table more quickly than does the DELETE statement because it drops the contents of the table page by page, while DELETE drops the contents row by row. Additionally, the TRUNCATE TABLE statement does not place the modifications of a table into the transaction log.

NOTE

The TRUNCATE TABLE statement is a Transact-SQL extension to the SQL standard.

The TRUNCATE TABLE statement has the form:

TRUNCATE TABLE table_name

Conclusion

Generally, there are only three SQL statements that can be used to modify a table: INSERT, UPDATE, and DELETE. (The Transact-SQL language supports one additional nonstandard statement: TRUNCATE TABLE.) They are generic in that for all types of row insertion, you use only one statement: INSERT. The same is true for the modification or deletion of rows with the UPDATE statement or DELETE statement.

Chapters 4 through 7 have introduced all SQL statements that belong to DDL and DML. Most of these statements can be grouped together to build a sequence of Transact-SQL statements. Such a sequence is the basis for *stored procedures*, which will be covered in the next chapter.

Exercises

E.7.1

Insert the data of a new employee called Julia Long, whose employee number is 11111. Her department number is not known yet.

E.7.2

Create a new table called **emp_d1_d2** with all employees who work for department d1 or d2, and load the corresponding rows from the **employee** table. Find two different, but equivalent, solutions.

E.7.3

Create a new table of all employees who entered their projects in 1998 and load it with the corresponding rows from the **employee** table.

E.7.4

Modify the job of all employees in project p1 who are managers. They have to work as clerks from now on.

E.7.5

The budgets of all projects are no longer determined. Assign all budgets the NULL value.

E.7.6

Modify the jobs of the employee with the employee number 28559. From now on, she will be the manager in all her projects.

E.7.7

Increase the budget of the project where the manager has the employee number 10102. The increase is 10 percent.

E.7.8

Change the name of the department for which the employee named James works. The new department name is Sales.

E.7.9

Change the enter date for the projects for those employees who work in project p1 and belong to department Sales. The new date is 12.12.1998.

CHAPTER 8

Stored Procedures and User-Defined Functions

his chapter introduces additional Transact-SQL statements, referred to as "SQL extensions." These extensions can be used to create powerful scripts and stored procedures (scripts that are stored on the server and that can be reused). Some stored procedures are written by users, and others are provided by Microsoft and are referred to as *system stored procedures*. Both kinds can be written either in Transact-SQL or programming languages, such as C# and Visual Basic 2005. System stored procedures will be mentioned in this chapter but covered in more detail later in the book. The last section of the chapter covers the use of user-defined functions.

SQL Extensions

The preceding four chapters introduced Transact-SQL statements that belong to the data definition language and the data manipulation language. Most of these statements can be grouped together to build a batch. A *batch* is a sequence of SQL statements and SQL extensions that are sent to SQL Server for execution together. The number of statements in a batch is limited by the size of the compiled batch object.

There are a number of restrictions concerning the appearance of different SQL statements inside a batch. The most important is that the data definition statements CREATE VIEW, CREATE PROCEDURE, CREATE RULE, CREATE TRIGGER, and CREATE DEFAULT must each be the only statement in a batch.

NOTE

To separate data definition language statements one from another, use the GO statement.

The following sections describe each SQL extension of the Transact-SQL language separately.

Block of Statements

A block allows the building of units with one or more SQL statements. Every block begins with the BEGIN statement and terminates with the END statement:

```
BEGIN
statement_1
statement_2
...
END
```

A block can be used inside the IF statement to allow the execution of more than one statement, depending on a certain condition (see Example 8.1).

IF Statement

The Transact-SQL statement IF corresponds to the statement with the same name that is supported by almost all programming languages. This statement executes one SQL statement (or more, enclosed in a block) *if* a Boolean expression, which follows the keyword IF, evaluates to true. If the IF statement contains an ELSE statement, a second group of SQL statements can be executed if the condition in the IF part evaluates to false.

NOTE

Before you start to execute batches, stored procedures, and user-defined functions in this chapter, please re-create the entire sample database.

EXAMPLE 8.1

```
USE sample
IF (SELECT COUNT(*)
        FROM works_on
        WHERE project_no = 'p1'
        GROUP BY project_no ) > 3
    PRINT 'The number of employees in the project p1 is 4 or more'
ELSE BEGIN
    PRINT 'The following employees work for the project p1'
    SELECT emp_fname, emp_lname
    FROM employee, works_on
    WHERE employee.emp_no = works_on.emp_no
    AND project_no = 'p1'
END
```

Example 8.1 shows the use of a block inside the IF statement. The Boolean condition:

```
(SELECT COUNT(*)
        FROM works_on
        WHERE project_no = 'p1'
         GROUP BY project_no) > 3
```

is evaluated to true for the sample database. Therefore, the single PRINT statement in the IF part is executed. Notice that this example uses a subquery to return the number of rows (using the aggregate function COUNT(*)) that satisfy the WHERE condition (project_no = 'p1'). The result of the example above is

The number of employees in the project p1 is 4 or more

NOTE

The ELSE part of the IF statement in Example 8.1 contains two SQL statements: PRINT and SELECT. Therefore, the block with the BEGIN and END statements is required to enclose the two statements. (The PRINT statement is another SQL extension. It returns a user-defined message.)

WHILE Statement

The WHILE statement repeatedly executes one SQL statement (or more, enclosed in a block) *while* the Boolean expression evaluates to true. In other words, if the expression is true, the statement (or block) is executed, and then the expression is evaluated again to determine if the statement(s) should be executed again. This process repeats until the expression evaluates to false.

A block within the WHILE statement can optionally contain one of two statements used to control the execution of the statements within the block: BREAK or CONTINUE. The BREAK statement stops the execution of the statements inside the block and starts the execution of the statement immediately following this block. The CONTINUE statement stops only the current execution of the statements in the block and starts the execution of the block from its beginning.

Example 8.2 shows the use of the WHILE statement.

EXAMPLE 8.2

```
USE sample
WHILE (SELECT SUM(budget)
        FROM project) < 500000
    BEGIN
      UPDATE project SET budget = budget*1.1
      IF (SELECT MAX(budget)
          FROM project) > 240000
      BREAK
    ELSE CONTINUE
    END
```

In Example 8.2, the budget of all projects will be increased by 10 percent until the sum of budgets is greater than $500,000. However, the repeated execution will be stopped if the budget of one of the projects is greater than $240,000. The execution of Example 8.2 gives the following output:

(3 rows affected)
(3 rows affected)
(3 rows affected)

Local Variables

Local variables are an important extension to the Transact-SQL language. They are used to store values (of any type) within a batch. They are "local" because they can only be referenced within the same block in which they were declared. SQL Server also supports global variables, which are described in Chapter 3.

Every local variable must be defined using the DECLARE statement. (For the syntax of the DECLARE statement, see Example 8.3.) The definition of each variable contains its name and the corresponding data type. Variables are always referenced in a batch using the prefix @. The assignment of a value to a local variable is done using the following:

▶ The special form of the SELECT statement

▶ The SET statement

The usage of both statements for a value assignment is demonstrated in Example 8.3.

EXAMPLE 8.3

```
USE sample
DECLARE @avg_budget MONEY, @extra_budget MONEY
     SET @extra_budget = 15000
     SELECT @avg_budget = AVG(budget) FROM project
     IF (SELECT budget
          FROM project
          WHERE project_no='p1') < @avg_budget
     BEGIN
      UPDATE project
          SET budget = budget + @extra_budget
```

```
              WHERE project_no ='p1'
               PRINT 'Budget for p1 increased by @extra_budget'
            END
            ELSE PRINT 'Budget for p1 unchanged'
```

The result is

Budget for p1 increased by @extra_budget

The batch in Example 8.3 calculates the average of all project budgets and compares this value with the budget of project p1. If the latter value is smaller than the calculated value, the budget of project p1 will be increased by the value of the local variable **@extra_budget**.

Miscellaneous Procedural Statements

The procedural extensions of the Transact-SQL language also contain the following statements:

- ► RETURN
- ► GOTO
- ► RAISEERROR
- ► WAITFOR

The RETURN statement has the same functionality inside a batch as the BREAK statement inside WHILE. This means that the RETURN statement causes the execution of the batch to terminate and the first statement following the end of the batch to begin executing.

The GOTO statement branches to a label, which stands in front of a Transact-SQL statement within a batch. The RAISEERROR statement generates a user-defined error message and sets a system error flag. A user-defined error number must be greater than 50000. (All error numbers <= 50000 are system defined and are reserved by SQL Server.) The error values are stored in the global variable @@ERROR (see Chapter 3). Example 21.2 shows the use of the RAISEERROR statement.

The WAITFOR statement defines either the time interval (if the DELAY option is used) or a specified time (if the TIME option is used) that the system has to wait before executing the next statement in the batch. The syntax of this statement is

WAITFOR {DELAY 'time' | TIME 'time' | TIMEOUT 'timeout' }

DELAY tells SQL Server to wait until the specified amount of time has passed. TIME specifies a time in one of the acceptable formats for date/time data. Example 14.4 shows the use of the WAITFOR statement. TIMEOUT specifies the amount of time, in milliseconds, to wait for a message to arrive on the queue.

Handling Events with TRY and CATCH Statements

Previous versions of SQL Server require that you include error handling code after every Transact-SQL statement that might produce an error. (You can handle errrors using the @@ERROR global variable. Example 14.1 shows the use of this variable.)

SQL Server 2005 introduces exception handling with two new statements, TRY and CATCH. We will first explain what exception means and then discuss how these two statements work.

An exception is a problem (usually an error) that prevents the continuation of a program. With such a problem you cannot continue program processing, because there is not enough information needed to handle the problem. For this reason, the existing problem will be relegated to another part of the program, which will handle the exception.

The role of the TRY statement is to capture the exception. (Because this process usually comprises several statements, we speak of the TRY block, instead of the TRY statement.) If an exception occurs within the TRY block, the part of the system called exception handler delivers the exception to the other part of the program, which will handle the exception. This program part is denoted by the keyword CATCH and is therefore called the CATCH block.

NOTE

Exception handling using the TRY and CATCH statements is the common way that modern programming languages like C# and Java treat errors.

Exception handling with the TRY and CATCH blocks gives a programmer a lot of benefits, such as:

▶ Exceptions provide a clean way to check for errors without cluttering code

▶ Exceptions provide a mechanism to signal errors directly rather than using some side effects

▶ Exceptions can be seen by the programmer and checked during the compilations process

We will use two examples to show how exception handling with the TRY/CATCH works. Both examples are based on the referential integrity between the **department** and **employee** tables. For this reason, you have to create both tables using the PRIMARY KEY and FOREIGN KEY constraints, as we have done it in Example 4.8. Also, the rows of these tables must be inserted using the INSERT statements in Examples 7.2 and 7.1, in this order.

EXAMPLE 8.4

```
USE sample
SET XACT_ABORT OFF
BEGIN TRANSACTION
insert into employee values(11111, 'Ann', 'Smith','d2')
insert into employee values(22222, 'Matthew', 'Jones','d4')  -- referential
constraint error
insert into employee values(33333, 'John', 'Barrimore', 'd2')
COMMIT TRANSACTION
```

Example 8.4 starts with the SET statement. When the SET XACT_ABORT option is set to OFF, only the Transact-SQL statement that raised the error is rolled back and the transaction continues processing. (Transaction specifies a sequence of Transact-SQL statements that build a logical unit. Transactions are covered in Chapter 14.) The second INSERT statement causes a referential constraint error, because the department 'd4' does not exist in the **department** table. After executing the batch in Example 8.4, the **employee** table will have two additional rows inserted with the first and third INSERT statements, because the XACT_ABORT option is set to OFF. This means that the subsequent statements after the failure execute successfully and the transaction is successfully committed.

The following example shows how you can use exception handling to insert all statements in a batch or to roll back the entire statement group if an error occurs.

EXAMPLE 8.5

```
USE sample
BEGIN TRY
  BEGIN TRANSACTION
  insert into employee values(11111, 'Ann', 'Smith','d2')
  insert into employee values(22222, 'Matthew', 'Jones','d4') -- referential
constraint error
  insert into employee values(33333, 'John', 'Barrimore', 'd2')
```

```
        COMMIT TRANSACTION
        PRINT 'Transaction committed'
    END TRY
    BEGIN CATCH
        ROLLBACK
        PRINT 'Transaction rolled back'
    END CATCH
```

After the execution of the batch in Example 8.5, all three statements in the batch won't be executed at all, and the output of this example is

```
(1 row(s) affected)
Transaction rolled back
```

The execution of Example 8.5 works as follows. The first INSERT statement will be executed successfully. (This is documented in the output result.) Then the second statement causes the referential constraint error. Because all three statements are written inside the TRY block, the exception is "thrown" and the exception handler starts the CATCH block. The CATCH rolls back all statements and prints the corresponding message. For this reason, the content of the **employee** table will not change. (The statements BEGIN TRANSACTION, COMMIT TRANSACTION, and ROLLBACK are Transact-SQL statements concerning transactions. These statements start, commit, and roll back transactions, respectively. See Chapter 14 for the discussion of these statements and transactions generally.)

Stored Procedures

A stored procedure is a special kind of batch written in Transact-SQL, using the SQL language and SQL extensions. It is saved on the database server to improve the performance and consistency of repetitive tasks. SQL Server supports stored procedures and system procedures. Stored procedures are created in the same way as all other database objects—that is, by using the Transact-SQL language. System procedures are provided with the product by Microsoft and can be used to access and modify the information in the system tables. This section describes the stored procedures, while the section later in this chapter is dedicated to the system procedures.

When a stored procedure is created, an optional list of parameters can be defined. The procedure accepts the corresponding arguments each time it is invoked. Stored procedures can optionally return a value, which displays the user-defined information or, in the case of an error, the corresponding error message.

A stored procedure is precompiled before it is stored as an object in the database. Therefore, the execution plan of a procedure is stored in the database and used whenever the stored procedure is executed. This property of stored procedures offers an important benefit: The repeated compilation of a procedure is (almost always) eliminated, and the execution performance is therefore increased.

The above property of stored procedures offers another benefit concerning the volume of data that must be sent to and from SQL Server. It might take less than 50 bytes to call a stored procedure containing several thousand bytes of statements. The accumulated effect of this savings when multiple users are performing repetitive tasks can be quite significant.

Stored procedures can also be used for the following purposes:

▶ To control access authorization

▶ To create an audit trail of activities in database tables

▶ To separate data definition and data manipulation statements concerning a database and all corresponding applications

The use of stored procedures provides security control above and beyond the use of the GRANT and the REVOKE statements (see Chapter 12), which define different access privileges for a user. This is because the authorization to execute a stored procedure is independent of the authorization to modify the objects that the stored procedure contains, as will be seen in the next section.

Stored procedures that audit write and/or read operations concerning a table are an additional security feature of the database. With the use of such procedures, the database administrator can track modifications made by users or application programs.

Creation and Execution of Stored Procedures

Stored procedures are created with the CREATE PROCEDURE statement, which has the following syntax:

```
CREATE PROC[EDURE] [schema_name.]proc_name [;number]
[({ @param1 } type1 [ VARYING] [= default1] [OUTPUT])]
          {[({ @param2 } type2 [ VARYING] [= default2] [OUTPUT])]}...
[WITH {RECOMPILE | ENCRYPTION | EXECUTE AS 'user_name'}]
[FOR REPLICATION]
AS batch | EXTERNAL NAME method_name
```

schema_name is the name of the schema to which the ownership of the created stored procedure is assigned. **proc_name** is the name of the new stored procedure. The optional specification **number** allows the owner of the stored procedure to group procedures with the same name. This means all stored procedures with the same name but with different numbers create a group. The benefit of such procedures is that all grouped procedures can be dropped using a single DROP statement.

NOTE

*The **number** specification is marked as a deprecated feature and will be removed in a future version of SQL Server.*

@**param1**, @**param2**,... are parameters, and **type1, type2**,... specify their data types, respectively. The parameter in a stored procedure has the same logical meaning as the local variable for a block. Parameters are values passed from the caller of the stored procedure and are used within the stored procedure. **default1** specifies the optional default value of the corresponding parameter. (Default can also be NULL.)

The OUTPUT option indicates that the parameter is a return parameter and can be returned to the calling procedure or to the system (see Example 8.9).

As stated previously, the execution plan for a stored procedure is generated once and can be executed many times. The WITH RECOMPILE option ignores the existing execution plan and generates a new one each time the procedure is executed.

NOTE

The use of the WITH RECOMPILE option destroys one of the most important benefits of the stored procedures: the performance advantage gained by a single precompilation. For this reason, the WITH RECOMPILE option should only be used when database objects used by the stored procedure are modified frequently or when the parameters used by the stored procedure are volatile.

The EXECUTE AS clause specifies the security context under which to execute the stored procedure after it is accessed. By specifying the context in which the procedure is executed, you can control which user account the database engine uses to validate permissions on objects referenced by the procedure. (See Chapter 12 for a detailed discussion of user permissions.)

The Transact-SQL statements CREATE DEFAULT, CREATE RULE, CREATE PROCEDURE, CREATE VIEW, and CREATE TRIGGER must each be defined as a single statement inside a batch.

By default, only the members of the **sysadmin** fixed server role, and the **db_owner** and **db_ddladmin** fixed database roles, can use the CREATE PROCEDURE statement. However, the members of these roles may assign this privilege to other users using the GRANT CREATE PROCEDURE statement.

EXAMPLE 8.6

```
USE sample
GO
CREATE PROCEDURE increase_budget (@percent INT=5)
      AS UPDATE project
            SET budget = budget + budget*@percent/100
```

The stored procedure **increase_budget** increases the budgets of all projects for a certain percentage value that is defined using the parameter **@percent**. The procedure also defines the default value (5), which is used if there is no argument at the execution time of the procedure.

> **NOTE**
>
> *It is possible to create stored procedures that reference nonexistent tables. This feature allows you to debug procedure code without creating the underlying tables first, or even connecting to the target server.*

In contrast to "base" stored procedures that are placed in the current database, it is possible to create temporary stored procedures that are always placed in the temporary **tempdb** database. You might create a temporary stored procedure to avoid executing a particular batch of statements repeatedly within a connection. You can create *local* or *global* temporary procedures by preceding the **procedure_name** with a single pound sign (**#procedure_name**) for local temporary procedures and a double pound sign (**##procedure_name**) for global temporary procedures. A local temporary stored procedure can only be executed by the user who created it, and only during the same connection. A global temporary procedure can be executed by all users, but only until the last connection executing it (usually the creator's) ends.

The EXECUTE statement executes an existing procedure. The execution of a stored procedure is allowed for each user who is either the owner or has the EXECUTE privilege for the procedure (see Chapter 12). The EXECUTE statement has the following syntax:

```
[[EXEC[UTE]] [@return_status =] {procedure_name
      [;number] | @procedure_name_var}
      {[[@parameter1 =] value | [@parameter1=] @variable [OUTPUT]] |
DEFAULT}..
      [WITH RECOMPILE]
```

All options in the EXECUTE statement, other than the **return_status**, have the equivalent logical meaning as the options with the same names in the CREATE PROCEDURE statement. **return_status** is an optional integer variable that stores the return status of a procedure. The value of a parameter can be assigned using either a value (**value**) or a local variable (@**variable**). The order of parameter values is not relevant if they are named, but if they are not named, parameter values must be supplied in the order defined in the CREATE PROCEDURE statement.

The DEFAULT clause supplies the default value of the parameter as defined in the procedure. When the procedure expects a value for a parameter that does not have a defined default and either a parameter is missing or the DEFAULT keyword is specified, an error occurs.

NOTE

When an EXECUTE statement is the first statement in a batch, the word "EXECUTE" can be omitted from the statement. Despite this, it would be safer to include this word in every batch you write.

EXAMPLE 8.7

```
USE sample
EXECUTE increase_budget 10
```

The EXECUTE statement in Example 8.7 executes the stored procedure **increase_budget** (Example 8.6) and increases the budgets of all projects by 10 percent each.

EXAMPLE 8.8

```
CREATE PROCEDURE modify_empno (@old_no INTEGER, @new_no INTEGER)
    AS UPDATE employee
        SET emp_no = @new_no
        WHERE emp_no = @old_no
    UPDATE works_on
        SET emp_no = @new_no
        WHERE emp_no = @old_no
```

The procedure **modify_empno** in Example 8.8 demonstrates using stored procedures as part of the maintenance of the referential constraint (in this case, between the tables **employee** and **works_on**). Such a stored procedure can be used inside the definition of a trigger, which actually maintains the referential constraint (see Example 13.3).

EXAMPLE 8.9

```
USE sample
GO
CREATE PROCEDURE delete_emp @employee_no INT, @counter INT OUTPUT
       AS SELECT @counter = COUNT(*)
           FROM works_on
            WHERE emp_no = @employee_no
       DELETE FROM employee
           WHERE emp_no = @employee_no
        DELETE FROM works_on
           WHERE emp_no = @employee_no
```

This stored procedure can be executed using the following statements:

```
DECLARE @quantity INT
       EXECUTE delete_emp @employee_no=28559, @counter=@quantity
OUTPUT
```

The batch in Example 8.9 contains the creation of the stored procedure **delete_emp** as well as its execution. The stored procedure **delete_emp** calculates the number of projects on which the employee (with the employee number **@employee_no**) works. The calculated value is then assigned to the parameter **@counter**. After the deletion of all rows with the assigned employee number from the tables **employee** and **works_on**, the calculated value will be assigned to the local variable **@quantity**.

NOTE

*The value of the parameter will be returned to the calling procedure if the OUTPUT option is used. In Example 8.9, the stored procedure **delete_emp** passes the parameter **@counter** to the calling statement, so the procedure returns the value to the system. Therefore, the parameter **@counter** must be declared with the OUTPUT option in the procedure as well as in the EXECUTE statement.*

SQL Server also supports a Transact-SQL statement, ALTER PROCEDURE, which modifies the structure of a stored procedure. The ALTER PROCEDURE statement is usually used to modify Transact-SQL statements in the batch of a stored procedure. All options of the ALTER PROCEDURE statement correspond to the options with the same name in the CREATE PROCEDURE statement. The main purpose of this statement is to avoid reassignment of existing privileges for the stored procedure.

A stored procedure (or a group of stored procedures with the same name) is removed using the DROP PROCEDURE statement. Only the owner of the stored procedure and the members of the **db_owner** and **sysadmin** fixed roles can remove the procedure (see Chapter 12).

The SQL Server system catalog contains two system tables related to stored procedures: **sys.objects** and **sys.sql_modules**. There are also two system procedures that provide relevant information about stored procedures: **sp_helptext** and **sp_depend**. For the definition of these views and system procedures, see Chapter 11.

System Stored Procedures

System stored procedures are special types of stored procedures that are automatically generated during installation and are therefore an integral part of the SQL Server system. Names of all system stored procedures begin with the prefix "sp_". System stored procedures are used for the following purposes:

▶   To directly access (with read and write operations) the system tables

▶   To retrieve and modify access privileges of a database

▶   To control and manage the memory used by each database

NOTE
The above list is neither complete nor exclusive. For example, some system stored procedures belong at the same time to the groups listed above.

We will discuss system procedures in different chapters, depending on their purpose. Most of them are described in Chapter 11 along with the SQL Server system tables.

Stored Procedures and CLR

In the previous versions of SQL Server you can use only Transact-SQL statements to create stored procedures. SQL Server 2005 introduces a new feature, Common

Language Runtime (CLR), which allows you to develop different database objects, such as stored procedures, user-defined functions, triggers, and user-defined types using C# and Visual Basic 2005. CLR also allows you to execute these database objects using the common run-time system.

NOTE

*You enable and disable the use of the CLR through the **clr_enabled** option of the **sp_configure** system procedure. After execution of the **sp_configure** system procedure, execute the RECONFIGURE statement to update the running configuration value. (The use of Common Language Runtime is disabled by default.)*

To implement, compile, and store procedures using CLR, you have to execute the following four steps in the given order:

▶ Implement a stored procedure using C# (or Visual Basic 2005) and compile the program, using the corresponding compiler

▶ Use the CREATE ASSEMBLY statement to create the corresponding executable file

▶ Store the procedure as a SQL Server object using the CREATE PROCEDURE statement

▶ Execute the procedure using the EXECUTE statement

NOTE

Microsoft suggests using Transact-SQL as the default language for creating objects in SQL Server.

Figure 8-1 shows how CLR works. You use a development environment such as Visual Studio 2005 to implement your program. After the implementation, start the C# or Visual Basic 2005 compiler to generate the object code. This code will be stored in a .dll file, which is the source for the CREATE ASSEMBLY statement. After the execution of this statement you get the intermediate code. In the next step you use the already-known statement CREATE PROCEDURE to store the executable as a database object. Finally, the stored procedure can be executed using the already-introduced EXECUTE statement.

The following five examples demonstrate the whole process, which we described above.

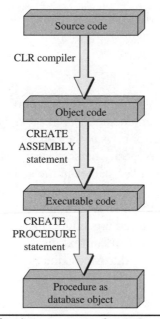

Figure 8-1   *The flow diagram for the execution of a CLR stored procedure*

EXAMPLE 8.10

```
using System;
using System.Data;
using System.Data.Sql;
using System.Data.SqlServer;
using System.Data.SqlTypes;
public partial class StoredProcedures
{
   [SqlProcedure]
   public static int GetEmployeeCount()
   {
      int iRows;
      SqlCommand sqlCmd = SqlContext.GetCommand();
      sqlCmd.CommandText = "select count(*) as 'Employee Count' " +
"from employee";
```

```
          iRows = (int)sqlCmd.ExecuteScalar();
          return iRows;
      }
  };
```

Example 8.10 shows the C# program, which will be used to demonstrate how you apply CLR to implement and deploy stored procedures. This program uses a query to calculate the number of rows in the **employee** table. The **using** directives at the beginning of the program specify namespaces, such as **System.Data**. These directives allow you to specify class names in the source program without referencing the corresponding namespace. After that we define the **StoredProcedures** class, which is written with a **[SqlProcedure]** attribute. The latter tells the compiler that the class is a SQL Server stored procedure. Inside that class we define a method called **GetEmployeeCount**. The **SqlContext** class, located in the **System.Data. SqlServer** namespace, is then used to access the **SqlCommand** object called **sqlCmd**.

The following lines of code:

```
sqlCmd.CommandText = "select count(*) as 'Employee Count' " + "from employee";
iRows = (int)sqlCmd.ExecuteScalar();
```

use the SELECT statement to find the number of rows in the **employee** table and to display the result. The command text is specified by setting the **CommandText** property of the **SqlCommand** object returned by the call to **SqlContext. GetCommand**. Next, the **ExecuteScalar** method of the **SqlCommand** object is called. This returns a scalar value, which is finally casted (converted) to **int** and assigned to the **iRows** variable.

The next example shows the first step in deploying stored procedures using CLR.

EXAMPLE 8.11

csc /target:library GetEmployeeCount.cs /reference:"c:\Program Files\ Microsoft SQL Server\MSSQL.1\MSSQL\Binn\sqlaccess.dll"

Example 8.11 demonstrates how to compile the C# program called **GetEmployeeCount** (Example 8.10). (Actually, this command can be used generally to compile any C# program, if you set the appropriate name for the source program.)

csc is the command that is used to invoke the C# compiler. You invoke the **csc** command at the Windows command line. Before starting the command, you have to specify the location of the compiler using the PATH environment variable.

The **/target** option specifies the name of the C# program, while the **/reference** option defines the .dll file, which is necessary for the compilation process.

Example 8.12 shows the next step in creating the stored procedure. (Use SQL Server Management Studio to execute this statement.)

EXAMPLE 8.12

```
USE sample
GO
create assembly GetEmployeeCount
FROM 'C:\GetEmployeeCount.dll' WITH PERMISSION_SET = SAFE
```

The CREATE ASSEMBLY statement uses the managed code as the source to create the corresponding object in SQL Server, against which CLR stored procedures, user-defined functions, and triggers can be created. This statement has the following syntax:

```
CREATE ASSEMBLY assembly_name [ AUTHORIZATION owner_name ]
FROM { dll_file}
[ WITH PERMISSION_SET = { SAFE | EXTERNAL_ACCESS | UNSAFE } ]
```

assembly_name is the name of the assembly. The optional AUTHORIZATION clause specifies the name of a particular owner of the assembly. The FROM clause specifies the path where the assembly being uploaded is located. (In Example 8.12 we copied the .dll file generated from the source program from the **Framework** directory to the root of drive C:.)

The WITH PERMISSION SET clause is a very important clause of the CREATE ASSEMBLY statement and should always be set. It specifies a set of code access permissions granted to the assembly. SAFE is the most restrictive permission set. Code executed by an assembly with this permission cannot access external system resources, such as files. EXTERNAL_ACCESS allows assemblies to access certain external system resources, while UNSAFE allows unrestricted access to resources, both within and outside the SQL Server system.

NOTE

In order to store the information concerning assembly code, a user must have the ability to execute the CREATE ASSEMBLY statement. The user (or role) executing the statement is the owner of the assembly. It is possible to assign an assembly to another user by using the AUTHORIZATION clause of the CREATE SCHEMA statement. (See Chapter 12 for more details concerning the ownership of an database object.)

SQL Server also supports the ALTER ASSEMBLY and DROP ASSEMBLY statements. You can use the ALTER ASSEMBLY statement to refresh the system catalog to the latest copy of .NET modules holding its implementation. This statement also adds or removes files associated with the corresponding assembly. Example 8.13 shows how the executable C# code can be stored as a procedure.

EXAMPLE 8.13

```
USE sample
GO
CREATE PROCEDURE GetEmployeeCount
AS EXTERNAL NAME GetEmployeeCount.StoredProcedures.
GetEmployeeCount
```

The CREATE PROCEDURE statement in Example 8.13 shows an extension to the AS clause as we used it in Examples 8.6 and 8.8. The EXTERNAL NAME option specifies that the code is generated using CLR. The name in this clause is a three-part name:

assembly_name.class_name.method_name

▶ **assembly_name** is the name of the assembly (see Example 8.12)

▶ **class_name** is the name of the public class defined in Example 8.10

▶ **method_name**, which is optional, is the name of the method, which is specified inside the class

Example 8.14 shows how an existing CLR stored procedure can be executed.

EXAMPLE 8.14

```
USE sample
DECLARE @ret INT
EXECUTE @ret=GetEmployeeCount
PRINT @ret
```

Example 8.14 shows the batch, which is used to execute the stored procedure. (The PRINT statement returns the value 7, because the **employee** table contains exactly seven rows.)

User-Defined Functions

In programming languages, there are generally two types of routines:

▶ Procedures

▶ Functions

Procedures are made up of several statements that have zero or more input parameters but do not return any output parameters. In contrast, functions generally return one or more parameters.

NOTE

As you will see below, SQL Server functions do not support output parameters but return a single data value.

Creation and Execution of User-Defined Functions

User-defined functions are created with the CREATE FUNCTION statement, which has the following syntax:

CREATE FUNCTION [*schema_name*.] *function_name*
　　[({ @param1 } type1 [= default1])] {[({ @param2 } type2 [= default2])]}...
　　RETURNS {scalar_type | [@variable] TABLE}
　　[WITH {ENCRYPTION | SCHEMABINDING}]
　　[AS] {block | RETURN (select_statement)}

schema_name is the name of the schema to which the ownership of the created user-defined function is assigned. **function_name** is the name of the user-defined function. **@param1, @param2,**... are input parameters, and **type1, type2,**... specify their data types, respectively. Parameters are values passed from the caller of the user-defined function and are used within the function. **default1, default2** specify the optional default value of the corresponding parameter. (Default can also be NULL.)

The RETURNS clause defines a data type of the value returned by the user-defined function. This data type can be any of the standard data types supported by SQL

Server, including the TABLE data type. (The only standard data types that you cannot use are the TIMESTAMP data type and **text/image** data.)

User-defined functions are either scalar-valued or table-valued. In the RETURNS clause of a scalar-valued function, you specify one of the standard data types. Functions are table-valued if the RETURNS clause contains the reserved word TABLE. Depending on how the body of the function is defined, table-valued functions can be classified as inline or multistatement functions. If the RETURNS clause specifies TABLE with no accompanying list of columns, the function is an inline function. Inline functions return the result set of a SELECT statement as a variable of the TABLE data type (see Example 8.17). A multistatement table-valued function includes a name followed by TABLE. The name defines an internal variable of the type TABLE. You can use this variable to insert rows into it and then return the variable as the return value of the function.

The WITH ENCRYPTION option encrypts the system table columns that contain the text of the CREATE FUNCTION statement. In that case, you cannot use the **sp_helptext** system procedure to view the text used to create the function. (Use this option to enhance the security of the SQL Server system.)

The alternative clause, WITH SCHEMABINDING, binds the user-defined function to the database objects that it references. Any attempt to modify the structure of the database object that the function references fails. (The binding of the function to the database object(s) it references is removed only when the function is altered so that the SCHEMABINDING option is not specified anymore.)

Database objects that are referenced by a function must fulfill certain conditions, if you want to use the SCHEMABINDING clause during the creation of that function. These are as follows:

▶ All views and user-defined functions referenced by the function must be schema-bound

▶ All objects (tables, views, or user-defined functions) must be in the same database as the function

block is the BEGIN-END block that contains the implementation of the function. The final statement of the block must be a RETURN statement with an argument. (The value of the argument is the value returned by the function.) In the body of a BEGIN-END block, only the following statements are allowed:

▶ Assignment statements such as SET

▶ Control-of-flow statements such as WHILE and IF

▶ DECLARE statements defining local data variables

▶ SELECT statements containing SELECT lists with expressions that assign to variables that are local to the function

▶ INSERT, UPDATE, and DELETE statements modifying variables of the TABLE data type that are local to the function

By default, only the members of the **sysadmin** fixed server role, and the **db_ owner** and **db_ddladmin** fixed database roles, can use the CREATE FUNCTION statement. However, the members of these roles may assign this privilege to other users using the GRANT CREATE FUNCTION statement (see Chapter 12).

Example 8.15 shows the creation of the function called **compute_costs**.

EXAMPLE 8.15

```
-- This function computes additional total costs that arise
-- if budgets of projects increase
USE sample
GO
CREATE FUNCTION compute_costs (@percent INT =10)
   RETURNS DECIMAL(16,2)
  BEGIN
   DECLARE @additional_costs DEC (14,2), @sum_budget dec(16,2)
   SELECT @sum_budget = SUM (budget) FROM project
   SET @additional_costs = @sum_budget * @percent/100
   RETURN @additional_costs
  END
```

The function **compute_costs** computes additional costs that arise when all budgets of projects increase. The only input variable, **@percent**, specifies the percentage of increase of budgets. In the BEGIN-END block, we first declare two local variables: **@sum_budget** and **@additional_costs**. The function assigns to the former the sum of all budgets, using the special form of the SELECT statement. After that, the function computes total additional costs and returns this value using the RETURN statement.

Each user-defined function can be invoked in Transact-SQL statements, such as SELECT, INSERT, UPDATE, or DELETE. To invoke a function, specify the name of it, followed by parentheses. Within the parentheses, you can specify one or more arguments. Arguments are values or expressions that are passed to the input parameters that are defined immediately after the function name. When you invoke a function, and all parameters have no default values, you must supply argument values for all of the parameters and you must specify the argument values in the same sequence in which the parameters are defined in the CREATE FUNCTION statement.

Example 8.16 shows the use of the function **compute_costs** (Example 8.15) in a SELECT statement.

EXAMPLE 8.16

```
USE sample
SELECT project_no, project_name
   FROM project
   WHERE budget < dbo.compute_costs(25)
```

The result is

project_no	project_name
p2	Gemini

The SELECT statement in Example 8.16 displays names and numbers of all projects where the budget is lower than the total additional costs of all projects for a given percentage.

 NOTE

*Each function used in a Transact-SQL statement must be specified using its two-part name — that is, **schema_name.function_name**.*

Example 8.17 shows a function that returns a variable of the type TABLE.

EXAMPLE 8.17

```
USE sample
GO
CREATE FUNCTION employees_in_project (@pr_number CHAR(4))
   RETURNS TABLE
AS RETURN (SELECT emp_fname, emp_lname
            FROM works_on, employee
            WHERE employee.emp_no = works_on.emp_no
         AND project_no = @pr_number)
```

The **employees_in_project** function is used to display names of all employees that belong to a particular project. The input parameter **@pr_number** specifies a project number. While the function generally returns many rows, the RETURNS clause contains the TABLE data type. (Note that the BEGIN-END block in Example 8.17 must be omitted, while the RETURN clause contains a SELECT statement.)

Example 8.18 shows the use of the function **employees_in_project**.

EXAMPLE 8.18

```
USE sample
SELECT *
    FROM employees_in_project('p3')
```

The result is

emp_fname	emp_lname
Ann	Jones
Elsa	Bertoni
Elke	Hansel

SQL Server also supports the Transact-SQL statement ALTER FUNCTION that modifies the structure of a user-defined function. The ALTER FUNCTION statement is usually used to remove the schema binding. All options of the ALTER FUNCTION statement correspond to the options with the same name in the CREATE FUNCTION statement.

A user-defined function is removed using the DROP FUNCTION statement. Only the owner of the function (or the members of the **db_owner** and **sysadmin** fixed database roles) can remove the function.

The system table **sysobjects** contains the information about existing user-defined functions. You can use the **sys.objects** catalog view and system procedure **sp_helptext** to display relevant information concerning stored procedures and user-defined functions. For the definition of the system table **sysobjects**, see Chapter 11.

User-Defined Functions and CLR

Everything we have already said about CLR in the stored procedure section is also valid for user-defined functions. The only difference is that you use the CREATE FUNCTION statement (instead of CREATE PROCEDURE) to store a user-defined function as database object. Also, user-defined functions are used in another context than procedures, because they always have a return value (see Example 8.22).

The following example shows the C# program, which we use to demonstrate how user-defined functions are compiled and deployed.

EXAMPLE 8.19

```
using System;
using System.Data.Sql;
```

```
using System.Data.SqlTypes;
public class budgetPercent
{ private const float percent = 10;
    public static SqlDouble computeBudget(float budget)
    { float budgetNew;
      budgetNew = budget * percent;
      return budgetNew;
    }
};
```

The C# source program in Example 8.19 shows a user-defined function, which calculates the new budget (of the project) using the old budget and the percentual increase. (We omit the description of the C# program, because this program is analog to the program in Example 8.10.) Example 8.20 shows the CREATE ASSEMBLY statement, which is necessary if you want to create an object in SQL Server. This example is analog to Example 8.12.

EXAMPLE 8.20

```
USE sample
GO
CREATE ASSEMBLY computeBudget
FROM 'C:\computeBudget.dll'
WITH PERMISSION_SET = SAFE
```

Example 8.21 creates the user-defined function called ReturncomputeBudget.

EXAMPLE 8.21

```
USE sample
GO
CREATE FUNCTION ReturncomputeBudget (@budget Real)
RETURNS FLOAT
AS EXTERNAL NAME computeBudget.budgetPercent.computeBudget
```

The CREATE FUNCTION statement in Example 8.21 stores the **computeBudget** assembly as a user-defined function, which can be used subsequently in data manipulation statements, such as SELECT, as shown in the following example.

EXAMPLE 8.22

```
USE sample
select dbo.ReturncomputeBudget (321.50)
```

Conclusion

A stored procedure is a special kind of batch, written in the Transact-SQL language. Stored procedures are used for the following purposes:

▶ To control access authorization

▶ To create an audit trail of activities in database tables

▶ To enforce consistency and business rules with respect to data modification

▶ To improve the performance of repetitive tasks

User-defined functions have a lot in common with stored procedures. The main difference is that user-defined functions do not support parameter but return a single data value, which can also be a table. SQL Server 2005 introduces a new feature, Common Language Runtime (CLR), which allows you to develop stored procedures and user-defined functions using C# and Visual Studio 2005.

In contrast to most other SQL dialects, Transact-SQL allows the use of SQL statements and procedural extensions inside a batch, rather than restricting their use to within a stored procedure. The next chapter discusses another database object: indices.

Exercises

E.8.1

Create a batch that inserts 3,000 rows in the **employee** table. The values of the **emp_no** column should be unique and between 1 and 3,000. All values of the columns **emp_lname**, **emp_fname**, and **dept_no** should be set to 'Jane', 'Smith', and 'd1', respectively.

E.8.2

Modify the batch E.8.1 so that the values of the **emp_no** column should be generated randomly using the RAND function. (Hint: Also use the datetime system functions DATEPART and GETDATE to generate the random values.)

Indices and Query Optimization

IN THIS CHAPTER

his chapter describes indices and their role in optimizing response time of queries. All Transact-SQL statements pertaining to indices are listed and explained. Additionally, general recommendations are given in cases where indices are appropriate. In the second part of the chapter, examples and comparisons of query optimizations show the performance benefits that can be achieved if the appropriate form of the SELECT statement is used. The final discussion highlights the role of SQL Server's query optimizer.

Indices

SQL Server uses indices to provide fast access to data. An index is in many ways analogous to a book index. When you are looking for a topic in a book, you use its index to find the page(s) where this topic is described. Similarly, when you search for a row of a table, SQL Server uses an index to find its physical location.

However, there are two main differences between a book index and a SQL Server index. First, you (as a book reader) can decide whether or not to use the book index. This possibility generally does not exist if you use SQL Server: The database system itself decides whether to use an existing index or not. Second, a particular book index is edited together with the book and does not change at all. This means that you can find a topic exactly on the page where it is determined in the index. In contrast to it, a SQL Server index changes each time when the corresponding data is changed. (Targeted retrieval of data using an index is called *index access*.)

In contrast to index access, SQL Server (and all other database systems) supports table scan. *Table scan* means that each row is retrieved and examined in sequence (from first to last) and returned in the result set if the search condition in the WHERE clause evaluates to true. Therefore, all rows are fetched according to their physical memory location.

Indices in SQL Server are constructed using the b-tree data structure. As its name suggests, a b-tree has a treelike structure in which all of the bottommost nodes (leaf nodes) are the same number of levels away from the top (root) of the tree. This property is maintained even when new data is added or deleted from the indexed column.

Figure 9-1 illustrates the structure of the b-tree and the direct access to the row of the **employee** table with the value 25348 in its **emp_no** column. (It is assumed that the **employee** table has an index on the **emp_no** column.) You can also see that each b-tree consists of a root node, leaf nodes, and zero or more intermediate nodes.

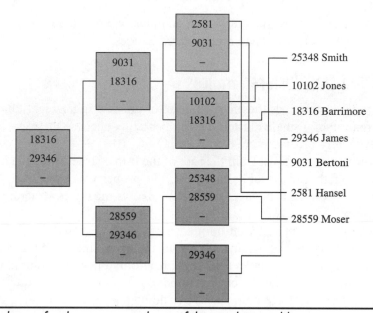

Figure 9-1   *b-tree for the emp_no column of the employee table*

Searching for the data value 25348 can be executed as follows: Starting from the root of the b-tree, a search proceeds for a value greater than or equal to the value to be retrieved. Therefore, the value 29346 is retrieved from the root node; then the value 28559 is fetched from the intermediate level, and the searched value, 25348, is retrieved at the leaf level. With the help of the respective pointers, the appropriate row is retrieved. (An alternative, but equivalent, search method would be to search for smaller or equal values.)

Index access is the preferred and obviously advantageous method for accessing tables with many rows. With index access, SQL Server generally takes only a few I/O operations to find any row of a table in a very short time, whereas sequential access requires much more time to find a row physically stored at the end of the table.

The system table that stores information about indices is **sysindexes**. **sysindexes** contains, among other things, a row for each index of the current database. (You use the **sys.indexes** catalog view to access information concerning indices.) There is also a system procedure, **sp_helpindex**, which lists indices of a table. (The **sysindexes** system table, the **sys.indexes** catalog view, and the **sp_helpindex** system stored procedure will be described in detail later in this chapter.)

Before we start to discuss the creation of an index, we will describe the two existing index types: clustered and nonclustered indices.

Clustered and Nonclustered Indices

A clustered index determines the physical order of the data in a table. SQL Server allows the creation of a single clustered index per table, because the rows of the table cannot be physically ordered more than one way.

SQL Server navigates down from the root of the b-tree structure to the leaf nodes that are linked together in a doubly linked list. The property of a clustered index is that its leaf nodes contain data pages. Figure 9-2 shows the b-tree structure of a clustered index.

A clustered index is implicitly built for each table, where you define the primary key using the primary key constraint. Also, each clustered index in SQL Server is per default unique—that is, each data value can appear only once in a column for which the clustered index is defined. If a clustered index is built on a nonunique column, the database system will force uniqueness by adding a 4-byte identifier to the rows that have duplicate values.

A nonclustered index has the same index structure as clustered index, with two important differences:

▶ Nonclustered indices do not change the physical order of the rows in the table.

▶ The leaf level of a nonclustered index consists of an index key plus a bookmark.

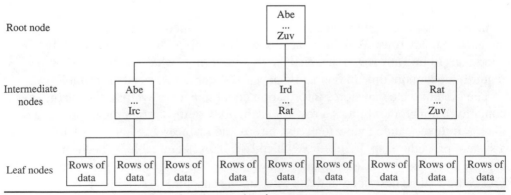

Figure 9-2 *Physical structure of a clustered index*

The physical order of rows in a table will not be changed if one or more nonclustered indices are defined for that table. For each (nonclustered) index, SQL Server creates an additional index structure that is stored in index pages.

A bookmark of a nonclustered index shows where to find the row corresponding to the index key. A bookmark part of the index key can have two forms, depending on the form of the table—that is, the table can be a clustered table or a heap. (A heap is a table without a clustered index, while each clustered table is so called because it contains a clustered index.) If a clustered index exists, the bookmark of the nonclustered index shows the b-tree structure of the table's clustered index. If the table has no clustered index, the bookmark is identical to the row identifier (RID). RID contains two parts: the address of the physical block, where the corresponding row is stored, and the position of the row inside the block.

As you can see from the discussion above, searching for data using a nonclustered index could be twofold. If you have a heap—that is, a table without clustered index— the traversing of the (nonclustered) index structure will be followed by the retrieval of the row using the row identifier. On the other hand, if you have a clustered table, the traversing operation of the index structure will be followed by the traversal of the corresponding clustered index. In both cases, the number of I/O operations is quite high, so you should design a nonclustered index with care and only when you are sure that there will be significant performance gains using it.

Figure 9-3 shows the b-tree structure of a nonclustered index.

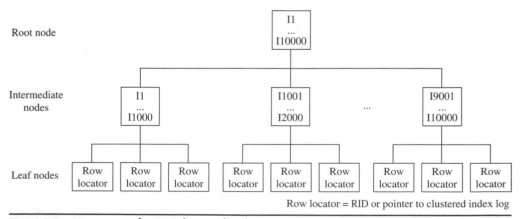

Figure 9-3   *Structure of a nonclustered index*

Indices and the Corresponding Transact-SQL Statements

The Transact-SQL language supports three DDL statements concerning indices:
CREATE INDEX, ALTER INDEX, and DROP INDEX. The CREATE INDEX
statement creates an index for the particular table. The general form of this statement is

```
CREATE [UNIQUE] [CLUSTERED |NONCLUSTERED] INDEX index_name
      ON {table_name| view_name}(column1 [ASC | DESC]
[{,column2[ASC|DESC]} ...])
[ INCLUDE (column_name1 [ ,...n ] ) ]
      [WITH
      [FILLFACTOR=n]
      [[,] IGNORE_DUP_KEY]
       [[,] PAD_INDEX]
      [[,] DROP_EXISTING]
      [[,] ONLINE = {ON | OFF}]
      [[,] ALLOW_ROW_LOCKS = {ON | OFF}]
      [[,]ALLOW_PAGE_LOCKS = {ON | OFF}]
      [[,] STATISTICS_NORECOMPUTE]]
      [ON file_group]
```

NOTE

*SQL Server 2005 also supports partitioned indices. A partitioned index is used with partitioned
tables and will be described in detail in Chapter 23.*

index_name specifies the name of the created index. An index can be established
for one or more columns of a single table called **table_name**. **column1, column2**,...
are names of the columns for which the index is created. As you can see from the
syntax of the CREATE INDEX statement, SQL Server supports indices on views.
(Indexed views are described in detail in the next chapter.)

NOTE

*Each column of a table or view, except those with text/images, can be indexed. That is, the
columns with data types BIGINT and SQL_VARIANT as well as XML columns can be indexed, too.*

An index can be either single or composite. In contrast to a single index, which has
one column, a composite index is built on more than one column. Each composite index
has certain restrictions concerning its length and the number of pertinent columns. The
maximum size of an index is 900 bytes, while the index can contain up to 16 columns.

The UNIQUE option specifies that each data value can appear only once in an indexed column(s). For a unique composite index, the combination of data values of all columns in each row must be unique. If UNIQUE is not specified, duplicate values are allowed.

The CLUSTERED option specifies a clustered index. The NONCLUSTERED option (the default) specifies that the index does not change the physical order of the rows in the table. SQL Server allows a maximum of 249 nonclustered indices per table.

The INCLUDE option allows you to specify the nonkey column(s) to be added to the existing columns of the nonclustered index. Significant performance gains can be achieved because the query optimizer can locate all of the required data values within the index and does not have to visit data pages. (This is called "covered index" of "index-only access.")

FILLFACTOR = n defines the storage percentage for each index page at the time the index is created. You can set the value of the FILLFACTOR from 1 to 100. If the value of **n** is set to 100, each index page will be 100 percent filled—that is, the existing index pages will have no space for the insertion of new rows. Therefore, this value is recommended only for static tables. (The default value 0 also indicates that the leaf index pages are filled and the intermediate nonleaf pages contain one free entry each.) Setting FILLFACTOR to a value between 1 and 99 causes a creation of the new index structure with leaf pages that are not completely full. The bigger the value of the FILLFACTOR option, the smaller the space that is left free on an index page. For instance, setting FILLFACTOR to 60 means that 40 percent of each leaf index page is left free for future UPDATE and INSERT statements. (The value 60 could be a reasonable value for tables with rather frequent data modification.) For all values of the FILLFACTOR option between 1 and 99, the intermediate nonleaf pages contain one free entry each.

NOTE

The FILLFACTOR value is not maintained — that is, it specifies only how much storage space is reserved with the existing data at the time the storage percentage is defined. If you want to reestablish the original value of the FILLFACTOR option, you need to use the DBCC DBREINDEX statement. (This statement is described at the end of this chapter.)

The PAD_INDEX option is tightly connected to the FILLFACTOR option. The FILLFACTOR option mainly specifies the percentage of space that is left free on leaf index pages. Despite it, the PAD_INDEX option specifies the place to leave open on each intermediate index page of the b-tree.

Besides the DBCC DBREINDEX statement, you can use the system procedure **sp_configure** to change the value of the FILLFACTOR option. The system procedure

sp_configure displays or changes several server configuration options. One of these options is FILLFACTOR.

> ### NOTE
>
> *The FILLFACTOR option of the system procedure **sp_configure** is an advanced option. If you use the **sp_configure** system stored procedure to change the value of index page fullness, you can change this option only when **show advanced options** is set to 1.*

The IGNORE_DUP_KEY option causes the system to ignore the attempt to insert duplicate values in the indexed column(s). This option should be used only to avoid the termination of a long transaction in cases when the INSERT statement inserts duplicate data in the indexed column(s). If this option is enabled and an INSERT statement attempts to insert rows that would violate the uniqueness of the index, SQL Server returns a warning rather than causing the entire statement to fail. SQL Server does *not* insert the rows that would add duplicate key values; it merely ignores those rows and adds the rest.

The DROP_EXISTING option allows you to enhance performance when re-creating a clustered index on a table that also has nonclustered indices. It specifies that the existing clustered or nonclustered index should be dropped and the specified index rebuilt. As you already know, each nonclustered index in a clustered table contains in its leaf nodes the corresponding values of the table's clustered index. For this reason, all nonclustered indices must be rebuilt when a table's clustered index is dropped. Using the DROP_EXISTING option, you can prevent the nonclustered indices to be rebuilt twice.

If you activate the ONLINE option, you can create, rebuild, or drop an index online. This option allows concurrent modifications to the underlying table or clustered index data and any associated indices during index execution. For example, while a clustered index is being rebuilt, you can continue to make updates to the underlying data and perform queries against the data. In earlier versions of SQL Server, index operations such as rebuilding index held exclusive locks on the underlying data and associated indices preventing modifications of queries until the index operation was complete.

The STATISTICS_NORECOMPUTE option specifies that statistics of the specified index should not be automatically recomputed. The ON **file_group** option creates the specified index on the given file group.

The ALLOW_ROW_LOCKS option specifies that the system uses row locks when this option is enabled. Similarly, the ALLOW_PAGE_LOCKS option specifies that the system uses page locks, when this option is set to ON. (For the description of page and row locks, see Chapter 14.)

SQL Server has been enhanced to support indices with descending order on column values. The ASC option after the column name specifies that the index is created on the ascending order of the column's values, while DESC specifies the descending order. This gives you more flexibility for using an index. (An index defined on ascending order of column values is generally useless if you search values in reverse order.)

NOTE

Before you start to execute the examples in this chapter, please re-create the entire sample database.

Example 9.1 shows the creation of a nonclustered index.

EXAMPLE 9.1

Create an index for the column **emp_no** of the table **employee**.

```
USE sample
CREATE INDEX i_empno    ON employee (emp_no)
```

Example 9.2 shows the creation of a unique index.

EXAMPLE 9.2

Create a composite index **i_empno_prno** for the columns **emp_no** and **project_no** on the **works_on** table. The compound values in both columns must be unique. Eighty percent of each index leaf page should be filled.

```
USE sample
CREATE UNIQUE INDEX i_empno_prno
ON works_on (emp_no, project_no)
WITH FILLFACTOR= 80
```

The creation of a unique index for a column is not possible if the column already contains duplicate values. The creation of such an index is possible if each existing data value (including the NULL value) occurs only once. Also, any attempt to insert or modify an existing data value into a column with an existing unique index will be rejected by the system.

Example 9.3 demonstrates how duplicate data can be located and deleted within a column to allow the creation of a unique index for the column.

EXAMPLE 9.3

For each employee, delete the rows of the **works_on** table that do not contain the most recent entry date for a project.

```
SELECT emp_no, MAX(enter_date) max_date
    INTO #works_on
    FROM works_on
    GROUP BY emp_no
    HAVING COUNT(*) > 1
DELETE works_on
    FROM works_on, #works_on
    WHERE works_on.emp_no = #works_on.emp_no
    AND works_on.enter_date < #works_on.max_date
```

The temporary **#works_on** table, created in Example 9.3, contains the rows of the **works_on** table that fulfill the two conditions: duplicate values of the **emp_no** column and its latest date.

The DELETE statement first retrieves all rows from the temporary table with the duplicate values in the **emp_no** column. The WHERE clause restricts the retrieval to only those rows that do not contain the latest date in the **enter_date** column. Hence, the DELETE statement deletes all rows from the **works_on** table that do not fulfill these two conditions.

After the execution of the Transact-SQL statements in Example 9.3, the **works_on** table contains the following rows:

emp_no	project_no	Job	enter_date
10102	p3	Manager	1999-01-01 00:00:00.000
25348	p2	Clerk	1998-02-15 00:00:00.000
18316	p2	NULL	1998-06-01 00:00:00.000
29346	p2	NULL	1997-12-15 00:00:00.000
2581	p3	Analyst	1998-10-15 00:00:00.000
9031	p1	NULL	1998-04-15 00:00:00.000
28559	p2	Clerk	1999-02-01 00:00:00.000
22334	p2	NULL	1998-01-15 00:00:00.000

As illustrated in the table, each data value in the **emp_no** column occurs only once. Therefore, it is now possible to create a unique index for the **works_on** table.

SQL Server is one of a few database systems that support the ALTER INDEX statement. Using this statement you can modify an existing index by disabling, rebuilding, or reorganizing the index or by setting options on the index. The syntax of the ALTER INDEX statement is very similar to the syntax of the CREATE INDEX statement. In other words, this statement supports all options that are part of the CREATE INDEX statement.

In addition to these, the ALTER INDEX statement supports three new options:

- ▶ REBUILD
- ▶ REORGANIZE
- ▶ DISABLE

With the REBUILD option you can rebuild an index for a table or all indices defined for a table. By allowing an index to be rebuilt dynamically, you don't have to drop and re-create it. (This option replaces the DBCC DBREINDEX statement, which is a deprecated feature in SQL Server 2005.)

The REORGANIZE option specifies that the leaf level of the corresponding index tree will be reorganized so that the physical order of the pages matches the left-to-right logical order of the leaf nodes, thus improving performance.

The DISABLE option disables an existing index. Each disabled index is unavailable for use until you enable it again. To enable an index, use the REBUILD option of the ALTER TABLE statement.

The DROP INDEX statement removes one or more existing indices from the current database. There are two different syntax forms to drop an index. Example 9.4 shows both possibilities of how the **i_empno** index can be dropped.

EXAMPLE 9.4

Remove the index created in Example 9.1.

```
USE sample
DROP INDEX employee.i_empno
-- The next statement is equivalent to the previous one
DROP INDEX i_empno ON employee
```

The first form of the DROP INDEX statement requires the specification of the qualified index name—that is, the index name must be written in the following form: tablename.indexname. This form is one of the features that will not be supported in a future version of SQL Server. Hence, we recommend that you use the second form of the DROP INDEX statement.

NOTE

The DROP INDEX statement cannot be used to remove indices that are implicitly generated by SQL Server for integrity constraints, such as PRIMARY KEY or UNIQUE. To remove such indices, you must drop the constraint.

Editing Index Information

To edit information about an existing index, you can use the following features of SQL Server:

▶ The **sys.indexes** catalog view

▶ System procedure **sp_helpindex**

▶ SQL Server Management Studio

The **sys.indexes** catalog view contains a row for each index and a row for each table without a clustered index. (It also contains a row for each table including **text/image** data.)

System stored procedure **sp_helpindex** displays all indices on a table as well as columns statistics. The syntax of this procedure is

sp_helpindex [@db_object =] 'name'
where **db_object** is the name of a table or a view.

To edit information about an existing index using SQL Server Management Studio, choose the database in the **Databases** folder and select **Tables**. Expand the table in which the index belongs, and expand the **Indexes** folder. The list of all existing indices for that table is shown. After you double-click one of the indices, the system shows you the **Index Properties** dialog box with all properties of that index.

To create a new index using SQL Server Management, right-click the **Indexes** folder and select **New Index**. In the **New Index** dialog box, choose the name of the new index and the type (clustered or nonclustered). In the Index key columns window, add one or more columns that will be indexed.

Indices and Keys

Just as indices are part of the Transact-SQL language, so are keys (as integrity constraints). Before considering the relationship between indices and keys, several key types must be explained. The following keys exist in the relational data model:

► Candidate key

► Primary key

► Foreign key

The primary key of a table is a column or group of columns whose values are different in every row. Sometimes more than one column or group of columns of the table have unique values. In that case, all columns or groups of columns that qualify to be primary keys are called candidate keys. A foreign key is a column or group of columns in one table that contain values that match the primary key values in the same or another table.

A unique index for each primary key and each candidate key of a table should exist. Also, each column representing a primary or a candidate key should contain the NOT NULL constraint. This requirement has its origins in the relational model: each primary or candidate key is viewed as a mathematical function that defines each element uniquely.

NOTE

You do not have to create a unique index for each primary key because SQL Server automatically generates an index for each primary key to enforce the uniqueness.

For each foreign key, the creation of a nonunique index is recommended. The creation of an index for a foreign key significantly reduces the execution time needed for the corresponding join operation. (The specification of UNIQUE in this case would be wrong, because a foreign key allows duplicate data values.)

Example 9.5 creates a nonunique index for each foreign key in the sample database.

EXAMPLE 9.5

```
CREATE INDEX i_emp_deptno ON employee(dept_no)
CREATE INDEX i_works_empno ON works_on(emp_no)
CREATE INDEX i_works_prno ON works_on(project_no)
```

Guidelines for Creating Indices

Although SQL Server does not have any practical limitations concerning the number of indices, it is advisable to limit them for a couple of reasons. First, each index uses a certain amount of disk space, so it is possible for the number of index pages to exceed the number of data pages within a database. Second, in contrast to the benefits of using an index for retrievals, inserting rows into a table with the indexed column causes a loss of performance because the index tree must be modified. (The same is true for deleting rows.)

The following sections give general recommendations for creating an index.

WHERE Clause

If the WHERE clause in a SELECT statement contains a search condition with a single column, an index on this column should be created. The use of an index is especially recommended if the selectivity of the condition is high (i.e., the ratio is small). (The *selectivity* of a condition is defined as the ratio of the number of rows satisfying the condition to the total number of rows in the table.) The most successful processing of a retrieval with the indexed column will be achieved if the selectivity of a condition is 5 percent or less.

The column should not be indexed if the selectivity of the condition is constantly 80 percent or more. In such a case, additional I/O operations will be needed for the existing index pages, which would eliminate any time savings gained by direct access. In this particular case, a table scan would be faster (and SQL Server query optimizer will usually choose to use a table scan, rendering the index useless).

AND Operator

If a search condition in an often-used WHERE clause contains one or more AND operators, it is best to create a composite index that includes all the columns of the table specified in the FROM clause of the SELECT statement. Example 9.6 shows the creation of a composite index that includes all the columns specified in the WHERE clause of the SELECT statement.

EXAMPLE 9.6

```
USE sample
CREATE INDEX i_works ON works_on(emp_no, enter_date)
SELECT *
```

```
FROM works_on
WHERE emp_no = 29346 AND enter_date='1.4.1997'
```

The AND operator in the SELECT statement in Example 9.6 contains two conditions. As such, both of the columns appearing in each condition should be indexed using a composite index.

Join Operator

In the case of a join operation, it is recommended that each join column be indexed. Join columns often represent the primary key of one table and the corresponding foreign key of the other or the same table. Both columns should be indexed according to the discussion in the previous sections.

The following example shows which indices should be used, if you have a query with a join operation and an additional filter.

EXAMPLE 9.7

```
USE sample
SELECT emp_lname, emp_fname
    FROM employee, works_on
    WHERE employee.emp_no = works_on.emp_no
    AND enter_date = '10.15.1998'
```

For Example 9.7, the creation of two separate indices for the **emp_no** column in both the **employee** and **works_on** tables is recommended. Also, an additional index should be created for the **enter_date** column.

These recommendations are general rules of thumb. They ultimately depend on how your database will be used in production and which columns are used most frequently. An index on a column that is never used will be counterproductive.

NOTE

A great new feature included in SQL Server is Database Tuning Advisor. This advisor will analyze a sample of your actual workload (supplied via either a script file from you or a captured trace file from SQL Profiler) and recommend indices for you to add or delete based on that workload. Use of Database Tuning Advisor is highly recommended. (Database Tuning Advisor replaces the well-known Index Tuning Wizard.) For more information on Database Tuning Advisor, see Chapter 22.

General Criteria to Improve Efficiency

Earlier sections have illustrated the efficiency of a database application and the possible improvements that can be made in response time using indices. This part of the chapter demonstrates how programming style can influence the efficiency of your database applications.

A component of SQL Server called the query optimizer provides solutions to the problem of how each query should be executed (for example, what indices should be used, in what order tables should be accessed, how joins should be implemented). These solutions are called query execution plans, and the main task of the optimizer is to select the optimal plan. (The SQL Server query optimizer is described in detail later in this chapter.) Sometimes the information available to the optimizer is not sufficient for it to determine the optimal plan. Therefore, it is very important to know how programmers can improve the efficiency of their applications. The following sections discuss some of these issues.

Join vs. Correlated Subquery

Each query can usually be expressed with one of the many different, but equivalent, SELECT statements. For example, each join operation can be expressed using the equivalent correlated subquery and vice versa. These methods differ in that a join operation is considerably more efficient than the corresponding correlated subquery. Example 9.8 shows the difference.

EXAMPLE 9.8

Get last names of all employees working on project p3.

Solution A:

```
USE sample
SELECT emp_lname
    FROM employee, works_on
    WHERE employee.emp_no = works_on.emp_no
    AND project_no = 'p3'
```

Solution B:

```
USE sample
SELECT emp_lname
    FROM employee
WHERE 'p3' IN (SELECT project_no
        FROM works_on
        WHERE employee.emp_no=works_on.emp_no)
```

The performance of solution A is better than the performance of solution B. The inner query in solution B of Example 9.8 must be evaluated several times because it contains the **emp_no** column, which belongs to the **employee** table in the outer query. Thus, the value of the **emp_no** column changes each time SQL Server examines a different row of the **employee** table in the outer query. The join in solution A works faster because it evaluates all values of the **project_no** column of the **works_on** table only once.

Incomplete Statements

In practice, it is possible for a programmer to specify an incomplete SQL statement. Such a statement is not only erroneous but strongly influences the efficiency of the whole application. A typical example is the Cartesian product of two tables.

The Cartesian product is described in detail in Chapter 6. The result of a Cartesian product contains each combination of rows of two tables. For example, if one table contains 10,000 and the other 100 rows, the result of the Cartesian product of both tables will be a table with 1 million rows.

The use of a Cartesian product in practice is highly unusual. Sometimes users accidentally generate the Cartesian product of two tables when they forget to include the join condition in the WHERE clause of the SELECT statement. In this case, users have an incomplete SELECT statement where the join condition is omitted. In general, if your query is accessing **n** different tables, you should have at least **n-1** join conditions relating all of the tables to avoid a Cartesian product.

NOTE

SQL Server supports the ROWCOUNT option in the SET statement, which restricts the display of selected rows to a certain amount. As such, the use of this option limits the number of rows that can be created by an unintentional Cartesian product. (ROWCOUNT is described in detail in the next section of this chapter.)

LIKE Operator

LIKE compares the values of a column with a specified pattern. If this column is associated with an index, the search for the character string is performed with the existing index. A condition based on a wildcard in the initial position forces SQL Server to examine each value in the column—that is, the existing index is of no use. The reason is that indices work by quickly determining whether the requested value is greater than or less than the values at various nodes of the b-tree. If the initial character(s) of the desired values are not specified, then these comparisons cannot be done.

EXAMPLE 9.9

Get employee numbers of all employees whose last names end with *es*.

```
USE sample
SELECT emp_no
    FROM employee
    WHERE emp_lname LIKE '%es'
```

For SQL Server query optimizer, it is not possible to apply index access in Example 9.9, even if the index for the **emp_lname** column exists. The reason is that the characters at the beginning of the data values are not known within the search condition in the WHERE clause.

Transact-SQL Statements for Query Optimization

SQL Server supports two statements that enable the optimization of queries:

▶ UPDATE STATISTICS

▶ SET

The statistics in the system tables are not constantly updated. (For the description of statistics that are used by the query optimizer, see "Optimizer Statistics" in the next section.) The UPDATE STATISTICS statement updates statistical information for the specified indices. The modification of information using the UPDATE STATISTICS statement should be processed by the user in the following cases:

▶ After the initial load of data

▶ After the execution of a DML statement (INSERT, UPDATE, or DELETE) that affects a large number of rows

On the other hand, the UPDATE STATISTICS statement is automatically run when you create or re-create an index on a table that already contains data. Also, the UPDATE STATISTICS statement is executed by SQL Server periodically as the data in the tables change. The frequency at which the statistical information is updated is determined by the volume of data in the index and the amount of changing data.

The second statement, SET, has several options. Some of these options are related to statistics, some of them are used for query execution, and some are used for other purposes. The first five options are used for query execution, while the last two are related to statistics:

- ► SHOWPLAN_TEXT
- ► SHOWPLAN_ALL
- ► SHOWPLAN_XML
- ► FORCEPLAN
- ► NOEXEC
- ► ROWCOUNT
- ► STATISTICS IO
- ► STATISTICS TIME
- ► STATISTICS XML

Generally, ON activates an option, whereas OFF turns it off.

Users running a query can display the textual execution plan for that query by activating either SHOWPLAN_TEXT or SHOWPLAN_ALL before they enter the corresponding SELECT statement. The SHOWPLAN_ALL option displays the same detailed information about the selected execution plan for the query as SHOWPLAN_TEXT with the addition of an estimate of the resource requirements for that statement. (Either one of these two options causes the SQL Server system not to execute the query.)

Example 9.10 shows the use of the SHOWPLAN_TEXT option. Please note that once you activate the SHOWPLAN_TEXT option, all consecutive Transact-SQL statements will not be executed, until you deactivate this option with SET SHOWPLAN_TEXT OFF. (The same is true for the SHOWPLAN_ALL option.)

EXAMPLE 9.10

```
USE sample
GO
SET SHOWPLAN_TEXT ON
GO
SELECT employee.dept_no
   FROM employee, works_on
   WHERE employee.emp_no = works_on.emp_no
   AND works_on.project_no = 'p1'
```

The result is

```
|--Nested Loops(Inner Join, OUTER REFERENCES:([sample].[dbo].[employee].[emp_no]))
    |--Table Scan(OBJECT:([sample].[dbo].[employee]))
            |--Index Seek(OBJECT:([sample].[dbo].[works_on].[i_empno_prno]),
SEEK:([sample].[dbo].[works_on].[emp_no]=[sample].[dbo].[employee].[emp_no] AND
[sample].[dbo].[works_on].[project_no]='p1') ORDERED FORWARD)
Scan(OBJECT:([sample1].[dbo].[works_on]),
```

The result of Example 9.10 shows the selected execution plan for the specified SELECT statement. (The textual output of a query plan will be read bottom-up.) The join column in the **works_on** table is indexed, so the query optimizer chooses the index seek as the access method to seek for the given filter (project_no = 'p1') table. After that, the table employee will be searched row by row. Finally, the query optimizer chooses in this case the nested-loop method to execute the join operation. (The nested-loop join method will be explained in detail later in this chapter.)

If you activate the SHOWPLAN_XML option of the SET statement, SQL Server returns detailed information about how the statements are going to be executed in the form of a well-formed XML document without executing them. That way, you can make the optimizer's execution plans portable.

The SHOWPLAN_XML option returns information as a set of XML documents. Each statement after activation of this option is reflected in the output by a single document. Each document contains the text of the statement, followed by the details of the execution steps. (For more information concerning XML, see Chapters 29 and 30.)

The NOEXEC option compiles all the statements but does not execute them. The NOEXEC option is set on until the statement SET NOEXEC OFF is executed. The option FORCEPLAN makes it possible for you to directly influence a query optimization. Using this option causes SQL Server to access the tables in the same order as they are listed in the FROM clause of the SELECT statement.

The option ROWCOUNT causes the system to stop processing a DML statement after the specified number of rows is returned. The activation of such an option can be very useful if the result of a query returns too many rows. The option ROWCOUNT is turned off with the statement SET ROWCOUNT 0. (This option is one of the deprecated features in SQL Server 2005. You can now use the TOP operator to limit the number of affected rows in UPDATE, DELETE, and INSERT statements. This allows the developer to avoid using SET ROWCOUNT for these statements, which forces a recompilation of a stored procedure.) The option STATISTICS IO causes the system to display statistical information concerning the amount of disk activity generated by the query—for example, the number of read and write I/O operations processed with the query. The option STATISTICS TIME causes the system to display the processing, optimization, and execution time of the query.

The STATISTICS XML is a new option in SQL Server 2005. The activation of this clause causes SQL Server to generate detailed statistics for the statements that have to be executed in a well-formed XML document. (For more on XML documents, see Chapters 29 and 30.)

Query Optimizer

A query can usually be performed in several different, but equivalent, ways. The query optimizer generates several query execution plans or specific steps to perform a query. After that, it assigns a cost to each plan and selects the plan with the lowest cost. (This is also called *systematic query optimization*.)

Besides using cost estimates to select the best solution, the query optimizer of SQL Server (and all other DBMSs) uses heuristic rules to improve the performance of the execution of a query. The existence of heuristic rules is based upon the fact that every query can be generated using several solutions. The main heuristic rule is to apply unary operations (selection and projection) *before* binary operations (mainly the join operation).

Optimizer Statistics

The existence of indices on columns in a query affects the choice of a particular execution plan and, therefore, the performance of the query. This is especially true for indices on filter columns—that is, columns that appear in conditions of the WHERE clause (see Example 9.11). The decision of whether an existing index will be used by the optimizer depends on its selectivity and its index type. If the selectivity of an index is high—that is, only a few rows are identified by the index key value—the index is usually used. The question is: How does the SQL Server optimizer determine the selectivity of an index?

The optimizer uses special statistics kept for an index to determine the selectivity. These statistics are called distribution statistics, and they describe the selectivity and distribution of the key values in an index. The following statistics kept for a table and its indices (among others) are used by the optimizer:

- ▶ Number of rows in the table
- ▶ Number of pages used to store the data
- ▶ Number of distribution steps
- ▶ Number of rows sampled for statistics

Example 9.11 shows how decisions of the SQL Server optimizer are influenced by the different selectivity of columns in the WHERE clause.

EXAMPLE 9.11

```
USE sample
select * from works_on
      where enter_date = '01/01/1998'
      and job = 'Analyst'
```

Assuming that the **works_on** table has an index on each of the columns **enter_date** and **job**, which index should be first used? For instance, say both indices have the following statistics:

```
Number of rows: 100,000
Estimated row count(for works_on.enter_date) = 100
Estimated row count(for works_on.job) = 40,000
```

Using these statistics, the optimizer estimates that the selectivity of the **enter_date** column is 0.1 percent (100/100,000) and the selectivity of the **job** column is 40 percent. From this calculation, the optimizer would usually choose the execution plan based on the index for the **enter_date** column, because the selectivity of that column is significantly higher than that of the **job** column.

NOTE

The example shown above simplifies the work of the optimizer. Generally, there are several other statistics that the optimizer takes into account when it chooses the appropriate execution plan.

The statistics that the optimizer needs to find the optimal execution plan are stored in the **statblob** column of the **sysindexes** system table. This column has the IMAGE data type; therefore, the information is stored as a bit string. To interpret the information, you have to use the DBCC SHOW_STATISTICS statement, which has the following syntax:

```
dbcc show_statistics (table_name, index_name)
```

table_name and **index_name** are the names of the table and corresponding index—that is, for which you want to display the statistics information.

Implementing the Join Operation

The join operation is the most time-consuming operation in query processing. For this reason, SQL Server supports three different processing techniques for join:

▶ Nested-loop join

▶ Merge join

▶ Hash join

Nested-Loop Join

The nested-loop join is the processing technique that works by "brute force." In other words, for each row of the outer table, each row from the inner table is retrieved and compared.

The pseudocode in Algorithm 9.1 demonstrates the nested-loop processing technique for two tables.

ALGORITHM 9.1

(A and B are two temporary tables.)

```
for each row in the outer table do:
    read the row into A
    for each row in the inner table do:
      read the row into B
        if A.join_column = B.join_column then
            accept the row and add it to the resulting set
        end if
    end for
end for
```

The nested-loop join is very slow if there is no index for one of the join columns. Without indices, SQL Server would have to scan the outer table once and the inner table **n** times, where **n** is the number of rows of the outer table. Therefore, the query optimizer chooses this method only if the join column of the *inner* table is indexed, so the inner table does not have to be scanned for each row in the outer table.

Merge Join

The merge join provides a cost-effective alternative to constructing an index for a nested-loop join. The rows of the joined tables must be physically sorted using the values of the join column. Both tables are then scanned in order of the join columns, matching the rows with the same value for the join columns.

No index is required when the query optimizer performs a merge join.

The pseudocode in Algorithm 9.2 demonstrates the merge join processing technique for two tables.

ALGORITHM 9.2

a. Sort the outer table in ascending order using the join column

b. Sort the inner table in ascending order using the join column

> for each row in the outer table do:
>   read the row into A
>   for each row from the inner table with a value less than or equal to the join
> column do:
>   read the row into B
>   if A.join_column = B.join_column then
>   accept the row and add it to the resulting set
>   end if
>   end for
> end for

The merge join processing technique has a high overhead if the rows from both tables are unsorted. However, this method is sometimes used when the values of at least one of the join columns are sorted.

Hash Join

A hash join is used when there is no ordered input. The rows of both tables are hashed to the same hash file, using the same hashing function on the join columns as hash keys. The hash join method requires no index. Therefore, this method is highly applicable for ad hoc queries (where indices cannot be expected).

Optimizer Hints

Optimizer hints are optional parts in a SELECT statement that instruct the SQL Server query optimizer to execute one specific behavior. In other words, using optimizer hints, you do not allow the query optimizer to search and find the way to execute a query because you tell it exactly what to do. For this reason, optimizer hints should be used when you think that the SQL Server optimizer does not choose the best execution plan to perform a query. Before using them, you have to understand some general issues as to how the optimizer makes its decisions.

The optimizer uses the following general guidelines to create an optimal execution plan for a query:

▶ An existing nonclustered index is not used when the large portion of a table is read. For instance, if the following query for the **works_on** table is executed:

```
select * from works_on
          where job = 'Analyst'
```

and the nonclustered index for the **job** column exists, the SQL Server optimizer will choose the table scan instead of index access, assuming that 40 percent of all employees have such a job. In that case, it is more efficient to read the data pages sequentially than to first traverse the b-tree structure and then read each row from data pages one after the other.

▶ A restrictive condition in the WHERE clause of a SELECT statement that filters rows will be performed first (or very early) in the execution plan of the optimizer. For instance, if the following query is executed:

```
select job
   from employee, works_on
   where employee.emp_no = works_on.emp_no
   and emp_fname = 'John'
```

the optimizer will first filter all details of employees that have the specified first name and then perform the join condition, because filtering rows in the **employee** table will reduce the number of input rows for the join operation, and this can then be executed more effectively.

▶ When the optimizer chooses between several indices to access a table, it will usually use the index for an expression that has the highest selectivity. For instance, if the following query is executed:

```
select emp_no
   from works_on
   where job = 'Manager'
   and project_no = 'p1'
```

and two nonclustered indices for the **job** and **project_no** columns exist, the optimizer will usually choose the index for the **job** column, assuming that this column has significantly higher selectivity.

► When neither column in the join condition has an index, the optimizer usually chooses the hash join method.

► When the cardinality of one table is small and the other table has an index on the join column, the optimizer usually chooses the nested-loop method.

SQL Server provides, among others, the following two types of optimizer hints:

► Index hints

► Join hints

Before introducing these hints, in the following sections you will find a discussion about the reasons to use them and the requirements for their demonstration.

Why to Use Optimizer Hints

In most cases, the SQL Server optimizer chooses the fastest execution plan. However, there are some special situations where the optimizer, for some particular reasons, cannot find the optimal solution. In such cases, you should use optimizer hints to force it to use a particular execution plan, which could perform better.

There are two reasons why the optimizer does not choose the fastest execution plan:

► It is not perfect.

► The system does not provide the optimizer with the appropriate information.

NOTE

Optimizer hints can help you only if the execution plan chosen by the optimizer is not optimal. In the second case, you have to create or modify statistics using the UPDATE STATISTICS statement.

As you already know, the UPDATE STATISTICS statement updates information concerning distribution of key values for a table. Although SQL Server updates statistics information automatically each time the optimizer determines that the information is out of date, you should execute this statement for a table any time the data in the table changes significantly. That way, you ensure that the optimizer generates the best execution plan based on the newest information concerning statistics.

NOTE

In most cases, you should use optimizer hints only temporarily and for testing. In other words, avoid using them as a permanent part of a query. There are two reasons for this statement. First, if you force the optimizer to use a particular index and later define an index that results in better performance of the query, the query and the application to which it belongs cannot benefit from the new index. Second, Microsoft continuously strives to make the optimizer better. If you bind a query to a specific execution plan, the query cannot benefit from new and improved features in the subsequent versions of SQL Server.

Requirements for a Demonstration of Query Hints

The sample database, as defined in the first chapter of this book, is not suitable for a practical demonstration of optimizer hints because all four tables contain just a few rows. Generally, if a table contains a few rows (not more than 200), there is no reason to define indices for such a table because in such a case a table scan always outperforms the corresponding index access. For this reason, you need all tables in the sample database with significantly more rows. Examples 9.12 and 9.13 show two batches that insert 3,000 and 12,000 rows in the **employee** and **works_on** tables, respectively. (Delete the content of both tables before you execute the batches in Examples 9.12 and 9.13.)

EXAMPLE 9.12

```
-- This procedure inserts 3000 row in the table employee
USE sample
GO
SET SHOWPLAN_TEXT OFF
GO
declare @i integer, @emp_no integer
declare @emp_lname char(20), @emp_fname char(20)
declare @dept_no char(4)
set @i = 1
set @emp_lname = 'Smith'
set @emp_fname = 'Jane'
set @dept_no = 'd1'
while @i < 3001
begin
insert into employee
   values (@i, @emp_fname, @emp_lname, @dept_no)
set @i = @i+1
end
```

EXAMPLE 9.13

```
-- This procedure inserts 12000 row in the table works_on
USE sample
declare @i integer, @j integer
declare @job char(20), @enter_date datetime
declare @project_no char(4)
declare @dept_no  char(4)
set @i = 1
set @j = 1
set @job = 'Analyst'
set @enter_date = GETDATE()
set @dept_no = 'd1'
while @i < 3001
begin
  while @j < 5
    begin
      if (@j = 1) set @dept_no = 'd1'
      else if (@j = 2) set @dept_no = 'd2'
       else if (@j = 3) set @dept_no = 'd3'
        else set @dept_no = 'd4'
    insert into works_on
        values (@i, @dept_no, @job, @enter_date)
   set @j = @j+1
  end
set @i = @i+1
set @j = 1
end
```

Index Hints

SQL Server supports two index hints:

- ▶ INDEX
- ▶ FASTFIRSTROW

NOTE

The FASTFIRSTROW index hint causes the optimizer to use the nonclustered index if one matches a column in the ORDER BY clause. This option is a deprecated feature and can be replaced by the FAST hint.

The INDEX hint is used to specify one or more indices that are then used in a query. This hint must be specified in the FROM clause of the query. You can use this hint to force index access if the optimizer for some reason chooses to perform a table scan for a given query.

NOTE

The following examples demonstrate the general use of query hints, but they don't give you any recommendations about using them in any particular queries. (In most cases shown below, the use of query hints would be counterproductive.)

Example 9.14 shows the use of the INDEX hint.

EXAMPLE 9.14

```
USE sample
GO
SET SHOWPLAN_TEXT ON
GO
select *
    from works_on  WITH (INDEX(i_works))
    where job  = 'Analyst'
    and enter_date='12/01/1998'
```

NOTE

In SQL Server 2005, with some exceptions, index and table hints are supported in the FROM clause only when the hints are specified with the WITH keyword.

The INDEX query hint in Example 9.14 (see Figure 9-4) forces the use of the **i_works** index, which was created in Example 9.6.

The other form of the INDEX query hint—INDEX(0)—forces the optimizer not to use any of the existing indices. Example 9.15 shows the use of this hint.

EXAMPLE 9.15

```
USE sample
GO
SET SHOWPLAN_TEXT ON
GO
select * from works_on  WITH (index(0))
    where emp_no = 10102
```

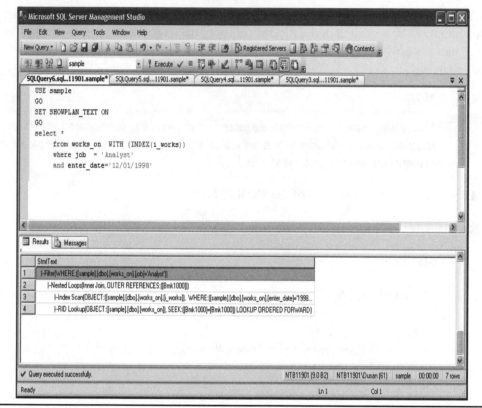

Figure 9-4 *The textual output of the execution plan for the query in Example 9.14*

NOTE

If a clustered index exists, INDEX(0) forces a clustered index scan and INDEX(1) forces a clustered index scan or seek. If no clustered index exists, INDEX(0) forces a table scan and INDEX(1) is interpreted as an error.

The textual form of the execution plan for the query in Example 9.15 (see Figure 9-5) shows that the optimizer does not use the existing index for the **emp_no** column of the **works_on** table, because the query hint forces the optimizer to perform a table scan for the given SELECT statement.

NOTE

You cannot specify INDEX(0) together with INDEX(index_name).

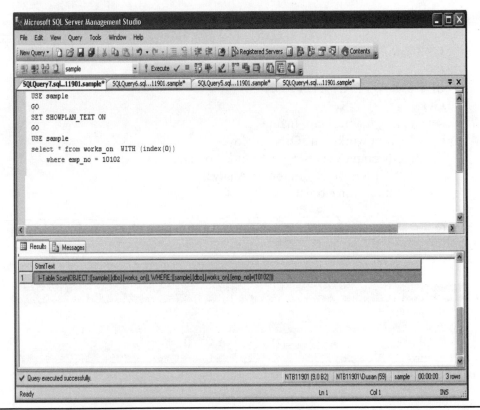

Figure 9-5   *The textual output of the execution plan forms the query in Example 9.15*

Join Hints

Join hints influence the SQL Server optimizer by performing the join operation in a query. They force the optimizer either to join tables in the order that the SELECT statement lists the tables or to use the join method explicitly specified in the statement. There are five join hints:

- ▶ FORCE ORDER
- ▶ LOOP JOIN
- ▶ HASH JOIN
- ▶ MERGE JOIN
- ▶ REMOTE

The FORCE ORDER hint forces the optimizer to join tables in the order in which they are specified in a query. Example 9.16 shows the use of this join hint.

EXAMPLE 9.16

```
USE sample
GO
SET SHOWPLAN_TEXT ON
GO
select emp_lname, emp_fname
     from works_on JOIN employee
     ON employee.emp_no = works_on.emp_no
     WHERE works_on.job = 'Analyst'
     option (force order)
```

Figure 9-6 shows the textual form of the execution plan for the query in Example 9.16.

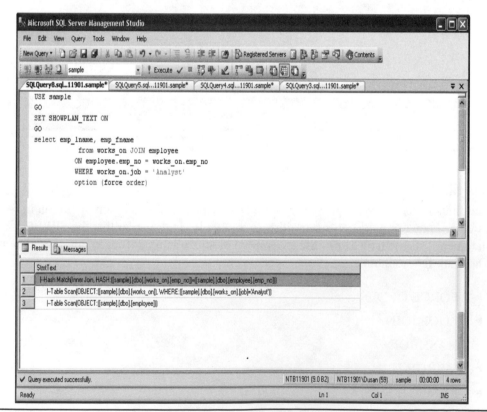

Figure 9-6 *The textual output of the execution plan for the query in Example 9.16*

As you can see from Example 9.16 and Figure 9-6, the optimizer performs the join operation in the order in which the **employee** and **works_on** tables appear in the query (from right to left). (Note that this does not necessarily mean that the new execution plan performs better than that chosen by the optimizer.)

The query hints LOOP JOIN, MERGE JOIN, and HASH JOIN force the optimizer to use the loop join, merge join, and hash join, respectively. These three join hints can be used only when the join operation conforms to the SQL92 standard—that is, when a join relationship is explicitly indicated with the JOIN and other keywords in the FROM clause instead of implicitly indicating it via the WHERE clause.

Examples 9.17 and 9.18 show a query that uses the hash join method, and the modification of the method after the MERGE JOIN hint is explicitly defined (in the same way you can apply the LOOP JOIN hint).

EXAMPLE 9.17

```
USE sample
GO
SET SHOWPLAN_TEXT ON
GO
select emp_lname, emp_fname
      from works_on JOIN employee
      ON employee.emp_no = works_on.emp_no
```

As you can see from Figure 9-7, the optimizer uses the existing index for the index scan of the **works_on** table. After that, the **employee** table will be searched using table scan and, finally, the hash join method will be applied against the selected rows from both tables.

EXAMPLE 9.18

```
USE sample
GO
SET SHOWPLAN_TEXT ON
GO
select emp_lname, emp_fname
      from works_on JOIN employee
      ON employee.emp_no = works_on.emp_no
  option (merge join)
```

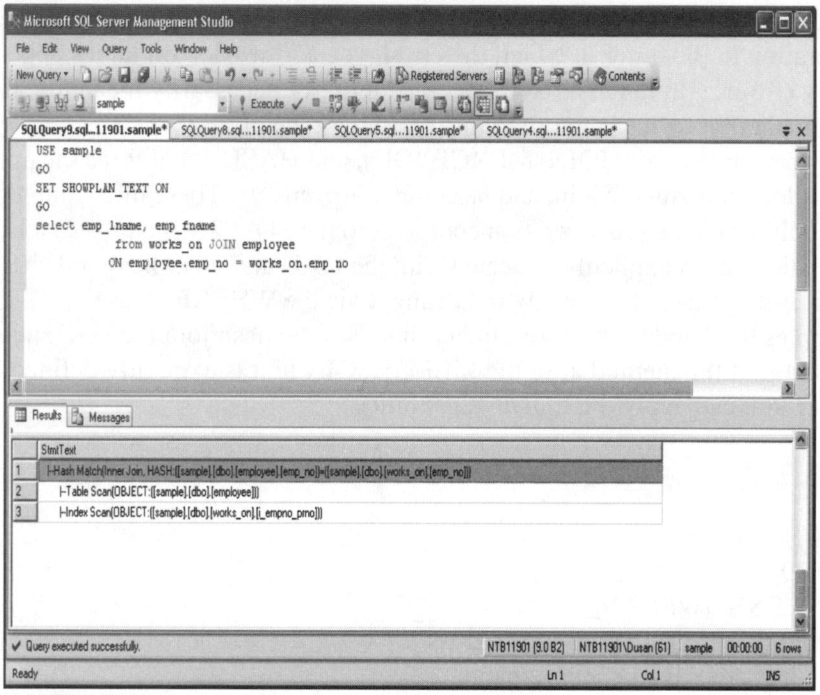

Figure 9-7   *The textual output of the execution plan for the query in Example 9.17*

Figure 9-8 shows the textual form of the execution plan for the query in Example 9.18. The SQL Server optimizer uses the merge join method, because the specification in the FROM clause contains such a join hint.

> **NOTE**
>
> *The specific join hint can be written either in the FROM clause of a query or using the OPTION clause at the end of it. (The use of the OPTION clause is recommended if you want to write several hints together.)*

The DBCC Command and Indices

DBCC specifies a group of statements that are used to check the physical and logical consistency of a database. (Some of them can also fix a database problem.) There are two DBCC statements concerning indices:

- ▶ DBCC DBREINDEX
- ▶ DBCC UPDATEUSAGE

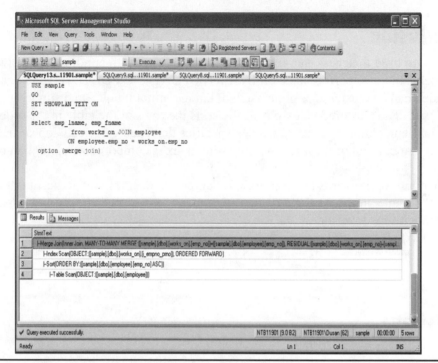

Figure 9-8   *The textual output of the execution plan for the query in Example 9.18*

The DBCC DBREINDEX statement rebuilds an index for a table or all indices defined for a table. By allowing an index to be rebuilt dynamically, you don't have to drop and re-create it. This is especially advantageous if an index is created implicitly using the PRIMARY KEY or UNIQUE integrity constraint. In such a case, you don't have to drop and re-create the defined constraint. (The DBCC DBREINDEX is a deprecated feature that will not be supported in a future version of SQL Server. Use the REBUILD option of the ALTER TABLE statement.)

The DBCC UPDATEUSAGE statement corrects pages and row count inaccuracies in the **sysindexes** table for tables and clustered indices. Size information is not maintained for nonclustered indices. If there are no inaccuracies in **sysindexes**, DBCC UPDATEUSAGE returns no data. If inaccuracies are found and corrected and the WITH NO_INFOMSGS option is not used, UPDATEUSAGE returns the rows and columns being updated in the **sysindexes** system table.

Conclusion

Indices are used to access data more efficiently. They can affect not only SELECT statements but also performance on INSERT, UPDATE, and DELETE statements. An index can be clustered or nonclustered, unique or nonunique, and single or composite. The clustered index physically sorts the rows of the table in the order of the specified column(s). A unique index specifies that each value can appear only once in that column of the table. A composite index is composed of more than one column.

The query optimizer is the part of SQL Server that decides how to best perform a query. It generates several query execution plans for the given query and selects the plan with the lowest cost.

The next chapter will discuss the system catalog of the SQL Server system, showing the structure of its most important system tables.

Exercises

E.9.1

Create a nonclustered index for the **enter_date** column of the **works_on** table. Sixty percent of each index leaf page should be filled.

E.9.2

Create a unique composite index for the **l_name** and **f_name** columns of the **employee** table. Is there any difference if you change the order of the columns in the composite index?

E.9.3

How can you drop the index that is implicitly created for the primary key of a table?

E.9.4

Discuss the benefits and disadvantages of an index.

 NOTE

In the following exercises, create indices that will improve performance of the queries. (We assume that all tables of the sample database that are used in the following exercises have a very large number of rows.)

E.9.5

SELECT emp_no, emp_fname, emp_lname
    FROM employee
    WHERE emp_lname = 'Smith'

E.9.6

SELECT emp_no, emp_fname, emp_lname
    FROM employee
    WHERE emp_lname = 'Hansel'
    AND emp_fname = 'Elke'

E.9.7

SELECT job
  FROM works_on, employee
  WHERE employee.emp_no = works_on.emp_no

E.9.8

SELECT emp_lname, emp_fname
    FROM employee, department
    WHERE employee.dept_no = department.dept_no
    AND dept_name = 'Research'

CHAPTER
10

Views

IN THIS CHAPTER

C hapter 10 is dedicated exclusively to the database object called a *view*. The structure of this chapter corresponds to the structure of Chapters 4 to 7, in which the DDL and DML statements for base tables were described. The first section of this chapter covers the DDL statements concerning views: CREATE VIEW, ALTER VIEW, and DROP VIEW. The second part of the chapter describes the DML statements SELECT, INSERT, UPDATE, and DELETE with views. The SELECT statement will be looked at separately from the other three statements. SQL Server 2000 supports the new form of a view called an *indexed view*. This new feature is also described in a section of this chapter.

In contrast to base tables, views cannot be used for modification operations without certain limitations. These limitations are described at the end of each corresponding section.

DDL Statements and Views

In the previous chapters, base tables were used to describe DDL and DML statements. A base table contains data stored on the disk. By contrast, views, by default, do not exist physically—that is, their content is not stored on the disk. (This is not true for so-called indexed views, which will be discussed later in this chapter.) Views are database objects that are always derived from one or more base tables using information stored in the system catalog. This information (including the name of the view and the way the rows from the base tables are to be retrieved) is the only information concerning views that is physically stored. Thus, views are called virtual tables.

sysobjects is the most important system table concerning views. (This system table contains a row for every database object of the current database.) The **type** column of this system table describes the type of the object, whereby the character *V* stands for view. (Similarly, *S* denotes a system table and *U* a user table.) The other two important columns of **sysobjects** are **name** and **id**. These specify the object name and the object identifier, respectively, and are unique within the entire database. You can use the **sys.objects** catalog view to access information from the **sysobjects** system table.

The second catalog view concerned with views is **sys.views**. The **with_check_ option** column contains the information that specifies whether the WITH CHECK OPTION clause is enabled. (This option will be described later in this chapter.)

There are also two system procedures concerning views. **sp_helptext** displays the SELECT statement belonging to a particular view, and **sp_rename** renames, if necessary, the name of a view (or any other database object).

Creating a View

A view is created using the CREATE VIEW statement. The general form of this statement is

    CREATE VIEW view_name [(column_list)]
        [WITH {ENCRYPTION | SCHEMABINDING | VIEW METADATA}]
        AS select
        [WITH CHECK OPTION]

NOTE

The CREATE VIEW statement must be the only statement in a batch.

view_name is the name of the defined view. **select** specifies the SELECT statement that retrieves rows and columns from one or more tables. **column_list** declares column names from the underlying tables. If this optional specification is omitted, column names of the underlying base tables are used (or they can be specified in the SELECT statement). The WITH ENCRYPTION option encrypts the SELECT statement in the system table **syscomments**. Therefore, this option can be used to enhance the security of the SQL Server system.

The SCHEMABINDING clause binds the view to the schema (i.e., structure) of the underlying table. When SCHEMABINDING is specified, tables, views, and user-defined functions referenced in the SELECT statement must include the two-part names in the form **schema_name.db_object**, where **db_object** may be a table, a view, or a user-defined function.

Any attempt to modify the structure of views or tables that participate in a view created with this clause fails. (You have to drop the view or change it so that it no longer has the SCHEMABINDING clause if you want to apply the ALTER or DROP statement to the referenced objects.)

When a view is created with the VIEW_METADATA option, all of its columns (except **timestamp** columns) can be updated if the view has INSERT or UPDATE INSTEAD OF triggers.

NOTE

The SELECT statement in a view cannot include the ORDER BY, INTO, or COMPUTE clauses. Additionally, a temporary table cannot be referenced in the query.

Views can be used for different purposes:

▶ To restrict the use of particular columns and/or rows of tables. Therefore, views can be used for controlling access to a particular part of one or more tables. (Chapter 12 describes in detail the use of views for security purposes.)

▶ To hide the details of complicated queries. If database applications need queries that involve complicated join operations, the creation of corresponding views can simplify the use of such queries.

▶ To restrict inserted and updated values to certain ranges (see the description of the option WITH CHECK OPTION later in the chapter).

A limited number of users have the authorization to create a view. After the installation of the system and the creation of the database, only the system administrator and the database owner have this privilege. They can then grant this privilege to other users using the GRANT CREATE VIEW statement. Additionally, the creator of a view must have read access for each column that is contained within the view query. (Granting and revoking database privileges is discussed in detail in Chapter 12.)

Example 10.1 shows the view called **v_clerk**.

EXAMPLE 10.1

```
USE sample
GO
CREATE VIEW v_clerk
  AS SELECT emp_no, project_no, enter_date
     FROM works_on
     WHERE job = 'Clerk'
```

The query in Example 10.1 retrieves the rows of the **works_on** table, for which the condition job = 'Clerk' evaluates to true. **v_clerk** is defined as the rows and columns returned by this query. Table 10-1 shows the **works_on** table with the rows that belong to the **v_clerk** view bolded.

A view is used exactly like any base table of a database. You can think about selecting from a view as if the statement were transformed into an equivalent operation on the underlying base table(s). Hence, the following query:

```
SELECT emp_no
  FROM v_clerk
  WHERE project_no = 'p2'
```

emp_no	project_no	job	enter_date
10102	p1	Analyst	1997.10.1 00:00:00
10102	p3	Manager	1999.1.1 00:00:00
25348	**p2**	**Clerk**	**1998.2.15 00:00:00**
18316	p2	NULL	1998.6.1 00:00:00
29346	p2	NULL	1997.12.15 00:00:00
2581	p3	Analyst	1998.10.15 00:00:00
9031	p1	Manager	1998.4.15 00:00:00
28559	p1	NULL	1998.8.1. 00:00:00
28559	**p2**	**Clerk**	**1999.2.1 00:00:00**
9031	**p3**	**Clerk**	**1997.11.15 00:00:00**
29346	**p1**	**Clerk**	**1998.1.4 00:00:00**

Table 10-1 *The base table **works_on***

is converted into the equivalent SELECT statement that uses the base table **works_on**:

```
SELECT emp_no
  FROM works_on
  WHERE job = 'Clerk'
    AND project_no = 'p2'
```

All modification operations are treated in a manner similar to queries. This means that an update of a view actually updates the table that it depends on. (The same is true for an insert or a delete operation.) The modification operations have some restrictions, which are described later in corresponding sections of this chapter.

Example 10.1 specifies the selection of rows—that is, it creates a horizontal subset from the base table **works_on**. It is also possible to create a view that limits the columns as well as the rows to be included in the view. Example 10.2 shows the creation of such a view.

EXAMPLE 10.2

```
USE sample
GO
CREATE VIEW v_without_budget
  AS SELECT project_no, project_name
      FROM project
```

The **v_without_budget** view in Example 10.2 contains all columns of the **project** table, but not the **budget** column.

As we already stated, specifying column names with a view in the general format of the CREATE VIEW statement is optional. On the other hand, there are also two cases in which the explicit specification of column names is required:

▶ If a column of the view is derived from an expression or an aggregate function

▶ If two or more columns of the view have the same name in the underlying tables

EXAMPLE 10.3

```
USE sample
GO
CREATE VIEW v_count(project_no, count_project)
  AS SELECT project_no, COUNT(*)
        FROM works_on
        GROUP BY project_no
```

The column names of the **v_count** view in Example 10.3 must be explicitly specified because the SELECT statement contains the aggregate function COUNT(*), and all columns in a view must be named.

EXAMPLE 10.4

```
USE sample
GO
CREATE VIEW v_seattle (emp_no,f_name,l_name, dept_no, no, dept_name,
location)
  AS SELECT employee.*, department.*
    FROM employee, department
    WHERE employee.dept_no = department.dept_no
    AND location = 'Seattle'
```

The SELECT list in Example 10.4 contains two columns with the same name— **dept_no**—so the explicit specification of the column list is required in the CREATE VIEW statement. (The alternative would be to list the columns in the SELECT statement and exclude the redundant **department.dept_no** column from the view.)

NOTE

The explicit specification of the column list in the CREATE VIEW statement can be avoided if you use column headers (see Example 10.5).

EXAMPLE 10.5

```
USE sample
GO
CREATE VIEW v_count1
  AS SELECT project_no, COUNT(*) count_project
      FROM works_on
      GROUP BY project_no
```

A view can be derived from another existing view.

EXAMPLE 10.6

```
USE sample
GO
CREATE VIEW v_project_p2
 AS SELECT emp_no
      FROM v_clerk
      WHERE project_no ='p2'
```

The **v_project_p2** view in Example 10.6 is derived from the **v_clerk** view (Example 10.1). Every query using the **v_project_p2** view is converted into the equivalent query on the underlying base table **works_on**.

Altering and Removing Views

SQL Server supports the ALTER VIEW statement that modifies the structure of a view. The ALTER VIEW statement is usually used to modify the definition of the view query. The syntax of ALTER VIEW is identical to that of the CREATE VIEW statement.

You can use the ALTER VIEW statement to avoid reassigning existing privileges for the view. Also, altering an existing view using this statement does not affect the stored procedures that depend upon the view. Otherwise, if you use the DROP VIEW and CREATE VIEW statements to remove and re-create a view, any stored procedure (or any other application) that uses the view will not work properly, at least in the time period between removing and re-creating the view. The following example shows the use of the ALTER VIEW statement.

EXAMPLE 10.7

```
USE sample
GO
ALTER VIEW v_without_budget
  AS SELECT project_no, project_name
      FROM project
      WHERE project_no >= 'p3'
```

The ALTER VIEW statement in Example 10.7 extends the SELECT statement of the **v_without_budget** view (Example 10.2) with the new condition in the WHERE clause.

> **NOTE**
>
> *With SQL Server, the ALTER VIEW statement can also be applied to indexed views. This statement removes all indices that exist for such a view. (Indexed views are explained in detail at the end of this chapter.)*

The DROP VIEW statement removes the definition of the specified view from the system catalog. Only the creator of the view, the system administrator, or the database owner can remove a view.

EXAMPLE 10.8

```
USE sample
GO
DROP VIEW v_count
```

The DROP VIEW statement in Example 10.8 removes the **v_count** view (Example 10.3). If the DROP VIEW statement removes a view, all other views derived from it will be dropped, too.

EXAMPLE 10.9

```
USE sample
GO
DROP VIEW v_clerk
```

The DROP VIEW statement in Example 10.9 also implicitly removes the **v_project_p2** view (Example 10.6).

NOTE

A view is not automatically dropped if the underlying table is removed. This means that any view from the removed table must be exclusively removed using the DROP VIEW statement. On the other hand, if a table with the same logical structure as the removed one is subsequently created, the view can be used again.

DML Statements and Views

Views are retrieved and modified with the same Transact-SQL statements that are used to retrieve and modify base tables.

View Retrieval

A query (SELECT statement) on a view is always transformed into the equivalent query on the base table(s) that it depends on.

EXAMPLE 10.10

```
USE sample
GO
CREATE VIEW v_d2
  AS SELECT emp_no, emp_lname
      FROM employee
      WHERE dept_no ='d2'
GO
SELECT emp_lname
    FROM v_d2
    WHERE emp_lname LIKE 'J%'
```

The result is

emp_lname
James

NOTE

Both Transact-SQL statements in Example 10.10 have to be executed in separate batches because the CREATE VIEW statement must be the only statement in a batch. The GO statement can be used to indicate the end of a batch.

The SELECT statement in Example 10.10 is transformed into the following equivalent form, using the underlying table of the **v_d2** view:

```
SELECT emp_lname
   FROM employee
   WHERE emp_lname LIKE 'J%'
   AND dept_no ='d2'
```

The next three sections describe the use of views with the three other DML statements: INSERT, UPDATE, and DELETE. Data modification with these statements is treated in a manner similar to a retrieval. The only difference is that there are some restrictions on a view used for insertion, modification, and deletion of data from the table that it depends on.

INSERT Statement and a View

A view can be used with the INSERT statement as if it were a base table. When a view is used to insert rows, the rows are actually inserted into the underlying base table.

EXAMPLE 10.11

```
USE sample
GO
CREATE VIEW v_dept
   AS SELECT dept_no, dept_name
         FROM department
GO
INSERT INTO v_dept
     VALUES ('d4', 'Development')
```

The **v_dept** view, which is created in Example 10.11, contains the first two columns of the **department** table. The subsequent INSERT statement inserts the row into the underlying table using the values 'd4' and 'Development'. The **location** column, which is not referenced by the **v_dept** view, is assigned a NULL value.

Using a view, it is generally possible to insert a row that does not satisfy the conditions of the view query's WHERE clause. The option WITH CHECK OPTION is used to restrict the insertion of only such rows that satisfy the conditions of the query. If this option is used, SQL Server tests every inserted row to ensure that the conditions in the WHERE clause are evaluated to true. If this option is omitted, there is no check of conditions in the WHERE clause, and therefore every row is inserted into the underlying table. This could lead to the confusing situation of a row being inserted into a view but subsequently not being returned by a SELECT statement against that view, because the WHERE clause is enforced for the SELECT. WITH CHECK OPTION is also applied to the UPDATE statement.

EXAMPLE 10.12

```
USE sample
GO
CREATE VIEW v_1997_check
  AS SELECT emp_no, project_no, enter_date
     FROM works_on
     WHERE enter_date BETWEEN '01.01.1997' AND '12.31.1997'
     WITH CHECK OPTION
GO
INSERT INTO v_1997_check
  VALUES (22334, 'p2', '1.15.1998')
```

Example 10.12 shows the use of WITH CHECK OPTION. SQL Server tests whether the inserted value of the **enter_date** column evaluates to true for the condition in the WHERE clause of the SELECT statement. The attempted insert fails because the condition is not met. The following example shows the view with the same structure as the previous one, but without the WITH CHECK OPTION clause.

EXAMPLE 10.13

```
USE sample
GO
CREATE VIEW v_1997_nocheck
  AS SELECT emp_no, project_no, enter_date
     FROM works_on
     WHERE enter_date BETWEEN '01.01.1997' AND '12.31.1997'
```

```
GO
INSERT INTO v_1997_nocheck
    VALUES (22334, 'p2', '1.15.1998')
SELECT *
    FROM v_1997_nocheck
```

The result is

emp_no	project_no	enter_date
10102	p1	1997-10-01 00:00:00.000
29346	p2	1997-12-15 00:00:00.000
9031	p3	1997-11-15 00:00:00.000

In Example 10.13, there is no WITH CHECK OPTION. Therefore, the INSERT statement is executed and the row is inserted into the underlying **works_on** table. Notice that the subsequent SELECT statement does not display the inserted row because it cannot be retrieved using the **v_1997_nocheck** view.

The insertion of rows into the underlying tables is *not* possible if the corresponding view contains any of the following features:

▶ If the FROM clause in the view definition involves two or more tables and the column list includes columns from more than one table

▶ If a column of the view is derived from an aggregate function

▶ If the SELECT statement in the view contains the GROUP BY clause or the DISTINCT option

▶ If a column of the view is derived from a constant or an expression

Example 10.14 shows a view that cannot be used to insert row(s) in the underlying table.

EXAMPLE 10.14

```
USE sample
GO
CREATE VIEW v_sum(sum_of_budget)
    AS SELECT SUM(budget)
        FROM project
```

```
GO
SELECT *
  FROM v_sum
```

Example 10.14 creates the **v_sum** view that contains an aggregate function in its SELECT statement. Because the view in Example 10.14 represents the result of an aggregation of many rows (and not a single row of the **project** table), it does not make sense to try to insert a row into the underlying table using the **v_sum** view.

UPDATE Statement and a View

A view can be used with the UPDATE statement as if it were a base table. When a view is used to modify rows, the content of the underlying base tables is actually modified. The following example shows a view that is used to update the underlying table.

EXAMPLE 10.15

```
USE sample
GO
CREATE VIEW v_p1
  AS SELECT emp_no, job
      FROM works_on
     WHERE project_no = 'p1'
GO
UPDATE v_p1
   SET job = NULL
   WHERE job = 'Manager'
```

You can think about updating the view in Example 10.15 as if the UPDATE statement were transformed into the following equivalent statement:

```
UPDATE works_on
   SET job = NULL
   WHERE job = 'Manager'
   AND project_no = 'p1'
```

The WITH CHECK OPTION clause has the same logical meaning for the UPDATE statement as for the INSERT statement. The following example shows the use of the clause for a view that is used to update the underlying table.

EXAMPLE 10.16

```
USE sample
GO
CREATE VIEW v_100000
  AS SELECT project_no, budget
      FROM project
        WHERE budget > 100000
        WITH CHECK OPTION
GO
UPDATE v_100000
  SET budget = 93000
  WHERE project_no = 'p3'
```

Example 10.16 shows the use of WITH CHECK OPTION with the UPDATE statement. SQL Server tests whether the modified value of the **budget** column evaluates to true for the condition in the WHERE clause of the SELECT statement. The attempted modification fails because the condition is not met—that is, the value 93000 is not greater than the value 100000.

The modification of columns in the underlying tables is *not* possible if the corresponding view contains the following features:

▶ If the FROM clause in the view definition involves two or more tables and the column list includes columns from more than one table

▶ If a column of the view is derived from an aggregate function

▶ If the SELECT statement in the view contains the GROUP BY clause or the DISTINCT option

▶ If a column of the view is derived from a constant or an expression

Example 10.17 shows a view that cannot be used to update the underlying table.

EXAMPLE 10.17

```
USE sample
GO
CREATE VIEW v_uk_pound (project_number, budget_in_pounds)
  AS SELECT project_no, budget*0.65
      FROM project
        WHERE budget > 100000
```

```
GO
SELECT *
   FROM v_uk_pound
```

The result is

project_number	budget_in_pounds
p1	78000.0
p3	121225.0

The **v_uk_pound** view in Example 10.17 cannot be used with an UPDATE statement (nor with an INSERT statement) because the **budget_in_pounds** column is calculated using an arithmetic expression.

DELETE Statement and a View

A view can be used to delete rows of a table that it depends on.

EXAMPLE 10.18

```
USE sample
GO
CREATE VIEW v_project_p1
   AS SELECT emp_no, job
        FROM works_on
        WHERE project_no = 'p1'
GO
DELETE FROM v_project_p1
   WHERE job = 'Clerk'
```

Example 10.18 creates a view that is then used to delete several rows from the **works_on** table.

The deletion of rows in the underlying tables is *not* possible if the corresponding view contains the following features:

▶ If the FROM clause in the view definition involves two or more tables and the column list includes columns from more than one table

▶ If a column of the view is derived from an aggregate function

▶ If the SELECT statement in the view contains the GROUP BY clause or the DISTINCT option

In contrast to the INSERT and the UPDATE statements, the DELETE statement allows the existence of a constant or an expression in a column of the view that is used to delete rows from the underlying table. Example 10.19 shows the use of such a view.

EXAMPLE 10.19

```
USE sample
GO
CREATE VIEW v_budget (budget_reduction)
   AS SELECT budget*0.9
        FROM project
GO
DELETE FROM v_budget
```

The DELETE statement in Example 10.19 deletes all rows of the **project** table, which is referenced by the **v_budget** view.

Indexed Views

As you already know, a view always contains a query that acts as a filter. SQL Server builds dynamically the result set from each query that references a view. ("Dynamically" means that if you modify a table, the corresponding view will always show the updated content of that table.) Also, if the view contains computations based on one or more columns of the table, the computations are performed each time you access the view.

Building dynamically the result set of a query can decrease performance, if the view with its SELECT statement processes many rows from one or more tables. If such a view is frequently used in queries, you could significantly increase performance by creating an index on the view.

SQL Server allows you to create indices on views. Such views are called indexed or materialized views. When a unique clustered index is created on a view, the view is executed and the result set is stored in the database in the same way a table with a clustered index is stored. (Clustered indices are described in detail in Chapter 9.)

> **NOTE**
>
> *Indexed views are implemented through syntax extensions to the CREATE INDEX and CREATE VIEW statements. In the CREATE INDEX statement, you can also specify the name of a view. The syntax of the CREATE VIEW statement is extended with the SCHEMABINDING clause. For more information on extensions to both statements, see their descriptions in this chapter.*

Creating an Indexed View

An indexed view is created using the CREATE VIEW statement with the WITH SCHEMABIDNIG clause. Example 10.20 shows a typical view that can be indexed to gain performance.

EXAMPLE 10.20

```
USE sample
GO
CREATE VIEW v_enter_month
  WITH SCHEMABINDING
  AS SELECT emp_no, DATEPART(MONTH, enter_date)  AS enter_month
     FROM dbo.works_on
```

The **employee** table in the sample database contains the **enter_date** column, which represents the starting date of an employee in the corresponding project. If you want to retrieve all employees that entered their projects in a specified month, you can use the view in Example 10.20. To retrieve such a result set using index access, SQL Server cannot use a table index, because an index on the **enter_date** column would locate the values of that column by the date, and not by the month. In such a case, SQL Server indexed views can help.

To make a view indexed, you have to first create a unique clustered index on the column(s) of the view. (As we already stated, a clustered index is the only index type that contains the data values in leafs of the corresponding b-tree structure.) After you create that index, SQL Server allocates storage for the view, and then you can create any number of nonclustered indices because the view is treated as a (base) table.

An indexed view can be created only if the following options of the SET statement are set to ON.

- ▶ QUOTED_IDENTIFIER
- ▶ ANSI_NULLS

Also, the NUMERIC_ROUNDABORT option must be set to OFF (the default value).

To create an indexed view, the view definition has to meet the following requirements:

▶ All referenced (system and user-defined) functions used by the view have to be deterministic—that is, they must always return the same result for the same arguments.

▶ The view must reference only base tables.

▶ The view and the referenced base table(s) must have the same owner and belong to the same database.

▶ The view must be created with the SCHEMABINDING option. SCHEMABINDING binds the view to the schema of the unerlying base tables.

▶ The referenced user-defined functions must be created with the SCHEMABINDING option.

▶ The SELECT statement in the view cannot contain the following clauses and options: DISTINCT, UNION, COMPUTE, TOP, ORDER BY, MIN, MAX, COUNT, SUM (on a nullable expression), subqueries, and OUTER.

SQL Server allows you to verify all of the above requirements with the **isindexable** parameter of the **objectproperty** function. If the value of the function is 1, all requirements are met and you can create the clustered index. Example 10.21 shows the execution of the **objectproperty** function, and Example 10.22 shows the creation of a unique clustered index on the columns **enter_month** and **emp_no** of the **v_enter_month** view.

EXAMPLE 10.21

```
USE sample
SELECT objectproperty(object_id('v_enter_month'), 'isindexable')
```

EXAMPLE 10.22

```
USE sample
GO
CREATE  UNIQUE CLUSTERED INDEX
     c_workson_deptno ON v_enter_month (enter_month, emp_no)
```

After creation of the unique clustered index, you can create any number of nonclustered indices for that view.

The **sp_spaceused** system procedure allows you to check whether the view is materialized—that is, whether it uses the storage space or not. The result of Example 10.23 shows that the **v_enter_month** view uses storage space for the data as well as for the defined index.

EXAMPLE 10.23

```
USE sample
EXEC sp_spaceused 'v_enter_month'
```

The result is

name	rows	reserved	data	index_size	unused
v_enter_month	11	16KB	8KB	8KB	0KB

Modifying an Indexed View

If you drop the unique clustered index on an indexed view, all nonclustered indices on the view are dropped, too. After dropping its clustered index, the view is treated by the system as a standard view.

NOTE

If you drop an indexed view, all indices on that view are dropped.

If you want to change a standard view to an indexed one, you have to create a unique clustered index on it. To do it, you must first specify the SCHEMABINDING option for that view. You can either drop the view and re-create it, specifying the SCHEMABINDING clause in the CREATE SCHEMA statement, or you can create another view that has the same text as the existing view but a different name.

NOTE

If you create a new view with a different name, you must ensure that the new view meets all of the requirements for an indexed view that are described above.

Benefits of Indexed Views

Besides possible performance gains for complex views that are frequently referenced in queries, the use of indexed views has two other advantages:

▶ All modifications to data are reflected in the corresponding indexed view.

▶ Index of an indexed view can be used even if the view is not explicitly referenced in the FROM clause.

When you create an indexed view, the result set of the view (at the time the index is created) is stored on the disk. Therefore, all data that are modified in the base table(s) will also be modified in the corresponding result set of the indexed view.

A use of the index of an indexed view is possible even if the view name does not appear in the FROM clause of a query.

Besides all the benefits that you can gain using indexed views, there is also a (possible) disadvantage: Indices for indexed views are usually more complex to maintain than indices on base tables. The maintenance of indices on indexed views is generally higher than the maintenance of indices on base tables, because the structure of a unique clustered index on an indexed view is more complex than a structure of the corresponding index on a base table. For this reason, there are additional requirements when indices should be created for a view. (See also "Guidelines for Creating Indices" in Chapter 9.)

There are several types of queries that can achieve significant performance benefits if a view that is referenced by the corresponding query is indexed. These are as follows:

▶ Queries that process many rows and contain join operations or aggregate functions

▶ Join operations and aggregate functions that are frequently performed by one or several queries

If a query references a (standard) view and the database system has to process many rows using join, the SQL Server optimizer will usually use the hash join method. However, if you define a clustered index on that view, the performance of the query could be significantly enhanced, because the optimizer can use the nested loop join instead of the hash join. (The same is true for aggregate functions.)

If a query that references a standard view does not process many rows, the use of an indexed view could still be beneficial if the query is used very frequently. (The same is true for groups of queries that join the same tables or use the same type of aggregates.)

If the restrictions on the types of views that can be indexed may prevent you from using an indexed view in a particular query, you may try to create partial solutions—each with the corresponding indexed view—and after that, union all partial solutions to an entire one. For instance, you cannot design an indexed view to process the aggregation of data in tables from different databases and with the subsequent join of their results, because an indexed view cannot reference tables from several databases. You can, however, create an indexed view in each database that does the aggregation of data. If the optimizer can match the indexed view against all partial queries, at least the aggregation processing will speed up. While the join processing is not faster, the overall query is faster because it uses the aggregations stored in the indexed view.

Using Indexed Views

Probably the most important property of indexed views is that a query does not have to explicitly reference a view to use the index on that view. In other words, if the query contains references to columns in the base table(s), which exist also in the indexed views, and the optimizer estimates that using the indexed view is the best choice, it chooses the view indices (in the same way it chooses table indices when they are not directly referenced in a query).

Example 10.24 shows the query that uses the indexed view defined in Example 10.20, where the query optimizer chooses to access rows using the existing clustered index of the view. Figure 10-1 represents the textual output of the query execution.

EXAMPLE 10.24

```
SET SHOWPLAN_TEXT ON
GO
select * from v_enter_month
        where enter_month = 6
```

Optimizer Hints Concerning Indexed Views

As you already know from Chapter 9, optimizer hints are optional parts of a SELECT statement that instruct different components of SQL Server (usually the query optimizer) to execute one specific behavior. SQL Server supports two optimizer hints concerning indexed views:

▶   EXPAND VIEWS
▶   NOEXPAND

```
Microsoft SQL Server Management Studio
File   Edit   View   Query   Tools   Window   Help

New Query ▾  [icons]  Registered Servers  [icons]  Contents

[icons]  sample         ▾  Execute ✓ [icons]

SQLQuery2.sql...11901.sample*  SQLQuery1.sql...11901.sample*  Summary        ▾ X

SET SHOWPLAN_TEXT ON
GO
select * from v_enter_month
              where enter_month = 6

Results  Messages
    StmtText
1   select * from v_enter_month         where enter_month = 6

    StmtText
1   |-Compute Scalar(DEFINE:[[Expr1003]=datepart(month,[sample].[dbo].[works_on].[enter_date]]))
2     |-Clustered Index Scan(OBJECT:[[sample].[dbo].[works_on].[PK_works_on]], WHERE:(datepart(month,[sample].[dbo].[works_on].[enter_date])=CONVERT_IMPLICIT(int,[@1],0)))

✓ Query executed successfully.         NTB11901 (9.0 B2)   NTB11901\Dusan (56)   sample   00:00:00   3 rows
Ready                                                      Ln 1                  Col 1
```

Figure 10-1 *The textual output of the query execution plan for Example 10.24*

With the EXPAND VIEWS hint, you do not allow the query optimizer to create an execution plan using the existing view indices. Therefore, if you specify this hint in the SELECT statement, the SQL Server query optimizer ignores all indices on a view when estimating the best execution plan for covering columns referenced in the query—that is, it treats the indexed view as a standard one.

You can use the other hint—NOEXPAND—to force the optimizer to consider the use of any indices defined on the view. If you want to instruct the optimizer to use one or more indices, use the NOEXPAND hint together with the INDEX hint. (The NOEXPAND hint cannot be specified for a standard view.)

NOTE

Use optimizer hints only temporarily and for testing. This is also valid for the EXPAND VIEWS and NOEXPAND hints.

Conclusion

Views can be used for different purposes:

▶ To restrict the use of particular columns and/or rows of tables—that is, to control access to a particular part of one or more tables

▶ To hide the details of complicated queries

▶ To restrict inserted and updated values to certain ranges

Views are created, retrieved, and modified with the same Transact-SQL statements that are used to create, retrieve, and modify base tables. The query on a view is always transformed into the equivalent query on an underlying base table. Update operations are treated in a manner similar to a retrieval. The only difference is that there are some restrictions on a view used for insertion, modification, and deletion of data from a table that it depends on. Even so, SQL Server handles the modification of rows and columns in a more systematic way than other relational DBMSs.

The next chapter will introduce the system catalog of the SQL Server system, showing the structure of its most important system tables.

Exercises

E.10.1

Create a view that comprises the data of all employees that work for the department d1.

E.10.2

For the **project** table, create a view that can be used by employees who are allowed to view all data of this table except the **budget** column.

E.10.3

Create a view that comprises the first and last names of all employees who entered their projects in the second half of the year 1988.

E.10.4

Solve the previous exercise so that the original columns **f_name** and **l_name** have new names in the view: **first** and **last**, respectively.

E.10.5

Use the view in E.10.1 to display full details of all employees whose last names begin with the letter *M*.

E.10.6

Create a view that comprises full details of all projects on which the employee named Smith works.

E.10.7

Using the ALTER VIEW statement, modify the condition in the view in E.10.1. The modified view should comprise the data of all employees that work either for the department d1 or d2, or both.

E.10.8

Delete the view created in E.10.3. What happens with the view created in E.10.4?

E.10.9

Using the view from E.10.2, insert the details of the new project with the project number p2 and the name Moon.

E.10.10

Create a view (with the WITH CHECK OPTION clause) that comprises the first and last names of all employees whose employee number is less than 10,000. After that, use the view to insert data for a new employee named Kohn with the employee number 22123, who works for the department d3.

E.10.11

Solve the exercise E.10.10 without the WITH CHECK OPTION clause and find the differences in relation to the insertion of the data.

E.10.12

Create a view (with the WITH CHECK OPTION clause) with full details from the **works_on** table for all employees that entered their projects during the years 1998 and 1999. After that, modify the entering date of the employee with the employee number 29346. The new date is 06/01/1997.

E.10.13

Solve the exercise E.10.12 without the WITH CHECK OPTION clause and find the differences in relation to the modification of the data.

CHAPTER
11

System Catalog

Thistory chapter will discuss SQL Server's system catalog. The introduction is followed by a description of the structure of several system tables, each of which is part of the system catalog. The retrieval of information from system tables using the SELECT statement is also covered in this chapter. Four alternate ways of retrieving information from system tables are provided by the use of system procedures, system and property functions, as well as information schema, which are described at the end of the chapter.

System Tables

The system catalog consists of system tables describing the structure of objects such as databases, base tables, views, and indices in the SQL Server system. SQL Server frequently accesses the system catalog for information that is essential for the system to function properly.

NOTE

*SQL Server distinguishes the system tables of the **master** database from those of a particular user-defined database. The former is called a system catalog, the latter a database catalog. Therefore, system tables occur only once in the entire system (if they belong exclusively to the system catalog), while others occur once in each database, including the **master** database.*

In SQL Server and other relational database systems, all the system tables have the same logical structure as base tables. As a result, the same Transact-SQL statements used to retrieve and modify information in the base tables can also be used to retrieve and modify information in the system tables.

NOTE

Modifying system information using the DDL statements INSERT, UPDATE, and DELETE can be very dangerous for the entire system. Microsoft also discourages the direct querying of system tables in scripts or user-defined procedures. In both cases, you should use system procedures instead.

The following sections describe the structure of the most important system tables.

Sysobjects

The main system table of SQL Server, **sysobjects**, appears in the master database and in every user-defined database. **sysobjects** contains a row for each database object. Table 11-1 shows the most important columns of this system table.

Column	Description
id	The unique identification number of a database object
name	The name of a database object
uid	The identification number of the object owner
type	The type of a database object. Can be one of the following strings: C = check constraint; D = default; F = foreign key constraint; L = transaction log; P = stored procedure; K = primary key or unique constraint; R = rule; RF = replication stored procedure; S = system table; TR = trigger; U = user table; V = view; X = extended stored procedure
crdate	The creation date of a database object

Table 11-1 *Selected Columns of the System Table **sysobjects***

Syscolumns

The system table **syscolumns** appears in the **master** database and in every user-defined database. It contains a row for every column of a base table or a view and a row for each parameter in a stored procedure. Table 11-2 shows the most important columns of **syscolumns**.

Sysindexes

The system table **sysindexes** appears in the **master** database and in every user-defined database. It contains a row for each index and a row for each table without a clustered index. (It also contains a row for each table including **text/image** data.) This system table is described in detail in Chapter 9.

Column	Description
id	The identification number of the table to which this column belongs or the identification number of the stored procedure to which the parameter belongs
colid	The identification number of a column or parameter
name	Name of a column or a procedure parameter

Table 11-2 *Selected Columns of the System Table syscolumns*

Column	Description
uid	The identification number of a user, unique in the entire database
sid	The system ID of the corresponding database creator
name	The user name or the group name, unique in the entire database

Table 11-3   *Selected Columns of the System Table sysusers*

Sysusers

The system table **sysusers** appears in the **master** database and in every user-defined database. It contains a row for each Windows user account, Windows group, SQL Server login, or SQL Server role in the entire database. (For the definition of users, groups, and roles, see Chapter 12.) Table 11-3 shows the most important columns of **sysusers**.

Sysdatabases

The system table **sysdatabases** contains a row for every system and user-defined database on the SQL Server system. It appears only in the **master** database. Table 11-4 shows the most important columns of **sysdatabases**.

Sysdepends

The system table **sysdepends** contains a row for every dependency relationship between tables, views, and stored procedures. It appears in the **master** database and in every user-defined database. Table 11-5 shows the most important columns of **sysdepends**.

Column	Description
dbid	The unique identification number of the database
name	The unique name of the database
sid	The system ID of the database creator
crdate	The creation date
filename	The operating system path and the name of the primary file of the database

Table 11-4   *Selected Columns of the System Table sysdatabases*

Column	Description
id	The identification number of the table, view, or stored procedure
number	The number of the stored procedure (otherwise NULL)
depid	The identification number of the dependent object

Table 11-5 *Selected Columns of the System Table sysdepends*

Sysconstraints

The system table **sysconstraints** contains one row for every integrity constraint that is defined for a database object using the CREATE TABLE or ALTER TABLE statement. It appears in the **master** database and in every user-defined database. Table 11-6 shows the most important columns of **sysconstraints**.

Catalog Views

SQL Server 2005 introduces catalog views as a new interface to retrieve system information from the catalog metadata. Catalog views are, together with the information schema views, the most general interface to the system catalog and provide the most efficient way to obtain, transform, and present customized forms of this information (see Examples 11.1 to 11.3.)

NOTE

Catalog views are the common interface that is used by other enterprise database systems, like IBM DB2 and Oracle, to access metadata.

Column	Description
constid	The identification number of the integrity constraint
id	The identification number of the table with the integrity constraint
colid	The identification number of the column on which the integrity constraint is defined; 0 specifies that the constraint is defined as a table constraint
status	The type of the integrity constraint: 1 = PRIMARY KEY constraint; 2 = UNIQUE KEY constraint; 3 = FOREIGN KEY constraint; 4 = CHECK constraint; 5 = DEFAULT constraint; 16 = column-level constraint; 32 = table-level constraint

Table 11-6 *Selected Columns of the System Table sysconstraints*

Table	Catalog view
sysdatabases	Sys.databases
sysobjects	Sys.objects
syscolumns	Sys.columns
syslogins	Sys.server_principals
sysusers	Sys.database_principals

Table 11-7   *Most Important Catalog Views*

All user-available data in the system catalog is exposed through catalog views. Table 11-7 shows the most important system tables and the corresponding system views. (For each existing SQL Server 2000 system table there is now a view with the same name. That way, SQL Server 2005 supports existing applications that access tables directly. Such views are called *compatiblity views*.)

NOTE

In previous versions of SQL Server, it is possible to query information on other database objects. The introduction of catalog views remedies this problem, because you can use the VIEW DEFINITION privilege to grant or deny access to metadata. (For more information concerning the VIEW DEFINITION privilege, see Chapter 12.)

In the following subsections we will show the structure of the three most important catalog views. The description of all other views can be found in Books Online.

Sys_objects

The **sys.objects** catalog view contains a row for each object in the database. The analog catalog view that shows system objects is called **sys.system_objects**. There is another view named **sys.all_objects** that shows both system and user objects. All three catalog views have the same structure.

Table 11-8 shows the most important columns of the **sys.objects** catalog view.

Column Name	Description
name	Object name
object_id	Object identification number, unique within a database
schema_id	ID of the schema in which the object is contained
type	Object type

Table 11-8   *Selected Columns of the Catalog View **sys.objects***

Column Name	Description
object_id	ID of the object to which this column belongs
name	Column name (unique within the object)
column_id	ID of the column (unique within the object)

Table 11-9   *Selected Columns of the Catalog View sys.columns*

Sys.columns

The **sys.columns** catalog view contains a row for each column of an object that has columns, such as tables and views.

Table 11-9 shows the most important columns of the **sys.columns** catalog view.

Sys.database_principals

The **sys.database_principals** catalog view contains a row for each security principal, i.e., user, group, or role in a database.

Table 11-10 shows the most important columns of the **sys.database_principals** catalog view.

Querying Catalog Views

As already stated in this chapter, all SQL Server system tables have the same structure as base tables. Therefore, each system table, like base tables, can be queried by using the SELECT statement. We will use existing catalog views to demonstrate how information concerning database objects can be queried. Examples 11.1, 11.2, and 11.3 show queries using the catalog views for our sample database.

Column Name	Description
name	Name of principal (unique within the database)
principal_id	ID of principal (unique within the database)
type	Principal type

Table 11-10   *Selected Columns of the catalog view sys.database_principals*

NOTE

Beginning with SQL Server 2005, you can query system information only indirectly. This means that if you query system information using system table names, you actually use corresponding compatibility views (i.e., views with the same names as the corresponding system tables).

EXAMPLE 11.1

Get the table ID, the user ID, and the table type of the **employee** table.

```
USE sample
select object_id, principal_id, type
   from sys.objects
   where name = 'employee';
```

The result is

Object_id	Principal_id	type
530100929	NULL	U

EXAMPLE 11.2

Get the names of all tables of the sample database that contain the **project_no** column.

```
SELECT sys.objects.name
   FROM sys.objects INNER JOIN sys.columns
   ON sys.objects.object_id = sys.columns.object_id
   WHERE sys.objects.type = 'U'
   AND sys.columns.name = 'project_no';
```

The result is

Name
Project
works_on

EXAMPLE 11.3

Who is the owner of the **employee** table?

```
SELECT sys.database_principals.name
FROM sys.database_principals INNER JOIN sys.objects
ON sys.database_principals.principal_id = sys.objects.schema_id
WHERE sys.objects.name = 'employee'
AND sys.objects.type = 'U';
```

The result is

Name
dbo

By default, SQL Server system tables cannot be modified using the Transact-SQL statements INSERT, UPDATE, and DELETE. The only way to do this is to change the corresponding configuration variable using the RECONFIGURE WITH OVERRIDE statement and to set the option ALLOW UPDATE of the **sp_configure** system procedure to 1. (Only the system administrator can execute the RECONFIGURE statement.) After that, only authorized users are allowed to modify system tables.

NOTE

Do not modify the value of ALLOW UPDATE in the RECONFIGURE statement! Updating system information using the DDL statements INSERT, UPDATE, and DELETE can be very dangerous for the entire system. For example, should any information about a base table in the system catalog be dropped, any further use of that table (and of the database to which it belongs) will not be possible. To modify system information, use only system procedures, which are described in the next section.

Other Ways to Access System Information

You can also retrieve system information using one of the following four mechanisms:

- ▶ System stored procedures
- ▶ System functions

▶ Property functions

▶ Information schema

The following sections describe these mechanisms.

System Procedures

System procedures are used to provide many administrative and end-user tasks, such as renaming database objects, identifying users, and monitoring authorization and resources. Almost all existing system procedures access system tables to retrieve and modify system information.

NOTE

In contrast to the direct modification of system tables, system procedures can be used for easy and reliable modification of system tables.

Some procedures are described and explained in this chapter. Depending on the subject matter of the chapters, certain system procedures were discussed in previous chapters, and additional procedures will be discussed in later chapters of the book.

sp_help

The system procedure **sp_help** displays information about one or more database objects. The name of any database object or data type can be used as a parameter of this procedure. If **sp_help** is executed without any parameter, information on all database objects of the current database will be displayed. Example 11.4 displays all information for the **sales** table (Example 4.23) of the sample database.

EXAMPLE 11.4

```
USE sample
exec sp_help sales
```

The result is

Name		Owner		Type		Created_datetime	
Sales		Dbo		User table		1998-06-11 09:30:36.807	

Column_name	Type	Computed	Length	Prec	Scale	Nullable
Order_no	int	no	4	10	0	No
Order_date	datetime	no	8	0	0	No
ship_date	datetime	no	8	0	0	No

Identity	Seed	Increment	Not for replication
No identity column defined	NULL	NULL	NULL

Index_name	index_description	index_keys
PK__sales__OEA330E9	clustered, unique, primary key located on default	order_no

Constraint_type	Constraint_name	Status_enabled	Status_for_replication	Constraint_keys
CHECK Table Level	order_check	Enabled	Is_For_Replication	([order_date] <= [ship_date])
PRIMARY KEY (clustered)	PK__sales__OEA330E9	(n/a)	(n/a)	order_no

No foreign keys reference this table.

sp_depends

The system procedure **sp_depends** displays the dependency information among tables, views, triggers, and stored procedures.

Example 11.5 displays the dependency information for the **v_clerk** view (Example 9.1).

EXAMPLE 11.5

```
USE sample
EXEC sp_depends v_clerk
```

The result is that in the current database, the specified object references the following:

Name	type	Updated	Selected	Column
dbo.works_on	user table	No	No	emp_no
dbo.works_on	user table	No	No	project_no
dbo.works_on	user table	No	No	Job
dbo.works_on	user table	No	No	enter_date

In the current database, the specified object is referenced by the following:

Name	Type
dbo.v_project_p2	View

The system procedure **sp_depends** in Example 11.5 displays the dependency information of the **v_clerk** view. This information contains the name of the underlying table (**works_on**) and the name of the view (**v_project_p2**), which is created using the **v_clerk** view.

sp_helptext

The system procedure **sp_helptext** displays the contents of a stored procedure, a trigger, or a view.

Example 11.6 displays the contents of the stored procedure **increase_budget** (see Example 8.4).

EXAMPLE 11.6

```
sp_helptext increase_budget
```

The result is

Text
CREATE PROCEDURE increase_budget (@percent INT=5) AS UPDATE project SET budget = budget + budget*@percent/100

System Functions

All system functions are described in Chapter 3. Some of them access system tables and can therefore be used to retrieve system information. Example 11.7 shows two SELECT statements that query the same information from the **sysobjects** system table.

(The first one uses the compatibility views with the same name as the system table, while the second one uses the OBJECT_ID system function.)

EXAMPLE 11.7

```
USE sample
SELECT id
  FROM sysobjects
  WHERE name = 'employee'
SELECT object_id('employee')
```

The second SELECT statement in Example 11.7 uses the system function OBJECT_ID to retrieve the ID of the **employee** table. (This information can be stored in a variable and used when calling a command (or system procedure) with the object's ID as parameter.)

The following system functions, among others, access system tables:

- ▶ OBJECT_ID (object_name)
- ▶ OBJECT_NAME (object_id)
- ▶ USER_ID ([user_name])
- ▶ USER_NAME ([user_id])
- ▶ DB_ID ([db_name])
- ▶ DB_NAME ([db_id])
- ▶ INDEX_COL (table, index_id, col_id)

Using Example 11.8, you will see that the INDEX_COL system function is much easier to use than retrieving the same information using catalog views. (The INDEX_COL function displays the name of the column on which an index key is based.)

EXAMPLE 11.8

```
select index_col ('employee', 1,1) AS Index_Col_1
```

If there is a clustered index for the **emp_no** column of the **employee** table, the result is the following:

Index_col_1

emp_no

Example 11.8 retrieves the clustered index (index_id = 1) of the first column (col_id = 1) of the **employee** table. (To display the same information using catalog views, you have to join three compatibility views: **sysobjects, syscolumns**, and **sysindexes**.)

Property Functions

Property functions return properties of database objects, data types, or files. Generally, property functions can return more information than system functions, because they support dozens of properties (as parameters), which you can explicitly specify.

Almost all property functions are threefold (i.e., return one of the following three values): 0, 1, or NULL. If the value is 0, the object does not have the specified property. If the value is 1, the object has the specified property. Similarly, the value NULL specifies that the existence of the specified property for the object is unknown to the system.

SQL Server supports, among others, the following property functions:

- ▶ OBJECTPROPERTY (id, property)
- ▶ COLUMNPROPERTY (id, column, property)
- ▶ FILEPROPERTY (filename, property)
- ▶ TYPEPROPERTY (type, property)

The OBJECTPROPERTY function returns information about objects in the current database (see Example 10.21). The COLUMNPROPERTY function returns information about a column or procedure parameter. The FILEPROPERTY function returns the specified file name property value for a given file name and property name. The TYPEPROPERTY function returns information about a data type. (The description of existing properties for each property function is beyond the scope of this book.)

Information Schema

The information schema consists of read-only views that provide information about all tables, views, and columns of SQL Server to which you have access. In contrast to the system catalog that manages the metadata applied to the system as a whole, the information schema primarily manages the environment of a database.

NOTE

The information schema was originally introduced in the SQL92 standard. SQL Server provides the information schema views so applications developed on other database systems can obtain the SQL Server system catalog without having to use it directly. These standard views use different terminology from SQL Server, so when you interpret the column names, be aware that catalog corresponds to database and domain is the same as user-defined data type.

The following sections provide a description of the most important information schema views.

Information_schema.tables

The **Information_schema.tables** view contains one row for each table in the current database to which the user has access. The view retrieves the information from the system table **sysobjects**. Table 11-11 shows the four columns of this view.

Information_schema.views

The **Information_schema.views** view contains one row for each view in the current database accessible by the user. The view retrieves information from the system tables **sysobjects** and **syscomments**. Table 11-12 shows the five columns of this view.

Information_schema.columns

The view **Information_schema.columns** contains one row for each column in the current database accessible by the user. The view retrieves the information from the system tables **sysobjects**, **systypes**, **syscolumns**, and **syscomments**. Table 11-13 shows the six selected columns of this view.

Information_schema.referential_constraints

The **information_schema.referential_constraints** view contains one row for each referential constraint owned by the current user and defined in the current database. The view retrieves the information from the system tables **sysreferences**, **sysindexes**, and **sysobjects**. Table 11-14 shows the most important columns of this view.

Information_schema.routines

The **information_schema.routines** view contains one row for each user-defined function or stored procedure accessible by the current user and defined in the current database. The view retrieves the information from the system tables **syscolumns** and **sysobjects**. Table 11-15 shows the most important columns of this view.

Column	Description
TABLE_CATALOG	The name of the catalog (database) to which the view belongs
TABLE_SCHEMA	The name of schema (owner) to which the view belongs
TABLE_NAME	The table name
TABLE_TYPE	The type of the table (can be "BASE TABLE" or "VIEW")

Table 11-11 *The View Information_schema.tables*

Column	Description
TABLE_CATALOG	The name of the catalog (database) to which the view belongs
TABLE_SCHEMA	The name of schema (owner) to which the view belongs
VIEW_NAME	The name of the underlying table
VIEW_DEFINITION	The text of the view definition
CHECK_OPTION	Specifies whether the check option is set to ON; if so, "CASCADE" is returned; otherwise, "NONE" is returned

Table 11-12   *The View Information_schema.views*

Column	Description
TABLE_CATALOG	The name of the catalog (database) to which the column belongs
TABLE_SCHEMA	The name of schema to which the column belongs
TABLE_NAME	The name of the table to which the column belongs
COLUMN_NAME	The column name
ORDINAL_POSITION	The column identification number
DATA_TYPE	The data type of the column

Table 11-13   *The View Information_schema.columns*

Column	Description
CONSTRAINT_CATALOG	The name of the catalog (database) to which the referential constraint belongs
CONSTRAINT_SCHEMA	The name of schema (owner) to which the referential constraint belongs
CONSTRAINT_NAME	The constraint name
DELETE_RULE	The action that is taken if a DELETE statement violates referential integrity defined by this constraint (could be NO ACTION, CASCADE, SET NULL, and SET DEFAULT)
UPDATE_RULE	The action that is taken if an UPDATE statement violates referential integrity defined by this constraint (could be NO ACTION, CASCADE, SET NULL, and SET DEFAULT)

Table 11-14   *The View Information_schema.referential_constraints*

Column	Description
ROUTINE_CATALOG	The name of the catalog (database) to which the routine (function of stored procedure) belongs
ROUTINE_SCHEMA	The name of schema (owner) to which the routine belongs
ROUTINE_NAME	The name of the function or stored procedure
ROUTINE_TYPE	The type of the routine. Returns PROCEDURE for a stored procedure and FUNCTION for a user-defined function
ROUTINE_DEFINITION	Definition text of the function or stored procedure if the function or stored procedure is not encrypted. Otherwise, NULL
ROUTINE_BODY	Returns "SQL" (for a user-defined function implemented using SQL). Also, returns "EXTERNAL" (for CLR functions).

Table 11-15   *The View Information_schema.routines*

Conclusion

The SQL Server catalog contains a single system catalog and several database catalogs. The system catalog is a collection of system tables belonging to the **master** database. Each database catalog contains system tables of the user-defined database.

SQL Server 2005 system information can be queried only indirectly, that is, by using catalog views or system procedures. Catalog views are the general interface to the system information. They also comprise compatibility views, which are views that have the same names as the corresponding system tables.

The benefit of using system procedures is that they provide easy and reliable access to system tables. It is also strongly recommended to exclusively use system procedures for modification of system tables.

There are other interfaces that you can use to access system information. The information schema is a collection of views defined on system tables that provide unified access to the SQL Server system catalog for all database applications developed on other database systems. Some property functions, such as OBJECTPROPERTY and COLUMNPROPERTY, can also be used to display system information.

The next chapter introduces you to database security and the two existing authentication modes: Windows security mode and Mixed mode.

Exercises

E.11.1

Using compatibility views, find the operating system path and the name of the file of the **sample** database.

E.11.2

Using compatibility views, find the name of the clustered index (if it exists) that is defined for the **employee** table of the sample database.

E.11.3

Using compatibility views, find how many integrity constraints are defined for the **employee** table of the sample database.

E.11.4

Using compatibility views, find out if there is any integrity constraint defined for the **dept_no** column of the **employee** table.

E.11.5

Which system table is used by the system procedure **sp_depends** to display the dependency information among tables and other database objects?

E.11.6

Find the name of the column that has the user-defined data type **western_countries** (E.4.16). Hint: Use the compatibility views **systypes** and **syscolumns**. These two views have to be joined together using three columns: **xtype**, **type**, and **usertype**.

E.11.7

Using the information schema, display all user tables that belong to the **AdventureWorks** database.

E.11.8

Using the information schema, find all columns of the **employee** table with their ordinal positions and the corresponding data types.

CHAPTER
12

SQL Server Security

S QL Server security protects data in the database against unauthorized access. This important feature of every database system (see Chapter 1) requires the evaluation of two primary questions:

▶ Which user has been granted legitimate access to the SQL Server system (authentication)?

▶ Which access privileges are valid for a particular user (authorization)?

The following sections discuss these two issues and describe the Transact-SQL statements that grant and limit access to users. Later in the chapter, views and stored procedures are shown, which can also be used to protect data in databases and restrict the access to data by unauthorized users.

Authentication

Authentication prevents unauthorized users from using a system by checking their identity through:

▶ Something a user is acquainted with (usually passwords)

▶ Something the user owns, such as magnetic cards or badges

▶ Physical characteristics of the user, such as signature or fingerprints

SQL Server has two kinds of authentication:

▶ Windows authentication

▶ SQL Server authentication

Windows authentication defines a user account that exists at the operating system level. SQL Server authentication defines a login that is created within SQL Server and is associated with a password. (Some SQL Server logins are identical to the existing Windows user accounts.)

NOTE

In addition to Windows user accounts and SQL Server logins, there are also Windows groups and SQL Server roles. A Windows group is a collection of Windows user accounts. Assigning a user account membership to a group gives the user all the permissions granted to the group. Similarly, a SQL Server role is a collection of SQL Server logins. (Roles are discussed in detail later in this chapter.)

SQL Server security includes two different security subsystems:

► Windows security
► SQL Server security

Windows security specifies security at the operating system level—that is, the method by which users connect to Windows using their Windows *user accounts*. SQL Server security specifies the additional security necessary at the SQL Server system level—that is, how users who have already logged on to the operating system can subsequently connect to SQL Server.

Based on these two security subsystems, SQL Server can operate in one of these two authentication modes:

► Windows mode
► Mixed mode

Windows mode exclusively uses Windows user accounts to log in to the SQL Server system. SQL Server accepts the user account, assuming it has already been validated at the operating system level. This kind of connection to a database system is called a *trusted connection*, because SQL Server trusts that the operating system already validated the account and the corresponding password.

Mixed mode allows users to connect to SQL Server using Windows authentication or SQL Server authentication. This means some user accounts can be set up to use Windows security subsystem, while others can use SQL Server security subsystem additionally to Windows security subsystem.

NOTE
SQL Server Authentication is provided for backward compatibility only. For this reason, use Windows Authentication instead.

Before we discuss how you can set SQL Server security, we have to describe the SQL Server encryption policy and mechanisms.

SQL Server Encryption Policy and Mechanisms

SQL Server secures data with hierarchical encryption layers and a key management infrastructure. Each layer secures the layer beneath it, using a combination of certificates, asymmetric keys, and symmetric keys. There are two layers (see Figure 12-1):

► Service Master Key
► Database Master Key

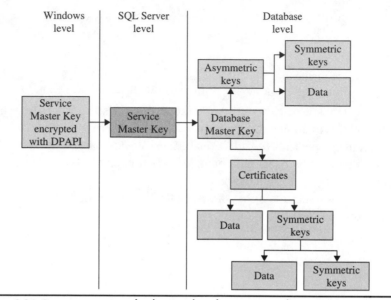

Figure 12-1 *SQL Server security: the hierarchical encryption layers*

The top layer, Service Master Key, is encrypted using the Windows data protection API. As you can see from Figure 12-1, Database Master Key depends on the encryption mechanisms, such as certificates and keys, which will be explained next.

Certificates

A public key certificate, usually just called a certificate, is a digitally signed statement that binds the value of a public key to the identity of the person, device, or service that holds the corresponding private key. Certificates are issued and signed by a certification authority (CA). The entity that receives a certificate from a CA is the subject of that certificate. Certificates contain the following information, among others:

▶ The subject's public key value

▶ The subject's identifier information

▶ Issuer identifier information

▶ The digital signature of the issuer

A primary benefit of certificates is that they relieve hosts of the need to maintain a set of passwords for individual subjects. When a host, such as a secure web server, designates an issuer as a trusted authority, the host implicitly trusts that the issuer has verified the identity of the certificate subject.

Symmetric and Asymmetric Keys

A symmetric key is an encryption system in which the sender and receiver of a message share a common key that is used to encrypt and decrypt the message. Thus, this single key is used for encryption as well as decryption. Encryption and decryption with a symmetric key is fast and suitable for routine use with sensitive data in the database.

An asymmetric key consists of a private key and the corresponding public key. Each key can decrypt data encrypted by the other key. Asymmetric encryption is used, because it provides a higher level of security than symmetric encryption. An asymmetric key can be used to encrypt a symmetric key for storage in a database.

Setting Up SQL Server Security Using DDL

SQL Server security can be set up using either data definition language (DDL) statements or SQL Server system procedures. In this section we discuss data definition statements, while the next section describes all system procedures concerning security.

The first statement to be considered is CREATE LOGIN. This statement creates a new SQL Server login. The syntax of the CREATE LOGIN statement is as follows:

```
CREATE LOGIN login_name
{ WITH option_list1  |
FROM {WINDOWS [ WITH option_list2 [,...] ]
| CERTIFICATE certname  |   ASYMMETRIC KEY key_name } }
```

login_name specifies the name of the SQL Server login that is being created. As you can see from the syntax of the statement, you can use the WITH clause to specify one or more options for the login or use the FROM clause to define certificate, asymmetric key, or Windows login associated with the corresponding SQL Server login.

options_list1 contains several options. The most important one is the PASSWORD option. Using this option you specify the password of the login (see Example 12.1). (Among the other possible options are: DEFAULT_DATABASE, DEFAULT_ LANGUAGE and CHECK_EXPIRATION.) The FROM clause comprises three different options:

- ► CERTIFICATE
- ► WINDOWS
- ► ASYMMETRIC KEY

The CERTIFICATE option specifies the name of the certificate to be associated with this login (see Example 12.2). The WINDOWS clause specifies that the login will be mapped to an existing Windows user account (see Example 12.3). This clause can be specified with other suboptions, such as DEFAULT_DATABASE and DEFAULT_LANGUAGE. Finally, the ASYMMETRIC KEY option specifies the name of the asymmetric key to be associated with this login. The certificate as well as the asymmetric key must already exist in the **master** database.

EXAMPLE 12.1

```
USE sample
CREATE CREDENTIAL DbLabor with identity = 'dusan'
CREATE LOGIN dusan WITH PASSWORD = 'you1know4it9',
CREDENTIAL= DbLabor
```

In Example 12.1 we specify the SQL Server login called **dusan**, with the password **you1know4it9** and credential called **DbLabor**. Before the CREATE LOGIN statement is executed, the credential used with it must be created (using the CREATE CREDENTIAL statement).

EXAMPLE 12.2

```
USE sample
CREATE CERTIFICATE cert02
  WITH SUBJECT = 'SQL Server 2005',
  ENCRYPTION_PASSWORD = 'pGFD4bb925DGvbd2439587y';
GO
 CREATE LOGIN claudia FROM CERTIFICATE cert02;
```

Example 12.2 first creates the new certificate called **cert02**, and then it creates the new login **claudia** using the certificate **cert02**.

EXAMPLE 12.3

```
USE sample
CREATE LOGIN [NTB11901\pete] FROM WINDOWS;
```

In Example 12.3 we specify the SQL Server login called **pete**, which will be mapped to a Windows user account with the same name.

SQL Server also supports the ALTER LOGIN statement. This statement changes the properties of a SQL Server login. Using the ALTER LOGIN statement, you can change the current password and its expiration properties, credentials, default database, and default language. You can also enable or disable the specified login.

The DROP LOGIN statement drops an existing SQL Server login. A login cannot be dropped if it owns any objects.

Setting Up SQL Server Security Using System Procedures

The following system procedures are used to set up SQL Server security:

- ▶ sp_addlogin
- ▶ sp_droplogin
- ▶ sp_password
- ▶ sp_grantlogin
- ▶ sp_revokelogin
- ▶ sp_denylogin

The first three procedures, which concern SQL Server logins, will be explained in the following section, while the last three, which concern Windows user accounts and groups, will be discussed in the subsequent section.

System Procedures Concerning Logins

The **sp_addlogin** system procedure has the same effect as the CREATE LOGIN statement. This means that it creates a new SQL Server login, which can subsequently be used by the user to log in to the SQL Server system using SQL Server Authentication.

Example 12.4 shows the use of the **sp_addlogin** system procedure.

EXAMPLE 12.4

```
USE sample
sp_addlogin 'peter', 'xxyyzz', 'sample'
GO
sp_addlogin 'mary', 'zzyyxx', 'sample'
GO
sp_addlogin 'paul', 'xyz123', 'sample'
```

The **sp_addlogin** system procedure in Example 12.4 creates three new SQL Server logins: **peter, paul**, and **mary**. The default database for all three logins is **sample**.

NOTE

*The **sp_addlogin** system procedure will be removed in a future version of SQL Server. Use the CREATE LOGIN statement instead.*

The **sp_droplogin** system procedure drops an existing SQL Server login. It is not possible to remove a SQL Server login that still has access to any database of the SQL Server system. The user must first be removed using the DROP USER statement (discussed a bit later in the chapter).

NOTE

*The **sp_droplogin** system procedure will be removed in a future version of SQL Server. Use the DROP LOGIN statement instead.*

The **sp_password** system procedure adds a new password to a SQL Server login or replaces the existing one. Users can change their own password at any time by using this system procedure. The system administrator can change any password by using **sp_password** and specifying NULL as the parameter for the old password.

System Procedures Concerning Windows Users

There are also three system procedures concerning Windows users and groups: **sp_grantlogin, sp_revokelogin**, and **sp_denylogin**. The system procedure **sp_grantlogin** allows a Windows user or group to connect to SQL Server or resets previous **sp_denylogin** restrictions for users within the group. The system procedure **sp_revokelogin** removes the login entries for a Windows user or group from SQL Server. The system procedure **sp_denylogin** prevents a Windows user or group from connecting to SQL Server (even if a group that contains this user or group is granted access). Only the system or security administrators can execute these three system procedures.

Schema

We described schema already in Chapter 4, where we introduced the CREATE SCHEMA statement as one of the DDL statements of Transact-SQL language. The notion of schema has very big impact in SQL Server 2005, because SQL Server uses schema in its security model to simplify the relationship between users and objects. The following sections are dedicated to this feature and its role in SQL Server security. First we describe the relationship between schemas and users; then we discuss all three Transact SQL statements concerning schema creation and modification.

User-Schema Separation

Schema is a collection of database objects that are owned by a single person and form a single namespace. (Two tables in the same schema cannot have the same name.)

> **NOTE**
>
> *SQL Server 2000 does not separate users and schemas, because it supports only unnamed schemas and the AUTHORIZATION clause specifies the owner (see Example 4.12). In SQL Server 2000, database users and schemas are implicitly connected. Also, this connection is fixed and cannot be modified. For that reason, every database user is the owner of a schema that has the same name as the user.*

SQL Server 2005 breaks the tight relationship between users and schemas, which existed in the previous version. Now, SQL Server 2005 supports named schemas using the notion of principal. A principal is an entity that can access objects. A principal can be

- ▶ Indivisible principal
- ▶ Group principal

An indivisible principal represents a single user, such as a SQL Server login or Windows user account. A group principal can be a group of users, such as a SQL Server role or Windows group. Principals are ownerships of schemas, but the ownership of a schema can be transferred easily to another principal and without changing the schema name.

The separation of database users from schemas provides significant benefits, such as:

- ▶ One principal can own several schemas
- ▶ Several indivisible principals can own a single schema via membership in SQL Server roles or Windows groups
- ▶ Droppping a database user does not require the renaming of objects contained by that user's schema

SQL Server 2005 introduces the notion of default schema, which is used to resolve the names of objects that are referred to without their fully qualified names. The default schema specifies the first schema that will be searched by the server when it resolves the names of objects. The default schema can be set and changed using the DEFAULT_SCHEMA option of the CREATE USER or ALTER USER statement.

If the DEFAULT_SCHEMA option is left undefined, the database user will have **dbo** as its default schema. (All default schemas will be described in detail in the section "Default Database Schemas" later in this chapter.)

DDL Statements Concerning Schema

Because SQL Server 2005 separates users from schemas, we will discuss the Transact SQL statements concerning schemas first and then discuss those concerning users.

There are three statements concerning schemas:

▶ CREATE SCHEMA

▶ ALTER SCHEMA

▶ DROP SCHEMA

We will use the slightly modified example from Chapter 4 (Example 4.12) to explain how SQL Server 2005 uses schemas to control security of databases.

EXAMPLE 12.5

```
USE sample
GO
CREATE SCHEMA my_schema AUTHORIZATION peter
CREATE TABLE product
    (product_no CHAR(10) NOT NULL UNIQUE,
     product_name CHAR(20) NULL,
      price MONEY NULL)
CREATE VIEW product_info
   AS SELECT product_no, product_name
      FROM product
GRANT SELECT TO mary
DENY UPDATE TO mary
```

NOTE

*Before you start Example 12.5, you have to create database users **peter** and **mary**. For this reason, first execute the Transact-SQL statements in Example 12.8.*

In Example 12.5 we create the schema called **my_schema**, which comprises the **product** table and a view (**product_info**). The user called **peter** is the database-level principal that owns the schema. You use the AUTHORIZATION option to define the principal of a schema. (The principal may own other schemas and may not use the current schema as his default schema.) Also, there are two other statements concerning permissions of database objects, and they are called GRANT and DENY. The first one grants the SELECT permissions for all objects created in the schema, while the second one denies the UPDATE permissions for all objects of the schema. (The GRANT and DENY statements are discussed in detail at the end of this chapter.)

The CREATE SCHEMA statement can create a schema, the tables and views it contains, and grant, revoke, or deny permissions on a securable in a single statement. (Securables are resources to which the SQL Server authorization system regulates access. There are three securable scopes, server, database, and schema, which contain other securables, such us SQL Server login, database users, tables, and stored procedures.)

The CREATE SCHEMA is atomic. In other words, if any error occurs during the execution of a CREATE SCHEMA statement, none of the Transact-SQL statements specified in the schema will be executed.

Database objects that are created in a CREATE SCHEMA statement can be specified in any order, with one exception: A view that references another view must be specified after the referenced view.

A database-level principal could be either database user, role, or application role. (Roles and application roles will be discussed in a moment.) The principal that is specified in the AUTHORIZATION clause of the CREATE SCHEMA statement is the owner of all objects created within a schema. Ownership of schema-contained objects can be transferred to any other database-level principal using the ALTER AUTHORIZATION statement (see Example 12.7).

The user needs the CREATE SCHEMA permission on the database to execute the CREATE SCHEMA statement. Also, to create the objects specified within the CREATE SCHEMA statement, the user needs the corresponding CREATE permissions.

The ALTER SCHEMA statement transfers an object between different schemas of the same database. The syntax of the ALTER SCHEMA statement is as follows:

ALTER SCHEMA schema_name TRANSFER object_name

The following example shows the use of the ALTER SCHEMA statement.

EXAMPLE 12.6

```
USE AdventureWorks
ALTER SCHEMA humanresources TRANSFER person.address
```

In Example 12.6 we alter the schema called **humanresources** of the **AdventureWorks** database by transferring into it the **address** table from the **person** schema of the same database.

The ALTER SCHEMA statement can only be used to transfer objects between different schemas in the same database. (Single objects within a schema can be altered using the ALTER TABLE statement, i.e., ALTER VIEW statement, as described in Chapter 4.)

The DROP SCHEMA statement removes a schema from the database. You can successfully execute the DROP SCHEMA statement for a schema, only if the schema does not contain any objects. Otherwise, the DROP SCHEMA statement will be rejected by the system.

As we already stated, SQL Server 2005 allows you to change the ownership of a schema. You can do this using the ALTER AUTHORIZATION statement. The ALTER AUTHORIZATION statement modifies the ownership of an entity.

NOTE

SQL Server does not support CREATE AUTHORIZATION or DROP AUTHORIZATION statements. You specify the ownership of an entity using the CREATE SCHEMA statement.

Example 12.7 shows the use of the CREATE AUTHORIZATION statement to change the ownership of the schema called **my_schema** (Example 12.5).

EXAMPLE 12.7

```
USE sample
ALTER AUTHORIZATION ON SCHEMA ::my_schema TO mary;
```

Database Security

A Windows user account or a SQL Server login allows a user to log in to the SQL Server system. A user who subsequently wants to access a particular database of the system also needs a database user account to work in the database. Therefore, users must have a database user account for each database they want to use. The database user account can be mapped from the existing Windows user accounts, Windows groups (of which the user is a member), SQL Server logins, or roles.

Setting Up Database User Accounts with DDL

Database security permissions can be set up using either Transact-SQL statements or system procedures. In this section we will explain how to set up user accounts with Transact-SQL statements.

The CREATE USER statement adds a user to the current database. The syntax of this statement is

```
CREATE USER user_name
    [FOR {LOGIN login_name | CERTIFICATE cert_name |
    ASYMMETRIC KEY key_name}]
        [ WITH DEFAULT_SCHEMA = schema_name ]
```

user_name is the name that is used to identify the user inside the database. **login_name** specifies the SQL Server login for which the user is being created. **cert_name** and **key_name** specify the corresponding certificate and asymmetric key, respectively. Finally, the WITH DEFAULT SCHEMA option specifies the first schema that will be searched by the server when it resolves the names of objects for this database user.

Example 12.8 demonstrates the use of the CREATE USER statement.

EXAMPLE 12.8

```
USE sample
CREATE USER peter FOR LOGIN [NTB11901\pete]
CREATE USER mary FOR LOGIN mary
WITH DEFAULT_SCHEMA = my_schema;
```

NOTE

*To execute the first statement successfully, create the Windows account named **pete** and change the server name NTB11901.*

The first CREATE USER statement creates the database user called **peter** for the Windows login with the name **pete** (see Example 12.3). The database user **peter** will use **dbo** as its default schema, because the DEFAULT SCHEMA option is omitted. (All default schemas will be described later in this chapter.)

The second statement creates a new database user with the name **mary**. This user has **my_schema** as her default schema. (The DEFAULT_SCHEMA option can be set to a schema that does not currently exist in the database.)

NOTE

Each database of the SQL Server system has its own specific users. Therefore, the CREATE USER statement must be executed once for each database where a user account should exist for a database login. Also, a SQL Server login can have only a single database user for a given database.

The ALTER USER statement either modifies a database user name or changes its default schema. Similar to the CREATE USER statement, it is possible to assign a default schema to a user before the creation of the schema.

The DROP USER statement removes a user from the current database. Users that own securables, i.e., database objects, cannot be dropped from the database.

Setting Up Database User Accounts Using System Procedures

The following system procedures can also be used to establish database security permissions:

▶ sp_grantdbaccess

▶ sp_revokedbaccess

▶ sp_helpuser

▶ sp_changedbowner

 NOTE

*Generally, you should not use the system procedures **sp_grantdbaccess** and **sp_revokedbaccess** to set up database user accounts. These system procedures will be removed in a future version of SQL Server. Use CREATE USER and DROP USER instead.*

The **sp_grantdbaccess** system procedure adds a new database user to the current database and associates it with an existing security account (login). The login can be a Windows user, Windows group, or SQL Server login.

Example 12.9 shows the use of the **sp_grantdbaccess** system procedure. (Before the execution of Example 12.9, you have to drop the existing database users **peter** and **mary** using the DROP USER statement.)

EXAMPLE 12.9

```
USE sample
GO
sp_grantdbaccess 'peter', 'peter'
GO
sp_grantdbaccess 'mary', 'mary'
GO
sp_grantdbaccess 'paul', 'paul'
```

In Example 12.9, the **sp_grantdbaccess** system procedure creates the database users, which are identical to the corresponding logins created in Example 12.4.

The **sp_revokedbaccess** system procedure removes an existing database user from the current database. (The database user can be a Windows user account, Windows group, or Microsoft SQL Server login.)

The **sp_helpuser** system procedure displays information about one or more database users in the current database. If the user is omitted, **sp_helpuser** displays the information about all existing database users and roles in the current database.

The **sp_changedbowner** system procedure changes the owner of the current database. After the execution of the procedure, the specified login is the new database owner (**dbo**) of the current database. All members of the **sysadmin** fixed server role and the owner of the current database can execute this system procedure.

Default Database Schemas

Each database within the SQL Server 2005 system contains the following default database schemas:

- ▶ guest
- ▶ dbo
- ▶ INFORMATION_SCHEMA
- ▶ sys

The SQL Server system allows users without user accounts to access database objects belonging to the **guest** schema. (After creation, each database contains this schema.) You can apply permissions to the **guest** schema in the same way as to any other schema. Also, you can drop and add the guest schema from any database except the **master** and **tempdb** system databases.

Each database object belongs to one and only one schema, which is default schema for that object. The default schema can be defined explicitly or implicitly. If the default schema isn't defined explicitly during the creation of an object, that object has the **dbo** schema as its default schema.

The INFORMATION_SCHEMA schema contains all information schema views (see Chapter 11). The **sys** schema, as you may have already guessed, contains system objects, such as catalog views.

Roles

When several users need to perform similar activities in a particular database (and there is no corresponding Windows group), it is possible to add a *role* in this database. A database role specifies a group of database users that can access the same objects of the database.

Members of a database role can be any of the following:

▶ Windows groups and user accounts

▶ SQL Server logins

▶ Other roles

The security architecture in SQL Server includes several roles that have special implicit permissions. There are two types of predefined roles in addition to roles that can be created by the database owner. These roles are classified as follows:

▶ Fixed server

▶ Fixed database

▶ User-defined

Fixed Server Roles

Fixed server roles are defined at the server level and therefore exist outside of databases belonging to the database server. Table 12-1 lists all existing fixed server roles.

Fixed Server Role	Description
sysadmin	Performs any activity in SQL Server
serveradmin	Configures server settings
setupadmin	Installs replication and manages extended procedures
securityadmin	Manages logins and CREATE DATABASE permissions and reads audits
processadmin	Manages SQL Server processes
dbcreator	Creates and modifies databases
diskadmin	Manages disk files

Table 12-1   *Fixed Server Roles*

The following two system procedures are used to add or delete members to a fixed server role:

▶ sp_addsrvrolemember

▶ sp_dropsrvrolemember

NOTE

You cannot add, modify, or remove fixed server roles. Additionally, only the members of fixed server roles can execute both system procedures to add or remove login accounts to/from the role.

The sa Login

The **sa** login is the login of the system administrator. In previous versions, where roles did not exist, the **sa** login was granted all possible permissions concerning system administration tasks. In SQL Server 2005, the **sa** login is included for backward compatibility. The **sa** login is always a member of the **sysadmin** fixed server role and cannot be dropped from the role.

NOTE

*Use the **sa** login only when there is not another way to log in to the SQL Server system.*

Fixed Server Roles and Their Permissions

Each fixed server role has its implicit permissions within a SQL Server system. You can view the permissions for each fixed server role using the **sp_srvrolepermission** system procedure. The syntax of this procedure is

    sp_srvrolepermission [[@srvrolename =] 'role']

If you do not specify the value for **role**, the permissions for all fixed server roles are displayed. The following sections discuss permissions of each fixed server role.

sysadmin

Members of the **sysadmin** fixed server role are granted all possible permissions for the SQL Server system. For example, only someone with this role (or a user who has been granted the CREATE DATABASE permission from a member of this role) can create databases.

This fixed server role has special relationships with the **sa** login. The **sa** login is always a member of this role and cannot be dropped from the role.

serveradmin

Members of the **serveradmin** fixed server role can perform the following activities:

- Add other logins to this server role
- Run the **dbcc pintable** command (to pin a table in the main memory)
- Run the **sp_configure** system procedure (to display or change system options)
- Run the **reconfigure** option (to update all modifications made with the **sp_configure** system procedure)
- Shut down the database server using the **shutdown** command
- Run the **sp_tableoption** system procedure to set option values for a user-defined table

setupadmin

Members of the **setupadmin** fixed server role can perform the following activities:

- Add other logins to this server role
- Add, drop, or configure linked servers
- Execute some system stored procedures, such as **sp_serveroption**

securityadmin

Members of the **securityadmin** fixed server role perform all activities in relation to server access and its security. They may perform the following system activities:

- Add other logins to this server role
- Read the SQL Server error log
- Run the following system procedures: **sp_addlinkedsrvlogin, sp_addlogin, sp_defaultdb, sp_defaultlanguage, sp_denylogin, sp_droplinkedsrvlogin, sp_droplogin, sp_grantlogin, sp_helplogins, sp_remoteoption**, and **sp_revokelogin**. (All these system procedures are related to the system security.)

processadmin

Members of the **processadmin** fixed server role manage SQL Server processes, such as aborting the user's runaway queries. They can perform the following activities:

- Add other logins to this server role
- Execute the KILL command (to kill user processes)

dbcreator

Members of the **dbcreator** fixed server role manage all activities concerning the creation and modification of a database. They can perform the following activities:

▶ Add other logins to this server role

▶ Run the CREATE DATABASE and ALTER DATABASE statements

▶ Modify the name of a database using the **sp_renamedb** system procedure

diskadmin

Members of the **diskadmin** fixed server role can perform the following activities concerning files and file groups that are used to store database objects:

▶ Add other logins to this server role

▶ Run the following system procedures: **sp_addumpdevice** and **sp_dropdevice**

▶ Run the DISK INIT statement

Fixed Database Roles

Fixed database roles are defined at the database level and therefore exist in each database belonging to the database server. Table 12-2 lists all of the fixed database roles.

Fixed Database Role	Description
db_owner	Users who can perform almost all activities in the database
db_accessadmin	Users who can add or remove users
db_datareader	Users who can see data from all user tables in the database
db_datawriter	Users who can add, modify, or delete data in all user tables in the database
db_ddladmin	Users who can perform all DDL operations in the database
db_securityadmin	Users who can manage all activities concerning security permissions in the database
db_backupoperator	Users who can back up the database (and issue DBCC and CHECKPOINT statements, which are often performed before a backup)
db_denydatareader	Users who cannot see any data in the database
db_denydatawriter	Users who cannot change any data in the database

Table 12-2 *Fixed Database Roles*

Besides the fixed database roles listed in Table 12-2, there is a special fixed database role called **public**, which will be explained first.

public Role

The **public** role is a special fixed database role to which every legitimate user of a database belongs. It captures all default permissions for users in a database. This provides a mechanism for giving all users without appropriate permissions a set of (usually limited) permissions. The **public** role maintains all default permissions for users in a database and cannot be dropped. This role cannot have users, groups, or roles assigned to it because they belong to the role by default. (Example 12.21 shows the use of the **public** role.)

By default, the **public** role allows users to do the following:

► View system tables and display information from the **master** database using certain system procedures

► Execute statements that do not require permissions—for example, PRINT

Fixed Database Roles and Their Permissions

Each fixed database role has its specific permissions within a database. This means that permissions of a member of a fixed database role are limited to a specific database. You can view the permissions for each fixed database role using the **sp_dbfixedrolepermission** system procedure. The syntax of this procedure is

```
sp_dbfixedrolepermission [[@rolename =] 'role']
```

If you do not specify the value for **role**, the permissions for all fixed database roles are displayed. In the following sections, permissions of each fixed database role are discussed.

db_owner

Members of the **db_owner** fixed database role may perform the following activities in the specific database:

► Add members to or remove members from any other fixed database role

► Run all DDL statements

► Run BACKUP DATABASE and BACKUP LOG statements

► Explicitly start the checkpoint process using the CHECKPOINT statement

▶ Run the following **dbcc** commands: **dbcc checkalloc, dbcc checkcatalog, dbcc checkdb, dbcc updateusage**

▶ Grant, revoke, or deny the following permissions on every database object: SELECT, INSERT, UPDATE, DELETE, and REFERENCES

▶ Add users or roles to a database with the following system procedures: **sp_addapprole, sp_addrole, sp_addrolemember, sp_approlepassword, sp_changeobjectowner, sp_dropapprole, sp_droprole, sp_droprolemember, sp_dropuser, sp_grantdbaccess**

▶ Rename any database object using the **sp_rename** system procedure

db_accessadmin

Members of the **db_accessadmin** fixed database role perform all activities in relation to database access. They may perform the following activities in the specific database:

▶ Run the following system procedures: **sp_addalias, sp_dropalias, sp_dropuser, sp_grantdbaccess, sp_revokedbaccess**

▶ Add or remove access for Windows user accounts, Windows groups, and SQL Server logins

db_datareader

Members of the **db_datareader** fixed database role have SELECT permissions on any database object (table or view) in a database. However, they cannot grant this permission to any other user or role. (The same is true for the REVOKE statement.)

db_datawriter

Members of the **db_datawriter** fixed database role have INSERT, UPDATE, and DELETE permissions on any database object (table or view) in a database. However, they cannot grant the permission to any other user or role. (The same is true for the REVOKE statement.)

db_ddladmin

Members of the **db_ddladmin** fixed database role can perform the following activities:

▶ Run all DDL statements

▶ Grant the REFERENCES permission on any table

▶ Modify the structure of any stored procedures with the **sp_procoption** and **sp_recompile** system procedures

▶ Rename any database object using the **sp_rename** system procedure

▶ Modify table options and the owner of any database object using the system procedures **sp_tableoption** and **sp_changeobjectowner**, respectively

db_securityadmin

Members of the **db_securityadmin** fixed database role manage security in the database. They can perform the following activities:

▶ Run all Transact-SQL statements concerning security (GRANT, DENY, and REVOKE)

▶ Run the following system procedures: **sp_addapprole, sp_addrole, sp_addrolemember, sp_approlepassword, sp_changeobjectowner, sp_dropapprole, sp_droprole, sp_droprolemember**

db_backupoperator

Members of the **db_backupoperator** fixed database role manage the process of backing up a database. They can perform the following activities:

▶ Run BACKUP DATABASE and BACKUP LOG statements

▶ Explicitly start the checkpoint process using the CHECKPOINT statement

▶ Run the following **dbcc** commands: **dbcc checkalloc, dbcc checkcatalog, dbcc checkdb, dbcc updateusage**

db_denydatareader and db_denydatawriter

As the name states, members of the **db_denydatareader** fixed database role do not have the SELECT permission on any database object (table or view) in the database. You should use this role if your database contains sensitive data that should not be read by some users.

Members of the **db_denydatawriter** fixed database role do not have the INSERT, UPDATE, and DELETE permissions on any database object (table or view) in the database.

Application Roles

Application roles allow you to enforce security for a particular application. In other words, they allow the application itself to accept the responsibility of user authentication, instead of SQL Server. For instance, if clerks in your company change an employee's data only using an existing application (and not Transact-SQL statements or any other tool), you can create an application role for it.

Application roles differ significantly from all other role types. First, application roles have no members, because they use the application only and therefore do not need to grant permissions directly to users. Second, you need a password to activate an application role.

When an application role is activated for a session by the application, the session loses all permissions applied to logins, user accounts, or roles in all databases for the duration of the session.

Creating Application Roles

You can create application roles using:

▶ CREATE APPLICATION ROLE statement

▶ **sp_addapprole** system procedure

The CREATE APPLICATION ROLE statement creates an application role to the current database. This statement has two options: one concerning the specification of the password and one for the definition of the default schema, i.e., first schema that will be searched by the server, when it resolves the names of objects for this role.

Example 12.10 shows the creation of an application role.

EXAMPLE 12.10

```
USE sample
CREATE APPLICATION ROLE weekly_reports WITH PASSWORD
='x1y2z3w4',
DEFAULT_SCHEMA =my_schema
```

Example 12.10 adds a new application role called **weekly_reports** to the current database.

The second way to create a new application role is by using the **sp_addapprole** system procedure. Using the **sp_addapprole** system procedure, you can create application roles and assign permissions to them. This procedure has the following syntax:

```
sp_addapprole [@rolename =] 'role', [@passwd_name =] 'password'
```

role specifies the name of the application role, while **password** is the corresponding password. (The value for **password** is required to activate the role.)

> **NOTE**
>
> *The **sp_addapprole** system procedure will be removed in a future version of SQL Server. Avoid using this feature. Use the CREATE APPLICATION ROLE statement instead.*

Activating Application Roles

After a connection is started, it must execute the **sp_setapprole** system procedure to activate the permissions that are associated with an application role. This procedure has the following syntax:

$$\text{sp\_setapprole } [@\text{rolename} =] \text{ 'role' }, [@\text{password} =] \text{ 'password'}$$
$$[,[@\text{encrypt} =] \text{ 'encrypt\_style'}]$$

role is the name of the application role defined in the current database. **password** specifies the corresponding password, while **encrypt_style** defines the encryption style specified for the password.

When you activate an application role using the **sp_setapprole** system procedure, you have to know the following:

▶ After the activation of an application role, you cannot deactivate it in the current database until the session is disconnected from SQL Server.

▶ An application role is always database bound—that is, its scope is the current database. If you change the current database within a session, you are allowed to perform (other) activities based on the permissions in that database.

> **NOTE**
>
> *Any user can execute the **sp_setapprole** system procedure by providing the correct password for the application role.*

Modifying Application Roles

You can modify application roles using the following Transact SQL statements:

▶ ALTER APPLICATION ROLE

▶ DROP APPLICATION ROLE

The ALTER APPLICATION ROLE statement changes the name, password, or default schema of an existing application role. The syntax of this statement is similar to the syntax of the CREATE APPLICATION ROLE statement. To execute the ALTER APPLICATION ROLE statement, you need the ALTER permission on the role.

The DROP APPLICATION ROLE statement removes the application role from the current database. If the application role owns any objects (securables), it cannot be dropped.

NOTE

*You can also use the **sp_dropapprole** system procedure to drop an application role, but this procedure will be removed in a future version of SQL Server.*

User-Defined Database Roles

Generally, user-defined database roles are applied when a group of database users need to perform a common set of activities within a database and no applicable Windows group exists. These roles are managed using the Transact-SQL statements or SQL Server system procedures. Next we will discuss Transact-SQL statements and then the corresponding system procedures.

Roles and Transact-SQL

The CREATE ROLE statement creates a new database role in the current database. The syntax of this statement is

    CREATE ROLE role_name [AUTHORIZATION owner_name]

role_name is the name of the user-defined role to be created. **owner_name** specifies the database user or role that will own the new role. (If no user is specified, the role will be owned by the user that executes the CREATE ROLE statement.)

The ALTER ROLE statement changes the name of a user-defined database role. Similarly, the DROP ROLE statement drops a role from the database. Roles that own database objects (securables) cannot be dropped from the database. To drop such a role, you must first transfer ownership of those objects. The syntax of the DROP ROLE statement is as follows:

    DROP ROLE *role_name*

Roles and System Procedures

The alternative way to create or modify user-defined roles is to use SQL Server system procedures. The following system procedures are used to set up and display the user-defined database roles:

- sp_addrole
- sp_addrolemember
- sp_droprolemember
- sp_droprole
- sp_helprole

The **sp_addrole** system procedure creates a new role in the current database. Only members of the **db_securityadmin** or **db_owner** database roles can execute this system procedure.

NOTE

*The **sp_addrole** system procedure is included in SQL Server 2005 only for backward compatibility and may not be supported in a future release. Use the CREATE ROLE statement instead.*

After adding a role to the current database, you can use the system procedure **sp_addrolemember** to add members of the role. The member of the role can be any valid SQL Server user, Windows group or user, or another SQL Server role. Only members of the **db_owner** database role can execute this system procedure. Additionally, role owners can execute **sp_addrolemember** to add a member to any role that they own.

The **sp_droprolemember** system procedure removes an existing member from the role. (It is not possible to use this system procedure to remove an existing Windows user from a Windows group.) Only members of the **db_owner** or **db_securityadmin** database roles can execute this system procedure.

After removing all members from the role using the system procedure **sp_droprolemember**, you can use the **sp_droprole** system procedure to remove a role from the current database. (A role with existing members cannot be dropped.) Only members of the **db_owner** or **db_securityadmin** database roles can execute this system procedure.

NOTE

*The **sp_droprole** system procedure is included in SQL Server 2005 only for backward compatibility and may not be supported in a future release. Use the DROP ROLE statement instead.*

The **sp_helprole** system procedure displays information (role name and role ID number) about a particular role or all roles in the current database if no role name is provided. Only the members of the **db_owner** or **db_securityadmin** roles can execute this system procedure.

Authorization

Only authorized users are able to execute statements or perform operations on a securable. Otherwise, the execution of the Transact-SQL statement or the operation on the database object will be rejected.

SQL Server supports three Transact-SQL statements concerning authorization:

▶ GRANT

▶ DENY

▶ REVOKE

Before we describe these three statements, we will state one of the most important properties of SQL Server 2005 concerning security: SQL Server 2005 introduces multiple scopes and permissions to help database administrators handle permissions. The new authorization model separates the world into principals and securables. Every SQL Server securable has associated permissions that can be granted to a principal. Principals, such as individuals, groups, or applications can access securables. Securables are the resources to which the SQL Server authorization system regulates access. As we already stated, there are three securable scopes: server, database, and schema, which contain other securables, such as SQL Server login, database users, tables, and stored procedures.

GRANT Statement

The GRANT statement grants permissions to SQL Server securables. The syntax of the GRANT statement is

```
GRANT permission_list [ON scope]
  TO principal_list [WITH GRANT OPTION]
  [ AS  {windows_group | sqlserver_login | db_user |db_role | appl_role } ]
```

permission_list specifies either statements or objects (separated by commas) for which the permissions are granted. **scope** specifies either a securable class or a securable name for which permission will be granted. **principal_list** lists all accounts (separated by commas) to which permissions are granted. The components of **principal_list** can be a Windows user account, SQL Server login, login or user account mapped to certificate, login mapped to asymmetric key, database user, database role, or application role.

NOTE

SQL Server 2000 divides all permissions into two permission groups: statement permissions and object permissions, which use slightly different syntax of the GRANT statement to grant permissions to Transact-SQL statements and database objects. SQL Server 2005 has a uniform syntax of the GRANT statement for both permission groups.

Table 12-3 shows all permissions with their description, as well as the list of the corresponding securables that you can apply to them.

NOTE

Table 12-3 shows only the most important permissions. SQL Server 2005 security model is hierarchical. Hence, there are many granular permissions that are not listed in the table. You can find the description of these permissions in Books Online.

Next we will demonstrate the use of the GRANT statement with several examples.

EXAMPLE 12.11

```
USE sample
GRANT CREATE TABLE, CREATE PROCEDURE
   TO peter, paul, mary
```

Example 12.11 demonstrates the use of the CREATE permission. In this example, the users **peter, paul**, and **mary** can execute the Transact-SQL statements CREATE TABLE and CREATE PROCEDURE. (As you can see from this example, the GRANT statement with the CREATE permission does not include the ON option.)

Example 12.12 allows the user **mary** to create user-defined functions in the sample database.

Permission	Applies to	Description
SELECT	Tables + columns, synonyms, views + columns, table-valued functions	Provides the ability to select (read) rows. You can restrict this permission to one or more columns by listing them. (If the list is omitted, all columns of the table can be selected.)
INSERT	Tables + columns, synonyms, views + columns	Provides the ability to insert rows.
UPDATE	Tables + columns, synonyms, views + columns	Provides the ability to modify column values. You can restrict this permission to one or more columns by listing them. (If the list is omitted, all columns of the table can be modified.)
DELETE	Tables + columns, synonyms, views + columns	Provides the ability to delete rows.
REFERENCES	User-defined functions (SQL and CLR), tables + columns, synonyms, views + columns	Provides the ability to reference columns of the foreign key in the referenced table when the user has no SELECT permission for the referenced table.
EXECUTE	Stored procedures (SQL and CLR), user-defined functions (SQL and CLR), synonyms	Provides the ability to execute the specified stored procedure or user-defined functions.
CONTROL	Stored procedures (SQL and CLR), user-defined functions (SQL and CLR), synonyms	This permission grants ownership-like capabilities on the grantee; the grantee effectively has all defined permissions on the securable. A principal that has been granted CONTROL also has the ability to grant permissions on the securable. CONTROL at a particular scope implicitly includes CONTROL on all the securables under that scope (see Example 12.17).
ALTER	Stored procedures (SQL and CLR), user-defined functions (SQL and CLR), tables, views	The ALTER permissions grant the ability to alter the properties (except ownership) of a particular securable. When granted on a scope, it also bestows the ability to ALTER, CREATE, or DROP any securable contained within that scope.
TAKE OWNERSHIP	Stored procedures (SQL and CLR), user-defined functions (SQL and CLR), tables, views, synonyms	The TAKE OWNERSHIP permission allows the grantee to take ownership of the securable on which it is granted.

Table 12-3 *Permissions with Corresponding Securables*

Permission	Applies to	Description
VIEW DEFINITION	Stored procedures (SQL and CLR), user-defined functions (SQL and CLR), tables, views, synonyms	The VIEW DEFINITION permission controls the ability for the grantee to see the metadata of the securable (see Example. 12.16).
CREATE (Server securable)	n/a	Transfers to the grantee the ability to create the server securable.
CREATE (DB securable)	n/a	Transfers to the grantee the ability to create the database securable.

Table 12-3   *Permissions with Corresponding Securables* (continued)

EXAMPLE 12.12

```
USE sample
GRANT CREATE FUNCTION
    TO mary
```

The following example shows the use of the ALL clause. This clause indicates that all permissions applicable to the specified securable will be granted to the specified principal.

EXAMPLE 12.13

```
USE sample
GRANT ALL
    TO mary
```

In Example 12.13, the user **mary** can use all allowed Transact-SQL statements in the sample database.

The following example shows the use of the SELECT permission within the GRANT statement.

EXAMPLE 12.14

```
USE sample
GRANT SELECT ON employee
    TO peter, mary
```

In Example 12.14, the users **peter** and **mary** can read rows from the **employee** table.

> **NOTE**
>
> *When a permission is granted to a Windows user account or a database user account, this account is the only account affected by the permission. On the other hand, if a permission is granted to a group or role, the permission affects all users belonging to the group (role).*

By default, if user A grants a permission to user B, then user B can only use the permission to execute the Transact-SQL statement listed in the GRANT statement. The WITH GRANT OPTION gives user B the additional capability of granting the privilege to other users (see Example 12.18).

The following example shows the use of the UPDATE permission within the GRANT statement.

EXAMPLE 12.15

```
USE sample
GRANT UPDATE ON works_on (emp_no, enter_date)
   TO paul
```

In Example 12.15, the user **paul** can modify two columns of the **works_on** table: **emp_no** and **enter_date**.

The following example shows the use of the VIEW DEFINITION permission.

EXAMPLE 12.16

```
USE sample
GRANT VIEW DEFINITION ON OBJECT::employee TO peter
GRANT VIEW DEFINITION ON SCHEMA::dbo to peter
```

Example 12.16 shows two GRANT statements concerning the VIEW DEFINITION permission. The first one allows the user **peter** to see metadata concerning the **employee** table of the sample database. (The OBJECT securable is one of the base securables, and you can use this securable to give permissions for specific objects, such as tables, views, and stored procedures.) Because of the hierarchical structure of securables, you can use a "higher" securable to extend the VIEW DEFINITION (or any other base) permission. The second statement in Example 12.16 gives the user **peter** access to metadata of all the objects of the **dbo** schema of the sample database.

> **NOTE**
> *In previous versions of SQL Server, it is possible to query information on all database objects, even if these objects are owned by another user. The VIEW DEFINITION permission now allows you to grant or deny access to different pieces of your metadata and hence to decide which part of metadata is visible for other users.*

The following example shows the use of the CONTROL permission.

EXAMPLE 12.17

```
USE sample
GRANT CONTROL ON DATABASE::sample TO peter
```

In Example 12.17 the user **peter** effectively has all defined permissions on the securable (in this case, the sample database.). A principal that has been granted CONTROL also implicitly has the ability to grant permissions on the securable, i.e., the CONTROL permission includes the WITH GRANT OPTION clause (see the following example). The CONTROL permission is the highest permission in relation to several base securables. For this reason, CONTROL at a particular scope implicitly includes CONTROL on all the securables under that scope. Therefore, **peter's** CONTROL permission on the sample database implies all permissions on this database, all permissions on all assemblies in the database, all permissions on all schemas in the sample database, and all permissions on objects within the sample database.

The following example shows the use of the WITH GRANT OPTION clause of the GRANT statement.

EXAMPLE 12.18

```
USE sample
GRANT SELECT ON works_on
  TO mary
  WITH GRANT OPTION
```

In Example 12.18, the user **mary** can use the SELECT statement to retrieve rows from the **works_on** table and also may grant this privilege to other users of the current database.

DENY Statement

The DENY statement prevents users from performing actions. This means that it removes existing permissions from user accounts or prevents users from gaining permissions through their group/role membership that might be granted in the future. This statement has the following syntax form:

```
DENY permission_list [ON scope]
    TO principal_list [CASCADE]
    [ AS  {windows_group | sqlserver_login | db_user |db_role | appl_role } ]
```

All options of the DENY statement have the same logical meaning that the options with the same name in the GRANT statement. The only difference is the CASCADE option. This option specifies that permissions will be denied to user A and any other users to whom user A passed this permission. (If the CASCADE option is not specified in the DENY statement and the corresponding object permission was granted with the WITH GRANT OPTION, an error is returned.)

The DENY statement prevents the user, group, or role from gaining access to the permission granted through their group or role membership. This means that if a user belongs to a group (or role) and the granted permission for the group is denied to him or her, this user will be the only one of the group who cannot use this permission. On the other hand, if a permission is denied for a whole group, all members of the group will be denied the permission.

NOTE

You can think of the GRANT statement as a "positive" and the DENY statement as a "negative" user authorization. Usually, the DENY statement is used to deny already-existing permissions for groups (roles) to a few members of the group.

EXAMPLE 12.19

```
USE sample
DENY CREATE TABLE, CREATE PROCEDURE
    TO peter, paul
```

The DENY statement in Example 12.19 denies two already-granted statement permissions (Example 12.12) to the users **peter** and **paul**.

EXAMPLE 12.20

```
USE sample
GRANT SELECT ON project
  TO PUBLIC
DENY SELECT ON project
    TO peter, mary
```

Example 12.20 shows the negative authorization of some users of the current database. First, the retrieval of all rows of the **project** table is granted to all users of the sample database. After that, this permission is denied to two users: **peter** and **mary**.

REVOKE Statement

The REVOKE statement removes one or more already-granted (or denied) permissions. This statement has the following syntax:

```
REVOKE [GRANT OPTION FOR] permission_list [ON scope]
  FROM principal_list [CASCADE]
  [ AS  {windows_group | sqlserver_login | db_user |db_role | appl_role } ]
```

The only new option in the REVOKE statement is GRANT OPTION FOR. (All other options have the same logical meaning as the options with the same names in the GRANT or DENY statement.) GRANT OPTION FOR is used to remove the effects of the WITH GRANT OPTION in the corresponding GRANT statement. This means that the user will still have the previously granted permissions but will no longer be able to grant the permission to other users.

NOTE

The REVOKE statement revokes "positive" permissions specified with the GRANT statement as well as "negative" permissions generated by the DENY statement. Therefore, its function is to neutralize the specified (positive or negative) permissions.

EXAMPLE 12.21

```
USE sample
REVOKE SELECT ON project
  FROM PUBLIC
```

The REVOKE statement in Example 12.21 revokes the granted permission for the **public** role. At the same time, the existing "negative" permissions for the users **peter** and **mary** are not revoked (Example 12.20), because the explicitly granted or denied permissions are not affected by revoking permissions from roles or groups.

Views and Data Access

As already stated in Chapter 10, views can be used for the following purposes:

- ▶ To restrict the use of particular columns and/or rows of tables
- ▶ To hide the details of complicated queries
- ▶ To restrict inserted and updated values to certain ranges

Restricting the use of particular columns and/or rows means that the view mechanism of SQL Server provides itself with the control of data access. For example, if the table with employee data also contains the salaries of each employee, then access to these salaries can be restricted using a view that accesses all columns of the table except the **salary** column. Subsequently, retrieval of data from the table can be granted to all users of the database using the view, while only a small number of (privileged) users will have the same permission for all data of the table.

Examples 12.22, 12.23, and 12.24 show the use of views to restrict the access to data.

EXAMPLE 12.22

```
USE sample
GO
CREATE VIEW v_without_budget
   AS SELECT project_no, project_name
         FROM project
```

Using the **v_without_budget** view, it is possible to divide users into two groups: first, the group of privileged users who can read (write) the budget of all projects and second, the group of common users who can read all rows from the **projects** table, but not the data from the **budget** column.

EXAMPLE 12.23

```
USE sample
GO
ALTER TABLE employee
```

```
        ADD user_name CHAR(60) DEFAULT SYSTEM_USER
GO
CREATE VIEW v_my_rows
      AS SELECT emp_no, emp_fname, emp_lname, dept_no
          FROM employee
          WHERE user_name = SYSTEM_USER
```

NOTE

The Transact-SQL statements in Example 12.23 must be separately executed, because the CREATE VIEW statement must be the first statement in the batch. That is why the GO statement is used (to mark the end of the first batch).

The schema of the **employee** table is modified in Example 12.23 by adding the new column **user_name**. Every time a new row is inserted into the **employee** table, the current value of the system user name is inserted into the **user_name** column. After the creation of the corresponding view **v_my_rows**, a user can retrieve only the rows that she inserted into the table. (The same is true for the UPDATE statement.)

EXAMPLE 12.24

```
        USE sample
GO
CREATE VIEW v_analyst
  AS SELECT employee.emp_no, emp_fname, emp_lname
         FROM employee, works_on
         WHERE employee.emp_no = works_on.emp_no
         AND job = 'Analyst'
```

The **v_analyst** view represents a horizontal and a vertical subset (in other words, it limits the rows and columns that can be accessed) of the **employee** table.

Stored Procedures and Data Access

Stored procedures can also be used to restrict data access. The restriction of data access using stored procedures is based upon the property that the permission to execute a stored procedure is independent of any permissions for database objects that are referenced by the stored procedure. More precisely, granting permission to execute a stored procedure suffices if the owner of the stored procedure is also the owner of all the referenced database objects.

EXAMPLE 12.25

```
USE sample
GO
CREATE PROCEDURE analyst_data
AS SELECT employee.emp_no, emp_fname, emp_lname
      FROM employee, works_on
      WHERE employee.emp_no = works_on.emp_no
      AND job = 'Analyst'
```

In Example 12.25, users of the **analyst_data** stored procedure see a horizontal and a vertical subset of the **employee** table. Neither the SELECT permission for the **employee** table nor the same permission for the **works_on** table is needed to use this procedure. (The user must have only the EXECUTE permission for the **analyst_data** procedure.)

Conclusion

Security of a database system always concerns two topics:

► Authentication

► Authorization

Authentication specifies which user has been granted legitimate access to the database system. *Authorization* defines which privileges are valid for a particular user.
SQL Server can operate in one of two authentication modes:

► Windows

► Mixed

Windows authentication mode exclusively uses Windows user accounts to log in to the SQL Server system. Mixed mode allows users to connect to SQL Server using the Windows authentication or the SQL Server authentication.
SQL Server supports authorization with the following Transact-SQL statements: GRANT, DENY, and REVOKE.

SQL Server 2005 contains several new features in relation to security. The most important ones are the following:

► Separation of schemas and users

► New Transact-SQL statements, such as CREATE LOGIN, CREATE USER, and CREATE ROLE. (The corresponding ALTER and DROP statements exist, too.)

► Encryption hierarchy, with Service Master Key and Database Master Key

► The new authorization model that separates the world in principals end entities. Every SQL Server entity, i.e., securable has associated permissions that can be granted to a principal.

► Permissions hierarchy, with new permissions such as CONTROL, ALTER, and VIEW DEFINITION.

SQL Server provides a mechanism called a **trigger** that enforces general integrity constraints. This mechanism is discussed in detail in the next chapter.

Exercises

E.12.1

What is a difference between Windows authentication mode and Mixed mode?

E.12.2

What is a difference between a SQL Server login and database user account?

E.12.3

Create three new SQL Server logins called **ann, burt**, and **chuck**. The corresponding passwords are **abc, def**, and **fgh**, respectively. The default database is the sample database. After creating the logins, check their existence using SQL Server catalog views.

E.12.4

Using system procedures, create three new database names for the logins in E.12.3. The new names are **s_ann, s_burt**, and **s_chuck**.

E.12.5

Create a new user-defined database role called **managers** and add three members (see E.12.4) to the role. After that, display the information concerning this role and its members.

E.12.6

Using the GRANT statement, allow the user **s_peter** to create tables and the user **s_mary** to create stored procedures in the sample database.

E.12.7

Using the GRANT statement, allow the user **s_paul** to update the columns **lname** and **fname** of the **employee** table.

E.12.8

Using the GRANT statement, allow the users **s_peter** and **s_mary** to read the values from the columns **emp_lname** and **emp_fname** of the **employee** table. (Hint: create the corresponding view first.)

E.12.9

Using the GRANT statement, allow the user-defined role **managers** to insert new rows in the projects table.

E.12.10

Revoke the SELECT rights from the user **s_peter**.

E.12.11

Using Transact-SQL, do not allow the user **s_mary** to insert the new rows in the **projects** table either directly or indirectly (using roles).

E.12.12

Discuss the difference between the use of views and Transact-SQL statements in relation to SQL Server security.

E.12.13

Display the existing information about the user **s_mary** in relation to the sample database. (Hint: use the system procedure **sp_helpuser**.)

CHAPTER
13

Triggers

S QL Server provides a mechanism called a *trigger* for enforcing procedural integrity constraints. The introductory notes are followed by a description of triggers, which can be used to implement general constraints. Several examples show the main application areas for triggers. This chapter also describes how triggers can be implemented using Common Language Runtime (CLR).

Introduction

As previously stated in Chapter 4, a DBMS handles two types of integrity constraints:

▶ Declarative integrity constraints, defined by using the CREATE TABLE and ALTER TABLE statements

▶ Procedural integrity constraints (handled by triggers)

The use of the CREATE TABLE or ALTER TABLE statement in relation to triggers has several benefits, with simplicity as the most important one. This means, to implement a constraint using declarative constraints, only a few lines of code are necessary. On the other hand, to implement the same constraint using a trigger, some dozen (or more) lines of code are required (see Examples 4.7 and 13.4).

Another advantage of declarative integrity constraints occurs when a trigger is created after data is loaded into the table. In this case, the trigger checks only the subsequent violations of the specified integrity constraint. (The equivalent declarative constraint checks per default also if the existing data in the table violates the constraint.) Otherwise, triggers are more flexible than the declarative constraints, because *every* integrity constraint can be implemented using triggers. (The same is not true for declarative constraints.)

How Triggers Work

A trigger is a mechanism that is invoked when a particular action occurs on a particular table. Each trigger has three general parts:

▶ A name

▶ The action

▶ The execution

The action of a trigger can either be an INSERT, an UPDATE, or a DELETE statement. (Since SQL Server 2005, you can define an action for a data definition language statement, too.) The execution part of a trigger usually contains a stored procedure or a batch.

NOTE

SQL Server 2005 allows you to create triggers using either Transact-SQL or CLR programming languages such as C# and Visual Basic 2005. In this section we will describe the use of Transact-SQL to implement triggers. The implementation of triggers using CLR programming languages is shown at the end of the chapter.

A trigger is created using the CREATE TRIGGER statement, which has the following form:

```
CREATE TRIGGER [schema_name.]trigger_name
   ON table_name | view_name
 [WITH dml_trigger_option]
   {FOR | AFTER | INSTEAD OF} { [INSERT] [,] [UPDATE] [,] [DELETE]}
   [WITH APPEND]
   AS  sql_statement  | EXTERNAL NAME method_name
```

NOTE

The syntax shown above concerns only DML triggers. The DDL triggers have a slightly different syntax, which will be shown later in this chapter.

schema_name is the name of the schema to which the trigger belongs. **trigger_name** is the name of the trigger. **table_name** (**view_name**) is the name of the table (**view**) for which the trigger is specified.

The AFTER and INSTEAD OF are two additional options, which you can define for a trigger. (The FOR clause is the synonym for AFTER.) AFTER triggers fire after the triggering event occurs. INSTEAD OF triggers are executed instead of the corresponding triggering event. AFTER triggers can be created only on tables, while INSTEAD OF triggers can be created on both tables and views. For more information on using these two trigger types, see the corresponding sections later in this chapter.

The options INSERT, UPDATE, and DELETE specify the trigger action. (The trigger action is the type of Transact-SQL statement that activates the trigger.) These three statements can be written in any possible combination. (The DELETE statement is not allowed if the IF UPDATE is used.)

As can be seen from the syntax of the CREATE TRIGGER statement, the AS **sql_statement** specification is used to determine the action(s) of the trigger using the Transact-SQL language. (You can also use the EXTERNAL NAME option, which will be explained later in this chapter.)

NOTE

SQL Server allows multiple triggers to be created for each table and for each modification action (INSERT, UPDATE, and DELETE). By default, there is no defined order in which multiple triggers for a given modification action are executed. (See also the section "First and Last Triggers" at the end of this chapter.)

After the creation of the database, only the database owner, DDL administrators, and the table owner on which the trigger is defined have the authority to create a trigger for the current database.

When creating a triggered action, you usually must indicate whether you are referring to the value of a column before or after the effect of the triggering statement. For this reason, two virtual tables with special names are used to test the effect of the triggering statement:

- **deleted**
- **inserted**

The structure of these tables is equivalent to the structure of the table for which the trigger is specified. The **deleted** table contains copies of rows that are deleted from the triggered table. Similarly, the **inserted** table contains copies of rows that are inserted into the triggered table. If the trigger operates on an UPDATE statement, then the **deleted** table represents the data *before* modification, and the **inserted** table represents the data *after* modification.

The **deleted** table is used if the DELETE or UPDATE clause is specified in the CREATE TRIGGER statement. The **inserted** table is used if the INSERT or UPDATE clause is specified in the CREATE TRIGGER statement. This means that for each DELETE statement executed in the triggered action, the **deleted** table is created.

Similarly, for each INSERT statement executed in the triggered action, the **inserted** table is created.

An UPDATE statement is treated as a DELETE, followed by an INSERT. Therefore, for each UPDATE statement executed in the triggered action, the **deleted** and the **inserted** tables are created (in this sequence).

Application Areas for AFTER Triggers

As you already know, AFTER triggers fire after the triggering event has been processed. You can specify an AFTER trigger either by using the AFTER or FOR reserved keyword. AFTER triggers can be created only on base tables.

AFTER triggers can be used to perform the following actions, among others:

▶ Create an audit trail of activities in one or more tables of the database (see Example 13.1)

▶ Implement a (business) rule (see Example 13.2)

▶ Enforce referential integrity (see Examples 13.3 and 13.4)

EXAMPLE 13.1

```
/* The table audit_budget is used as an audit trail of activities
   in the table project */
    USE sample
    GO
    CREATE TABLE audit_budget
      (project_no CHAR(4) NULL,
       user_name CHAR(16) NULL,
       time DATETIME NULL,
       budget_old FLOAT NULL,
       budget_new FLOAT NULL)
    GO
    CREATE TRIGGER modify_budget
      ON project AFTER UPDATE
      AS IF UPDATE(budget)
      BEGIN
      DECLARE @budget_old FLOAT
      DECLARE @budget_new FLOAT
```

```
DECLARE @project_number CHAR(4)
SELECT @budget_old = (SELECT budget FROM deleted)
SELECT @budget_new = (SELECT budget FROM inserted)
SELECT @project_number = (SELECT project_no FROM deleted)
INSERT INTO audit_budget VALUES
(@project_number,USER_NAME(),GETDATE(),@budget_old, @budget_
new)
END
```

Example 13.1 shows how triggers can be used to implement an audit trail of the activity within a table. This example creates the **audit_budget** table, which stores all modifications of the **budget** column of the **project** table. Recording all the modifications of this column will be executed using the **modify_budget** trigger.

Every modification of the **budget** column using the UPDATE statement activates the trigger. In doing so, the values of the rows of the virtual tables **deleted** and **inserted** are assigned to the corresponding variables @**budget_old**, @**budget_new**, and @**project_number**. The assigned values, together with the user name and the current time, will be subsequently inserted into the **audit_budget** table.

NOTE

Example 13.1 assumes that only one row will be updated at a time. Therefore, it is a simplification of a general case in which a trigger handles multirow updates. The implementation of such a general (and complicated) trigger is beyond the introductory level of this book.

If the following Transact-SQL statement:

```
UPDATE project
SET budget = 200000
WHERE project_no = 'p2'
```

is executed, the content of the **audit_budget** table is as follows:

project_no	user_name	time	budget_old	budget_new
p2	Dbo	1997-06-06 11:51	95000.00	200000.00

EXAMPLE 13.2

-- The trigger total_budget is an example of using a trigger to implement a business
rule

```
USE sample
GO
CREATE TRIGGER total_budget
  ON project AFTER UPDATE
  AS IF UPDATE (budget)
   BEGIN
   DECLARE @sum_old FLOAT
   DECLARE @sum_new FLOAT
   SELECT @sum_old = (SELECT SUM(budget) FROM deleted)
   SELECT @sum_new = (SELECT SUM(budget) FROM inserted)
   IF @sum_new < @sum_old*1.5
     BEGIN
     PRINT 'The modification of budgets executed'
     END
   ELSE
     BEGIN
     PRINT 'No modification of budgets'
     ROLLBACK TRANSACTION
     END
   END
```

Example 13.2 creates the rule controlling the modification of the budget for
the projects. The **total_budget** trigger tests every modification of the budgets and
executes only such UPDATE statements where the modification does not increase
the sum of all budgets by more than 50 percent. Otherwise, the UPDATE statement
is rolled back using the ROLLBACK TRANSACTION statement. (This statement is
described in Chapter 14.)

EXAMPLE 13.3

```
USE sample
GO
CREATE TRIGGER workson_integrity
  ON works_on AFTER INSERT, UPDATE
  AS IF UPDATE(emp_no)
```

```
BEGIN
IF (SELECT employee.emp_no
    FROM employee, inserted
    WHERE employee.emp_no = inserted.emp_no) IS NULL
  BEGIN
  ROLLBACK TRANSACTION
  PRINT 'No insertion/modification of the row'
  END
ELSE PRINT 'The row inserted/modified'
END
```

The **workson_integrity** trigger in Example 13.3 checks the referential integrity for the **employee** and **works_on** tables. This means that every modification of the **emp_no** column in the referenced **works_on** table is checked, and any violation of the constraint is rejected. (The same is true for the insertion of new values into the **emp_no** column.) The ROLLBACK TRANSACTION in the second BEGIN block rolls back the INSERT or UPDATE statement after a violation of the referential constraint.

The trigger in Example 13.3 checks case 1 and case 2 for referential integrity between the **employee** and **works_on** tables. Example 13.4 introduces the trigger that checks for the violation of integrity constraints between the same tables in case 3 and case 4.

EXAMPLE 13.4

```
USE sample
GO
CREATE TRIGGER refint_workson2
  ON employee AFTER DELETE, UPDATE
  AS IF UPDATE (emp_no)
  BEGIN
  IF (SELECT COUNT(*)
     FROM WORKS_ON, deleted
     WHERE works_on.emp_no = deleted.emp_no) > 0
    BEGIN
    ROLLBACK TRANSACTION
    PRINT 'No modification/deletion of the row'
    END
  ELSE PRINT 'The row is deleted/modified'
  END
```

Application Areas for INSTEAD OF Triggers

INSTEAD OF triggers fire instead of the triggering event. They are executed after the corresponding **inserted** and **deleted** tables are created, but before any integrity constraint or any other action is performed.

INSTEAD OF triggers can be created on tables as well as on views. When a Transact-SQL statement references a view that has an INSTEAD OF trigger, SQL Server executes the trigger instead of taking any action against any table. The trigger always uses the information in the **inserted** and **deleted** tables built for the view to create any statements needed to build the requested event.

There are certain requirements on column values that are supplied by an INSTEAD OF trigger combined with an INSERT or UPDATE statement:

- ► Values cannot be specified for computed columns.

- ► Values cannot be specified for columns with the TIMESTAMP data type.

- ► Values cannot be specified for columns with an IDENTITY property, unless the IDENTITY_INSERT option is set to ON.

These requirements are valid only for INSERT and DELETE statements that reference a base table. An INSERT statement that references a view that has an INSTEAD OF trigger must supply values for all non-nullable columns of the underlying table. (The same is true for an UPDATE statement: An UPDATE statement that references a view that has an INSTEAD OF trigger must supply values for each view column that does not allow nulls and that is referenced in the SET clause.)

Example 13.5 shows the different behavior during insertion of values for computed columns using a table and its corresponding view.

EXAMPLE 13.5

```
USE sample
GO
CREATE TABLE orders
    (orderid INT NOT NULL,
     price MONEY NOT NULL,
     quantity INT NOT NULL,
     orderdate DATETIME NOT NULL,
     total AS price * quantity,
     shippeddate AS DATEADD (DAY, 7, orderdate))
GO
```

```
CREATE VIEW all_orders
  AS SELECT orderid, price, quantity, orderdate, total, shippeddate
  FROM orders
GO
CREATE TRIGGER tr_orders
  ON all_orders INSTEAD OF INSERT
  AS BEGIN
    INSERT INTO orders
      SELECT  orderid, price, quantity, orderdate
        FROM inserted
    END
```

An INSERT statement must specify a value for a view column that maps to a computed column in a base table. This can be avoided if you use an INSTEAD OF trigger (as in Example 13.5), because it can ignore this value by using an INSERT statement that inserts the values into the base table. (An INSERT statement that refers directly to the base table cannot supply a value for a computed column.)

First and Last Triggers

SQL Server allows multiple triggers to be created for each table or view and for each modification action (INSERT, UPDATE, and DELETE) on them. Additionally, you can specify the order of multiple triggers defined for a given event. Using the system stored procedure **sp_settriggerorder**, you can specify that one of the AFTER triggers associated with a table be either the first AFTER trigger or the last AFTER trigger executed for each triggering action. This system procedure has a parameter called **@order** that can contain three values:

▶ **first**

▶ **last**

▶ **none**

The value **first** for the parameter **@order** specifies that the trigger is the first AFTER trigger fired for a modification action. **last** specifies that the trigger is the last AFTER trigger fired for a triggering action. The value **none** specifies that there is no specific order in which the trigger should be fired. (This value is generally used to reset a trigger from being either first or last.)

Example 13.6 shows the use of the system stored procedure **sp_settriggerorder**.

EXAMPLE 13.6

> EXECUTE sp_settriggerorder @triggername = 'modify_budget',
> @order = 'first', @stmttype='update'

NOTE

There can be only one first and one last AFTER trigger on a table. The sequence in which all AFTER triggers, other than the first and last triggers, fire is undefined.

To display the order of a trigger, you can use the following:

▶ **sp_helptrigger**

▶ OBJECTPROPERTY function

The system procedure **sp_helptrigger** contains the **order** column, which displays the order of the specified trigger. Using the OBJECTPROPERTY function, you can specify one of the two following properties: **ExecIsFirstTrigger** and **ExecIsLastTrigger** as the value of the second parameter of this function. (The first parameter is always the identification number of the database object.)

NOTE

Because an INSTEAD OF trigger is fired before data modifications are made to the underlying table, INSTEAD OF triggers cannot be specified as first or last triggers.

DDL Triggers

SQL Server 2005 allows you to define triggers for DDL, and you can optionally define the scope to be an entire database or even an entire server, not just a single object. The syntax for DDL triggers is

```
CREATE TRIGGER [schema_name.]trigger_name
  ON { ALL SERVER | DATABASE }
  [WITH {ENCRYPTION | EXECUTE AS clause_name]
  {FOR | AFTER } { event_group | event_type}
  AS {batch  | EXTERNAL NAME method_name}
```

We will describe only those options that are new in the syntax of a DDL trigger. The DATABASE clause specifies that the scope of a DDL trigger is the current database. If specified, the trigger fires whenever **event_type** of **event_group** happens in the current database. The ALL SERVER option specifies that the scope of a DDL trigger is the current server.

event_group specifies a name of a predefined grouping of Transact-SQL language events. The DDL trigger fires after execution of any Transact-SQL language event belonging to **event_group**. **event_type** is the name of a Transact-SQL language event that, after execution, causes a DDL trigger to fire. You can find the list of all event groups and types in Books Online.

Example 13.7 shows a DDL trigger.

EXAMPLE 13.7

```
USE sample
GO
CREATE TRIGGER prevent_drop_triggers
  ON DATABASE  FOR DROP_TRIGGER
  AS PRINT 'You must disable "prevent_drop_triggers" to drop any trigger'
  ROLLBACK
```

The trigger in Example 13.7 prevents all users from deleting any trigger that belongs to the sample database. The ON DATABASE clause contains the DROP_TRIGGER event type, which prevents a deletion of any trigger.

Triggers and CLR

Triggers, as well as stored procedures and user-defined functions, can be implemented using Common Language Runtime (CLR). The following steps are necessary if you want to implement, compile, and store CLR triggers:

▶ Implement a trigger using C# (or Visual Basic 2005) and compile the program, using the corresponding compiler

▶ Use the CREATE ASSEMBLY statement to create the corresponding executable file

▶ Store the executable file as a SQL Server database object using the CREATE TRIGGER statement

The following examples demonstrate the steps listed above. Example 13.8 shows the C# source program, which will be used to implement the trigger from Example 13.1.

EXAMPLE 13.8

```csharp
using System;
using System.Data;
using System.Data.SqlClient;
using Microsoft.SqlServer.Server;
public class StoredProcedures
{
  public static void Modify_Budget()
  {
     SqlTriggerContext context = SqlContext.TriggerContext;
     if(context.IsUpdatedColumn(2)) //Budget
     {
        float budget_old;
        float budget_new;
        string project_number;
        SqlConnection conn = new SqlConnection("context
connection=true");
        conn.Open();
        SqlCommand cmd = conn.CreateCommand();
        cmd.CommandText = "SELECT budget FROM DELETED";
        budget_old = (float)Convert.ToDouble(cmd.ExecuteScalar());
        cmd.CommandText = "SELECT budget FROM INSERTED";
        budget_new = (float)Convert.ToDouble(cmd.ExecuteScalar());
        cmd.CommandText = "SELECT project_no FROM DELETED";
        project_number = Convert.ToString(cmd.ExecuteScalar());
        cmd.CommandText = @"INSERT INTO audit_budget
                VALUES(@project_number, USER_NAME(), GETDATE(),
                    @budget_old, @budget_new)";
        cmd.Parameters.AddWithValue("@project_number",project_number);
        cmd.Parameters.AddWithValue("@budget_old",budget_old);
        cmd.Parameters.AddWithValue("@budget_new",budget_new);
        cmd.ExecuteNonQuery();
     }
  }
}
```

NOTE

*You have to drop the trigger called **modify_budget** (see Example 13.1) using the DROP TRIGGER statement before you create the CLR trigger with the same name in Example 13.10.*

The **Microsoft.SQLServer.Server** namespace comprises all client classes that a C# program needs. **SqlTriggerContext** and **SqlFunction** are examples of the classes that belong to this namespace. Also, the **System.Data.SqlClient** namespace contains classes such as **SQLConnection** und **SQLCommand**, which are used to establish the connection and communication between the client and a database server. The connection will be established using the connection string "context connection = true":

> SqlConnection conn = new SqlConnection("context connection=true");

The instance of the SQL **TriggerContext** class called **context** allows the program in Example 13.8 to access the virtual table that is created during the execution of the trigger. The table stores the data that caused the trigger to fire. The **IsUpdatedColumn**() method of the **TriggerContext** class allows you to find out whether the specified column of the table is modified.

The C# program contains two other important classes: **SQLConnection** and **SQLCommand**. An instance of the former class is generally used to establish the connection to a database, while an instance of the latter class allows you to execute an SQL statement.

The statements

> cmd.Parameters.AddWithValue("@project_number",project_number);
> cmd.Parameters.AddWithValue("@budget_old",budget_old);
> cmd.Parameters.AddWithValue("@budget_new",budget_new);

use the **Parameters** property of the **SQLCommand** class to display parameters and the **AddWithValue**() method to insert the value in the specified parameter.

Example 13.9 shows the execution of the **csc** command. Using this command, you can compile the C# program in Example 13.8.

EXAMPLE 13.9

```
csc /target:library Example13_8.cs
/reference:"c:\Program Files\Microsoft SQL Server\MSSQL.1\MSSQL\Binn\
sqlaccess.dll"
```

You can find the detailed description of the **csc** command in Chapter 8 (see Example 8.11).

NOTE

*You enable and disable the use of the CLR through the **clr_enabled** option of the **sp_configure** system procedure. Execute the RECONFIGURE statement to update the running configuration value. (The **clr_enabled** option is disabled by default.)*

Example 13.10 shows the next two steps in creating the **modify_budget** trigger. (Use SQL Server Management Studio to execute these statements.)

EXAMPLE 13.10

```
CREATE ASSEMBLY Example13_8 FROM 'C:\Programs\Microsoft SQL
Server\assemblies\Example13_8.dll'
WITH PERMISSION_SET=EXTERNAL_ACCESS
GO
CREATE TRIGGER modify_budget ON project
AFTER UPDATE AS
EXTERNAL NAME Example13_8.StoredProcedures.Modify_Budget
```

The CREATE ASSEMBLY statement was explained in Chapter 8 (see Example 8.12). The CREATE TRIGGER statement differs from the same statement used in Examples 13.1 to 13.5, because it uses the EXTERNAL NAME option.

The EXTERNAL NAME option specifies that the code is generated using CLR. The name in this clause is a three-part name. The first-part name (**Example 13_8**) is the name of the assembly. The next one (**StoredProcedures**) is the name of the public class defined in Example 13.8, while **Modify_Budget** is the name of the method, which is specified inside the class.

The following example shows how the trigger in Example 13.2 can be implemented using the C# language.

NOTE

*You have to drop the trigger called **total_budget** (see Example 13.2) using the DROP TRIGGER statement before you create the CLR trigger with the same name in Example 13.12.*

EXAMPLE 13.11

```
using System;
using System.Data;
using System.Data.SqlClient;
using Microsoft.SqlServer.Server;
public class StoredProcedures
{
  public static void Total_Budget()
  {
    SqlTriggerContext context = SqlContext.TriggerContext;
    if(context.IsUpdatedColumn(2)) //Budget
    {
      float sum_old;
      float sum_new;
      SqlConnection conn = new SqlConnection("context
connection=true");
      conn.Open();
      SqlCommand cmd = conn.CreateCommand();
      cmd.CommandText = "SELECT SUM(budget) FROM DELETED";
      sum_old = (float)Convert.ToDouble(cmd.ExecuteScalar());
      cmd.CommandText = "SELECT SUM(budget) FROM INSERTED";
      sum_new = (float)Convert.ToDouble(cmd.ExecuteScalar());
      SqlPipe pipe = SqlContext.Pipe;
      if(sum_new < sum_old * 1.5)
        pipe.Send("The modification of budgets executed");
      else
      {
        System.Transactions.Transaction.Current.Rollback();
        pipe.Send("No modification of budgets");
      }
    }
  }
}
```

We will describe in detail only two new features, which are used in Example 13.11. The **SqlPipe** class belongs to the **Microsoft.SQLServer.Server** namespace and allows you to send messages to the caller, such as:

```
pipe.Send("The modification of budgets executed");
```

To set (or get) the current transaction inside a trigger you use the **Current** property of the **Transaction** class. In Example 13.11 we use the **Rollback**() method to roll back the whole transaction if the UPDATE statement increases the sum of all budgets by more than 50 percent.

The following example shows the creation of the assembly and the corresponding trigger based upon the C# program in Example 13.11. (The compilation of the C# program using the **csc** command as the intermediate step is necessary, but we omit it here, because it is analog to the same command in Example 13.9.)

EXAMPLE 13.12

```
CREATE ASSEMBLY Example13_11 FROM 'C:\Programs\Microsoft SQL
Server\assemblies\Example13_11.dll'
WITH PERMISSION_SET=EXTERNAL_ACCESS
GO
CREATE TRIGGER total_budget ON project
AFTER UPDATE AS
EXTERNAL NAME Example13_11.StoredProcedures.Total_Budget
```

The OUTPUT Clause

If you execute any of the statements in Chapter 7 concerning INSERT, UPDATE, and DELETE, you will see that the corresponding results contain only the text concerning the number of modified rows ("3 rows deleted", for instance). SQL Server 2005 supports the new OUTPUT clause, which can be used with the INSERT, UPDATE, and DELETE statements to display explicitly the rows, which are inserted or updated in the table or deleted from it.

The OUTPUT clause uses the **inserted** and **deleted** tables the same way triggers use them. This means that the **deleted** table is used with the DELETE or UPDATE statement, while the **inserted** table is used with the INSERT or UPDATE statement. Also, the OUTPUT clause must be used with the INTO clause to fill a table. For this reason, you use a table variable to store the result.

Example 13.13 shows how the OUTPUT clause works with a DELETE statement.

EXAMPLE 13.13

```
USE sample
DECLARE @del_table TABLE (emp_no INT, emp_lname CHAR(20));
DELETE employee
```

```
OUTPUT DELETED.emp_no, DELETED.emp_lname INTO @del_table
WHERE emp_no > 15000
SELECT * FROM @del_table
```

The result is

emp_no	emp_lname
25348	Smith
18316	Barrimore
29346	James
28559	Moser

First, we declare the table variable **del_table** with two columns: **emp_no** and **emp_lname**. This table will be used to store the deleted rows. The standard syntax of the DELETE statement is enhanced with the OUTPUT option:

```
OUTPUT DELETED.emp_no, DELETED.emp_lname INTO @del_table
```

Using this option, the system stores the deleted rows in the **deleted** table, which is then copied in the **@del** table variable. The final SELECT statement displays the result.

The following example shows the use of the OUTPUT option in an UPDATE statement.

EXAMPLE 13.14

```
USE sample
DECLARE @update_table TABLE
 (emp_no INT, project_no CHAR(20),old_job CHAR(20),new_job
CHAR(20));
UPDATE works_on
SET job = NULL
OUTPUT DELETED.emp_no, DELETED.project_no,
    DELETED.job, INSERTED.job INTO @update_table
WHERE job = 'Clerk'
SELECT * FROM @update_table
```

The result is

emp_no	project_no	old_job	new_job
25348	p2	Clerk	NULL
28559	p2	Clerk	NULL
9031	p3	Clerk	NULL
29346	p1	Clerk	NULL

In contrast to the previous example, Example 13.14 uses the values of the **deleted** table as well as the values of the **inserted** table to display the result of the UPDATE statement. The former is used to display the old values of the columns **emp_no**, **project_no**, and **job**, while the latter is used to display the modified values of the **job** column.

Modifying Trigger's Structure

SQL Server also supports the Transact-SQL statement ALTER TRIGGER that modifies the structure of a trigger. The ALTER TRIGGER statement is usually used to modify the body of the trigger. All clauses and options of the ALTER TRIGGER statement correspond to the clauses and options with the same name in the CREATE TRIGGER statement.

If you use the ALTER TRIGGER statement to alter an ordered trigger, the order of the (first or last) trigger is dropped. Use the **sp_settriggerorder** system procedure to specify the order of the trigger again.

The ALTER TRIGGER permissions default to members of the **db_owner** and **db_ddladmin** fixed database roles and to the table owner. In contrast to the permissions of the CREATE object statements, these permissions cannot be transferred.

The DROP TRIGGER statement removes one or more existing triggers from the current database.

Conclusion

A Transact-SQL trigger is a mechanism that resides in the database server and offers an alternative to the CREATE TABLE and ALTER TABLE statements for the implementation of integrity constraints. It specifies that when a modification of the table using an INSERT, an UPDATE, or a DELETE statement is executed, the database server should automatically perform one or more additional actions. (A trigger cannot be used with the SELECT statement.)

The next chapter discusses the features concerning SQL Server as a multiuser software system and describes the notions of transaction and locking.

Exercises

E.13.1

Using triggers, define the referential integrity for the primary key of the **department (dept_no)** table and the column with the same name, which is the foreign key of the **works_on** table.

E.13.2

With the help of triggers, define the referential integrity for the primary key of the **project (project_no)** table and the column with the same name, which is the foreign key of the **works_on** table.

E.13.3

Using CLR, implement the trigger from Example 13.3.

E.13.4

Using CLR, implement the trigger from Example 13.4.

14

Transactions

Transact-SQL Statements and Transactions

This chapter describes two related concepts: concurrency control and transactions. The chapter begins by explaining what a transaction is and by defining the Transact-SQL statements related to it. Locking, as a method to solve the problem of concurrency control, is discussed, along with the notions of isolation levels and deadlocks, which arise from the use of locking.

Introduction

If your SQL Server system is a single-user system, your database application programs can retrieve and modify data in the database without any restrictions. A single-user system is a special case of a DBMS, because usually many users and programs retrieve and modify data from a particular database. The situation in which several user application programs read and write the same data at the same time is called *concurrency*. Thus, each DBMS must have some kind of control mechanism to solve concurrency problems.

To demonstrate the possible concurrency problems, let's revisit the scenario from Chapter 1, which shows a problem that can arise if a DBMS does not contain such control mechanisms:

1. The owners of bank account 4711 at bank X have an account balance of $2,000.

2. The two joint owners of this bank account, Mrs. A and Mr. B, go to two different bank tellers, and each withdraws $1,000 *at the same time.*

3. After these transactions, the amount of money in bank account 4711 should be $0 and not $1,000.

Another general problem that can arise for a database system is different software and hardware errors. Every DBMS has a *recovery subsystem*, which is responsible for recovery from all kinds of software and hardware errors. This means that the recovery subsystem must return data in the database to a consistent state.

Both of these problems, concurrency and data recovery, are solved using transactions. (The recovery of data will be discussed in detail in Chapter 20.) A transaction specifies a sequence of Transact-SQL statements that build a logical unit. The following example will explain what a transaction is. In the sample database, the employee Ann Jones should be assigned a new employee number. The employee number must be modified in two different tables at the same time. The row in the **employee** table and all corresponding rows in the **works_on** table must be modified at the same time. (If only one of these tables is modified, data in the sample database would be inconsistent because the values of the primary key in the **employee** table and the corresponding values of the foreign key in the **works_on** table for Mrs. Jones would not match.)

EXAMPLE 14.1

```
USE sample
BEGIN TRANSACTION /* The beginning of the transaction */
UPDATE employee
   SET emp_no = 39831
   WHERE emp_no = 10102
   IF (@@error <> 0)
      ROLLBACK TRANSACTION /* Rollback of the transaction */
UPDATE works_on
   SET emp_no = 39831
   WHERE emp_no = 10102
   IF (@@error <> 0)
      ROLLBACK TRANSACTION
COMMIT TRANSACTION /*The end of the transaction */
```

The consistent state of data in Example 14.1 can be obtained only if both UPDATE statements or neither of them are executed. The global variable @@**error** is used to test the execution of each Transact-SQL statement. If an error occurs, @@**error** is set to a negative value and the execution of all statements is rolled back. (Definitions of the Transact-SQL statements BEGIN TRANSACTION, COMMIT TRANSACTION, and ROLLBACK TRANSACTION are given in the next section.)

NOTE

SQL Server 2005 supports exceptions. Instead of the global variable @@error, which we used in Example 14.1, you can use TRY and CATCH statements to implement exception handling in a transaction (see also Example 8.4).

Transact-SQL Statements and Transactions

There are six Transact-SQL statements regarding transactions:

▶ BEGIN TRANSACTION

▶ BEGIN DISTRIBUTED TRANSACTION

► COMMIT TRANSACTION

► ROLLBACK TRANSACTION

► SAVE TRANSACTION

► SET IMPLICIT_TRANSACTION

The BEGIN TRANSACTION statement starts the transaction. It has the following syntax:

BEGIN TRANSACTION [transaction_name]
    [WITH MARK ['*description*']]

transaction_name is the name assigned to the transaction, which can be used only on the outermost pair of nested BEGIN...COMMIT or BEGIN...ROLLBACK statements. The WITH MARK option specifies that the transaction is to be marked in the log. **description** is a string that describes the mark. If WITH MARK is used, a transaction name must be specified. (For more information on transaction log marking for recovery, see Chapter 20.)

The BEGIN DISTRIBUTED TRANSACTION statement specifies the start of a distributed transaction managed by the Microsoft Distributed Transaction Coordinator (MS DTC). A *distributed* transaction is one that involves databases on more than one server. The server executing this statement is the transaction coordinator and therefore controls the completion of the distributed transaction. (See Chapter 24 for a detailed discussion of distributed transactions.)

The COMMIT TRANSACTION statement successfully ends the transaction started with the BEGIN TRANSACTION statement. This means all modifications made by the transaction are stored on the disk.

NOTE

SQL Server also supports the COMMIT WORK statement, which is functionally equivalent to COMMIT TRANSACTION, with the exception that COMMIT TRANSACTION accepts a user-defined transaction name. The COMMIT WORK statement is supported in the SQL standard.

In contrast to the COMMIT TRANSACTION statement, the ROLLBACK TRANSACTION statement reports an unsuccessful end of the transaction. Programmers use this statement if they assume that the database might be in an inconsistent state. In this case, all executed modification operations within the transaction are rolled back.

NOTE

SQL Server also supports the ROLLBACK WORK statement, which is functionally equivalent to ROLLBACK TRANSACTION, with the exception that ROLLBACK TRANSACTION accepts a user-defined transaction name. The ROLLBACK WORK statement is supported in the SQL standard.

The SAVE TRANSACTION statement sets a savepoint within a transaction. A *savepoint* marks a specified point within the transaction so that all updates that follow can be canceled without canceling the entire transaction. (To cancel an entire transaction, use the ROLLBACK TRANSACTION statement.)

NOTE

The SAVE TRANSACTION statement actually does not commit any modification operation; it only creates a target for the subsequent ROLLBACK statement with the label with the same name as the SAVE statement.

Example 14.2 shows the use of the SAVE TRANSACTION statement.

EXAMPLE 14.2

```
USE sample
BEGIN TRANSACTION
INSERT INTO department (dept_no, dept_name)
    VALUES ('d4', 'Sales')
SAVE TRANSACTION a
INSERT INTO department (dept_no, dept_name)
    VALUES ('d5', 'Research')
SAVE TRANSACTION b
INSERT INTO department (dept_no, dept_name)
    VALUES ('d6', 'Management')
ROLLBACK TRANSACTION b
INSERT INTO department (dept_no, dept_name)
    VALUES ('d7', 'Support')
ROLLBACK TRANSACTION a
COMMIT TRANSACTION
```

The only statement in Example 14.2 that is executed is the first INSERT statement. The third INSERT statement in the example is rolled back by the ROLLBACK TRANSACTION **b** statement, and the other two INSERT statements are rolled back by the ROLLBACK TRANSACTION **a** statement.

> **NOTE**
>
> *The SAVE TRANSACTION statement, in combination with the IF or WHILE statement, is a useful transaction feature for the execution of parts of an entire transaction. On the other hand, the use of this statement is contrary to the principle of operational databases that a transaction should be as short as possible, because long transactions generally reduce data availability.*

Each Transact-SQL statement always belongs implicitly or explicitly to a transaction. An explicit transaction is specified with the pair of statements BEGIN TRANSACTION and COMMIT TRANSACTION (or ROLLBACK TRANSACTION). If BEGIN and COMMIT are not used, every DML statement builds its own transaction implicitly.

SQL Server provides implicit transactions for compliance with SQL standard. When a session operates in implicit transaction mode, selected statements implicitly issue the BEGIN TRANSACTION statement. This means that you do nothing to start such a transaction. However, the end of each implicit transaction must be explicitly committed or rolled back using the COMMIT (i.e., ROLLBACK) statement. (If you do not explicitly commit the transaction, the transaction and all the data changes it contains are rolled back when the user disconnects.)

To enable an implicit transaction, you have to enable the IMPLICIT_TRANSAC-TIONS ON option of the SET statement. This statement sets implicit transaction mode for the current session. When a connection is in implicit transaction mode and the connection is not currently in a transaction, executing any of the following statements starts a transaction:

ALTER TABLE	FETCH	REVOKE
CREATE TABLE	GRANT	SELECT
DELETE	INSERT	TRUNCATE TABLE
DROP TABLE	OPEN	UPDATE

In other words, if you have a sequence of statements from the list above, each statement will represent a single transaction.

Explicit transactions can be nested. In this case, each pair of statements BEGIN/COMMIT or BEGIN/ROLLBACK is used inside one or more such pairs. (The nested transactions are usually used in stored procedures, which themselves contain transactions and are invoked inside another transaction.) The global variable @@**trancount** contains the number of active transactions for the current user.

BEGIN, COMMIT, and ROLLBACK can be specified using a name assigned to the transaction. (The named ROLLBACK TRANSACTION statement corresponds either to a named transaction or to the SAVE TRANSACTION statement with the same name.) You can use a named transaction only in the outermost statement pair of nested BEGIN/COMMIT or BEGIN/ROLLBACK statements.

Transaction Logging

SQL Server keeps a record of each change it makes to the database during a transaction. This is necessary in case an error occurs during the execution of the transaction. In this situation, all previously executed statements within the transaction have to be rolled back. As soon as SQL Server detects the error, it uses the stored records to return the database to the consistent state that existed before the transaction was started.

SQL Server keeps all those records, in particular the before and after values, in one or more files called the *transaction log*. Each database of the SQL Server system has its own transaction log. Thus, if it is necessary to roll back one or more modification operations executed on the tables of the current database, SQL Server uses the entries in the transaction log to restore the values of columns that the database had before the transaction was started.

The transaction log is used to roll back or restore a transaction. If an error occurs and the transaction does not completely execute, SQL Server uses all existing "before" values from the transaction log (called *before images*) to roll back all modifications since the start of the transaction. For further details concerning transaction logs, see Chapter 20.

Locking

Concurrency can lead to several negative effects, such as the reading of nonexistent data or loss of modified data. Consider this real-world example illustrating one of these negative effects, called *dirty read*: The user U_1 in the personnel department gets an address change for the employee Jim Smith. U1 does the address change, but when controlling the bank account of Mr. Smith in the consecutive dialog step, he realizes that he modified the address of the wrong person. (The enterprise employs two persons with the name Jim Smith.) Fortunately, the application allows the user to cancel this change by pressing a button. User U1 presses the button knowing that he has committed no error.

At the same time, the user U_2 in the technical department retrieves the data of the latter Mr. Smith to send the newest technical document to his home, because the employee seldom comes to the office. As the employee's address was wrongly changed just before the user U_2 retrieved the address, he prints out the wrong label address and sends the document to the wrong person.

To prevent errors like these, every DBMS must have mechanisms that control the access of data by all users at the same time. SQL Server, like almost all relational DBMSs, uses locks to guarantee the consistency of the database in case of multiuser access. SQL Server gives an application program the ability to lock the data it needs, guaranteeing that no other program can modify the same data. When another application program requests the modification of the locked data, SQL Server either stops the program with an error or makes a program wait.

Lock Granularity

You can apply locks to the following database objects:

- ▶ Row
- ▶ Page
- ▶ Index
- ▶ Extent
- ▶ Table
- ▶ Database itself

A row is the smallest database object that can be locked. The support of row-level locking includes both data rows and index entries. Row-level locking means that only the row that is accessed by an application will be locked. Hence, all other rows that belong to the same page are free and can be used by other applications. SQL Server can also lock the page on which the row that has to be locked is stored. A user can determine which database object will be locked using the PAGLOCK, TABLOCK, and ROWLOCK hints in the SELECT statement. (The type of the object that is being locked is called *lock granularity*.) SQL Server automatically chooses the appropriate lock granularity.

Locking is also done on disk units, called *extents*, that are 64K in size (see Chapter 15). Extent locks are set automatically when a table (or index) grows and the additional disk space is needed.

Lock granularity affects concurrency. In general, the larger the lock granularity used, the more concurrency is reduced. This means that row-level locking maximizes concurrency because it leaves all but one row on the page unlocked. On the other hand, system overhead is increased because each locked row requires one lock. Page-level locking (and table-level locking) restricts the availability of data but decreases the system overhead.

If many page locks are held during a transaction, SQL Server upgrades the lock into a table lock. This process of converting many page-level locks into one table lock (or many row-level locks into one page lock) is called *lock escalation*. The escalation threshold is the boundary at which SQL Server applies the lock escalation.

Escalation thresholds are determined dynamically by SQL Server and require no configuration.

Concerning locks, a user can explicitly affect only the behavior of transactions that acquire a lock that conflicts with the existing lock for the same object. The SET LOCK_TIMEOUT statement can be used to specify the number of milliseconds a transaction will wait for a lock to be released. The value of −1 (the default value) indicates no time-out.

Kinds of Locks

SQL Server uses different kinds of locks depending on the database object that needs to be locked. At the row level and page level, there are three different types of locks:

- ▶ Shared (S)
- ▶ Exclusive (X)
- ▶ Update (U)

A shared lock reserves a database object (page or row) for reading only. Other processes cannot modify the locked object while the lock remains. On the other hand, several processes can hold a shared lock for an object at the same time—that is, there can be several shared locks for an object.

An exclusive lock reserves a page or row for the exclusive use of a single transaction. It is used for DML statements that modify the object (INSERT, UPDATE, and DELETE). An exclusive lock cannot be set if some other process holds a shared or exclusive lock on the object—that is, there can be only one exclusive lock for an object. Once an exclusive object is set for the page (or row), no other lock can be placed on the same object.

An update lock can be placed only if no other update or exclusive lock exists. On the other hand, it can be placed on objects that already have shared locks. (In this case, the update lock acquires another shared lock on the same object.) If a transaction that modifies the object is committed, the update lock is changed to an exclusive lock if there are no other (shared or exclusive) locks on the object. There can be only one update lock for an object.

Page-level locking also allows an intent lock; this is described shortly.

NOTE

Update locks prevent certain common types of deadlocks. (Deadlocks are described at the end of this chapter.)

Table 14-1 shows the compatibility matrix for shared, exclusive, and update locks. The matrix is interpreted as follows: Suppose transaction T_1 holds a lock as specified in the first row of the matrix, and suppose some other transaction T_2 requests a lock as specified in the corresponding column heading. In this case, "yes" indicates that a lock of the transaction T2 is possible, whereas "no" indicates a conflict with the existing lock.

NOTE

SQL Server supports other lock types in addition to those already discussed. Because of their complexity, these locks will not be covered in this introductory book.

At the table level, there are five different types of locks:

► Shared (S)

► Exclusive (X)

► Intent share (IS)

► Intent exclusive (IX)

► Share with intent exclusive (SIX)

The first two locks correspond to the row-level (or page-level) lock with the same name, respectively. Generally, an *intent* lock shows an intention to lock the next-lower object in the hierarchy of the database objects (see Example 14.3). Therefore, intent locks are placed at a level in the hierarchy above that which the process intends to lock. This is an efficient way to tell whether such locks will be possible, and it prevents other processes from locking the higher level before the desired locks can be attained.

Table 14-2 shows the compatibility matrix for all kinds of table locks. The matrix is interpreted exactly as the matrix in Table 14-1.

	Shared	Update	eXclusive
Shared	Yes	Yes	No
Update	Yes	No	No
eXclusive	No	No	No

Table 14-1 *Compatibility Matrix for Shared, Exclusive, and Update Locks*

	S	X	IS	SIX	IX
S	Yes	No	Yes	No	No
X	No	No	No	No	No
IS	Yes	No	Yes	Yes	Yes
SIX	No	No	Yes	No	No
IX	No	No	Yes	No	Yes

Table 14-2 *Compatibility Matrix for All Kinds of Table Locks*

SQL Server supports a configuration option called LOCKS that specifies the number of locks for your system. The default value 0 means that SQL Server assigns 2 percent of the memory it uses to locks. To change this advanced configuration option, use the **sp_configure** system procedure.

The most important system procedure concerning locks is **sp_lock**. This procedure displays information about the processes that hold locks. The syntax of **sp_lock** is

```
sp_lock  [spid_list]
```

where **spid_list** is the list of the ID numbers (maximum two) of SQL Server processes. If the list is omitted, SQL Server displays information about all active SQL Server processes.

Example 14.3 shows the use of the **sp_lock** system procedure.

EXAMPLE 14.3

```
USE sample
GO
SET SHOWPLAN_TEXT ON
GO
BEGIN TRANSACTION
UPDATE employee SET emp_lname = 'Robinson'
  WHERE emp_no = 28559
```

If there is a clustered index on the **emp_no** column of the **employee** table and the batch in Example 14.3 is executed, the **sp_lock** system procedure displays the result similar to the following output:

spid	dbid	objId	type	resource	mode	status
6	8	0	DB		S	GRANT
6	8	0	DB		S	GRANT
6	8	117575457	PAG	1:291	IX	GRANT
6	8	117575457	TAB		IX	GRANT

spid and **dbid** specify the process and database ID, respectively. The **type** column defines the lock type (DB = database, PAG = page, and TAB = base table). The most important column concerning locks is **mode**. In Example 14.3, it specifies that there is a shared lock for the entire (sample) database, an intent exclusive lock for the page numbered 1:291, and the same type of lock for the entire **employee** table.

The SELECT Statement and Locking

The FROM clause of the DML statements contains, among others, the following options concerning locking:

- ▶ UPDLOCK
- ▶ TABLOCK
- ▶ TABLOCKX
- ▶ ROWLOCK
- ▶ PAGLOCK

NOTE
There are some other options concerning isolation levels. These options are described in the next section.

UPDLOCK places update locks for each row of the table during the read operation. All update locks are held until the end of the transaction. TABLOCK (TABLOCKX) places a shared (exclusive) table lock on the table. All locks are held until the end of the transaction. ROWLOCK replaces the existing shared table lock with shared row locks for each qualifying row of the table. Similarly, PAGLOCK replaces a shared table lock with shared page locks for each page containing qualifying rows.

NOTE

All of the above options can be combined in any order if the combination makes sense. (For example, the combination between TABLOCK and PAGLOCK is senseless, because both options are applied to different database objects.)

Isolation Levels

Generally, a SELECT statement causes a shared lock to be placed on a row or page. This lock can be acquired only if no other transaction already holds an exclusive lock for that object. The availability of data in this case is rather low, because each read operation has to wait for a while. (In this case, the SET LOCK_TIMEOUT statement is set to –1, and there is no time out for the transaction.)

If data availability is an important issue, the isolation of read operations from the concurrent actions of other transactions can be loosened using isolation levels. An *isolation level* specifies the degree to which read operations of a program are isolated from the concurrent actions of other transactions. (Therefore, isolation levels are related to shared locks.)

SQL Server supports five isolation levels:

▶ READ UNCOMMITTED

▶ READ COMMITTED

▶ REPEATABLE READ

▶ SNAPSHOT

▶ SERIALIZABLE

READ UNCOMMITTED is the simplest isolation level, because it does not isolate the read operations from other transactions at all. When a transaction retrieves a row at this isolation level, it acquires no locks and respects none of the existing locks. The data that is read by such a transaction may be inconsistent. In this case, a transaction reads data that is updated from some other active transaction. If the latter transaction rolls back later, the former reads data that never really existed.

NOTE

The isolation level READ UNCOMMITTED is usually very undesirable and should only be used when the accuracy of read data is not important or the data is seldom modified.

A transaction that reads a row and uses the isolation level READ COMMITTED tests only whether an exclusive lock is placed on the row. If no such lock exists, it fetches the row. (This action prevents reading data that is not committed and that can be subsequently rolled back.) After reading the data values, data can then be changed by some other transaction.

Using the isolation level REPEATABLE READ, shared locks are placed on all data that is read, preventing other transactions from updating the data. This isolation level does not prevent another transaction from inserting new rows, which are included in subsequent reads, so the same SELECT statement can display different results at different times.

The isolation level SERIALIZABLE acquires a range lock on all data that is read by the corresponding transaction. Therefore, this isolation level also prevents the insertion of new rows by another transaction until the former transaction is committed or rolled back. (The SNAPSHOT isolation level will be discussed in the following subsection.)

NOTE

The isolation level SERIALIZABLE is implemented by SQL Server using a key-range locking method. This method locks individual rows and the ranges between them. A key-range lock acquires locks for index entries rather than locks for the particular pages or the entire table. In this case, any modification operation of another transaction cannot be executed, because the necessary changes of index entries are not possible.

Each isolation level in the preceding description reduces the concurrency more than the previous one. Thus, the isolation level READ UNCOMMITTED reduces concurrency the least. On the other hand, it also has the smallest isolation from concurrent transactions. SQL Server's default isolation level is READ COMMITTED.

An isolation level can be set using the following:

▶ The SET TRANSACTION ISOLATION LEVEL statement
▶ Several options in the FROM clause of the SELECT statement

The SET TRANSACTION ISOLATION LEVEL statement has five options with the same names and meanings as the standard isolation levels just described. The FROM clause in the SELECT statement supports seven options concerning isolation levels:

▶ READUNCOMMITTED
▶ READCOMMITTED

- ▶ REPEATABLEREAD
- ▶ SNAPSHOT
- ▶ SERIALIZABLE
- ▶ NOLOCK
- ▶ HOLDLOCK

The first five options correspond to the isolation levels with the same name. NOLOCK and HOLDLOCK are synonyms for READUNCOMMITTED and REPEATABLEREAD, respectively. The specification of isolation levels in the FROM clause of the SELECT statement overrides the current value set by the SET TRANSACTION ISOLATION LEVEL statement.

The DBCC USEROPTIONS statement returns, among other things, the current isolation level of the SQL Server process.

Row Versioning and Snapshot Isolation Level

Generally, database systems support two different concurrency control mechanisms:

- ▶ Pessimistic
- ▶ Optimistic

Pessimistic concurrency control locks resources as they are required, for the duration of a transaction. This mechanism is used by SQL Server by default and is explained in the previous sections of this chapter.

Optimistic concurrency control works on the assumption that resource conflicts between multiple users are unlikely, and it allows transactions to execute without using locking mechanism. Only when attempting to change data are resources checked to determine if any conflicts have occurred. If a conflict did occur, the application must read the data and attempt the change again.

SQL Server 2005 supports an optimistic concurrency control mechanism based on row versioning. When data are modified using row versioning, logical copies are maintained for all data modifications performed in the database. Every time a row is modified, database system stores a before image of the previously committed row values in the **tempdb** system database. Each version is marked with the transaction sequence number of the transaction that made the change. (The transaction sequence number is a number that is used to uniquely identify each transaction.) The newest version is always stored in the database and chained to the corresponding versions stored in **tempdb**.

Row versioning is used, among other things, to:

▶ Support the snapshot isolation level

▶ Support the read committed isolation level when the READ_COMMITTED_SNAPSHOT database option is enabled

▶ Build the **inserted** and **deleted** tables in triggers. (For the definition of these tables, see Chapter 13.)

The following subsections describe the snapshot and read-committed isolation levels.

Snapshot Isolation Level

The snapshot isolation level uses optimistic concurrency control to provide an alternate form to control concurrent accesses to a database. It differs from all other isolation levels that were described in the previous section. This isolation level has its foundation in row versioning, while all other levels are based on locks.

To enable the snapshot isolation level on the database level, set the ALLOW_SNAPSHOT_ISOLATION database option to ON. (If you want to set this isolation level inside a session, set the SET TRANSACTION ISOLATION LEVEL statement to SNAPSHOT.) When the option is set, versions are built for all rows that are modified in the database. These versions are held long enough to satisfy the requirements of the snapshot isolation level.

Row versioning isolates transactions from the effects of modifications made by other transactions without the need for requesting share locks on rows that have been read. However, exclusive locks are still needed: Transactions using the snapshot isolation level request locks when they modify rows. This reduction in the total number of locks acquired by snapshot isolation level significantly increases availability of data.

READ_COMMITTED_SNAPSHOT

Besides snapshot isolation level, there is also a form of read committed isolation level called READ_COMMITTED_SNAPSHOT, which also uses row versioning. The difference between the snapshot and read-committed isolation level is that the read-committed transaction does not use its own transaction sequence number when choosing row versions. Each time a statement is started, the read-committed transaction reads the latest transaction sequence number issued for that instance of the database system and selects the row based on that number.

Another difference is that read-committed isolation level allows other transactions to modify the data before the row versioning transaction completes. This can lead to a conflict if another transaction modified the data between the time the row versioning transaction performs a read and subsequently tries to execute the corresponding write operation. (For an application based on snapshot isolation level, the system detects the possible conflicts and sends the corresponding error message.)

Deadlock

A *deadlock* is a special situation in which two transactions block the progress of each other. The first transaction has a lock on some database object that the other transaction wants to access and vice versa. (In general, there can be several transactions, causing a deadlock by building a circle of dependencies.) Example 14.4 shows the deadlock situation between two transactions.

NOTE

The parallelism of processes cannot be achieved naturally using our small sample database, because every transaction in it is executed very quickly. Therefore, Example 14.4 uses the WAITFOR statement to pause both transactions for ten seconds and to simulate the deadlock.

EXAMPLE 14.4

```
BEGIN TRANSACTION                BEGIN TRANSACTION
UPDATE works_on                  UPDATE employee
   SET job = 'Manager'              SET dept_no = 'd2'
   WHERE emp_no = 18316             WHERE emp_no = 9031
   AND project_no = 'p2'         WAITFOR DELAY '00:00:10'
WAITFOR DELAY '00:00:10'         DELETE FROM works_on
UPDATE employee                     WHERE emp_no = 18316
   SET emp_lname = 'Green'           AND project_no = 'p2'
   WHERE emp_no = 9031           COMMIT TRANSACTION
COMMIT TRANSACTION
```

If both transactions in Example 14.4 are executed at the same time, the deadlock appears and the system returns the following output:

Server: Msg 1205, Level 13, State 40001

Your server command (process id #6) was deadlocked with another process and has been chosen as deadlock victim. Rerun your command.

As can be seen from the output of Example 14.4, SQL Server handles a deadlock by choosing one of the transactions as a "victim" (actually, the one that closed the loop in lock requests) and rolling it back. (The other transaction is executed after that.) A programmer can handle a deadlock by implementing the conditional statement, which tests for the returned error number (−1205) and then executes the rolled-back transaction again.

Users can affect the determined behavior of the SQL Server system concerning the choice of the "victim" by using the SET DEADLOCK_PRIORITY statement. If you use the LOW option of this statement for your process, it will be chosen for the victim, even if it did not close the loop in lock requests. (The default option is NORMAL.)

Conclusion

SQL Server, like all other DBMSs, solves the concurrency control problem by using transactions. A transaction is a sequence of Transact-SQL statements that logically belong together. All statements inside a transaction build an atomic unit. This means that either all statements are executed or, in the case of failure, all statements are canceled.

Concurrency can lead to several negative effects that SQL Server prevents using locks. The effect of the lock is to prevent other transactions from changing the locked object. The decision as to which database object should be locked is called lock granularity. Lock granularity affects concurrency because the narrower lock (row lock, for example) maximizes concurrency.

The next chapter concludes the second part of the book. It describes the overall environment of the SQL Server system.

Exercises

E.14.1

What is a purpose of transactions?

E.14.2

What is the difference between a local and a distributed transaction?

E.14.3

What is the difference between implicit and explicit transaction mode?

E.14.4

What kinds of locks are compatible with an exclusive lock?

E.14.5

How can you test the successful execution of each Transact-SQL statement?

E.14.6

When will you use the SAVE TRANSACTION statement?

E.14.7

Discuss the difference between row-level and page-level locking.

E.14.8

Does a user have the possibility of explicitly influencing the locking behavior of the system?

E.14.9

What is a difference between two basic locks (i.e., S lock and X lock) and an intent lock?

E.14.10

What does lock escalation mean?

E.14.11

Discuss the difference between the READ UNCOMMITTED and SERIALIZABLE isolation levels.

E.14.12

What is deadlock?

E.14.13

Which process is used as a victim in a deadlock situation? Can a user influence the decision of the SQL Server system?

E.14.14

Discuss the difference between pessimistic and optimistic concurrency control.

SQL Server System Environment

IN THIS CHAPTER

his chapter describes several SQL Server features that belong to the system environment. First, there is a detailed description of the SQL Server disk storage elements, system databases, and utilities. Then Unicode and national language support are explained. Multiple instance support is also discussed in this chapter. Finally, the architecture of the SQL Server system is discussed and illustrated.

Disk Storage

The storage architecture of SQL Server contains two units for storing database objects:

▶ Page

▶ Extent

The main unit of data storage in SQL Server is the page. The size of pages in SQL Server is 8K. Each page has a 96-byte header used to store the system information. Data rows are placed on the page immediately after the header. In SQL Server, a row cannot span two or more pages. Therefore, the maximum size of a single row is 8,060 bytes.

SQL Server has six distinct types of pages:

▶ Data pages

▶ Index pages

▶ Text/image pages

▶ Global allocation map (GAM) pages

▶ Page free space (PFS) pages

▶ Index allocation map (IAM) pages

NOTE

Data and index pages are actually physical parts of a database where the corresponding tables and indices are stored. The content of a database is stored in one or more files, and each file is divided in page units. Therefore, each table or index page (as a database physical unit) can be uniquely identified using a database ID, database file ID, and a page number.

When you create a table or index, SQL Server allocates a fixed amount of space to contain the data belonging to the table or index. When the space fills, SQL Server must allocate space for additional storage. The physical unit of storage in which space is allocated to a table (index) is called an *extent*. An extent comprises eight contiguous pages, or 64K. SQL Server has two types of extents:

► Uniform extents
► Mixed extents

Uniform extents are owned by a single table or index, while mixed extents are shared by up to eight tables or indices. A new table or index is always allocated pages from mixed extents first. After that, if the size of the table (index) is greater than eight pages, it is switched to uniform extents.

The following sections describe the first three types of existing pages. The discussion of GAM, PFS, and IAM pages is beyond the scope of this book.

Data Pages

Data pages are used to store data of a table. (The only data types that are not directly stored in data pages are values of columns of VARCHAR(MAX), VARBINARY(MAX), and text/image data types.) Each data page has the following three parts:

► Page header
► Space for data
► Row offset table

NOTE

Transaction log files do not contain data pages. Instead of pages, they contain a series of log records.

Page Header

Each page has a 96-byte page header used to store the system information, such as page ID, the ID of the database object to which the page belongs, and previous and next page in a page chain. As you may have already guessed, the page header is stored at the beginning of each page. Table 15-1 shows the information stored in the page header.

Page Header Information	Description
pageId	Database file number plus number of the page.
level	For index pages, the level of the page. (Leaf level is level 0, the first intermediate level is level 1, and so on.)
flagBits	Additional information concerning the page.
nextPage	Database file number plus page number of the next page in the chain (if a table has a clustered index).
prevPage	Database file number plus page number of the previous page in the chain (if a table has a clustered index).
objId	ID of the database object to which the page belongs.
lsn	Log sequence number.
slotCnt	Total number of slots used on this page.
indexId	Index ID of the page (0, if the page is data page).
freeData	Byte offset of the first available free space on the page.
pminlen	Number of bytes in fixed-length part of rows.
freeCnt	Number of free bytes on page.
reservedCnt	Number of bytes reserved by all transactions.
xactReserved	Number of bytes reserved by the most recently started transaction.
xactId	ID of the most recently started transaction.
tornBits	One bit per sector for detecting torn page write.

Table 15-1   *Information Contained in the Page Header*

Space Reserved for Data

The part of the page reserved for data has a variable length that depends upon a number and length of rows stored on the page. For each row stored on the page, there is an entry in the space reserved for data and an entry in the row offset table at the end of the page. (A data row cannot span two or more pages, except for values of VARCHAR(MAX), VARBINARY(MAX), and text/image columns that are stored in their own specific pages.) Each row is stored subsequently after already-stored rows, until the page is filled. If there is not enough space for a new row of the same table, it will be stored on the next page in the chain of pages.

For all tables that have only fixed-length columns, the same number of rows is stored at each page. If a table has at least one variable-length column (a VARCHAR column, for instance), the number of rows per page may differ and SQL Server then stores as many rows per page as will fit on it.

Row Offset Table

The last part of a page is tightly connected to a space reserved for data, because each row stored on a page has a corresponding entry in the row offset table. The row offset table contains two byte entries consisting of the row number and the offset byte address of the row on the page. (The entries in the row offset table are in reverse order from the sequence of the rows on the page.) Suppose that each row of a table is fixed-length, 36 bytes in length. The first table row is stored at byte offset 96 of a page (because of page header). The corresponding entry in the row offset table is written in the last two bytes of a page indicating the row number (in the first byte) and the row offset (in the second byte). The next row is stored subsequently in the next 36 bytes of the page. Therefore, the corresponding entry in the row offset table is stored in the third and fourth but last bytes of the page, indicating again the row number (1) and the row offset (132) (see Figure 15-1).

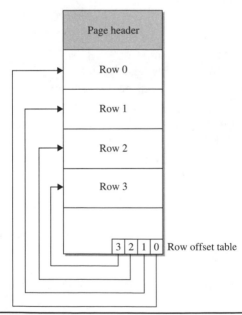

Figure 15-1   *The structure of a data page*

Large Objects

SQL Server supports five data types concerning large objects: VARCHAR(MAX), NVARCHAR(MAX), VARBINARY(MAX), TEXT, NTEXT, and IMAGE. A column of the VARCHAR(MAX), NVARCHAR(MAX), TEXT, or NTEXT data type contains values with textual data, and it is therefore used to store documents whose lengths exceed 8,000 bytes. The VARBINARY(MAX) and IMAGE data types can represent any data with a large amount of information, because they represent bit strings.

If a table contains one or more columns of these data types, the data are not stored with the data of other columns of the table. Only a pointer, which contains the physical address of the page where the text/image data is actually located, is stored with the data of other columns. All pages with the text/image data of a table are managed as a single unit and are therefore stored in one collection of pages. This means that one such page can hold data from different columns of a table if these columns contain text/image data.

A value of a column with large objects is stored in a collection of 8K pages that must not be located one after another. All pages are organized logically in a b-tree structure. The benefit of this implementation is that operations starting in the middle of the string perform better, because they can quickly move through the tree instead of making the scan through the page chain.

Index Pages

Index pages are used to store index values. An index page is almost identical to a data page. There are three kinds of index pages: leaf level for nonclustered indices, nonleaf level for clustered indices, and node level for nonclustered indices. The description of different forms of index pages is beyond the scope of this book. Although the structure of index pages is identical to the structure of data pages, they use a different locking mechanism. Locking of upper-level index pages is done by using latches, which are lightweight objects protecting actions that need not be locked for the duration of a transaction.

System Databases

During the installation of SQL Server, four system databases are generated:

▶   master

▶   model

▶   tempdb

▶   msdb

The **master** database is the most important database of the SQL Server system. It comprises all system tables that are necessary to work with the database system. For example, the **master** database contains information about all other databases managed by SQL Server, system connections to clients, and user authorizations.

The **model** database is used as a template when user-defined databases are created. It contains the subset of all system tables of the **master** database, which every user-defined database needs. The system administrator can change the properties of the **model** database to adapt it to the specific needs of his or her system.

The **tempdb** database provides the storage space for temporary tables and other temporary objects needed. For example, SQL Server stores intermediate results of the calculation of each complex expression in the **tempdb** database. The **tempdb** database is used by all the databases belonging to the entire system. Its content is destroyed every time the user process finishes or the system stops.

The information that allows SQL Server Agent to function is stored in the **msdb** database. This means the **msdb** database is used for storing alerts, jobs, and recording operators. (For a detailed description of the **msdb** database in relation to the SQL Server Agent, see Chapter 21.)

NOTE
*There is another system database, called the **distribution** database, that is installed on the distribution server in case data is replicated. (For more information on the distribution server and data replication, see Chapter 24.)*

Utilities

Utilities are components of SQL Server that provide different features such as data reliability, data definition, and statistics maintenance functions. All SQL Server utilities have two main properties:

▶ They are invoked using an operating system command.

▶ Each utility has several optional parameters.

This section describes the following SQL Server utilities:

▶ bcp

▶ osql

▶ sqlcmd

bcp Utility

bcp (Bulk Copy Program) is a useful utility that copies SQL Server data to/from a data file. Therefore, **bcp** is often used to transfer a large amount of data into a SQL Server database from another relational DBMS using a text file or vice versa. The syntax of the **bcp** utility is

> bcp [[db_name.]schema_name]table_name {IN | OUT|FORMAT} file_name
>   [{-option parameter} ...]

db_name is the name of the database to which the **table_name** table belongs. IN or OUT specifies the direction of data transfer. The IN option copies from the **file_name** file into the **table_name** table, and the OUT option copies from the **table_name** table to the **file_name** file. The FORMAT option creates a format file based on the options specified. If this option is used, the format option **–f** must also be used.

NOTE

The IN option appends the content of the file to the content of the database table, whereas the OUT option overwrites the content of the file.

Data to be copied can be either SQL Server-specific or ASCII text. The former is also called native mode and the latter the character mode. The parameter **–n** specifies the native mode, and the parameter **–c**, the character mode. The native mode is used to export and import data from one SQL Server system to another, and the character mode is commonly used to transfer data between SQL Server and other systems.

Example 15.1 shows the use of the **bcp** utility.

EXAMPLE 15.1

> bcp sample.dbo.department out empout.txt –c –U sa

The bcp command in Example 15.1 exports the data from the department table of the sample database in the output file empout.txt. The option –c specifies the character mode; thus, the data is stored in the ASCII file. The option –S specifies the server running the SQL Server system to connect to. (The default is the local server.) The option –U specifies the login ID used to connect to SQL Server. If the option –P (for password) is omitted, SQL Server prompts you to give the password for the specified login ID. Table following table shows the content of the file empout.txt:

d1	Research	Dallas
d2	Accounting	Seattle
d3	Marketing	Dallas

NOTE

*Be aware that the BULK INSERT Transact-SQL statement is an alternative to **bcp**. It supports all of the **bcp** options (although the syntax is a bit different) and offers much greater performance.*

To import data from a file to a database table, you must have INSERT and SELECT permissions on the table. To export data from a table to a file, you must have SELECT permission on the table. (For the description of INSERT and SELECT permissions, see Chapter 12.)

NOTE

*The **bcp** utility is an executable program that can be run from a command prompt. Hence, SQL Server Management Studio cannot be used to start this utility.*

osql Utility

The **osql** utility is an interactive Transact-SQL interface for SQL Server. It uses ODBC to communicate with the server. The general form of this utility is

    osql {option [parameter]} ...

where **option** is the specific option of the utility, while **parameter** specifies the value of the defined option. The **osql** utility has many options. The most important of these are described in Table 15-2.

EXAMPLE 15.2

    osql –S NTB11900 –U sa –i ms0510.sql –o ms0510.rpt

In Example 15.2, the system administrator of the SQL Server system named "NTB11900" executes the batch stored in the file "ms0510.sql" and stores the result in the output file "ms0510.rpt". The system prompts for the password of the system administrator because the option –P is omitted.

Option	Description
-S server_name	Specifies the name of SQL Server to which the connection is made. If this option is omitted, the connection is made to the database server set with the environment variable SQLSERVER. If this environment variable is not set, SQL Server tries to connect to the local machine.
-U login_id	Specifies the SQL Server login. The login must be created using the CREATE LOGIN statement. If this option is omitted, the value of the environment variable ISQLUSER is used.
-P password	Specifies a password corresponding to the SQL Server login. If this option is omitted, the value of the environment variable ISQLPASSWORD is used. If the variable is not set, the utility prompts for a password.
-c command_end	Specifies the command terminator. (The default value is "go".) This option can be used to set the command terminator to ";", which is the default terminator for almost all other database systems.
-i input_file	Specifies the name of the file that contains a batch or a stored procedure. The file must contain (at least one) command terminator. The sign "<"can be used instead of "-i".
-o output_file	Specifies the name of the file that receives the result from the utility. The sign ">" can be used instead of "-o".
-E	Uses a trusted connection (see Chapter 12) instead of requesting a password.
-e	Echoes each statement that runs as input.
-D option|datasource	Uses this option to connect to an ODBC data source. The option is either defined using the ODBC driver (**options**) or the connection uses the options defined in the data source (**datasource**).
-L	This option shows a list of all SQL Server instances found on the network.
-t seconds	This option specifies the number of seconds. The time interval defines how long the utility should wait before it considers the connection to the server to be a failure.
-?	Standard request for all options of the **osql** utility.
-p	Prints out the performance statistics for your queries.
-n	Removes numbering and the prompt symbol (>) from input lines.
-d dbname	Specifies which database should be a current database when **osql** is started.

Table 15-2   *Useful Options of the osql Utility*

sqlcmd Utility

sqlcmd is the new utility in SQL Server 2005. This utility allows you to enter T-SQL statements, system procedures, and script files at the command prompt. The general form of this utility is

        sqlcmd {option [parameter]} ...

where **option** is the specific option of the utility, while **parameter** specifies the value of the defined option. The **sqlcmd** utility has many options. The most important options are described in Table 15-3.

Option	Description
-S server_name[\instance_name]	Specifies the name of SQL Server and the instance to which the connection is made. If this option is omitted, the connection is made to the database server set with the environment variable SQLSERVER. If this environment variable is not set, SQL Server tries to connect to the local machine.
-U login_id	Specifies the SQL Server login. If this option is omitted, the value of the environment variable SQLCMDUSER is used.
-P password	Specifies a password corresponding to the SQL Server login. If neither the **-U** option nor the **-P** option is specified, **sqlcmd** attempts to connect by using Windows Authentication mode. Authentication is based on the account of the user who is running **sqlcmd**.
-c command_end	Specifies the batch terminator. (The default value is "go".) This option can be used to set the command terminator to ";", which is the default terminator for almost all other database systems.
-i input_file	Specifies the name of the file that contains a batch or a stored procedure. The file must contain (at least one) command terminator. The sign "<"can be used instead of "-i".
-o output_file	Specifies the name of the file that receives the result from the utility. The sign ">" can be used instead of "-o".
-E	Uses a trusted connection (see Chapter 12) instead of requesting a password.
-e	Echoes each statement that runs as input.
-D option|datasource	Uses this option to connect to an ODBC data source. The option is either defined using the ODBC driver (**options**) or the connection uses the options defined in the data source (**datasource**).
-L	This option shows a list of all SQL Server instances found on the network.
-t seconds	This option specifies the number of seconds. The time interval defines how long the utility should wait before it considers the connection to the server to be a failure.
-?	Standard request for all options of the **sqlcmd** utility.
-n	Removes numbering and the prompt symbol (>) from input lines.
-d dbname	Specifies which database should be a current database when **sqlcmd** is started.

Table 15-3 *Most Important Options of the sqlcmd Utility*

Command	Description
:ED	Starts the text editor. This editor can be used to edit the current batch or the last executed batch. The editor is defined by the SQLCMDEDITOR environment variable. For instance, if you want to set the text editor to Microsoft WordPad, type: SET SQLCMDEDITOR = wordpad.
:!!	Executes operating system commands. Example: :!! dir (Lists all files and directories in the current directory.)
:r filename	Parses additional Transact-SQL statements and **sqlcmd** commands from the file specified by **filename** into the statement cache. It is possible to issue multiple **:r** commands. Hence, you can use this command for chaining scripts with the **sqlcmd** utility.
:List	Prints the content of the statement cache.
:QUIT	Ends the session started by **sqlcmd**.
:EXIT [(statement)]	Allows you to use the result of a SELECT statement as the return value from **sqlcmd**.

Table 15-4   *Most Important Commands of the sqlcmd Utility*

The **sqlcmd** utility supports several specific commands that can be used within the utility, in addition to T-SQL statements. Table 15-4 describes the most important commands of the **sqlcmd** utility.

The following example shows the use of the **exit** command of the **sqlcmd** utility.

EXAMPLE 15.3

```
1>use sample
2>SELECT * FROM project
3>:EXIT(SELECT @@rowcount)
```

This example displays all rows from the **project** table and the number 3, if the **project** table contains three rows.

Instances of SQL Server

SQL Server supports multiple instances of the database engine. An instance is a database server that does not share its system and user databases with other servers running on the same computer.

SQL Server supports two instance types:

▶ Default

▶ Named

The *default instance* of the database server operates the same way as the database servers in earlier versions of SQL Server, where only one database server without instance support existed. The computer name on which the instance is running specifies solely the name of the default instance. Any instance of the database server other than the default instance is called a *named instance*. To identify a named instance, you have to specify its name as well as the name of the computer on which the instance is running: for example, NTB11901\INSTANCE1. On one computer, there can be any number of named instances of SQL Server (in addition to the default instance). Additionally, you can configure named instances on a computer that does not have the default instance.

Although all instances running on a computer do not share most system resources (SQL Server and SQL Server Agent services, system and user databases, as well as registry keys), there are some components that are shared among them:

▶ SQL Server program group

▶ Development libraries

The existence of only one SQL Server program group on a computer also means that only one copy of each utility exists, which is represented by an icon in the program group. (This includes SQL Server Books Online, too.) Therefore, each utility works with all instances configured on a computer.

You should consider using multiple instances if:

▶ You have different types of databases on your computer

▶ Your computer is powerful enough to manage multiple instances

The main purpose of multiple instances is to divide databases that exist in your organization into different groups. For instance, if SQL Server manages databases that are used by different users (production databases, test databases, sample databases), you should divide them to run under different instances. That way you can encapsulate your production databases from databases that are used by casual or inexperienced users. A single-processor machine will not be the right hardware platform to run multiple instances of SQL Server, because of limited resources. For this reason, you should consider the use of multiple instances only with multiprocessor or clustered computers.

Unicode

Because SQL Server is used around the world, it has to be able to process the specific data of any language (or country). This means that users outside the United States can use characters of their own writing system. These users expect SQL Server not only to support the same basic set of features as the native language edition of the system, but also to achieve the same level of quality. This entire process of supporting national languages is called the *internalization* of the software.

Generally, the internalization of SQL Server affects the following components of the system:

- ▶ Selection of the character set
- ▶ Selection of the collating sequence
- ▶ Installation of country-specific error messages
- ▶ Specification of date and money formats

Character Encoding

A mix of standards governs how characters can be encoded. Some standards are 7-bit, called single-byte character sets; others are 8-bit, called multibyte character sets. SQL Server uses Unicode for character encoding.

The Microsoft operating systems previously supported mainly English and a few Western European languages. All code pages at that time were composed of 256 characters. Each character was represented by a 1-byte numeric value. Twenty-six letters of the English alphabet (both uppercase and lowercase forms), punctuation marks, Greek letters, line drawing characters, and ligatures were available. (A *ligature* is a combination of two or more characters used to represent a single typographical character.)

Every code page consists of two parts. The ASCII (American Standard Code for Information Interchange) characters range with a code from 0 through 127, and the extended characters in a specific code range from 128 to theoretically any number. (The latter is called High-ASCII code range.) The High-ASCII code range comprises accented characters and various symbols in a Western character set and ideographs in a Far Eastern code page. (An *ideograph* is a character of Chinese origin representing a word or a syllable that is generally used in more than one Asian language.) Each country is assigned one code page that includes its native characters in the extended character range.

Character Encoding Using Unicode

Unicode is a 16-bit character encoding method adopted by Microsoft Windows. This character encoding was developed, maintained, and promoted by the Unicode Consortium. Unicode comprises almost all characters used in computers today. This includes most of the world's written scripts, publishing characters, and mathematical and technical symbols. Some 35,000 code points have already been assigned characters. In addition to modern languages, Unicode covers languages such as classical Greek and Hebrew. A private-use zone of 6,500 code points is available to applications for user-defined characters.

In contrast to the first code pages, which were not designed with expansion in mind, Unicode is a uniform character encoding method. This means that with Unicode it is possible to process characters of different writing systems in one document. Therefore, Unicode eliminates the need for code that handles multiple code pages.

The Unicode standard directly addresses only encoding and interpreting text and not any other actions performed on the text. This means the Unicode standard does not describe how the identified code value will be rendered on screen or paper. (The software- or hardware-rendering engine of a computer is responsible for the appearance of the character on the screen or on paper.)

SQL Server Architecture

SQL Server is a highly scalable database system. This means that the same database engine can be installed and used in the same way on any computer, from a mobile laptop computer to an SMP (symmetric multiprocessor) computer. The low memory footprint of SQL Server allows it to be used with laptop computers and the Windows operating system. On the other hand, the use of SQL Server with SMP computers takes advantage of its multithreaded architecture.

Before explaining the architecture of SQL Server, let's take a look at the existing multiprocessor hardware architectures.

Multiprocessor Hardware Architectures

There are three approaches to the architecture of multiprocessor computers:

- ▶ Symmetric multiprocessing (SMP)
- ▶ Clusters
- ▶ Massively parallel processors (MPP)

Symmetric multiprocessing specifies a system in which several processors share the main memory and disks. (Such systems are also called shared-disk systems, because they share a single operating system instance that manages one or more disks.) SMP systems usually have a high-speed interconnect that connects all processors. The benefits of SMP systems are as follows:

- ▶ Easy administration
- ▶ Little reprogramming of the DBMS

An SMP system is easy to administer because it looks like one computer with one instance of the operating system. On the other hand, if SMP systems are scaled to many CPUs, they become more difficult to administer.

Generally, the DBMS does not need to be reprogrammed at all to be used with an SMP system if different processes are simply assigned to different CPUs. However, the DBMS is reprogrammed to support the multithreaded architecture, where the processes are divided into threads that help the DBMS take better advantage of SMP systems. (For a definition of a thread, see the next section.)

The disadvantage of an SMP system is its restricted scalability. This means that the number of processors that can be synchronized together is limited by the amount of main memory, which provides this task.

A *cluster* usually specifies a group of SMP computers that are connected through a network. The benefits of clusters are better scalability and reliability (i.e., clusters can tolerate failures of single computers because the remaining computers in the cluster can take over the processing).

MPP systems offer the most scalability. As with clusters, an MPP system specifies many computers that are connected using a network. Those systems are also called *shared-nothing* systems, because each processor has its own main memory, its own operating system, and its own DBMS. Although MPP systems offer outstanding scalability, they are difficult to administer.

NOTE

SQL Server supports SMP systems and clusters with shared disks. Despite this, SQL Server with SMP hardware suits databases of almost all sizes, because SMP implementations are improving steadily. This means that the number of processors and the power of each of them is growing. Also, memory speed is increasing, and bus management is improving. Because of these factors, SQL Server can manage the largest databases that exist.

Multithreading Architecture of SQL Server

SQL Server supports SMP systems using two special architectural features:

▶ N:1-architecture

▶ Native multithreaded processing

N:1-architecture defines the architecture of a DBMS, where N user application programs are executed using a single process (see Figure 15-2). In addition to N:1-architecture, there is also 1:1-architecture, where each user application starts one process. The disadvantage of the latter is that if the number of users increases, the performance of the system degrades, because at some point the main memory cannot manage all existing processes. (N:1-architecture is also called single-process architecture.)

SQL Server supports SMP systems using threads rather than processes. A *thread* is a part of a process that can be executed on its own. Therefore, threads are sometimes called *lightweight* processes. With threads, it is possible for a DBMS to work efficiently on several database applications using just a few processors. The reason is that a switch from one thread to a thread of another process can be executed significantly faster than a switch from one process to another.

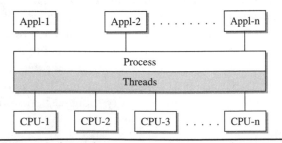

Figure 15-2   *The multithreaded, single-process architecture of SQL Server*

NOTE

Native multithreaded processing means that SQL Server supports multiprocessing using Windows threads. By using operating system threads, task scheduling within SQL Server is preemptive, and it allows dynamic load balancing across multiple CPUs.

SMP computers, together with SQL Server multithreaded architecture, are used to execute different database tasks in parallel. The following tasks, among others, can be parallelized using SQL Server:

▶ Data load

▶ Backup and recovery

▶ Query execution

▶ Index operations

SQL Server allows data to be loaded in parallel using the **bcp** utility or the BULK INSERT statement. The table into which the data is loaded must not have any indices, and the load operation must not be logged.

SQL Server can back up databases or transaction logs to multiple devices (tape or disk) using parallel striped backup. In this case, database pages are read by multiple threads one extent at a time.

SQL Server provides parallel queries to enhance the query execution. With this feature, the independent parts of a SELECT statement can be executed using several native threads on an SMP computer. Each query that is planned for the parallel execution contains an exchange operator in its query execution plan. (An *exchange operator* is an operator in a query execution plan that provides process management, data redistribution, and flow control.) For such a query, SQL Server generates a parallel query execution plan. Parallel queries significantly improve the performance of the SELECT statements that process very large amounts of data.

On multiple processor computers, Microsoft SQL Server 2005 automatically uses more processors to perform index operations, such as creation and rebuilding of an index. The number of processors employed to execute a single index statement is determined by the configuration option **max degree of parallelism** as well as the current workload. If the database engine detects that the system is busy, the degree of parallelism is automatically reduced before the statement is executed.

Conclusion

SQL Server is an enterprise relational DBMS that is superior to other DBMSs in two areas:

- ▶ Internalization of the database software
- ▶ Architecture of the database system

SQL Server is one of the first database systems to use Unicode as the future standard for the internalization of the software. Using Unicode, it is possible to process characters of different writing systems in one document, eliminating the need for code that handles multiple code pages. SQL Server also has a modern technology for using multiprocessor systems such as SMP computers. This technology is based upon the single-process architecture and native multithreaded processing.

This chapter closes the second part of the book. The next part is dedicated to system administration tasks of SQL Server. Chapter 16 introduces you to the general tasks of the system administrator and the SQL Server administration tools.

Exercises

E.15.1

What is a difference between a data and index page?

E.15.2

If you create a temporary database, where will its data be stored?

E.15.3

Discuss the benefits and disadvantages of multiple instances.

E.15.4

What does the notion of multithreading mean?

E.15.5

Which database management tasks can be parallelized using SQL Server?

SQL Server: System Administration

Overview of System Administration

T his chapter describes general issues concerning system administration and introduces you to the tools in the Microsoft SQL Server 2005 program group and tasks of the SQL Server administrator. At the end of the chapter we describe the new SQL Server 2005 component called SQL Computer Manager and dynamic management views.

Administration Tools

SQL Server is a high-performance DBMS that is scalable from laptops to clusters with shared disks. Additionally, SQL Server meets high-end requirements of distributed client/ server computing and supports both transactional as well as data warehouse database applications. SQL Server achieves all these goals by means of the following properties:

▶   Close integration with Windows operating systems

▶   Dynamic self-management and multisite management

▶   Job scheduling and alerting

As stated in the previous chapter, SQL Server supports multiprocessing using Windows threads. By using operating system threads, task scheduling within SQL Server is preemptive, and it allows dynamic load balancing across multiple CPUs. In addition, SQL Server uses several other Windows components, such as Performance Monitor and Event Viewer.

The system administrator's job in SQL Server has been significantly eased by the support of dynamic memory management and dynamic disk space management. The multisite management is supported through a Windows-based interface with visual drag-and-drop control that allows the creation and modification of server groups.

Using job scheduling and alerting, the system administrator can create different tasks (replication of data, command execution) and schedule them for execution at specified times. The execution of a task can be subsequently followed by e-mail and/or pager notification to one or more operators.

SQL Server also provides SQL Management Objects (SQL-SMO) to support enterprise-wide system administration. SQL-SMO (see Figure 16-1) is a collection of administration objects based on .NET Framework. SQL-SMO gives users full access to all features of SQL Server 2005. This new programming access layer is implemented as CLR managed code, so you can easily develop your solutions using Visual Basic 2005 or C#. (The previous programming access layer, SQL-DMO, remains in SQL Server 2005 for backward compatibility.)

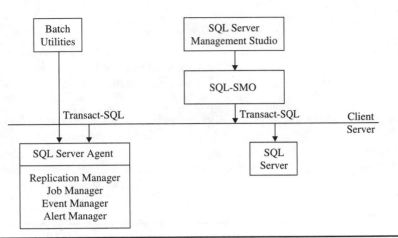

Figure 16-1   *Components of SQL-SMO*

MS SQL Server 2005 Program Group

SQL Server offers a lot of easy-to-use graphical interfaces that can be used by the system administrator to achieve administrative goals. These tools belong to the SQL Server program group. Table 16-1 describes all of the administration tools, which are covered in detail in other chapters as noted.

SQL Computer Manager

SQL Computer Manager is a new SQL Server 2005 tool. It is used to manage the services associated with several components of SQL Server and to configure the network protocols used by SQL Server. To start this tool, click Start | Microsoft SQL Server 2005 | Configuration Tools | SQL Computer Manager.

NOTE

SQL Computer Manager combines the functionality of the following SQL Server 2000 tools: Server Network Utility, Client Network Utility, and Service.

Starting, Pausing, and Stopping Services

You can use SQL Computer Manager to start, stop, pause, or resume different SQL Server services. The following services can be managed with this tool:

▶ Relational Database Services (MSSQLSERVER)

▶ SQL Server Agent

Tool	Description
SQL Server Management Studio	Used by both administrators and end users whose tasks are, among other things, to administer multiple servers, develop databases, and replicate data. (For more information on using Management Studio, see Chapter 2.)
Business Intelligence Development Studio	BI Development Studio is the main component of Analysis Services. Built on Visual Studio 2005, Development Studio supports an integrated development platform for system developers in the business intelligence area. Debugging, source control, and code development are available for all components of the BI application. This topic is discussed in detail in Chapter 27.
SQL Server Profiler	Used by the system administrator to monitor server activities such as connects and disconnects to the server and login attempts.
Database Engine Tuning Advisor	Database Engine Tuning Advisor is usually used together with Profiler to automate tuning process. This SQL Server component is described in detail in Chapter 22.
SQL Server Configuration Manager	SQL Server Configuration Manager is a tool to manage the services associated with SQL Server, to configure the network protocols used by SQL Server, and to manage the network connectivity configuration from SQL Server client computers.
SQL Server Surface Area Configuration	This tool helps you protect your server by allowing you to disable unnecessary services and protocols, as well as to disable unused features of SQL Server components.

Table 16-1 *SQL Server Administration Tools*

▶ Analysis Services

▶ Report Server

▶ Distributed Transaction Coordinator

To open a closed service (or vice versa), click **Services** and select the name of the service you want to open. Then right-click the service in the detail pane and select the status for the service you need. To view the properties of a service, right-click the service and select **Properties**.

Dynamic Management Views

Dynamic management views return server state information that can be used to monitor the status of a database server and to diagnose problems. All dynamic management views exist in the **sys** schema and have the same prefix: **dm_**. They provide information on internal disk structures and memory structures. There are two types of dynamic views:

- ▶ Server-scoped
- ▶ Database-scoped

Server-scoped dynamic views return information concerning the database server, while database-scoped views contain information in relation to the current database.

The most important property of dynamic management views is that they are continuously updated while a database is in use. In other words, such a view represents a pseudo table, which is built using internal system information each time it is accessed. (The most important dynamic management views are related to performance tuning. For this reason, we will describe several views in Chapter 22.)

Manage Network Protocols

SQL Computer Manager allows you to configure server and client network protocols, as well as connectivity options. This tool allows you to reconfigure the server connections so SQL Server listens on a particular network protocol and uses a proxy server to connect to SQL Server. Under Server Network Configuration you can select either **Protocols for MSSQLServer** or **Client Protocols**. To view one of the protocols (Shared Memory, TCP/IP, Named Pipes, VIA), right-click the protocol name in the detail pane and select **Properties**. To enable (disable) the protocol, select **Enable (Disable)**.

System Administrator

The system administrator's job consists of all tasks that are generally necessary to allow other users to work with the SQL Server system. These tasks are as follows:

- ▶ Planning the installation and installing SQL Server
- ▶ Starting and stopping the system
- ▶ Managing databases and transaction logs
- ▶ Backing up and restoring databases and transaction logs
- ▶ Troubleshooting SQL Server
- ▶ Tuning SQL Server
- ▶ Setting up and using data replication

These tasks are described in the following chapters of this part of the book. The next chapter explains the first two tasks: planning the installation and installing and starting the system. Managing databases and transaction logs is discussed in Chapter 18, while all aspects of system security (managing user accounts and assigning user permissions) are explained in Chapter 19. Chapter 20 discusses backing up and restoring databases and transaction logs. Job automation is explained in Chapter 21. SQL Server error messages and their resolution are also described in Chapter 21, while Chapter 22 discusses tuning and performance issues (also covered in Chapter 9). Chapter 23 covers another performance factor—table partitioning—while Chapter 24 explains all issues concerning data replication.

It can be difficult to separate system administration tasks from database administration tasks. For example, the deficit on disk storage space for a user-defined database can be either the task of the system administrator (if a new file has to be created for the database) or of the database administrator (if the ALTER DATABASE statement must be applied). Therefore, in this part of the book we shall make no distinction between system administration tasks and general database administration tasks.

Conclusion

The system administrator is primarily responsible for allowing all other database users the continuous use of SQL Server. On the other hand, SQL Server offers a lot of easy-to-use graphical utilities that can be used by the system administrator to achieve his or her goals.

The next chapter begins the discussion of singular administrative tasks. Before the installation of the system, the system administrator must plan this task very carefully. After that, the installation of the system must be done. The next chapter describes both of these tasks.

CHAPTER 17

Planning the Installation and Installing SQL Server

This chapter describes all tasks involved in the installation of the SQL Server system. First, the necessary steps in planning the installation are covered. This is followed by discussion of the actual installation of the database server. The last part of the chapter discusses several postinstallation steps and lists the different alternatives for starting, stopping, and pausing the system.

Planning the Installation

The specification of an installation plan should always precede the actual installation of the SQL Server system. Careful planning is absolutely necessary because several decisions have to be made before the installation of the system is started. The system administrator should have clear answers to the following questions before beginning the installation process:

- ▶ What is the purpose of the SQL Server system?
- ▶ What are the hardware and software requirements?
- ▶ How many users will be active at the same time?

Purpose of SQL Server

The purpose of the SQL Server system can be manifold. For example, you may use your system exclusively for education, or it may be a production system. In the case of production systems, you will need to make decisions concerning the number of users and amount of stored data, because these systems differ widely. Another decision concerning modern database systems is whether the system is used for operational or analytical tasks.

NOTE
SQL Server supports multiple instances of the database server. That way, you can use several instances for different purposes (production, education, testing).

If yours is a large database with a few hundred users, or if your system carries a heavy transaction load, performance of database operations will be an issue. In both cases, the use of symmetric multiprocessor (SMP) or cluster computers will be a general requirement to guarantee scalability and good response times of the relational DBMS. If you have a huge database, the purchase of enough disk storage could be the issue. In this case, SQL Server will usually perform better if you use several smaller disks instead of one or two large disks.

You must differentiate between systems used for operational goals (i.e., systems that require fast access and short transactions) and systems used for analytical goals (i.e., systems that use complex retrieval operations on huge databases), because both tasks cannot be optimally achieved using one database server. For this reason, SQL Server 2005 is bundled with Analysis Services. SQL Server is used for operational goals, whereas Analysis Services are used for analytical purposes. (For more information on Analysis Services, see Part IV of the book.)

Hardware and Software Requirements

The fact that SQL Server only runs on Microsoft operating systems simplifies decisions concerning hardware and system software requirements. The system administrator only has to meet the requirements concerning hardware and network.

Hardware Requirements

Windows operating systems are supported only on the Intel and compatible systems hardware platforms. Processor speed should be minimum 500MHz, but 1GHz or higher is recommended.

Officially, the minimum main memory is 512MB. However, almost everybody recognizes that such a minimal configuration will not perform very well, and as a general guideline, main memory of your computer should be at least 1GB.

Hard disk space requirements depend on your system configuration and the applications you choose to install.

Network Requirements

To connect to SQL Server Database Engine you must have a network protocol enabled. Microsoft SQL Server can serve requests on several protocols at once. Clients connect to SQL Server using a single protocol. If the client program does not know which protocol SQL Server is listening on, configure the client to sequentially attempt multiple protocols.

As a client/server database system, SQL Server allows clients to use different network protocols to communicate with the server and vice versa. During connectivity installation, the system administrator must decide which network protocols (as libraries) should be available to give clients access to the system. The following network protocols can be selected on the server side:

- ► Shared memory
- ► TCP/IP
- ► Named Pipes
- ► VIA (Virtual Interface Adapter) protocol

Connections to SQL Server from a client running on the same computer use the shared memory protocol. Shared memory has no configurable properties. This protocol is always tried first, and it cannot be moved from the top position of the **Enabled Properties** sublist in the **Client Protocols Properties** list.

Named Pipes is an alternative network protocol for SQL Server on the Windows platforms. After the installation process, you can drop the support for Named Pipes and use another network protocol for communication between the server and clients.

The Transmission Control Protocol/Internet Protocol (TCP/IP) network protocol allows SQL Server to communicate using standard Windows Sockets as the Internet protocol communication (IPC) method across the TCP/IP protocol.

NOTE

Microsoft SQL Server 2005 does not support the following protocols, which are supported by the previous version of the database system: Banyan Vines, Sequenced Packet Protocol (SPP), Multiprotocol, AppleTalk, or NWLink IPX/SPX. Clients previously connecting with these protocols must select one of the existing protocols to connect to SQL Server 2005.

SQL Server Editions

Before we start to discuss further installation steps, you have to know which kind of SQL Server 2005 exists. Microsoft supports four editions of SQL Server:

- ▶ SQL Server Express
- ▶ Workgroup Edition
- ▶ Standard Edition
- ▶ Enterprise Edition

SQL Server Express replaces Microsoft Desktop Engine (MSDE). This product should be used by application developers. For this reason, the product includes the basic Express Manager (XM) program and supports CLR integration and native XML. SQL Server Express is available as a free download at www.microsoft.com.

SQL Server 2005 Workgroup Edition is designed for small businesses and should also be used at the department level. Workgroup Edition provides relational database support without the business intelligence (BI) and high availability capabilities. This edition supports up to two processors and a maximum of 2 GB of RAM.

SQL Server 2005 Standard Edition includes support for clustering and database mirroring. Standard Edition provides a 32-bit version and 64-bit support for both x64 and Itanium-based systems. It also supports up to four processors and includes the full range of BI functionality: SQL Server Analysis Services, SQL Server Reporting Services, and Integration Services.

SQL Server 2005 Enterprise Edition is the special form of the SQL Server system, which is intended for time-critical applications with a huge number of users. In contrast to the Standard Edition, this edition contains additional features that can be useful for very high-end installations with symmetrical multiprocessors or clusters. The most important additional features of SQL Server 2005 Enterprise Edition are data partitioning, database snapshots, and online database maintenance.

Installation Recommendations

During the installation process, many specifications must be made. As a general guideline, it is better to familiarize yourself with their effects before running the Setup program. The following questions should be answered before the installation process is started:

- ▶ Where will the root directory be stored?
- ▶ Which security type will be used?

The root directory is where the Setup program stores all program files and those files that do not change as you use the SQL Server system. By default, SQL Server stores all program files in the subdirectory **Microsoft SQL Server**, although you can change this setting during the installation process. Using the default name is recommended.

As we already know from Chapter 12, there are two different authentication modes: Windows Authentication Mode and Mixed Mode. Windows Authentication Mode specifies security exclusively at the operating system level—that is, the way users connect to Windows operating system using their user accounts and group memberships. Mixed Mode allows users to connect to SQL Server using Windows security or SQL Server security.

Installing SQL Server

If you have done an installation of a complex software product before, you will probably recognize the uncertain feeling when starting the installation for the first time. This feeling comes from the complexity of the product to be installed and the diversity of questions to be answered during the installation process. Because you may not completely understand the product, you (or the person who installs the software) may be less than confident about giving accurate answers for the tasks that must be completed. This section will help you to find a way through your installation by giving you answers to most of the questions beforehand.

Beginning the Installation

To begin the installation, insert the SQL Server 2005 CD. Next, decide where you would like to save the extracted files. Then the **Install Shield** wizard extracts all necessary files from the CD and completes its task.

NOTE

If the Windows IIS is not installed on your computer, you must install it before continuing with the installation of the database system.

Before Starting the Setup Program

There are several tasks that you should complete before starting the Setup program. The best place to start is with the Release Notes. The benefit of Release Notes is that they contain the newest information, which is not provided in the Books Online. Read this information carefully to get a picture of features that are modified shortly before the delivery of the final release. (Release Notes also contain the list of bugs; it can be useful for you to know about some of them.)

Microsoft's web site could be an additional source for further information. As is the case with Release Notes, you can find many interesting documents on the web site. Especially important are white papers that Microsoft provides during the implementation of each new SQL Server version. On the Microsoft site, you can search for and download documents that are of interest to you.

Prerequisites

The prerequisites can be divided into hardware and software prerequisites. The hardware prerequisites were described at the beginning of this chapter. During the preinstallation phase, the Setup program checks to see which software prerequisites are missing and offers the installation of the missing ones (see Figure 17-1).

Potential Implementation Problems

In the next step, the SQL Server Installation wizard starts the system configuration check. During this step, the system is checked for potential installation problems, such as whether the minimum hardware requirements are fulfilled and IIS is installed (see Figure 17-2).

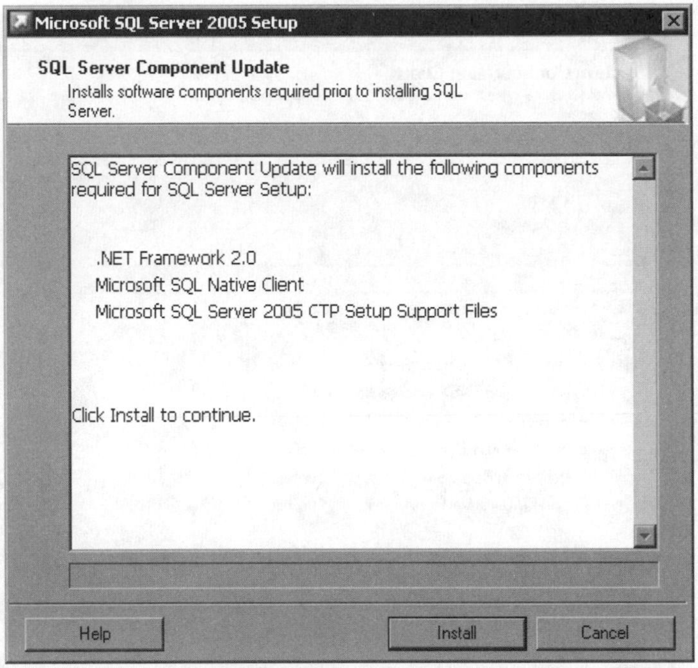

Figure 17-1   *SQL Server Component Update*

As you can see from Figure 17-2, the summary of all potential problems is reported. If any of the requirements is not fulfilled, the wizard reports whether the problem is a serious one or not. All errors as well as warnings are reported in the **Message** column of the window. If you click on the message, the system provides additional information concerning that potential problem. If an error is reported, you must follow the instructions in the corresponding message and then start the installation process again.

Install SQL Server 2005 Components

After you have installed all prerequisites, the Setup program prepares to continue with the installation. The next step requires the personalization of your installation—you must enter your name and the name of your company. Additionally, you must enter the Product key.

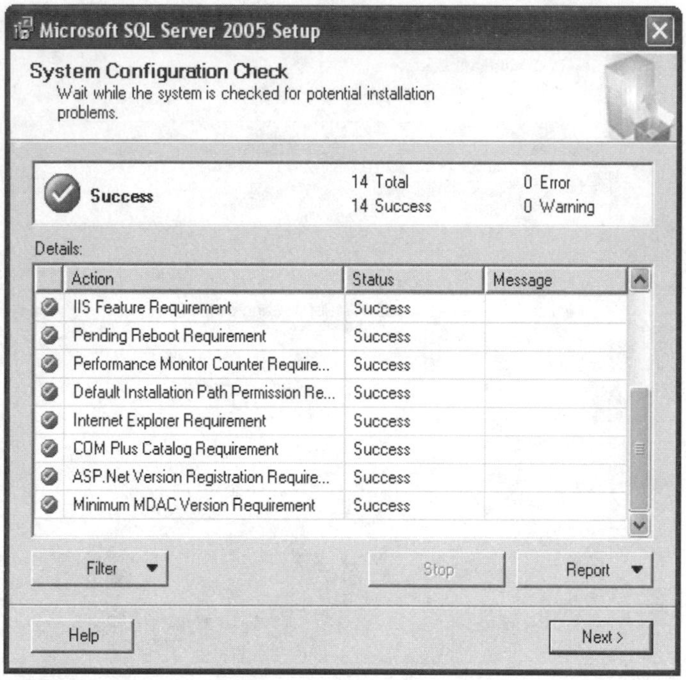

Microsoft SQL Server 2005 Setup ✕

System Configuration Check
Wait while the system is checked for potential installation problems.

✓ **Success**

| | 14 Total | 0 Error |
| | 14 Success | 0 Warning |

Details:

	Action	Status	Message	
◉	IIS Feature Requirement	Success		
◉	Pending Reboot Requirement	Success		
◉	Performance Monitor Counter Require...	Success		
◉	Default Installation Path Permission Re...	Success		
◉	Internet Explorer Requirement	Success		
◉	COM Plus Catalog Requirement	Success		
◉	ASP.Net Version Registration Require...	Success		
◉	Minimum MDAC Version Requirement	Success		

Filter ▼   Stop   Report ▼

Help   Next >

Figure 17-2 *System Configuration Check*

In the next step, you select all components that you want to install (see Figure 17-3). The following components can be installed:

▶ SQL Server Database Services

▶ Analysis Services

▶ Reporting Services

▶ Notification Services

▶ Integration Services

▶ Workstation components, Books Online, and development tools

NOTE

The list of components that displays may differ, depending on the SQL Server 2005 edition you want to install.

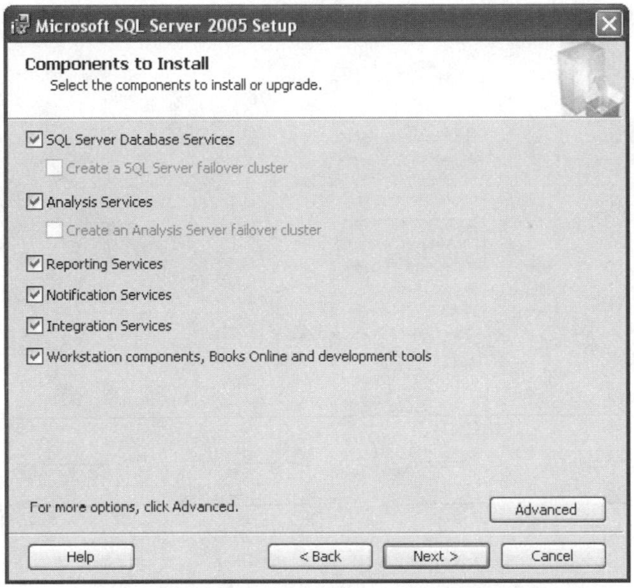

Figure 17-3 *Selection of components*

If you want to install additional components, such as sample database(s), click the **Advanced** button. The **Feature Selection** window appears (see Figure 17-4). Now you can make a refined selection of all components.

NOTE

*It is strongly recommended that you use the **Advanced** button. First, you should install at least both sample databases, **AdventureWorks** and **AdventureWorksDW,** by opening the **Feature Selection** window. Second, the system shows you how much KB (or MB) you need on your hard drive for the installation of each component. This information can help you decide what to install.*

In the next step, you can choose the folder where the root directory will be stored. We discussed this topic earlier in this chapter and recommended that you use the default directory. Next, the installation process allows you to install a default or named instance of the database server. SQL Server supports multiple instances, and each instance of the database server has its own set of database objects (system and user databases) that are not shared between different instances. Accept the installation of the default instance and continue the installation process with the assignment of Windows user accounts to different services (see Figure 17-5). All services can use either a local

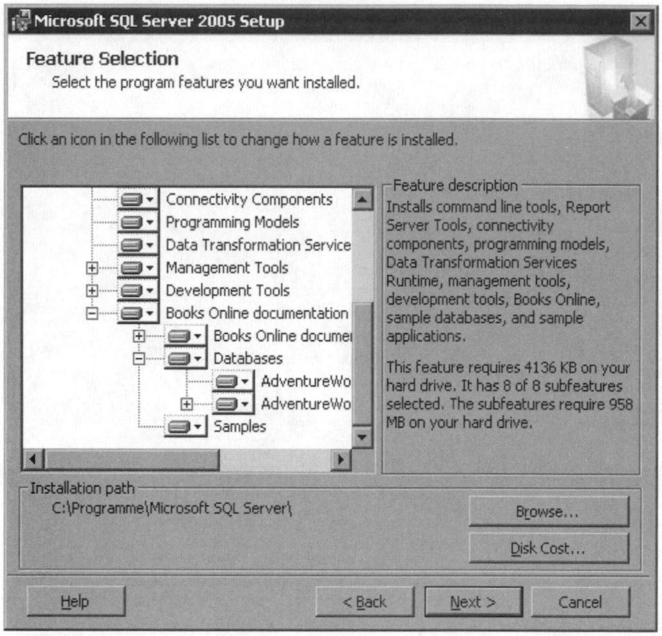

Figure 17-4 *The Feature Selection window*

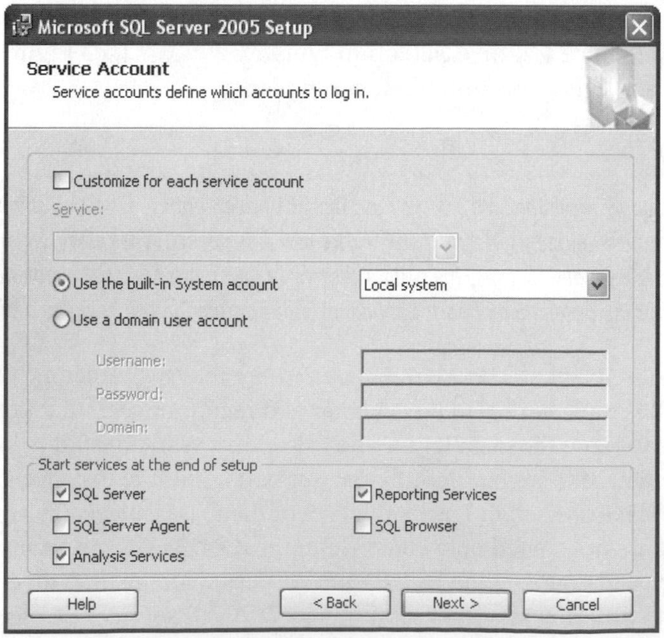

Figure 17-5 *The Service Account dialog box*

account or a domain account. If you select a domain user account, it allows the system to interact with different servers across a network and to perform such operations as data replication, which involves several computers. To specify different accounts for each service, click **Customize for each service account**, and then specify the corresponding account for the selected service.

In the same step, you may choose the **Auto-Start** service option, which allows you to change the running mode for the processes. By default, the processes must be manually started and stopped.

In the next step, you choose the authentication mode for your system. As we discussed earlier in this chapter, SQL Server 2005 supports Windows Authentication Mode and Mixed Mode. (Windows Authentication Mode is recommended, because it does not require passwords to be stored in connection strings.) If you choose Mixed Mode, you must enter the system administrator's password.

The choice of collation settings follows the selection of the authentication mode. Selection of the collating sequence defines the sorting behavior for your server. In the same step, you select one of the SQL collations, which are used for backward compatibility. In both cases we recommend that you select the default settings (Dictionary order, case-insensitive, for use with 1252 Character Set.)

If you selected Reporting Services as one of the components that must be installed, the next step is to specify how to install a report server instance. There are two alternatives:

▶ Install the default configuration

▶ Install but do not configure the server

In the former case, the report server is usable as soon as the Setup program is finished. In the latter case, you must configure the report server before you can use it. Figure 17-6 shows information about the default installation options.

The last step concerns error reports. You can automatically send error reports to Microsoft if you check the corresponding box. Also, you can send anonymous information about your hardware and software configuration by checking the Usage Report box.

At this time, the Setup program is ready to begin the installation. Figure 17-7 shows the components that will be installed. You can still change any of your installation settings by clicking **Back**.

The installation process is shown using the tabular representation. On the left side of the table, you can see the list of all products that will be installed. The second table

Figure 17-6 *Information concerning the default installation options*

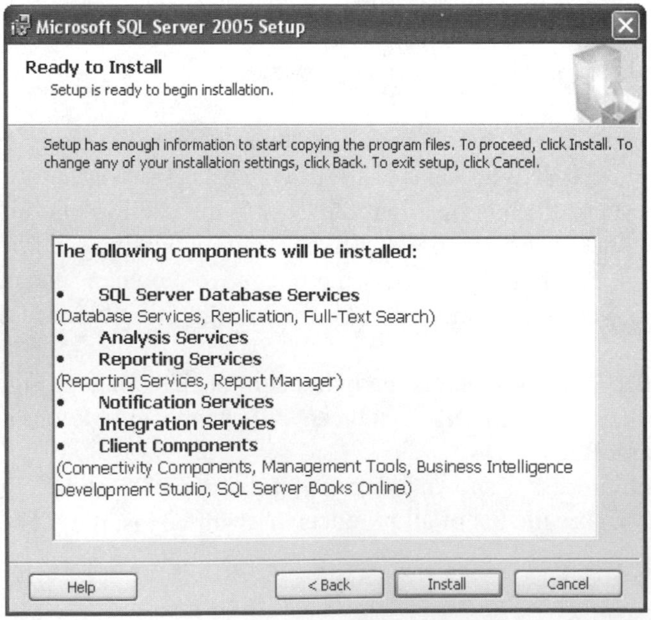

Figure 17-7 *The list of components that will be installed*

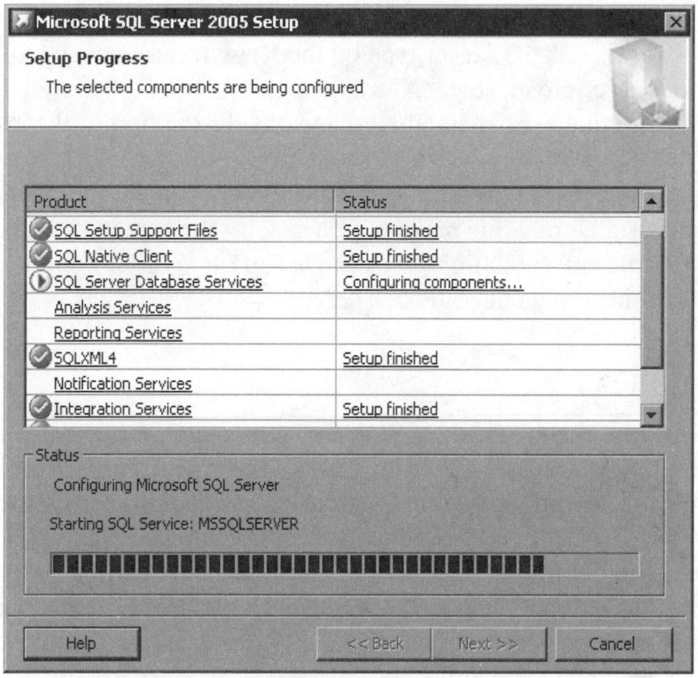

Figure 17-8   *The Setup Progress dialog box*

column lists the status of the components. As you can see from Figure 17-8, this representation allows you to follow the progress of your installation process.

Configuring SQL Server After Installation

After SQL Server is installed, you must perform several configuration tasks before you begin to use it. Generally, the following tasks are performed using SQL Server Management Studio:

- ▶ Create server groups and register the server
- ▶ Set server options

Create Server Groups and Register the Server

SQL Server can contain one or more server groups. A *server group* is a set of SQL Server systems that can be put together to specify the organizational structure of your company. Server groups are created using SQL Server Management Studio. In **Registered Servers**, click the server type on the **Registered Server** toolbar. Right-click a server or server group, select **New** and then click **Server Group**. In the **New Server Group** dialog box, enter the name, the description of the group, and a location.

Registering a server is the process where the server connection information is stored for future use. During this process, you specify the type and the name of the server, as well as the authentication type used to log on to the server. (Chapter 2 describes in detail how you can register a server.)

Set Server Options

One of the most important features of SQL Server is that it performs several standard system administration operations for you. Many server configuration options have been simplified and streamlined so that, in most cases, you do not have to set server options. However, if any of the default values are not appropriate for your situation, right-click the server and choose Properties. The Server Properties dialog box appears (Figure 17-9). In the dialog box, you can select between any tabs to change existing server options.

Starting and Stopping an Instance of SQL Server

The most convenient way to start an instance of SQL Server is automatically with the boot process of the computer. However, certain circumstances might require different handling of the system. Therefore, SQL Server offers several options for starting an instance:

- ▶ SQL Computer Manager (see Chapter 16)
- ▶ SQL Server Management Studio (see Chapter 2)
- ▶ The **sqlservr** application
- ▶ The **net** command

The **sqlservr** application can only be used to start SQL Server. This application is invoked using the following command:

```
sqlservr option_list
```

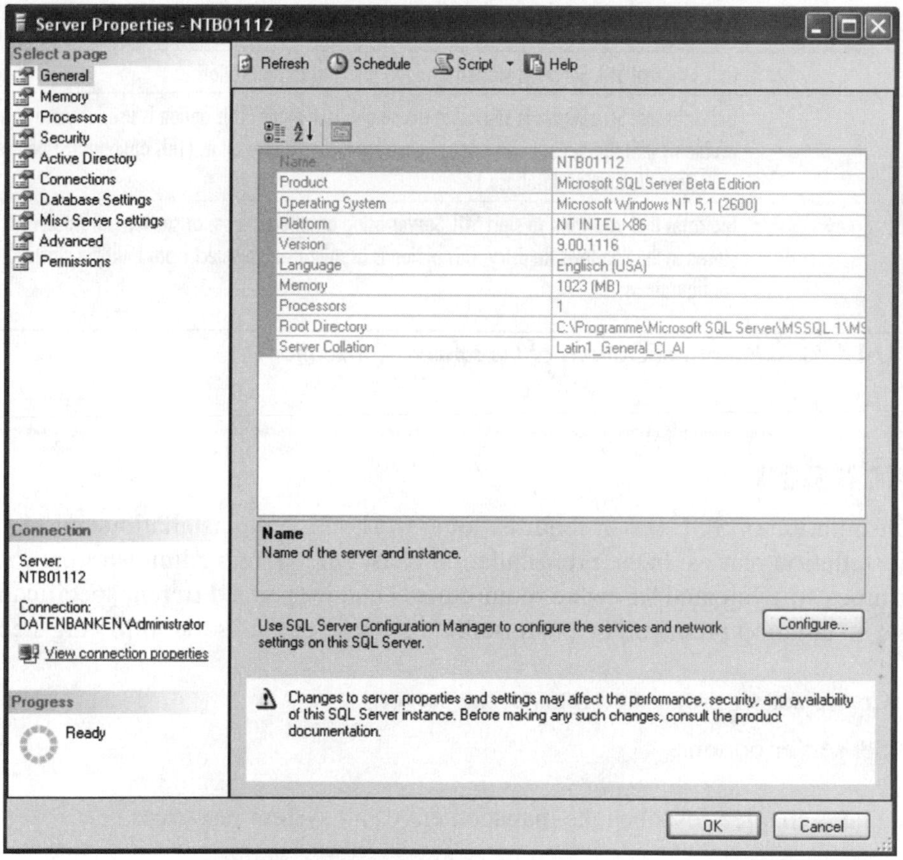

Figure 17-9   *The Server Properties dialog box*

option_list contains all options that can be invoked using the application. Table 17-1 describes the most important options.

The **net start**, **net stop**, and **net pause** commands start, stop, and pause the SQL Server system, respectively. The **net** command in Example 17.1 starts SQL Server.

EXAMPLE 17.1

    net start mssqlserver

Option	Description
-f	Indicates that SQL Server is started with the minimal configuration.
-m	Indicates that SQL Server is started in the single-user mode. This option is used if you have problems with the system and want to perform maintenance on it. (This option must be used to restore the master database.)
-s registry_key	Indicates that you want to start SQL Server using an alternate set of startup parameters stored in the Windows Registry. This option is usually used to select from multiple startup configurations.

Table 17-1   *Most Important Options of the* **sqlservr** *Application*

Conclusion

The installation of SQL Server requires some work in the preinstallation and postinstallation phases. In the preinstallation phase, the system administrator determines software and hardware requirements and prepares different specifications for the installation process. The postinstallation phase contains the following steps:

1. Create server groups and register the server.

2. Set server options.

The next chapter describes the management of all system resources.

Managing Databases and Database Files

This chapter describes how SQL Server stores data and how the system administrator manages it. The following tasks are part of data management:

▶ Managing filegroups

▶ Managing databases

▶ Managing transaction logs

Managing Filegroups

As stated in Chapter 15, SQL Server uses 8K contiguous blocks of disk space to store data. Such a block is called a *page*. When you create a table or index, SQL Server uses eight contiguous pages called an *extent* to store the data belonging to that table or index. (An extent can be used by more than one table or index.)

All databases have one "primary" file that has the same name as the corresponding database. Optionally, there can be one or more secondary data files, specified by the suffix .ndf. Similarly, each database has one or more transaction logs. The name of the "primary" log is dbname_log, where **dbname** is the name of the database (**sample_log**, for instance). All additional logs are specified by the suffix .ldf. (All suffixes are recommended extensions, but they can be modified if necessary.)

All files that are used to store databases and transaction logs have a physical name—the operating system file name—and a logical name that is used by SQL Server components. A collection of files belonging to a single disk can be grouped to build filegroups. With filegroups, you can locate different tables or indices on a specific file (or set of files). SQL Server supports three types of filegroups:

▶ Primary

▶ User-defined

▶ Default

The primary filegroup is implicitly created by the system during the creation of the database to which it belongs. All system tables are always in the primary filegroup, while user-defined tables can belong either to the primary filegroup or to any user-defined filegroup. This means that all user-defined tables, together with the corresponding indices, are placed in the primary filegroup if they are not explicitly assigned to another filegroup.

A user-defined filegroup must be explicitly created by the system administrator and subsequently attached to the corresponding database using the CREATE DATABASE or ALTER DATABASE statement (see Chapter 4).

NOTE

No file can belong to more than one filegroup.

The default filegroup indicates the filegroup used when no filegroup is specified as part of table or index creation. If no default filegroup is explicitly specified, the primary filegroup is the default filegroup. (You can use the ALTER DATABASE statement or SQL Server Management Studio if you want to change the default filegroup.)

Viewing Filegroups

All filegroups belonging to a database can be viewed using the following:

▶   SQL Server Management Studio

▶   System procedure **sp_helpfilegroup**

To display all filegroups with the corresponding files using SQL Server Management Studio, right-click the database and choose Properties. In the **Database Properties** dialog box, all existing filegroups of the current database are listed under the tab **Filegroups** (see Figure 18-1).

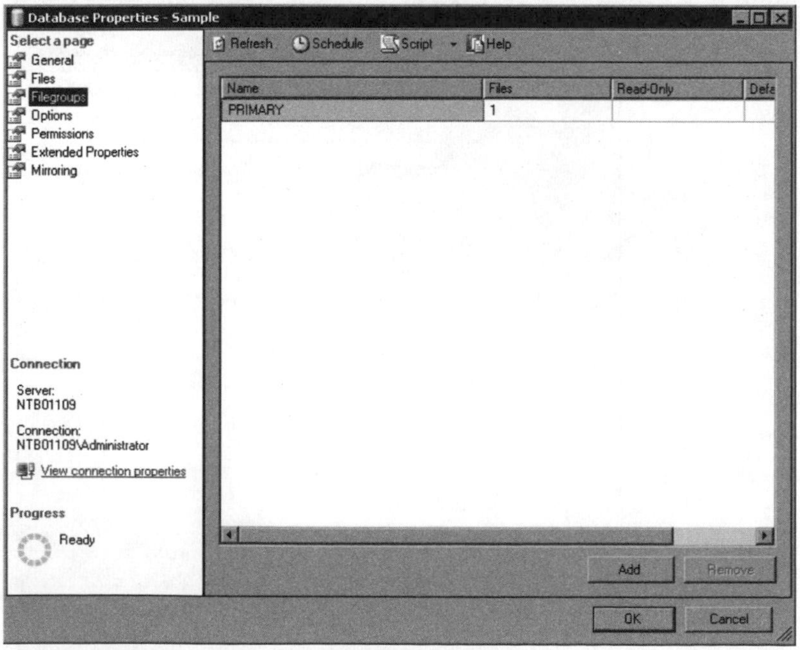

Figure 18-1   *Database Properties: The Filegroups page*

The system procedure **sp_helpfilegroup** displays the specified filegroup with all of its properties (file names and their sizes). If no filegroup name is specified, it displays the properties of all filegroups in the current database.

Managing Databases

Managing databases consists of the following tasks:

► Creating databases

► Viewing and modifying database options

► Modifying and removing databases

Creating Databases

In addition to the CREATE DATABASE statement (see Chapter 4), a database can be created using SQL Server Management Studio. Right-click the **Databases** folder of your SQL Server system in the console tree and choose **New Database**. The **Database Properties** dialog box appears (see Figure 18-2).

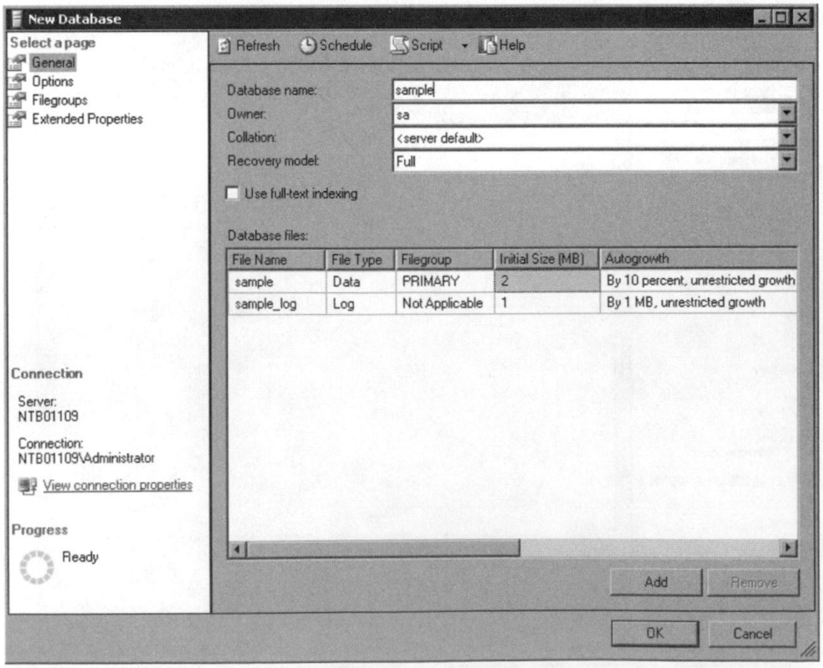

Figure 18-2 *Database Properties: The General page*

The name of the database must be specified in this dialog box. (All other specifications are optional.) In the same dialog box, you can view existing database files and create new ones. If you want to create a new file, click the **Add** button and specify the name and all attributes (Initial size, Autogrowth, and the Path) of the new file.

The . . . in the **Autogrowth** field must be selected in this dialog box if the growth of the file of the database should be managed through the administrator. The **Change Autogrowth** dialog box appears (see Figure 18-3). The additional portions of disk storage are assigned by checking the radio button **In Megabytes** and specifying the amount of storage. Two other radio buttons, **Unrestricted File Growth** and **Restrict File Growth**, specify whether the data file can grow without restrictions. (The specification **Unrestricted File Growth** corresponds to the value "UNLIMITED" of the option FILEGROWTH in the CREATE DATABASE statement.)

NOTE
The master database should be backed up each time you create, modify, or drop a database.

Viewing and Modifying Database Options

After the creation of a database, all database options are set by default (see Figure 18-4). Database options can be viewed and modified using the following:

▶ SQL Server Management Studio

▶ System procedure **sp_dboption**

▶ ALTER DATABASE statement

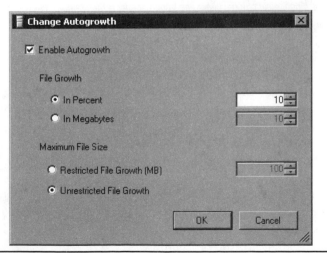

Figure 18-3   *The Change Autogrowth dialog box*

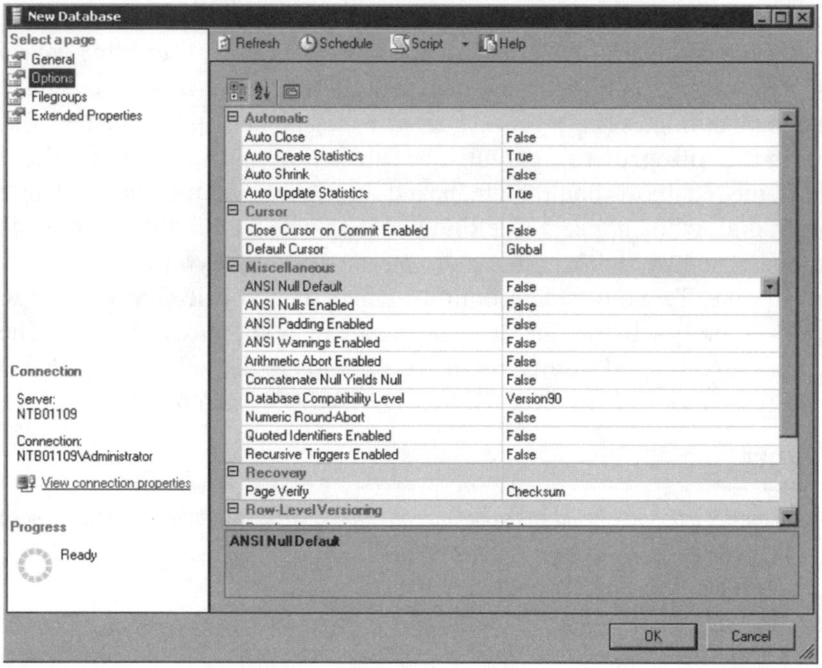

Figure 18-4 *Database dialog box: The Options page*

Also, you can use the DATABASEPROPERTYEX function to view all options.

NOTE

SQL Server Management Studio allows the setting of only certain options, but with **sp_dboption** *you can modify all options.*

To display or modify the database options of a database, right-click the name of the database and choose **Properties**. In the **Properties** dialog box, click the **Options** tab. Table 18-1 lists some of the database options.

The system procedure **sp_dboption** displays or changes database options. The general form of this procedure is

EXECUTE sp_dboption [db_name, option, {TRUE|FALSE}]

db_name is the name of the database for which the activate options are displayed. **option** specifies one of all possible options. (To display the list of all available options, use the **sp_dboption** system procedure without parameters.) Example 18.1 shows the use of the **sp_dboption** procedure.

Option	Description
Auto Close	When set to **true**, the database is shut down cleanly and its resources are freed after the last user logs off.
Auto Create Statistics	When set to **true** (the default value), any missing statistics needed by a query for optimization are automatically built during optimization (see also Chapter 9).
Auto Shrink	When this option is set, the size of database files could shrink periodically.
Auto Update Statistics	When set to **true** (the default value), any out-of-date statistics needed by a query for optimization are automatically built during optimization (see Chapter 9).
ANSI NULL Default	This option specifies whether a table column of the database will be defined as NULL or NOT NULL by default. (See also the discussion of the ANSI_NULL_DFLT_ON option at the end of Chapter 3.)
ANSI NULL Enabled	When set to **true**, all comparisons to a null value evaluate to UNKNOWN. When set to **false**, comparisons of non-UNICODE values to a null value evaluate to TRUE if both values are NULL (see Chapter 3).
Concatenate Null Yields Null	When set to **true**, anything you concatenate to a null value will yield NULL again (see Chapter 3).
Recursive Triggers Enabled	When this option is set, you can implement triggers that invoke other triggers (see Chapter 13).
Database Read Only	When this option is set to **true**, only read operations can be performed on the database.
Restrict Access	When set to **Restrict**, only the database owner and the system administrator can access the database. The current users of the database can continue to work with the database. When set to **Single**, only one user at a time can use the database. When set to **Multiple** (the default value), all users can use the database.

Table 18-1   *Database Options*

EXAMPLE 18.1

execute sp_dboption sample, 'read only', TRUE

In Example 18.1, the sample database is defined as read-only. (Because SQL Server understands any unique string that is part of the option name, you can write, for example, 'read' instead of 'read only'.)

NOTE

*The system procedure **sp_dboption** is a deprecated feature in SQL Server 2005 and is supported only for backward compatibility. Use the ALTER DATABASE statement instead.*

The DATABASEPROPERTYEX function

This function displays the current value of the specified database option or property. The syntax of this function is

DATABASEPROPERTYEX (db_name, property)

property specifies the name of the option or property for which a value should be returned. In most cases, the returned value can be either 1 (true) or 0 (false) or NULL (invalid input). Table 18-2 shows the list of selected properties with their descriptions.

Modifying Databases

The administrative tasks concerning the modification of a database in SQL Server are easy to perform. The only task you can do manually to modify a database is to expand or shrink its size by changing the size of the corresponding database files.

Property	Description
IsAnsiNullDefault	Returns 1 if the use of NULL values in the database complies with the ANSI SQL standard. (See also the explanation of NULL values at the end of Chapter 3.)
IsAnsiNullEnabled	Returns 1 if all comparisons to a NULL evaluate according to the ANSI SQL standard (i.e., to unknown).
IsAutoShrink	All files that belong to the database will be checked for automatic periodic shrinking.
IsAutoCreateStatistics	Existing statistics are implicitly updated by the system when they are out-of-date.
IsAutoUpdatedStatistics	Autoupdated statistics database option is enabled.
IsNullConcat	This database option influences the concatenation operation with a NULL value. The value 1 means that anything you concatenate to a NULL value will yield again NULL.
IsQuotedIdentifiersEnabled	Double quotation marks are used on identifiers.
IsInStandby	The database modus is read-only, with restore log allowed.
Status	Displays the status of the database. The values are ONLINE, OFFLINE, RESTORING, RECOVERING, and SUSPECT.
Updateability	Has two values: READ_ONLY (data can be read but not written) and READ_WRITE (data can be read and modified).
Collation	Default collation name for the database (see Chapter 16).

Table 18-2   *Database Options and Properties*

The task of expanding the database files can also be done automatically using SQL Server Management Studio or the ALTER DATABASE statement. In the first case, expand **Databases**, right-click the database, and select **Properties**. In the **Database Properties** dialog box, choose **Files** and right-click **. . .** in the **Autogrowth** column. The **Change Autogrowth** dialog box appears. Check the **Enable Autogrowth** option (see Figure 18-3). Using this method, the administrative tasks concerning a database can be significantly reduced. (The alternative way is to set the FILEGROWTH option of the MODIFY FILE clause in the ALTER DATABASE statement.)

If you do not set an existing database file to grow automatically, you can still expand the database size by either increasing the size of the file or adding new (secondary) file(s) to the database. The easiest way to increase the size of the existing file is to change the value in the **Space allocated** field for that file. A new file can be added to the database by using the ALTER DATABASE statement or by specifying a new database file in the **Database Properties** dialog box. In both cases, the name and the size of the file must be specified.

You can shrink the database size by shrinking the size of the entire database or by shrinking the size of the corresponding files. You can shrink a database automatically using SQL Server Management Studio or the system procedure **sp_dboption**. In the former case, right-click the database you want to shrink, choose the **Task** function, and then click **Shrink** and **Database**. In the **Shrink Database** dialog box, click OK. (You can also shrink the size of individual files of a database.) In the latter case, set the **Autoshrink** option of the system procedure **sp_dboption** to true.

NOTE

Automatic shrinking of a database occurs periodically, whenever a certain amount of free disk space is available in the database.

When the database should shrink immediately, use the DBCC SHRINKDATABASE command. After executing this command, the system tries to shrink all data files belonging to the database for the specific percentage. The used pages that are stored at the end of these disk files will be moved to the space on the disk that is below the percentage threshold. For instance, if your database is stored in 10MB and you shrink it to 70 percent, all database rows that are located in the last 3MB are moved to the 7MB disk space that is below the threshold, and the 3MB disk space at the end of the file will be released.

If your database needs more storage space than is specified with the DBCC SHRINKDATABASE command, the reallocation process will be performed, but only the existing part of free disk space will be released.

NOTE

You cannot shrink your database smaller than the ***model*** *database size.*

Example 18.2 uses the specified value (20 percent) as a target for free space that remains after shrinking the sample database.

EXAMPLE 18.2

DBCC SHRINKDATABASE (sample, 20)

The DBCC command with the SHRINKFILE option is used to shrink the size of a specific file of a database.

You can remove a database using the DROP DATABASE statement (see Chapter 4) or SQL Server Management Studio. Removing a database deletes all database objects within the database and removes all files used by the database. Additionally, all system tables in the **master** database concerning the database are modified to remove references to the database.

To remove a database using Management Studio, open the **Database** folder, right-click the database, and choose **Delete**. In contrast to the DROP DATABASE statement, with Management Studio you can remove only one database at a time.

Managing Transaction Logs

SQL Server records the changes that INSERT, UPDATE, or DELETE statements make during a transaction in one or more files called the transaction log. Each SQL Server database uses its own transaction log to record modifications to the data.

In the case of error, SQL Server starts the process called automatic recovery. During this process, SQL Server uses the records stored in the transaction log to roll back all incomplete transactions. Also, for all committed transactions, the changes are rolled forward so that all of the changes of the transaction are applied to the database. (For more information on transaction logs, see Chapter 14.)

Transaction log files are created at the same time that database files are created. You can use SQL Server Management Studio or the CREATE DATABASE statement to create file(s) for the transaction log. (See the description of the database creation at the beginning of this chapter.)

Using the ALTER DATABASE statement or Management Studio, you can modify transaction log files. (For the description of the ALTER DATABASE statement, see Chapter 4.) To modify (or view) transaction log files using Management Studio, right-click the database, choose **Properties**, and select the **Files** tab in the **Database Properties** dialog box.

The modification of existing files and the creation of new transaction log files can be done in the same way as the database files are modified or created.

NOTE

The size of the transaction log must be carefully planned, and its growth must be monitored, because there are some operations (such as loading the data into a table with existing indices) that fill the transaction log very quickly. For this reason, create an alert (see Chapter 21) to notify you when the transaction log threshold is reached.

Conclusion

The most significant property of SQL Server is its easy-to-manage features that are part of the database engine. The amount of time and effort that goes into managing databases and files is negligible compared with the previous versions.

All tasks concerning management of databases and their files can be done using either SQL Server Management Studio or the Transact-SQL statements CREATE DATABASE and ALTER DATABASE. For displaying database and file properties, some system procedures can also be used.

The next chapter discusses the SQL Server security system and how security issues can be managed.

Exercises

E.18.1

When is the primary filegroup of a database identical to its default file?

E.18.2

Discuss the differences in using the **sp_dboption** system stored procedure and the DATABASEPROPERTYEX function.

E.18.3

Which SQL Server utility would you prefer to use to modify database options?

E.18.4

How can you know whether SQL Server implicitly shrinks the size of database files?

E.18.5

Can data of a database and its transaction log use the same file?

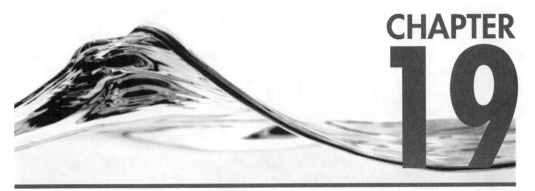

CHAPTER
19

Managing Security

This chapter discusses security issues in SQL Server from the system administrator's point of view. After a few introductory notes, the chapter describes the features of SQL Server Management Studio that allow users to access the database server and databases within it.

Introduction

SQL Server security is based on Windows authorization and optionally uses the SQL Server security subsystem. Therefore, SQL Server can operate in two different authentication modes:

▶ Windows Authentication mode

▶ Mixed mode

When a user connects to SQL Server in Windows Authentication mode, the SQL Server client starts a *trusted connection*, which means SQL Server searches for the Windows user account (or group account) in the list of SQL Server login accounts. If the account exists, the user's SQL Server login account is the operating system's user or group account. In this case, SQL Server does not verify a corresponding password because it "trusts" that the Windows operating system has verified it already.

Mixed mode allows users to connect to SQL Server using the Windows Authentication or SQL Server Authentication. This means that a user logs in to the Windows operating system using his or her account or logs in to the SQL Server system using his or her login name. In the latter case, SQL Server verifies that a login exists in the list of SQL Server login accounts and that the specified password matches the stored password for the same account.

Both modes have their specific benefits. Windows Authentication mode offers advanced security features, which are not implemented for the SQL Server security system. The most important features are the auditing and account lockout after the specification of an invalid password. Additionally, maintenance tasks are reduced, because you only have to maintain a Windows user account (or a Windows group) and the corresponding password. On the other hand, using SQL Server Authentication in a Mixed mode allows you to use two-level security and therefore to enhance the security of the overall system.

For more information on all features concerning SQL Server security issues, see the section "Authentication" in Chapter 12.

NOTE

SQL Server Authentication is provided for backward compatibility only. For this reason, use Windows Authentication instead.

Implementing a Security Mode

SQL Server Management Studio can be used to select the security mode. To set up Windows Authentication mode, right-click the server and click **Properties**. In the **Server Properties** dialog box, choose the **Security** page and click **Windows Authentication mode** (see Figure 19-1). Mixed mode can be selected similarly; the only difference is that you have to click **SQL Server and Windows Authentication mode** in the **SQL Server Properties** dialog box.

After successful connection to SQL Server, the access to database objects is independent of whether Windows or SQL Server Authentication is used.

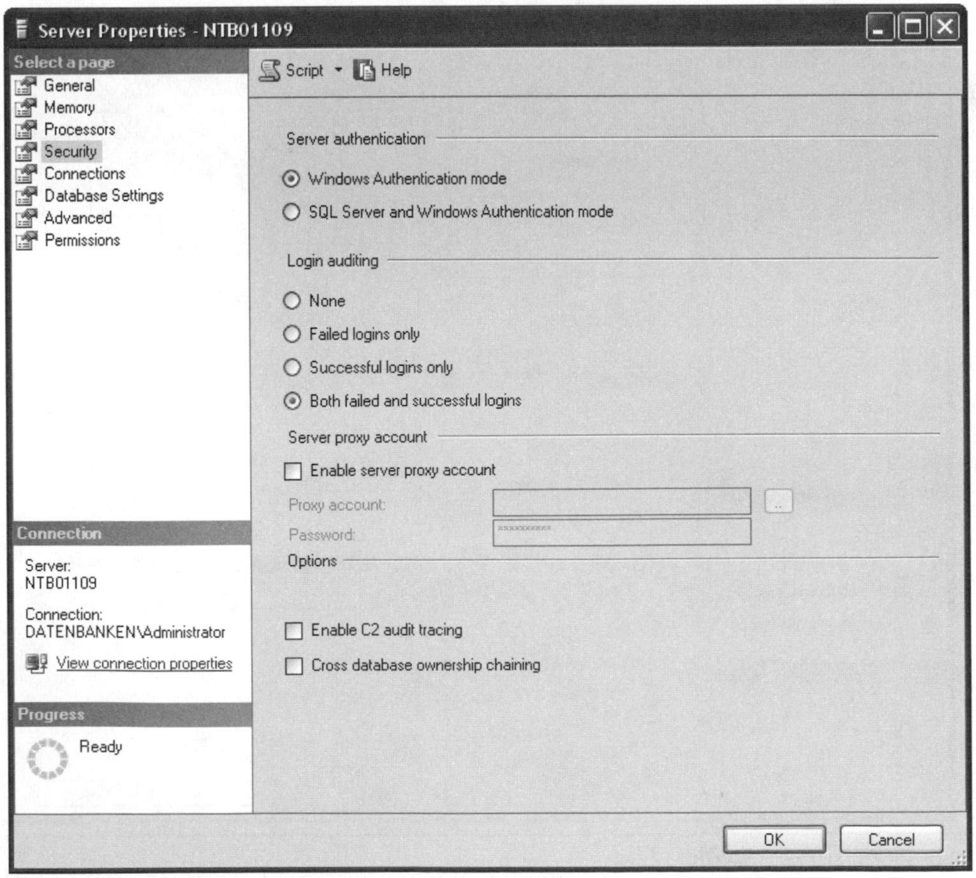

Figure 19-1   *The Server Properties dialog box*

Managing SQL Server Logins

SQL Server login can be created using the CREATE LOGIN statement (see Chapter 12) or SQL Server Management Studio.

To create a new login using Management Studio, expand the server, expand **Security**, right-click **Logins**, and click **New Login**. The **Login** dialog box (see Figure 19-2) appears. First, you have to decide between Windows and SQL Server Authentication. If you choose Windows Authentication, the login name must be a valid Windows name, which is written in the form domain\user_name. If you choose the SQL Server Authentication, you have to type the new login name and the corresponding password. Optionally, the default database and language can also be specified for the new login. (The default database is the database that the user is automatically connected to immediately after logging in to SQL Server.) After that, the user can log in to SQL Server under the new account.

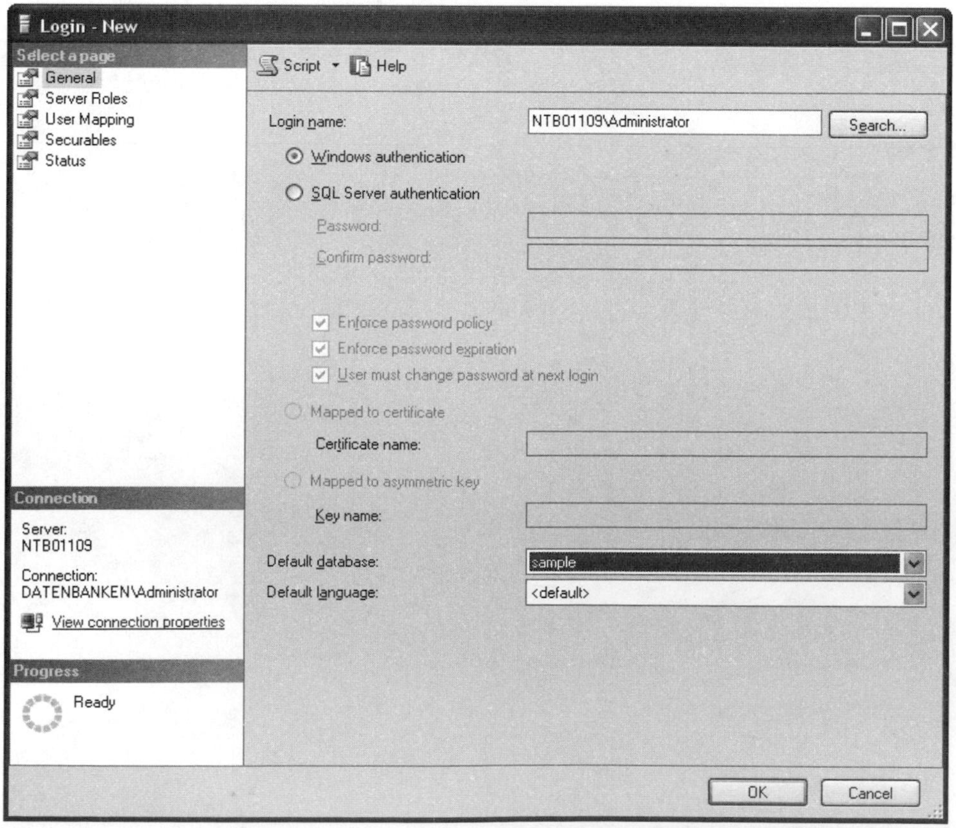

Figure 19-2 *The Login dialog box*

Database Security Permissions

To grant SQL Server login access to a database using SQL Server Management Studio, expand the server and the Databases folder. Then expand the database, click **Security**, right-click **Users**, and click **New User**. In the **Database User** dialog box (see Figure 19-3), enter a user name and select a corresponding login name. Optionally, you can select database role memberships and schemas owned by this user. An alternative method is to use the CREATE USER statement (see the section "Setting Database User Accounts" in Chapter 12).

Roles

A role groups database users into a single unit, providing the same permissions to all of them. The purpose of roles is to assign a name to each functional area in an organization.

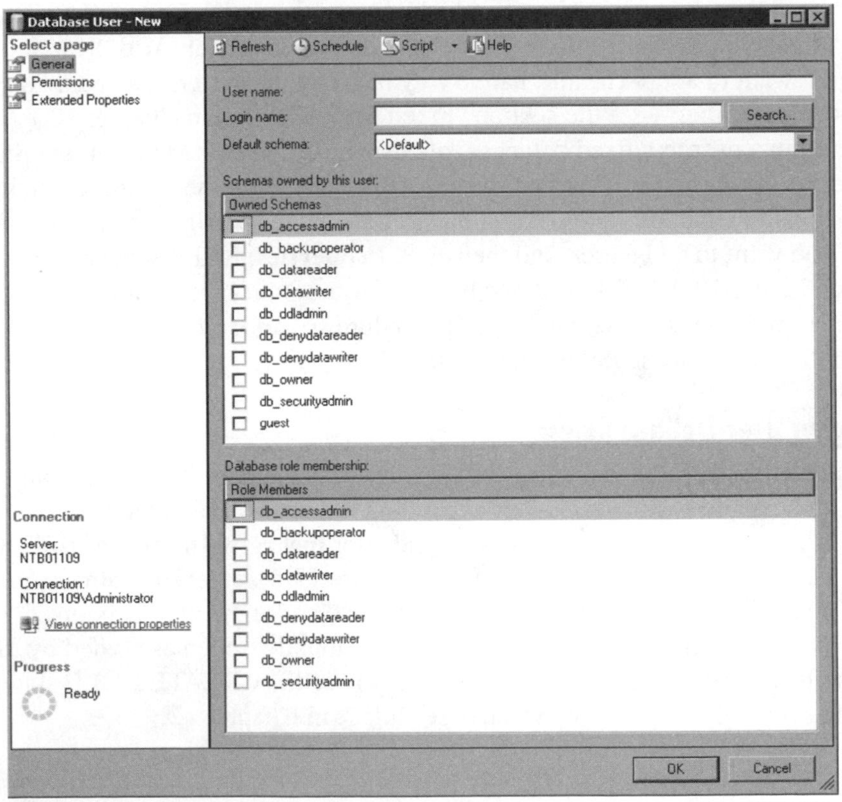

Figure 19-3   *The Database User dialog box*

As employees rotate into certain positions, you simply add them as members of the role. This way, you do not have to assign new permissions to them and revoke the old ones.

There are four types of roles:

▶ Fixed server roles

▶ Fixed database roles

▶ User-defined roles

▶ Application roles

The management of these roles will be described in the following sections.

Assigning a Login Account to a Fixed Role

To assign a login account to a fixed server role using SQL Server Management Studio, expand the server, expand **Security**, and expand **Server Roles**. Right-click the role to which you want to add a login and then click **Properties**. On the **General** page of the **Server Role Properties** dialog box, click **Add**. Search for the login you want to add. (The alternative way is to use the system procedure **sp_addsrvrolemember**—see the section "Fixed Server Roles" in Chapter 12.)

To assign a user to a fixed database role using SQL Server Management Studio, expand the server and expand **Databases**. After expanding the database, click **Security** and then click **Roles**. Expand **Database Role** and right-click the role to which you want to add a user, and then click **Properties**. In the **Server Role** dialog box (see Figure 19-4), click Add and browse for the user(s) you want to add. (An alternative method is to use the system procedure **sp_addrolemember**—see the section "Fixed Database Roles" in Chapter 12.)

Managing User-Defined Roles

To create a user-defined role using SQL Server Management Studio, expand the server and expand **Databases**. After expanding the database and the Security folder, right-click **Roles**, then click **New** and after that **New Database Role**. In the **Database Role Properties** dialog box (see Figure 19-5), enter the name of the new role. Click **Add** to add members to the new role. Choose the members (users and/or other roles) of the new role and click OK. (Additionally, schemas owned by this role can also be chosen.) An alternative method is to use the CREATE ROLE statement —see the section "User-Defined Database Roles" in Chapter 12.

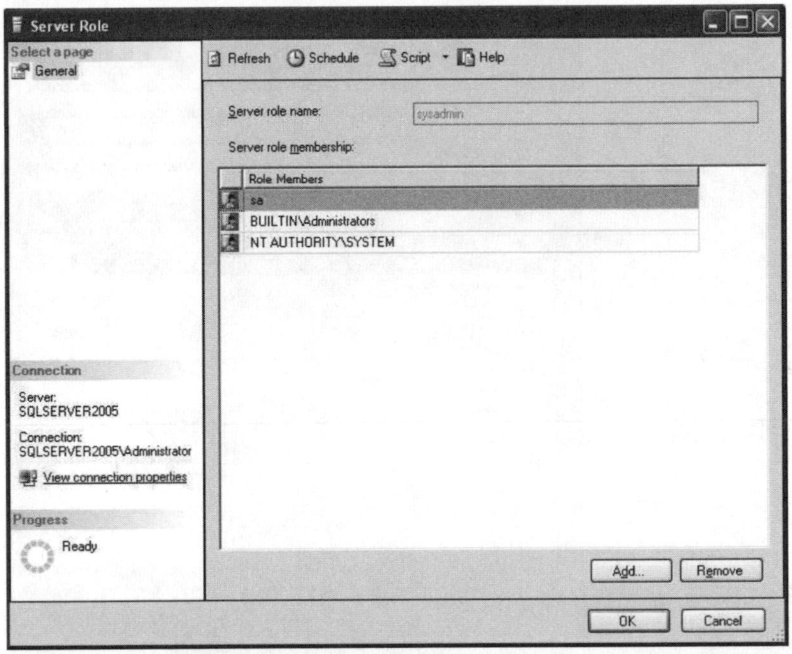

Figure 19-4   *The Server Role dialog box*

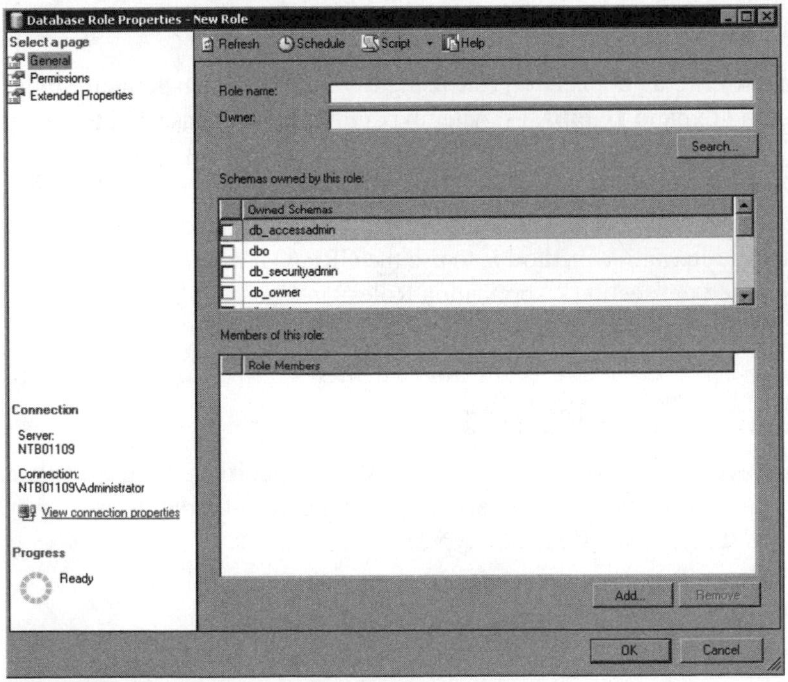

Figure 19-5   *The Database Role Properties dialog box*

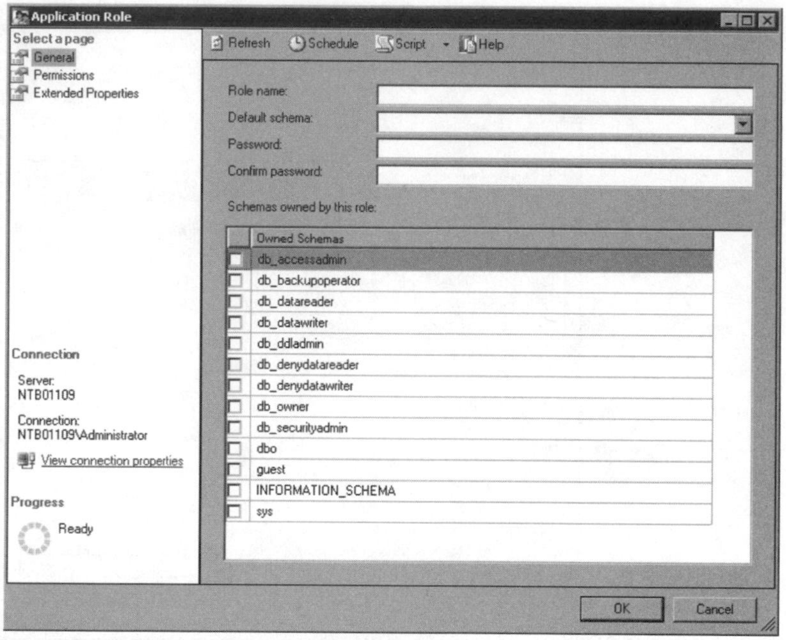

Figure 19-6   *The Application Role dialog box*

Managing Application Roles

To assign a user to an application role using SQL Server Management Studio, expand the server and expand **Databases**. After expanding the database and the **Security** folder, right-click **Roles**, then click **New** and after that **New Application Role**. In the **Application Role** dialog box (see Figure 19-6), enter the name of the new role. Additionally, you must enter the password and can enter the default schema for the new role. (An alternative method is to use the CREATE APPLICATION ROLE statement —see the section "Application Roles" in Chapter 12.)

Managing Permissions

After you have created database user accounts for specific databases, you must assign specific permissions to the security of the particular database.

There are three permission state types:

▶   Granted (or positive)

▶   Denied (or negative)

▶   None

Database users can perform activities that are granted to them. The negative entry in the system catalog prevents users from performing activities. This entry overrides a permission, which was granted to a user explicitly or implicitly using a role to which the user belongs. Therefore, the user cannot perform this activity in any case. In the last case (none), the user has no explicit privileges but can perform an activity if a role to which he or she belongs has the appropriate permission.

Permissions can be managed using either SQL Server Management Studio or the Transact-SQL statements GRANT, DENY, and REVOKE. To manage permissions for a user or role using Management Studio, expand the server and expand **Databases**. Right-click the database, and then click **Properties**. Choose the **Permission** page and click the **Add** button. In the **Select Users or Role** dialog box you can select one or more object types (users and/or roles) to which you want to grant or deny permissions. To grant a permission, check the corresponding box in the **Grant** column and click **OK**. To deny a permission, check the corresponding box in the **Deny** column. Blanks in both columns mean no permission (see Figure 19-7).

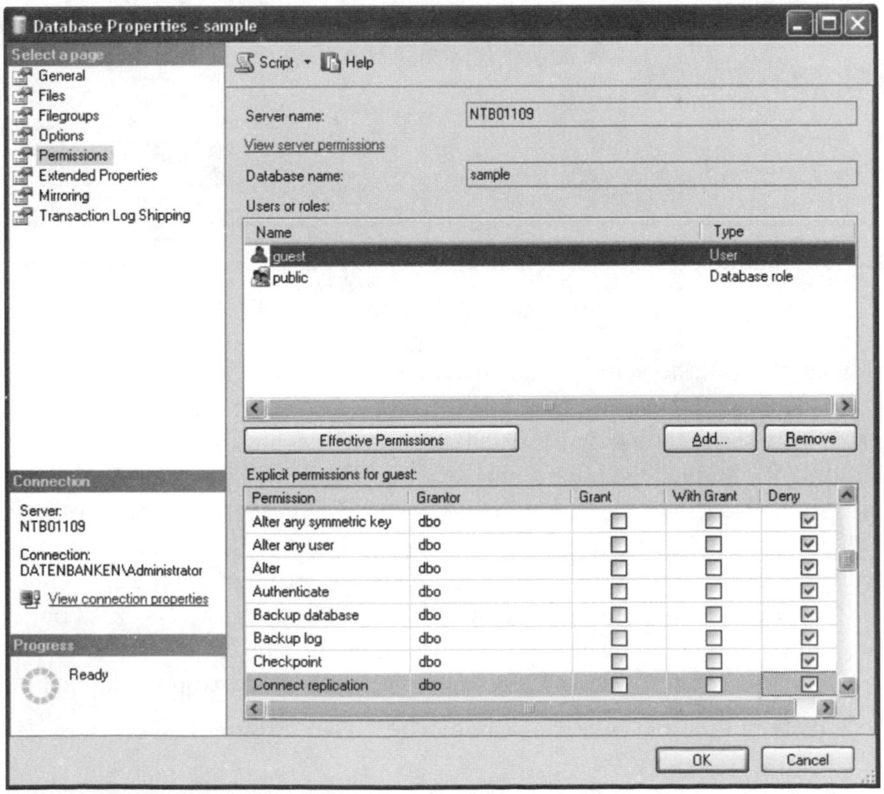

Figure 19-7   *Managing statement permissions using SQL Server Management Studio*

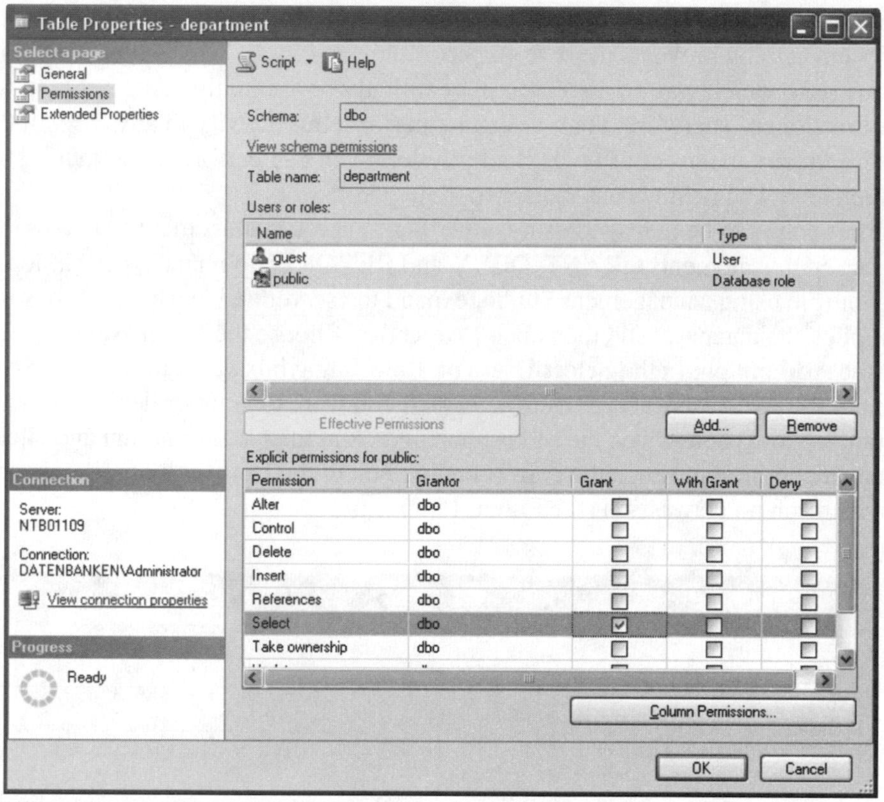

Figure 19-8 *Managing object permissions using SQL Server Management Studio*

To manage permissions for a single database object using SQL Server Management Studio, expand the server and expand **Databases**. Then expand the database and click **Tables** or **Views**, depending on the database object for which you want to manage permissions. Right-click the object, choose **Properties**, and select the **Permissions** page. (Figure 19-8 shows the **Table Properties** dialog box for the **department** table.) After clicking the **Add** button, the **Select Users or Roles** dialog box appears. Click **Object Types** and select one or more object types (users, database roles, application roles). Click **Browse** in the **Select Users or Roles** dialog box and check all objects to which permissions should be granted. To allow a permission, check the corresponding box in the **Grant** column. To deny a permission, check the corresponding box in the **Deny** column.

Conclusion

All tasks concerning the management of SQL Server security can be done using either SQL Server Management Studio, Transact-SQL statements, or system procedures. Additionally, the Transact-SQL statements GRANT, DENY, and REVOKE allow you to manage permissions. Generally, Transact-SQL statements offer more possibilities for managing the security issues than SQL Server Management Studio.

Concerning security, you can use SQL Server Management Studio to do the following tasks:

► Implement a security mode

► Manage SQL Server logins

► Manage permissions

The next chapter introduces you to how SQL Server and the system administrator can prevent the loss of data.

Exercises

E.19.1

Using SQL Server Management Studio, create three new SQL Server logins called **peter1, paul1**, and **mary1**. The corresponding passwords are "abc," "def," and "fgh," respectively. The default database is the sample database where the user should have access. After creating the logins, check their existence using SQL Server Management Studio.

E.19.2

Using SQL Server Management Studio and the sample database, create three new database users for the logins in Exercise 19.1. The new names are **s_peter, s_paul**, and **s_mary**.

E.19.3

Using SQL Server Management Studio, create a new user-defined database role called **managers** and add the users from Exercise 19.2 to the role. After that, display the information concerning this role and its members.

E.19.4

Using SQL Server Management Studio, allow the database user **s_peter** to create tables and the user **s_mary** to create stored procedures in the sample database.

E.19.5

Is it possible to allow the database user **s_paul** to update the columns **lname** and **fname** of the **employee** table using the SQL Server Management Studio?

E.19.6

Using the SQL Server Management Studio, allow the user-defined-role **managers** to insert new rows into the **projects** table.

CHAPTER 20

Backup and Recovery

This chapter covers two of the most important tasks concerning system administration: backup and recovery. The introduction describes the different reasons for software and hardware failures and explains the transaction log—a vital part of the backup and recovery processes. Then the various forms of backups are discussed, followed by procedures for restoring databases (including system databases).

Introduction

Backup determines how a copy of the database(s) and/or transaction logs is made and which media are used for this process. All of these precautions have to be taken to prevent data loss. You can lose data as a result of different hardware or software errors, which are discussed next. Knowing something about the transaction log will help you understand how SQL Server (and all other DBMSs) keeps information that is needed to recover data from failures.

Software and Hardware Failures

The reasons for data loss can be divided into five main groups:

- ▶ Program errors
- ▶ Administrator (human) errors
- ▶ Computer failures (system crash)
- ▶ Disk failures
- ▶ Catastrophes (fire, earthquake) or theft

During execution of a program, conditions may arise that abnormally terminate the program. Such program errors concern only the database application and usually have no impact on the entire database system. As these errors are based on faulty program logic, the database system cannot recover in such situations. The recovery should therefore be done by the programmer, who has to handle such exceptions using the COMMIT and ROLLBACK statements. (Both of these Transact-SQL statements are described in Chapter 14.)

Another source of data loss is human error. Users with sufficient permissions, or the database administrator, may accidentally lose or corrupt data (people have been known to drop the wrong table, update or delete data incorrectly, and so on). Of course, we would prefer that this never happen, and we can establish practices that make it unlikely that production data is compromised in this way, but we have to recognize that people make mistakes, and data can be affected. The best we can do is try to avoid it, and be prepared to recover when it happens.

A computer failure specifies different hardware or software errors. A hardware crash is an example of a system failure. In this case, the contents of the computer's main memory may be lost. A disk failure occurs either when a read/write head of the disk crashes or when the I/O system discovers corrupted disk blocks during I/O operations.

In the case of catastrophes or theft, the system must keep enough information to recover from the failure. This is normally done by means of media that offer the needed recovery information on a piece of hardware that has not been damaged by the failure.

Transaction Log

SQL Server keeps an image of the old contents of the record of each row that has been changed during a transaction. (A transaction specifies a sequence of Transact-SQL statements that build a logical unit; see also Chapter 14.) This is necessary in case an error occurs later during the execution of the transaction and all executed statements inside the transaction have to be rolled back. As soon as SQL Server detects such a situation, it uses the stored records to bring the database back to the consistent state it was in before the transaction was started.

SQL Server keeps all those records in one or more system files, called the transaction log. In particular, this log contains the "before" and "after" values of each changed column during transactions. The transaction log can then be used to perform automatic recovery or a restore process. (The notion of automatic recovery is described later in this chapter.) After a failure, SQL Server uses stored values from the transaction log (called *before images*) to restore all pages on the disk to their previous consistent state. In the case of a restore, the transaction log is always used together with a database backup copy to recover the database. The transaction log is generally needed to prevent a loss of all changes that have been executed since the last database backup. (The use of transaction logs, together with database backups, is explained further in "Transaction Log Backup" later in this chapter.)

Backup

SQL Server provides static as well as dynamic backup. (Dynamic backup means that a database backup can be performed while users are working on data.) In contrast to some other DBMSs, which back up all databases together, SQL Server does the backup of each database separately. This method increases security when it comes time to restore each database, because a restoration of each database separately is more secure than restoring all databases at once.

SQL Server provides four different backup methods:

▶ Full database backup

▶ Differential database backup

▶ Transaction log backup

▶ Database file (or filegroup) backup

Full Database Backup

A full database backup captures the state of the database at the time the backup is started. During the full database backup, the system copies the data as well as the schema of all tables of the database and the corresponding file structures. If the full database backup is executed dynamically, SQL Server records any activity that took place during the backup. Therefore, even all uncommitted transactions in the transaction log are written to the backup media.

Differential Backup

Using differential backup, only the parts of the database that have changed since the last full database backup are read and then written to the copy. (As in the full database backup, any activity that took place during the differential backup is backed up, too.) The advantage of a differential backup is speed. It minimizes the time required to back up a database, because the amount of data to be backed up is considerably smaller than in the case of the full backup. (Remember that a full database backup includes a copy of all database pages.)

Transaction Log Backup

A transaction log backup considers only the changes recorded in the log. This form of backup is therefore not based on physical parts (pages) of the database, but on logical operations—that is, changes executed using the DML statements INSERT, UPDATE, and DELETE. Again, because the amount of data is smaller, this process can be performed significantly quicker than the full database backup and quicker than a differential backup.

NOTE

It does not make sense to back up a transaction log unless a full database backup is performed at least once!

There are two main reasons to perform the transaction log backup: first, to store the data that has changed since the last transaction log backup or database backup on a secure medium; second (and more importantly), to properly close the transaction log up to the beginning of the active portion of it. (The active portion of the transaction log contains all uncommitted transactions.)

Using the full database backup and the valid chain of all closed transaction logs, it is possible to propagate a database copy on a different computer. This database copy can then be used to replace the original database in case of a failure. (The same scenario can be established using a full database backup and the last differential backup.)

SQL Server does not allow you to store the transaction log in the same file in which the database is stored. One reason for this is that if the file is damaged, the use of the transaction log to restore all changes since the last backup will not be possible.

Using a transaction log to record changes in the database is a common feature used by nearly all existing relational DBMSs. Nevertheless, situations may arise when it becomes helpful to switch this feature off. For example, the execution of a heavy load can last for hours. Such a program runs much faster when the logging is switched off. On the other hand, switching off the logging process is dangerous, as it destroys the valid chain of transaction logs. To ensure the database recovery, it is strongly recommended that you perform full database backup after the successful end of the load.

One of the most common system failures occurs because the transaction log is filled up. Be aware that the use of a transaction log in itself may cause a complete standstill of the system. If the storage used for the transaction log fills up to 100 percent, SQL Server must stop all running transactions until the transaction log storage is freed again. This problem can only be avoided by making frequent backups of the transaction log: each time you close a portion of the actual transaction log and store it to a different storage media, this portion of the log becomes reusable, and SQL Server thus regains disk space.

NOTE

A differential backup and a transaction log backup both minimize the time required to back up the database. But there is one significant difference between them: the transaction log backup contains all changes of a row that has been modified several times since the last backup, while a differential backup contains only the last modification of that row.

Some differences between transaction log backups and differential backups are worth noting. The benefit of differential backups is that you save time in the restore process, because to recover a database completely, you need a full database backup and only the *latest* differential backup. If you use transaction logs for the same scenario, you have to apply the full database backup and *all* transaction logs made since last full database backup to bring the database to a consistent state. A disadvantage of differential backups is that you cannot use them to recover data to a specific point in time because they do not store intermediate changes to the database. (See the description of the STOPAT option of the RESTORE LOG statement later in this chapter.)

NOTE

The time of finishing is significant for backup. This means that the process of backing up a database is consistent with the end of the backup.

Database File Backup

Database file backup allows you to back up specific database files (or filegroups) instead of the entire database. In this case, SQL Server backs up only files you specify. Individual files (or filegroups) can be restored from database backup, allowing recovery from a failure that affects only a small subset of the database files. Individual files or filegroups can be restored from either a database backup or a filegroup backup. This means that you can use database and transaction log backups as your backup procedure and still be able to restore individual files (or filegroups) from the database backup.

NOTE

The database file backup is recommended only when a database that should be backed up is very large and there is not enough time to perform a full database backup.

Performing Backup

You can perform backup operations using the following:

▶ SQL Server Management Studio
▶ Transact-SQL statements

Each of these backup methods is described in the following sections.

Backup Using Management Studio

Before a database or transaction log backup can be done, it is necessary to specify (or create) backup devices. SQL Server Management Studio allows you to create disk devices and tape devices in a similar manner. In both cases, expand the server, expand **Server Objects**, right-click **Backup Devices**, and choose **New Backup Device**. In the **Backup Device** dialog box (see Figure 20-1), either enter the name of the disk device (if you clicked **File**) or the name of the tape device (if you clicked **Tape**). In the former case, you can click the button with the ... on the right side of the field to display existing backup device locations. In the latter case, if **Tape** cannot be activated, then no tape devices exist on the local computer.

After you specify backup devices, a database backup can be done. Expand the server, expand **Databases**, and right-click the database. After pointing to **Tasks**, choose **Back Up**. The **Back Up Database** dialog box appears (see Figure 20-2). On the **General** tab of the dialog box, choose the backup type (Full, Differential, or Transaction Log) and enter the backup set name in the **Name** field and, in the **Description** field, an optional description of this set. In the same dialog box, you can choose an expiration date for the backup. (The alternative way is to expand the server, expand **Server Objects**, right-click **Backup Devices**, and choose **Back Up a Database**.)

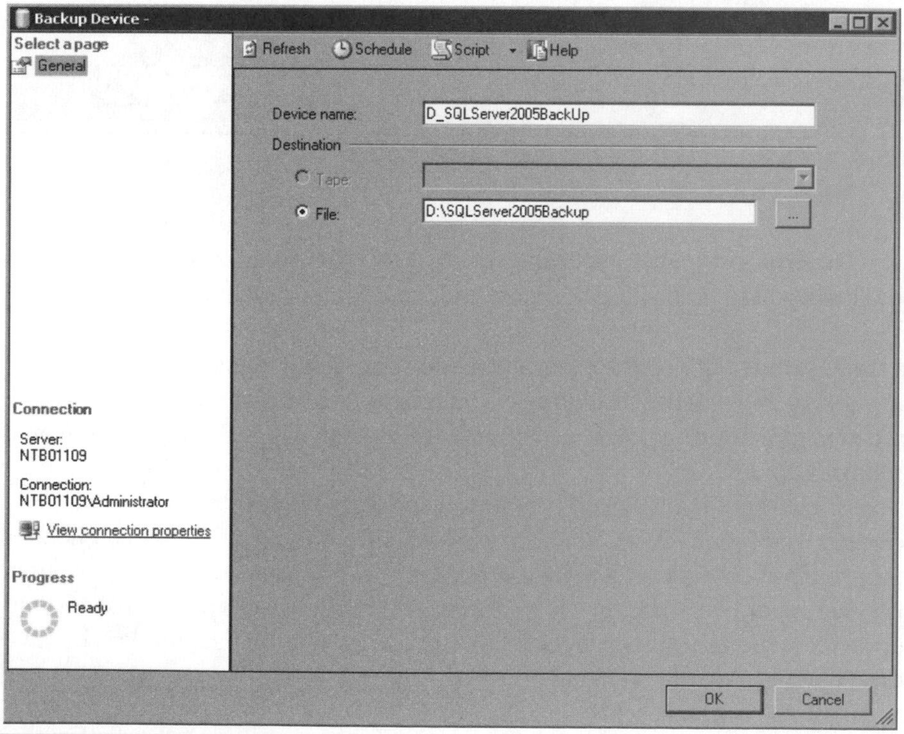

Figure 20-1 *The Backup Device dialog box*

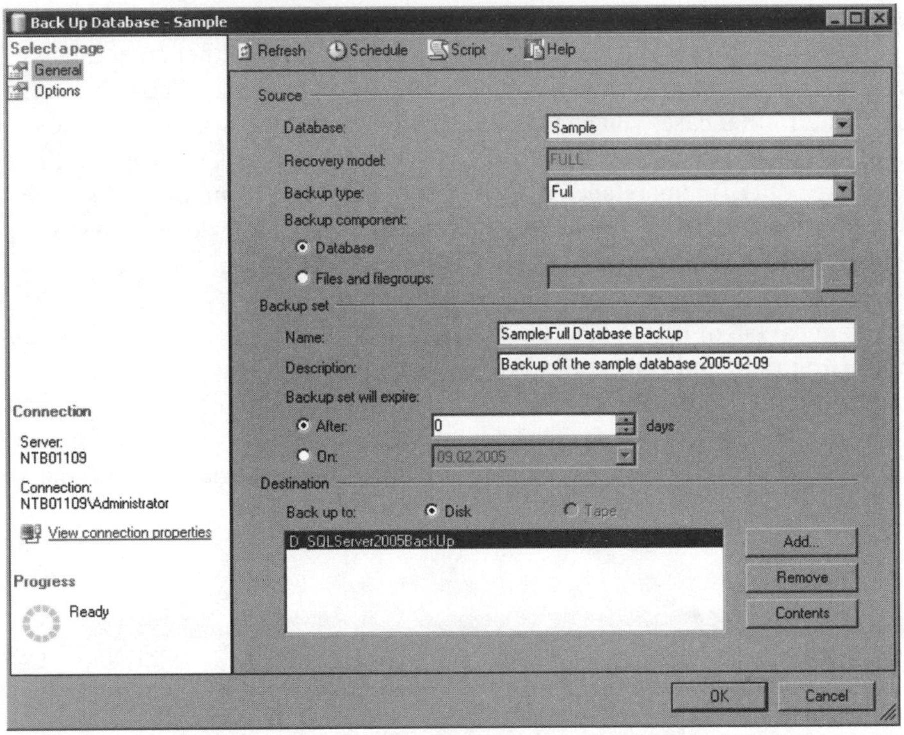

Figure 20-2 *The Back Up Database dialog box*

In the **Destination** frame, select an existing device by clicking **Add**. (The **Remove** button allows you to remove one or more backup devices from the list of devices to be used.)

On the **Options** tab, to append to an existing backup on the selected device, check the **Append to the existing backup set** radio button. The **Overwrite all existing backup sets** radio button in the same frame overwrites any existing backups on the selected backup device.

For verification of the database backup, click **Verify backup** when finished. On the **Options** tab (see Figure 20-3), you can also back up to a new media set by clicking **Back up to a new media set** and then entering the media set name and description.

For creation and verification of a differential database backup or transaction log backup, follow the same steps, but choose the corresponding backup type in the **Backup type** field on the **General** tab.

After all options have been selected, click **OK**. The database or the transaction log is then backed up. The name, physical location, and the type of the backup devices

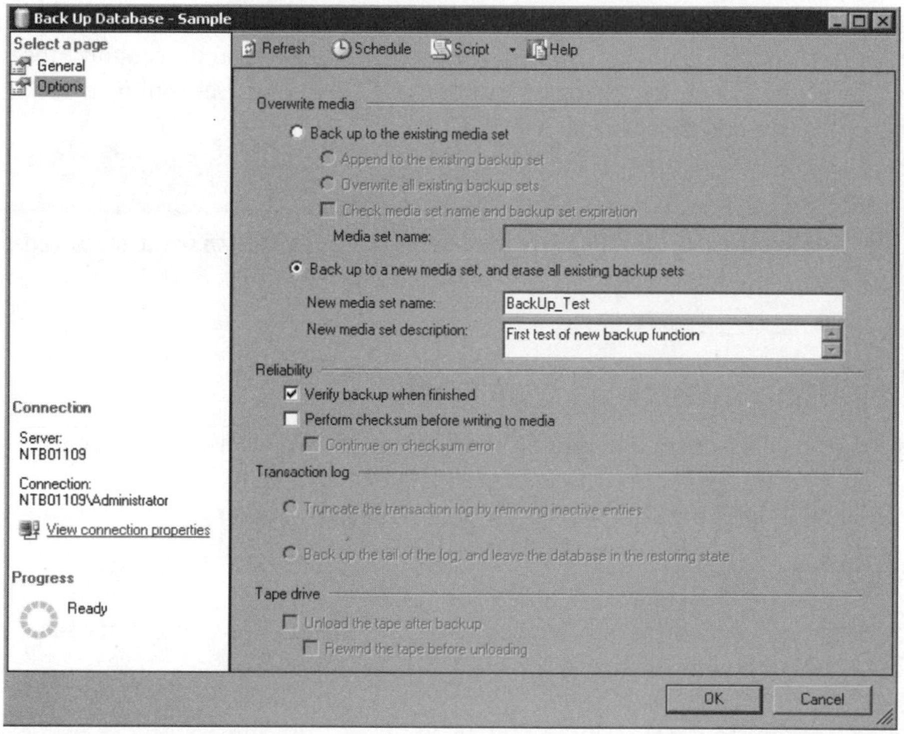

Figure 20-3 *The Options tab*

can be shown by selecting the server, expanding the **Server Objects** folder, and finally expanding the **Backup Devices** folder.

Scheduling Backups with Management Studio

A well-planned timetable for the scheduling of backup operations will help you avoid system shortages when users are working. For example, dynamic backup is not recommended unless there are no times when users are not using the database system. SQL Server Management Studio supports this planning by offering an easy-to-use graphical interface for scheduling backups.

The backup operation can be executed at once or planned for later periodic execution. To plan a backup operation, you can use the following:

- ► SQL Server Management Studio
- ► Maintenance Plan Wizard

First, you have to choose the job and schedule name. Always choose a descriptive name for the scheduled job. Using a descriptive name allows you to recognize the job easily later in the Event Viewer log or error log of SQL Server. Scheduling a backup operation is described in detail in Chapter 21.

NOTE

To schedule backups, the SQL Server Agent service must be started. This service can be started manually or automatically.

Backup Using Transact-SQL Statements

All types of backup operations can be executed using two Transact-SQL statements:

▶ BACKUP DATABASE

▶ BACKUP LOG

Before we describe these two Transact-SQL statements, we will specify the existing types of backup devices.

Types of Backup Devices

SQL Server allows you to back up databases, transaction logs, and files to the following backup devices:

▶ Disk

▶ Tape

Disk files are the most common media used for storing backups. Disk backup devices can be located on a server's local hard disk or on a remote disk on a shared network resource. SQL Server allows you to append a new backup to a file that already contains backups from the same or different databases. By appending a new backup set to existing media, the previous contents of the media remain intact, and the new backup is written after the end of the last backup on the media. By default, SQL Server always appends new backups to disk files.

NOTE

Do not back up to a file on the same physical disk where the database or its transaction log is stored! If the disk with the database crashes, the backup that is stored on the same disk will also be damaged.

Tape backup devices are generally used in the same way as disk devices. However, when you back up to a tape, the tape drive must be attached locally to SQL Server. The advantage of tape devices in relation to disk devices is their simple administration and operation.

BACKUP DATABASE Statement

The BACKUP DATABASE statement is used to perform a full database backup or a differential database backup. This statement has the following syntax:

```
BACKUP DATABASE {db_name | @variable}
    TO device_list
    [MIRROR TO device_list2]
    [WITH option_list]
```

db_name is the name of the database that should be backed up. (The name of the database can also be supplied using a variable @**variable**.) **device_list** specifies one or more device names, where the database backup will be stored. **device_list** can be a list of names of disk files or tapes. The MIRROR TO option indicates that the accompanying set of backup devices is a mirror within a mirrored media set. The backup devices must be identical in type and number to the devices specified in the TO clause. In a mirrored media set, all the backup devices must have the same properties. (See also the description of mirrored media in the section "Log Shipping and Database Mirroring" later in this chapter.)

option_list comprises several options that can be specified for the different backup types. The most important options are the following:

- ► SKIP/NOSKIP
- ► INIT/NOINIT
- ► FORMAT
- ► DIFFERENTIAL
- ► UNLOAD/NOUNLOAD

The SKIP option disables the backup set expiration and name checking, which is usually performed by the BACKUP statement to prevent overwrites of backup sets. The NOSKIP option, which is a default, instructs the BACKUP statement to check the expiration date and name of all backup sets before allowing them to be overwritten.

The INIT option is used to overwrite any existing data on the backup media. This option does not overwrite the media header, if one exists. If there is a backup that has not yet expired, the backup operation fails. In this case, use the combination of

SKIP and INIT options to overwrite the backup device. The NOINIT option, which is a default, appends a backup to existing backups on the media.

The FORMAT option is used to write a header on all of the files (or tape volumes) that are used for a backup. Therefore, use this option to initialize a backup medium. When you use the FORMAT option to back up to a tape device, the INIT option and the SKIP option are implied. Similarly, the INIT option is implied if the FORMAT option is specified for a file device. The DIFFERENTIAL option specifies a differential database backup. If this option is omitted, a full database backup will be performed.

The UNLOAD and NOUNLOAD options are performed only if the backup medium is a tape device. The UNLOAD option, which is the default, specifies that the tape is automatically rewound and unloaded from the tape device after the backup is completed. Use the NOUNLOAD option if SQL Server should not rewind (and unload) the tape from the tape device automatically.

BACKUP LOG Statement

The BACKUP LOG statement is used to perform a backup of the transaction log. This statement has the following syntax:

        BACKUP LOG {db_name | @variable}
          TO device_list
            [MIRROR TO device_list2]
          [WITH option_list]

db_name, @variable, device_list, and **device_list2** have the same meanings as the parameters with the same names in the BACKUP DATABASE statement. **option_list** has the same options as the BACKUP DATABASE statement and also supports the additional option NO_TRUNCATE. You should use the NO_TRUNCATE option if you want to back up the transaction log without truncating it—that is, this option does not clear the committed transactions in the log. After the execution of this option, SQL Server writes all recent database activities in the transaction log. Therefore, the NO_TRUNCATE option allows you to recover data right up to the point of the database failure.

NOTE

SQL Server 2000 supports, besides the NO_TRUNCATE option, two other options: NO_LOG and TRUNCATE_ONLY. The options remove the inactive part of the log without making a backup copy of it. SQL Server 2005 does not support these options. Now the transaction log is automatically truncated when the database is using the simple recovery model. If you need to remove the log backup chain from a database, switch to the simple recovery model (see also the description of the simple recovery model in the section "Recovery Models" later in this chapter).

Which Databases to Back Up?

The following databases should be backed up regularly:

- ▶ The **master** database
- ▶ All production databases
- ▶ The **msdb** database

Back Up master Database

The **master** database is the most important database of the SQL Server system because it contains information about all of the databases in the system. Therefore, the **master** database should be backed up on a regular basis. Additionally, you should back up the **master** database anytime certain statements and stored procedures are executed, because the database server modifies the **master** database automatically.

NOTE
*You can perform full database backups of the **master** database only. (SQL Server does not support differential, transaction log, and file backups for the **master** database.)*

Many activities cause the modification of the **master** database. Some of them are listed here:

- ▶ The creation, alteration, and removal of a database
- ▶ The alteration of the transaction log

NOTE
*Without a backup of the **master** database, you must completely rebuild all system databases, because if the **master** database is damaged, all references to the existing user-defined databases are lost.*

Back Up Production Databases

Each production database should be backed up on a regular basis. Additionally, you should back up any production database when the following activities are executed:

- ▶ After creating it
- ▶ After creating indices
- ▶ After clearing the transaction log
- ▶ After performing nonlogged operations

Always make a full database backup after it has been created in case a failure occurs between the creation of the database and the first regular database backup. Remember that backups of the transaction log cannot be applied without a full database backup.

Backing up the database after creation of one or more indices saves time during the restore process, because the index structures are backed up together with the data. Backing up the transaction log after creation of indices does not save time during the restore process at all, because the transaction log only records the fact that an index was created (and does not record the modified index structure).

Backing up the database after clearing the transaction log is necessary because the transaction log no longer contains a record of database activity, which is used to recover the database. All operations that are not recorded to the transaction log are called nonlogged operations. Therefore, all changes made by these operations cannot be restored during the recovery process. The following Transact-SQL statements and utilities do not record changes in the transaction log:

▶ The WRITETEXT and UPDATETEXT statements without WITH LOG

▶ The SELECT INTO statement

▶ The bulk copy program (see the description of the **bcp** utility in Chapter 15)

Back Up msdb Database

The **msdb** database is used for storing alerts, jobs, and recording operators that are subsequently used by the SQL Server Agent service. Therefore, any modification of these operators changes the **msdb** database. Back up the **msdb** database after each modification of it. (If you do not have a current backup of the **msdb** database when a failure occurs, you can rebuild the **msdb** database by executing the **instmsdb.sql** script from the **install** directory.)

Minimizing System Downtime

You can use various strategies to avoid data loss and downtime due to disk failures. Two general strategies supported by SQL Server are discussed here:

▶ Standby server

▶ RAID technology

Using a Standby Server

A standby server is just what its name implies—another server that is standing by in case something happens to the production server (also called the primary server). The standby server also runs and contains files, databases (system and user-defined), and user accounts identical to those on the production server.

A standby server is implemented by initially restoring a full database backup of the database and applying transaction log backups to keep the database on the standby server synchronized with the production server. To set up a standby server, set the **read only** database option to true. This option prevents users from performing any write operations in the database.

The general steps to use a copy of a production database are as follows:

▶ Restore the production database using the RESTORE DATABASE statement with the STANDBY clause.

▶ Apply each transaction log to the standby server using the RESTORE LOG statement with the STANDBY clause.

▶ When applying the final transaction log backup, use the RESTORE LOG statement with the RECOVERY clause. (This final statement recovers the database without creating a file with before images, making the database available for write operations, too.)

After the database and transaction logs are restored, users can work with an exact copy of the production database. Only the noncommitted transactions at the time of failure will be permanently lost.

NOTE

If the production server fails, user processes are not automatically brought to the standby server. Additionally, all user processes need to restart any tasks with the uncommitted transactions due to the failure of the production server.

RAID

RAID (redundant array of inexpensive disks) is a special disk configuration in which multiple disk drives build a single logical unit. This process allows files to span multiple disk devices. RAID technology provides improved reliability at the cost of performance decrease. Generally, there are six RAID levels: 0 through 5. Only three of these levels, level 0, level 1, and level 5, are significant for database systems.

RAID can be hardware- or software-based. Hardware-based RAID is more costly (because you have to buy additional disk controllers), but it usually performs better. Software-based RAID can be supported either by the operating system or by the database system itself. SQL Server does not support software-based RAID, except for database mirroring, which is a form of RAID 1. Windows operating systems provide RAID levels 0, 1, and 5. The RAID technology has impacts on the following features:

▶ Fault tolerance

▶ Performance

The benefits and disadvantages of each RAID level in relation to these two features will be explained next.

Windows-Based RAID RAID provides protection from hard disk failure and accompanying data loss with three methods: disk striping, mirroring, and parity. These three methods correspond to RAID levels 0, 1, and 5, respectively. RAID 0 specifies disk striping without parity. Using RAID 0, the data is written across several disk drives in order to allow data access more readily, and all read and write operations can be speeded up. For this reason, RAID 0 is the fastest RAID configuration. The disadvantage of disk striping is that it does not offer fault tolerance at all. This means if one disk fails, all the data on that array become inaccessible.

Mirroring is the special form of disk striping that uses the space on a disk drive to maintain a duplicate copy of some files. Therefore, RAID 1, which specifies disk mirroring, protects data against media failure by maintaining a copy of the database (or a part of it) on another disk. If there is a drive loss with mirroring in place, the files for the lost drive can be rebuilt by replacing the failed drive and rebuilding the damaged files. The hardware configurations of mirroring are more expensive, but they provide additional speed. The advantage of the Windows solution for mirroring is that it can be configured to mirror disk partitions, while the hardware solutions are usually implemented on the entire disk.

In contrast to RAID 0, RAID 1 is much slower, but the reliability is higher. Also, RAID 1 costs much more than RAID 0, because each mirrored disk drive must be doubled. It can sustain at least one failed drive and may be able to survive failure of up to half of the drives in the set of the mirrored disks without forcing the system administrator to shut down the server and recover from file backup. (RAID 1 is the best-performing RAID option when fault tolerance is required.)

Mirroring also has performance impacts in relation to read and write operations. When mirroring is used, write operations decrease performance, because each such operation costs two disk I/O operations, once to the original and once to the mirrored disk drive. On the other hand, mirroring increases performance of read operations, because SQL Server will be able to read from either disk drive, depending on which one is least busy at the time.

Parity (i.e., RAID level 5) is implemented by calculating recovery information about data written to disk and writing this parity information on the other drives that form the RAID array. If a drive fails, a new drive is inserted into the RAID array and the data on that failed drive is recovered by taking the recovery information (parity) written on the other drives and using this information to regenerate the data from the failed drive.

The advantage of parity is that you need one additional disk drive to protect any number of existing disk drives. The disadvantages of parity concern performance and fault tolerance. Due to the additional costs associated with calculating and writing parity, additional disk I/O operations are required. (Read I/O operation costs are the same for mirroring and parity.) Also, using parity, you can sustain only one failed drive before the array must be taken offline and recovery from backup media must be performed. Because disk striping with parity requires additional costs associated with calculating and writing parity, RAID 5 requires four disk I/O operations, where RAID 0 requires only one operation and RAID 1 two.

High Availability

The techniques explained in the previous section concern mechanisms that minimize system downtime but are not implemented in SQL Server. The SQL Server system supports the following technologies:

- ▶ Log shipping and database mirroring
- ▶ Failover clustering
- ▶ Data replication

These technologies can be used to minimize system downtime, and consequently achieve high availability of the whole system.

The first two technologies will be described in the following sections, while Chapter 24 describes data replication in detail.

Log Shipping and Database Mirroring

Log shipping allows the transaction logs from one database to be constantly sent and used by another database. This allows you to have a warm standby server and also provides a way to offload data from the source machine to read-only destination computers. The target database is an exact copy of the primary database, because the former receives all changes from the latter. You have the ability to make the target database a new primary database if the primary server, which hosts the original database, becomes unavailable. When the primary server becomes available again, you can make it a new standby server by reversing the server roles.

SQL Server 2005 enhances the capabilities of log shipping by providing you with a database mirroring option. Database mirroring allows continuous streaming of the transaction log from a source server to a target server. If the primary server becomes unavailable, applications can reconnect to the database on the target server without waiting for recovery to finish. Unlike failover clustering, the mirrored server is fully cached and ready to accept workloads because of its synchronized state. It is possible to implement up to four mirrored backup sets. (To implement mirroring, use the MIRROR TO option in the BACKUP DATABASE, e.g., BACKUP LOG statement.)

A database mirroring system requires three servers:

▶ Principal server

▶ Mirror server

▶ Witness server

The principal server is the primary server, i.e., the server where applications connect and where transactions are processed. The mirroring server is the target of transaction log records. This server exists in a state that does not allow direct read access to the data. As transaction log records are generated on the principal server, they are continuously replayed on the mirroring server. The witness server determines which server is the principal server and which is the mirror server. This server is only needed when automatic failover is required. (Database mirroring is not implemented in the first release of SQL Server 2005.)

NOTE

Both technologies, database mirroring and log shipping, are similar. On the other hand, database mirroring extends the capabilities of log shipping because it allows you to update the target database through a direct connection and in real time.

Failover Clustering

Failover clustering is probably the most important technology in SQL Server to achieve high availability. It is a process in which the operating system and SQL Server work together to provide availability in the event of failures. When a piece of hardware (called a node) with the SQL Server system fails, SQL Server on that machine shuts down. The Microsoft Cluster service transfers resources from a failing machine to an equally configured target node automatically. The transfer of resources from one node to the other node in a cluster occurs very quickly.

The advantage of failover clustering is that it protects your system against hardware failures, because it provides a mechanism to automatically restart the SQL Server system on another node of the cluster. On the other hand, this technology has a single point of failure in the set of disks, which cluster nodes share and cannot protect from data errors. Another disadvantage of this technology is that it does not increase performance or scalability, i.e., an application cannot scale any further on a cluster than it can on one node.

Recovery

Whenever a transaction is submitted for execution, SQL Server is responsible either for executing the transaction completely and recording its changes permanently in the database or for guaranteeing that the transaction has no effect at all on the database. This approach ensures that the database is consistent in case of a failure, because failures do not damage the database itself, but instead affect transactions that are in progress at the time of the failure. SQL Server supports both automatic and manual recovery.

Automatic Recovery

Automatic recovery is a fault-tolerant feature that SQL Server executes every time it is restarted after a failure or shutdown. The automatic recovery process checks to see if the restoration of databases is necessary. If it is, each database is returned to its last consistent state using the transaction log.

SQL Server examines the transaction log from the last checkpoint to the point at which the system failed or was shut down. (A *checkpoint* is the most recent point at which all data changes are written permanently to the database from memory. Therefore, a checkpoint ensures the physical consistency of the data.) The transaction log contains committed transactions (transactions that are successfully executed, but their changes have not yet been written to the database) and uncommitted transactions (transactions that are not successfully executed before a shutdown or failure occurred). SQL Server rolls forward all committed transactions, thus making permanent changes to the database, and undoes the part of the uncommitted transactions that occurred before the checkpoint.

SQL Server first performs the automatic recovery of the **master** database, followed by the recovery of all other system databases. Then, all user-defined databases are recovered.

Manual Recovery

A manual recovery of a database specifies the application of the backup of your database and subsequent application of all transaction logs in the sequence of their creation. After this, the database is in the same (consistent) state as it was at the point when the transaction log was backed up for the last time.

When you recover a database using a full database backup, SQL Server first re-creates all database files and places them in the corresponding physical locations. After that, the system re-creates all database objects.

In contrast to the previous versions, SQL Server 2005 processes certain forms of recovery process dynamically, i.e., while an instance of the database system is running. Dynamic recovery improves the availability of the system, because only the data being restored is unavailable. Dynamic recovery allows you to restore either an entire database file or a single page of data. SQL Server 2005 also supports the dynamic restore of a filegroup, because a filegroup is a collection of files. (Microsoft calls dynamic recovery "online restore.")

Is My Backup Set Ready for Recovery?

After executing the BACKUP statement, the selected device (tape or disk) contains all data of the object you choose to back up. The stored data is called a *backup set*. Before you start a recovery process, you should be sure that

▶ The backup set contains the data you want to restore

▶ The backup set is usable

SQL Server supports four Transact-SQL statements that allow you to get the answers to the two questions previously formulated. They are as follows:

▶ RESTORE LABELONLY

▶ RESTORE HEADERONLY

▶ RESTORE FILELISTONLY

▶ RESTORE VERIFYONLY

RESTORE LABELONLY   This statement is used to display the header information of the media (disk or tape) used for a backup process. The output of the RESTORE LABELONLY statement is a single row that contains the summary of the header information (name of the media, the description of the backup process, and the date of a backup process). The syntax of this statement is

RESTORE LABELONLY
    FROM device_name
    [WITH {UNLOAD | NOUNLOAD}]

device_name is the name of either a specific backup device or a variable that is used as the placeholder for the backup device. The UNLOAD option specifies that the tape device is automatically rewound and unloaded at the end of the recovery process. The other option—NOUNLOAD—leaves the tape device unwound after the recovery process.

NOTE

The RESTORE LABELONLY reads just the header file, so use this statement if you want to get a quick look at what your backup media contains.

RESTORE HEADERONLY   The former statement—RESTORE LABELONLY—gives you the concise information concerning the header file of your backup device. If you want to get the information concerning backups that are stored on a backup device, you should use the RESTORE HEADERONLY statement. This statement displays a one-line summary for each backup on a backup device. In contrast to the RESTORE LABELONLY statement, the RESTORE HEADERONLY statement can be time-consuming if the device contains several backups.

NOTE

This statement has the same options as the RESTORE LABELONLY statement.

RESTORE FILELISTONLY   The RESTORE FILELISTONLY statement returns a result set with a list of the database and log files contained in the backup set. You can display the information concerning only one backup set at a time. For this reason, if the specified backup device contains several backups, you have to specify the position of the backup set to be processed. The syntax of this statement is

RESTORE FILELISTONLY
    FROM device_name
    [WITH [FILE = number] [,{UNLOAD | NOUNLOAD}]]

The only additional option (in contrast to the previous statements) is the FILE option. It specifies the position of the backup set on the device. The default value is 1, specifying the first backup on the device.

You should use the RESTORE FILELISTONLY statement if you don't know exactly either which backup sets exist or where the files of a particular backup set are stored. In both cases, you can check all or part of the devices to make a global picture of existing backups.

RESTORE VERIFYONLY   After you have found your backup, you can do the next step: Verify the backup without using it for the restore process. The verification can be done with the RESTORE VERIFYONLY statement. This statement checks the existence of all backup devices (tapes or files) and whether the information can be read. The syntax of this statement is:

```
RESTORE VERIFYONLY
   FROM device_name
   [WITH  [FILE = number] [,{UNLOAD | NOUNLOAD}]
   [, STATS = [percentage]]
   [, LOADHISTORY]]
```

As you can see from the syntax, the options of the RESTORE VERIFYONLY correspond to the options of the RESTORE FILELISTONLY statement. There are two additional options:

▶ LOADHISTORY

▶ STATS

The LOADHISTORY option causes the backup information to be added to the backup history tables. The STATS option displays a message each time another percentage of the reading process completes and is used to gauge progress. If *percentage* is omitted, SQL Server displays a message after each 10 percent of the information is read.

Restoring Databases and Logs Using Management Studio

To restore a database from a full database backup, expand the server, choose **Databases**, and right-click the database. After pointing to **Tasks**, choose **Restore** and then **Database**. The **Restore Database** dialog box appears (see Figure 20-4). On the **General** tab, select databases to which and from which you want to restore. Then check the type of a backup that you want to process (in this case, Full Database Backup).

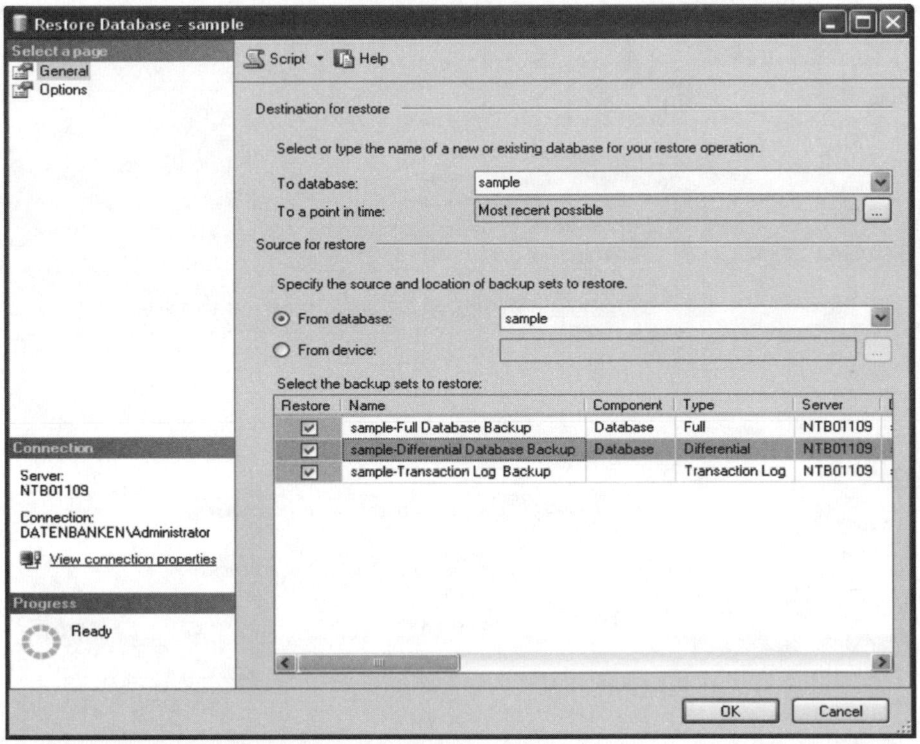

Figure 20-4 in the Restore Database dialog box appears here:

Restore	Name	Component	Type	Server	
✓	sample-Full Database Backup	Database	Full	NTB01109	
✓	sample-Differential Database Backup	Database	Differential	NTB01109	
✓	sample-Transaction Log Backup		Transaction Log	NTB01109	

Figure 20-4 *The Restore Database dialog box*

NOTE

Do not forget the sequence of restoring different types of backups! First restore the full database backup. Then restore all corresponding transaction logs in the sequence of their creation.

To select the appropriate restore options, choose the **Options** tab (see Figure 20-5) of the **Restore Database** dialog box. In the upper part of the window, choose one or more restore types. In the lower part of the **Restore database** window, you can choose one of the three existing options. The first option **(Leave the database ready to use by rolling back uncommitted transactions)** instructs SQL Server to roll forward any committed transaction and to roll back any uncommitted transaction. After applying this option, the database is in a consistent state and is ready for use. This option is equivalent to the RECOVERY option of the RESTORE DATABASE statement. (The RESTORE DATABASE statement is described in the next section.)

NOTE

Use this option only with the last transaction log to be restored or with a full database restore when no subsequent transaction logs need to be applied.

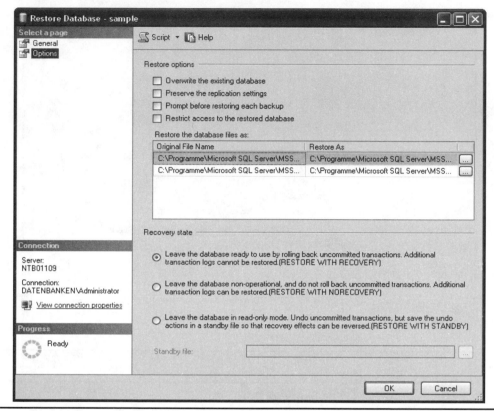

Figure 20-5 *The Options tab of the Restore Database dialog box*

If you click the second option (**Leave the database non-operational, and do not roll back uncommitted transactions**), SQL Server does not roll back uncommitted transactions because you will be applying further backups. After this option is applied, the database is unavailable for use, and additional transaction logs should be restored. This option is equivalent to the NORECOVERY option of the RESTORE DATABASE statement.

NOTE

Use this option with all but the last transaction log to be restored or with a differential database restore.

The third option (**Leave the database in read-only mode**) specifies the file (in the **Standby file** dialog box) that is subsequently used to roll back the recovery effects. (See also the STANDBY option in the RESTORE DATABASE statement.)

The process of a database restoration from a differential database backup is equivalent to the process of a restoration from a full database backup. In this case, you have to check the corresponding backup set in the list of all backup sets (see Figure 20-4).

NOTE

If you restore from a differential backup, first restore the full database backup before you restore a differential one. In contrast to transaction log backups, only the latest differential backup is applied because it includes all changes since the full backup!

If you want to restore a transaction log backup, follow the same steps as for the restoration of a full database backup and choose the corresponding backup set(s) from the list of all backup sets (see Figure 20-4).

To restore a database with a new name, expand the server, expand **Databases**, and right-click the database. After pointing to **Tasks**, choose **Restore** and then **Database**. In the **Restore database** dialog box on the **General** tab, in the **To database** dialog box, enter the name of the database you want to create, and in the **From database** dialog box, the name of the database whose backup is used.

Restoring Databases and Logs Using Transact-SQL Statements

All restore operations can be executed using two Transact-SQL statements:

▶ RESTORE DATABASE

▶ RESTORE LOG

The RESTORE DATABASE statement is used to perform the restore process for a database. The general syntax of this statement is

```
RESTORE DATABASE {db_name | @variable}
    [FROM device_list]
    [WITH option_list]
```

db_name is the name of the database that will be restored. (The name of the database can be supplied using a variable @**variable**.) **device_list** in the FROM clause specifies one or more device names where the database backup is stored. (If the FROM clause is not specified, the restore of a backup does not take place, but only the process of automatic recovery takes place, and you must specify either the RECOVERY, NORECOVERY, or STANDBY option. This action can take place if you want to switch over to a standby server.) **device_list** can be a list of names of disk files or tapes. **option_list** comprises several options that can be specified for the different backup forms. The most important options are

- ▶ RECOVERY/NORECOVERY/STANDBY
- ▶ CHECKSUM/NO_CHECKSUM
- ▶ REPLACE
- ▶ PARTIAL
- ▶ STOPAT
- ▶ STOPATMARK
- ▶ STOPBEFOREMARK

The RECOVERY option instructs SQL Server to roll forward any committed transaction and to roll back any uncommitted transaction. After the RECOVERY option is applied, the database is in a consistent state and is ready for use. This option is the default.

NOTE

Use the RECOVERY option only with the last transaction log to be restored or with a full database restore with no subsequent transaction log backups to restore.

With the NORECOVERY option, SQL Server does not roll back uncommitted transactions because you will be applying further backups. After the NORECOVERY option is applied, the database is unavailable for use.

NOTE

Use the NORECOVERY option either with all but the last transaction log to be restored or with a differential database restore.

The STANDBY option is an alternative to the RECOVERY/NORECOVERY options and is used with the standby server. In order to access data stored on the standby server, you usually recover the database after a transaction log is restored. On the other hand, if you recover the database on the standby server, you cannot apply additional logs from the production server for the restore process. In that case, you use the STANDBY option to allow users read access to the standby server. Additionally, you allow the system the restoration of additional transaction logs.

The STANDBY option implies the existence of the undo file that is used to roll back changes when additional logs are restored.

The CHECKSUM option initiates the verification of both the backup checksums and page checksums, if present. If checksums are absent, RESTORE proceeds without verification. The NO_CHECKSUM option explicitly disables the validation of checksums by the restore operation.

The REPLACE option replaces an existing database with data from a backup of a different database. In this case, the existing database is first destroyed, and the differences regarding the names of the files in the database and the database name are ignored. (If you do not use the REPLACE option, the database server performs a safety check that guarantees an existing database is not replaced if the names of files in the database or the database name itself differs from the corresponding names in the backup set.)

The PARTIAL option specifies a partial restore operation. With this option you can restore a portion of a database, consisting of its primary filegroup and one or more secondary filegroups, which are specified in an additional option called FILEGROUP. (The PARTIAL option is not allowed with the RESTORE LOG statement.)

The STOPAT option allows you to restore a database to the state it was in at the exact moment before a failure occurred by specifying a point in time. SQL Server restores all committed transactions that were recorded in the transaction log before the specified point in time. If you want to restore a database by specifying a point in time, execute the RESTORE DATABASE statement using the NORECOVERY clause. After that, execute the RESTORE LOG statement to apply each transaction log backup, specifying the name of the database, the backup device from where the transaction log backup will be restored, and the STOPAT clause. (If the backup of a log does not contain the requested time, the database will not be recovered.)

The STOPATMARK and STOPBEFOREMARK options specify recovering to a mark. This topic is described at the end of this chapter.

The RESTORE DATABASE statement is also used to restore a database using a differential backup. The syntax and the options for restoring a differential backup are the same as for restoring from a full database backup. During a restoration from a differential backup, the database server restores only that part of the database that has changed since the last full database backup. Therefore, restore your database using the full database backup *before* you restore it using a differential backup!

The RESTORE LOG statement is used to perform a restore process for a transaction log. This statement has the same syntax form and the same options as the RESTORE DATABASE statement.

Restoring master Database

The corruption of the **master** database can be devastating for the whole system, because it comprises all system tables that are necessary to work with the database system. (This makes a file with the **master** database a good candidate for mirroring using RAID 1.) The restore process of the **master** database is quite different from the same process concerning user-defined databases, as you will see.

A damaged **master** database makes itself known through different failures. These failures include the following:

► Inability to start the relational database server

► An input/output error

► The execution of the DBCC utility points to such a failure

There are two different ways you have to go to recover the **master** database. The easier way is when you can start your database system. In that case, you just restore the **master** database from the full database backup.

To restore your **master** database, start the database server in single-user mode. As you already know from Chapter 17, there are several ways to do it. My favorite way is to use the command window and execute the **sqlservr** application with the option **–m**. In the second step, you restore the **master** database together with all other databases using the last full database backup.

NOTE
*If there have been any changes to the **master** database since the last full database backup, you will need to re-create those changes manually.*

Restoring Other System Databases

The restore process for all system databases other than **master** is similar. Therefore, we will explain this process using the **msdb** database. The **msdb** database needs to be restored from a backup when either the **master** database has been rebuilt or the **msdb** database itself has been damaged. If the **msdb** database is damaged, restore it using the existing backups. If there have been any changes after the **msdb** database backup was created, re-create those changes manually.

NOTE
*You cannot restore a database that is being accessed by users. Therefore, when restoring the **msdb** database, the SQL Server Agent service should be stopped. (The SQL Server Agent service accesses the **msdb** database.)*

Recovery Models

SQL Server supports the database recovery models, which allow you to control to what extent you are ready to risk losing committed transactions if a database is damaged. Additionally, the choice of a recovery model has an impact on the size of the transaction log therefore on the time period needed to back up the log. The database server supports three recovery models:

▶ Full

▶ Bulk-logged

▶ Simple

The following sections describe the three recovery models.

Full Recovery

During full recovery, all operations are written to the transaction log. Therefore, this model provides complete protection against media failure. This means that you can restore your database up to the last committed transaction that is stored in the log file. Additionally, data can be recovered to any point in time (prior to the point of failure). To guarantee this, such operations as SELECT INTO and the execution of the **bcp** utility are fully logged, too.

Besides point-in-time recovery, the full recovery model allows you also to recover to a log mark. Log marks correspond to a specific transaction and are inserted only if the transaction commits. (For more information on log marks, see the corresponding section later in this chapter.)

The full recovery model also logs all operations concerning the CREATE INDEX statement, implying that the process of data recovery now includes the restoration of index creations. That way, the re-creation of the indices is faster, because you do not have to rebuild them separately.

The disadvantage of this recovery model is that the corresponding transaction log may be very voluminous and the files on the disk containing the log will be filled up very quickly. Also, for such a voluminous log you will need significantly more time for backup.

NOTE

If you use the full recovery model, the transaction log must be protected from media failure. For this reason, using RAID 1 to protect transaction logs is strongly recommended.

Bulk-Logged Recovery

Bulk-logged recovery supports log backups by using minimal space in the transaction log for certain large-scale or bulk operations. The logging of the following operations is minimal and cannot be controlled on an operation-by-operation basis:

- ▶ SELECT INTO
- ▶ CREATE INDEX (including indexed views)
- ▶ **bcp** utility and BULK INSERT
- ▶ WRITETEXT and UPDATETEXT

Although bulk operations are not fully logged, you do not have to perform a full database backup after the completion of such an operation. During bulk-logged recovery, transaction log backups contain both the log as well as the results of a bulk operation. This simplifies the transition between full and bulk-logged recovery models.

The bulk-logged recovery model allows you to recover a database to the end of a transaction log backup (i.e., up to the last committed transaction). In contrast to the full recovery model, bulk-logged recovery does not support generally point-in-time recovery. (You can use bulk-logged recovery for the point-in-time recovery if no bulk operations have been performed.)

The advantage of the bulk-logged recovery model is that bulk operations are performed much faster than under the full recovery model, because they are not fully logged.

Simple Recovery

In the simple recovery model, the transaction log is not used to protect your database against any media failure. Therefore, you can recover a damaged database only using full database or differential backup. Backup strategy for this model is very simple: Restore the database using existing database backups and, if differential backups exist, apply the most recent one.

The advantages of the simple recovery model are that the performance of all bulk operations is very high and requirements for the log space very small. On the other hand, this model requires the most manual work because all changes since the most recent database (or differential) backup must be redone. Point-in-time as well as page restore are not allowed with this recovery model. Also, file restore is available only for read-only secondary filegroups.

Recovery Models and Backward Compatibility

You can change the recovery model using the RECOVERY option of the ALTER DATABASE statement. The part of the syntax of the ALTER DATABASE statement concerning recovery models is

ALTER DATABASE db_name
　　　　SET RECOVERY [FULL | BULK_LOGGED | SIMPLE]
　　　　...

If you want to display the current model of your database, use the RECOVERY clause of the DATABASEPROPERTYEX function. Example 20.1 shows the SELECT statement that displays the recovery model for the sample database.

EXAMPLE 20.1

SELECT databasepropertyex('sample', 'recovery')

Recovery to a Mark

The database server allows you to use the transaction log to recover to a specific mark. Log marks correspond to a specific transaction and are inserted only if the transaction commits. This allows the marks to be tied to specific work and provides the ability to recover to a point that includes or excludes this work.

NOTE

If a marked transaction spans multiple databases on the same database server, the marks are recorded in the logs of all the affected databases.

The BEGIN TRANSACTION statement is enhanced to support transaction log marking. Use the WITH MARK clause to insert marks into the logs. Because the name of the mark is the same as its transaction, a transaction name is required. (The **description** option specifies a textual description of the mark.)

The transaction log records the mark name, description, database, user, date and time information, and the unique log sequence number (LSN). To allow their reuse, the transaction names are not required to be unique. The date and time information is used along with the name to uniquely identify the mark.

You can use the RESTORE LOG statement (either with the STOPATMARK clause or the STOPBEFOREMARK clause) to specify recovering to a mark. The STOPATMARK clause causes the recover process to roll forward to the mark and include the transaction that contains the mark. If you specify the STOPBEFOREMARK clause, the recover process excludes the transaction that contains the mark.

Both clauses just described support an optional AFTER **datetime** clause. If this clause is omitted, recovery stops at the first mark with the specified name. If the clause is specified, recovery stops at the first mark with the specified name exactly at or after **datetime**.

Conclusion

The system administrator or database owner should periodically make a backup copy of the database and its transaction log to allow for recovery in the event of system errors, media failures, or a combination of other reasons (such as fire or theft). The database server provides two kinds of backup copies of the database: full and differential. A full backup captures the state of the database at the time the statement is issued and copies it to the backup media (file or tape device). A differential backup copies the parts of the database that have changed since the last full database backup. The benefit of the differential backup is that it completes more rapidly than the full database backup for the same database.

The database server performs automatic recovery each time a system failure occurs that does not cause any media failure. (The automatic recovery is also performed when the system is started after each shutdown of the system.) During automatic recovery, any committed transaction found in the transaction log is written to the database, and any uncommitted transaction is rolled back. After any media failure, it may be necessary to recover the database from the archived copy of it and its transaction logs. To recover a database, a full database backup and only the latest differential backup must be used. If you use transaction logs to restore a database, use the full database backup first, and after that, apply all existing transaction logs in the sequence of their creation to bring the database to the consistent state that it was in before the last transaction log backup was created.

The next chapter describes all SQL Server tools and features that you can use for data transfer and data transformation.

Exercises

E.20.1

Discuss the differences between the differential and transaction log backup.

E.20.2

When should you back up your production database?

E.20.3

How can you make a differential backup of the **master** database?

E.20.4

Discuss the use of different RAID technologies concerning fault tolerance of a database and its transaction log.

E.20.5

What are the main differences between manual and automatic recovery?

E.20.6

Which statement should you use to verify your backup, without using it for the restore process?

E.20.7

Discuss the use of the three recovery models.

Automating System Administration Tasks

The system administrator has many different tasks to perform: surveying one or more databases, tuning and optimizing them, and tailoring database layouts and database tables to fulfill actual and future needs. Generally, a database environment that works optimally during all working hours is the system administrator's goal. To achieve this, he or she has to organize all tasks very efficiently. The service tools provided by SQL Server, and especially SQL Server Agent, help the system administrator reach this goal.

This chapter describes, first, how SQL Server Agent can be used to automate the daily work of the system administrator. In the second part of the chapter, the creation of jobs and the definition of alerts, which are used to respond to system- or user-defined errors, are discussed.

Introduction

The most important advantages of the SQL Server system in relation to other relational DBMSs are as follows:

▶ The graphical user interfaces adapted and integrated into the well-known MS Windows standard interface make it easy for the system administrator to build and manage databases and all database objects.

▶ The ability to automate administrative tasks and hence to reduce costs.

Here are some important administrative tasks that are performed frequently and therefore could be automated:

▶ Backing up the database and transaction log

▶ Transferring data

▶ Dropping and re-creating indices

▶ Checking data integrity

You can automate all these tasks so they occur on a regular schedule. For example, you can set the database backup task to occur every Friday at 8:00 P.M. and the transaction log backup task to occur daily at 12:00 P.M.

SQL Server components used in automation include the following:

▶ MSSQLServer service

▶ Event log

▶ SQL Server Agent

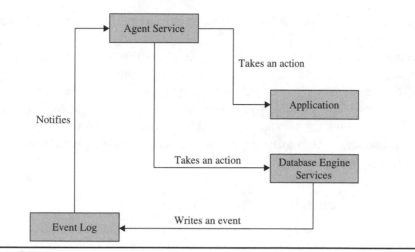

Figure 21-1   *SQL Server automation components*

Why does SQL Server need these three components to automate processes? In relation to automation of administration tasks, the MSSQLServer service is needed to write events to the event log. Some events are written automatically, and some must be raised by the system administrator (see the detailed explanation later in this chapter).

The event log is where all operating system messages of Windows operating systems and messages of its components are written. (For example, SQL Server errors with severity levels between 19 and 25 are always stored in the Windows event log.) The role of the event log in the automation process is to notify SQL Server Agent about existing events.

SQL Server Agent is another service that connects to the event log and the MSSQLServer service. The role of SQL Server Agent in the automation process is to take an action after a notification through event log. The action can be performed in connection with the MSSQLServer service or some other application. Figure 21-1 shows how these three components work together.

SQL Server Agent

SQL Server Agent executes jobs and fires alerts. As you will see in the upcoming sections, jobs and alerts are defined separately and can be executed independently. Nevertheless, jobs and alerts may also be complementary processes, because a job can invoke an alert and vice versa.

Consider an example: A job is executed to inform the system administrator about an unexpected filling of the transaction log that exceeds a tolerable limit. When this event occurs, the associated alert is invoked and, as a reaction, the system administrator may be notified by e-mail or pager.

Another critical event is a failure in backing up the transaction log. When this happens, the associated alert may invoke a job that truncates the transaction log (see also Chapter 20). This reaction will be appropriate if the reason for the backup failure is an overflow (filling up) of the transaction log. In other cases (for example, the target device for the backup copy is full), such a truncation will have no effect. This example shows the close connection that may exist between events that have similar symptoms.

Running and Configuring SQL Server Agent

SQL Server Agent allows you to automate different administrative tasks. Before you can do this, of course, it must be started. SQL Server Agent can be started in the same way as the MSSQLServer service.

As already stated, the invocation of an alert can also include the notification of the operator by e-mail. SQL Server uses a mail session called SQLiMail to send text strings, files, or query results to other computers.

Creating Jobs and Operators

Generally, there are three steps to follow if you want to create a job:

► Create a job and its steps

► Create a schedule of the job execution if the job is not to be executed by the user on demand

► Notify operators about the status of the job

The following sections explain these steps using an example job.

Job Steps

A job may contain one or more steps. There are different ways in which a job step can be defined:

► Using Transact-SQL statements

► Executing a utility

► Invoking a program

► Executing replication or Analysis Services tasks

Many job steps contain Transact-SQL statements. For example, if you want to automate database or transaction log backups, you will use the BACKUP DATABASE statement or BACKUP LOG statement, respectively. Some other jobs may require the execution of a SQL Server utility, which usually will be started with the corresponding command. For example, if you want to automate the data transfer from SQL Server to a data file, or vice versa, you will use the **bcp** command.

As a third alternative, it may be necessary to execute a program that has been developed using Visual Basic or some other programming language. In this case, you should always include the path drive letter in the **Command** text box when you start such a program. This is necessary because SQL Server Agent has to find the executable file.

If the job contains several steps, it is important to determine what actions should be taken in case of a failure. Generally, the database server will start the next job step if the previous one was successfully executed. However, if a job step fails, any job steps that follow will not be executed. Therefore, you should always specify how often each step should be retried in the case of failure. And, of course, it will be necessary to eliminate the reason for the abnormal termination of the job step (obviously, a repeated job execution will always lead to the same error if the error is not repaired).

NOTE

The number of attempts depends on the type and content of the executed job step (batch, command, or application program).

Creating a Job Using SQL Server Management Studio

You can create a job using the following:

▶ SQL Server Management Studio

▶ System stored procedures

This section illustrates the creation of a job using SQL Server Management Studio. The job backs up a sample database. To create this job, expand SQL Server Agent under the database server, right-click **Jobs**, and then click **New Job**. The **New Job** dialog box appears (see Figure 21-2). On the **General** page, enter a name for the job (as you can see in Figure 21-2, the name of the job for backing up the sample database is **backup_sample**).

In the **Owner** list, click the owner responsible for performing the job, and in the **Category** list, choose the category to which the job belongs. In the example in Figure 21-2, the job **backup_sample** is not categorized, and the owner is the user

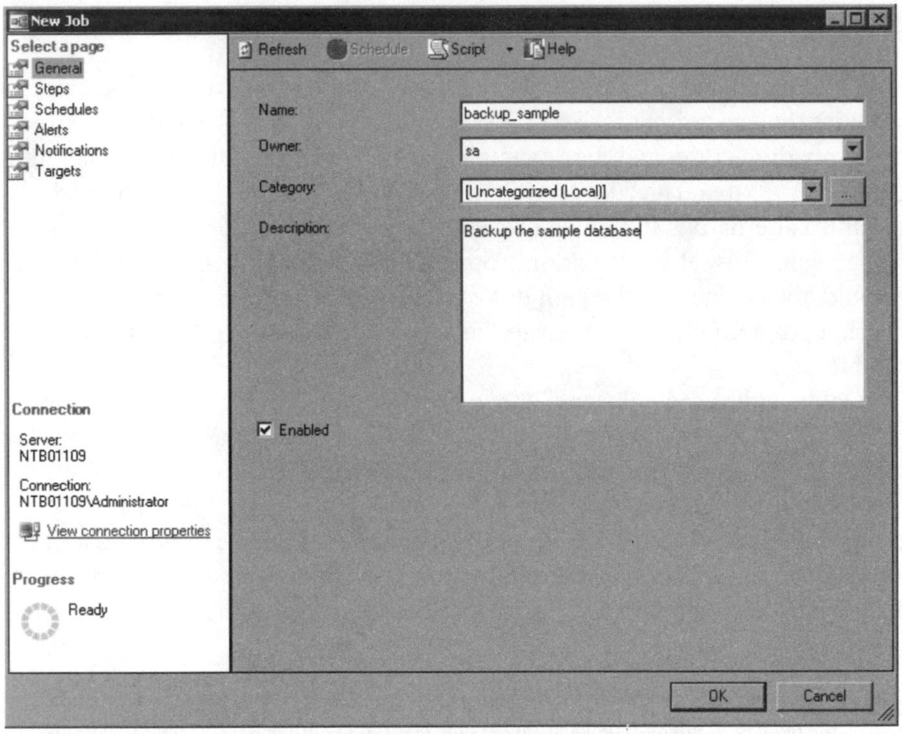

Figure 21-2 *The New Job dialog box*

who creates the job. You can add a description of the job in the **Description** box, if you wish.

NOTE

If you have to manage several jobs, categorizing them is recommended. This is especially useful if your jobs are executed in a multiserver environment.

Check the **Enabled** check box to enable the job.

NOTE

All jobs are enabled by default. SQL Server Agent disables jobs if the job schedule is defined either at a specific time that has passed or on a recurring basis with an end date that has also passed. In both cases, you must re-enable the job manually.

Each job must have one or more steps. Therefore, in addition to the definition of job properties, at least one step must be created before the job can be saved.

To define one or more steps, click the **Steps** page in the **New Job** dialog box and choose **New**. The **New Job Step** dialog box appears. Enter a name for the job step. (It is called **backup** in the example.) In the **Type** list, choose Transact-SQL script, because the backup of the sample database will be executed using the Transact-SQL statement BACKUP DATABASE (see below).

In the **Database** list, choose the **master** database, because this system database must be the current database in case you want to back up a database.

The Transact-SQL statement can either be directly entered in the **Command** box or invoked from a file. In the former case, write the following statements (the file C:\xxx must exist):

        EXEC sp_addumpdevice 'disk', 'backup_file1', 'C:\xxx'
    backup database sample to backup_file1

In the latter case, click **Open** and select the file (see Figure 21-3). (The syntax of the statement(s) can be checked by clicking **Parse**.)

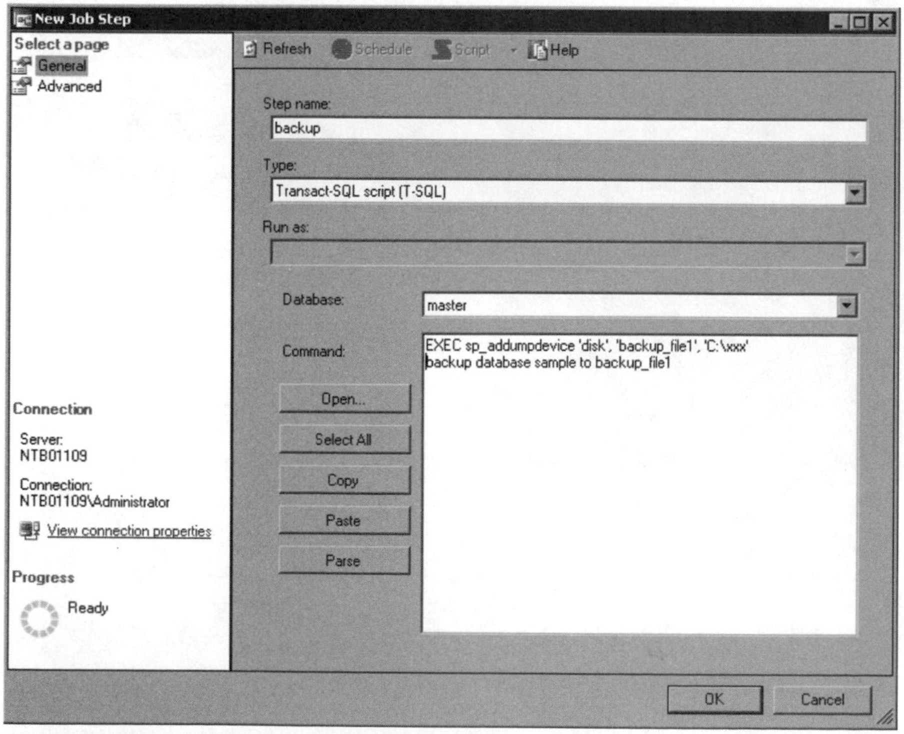

Figure 21-3 *The New Job Step dialog box: The General page*

Creating Job Schedules

Each created job can be executed on demand (i.e., manually by the user) or by using one or more schedules. A scheduled job can occur at a specific time or on a recurring schedule.

NOTE

Each job can have multiple schedules. For example, the backup of the transaction log of a production database can be executed with two different schedules, depending on time of day. This means that during peak business hours, you can execute the backup more frequently than during nonpeak hours.

To create a schedule for an existing job using SQL Server Management Studio, select the **Schedules** page in the **New Job Properties** dialog box and click **New**. The **New Job Schedule** dialog box appears (see Figure 21-4). If the **New Job Properties** dialog box is not active, expand **SQL Server Agent**, expand **Jobs**, right-click the job, and click **Properties**.

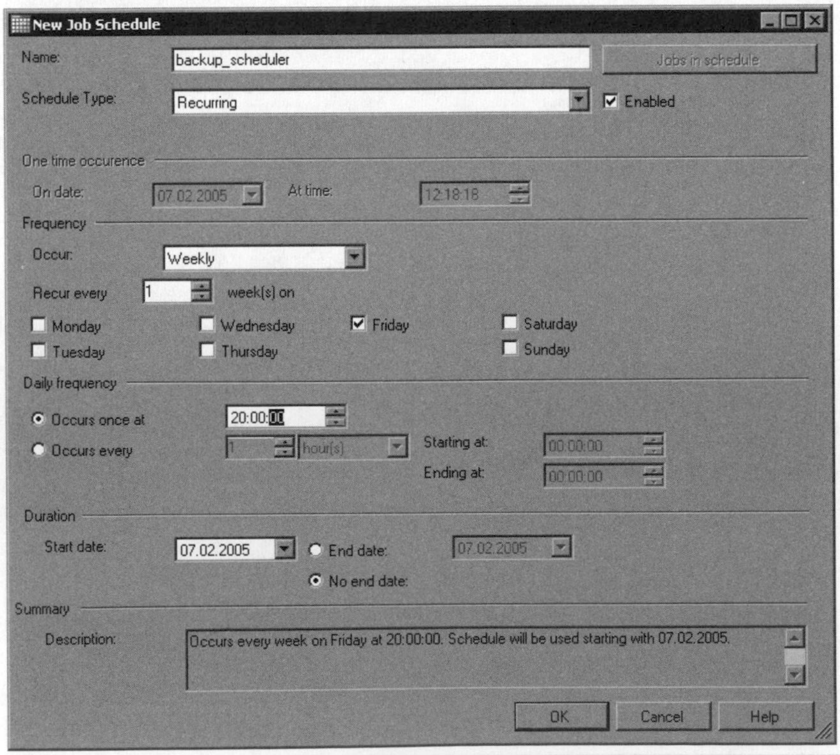

Figure 21-4   *The New Job Schedule dialog box*

For the sample database, let's set the schedule for the backup to be executed every Friday at 8:00 P.M. To do this, enter the name in the **Name** dialog box and choose **Recurring** in the **Schedule Types** list. Select **Weekly** in the **Occur** box, and check **Friday**. In the **Daily frequency** frame, check **Occurs once at** and enter the time (**8:00 PM**). In the **Duration** frame, enter the **start** and **end** dates. (If the job should be scheduled without the end date, check **No end** date.)

Creating Operators for Notification

When a job completes, several methods of notification are possible. For example, you can instruct the system to write a corresponding message to the event log, hoping that the system administrator reads this log from time to time. A better choice is to explicitly notify one or more operators using e-mail, pager, and/or the **net send** command.

Before an operator can be assigned to a job, you have to create an entry for it. To create an operator using SQL Server Management Studio, expand **SQL Server Agent**, right-click **Operators**, and then click **New Operator**. The **New Operator Properties**

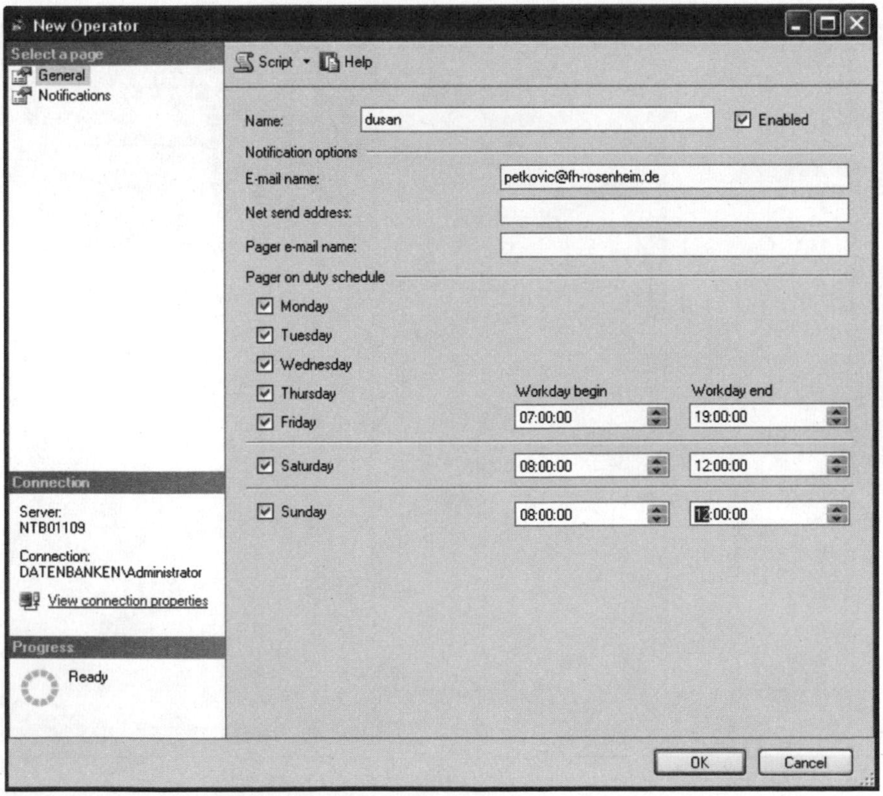

Figure 21-5 *The New Operator Properties dialog box*

dialog box appears (see Figure 21-5). On the **General** tab, enter the name of the operator in the **Name** box. Specify one or more methods of notifying the operator (via e-mail, pager, or the **net send** address). In the **Pager on duty schedule** frame, enter the working hours of the operator.

To notify one or more operators after the job finishes (successfully or unsuccessfully), open again the **Job Properties** dialog box, select the **Notifications** page, and check the corresponding boxes. (Besides e-mail, pager, or the **net send** command notification, in this dialog box you also have the option of writing the message to the event log and/or deleting the job.)

Viewing the Job History Log

The SQL Server system stores the information concerning all job activities in the system catalog of the **msdb** system database. You can view the information using SQL Server Management Studio. To do this, expand SQL Server Agent, click **Jobs**, right-click the job, and click **View History**. The **Log File Viewer** dialog box appears.

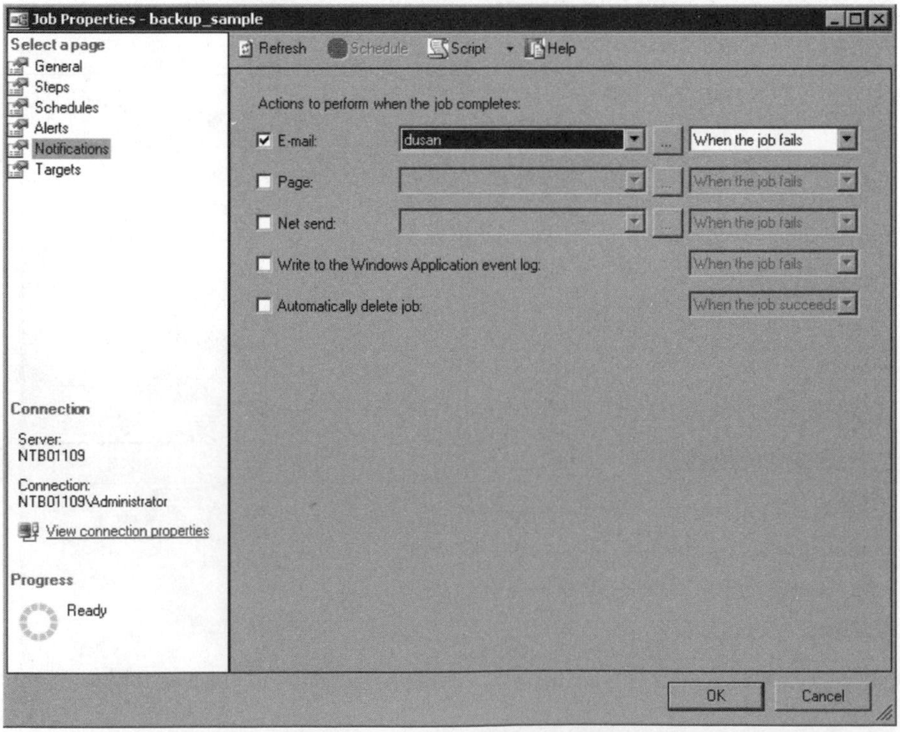

Figure 21-6   *The Job Properties dialog box: The Notifications page*

Each row of the job history log is displayed in the details pane of SQL Server Management Studio, and it contains the following information, among others:

▶ Date and time when the job step occurred

▶ Whether the job step completed successfully or unsuccessfully

▶ Operators who were notified

▶ Duration of the job

▶ Errors or messages concerning the job step

By default, the maximum size of the job history log is 1,000, while the number of rows for a job is limited to 100. (The job history log is automatically cleared when the maximum size of rows is reached.) If you want to store the information about each job and there are several jobs for your system, increase the size of the job history log and/or the amount of rows per job. Using SQL Server Management Studio, right-click **SQL Server Agent** and click **Properties**. In the **SQL Server Agent Properties** dialog box, select the **History** page and enter the new values for the maximum job history log size and maximum job history rows per job. You can also check **Automatically remove agent history** and select a time interval when logs should be deleted.

Alerts

The information about execution of jobs and SQL Server error messages is stored in the event log. SQL Server Agent reads this log and compares the stored messages with the alerts defined for the system. If there is a match, SQL Server Agent fires the alert. Therefore, the alerts can be used to respond to potential problems (such as filling up the transaction log), different SQL Server errors, or user-defined errors. Before we explain how alerts can be created, we will discuss SQL Server error messages and two logs, SQL Server log and event log, which are used to capture all system messages (and thus most of the errors).

Error Messages

As explained at the beginning of Chapter 20, there are four different groups of errors that might occur in a SQL Server system. SQL Server provides extensive information about each error. The information is structured and includes the following:

- ▶ A unique error message number
- ▶ An additional number between 0 and 25, which represents the error's severity level
- ▶ A line number, which identifies the line where the error occurred
- ▶ The error text

NOTE

The error text not only describes the detected error but also may recommend how to resolve the problem, which can be very helpful to the user.

Example 21.1 queries a nonexistent table in the sample database.

EXAMPLE 21.1

    USE sample
    SELECT * FROM authors

The result is

    Msg 208, Level 16, State 1, Line 1
    Invalid object name 'authors'.

All error messages are stored in the system table **sysmessages** of the **master** database. To view the information from this table, use the **sys.messages** catalog view. The three most important columns of this catalog view are **message_id, severity**, and **text**, which are described below.

Each unique error number has a corresponding error message. (The error message is stored in the **text** column, and the corresponding error number is stored in the **message_id** column of the **sys.messages** catalog view.) In Example 21.1, the message concerning the nonexistent or incorrectly spelled database object corresponds to error number -208.

The severity level of an error (the **severity** column of the **sys.messages** catalog view) is represented in the form of a number between 0 and 25. The levels between

0 and 10 are simply informational messages, where nothing needs to be fixed. All levels from 11 through 16 indicate different program errors and can be resolved by the user. The values 17 and 18 indicate software and hardware errors that generally do not terminate the running process. All errors with a severity level of 19 and greater are fatal system errors. The connection of the program generating such an error is closed, and its process will then be removed.

The messages relating to program errors (that is, the levels between 11 and 16) are shown on the screen only. All system errors (errors with a severity level of 19 or greater) will also be written to the error log file.

In order to resolve an error, you usually need to read the detailed description of the corresponding error. You can also find detailed error descriptions in Books Online.

SQL Server error messages are written to the SQL Server error log and to the event log. The following two sections describe these two components.

SQL Server Error Log

Each database server has an error log in the form of several text files. In addition to system errors, the error log records system activities such as starting, archiving, recovering, and stopping the system. SQL Server always maintains several files, which are all part of the error log. The current error log file name is **Current**, and the other file names are **Archive #1** (the most recent file) up to **Archive #6** (the oldest file).

The error log is an important source of information for the system administrator. With it, he or she can trace the progress of the system and determine which corrective actions to take. To view the SQL Server error logs from Management Studio, expand the server and the **SQL Server Agent** folder, and then expand **Error logs**. Click one of the error logs to view the desired log. The log details appear in the details pane.

Event Log

The database server also writes system messages to the event log. The event log is the location of all operating system messages for the Windows operating systems, and it is where all application messages are stored. You can view the event log using the Windows Event Viewer.

Using the event log for viewing errors has some advantages compared to the error log. First, the event log marks all errors with a red stop sign at the beginning of the line.

Thus, the system administrator can recognize them immediately. Second, the event log provides an additional component for the search for desired strings.

To view information stored in the event log, click **Start**, select **Settings** and then **Control Panel**, choose **Administrative Tools**, and select **Event Viewer**. In the **Event Viewer** dialog box, you can choose between system, security, and application messages.

Defining Alerts to Handle SQL Server Errors

An alert can be defined to raise a response to a particular error number or to the group of errors that belong to a specific severity code (see Chapter 22). Furthermore, the definition of an alert for a particular error is different for system errors and user-defined errors. (The creation of alerts on user-defined errors is described later in this chapter.)

Alerts can be defined using SQL Server Management Studio. The next sections show this.

Creating Alerts on SQL Server Error Numbers

Example 14.4, where one transaction was deadlocked by another transaction, will be used to show how to create an alert on a SQL Server error number using SQL Server Management Studio. If a transaction was deadlocked by another transaction, the victim must be executed again. This can be done, among other ways, by using an alert.

To create the deadlock (or any other) alert, expand SQL Server Agent, right-click **Alerts**, and click **New Alert**. In the **New Alert** dialog box (see Figure 21-7), enter the name of the alert in the **Name** box, select the alert type (**SQL Server event alert**), and choose the **sample** database from the **Database name** list. Click **Error number**, and enter **1205**. (This error number indicates that SQL Server found a deadlock and the process was selected as the "victim.")

The second step defines the response for the alert. In the same dialog box, click the **Response** page (see Figure 21-8). First select **Execute job**, and then select the job to execute when the alert occurs. (In the example here, we defined a new job called **deadlock_all_db**, which restarts the victim transaction.) In the **Notify operators** frame, you can select operators and the methods of their notifications (e-mail, pager, and/or the **net send** command).

NOTE

In the example, it is assumed that the victim transaction will be terminated. Actually, after receiving the deadlock error 1205, the program resubmits the failed transaction on its own.

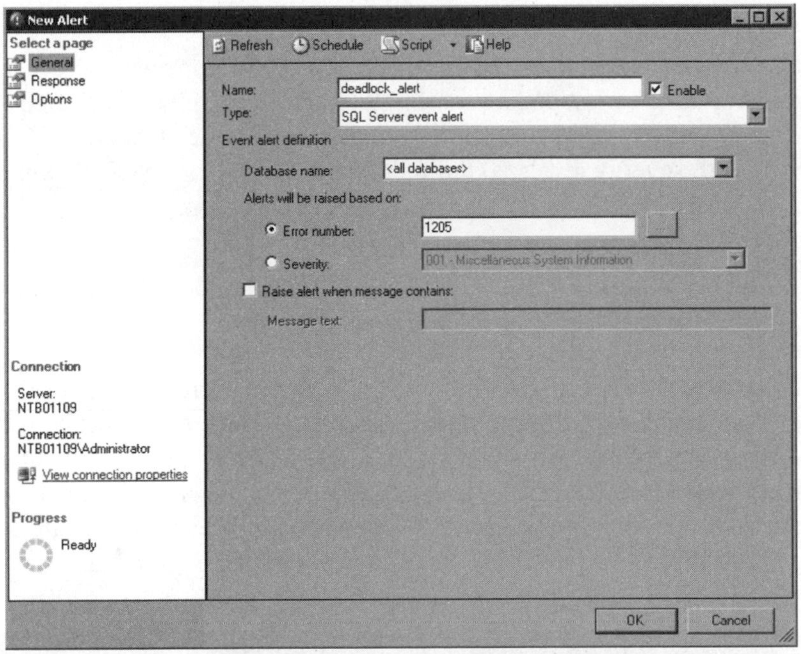

Figure 21-7   *The New Alert dialog box: The General page*

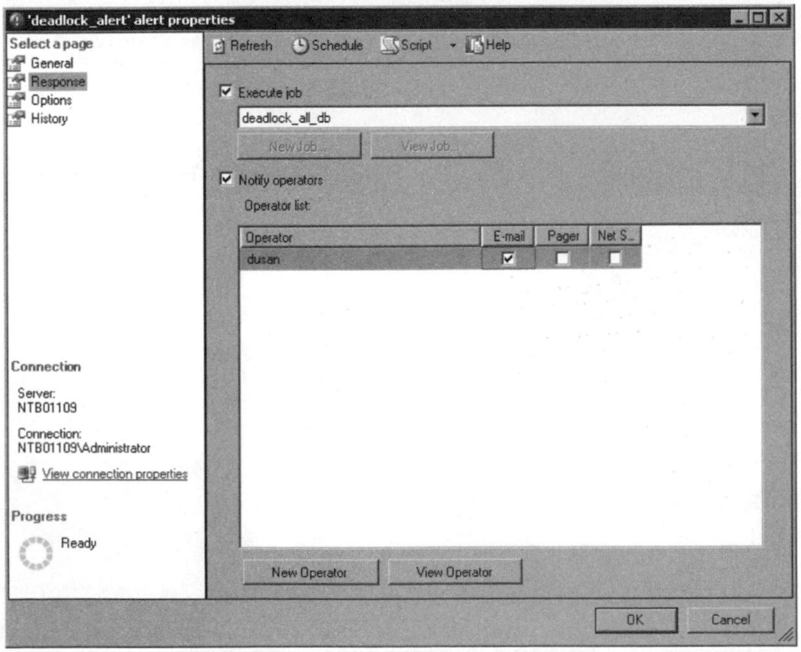

Figure 21-8   *The deadlock alert properties dialog box: The Response page*

Creating Alerts on SQL Server Severity Level

You can also define an alert that will raise a response on error severity levels. Each SQL Server error has a corresponding severity level that is a number between 0 and 25. The higher the severity level is, the more serious the error (see Chapter 22). SQL Server errors with severity levels 20 through 25 are fatal errors. SQL Server errors with severity levels 19 through 25 are written to the event log.

NOTE

Always define an operator to be notified when a fatal error occurs.

We will use severity level 25 to show how an alert can be created for error severity levels. Expand **SQL Server Agent**, right-click **Alert**, and select **New Alert**. On the **General** page of the **New Alert** dialog box, check **Severity** and select **"025 - Fatal Error"** (see Figure 21-9). Optionally, give a new name to the alert and enter the name of the database for which this alert should be valid. (You can create an alert to be raised when an error occurs on all databases or on a particular database.)

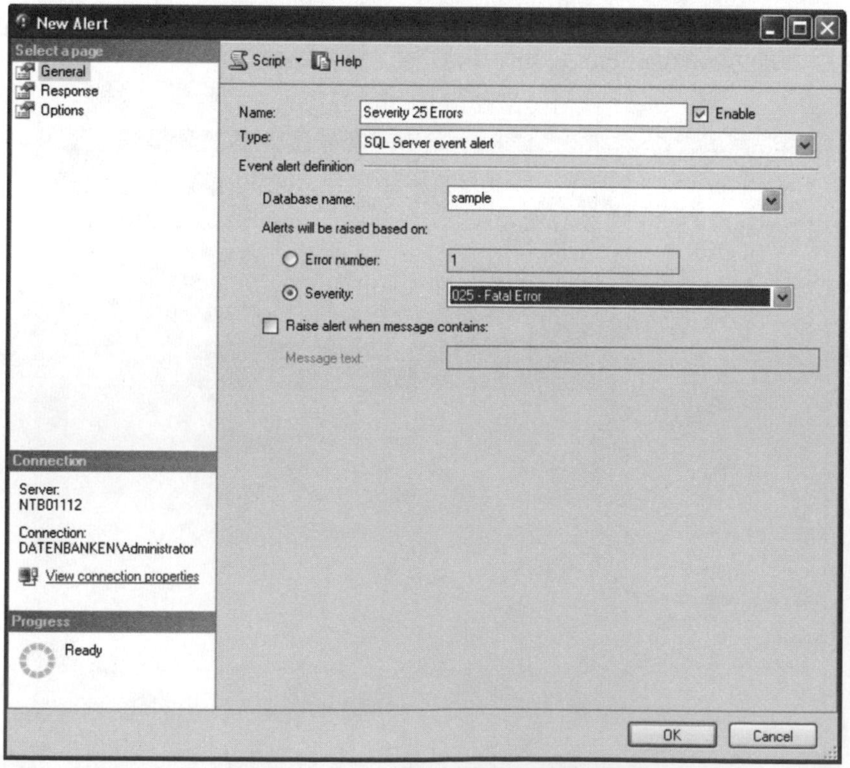

Figure 21-9 *The Demo: Sev. 25 Errors alert properties dialog box*

On the **Response** page, enter one or more operators to be notified via e-mail and/ or pager when an error of severity level 25 occurs.

Defining Alerts to Handle User-Defined Errors

In addition to creating alerts on SQL Server errors, you can create alerts on customized error messages for individual database applications. Using such messages (and alerts), you can define solutions to problems that can occur in an application.

The following steps are necessary if you want to create an alert on a user-defined message:

1. Create the error message.
2. Raise the error from a database application.
3. Define an alert on the error message.

An example is the best way to illustrate the creation of such an alert: the alert is fired if the shipping date of a product is earlier than the order date. (For the definition of the table **sales**, which contains those two columns, see Example 4.21.)

Creating the Error Message

To create user-defined errors, you can use SQL Server Management Studio or the **sp_addmessage** stored procedure. Example 21.2 creates the error message for the example using the **sp_addmessage** stored procedure.

EXAMPLE 21.2

```
sp_addmessage 50010, 16, 'The shipping date of a product is earlier than the
order date', 'us_english', 'true'
```

The **sp_addmessage** stored procedure in Example 21.2 creates a user-defined error message with error number 50010 and severity level 16. The error number in Example 21.2 is 50010 because all user-defined errors must be greater than 50000. (All error numbers less than 50000 are reserved for the SQL Server system.)

For each user-defined error message, you can optionally specify the language in which the message is displayed. The specification can be necessary if multiple languages are installed on your computer. (When language is omitted, the session language is the default language.)

By default, user-defined messages are not written to the event log. On the other hand, you must write the message to the event log if you want to raise an alert on it. Therefore, the corresponding parameter of the **sp_addmessage** system procedure in Example 21.2 must be set to true.

Raising the Error from a Database Application

To raise an error from a database application, you invoke the RAISERROR statement. This statement returns a user-defined error message and sets a system flag in the @@**error** global variable.

Example 21.3 creates the trigger **t_date_comp** that returns a user-defined error 50010 if the shipping date of a product is earlier than the order date.

EXAMPLE 21.3

```
USE sample
GO
CREATE TRIGGER t_date_comp
   ON sales
   FOR INSERT AS
   DECLARE @order_date DATETIME
   DECLARE @ship_date DATETIME
SELECT @order_date=order_date, @ship_date=ship_date FROM
INSERTED
   IF @order_date > @ship_date
        RAISERROR (50010, 16, -1)
```

Defining an Alert on the Error Message

An alert on the user-defined message is defined in the same way as the alert on a SQL Server error message. This means that in the **New Alert** dialog box (see Figure 21-7) you should enter the name of the alert in the **Name** box. Click **Error number**, and enter user-defined error (in our case the error number is 50010).

Conclusion

SQL Server allows you to automate and streamline administrator tasks, such as database backup, data transfer, and maintenance of indices. For the execution of such tasks, SQL Server Agent must be running. The easiest way to create tasks is to use SQL Server Management Studio, which allows you to define one or more job steps, creates an execution schedule, and optionally notifies operators by e-mail and/or pager.

Alerts are defined separately and can also be executed independently of jobs. An alert can handle individual SQL Server errors, user-defined errors, or groups of errors belonging to one of 25 severity levels in the SQL Server system.

The next chapter discusses performance issues concerning the relational database engine of SQL Server.

Exercises

E.21.1

Name several administrative tasks that could be automated.

E.21.2

You want to back up the transaction log of your database every hour during peak business hours and every four hours during nonpeak hours. What should you do?

E.21.3

You want to test performance of your production database in relation to locks and want to know whether the lock wait time is more than 30 seconds. How could you be notified automatically when this event occurs?

E.21.4

Specify all parts of a SQL Server error message.

E.21.5

Which are the most important columns of the **sys.messages** catalog view concerning errors?

CHAPTER

22

Performance and Tuning

IN THIS CHAPTER
Introduction
Factors that Affect Performance
Monitoring Tools
Choose the Right Tool

This chapter discusses performance issues and the tools for tuning the database server that are relevant to daily administration of the system. After introductory notes concerning the measurements of performance, the factors that affect performance are described and the tools for monitoring the database server are presented. Some tips on how to choose the right tool for the job are given at the end of the chapter.

Introduction

Improving the performance of the database server requires many decisions, such as where to store data and how to access the data. This task is different from other administrative tasks because it comprises several different steps that concern all aspects of software and hardware. If the SQL Server system is not performing optimally, the system administrator must check many factors and possibly tune software (operating system, database system, database applications) as well as hardware.

The performance of the SQL Server system (and any other relational DBMS) is measured by two criteria:

▶ Response time

▶ Throughput

Response time measures the performance of an individual transaction or program. Response time is treated as the length of time from the moment a user enters a command or statement until the time the system indicates that the command (statement) has completed. To achieve optimum response time of an overall system, almost all existing commands and statements (80 percent to 90 percent of them) must not cross the specified response time limit.

Throughput measures the overall performance of the system by counting the number of transactions that can be handled by the database server during the given time period. (The throughput is typically measured in transactions per second.) Therefore, there is a direct relation between response time of the system and its throughput: when the response time of a system degrades (for example, because many users concurrently use the system), the throughput of the system degrades, too.

Factors that Affect Performance

Factors affecting performance fall into three general categories:

- ▶ Database applications
- ▶ Database systems
- ▶ System resources

They in turn can be affected by several factors, which are discussed in the following sections.

Database Applications and Performance

The following factors can affect the performance of the database application:

- ▶ Application-code efficiency
- ▶ Physical design

Application-Code Efficiency

Applications introduce their own load on the system software and on the database server. For this reason, they can contribute to performance problems if you make poor use of system resources. Most performance problems in application programs are caused by the improper choice of Transact-SQL statements and their sequence in an application program.

The following list gives some of the ways you can improve overall performance by modifying code in an application:

- ▶ Use clustered indices (examples will be given in the discussion of monitoring tools later in the chapter).
- ▶ Do not use the NOT IN predicate.
- ▶ Use the Parallel Query option to distribute execution of complex and long-lasting queries over several processors, if possible (see also the description of parallel queries in Chapter 15).

NOTE

More hints on how code modification can improve overall performance are given in Chapter 9.

Physical Design

During physical database design, you choose the specific storage structures and access paths for the database files. In this design step, it is sometimes recommended that you denormalize some of the tables in the database to achieve good performance for various database applications. Denormalizing tables means that two or more normalized tables are coupled together, resulting in one table with some redundant data.

Let us take an example to demonstrate the process of denormalization. Figure 22-1 shows two tables from the sample database: **department** and **employee**. These two tables are normalized. (For more information on data normalization, see Chapter 1.) Data in those two tables can be specified using just one table: **dept_emp** (see Figure 22-2). The table **dept_emp** shows the denormalized form of data stored in the tables **department** and **employee**. In contrast to the tables **department** and **employee**, which do not contain any data redundancies, the **dept_emp** table contains a lot of redundancies, because two columns of this table (**dept_name**, **location**) are dependent on the **dept_no** column.

Data denormalization has two benefits and one disadvantage. First, if you have a column that is dependent on another column of the table (such as the **dept_name** column in the **dept_emp** table, which is dependent on the **dept_no** column), you can avoid the use of the join operation, which would affect the performance of applications. Second, denormalized data requires fewer tables than normalized data.

emp_no	emp_fname	emp_lname	dept_no
25348	Matthew	Smith	d3
10102	Ann	Jones	d3
18316	John	Barrimore	d1
29346	James	James	d2
9031	Elke	Hansel	d2
28559	Sybill	Moser	d1

dept_no	dept_name	location
d1	Research	Dallas
d2	Accounting	Seattle
d3	Marketing	Dallas

Figure 22-1 *The tables **department** and **employee***

emp_no	emp_fname	emp_lname	dept_no	dept_name	location
25348	Matthew	Smith	d3	Marketing	Dallas
10102	Ann	Jones	d3	Marketing	Dallas
18316	John	Barrimore	d1	Research	Dallas
29346	James	James	d2	Accounting	Seattle
9031	Elke	Hansel	d2	Accounting	Seattle
28559	Sybill	Moser	d1	Research	Dallas

Figure 22-2   *The **dept_emp** table*

On the other hand, a denormalized table requires additional amounts of disk space, and data modification is difficult because of data redundancy.

Another option in the physical database design that contributes to good performance is the creation of indices. Chapter 9 gives several guidelines for the creation of indices, and examples are given later in this chapter.

The Database Server and Performance

The database server can substantially affect the performance of an entire system. The two most important SQL Server components that affect performance are

▶ Optimizer

▶ Locks

Optimizer

The optimizer formulates several query execution plans for fetching the data rows that are required to process a query and then decides which plan should be used. The decision concerning the selection of the most appropriate execution plan includes which indices should be used, how to access tables, and the order of joining tables. All of these decisions can significantly affect the performance of database applications. The optimizer is discussed in detail in Chapter 9.

Locks

The database system uses locks as the mechanism for protecting one user's work from another's. Therefore, locks are used to control the access of data by all users at the same time and to prevent possible errors that can arise from the concurrent access of the same data.

Locking affects the performance of the system through its granularity—that is, the size of the object that is being locked and the isolation level. Row-level locking provides the best system performance, because it leaves all but one row on the page unlocked and hence allows more concurrency than page-level or table-level locking.

Isolation levels affect the duration of the lock for SELECT statements. Using the lower isolation levels, such as READ UNCOMMITTED and READ COMMITTED, the data availability and hence the concurrency of the data can be improved. (Locking and isolation levels are explained in detail in Chapter 14.)

System Resources and Performance

The SQL Server system runs on the Windows operating systems, which in themselves use underlying system resources. These resources have a significant impact on the performance of the operating system as well as the database system. Performance of any database system depends on four main system resources:

▶ CPU

▶ Memory

▶ Disk I/O

▶ Network

The CPU of your computer executes user processes and interacts with other resources of your system. Performance problems in relation to the CPU can occur when the operating system and user programs are making too many requests on it. There are many ways you can increase the performance of your system concerning the CPU, and these will be discussed later in this chapter. Generally, the more CPU power available for your computer, the better the overall system is likely to perform.

The database server dynamically acquires and frees memory as needed. Performance problems concerning memory can occur only if there is not enough of it to do the required work. When this occurs, many memory pages are written to a pagefile. (The notion of a *pagefile* is explained in detail later in this chapter.) If the process of writing to a pagefile happens very often, the performance of the system can degrade. Therefore, similarly to the CPU rule, the more memory available for your computer, the better the system is likely to perform.

There are two issues concerning disk I/O: disk speed and disk transfer rate. The disk speed determines how fast read and write operations to disk are executed. The disk transfer rate specifies how much data can be written to disk during a time unit (usually measured in seconds). Obviously, the faster the disk, the larger the amount of data is being processed. Also, more disks are generally better than a single disk when many users are using the database system concurrently. (In this case, access to data is usually spread across many disks, thus improving the overall performance of the system.) Note that disk controllers can reduce the performance of the system if they control access to multiple disks.

For a client/server configuration, the database system sometimes performs poorly if there are many client connections. In that case, the amount of data that needs to be transferred across the network possibly exceeds the network capacity. Another performance issue concerning networks can be the choice of network libraries that enable the database server to communicate with its clients.

All of these four system resources are dependent on each other. This means that performance problems in one resource can cause performance problems in the other resources. Similarly, an improvement concerning one resource can significantly increase performance of some other (or even all) resources. For example:

▶   If you increase the number of CPUs, each CPU can share the load evenly and therefore can remedy the disk I/O bottleneck. On the other hand, the inefficient use of the CPU is often the result of a preexisting heavy load on disk I/O and/or memory.

▶   Also, if more memory is available, there is more chance of finding a page needed by the application in the memory (rather than reading the page from disk), which results in a performance gain. In contrast to it, reading from the disk drive, instead of drawing from the immensely faster memory, slows the system down considerably, especially if there are many concurrent processes.

The following sections describe in detail the main system resources.

CPU

The CPU (central processing unit), together with memory, is the key component for marking the speed of a computer. It is also the key to the performance of a system, because it manages other resources of the system and executes all applications. The database server can run on single-processor systems (i.e., a system with one CPU) or on a special class of multiprocessor systems called symmetric multiprocessing (SMP) systems.

Symmetric multiprocessing specifies a system in which several processors share the main memory and disks. (Such systems are also called shared-disk systems, because they share a single operating system instance that manages one or more disks.) SMP systems usually have a high-speed interconnect that connects all processors.

The benefits of SMP systems are easy administration and the need to reprogram the DBMS only slightly.

The database server was reprogrammed to be used with an SMP system because different processes had to be assigned parallel to more than one CPU. The system supports the multithreaded architecture, where the processes are divided into threads that help the system take better advantage of SMP systems. (The database server simply starts each thread and the Windows operating system assigns to each of them a specific CPU.)

The disadvantage of an SMP system is its restricted scalability. This means the number of processors that can be synchronized together is limited by the amount of main memory, which provides this task. For this reason, a new hardware architecture called a *cluster* was introduced.

A cluster specifies a group of computers that are connected through a network. In contrast to SMP systems, all processors within the cluster share a disk subsystem. The benefits of clusters are better scalability and reliability (i.e., clusters can tolerate failures of single computers because the remaining computers in the cluster can take over the processing).

NOTE

There is another hardware architecture called MPP (massively parallel processing). This hardware architecture offers the most scalability, because it does not share anything. For this reason those systems are also called shared-nothing systems, because each processor has its own main memory, its own disk subsystem, its own operating system, and its own DBMS. Although MPP systems offer outstanding scalability, they are difficult to administer.

Disk I/O

A purpose of a database is to store, retrieve, and modify data. Therefore, the database server, like any other database system, must perform a lot of disk activity. In contrast to other system resources, a disk subsystem has two moving parts: the disk itself and the disk head. The rotation of the disk and the movement of the disk head need a great deal of time; therefore, disk reads and writes are two of the highest-cost operations that a database system performs. (For instance, access to a disk is usually slower than memory access by a factor of two.)

The data in a SQL Server system is stored in 8K pages. The buffer cache of the RAM is also divided into 8K pages. The database server reads data in units of pages. Reads occur not only for data retrieval, but also for any modification operations such as UPDATE and DELETE, because the database system must read the data before it can be modified.

If the needed page is in the buffer cache, it will be read from memory. This I/O operation is called logical I/O or logical read. If it is not in memory, the page is read from disk and put in the buffer cache. This I/O operation is called physical I/O or physical read. Because the buffer cache is shared (because the database server uses the architecture with only one memory address space), many users can access the same page. A logical write occurs when data is modified in the buffer cache. Similarly, a physical write occurs when the page is written from the buffer cache to disk. Therefore, more logical write operations can be made on one page before it is written to disk.

The database server has several components that have great impact on performance, because they significantly consume the I/O resources. These components are as follows:

▶   Read ahead

▶   Checkpoint

The first component will be described in the following section, while the second one is explained in detail in Chapter 20.

Read Ahead   The optimal behavior of the SQL Server system would be to read data and never have to wait for a disk read request. The best way to perform this task for a database system is to know the next several pages that the user will need and to read them from the disk into the buffer pool *before* they are requested by the user process. This mechanism is called *read ahead*, and it allows the system to optimize performance by processing large amounts of data effectively.

The component of SQL Server called Read Ahead Manager manages the read-ahead processes completely internally, so a user has no way to influence this process. Instead of using the usual 8K pages, the database server uses 64K blocks of data as the unit for read-ahead reads. That way, the throughput for I/O requests is significantly increased. The read-ahead mechanism is used by a database system to perform large table scans and index range scans. Table scans are performed using the information that is stored in IAM pages to build a serial list of the disk addresses that must be read. This allows the database system to optimize its I/O as large sequential reads in disk order. Read Ahead Manager reads up to 2MB of data at a time. Each extent is read with a single operation.

NOTE

The SQL Server system provides multiple serial read-ahead operations at once for each file involved in the table scan. This feature can take advantage of striped disk sets.

For index ranges, the database server uses the information in the intermediate level of index pages immediately above the leaf level to determine which pages to read. SQL Server scans all these pages and builds a list of the leaf pages that must be read. During this operation, the contiguous pages are recognized and read in one operation. When there are many pages to be retrieved, the system schedules a block of reads at a time.

The read-ahead mechanism can also have negative impacts on performance if too many pages for a process are read and the buffer cache is unnecessarily filled up. The only thing you can do in this case is create the indices you will actually need.

The read-ahead activity of the system can be monitored using the Performance counter called **Buffer Manager–Readahead Pages**. (The Performance monitor, together with its counters, will be described in detail later in this chapter.)

Memory

Memory is a crucial resource component, not only for the running applications but also for the operating system. When an application is executed, it is loaded into memory and a certain amount of memory is allocated to the application. (In Microsoft terminology, the total amount of memory available for an application is called its *address space*.)

Windows operating systems support virtual memory. This means that the total amount of memory available to applications is the amount of physical memory (or RAM) in the computer plus the size of the specific file on the disk drive called pagefile. (The name of the pagefile on Windows operating systems is **pagefile.sys**.) Once data is moved out of its location in the RAM, it resides in the pagefile. If the system is asked to retrieve data that is not in the proper RAM location, it will load the data from the location where it is stored and additionally produce a so-called page fault.

NOTE

pagefile.sys should be placed on a different drive than the files used by the database server, because the paging process can have an impact on disk I/O activities.

For an entire application, only a portion of it resides in the RAM of the computer. (Recently referenced pages can usually be found in the RAM.) When the information the application needs is not in the RAM, the operating system must page (i.e., read the page from the pagefile into the RAM). This process is called demand paging. The more the system has to page, the worse the performance is.

NOTE

When a page is required, the oldest page of the address space for an application is moved to the pagefile to make room for the new page. The replacement of pages is always limited to the address space of the current application. Therefore, there is no chance that pages in the address space of other running applications will be replaced.

As you already know, a page fault occurs if the application makes a request for information and the data page that contains that information is not in the proper RAM location of the computer. The information may either have been paged out to the pagefile or be located somewhere else in the RAM. Therefore, there are two types of page fault: a hard page fault and a soft page fault. A hard page fault means that the page had been paged out (to the pagefile) and has to be brought into the RAM from the disk drive. The soft page fault occurs when the page is found in another location in RAM. Soft page faults consume only CPU resources. Therefore, they are better for performance than hard page faults, which cause disk reads and writes to occur.

NOTE

Page faults are normal in a Windows operating system environment, because the operating system requires pages from the running applications to satisfy the need for memory of the starting ones. However, excessive paging (especially with hard page faults) is a serious performance problem, because it can cause disk bottlenecks and start to consume the additional power of the processor.

Network

For client/server configuration, a database system sometimes performs poorly if there is a large number of client connections. To avoid such a performance bottleneck, the following general recommendations should be taken into account:

▶ If a database server sends any rows to an application, only the rows needed by the application should be sent. (In addition, use the ROWCOUNT option in the SET statement to restrict the display of selected rows to a certain amount.)

▶ If a long-lasting user application executes strictly on a client side, move it to a server side (by executing it as a stored procedure, for example).

Monitoring Tools

All the factors that affect performance can be monitored using different SQL Server and Windows tools. These tools can be grouped into three categories:

► Application performance tools

► SQL Server–specific monitoring

► System resource tools

The following sections describe the tools for dealing with performance factors, which we discussed in the first part of this chapter.

Application Performance Tools

As already stated, most performance problems in applications are caused by the improper choice of Transact-SQL statements and/or the inappropriate use of indices. Therefore, you will gain a thorough understanding of the performance of an application by examining each query executed in it. SQL Server Management Studio is the most suitable tool for this task.

As you know by now, Management Studio is a tool used to generate, execute, and store Transact-SQL statements. Besides these features, which are described in detail in Chapter 2, you can use this tool to show the execution plan of a query, either in the form of text or graphics. This allows you to examine the plan and to make corrections concerning indices of the query if the performance of the query is inefficient. The SQL Server optimizer provides several different solutions (called *query execution plans*) for executing a query of an application program. After that, the optimizer chooses the best plan and executes the query.

When you run the query, you can display the textual execution plan for the query by activating the SHOWPLAN_TEXT or SHOWPLAN_ALL option of the SET statement. Both options display detailed information about the selected execution for the query. (The optimizer, the SHOWPLAN_TEXT, and the SHOWPLAN_ALL options are described in detail in Chapter 9.)

Using an example, you will see how the performance of a query can be improved by modifying the index of the query. This modification will be shown by the graphical features of SQL Server Management Studio.

The database server uses two different data organization forms to store data of a table on the disk: heaps and clustered tables. A *heap* is a form of data organization in which table data are not stored in any particular order and there is no particular order to the sequence of the data pages. Tables that have no clustered index are stored in heaps. (For this reason, such a table is called a heap in SQL Server terminology.)

The data rows of a *clustered table* are stored in order based on the clustered index, and the data pages are linked using the linked list. Which physical data structure the database server chooses depends on the form of the CREATE INDEX statement. (Tables without any index as well as tables with only nonclustered indices are stored using heaps.)

Example 22.1 shows two tables that are used to demonstrate the way to improve performance of a query by using clustered indices.

EXAMPLE 22.1

```
USE sample
CREATE TABLE orders
  (orderid INTEGER NOT NULL,
   orderdate DATETIME,
   shippeddate DATETIME,
   freight money)

CREATE TABLE order_details
  (productid INTEGER NOT NULL,
   orderid INTEGER NOT NULL,
   unitprice money,
   quantity INTEGER)
```

Suppose the **orders** table contains 3,000 rows, and the **order_details** table contains on average ten rows per row of the **orders** table. (There is a 1:N relationship between the **orders** table and the **order_details** table; that is, for each row of the former table, there are zero, one, or more rows in the latter table.) The following two examples show the batches that can be used to load data into those two tables.

EXAMPLE 22.2

```
USE sample
declare @i int , @order_id integer
        declare @orderdate datetime
        declare @shipped_date datetime
        declare @freight money
        set @i = 1
        set @orderdate = getdate()
        set @shipped_date = getdate()
```

```
set @freight = 100.00
while @i < 3001
begin
insert into orders (orderid, orderdate, shippeddate, freight)
  values( @i, @orderdate, @shipped_date, @freight)
set @i = @i+1
end
```

EXAMPLE 22.3

-- This procedure inserts 30,000 rows in the table order_details

```
USE sample
declare @i int, @j int
      set @i = 3000
      set @j = 10
      while @j > 0
      begin
      if @i > 0
        begin
        insert into order_details (productid, orderid, quantity)
             values (@i, @j, 5)
        set @i = @i –1
        end
      else begin
         set @j = @j - 1
         set @i = 3000
         end
      end

      go
update order_details set quantity = 3
      where productid in (1511, 2678)
```

Example 22.4 shows the query used to demonstrate the possible performance issues.

EXAMPLE 22.4

```
USE sample
SELECT orders.orderid, orders.orderdate, order_details.unitprice
          FROM orders, order_details
          WHERE orders.orderid = order_details.orderid
          AND order_details.quantity = 3
```

By creating the indices shown in Example 22.5, both tables are stored in heaps.

EXAMPLE 22.5

```
USE sample
CREATE UNIQUE INDEX i_order_orderid ON orders(orderid)
CREATE INDEX i_details_prodid ON order_details(productid)
CREATE INDEX i_details_orderid ON order_details(orderid)
```

Figure 22-3 shows the graphical form of the execution plan for the query in Example 22.4. (To display the graphical execution plan of a query, you must click **Query** in the toolbar of SQL Server Management Studio and select **Display Estimated Execution Plan**.)

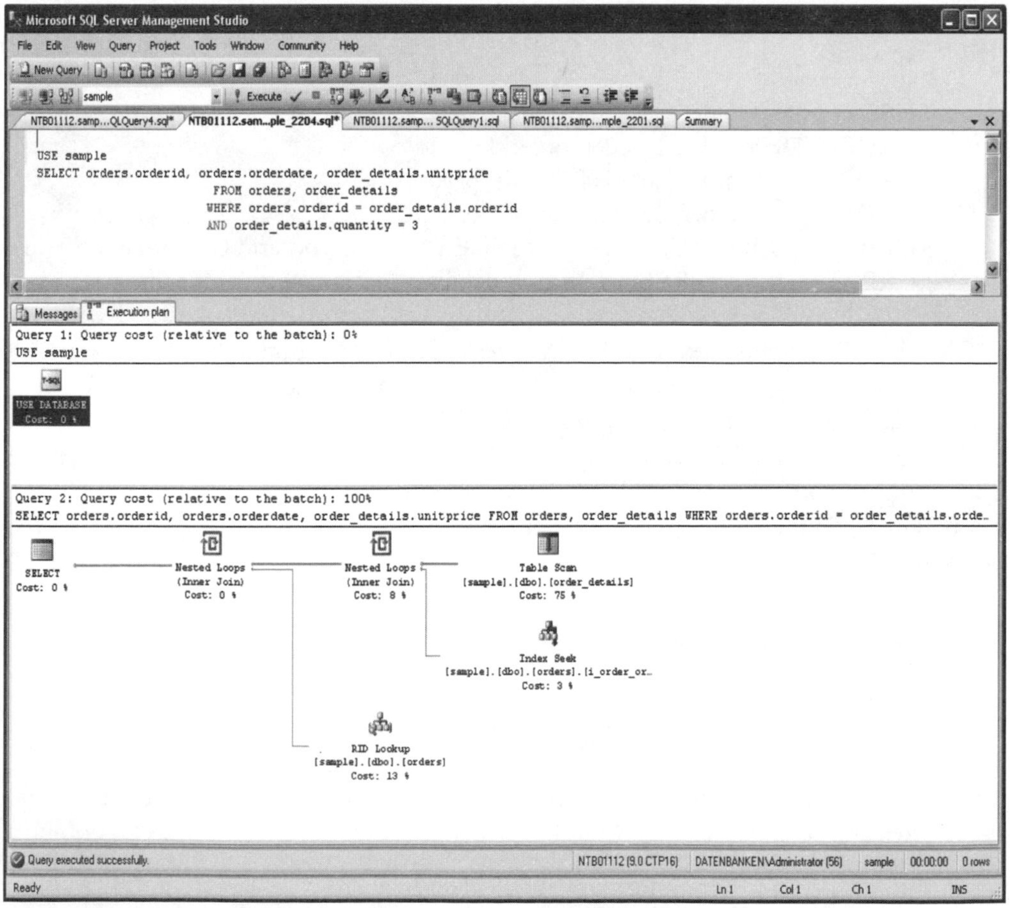

Figure 22-3 *The graphical form of the execution plan for the query in Example 22.4*

The query execution plan of Figure 22-3 is read from left to right and from the *bottom up*. Therefore, the SQL Server optimizer first uses index **i_order_orderid** for the index search on the **orderid** column in the **orders** tables and a sequential scan on the **quantity** column. After that, the nested-loop method for the join operation in Example 22.4 is applied.

As the next operator, the bookmark lookup is executed. Bookmark Lookup represents the RID (row identifier) that is used to look up the row that corresponds to the selected index value. Therefore, a bookmark specifies a value that is used to identify the corresponding row.

The physical structure of the tables **orders** and **order_details** can be modified if clustered indices are created (instead of nonclustered ones). Example 22.6 creates two clustered indices for these tables. (The existing indices for the **orderid** column in both tables, **orders** and **order_details**, must be dropped before you create the new indices.)

EXAMPLE 22.6

```
USE sample
DROP INDEX orders.i_order_orderid
DROP INDEX order_details.i_details_prodid
DROP INDEX order_details.i_details_orderid
CREATE UNIQUE CLUSTERED INDEX ci_order_orderid ON orders(orderid)
CREATE  CLUSTERED INDEX ci_details_orderid ON order_details(orderid)
```

The creation of clustered indices in Example 22.6 stores both tables as clustered tables; that is, the rows of each table are stored in order based on the clustered index, and the data pages are linked using the linked list.

Figure 22-4 shows the graphical form of the execution plan of the query in Example 22.4. If clustered indices are used, the optimizer will perform two clustered index scans. This change will result in significant improvements of the execution time for the query in Example 22.4.

SQL Server–Specific Monitoring

In addition to locking, which has already been described, the number of user connections and logging activities are performance factors specific for the database server. You can monitor these performance factors using SQL Profiler, several system procedures, Transact-SQL statements, and the **dbcc** utility. In this section, we will describe several procedures and statements except SQL Profiler. This tool is described at the end of this chapter.

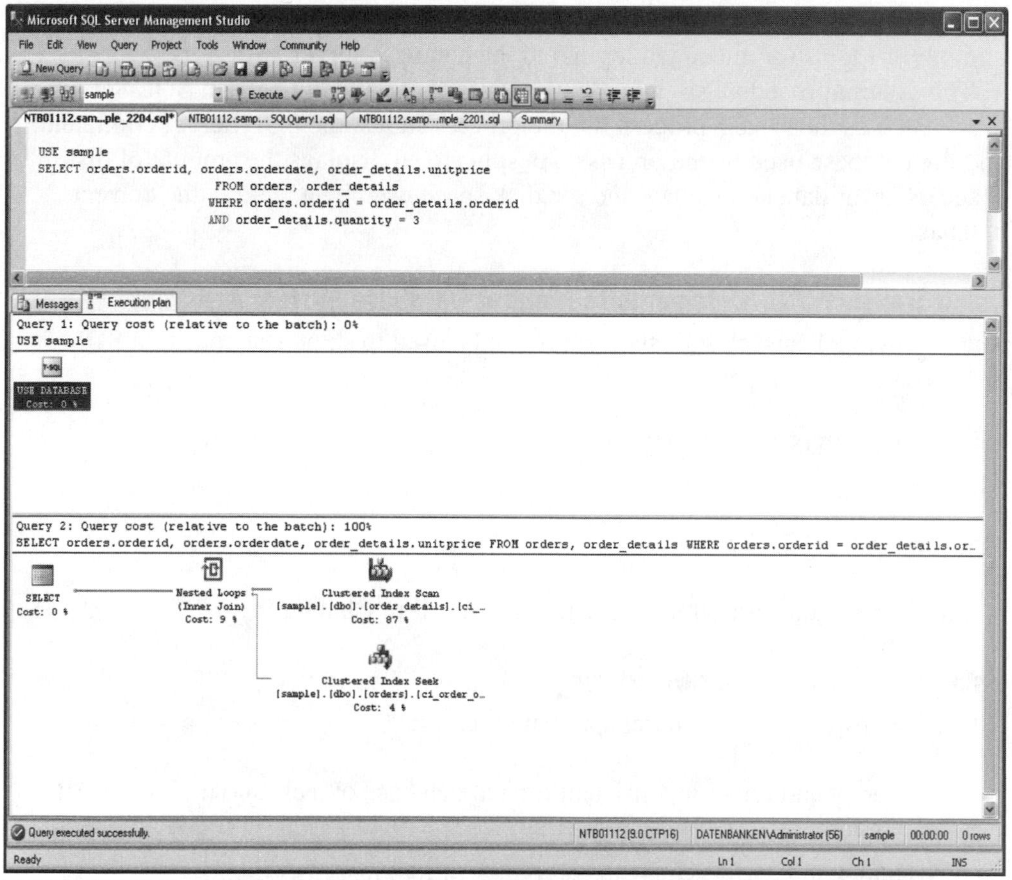

Figure 22-4   *The graphical form of the execution plan after creating clustered indices*

Using System Procedures to Monitor SQL Server Activities

The following system procedures can be used to monitor database system activities:

▶ sp_helpindex

▶ sp_monitor

▶ sp_who

▶ sp_spaceused

The system procedure **sp_helpindex** displays the overall information about indices. This procedure is covered in more detail in Chapter 9.

The system procedure **sp_monitor** displays optimizer statistics—for example, the number of seconds the CPU has been doing system activities, the number of seconds the database server has been idle, the number of read/write operations, and the number of logins (or attempted logins) to the database server.

The system procedure **sp_who** displays information about current SQL Server users, such as the system process ID, the process status, the SQL Server command, and the database used by the process. **sp_spaceused** displays the amount of disk space used for data and indices and the disk space used by a table in the current database.

Using Transact-SQL Statements to Monitor Database System Activities

The following Transact-SQL statements can be used to show statistics of a SQL Server database system:

▶ SET STATISTICS TIME

▶ SET STATISTICS I/O

▶ SET STATISTICS XML

These statements are already described in detail in Chapter 9.

Using the dbcc utility for Monitoring

The **dbcc** utility has two general application areas:

▶ To verify and repair inconsistent logical database objects and their physical data structures

▶ To check the performance and activities of the overall system

The options of the **dbcc** utility that apply to the first application area are, among others:

▶ CHECKTABLE

▶ CHECKDB

▶ CHECKALLOC

▶ CHECKCATALOG

The CHECKTABLE specification verifies the consistency of the data and index pages, the consistency of the pointers, and the correct sequence of the indices for the specified table. The most important options of this specification are three forms of the

REPAIR option: REPAIR_FAST, REPAIR_REBUILD, and REPAIR_ALLOW_DATA_LOSS. Using them, you can instruct the system to repair the errors you have found.

The second specification—CHECKDB—is identical to the CHECKTABLE specification except that it verifies all tables of the specified or current database. (The most important options of this specification are, again, REPAIR_FAST, REPAIR_REBUILD, and REPAIR_ALLOW_DATA_LOSS.)

Use the CHECKALLOC option to check the allocation of data pages and index pages for each table within its extents.

The CHECKCATALOG option verifies the consistency of each system table of the specified database as well as the consistency of the existing links between different system tables. When no database name is specified, the system tables of the current database will be verified.

The CHECKFILEGROUP option checks the structural integrity of all tables and indices that belong to the current database and are stored in the specified filegroup. During the structural integrity check, SQL Server verifies the existing links between data pages and index pages and also checks the consistency of pointers. If the filegroup is not specified, SQL Server checks all tables stored in the PRIMARY filegroup.

The following options of the **dbcc** utility concern system performance:

► SHOW_STATISTICS

► SQLPERF

The SHOW_STATISTICS option computes the current distribution statistics for an index (or a column) of a table. It displays the number of rows, the number of rows sampled for statistics information, the selectivity of the index, and the number of histogram values in the current distribution statistics.

The SQLPERF option provides statistics about the use of transaction-log space in all databases. Therefore, this option can inform you when to back up or truncate the transaction log.

Dynamic Management Views

Instead of DBCC commands to return information concerning performance, SQL Server 2005 allows you to use several dynamic performance views. The system now contains a set of underlying views that are maintained by the database server. These views are called *dynamic management views*, because they are continuously updated while a database is in use.

The two dynamic views that are most relevant to performance are **dm_exec_query_plan** and **dm_exec_query_optimizer_info**. The former returns the showplan in XML format for a Transact-SQL batch whose query execution plan resides in the plan cache. The latter returns detailed statistics about the operator of the query optimizer.

Tools for Monitoring System Resources

System resources such as memory and disk I/O can be examined using the following:

▶   Windows Event Viewer

▶   Performance monitor

Event Viewer is used to view the event log. (The event log is where all system messages of a Windows operating system and all application messages are stored.) For more information on Event Viewer and the event log, see Chapter 21.

The Performance Monitor

The Performance monitor is the Windows component that provides the ability to monitor Windows as well as database system activities. The benefit of this tool is that it is tightly integrated with Windows operating systems and therefore displays reliable values concerning different performance issues.

To start the Performance monitor, click **Start** | **Programs** | **Administrative Tools**, and finally, **Performance Monitor**. The **Performance** dialog box appears (Figure 22-5).

The Performance monitor provides a lot of performance objects, and each performance object contains several counters. (To add a counter for monitoring, click the plus sign in the tool bar of the Performance monitor, select the performance object to which the counter belongs, choose the counter, and click **Add**.)

We will list and describe several counters that belong to different performance objects:

▶   Pages/sec (Object: Memory)

▶   % Processor Time (Object: Processor)

▶   Full Scans/sec (Object: SQL Server:Access Methods)

▶   Buffer Cache Hit Ratio (Object: SQL Server:Buffer Manager)

▶   Bytes total/sec (Object: Network Interface)

▶   Disk Transfers/sec (Object: Physical Disk)

▶   Transactions/sec (Object: SQLServer:Databases)

The **Pages/sec** counter displays the amount of paging (that is, the number of pages read or written to disk per second). The counter is an important indicator of the types of faults that cause performance problems. If the value of this counter is too high, you should consider adding more physical memory.

The **% Processor Time** counter displays system-wide CPU usage and, therefore acts as the primary indicator of processor activity. The value of this counter should be

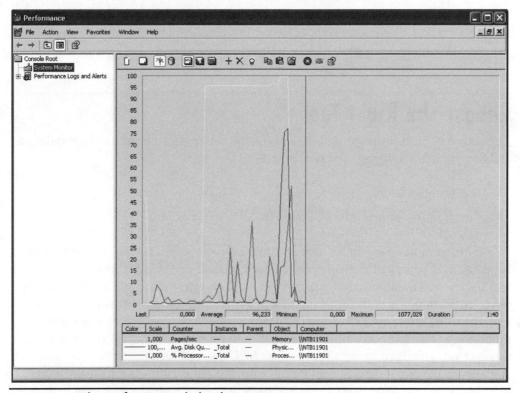

Figure 22-5   *The Performance dialog box*

between 80 and 90 percent). You should try to reduce CPU usage if the value of the counter is constantly greater than 90 percent). (CPU usage of 100 percent is acceptable only if it happens for short periods of time.)

The **Full Scans/sec** counter monitors the number of unrestricted table scans or index scans per second. The value of this counter should be low because scans (particularly table scans) often cause bottlenecks.

The **Buffer Cache Hit Ratio** counter displays the percentage of pages that did not require a read from disk. Note that there is no right value for this counter because it is application specific.

The **Bytes total/sec** counter monitors the number of bytes that are sent over the network per second. The consistently low value of the counter specifies that network problems may be interfering with your application.

The **Disk Transfers/sec** counter monitors the rate of disk read/write operations for all activities on your computer. You can set up an instance for each disk in the system or watch it for all disks. (It is recommended to define a counter for each physical disk on the system.)

The **Transactions/sec** counter displays the number of transactions started for the current database. There is no right value for this counter: The higher the value, the better. (You cannot keep track of total transactions for the whole system.)

Choose the Right Tool

The choice of an appropriate tool depends on the performance factors to be monitored and the type of monitoring. The type of monitoring can be

▶ Real time

▶ Delayed (by saving information in the file, for example)

Real-time monitoring means that performance issues are investigated as they are happening. If you want to display the actual values of one or a few performance factors, such as number of users or number of attempted logins, use the **dbcc** utility or the corresponding dynamic management views, because of their simplicity. In fact, the **dbcc** utility as well as system procedures can only be used for real-time monitoring. Therefore, if you want to trace performance activities during a specific time period, you have to use a tool such as SQL Server Profiler.

Probably the best all-around tool for monitoring is the Performance monitor, because of its many options. First, you can choose the performance activities you want to track and display them simultaneously. Second, the Performance monitor allows you to set thresholds on specific counters (performance factors) to generate alerts that notify operators. This way, you can react promptly to any performance bottlenecks. Third, you can report performance activities and investigate the resulting chart log files later.

In this section, I'll describe the following tools that are relevant to performance issues:

▶ SQL Server Profiler

▶ Database Tuning Advisor

SQL Server Profiler

SQL Server Profiler is a graphical tool that lets system administrators monitor and record database and server activities, such as login, user, and application information. Profiler can display information about several server activities in real time, or it can create filters to focus on particular events of a user, types of commands, or types of Transact-SQL statements. Among others, you can monitor the following events using Profiler:

▶ Login connections, attempts, failures, and disconnections

▶ CPU use of a statement

▶ Deadlock problems

▶ All DML statements (SELECT, INSERT, UPDATE, and DELETE)

▶ The start or end of a stored procedure

The most useful feature of this tool is the possibility of capturing activities in relation to queries. These activities can be used as input for Database Engine Tuning Advisor that allows you to select indices and indexed views for one or more queries. The following section describes this important tuning tool.

Database Engine Tuning Advisor

In this section, you will find a discussion about Database Tuning Advisor, which is part of the SQL Server system and allows you to automate the physical design of your databases. Database Engine Tuning Advisor is tightly connected to another SQL Server tool called Profiler. As you already know, Profiler can display information about several server activities in real time, or it can create filters to focus on particular events of a user, types of commands, or Transact-SQL statements.

The specific feature of SQL Server Profiler that is used by Database Engine Tuning Advisor is to watch and record batches executed by users and to provide performance information, such as CPU use of a batch and corresponding I/O statistics.

Providing Information for Database Engine Tuning Advisor

Database Tuning Advisor is usually used together with Profiler to automate tuning process. You use SQL Server Profiler to record information about the workload being examined into a trace file. (As an alternative to a workload file, you can use any file that contains a set of Transact-SQL statements. In this case, you do not need Profiler.) The file can be read by Database Engine Tuning Advisor, and the advisor recommends several physical objects, such as indices, indexed views, and partitioning schema that should be created for the given workload.

Let us use an example to see how the Database Engine Tuning Provider evaluates the file created by SQL Server Profiler. I'll use the tables **orders** and **order_details** (see Examples 22.1 through 22.3) to demonstrate the recommendation of physical objects by

Database Engine Tuning Advisor. To demonstrate the use of the advisor, we need many more rows in both tables. Examples 22.2 and 22.3 insert 3,000 rows in the **orders** table and 30,000 rows in the **order_details** table. The query in Example 22.7 will be used as an input file for Profiler. (We suppose that no indices for the columns that appear in the SELECT statement are created.)

EXAMPLE 22.7

```
USE sample
SELECT orders.orderid, orders.shippeddate
    FROM orders
    WHERE orders.orderid between 806 and 1600
    and not exists (SELECT order_details.orderid
                    FROM order_details
                    WHERE order_details.orderid = orders.orderid)
```

First, set up SQL Server Profiler by clicking **Programs | Microsoft SQL Server 2005 | Performance Tools | SQL Server Profiler**. On the **File** menu, select **New Trace**. After connecting to the server, the **Trace Properties** dialog box appears. In this dialog box, type a name for the trace and select an output .trc file for the Profiler information (in the **Save to file** field). Click **Run** to start the capture and use SQL Server Management Studio to execute the query in Example 22.7. Finally, stop Profiler by clicking **Stop Traces** on the **File** menu and select the corresponding trace.

Working with Database Tuning Advisor

Database Tuning Advisor analyzes a workload and recommends the physical design of one or more databases. The analysis will include recommendations to add, remove or modify the physical database structures, such as indices, indexed views, and partitions. Database Tuning Advisor will recommend a set of physical database structures that will optimize the tasks included in the workload.

To use the advisor, click **Start | Programs**, select **Microsoft SQL Server 2005**, choose **Performance Tools**, and select **Database Engine Tuning Advisor**; see Figure 22-6. (The alternative way is to start SQL Server Profiler, click **Tools**, and select **Database Engine Tuning Advisor**.)

In the **Session Name** field, type the name of the session for which the tool will create tuning recommendations. In the **Workload** frame, select either **File** or **Table**. If you select **File**, enter the name of the trace file. If you choose **Table**, the name of the table that is created by SQL Server Profiler must be entered. (Using Profiler, you can capture and save data about each workload to a file or to a table.)

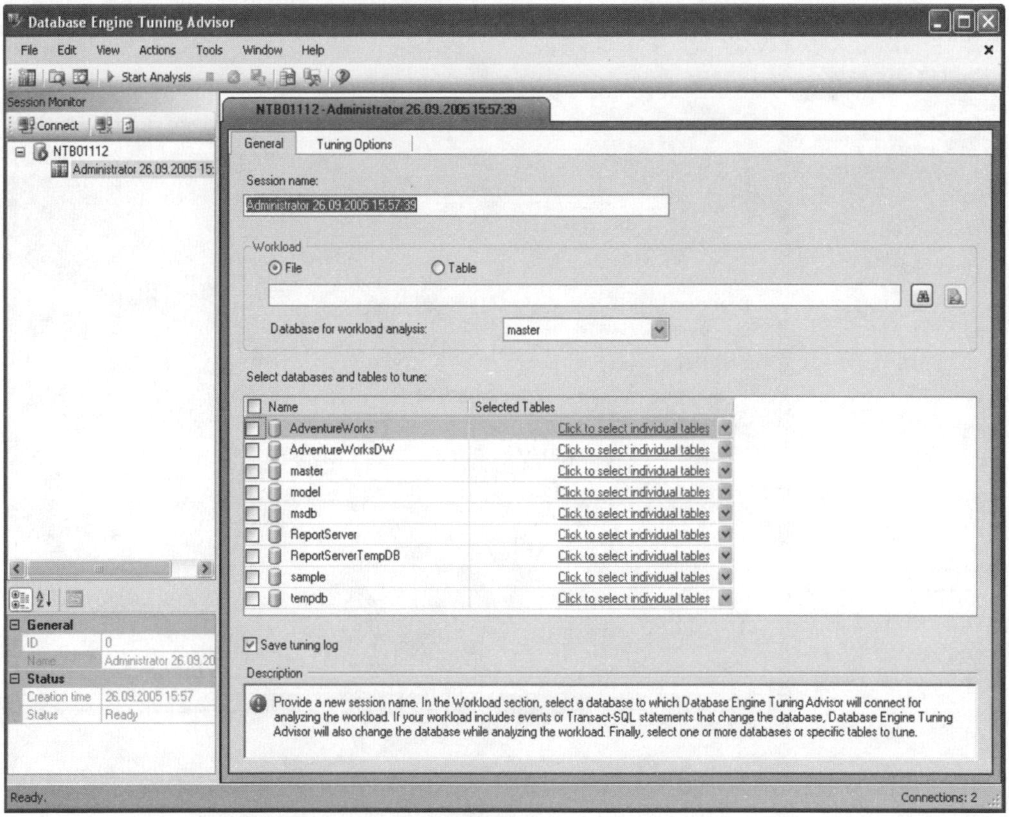

Figure 22-6   *Database Tuning Advisor*

In the **Select databases and tables to tune** frame, choose one or more databases and/or one or more tables that you want to tune. (Database Engine Tuning Advisor can tune a workload that involves multiple databases. This means that the tool can recommend indices, indexed views, and partitioning schema on any of the databases in the workload.)

To choose options for tuning, click **Tuning Options** in the toolbar of the advisor (see Figure 22-7). All options in this dialog box are divided into three groups:

▶ Physical Design Structures (PDS) to use in database

▶ Partitioning strategy to employ

▶ Physical Design Structures (PDS) to keep in database

The first group of options allows you to choose which physical structures (indices and/or indexed views) should be recommended by the tool, after tuning the existing

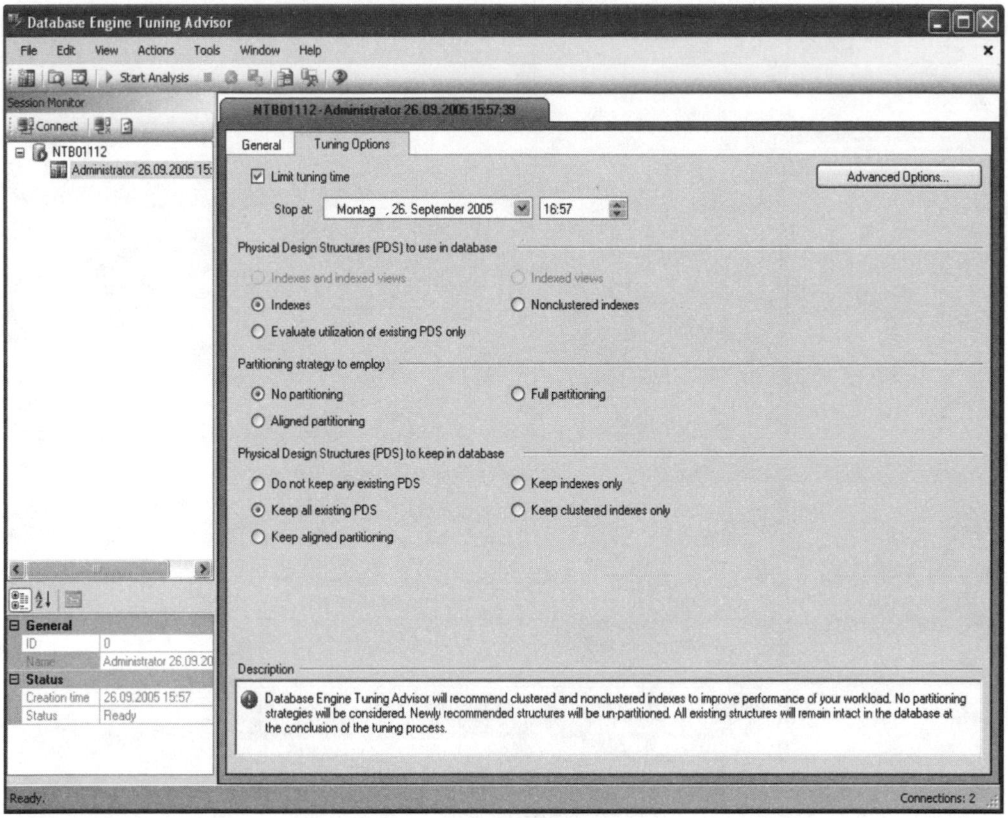

Figure 22-7 *Database Tuning Advisor: Tuning Options*

workload. (The **Evaluate utilization of existing PDS only** option causes Database
Engine Tuning Advisor to analyze the existing physical structures and gives the
recommendation of which of them should be deleted.)

The **Partitioning strategy to employ** option allows you to choose whether
partitioning recommendations should be made or not. In the former case, the type
of partitioning (full or aligned) can be selected, too. (The next chapter discusses
partitioning in detail.)

The last option group, **Physical Design Structures (PDS) to keep in database**,
gives you a possibility to decide which existing structures should remain intact in the
database after the tuning process.

NOTE

Be aware that the selection of some option sets from these three groups can be invalid.

For large databases, tuning physical structures usually requires a significant amount of time and resources. Instead of starting an exhaustive search for possible indexes, Database Tuning Advisor offers (by default) the restrictive use of resources. This operation mode still gives very accurate results, although the resources are significantly lessened.

During the specification of the options, you can define additional customization options by clicking **Advanced Options**. The **Advanced Tuning Options** dialog box (see Figure 22-8) has two parts. In the above part of the dialog box you can define maximum space for recommendations. (For large databases, selection of physical structures usually requires a significant amount of resources. Instead of starting an exhaustive search, Database Tuning Advisor allows you to restrict the space used for tuning.)

Of all index tuning options, one of the most interesting is the option to determine the maximum number of columns per index. A single-column index or a composite index built on two columns can be used several times for a workload with many queries and requires less storage space than a composite index built on four or more columns. (This is in the case where you use a workload file on your own instead of using Profiler's trace for the specific workload.) On the other hand, the latter index may be used as a covering index to enable index-only access for some of the queries in the workload. (For more information on index-only access, see Chapter 9.)

In the **Online index recommendation** frame, you can choose whether the tuning recommendations of Database Tuning Advisor should be offline or online.

After the selection of options, the analysis of the workload can be started. To start the tuning process, choose **Actions** in the toolbar and select **Start Analysis**.

After starting the tuning process for the trace file of the query in Example 22.7, Database Engine Tuning Advisor creates tuning recommendations, which can be seen after you click **Recommendations** (see Figure 22-9). As you can see from the figure, the tool recommends the creation of two indices.

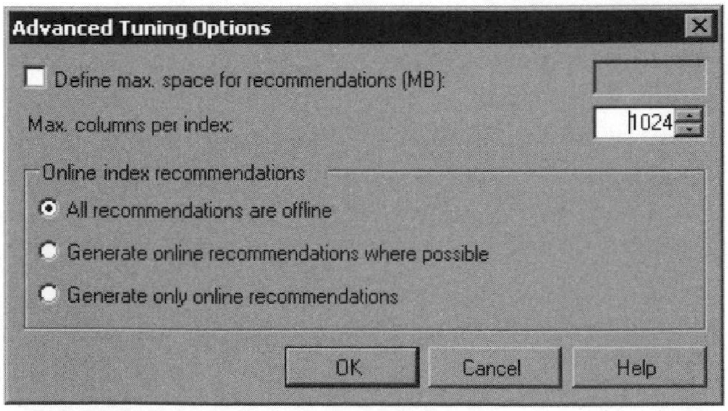

Figure 22-8 *The Advanced Tuning Options dialog box*

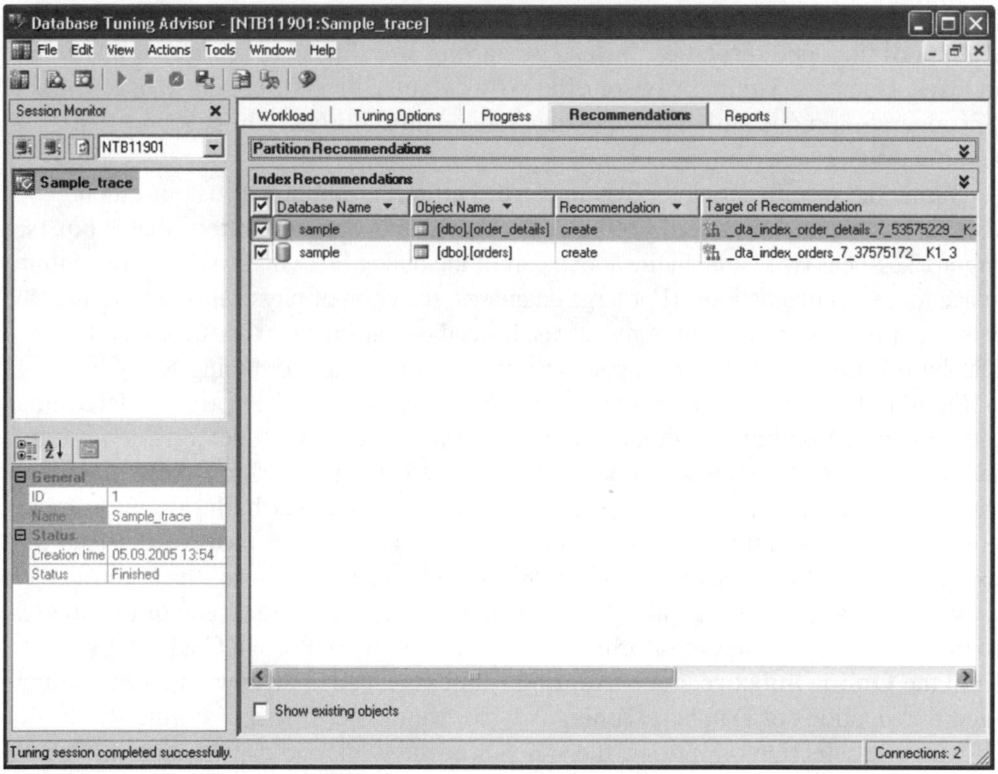

Figure 22-9 *Database Index advisor: Index Recommendations*

Database Tuning Advisor recommendations concerning physical structures are expanded by a series of reports that provide information about very interesting options, which let you see how the advisor evaluated the workload. These reports can be seen by clicking the **Reports** check box in the **Database Engine Tuning Advisor** dialog box after the tuning process is finished. The following reports, among others, can be seen:

▶ Index usage report

▶ Index detail report

▶ Table access report

▶ Workload analysis report

Index usage report (recommended) displays information concerning the expected usage of the recommended indexes and their estimated sizes. In contrast to it, **Index Usage Report** (current) presents the same information for the existing configuration.

Index detail report (recommended) displays information concerning the names of all recommended indices and their types. **Index detail report** (current) presents the same information for the actual configuration, before the tuning process was started.

Table access report displays information about the costs of all queries in the workload (using tables in the database).

Workload analysis report provides information about the relative frequencies of all data modification statements. (Costs are calculated relative to the most expensive statement with the current index configuration.)

There are three alternatives for how you can apply recommendations: immediately, scheduled, or after saving to the file. If you select **Actions** and then **Apply Recommendations**, the recommendations will be applied immediately. Similarly, if you select **Actions** and then **Save Recommendations**, the recommendations will be saved to the file. (This alternative is useful if you generate the script with one (test) system and intend to use the tuning recommendation with another (production) system.) Figure 22-10 shows SQL Server Management Studio with the script that creates both recommended indices.

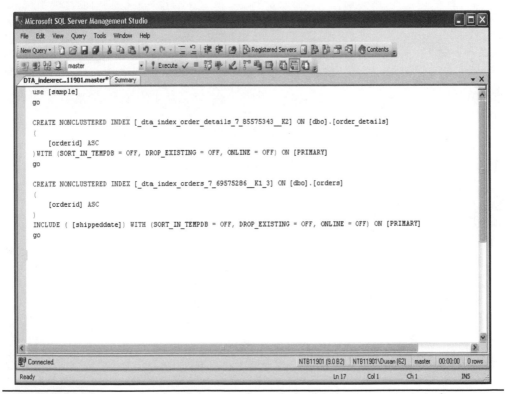

Figure 22-10 *SQL Server Management Studio with the SQL script to create indices*

Conclusion

Performance issues can be divided into proactive and reactive. Proactive issues concern all activities that affect performance of the overall system and that will affect future systems of an organization. Proper database design and proper choice of the form of Transact-SQL statements in application programs belong to the proactive issues. Reactive performance issues concern activities that are undertaken after the performance bottleneck occurs. The SQL Server system offers a variety of tools (graphical components, Transact-SQL statements, and stored procedures) that can be used to view and trace performance problems.

Of all components, the Performance monitor is the best tool for monitoring, because you can use it to track, display, report, and trace any performance bottlenecks.

The next chapter discusses another feature concerning performance of the SQL Server system: table partitioning.

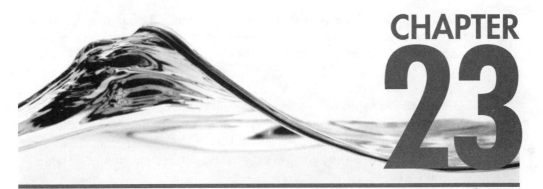

Data Partitioning

ach table of a database is by default one logical unit. This means that each table contains information concerning an entity (employees or orders, for instance). Although a single table is the easiest way to represent an entity, it is not always the best approach. This chapter discusses when it is reasonable to store all entity instances in a single table.

The easiest and most natural way to design an entity is to use a single table. Also, if all instances of an entity belong to a table, you don't need to decide where to store its rows physically, because the database server does this for you. For this reason there is no need for you to do any administrative tasks concerning storage of table data, if you don't want to.

On the other hand, one of the most frequent causes of poor performance in relational database systems is contention for data that resides on a single I/O device. This is especially true if you have one or more very large tables with several hundred, thousands, or millions of rows. In that case, on a system with multiple CPUs, partitioning the table can lead to better performance through parallel operations.

SQL Server supports data partitioning since SQL Server 7. The main drawback of the existing solutions for data partitioning in SQL Server 7 and SQL Server 2000 is that they are not transparent to the application. (SQL Server 2000 solution was not transparent to the application, because you had to create a table for each partition and define the integrity rules that partition the data. Then you had to design the view, which unified all tables.) The solution in SQL Server 2005 is transparent to the application, because the only thing you must do is define the table and the corresponding partition rules.

Introduction

Using data partitioning you can divide very large tables (and indices, too) into smaller parts that are easier to manage. If the partitioning is done, many operations can be done in parallel, such as loading data, backup and recovery, and query processing.

Partitioning also improves the availability of the entire table. By placing each partition on its own disk, you can still access data, even if one or more disks are unavailable. In that case, all data in the available partitions can be used for read and write operations. The same is true for maintenance operations.

If a table is partitioned, the optimizer can recognize when the search condition in a query references only rows in certain partitions and therefore limits its search to those partitions. That way, you can achieve significant performance gains.

Ways to Partition Your Data

A table can be partitioned using any column of the table. This column is called the *partition key*. (It is also possible to use a group of columns for the particular partition key.) The values of the partition key are used to partition table rows to different filegroups.

Beside partition key, the database server introduces two other important notions: partition scheme and partition function. The partition scheme maps the table rows to one or more filegroups. The way this mapping is done is described using the partitioning function. In other words, the partition function defines the algorithm that is used to direct the rows to their physical location.

SQL Server supports only one form of partitioning: range partitioning. *Range partitioning* divides table rows into different partitions based on the value of the partition key. Hence, by applying range partitioning you will always know in which partition a particular row will be stored.

NOTE

Hash partitioning was on the Microsoft feature list for SQL Server 2005, but it was deleted from the list later. (In contrast to range partitioning, hash partitioning places rows one after another in partitions by applying a hashing function to the partition key.)

Before we define range partitioning, we will look at the steps for creating partitioned tables.

Steps for Creating Partitioned Tables

Before you start to partition database tables, you have to complete the following steps:

► Set partition goals
► Determine partitioning key and number of partitions
► Create a filegroup for each partition
► Create partition function and partition scheme
► Create partitioned indices (if necessary)

All of these steps will be explained in the following sections.

Set Partition Goals

Partition goals depend on the type of applications that access the table that should be partitioned. There are many different goals, and each of them could be a single reason to partition a table:

▶ Improved performance for individual queries

▶ Reduced contention

▶ Improved data availability

If the primary goal of table partitioning is improved performance for individual queries, distribute all table rows evenly. The reason is that the database server does not have to wait for data retrieval from a partition that has more rows than other partitions. Also, if such queries access data by performing table scan against significant portions of a table, partition the table rows only. (The partition of the corresponding index will just make the overhead in such a case.)

Data partitioning can reduce contention when many simultaneous queries perform index scan to return just a few rows from a table. In this case, partition the table and index with a partition scheme that allows each query to eliminate unneeded partitions from its scan. To reach this goal, start by investigating which queries access which parts of the table. Then partition table rows so that different queries access different partitions. If you want to reduce contention, apply the range partitioning.

Partitioning improves the availability of the database. By placing each partition on its own filegroup and locating each filegroup on its own disk, you can increase the data availability, because if one disk fails and is no longer accessible, only the data in that partition is unavailable. While the system administrator services the corrupted disk, other users can continue to access data from the other partitions of the table.

Determine Partitioning Key and Number of Partitions

A table can be partitioned using any table column. The values of the partition key are used to partition table rows to different filegroups. For the best performance, each partition should be stored in a separate filegroup, and each filegroup should be stored on one separate disk device. By spreading the data across several disk devices, you can balance the I/O and improve query performance, availability, and maintenance.

You should partition the data of a table using a column that does not frequently change. If the partitioning is done by a column that changes often, any update operation of that column can force the system to move the modified rows from one partition to the other, and this could be time consuming.

Create a Filegroup for Each Partition

To achieve better performance, higher data availability, and easier maintenance, you will use different filegroups to separate table data. The number of filegroups depends mostly on the hardware you have. When you have multiple CPUs, partition your data so that each CPU can access data on one disk device. If SQL Server can process multiple partitions in parallel, the processing time of your application will be significantly reduced.

Each data partition must map to a filegroup. To create a filegroup, you use either the CREATE DATABASE or ALTER DATABASE statement. The following example shows the creation of a database called **test_partitioned** with two filegroups.

EXAMPLE 23.1

```
CREATE DATABASE test_partitioned
ON PRIMARY
 ( NAME='MyDB_Primary',
   FILENAME=
     'd:\mssql\PT_Test_Partitioned_Range_df.mdf',
   SIZE=2000,
   MAXSIZE=5000,
   FILEGROWTH=1 ),
FILEGROUP MyDB_FG1
 ( NAME = 'FirstFileGroup',
   FILENAME =
     'd:\mssql\MyDB_FG1.ndf',
   SIZE = 1000MB,
   MAXSIZE=2500,
   FILEGROWTH=1 ),
FILEGROUP MyDB_FG2
 ( NAME = 'SecondFileGroup',
   FILENAME =
     'f:\mssql\MyDB_FG2.ndf',
   SIZE = 1000MB,
   MAXSIZE=2500,
   FILEGROWTH=1 )
```

In Example 23.1 we create a database called **test_partitioned**, which contains a primary filegroup **MyDB_Primary** and two other filegroups: **MyDB_FG1** and **MyDB_FG2**. The **MyDB_FG1** filegroup is stored on the D drive, while the **MyDB_FG2** filegroup is stored on the F drive.

In case you want to add filegroups to an existing database, use the ALTER DATABASE statement. The following example shows how to create another filegroup for the **test_partitioned** database. (All directories used in Example 23.2 must be created before you execute the example.)

EXAMPLE 23.2

```
ALTER DATABASE test_partitioned
  ADD FILEGROUP MyDB_FG3
GO
ALTER DATABASE test_partitioned
ADD FILE
  ( NAME = 'ThirdFileGroup',
    FILENAME =
      'G:\mssql\MyDB_FG3.ndf',
    SIZE = 1000MB,
    MAXSIZE=2500,
    FILEGROWTH=1)
TO FILEGROUP MyDB_FG3;
```

In Example 23.2 we use the ALTER DATABASE statement to create an additional filegroup called **MyDB_FG3**. With the second ALER DATABASE statement, we add a new file to the created filegroup. Notice that the TO FILEGROUP option specifies the name of the filegroup to which the new file will be added.

Create Partition Function and Partition Scheme

The next step after creating filegroups is to create the partition function. The partition function is created with the CREATE PARTITION FUNCTION statement. The syntax of the CREATE PARTITION FUNCTION concerning the range partitioning type is as follows:

```
CREATE PARTITION FUNCTION function_name(param_type)
  AS RANGE [ LEFT | RIGHT ]
    FOR VALUES ( [ boundary_value [ ,...n ] ] )
```

function_name defines the name of the partition function, while **param_type** specifies the data type of the partition key. **boundary_value** specifies the boundary values for each partition of a partitioned table or index that uses the partition function.

The CREATE PARTITION FUNCTION supports two forms of the RANGE option—RANGE LEFT and RANGE RIGHT. RANGE LEFT determines that the boundary condition is the upper boundary in the first partition. According to this, RANGE RIGHT specifies that the boundary condition is the lower boundary in the last partition. If not specified, RANGE LEFT is the default.

Before we define the partition function, we must specify the table that we want to partition. In this chapter's examples, we will use the tables **orders** and **order_ details**, which were defined in Chapter 22 (see Example 22.1). For the definition of the partition function in the following example, we will use the **orders** table and suppose that this table contains 1,000,000 rows. You can load one million rows in the **orders** table if you execute the batch in Example 22.2 after modifying the **while** statement in it:

> while @i < 1000001

The following example shows the definition of the partition function for the **orders** table with 1.000.000 rows.

EXAMPLE 23.3

```
USE test_partitioned
CREATE PARTITION FUNCTION myRangePF1 (int)
    AS RANGE LEFT FOR VALUES (500000) ;
```

Example 23.3 creates the partition function called **myRangePF1**. The number and values of parameters of the RANGE FOR VALUES clause specify the number of partitions and their boundaries. The number of parameters (say n) specifies $n + 1$ partitions. (Hence, one parameter in Example 23.3 defines two partitions.) The boundary value is 500,000. This means that all values of the partition key that are smaller than 500,000 will be placed in the first partition, while all values greater than 500,000 will be stored in the second partition. (Note that the boundary value is related to the values in the partition key, which in our example is the column **orderid** of the **orders** table. As you will see, we specify the name of the partition key in the corresponding CREATE TABLE statement.)

The created partition function is useless if we don't associate it with specific filegroups. This process is called partition scheme, and you use the CREATE PARTITION SCHEME statement to specify the association between a partition scheme and the corresponding filegroups. The following example shows the creation of the partition scheme for the partition function in Example 23.3.

EXAMPLE 23.4

```
USE test_partitioned
CREATE PARTITION SCHEME myRangePS1
    AS PARTITION myRangePF1
    TO (MyDB_FG1, MyDB_FG2);
```

Example 23.4 creates the partition scheme called **myRangePS1**. According to this scheme, all values to the left of the boundary value (i.e., all values < 500,000) will be stored in the **MyDB_FG1**filegroup. Also, all values to the right of the boundary value will be stored in the **MyDB_FG2** filegroup.

NOTE

When you define a partition scheme, you must be sure to specify a filegroup for each partition, even if multiple partitions will be stored on the same filegroup.

The creation of a partitioned table is slightly different from the creation of a nonpartitioned one. As you might guess, the CREATE TABLE statement must contain the name of the partition scheme and the name of the table column, which will be used as partition key. The following example shows the enhanced form of the CREATE TABLE statement, which is used to define partitioning of a table.

EXAMPLE 23.5

```
USE test_partitioned
CREATE TABLE orders
    (orderid INTEGER NOT NULL,
     orderdate DATETIME,
     shippeddate DATETIME,
     freight money)
ON myRangePS1 (orderid);
```

The ON clause at the end of the CREATE TABLE statement is used to specify the already-defined partition scheme (see Example 23.4). Using this scheme, the specified partition schema ties together the column of the table (**orderid**) with the partitioning function where the data type (**int**) of the partition key is specified (see Example 23.3).

Create Partitioned Index

When you partition table data, the indices that are associated with that table can be partitioned, too. You can partition table indices using the existing partition schema for that table or a different one. When both the indices and the table use the same partitioning function and the same partitioning columns (in the same order), the table and index are said to be aligned. When a table and its indices are aligned, the database server can move partitions in and out of partitioned tables very effectively, because the partitioning of both database objects is done with the same algorithm. For this reason, in the most practical cases it is recommended that you use aligned indices.

The following example shows the creation of a clustered index for the **orders** table. This index is aligned, i.e., it is partitioned using the partition scheme of the **orders** table.

EXAMPLE 23.6

```
USE test_partitioned
CREATE UNIQUE CLUSTERED INDEX CI_orders
 ON orders(orderid)
 ON myRangePS1(orderid)
```

As you can see from Example 23.6, the creation of the partitioned index for the **orders** table is done using the enhanced form of the CREATE INDEX statement. This form of the CREATE INDEX statement contains an additional ON clause that specifies the partitioning scheme. If you want to align the index with the table, specify the same partition scheme as for the corresponding table. (The first ON clause is part of the standard syntax of the CREATE INDEX statement and specifies the column for partitioning.)

Collocating Objects

Besides the partitioning of a table together with the corresponding indices, the database server also supports the partitioning of two tables using the same partition function. This partition form means that rows of both tables that have the same value for the partitioning key are stored together on a specific location. This concept of data partitioning is called collocation.

Let's use the tables **orders** and **order_details** (see Example 22.1) again to explain collocation. If you partition these tables using the same partition function on the join columns **orders.orderid** and **order_details.orderid**, the rows of both tables with the same value for the **orderid** columns will be stored together on the disk. Suppose there is a unique order with the identification number 49031 in the **orders** table and five corresponding rows in the **order_detail** table. In the case of collocation, all six rows will be stored side by side on the disk. (The same procedure will be applied to all rows of these tables with the same value for the **orderid** column.)

Guidelines for Partitioning Tables and Indices

The following suggestions are guidelines for partitioning tables and indices:

▶ For best performance in transactional systems, use partitioned indices to reduce contention between sessions.

▶ Do not partition every table. Partition only those tables that are accessed most frequently.

▶ Balance the number of partitions with the number of processors on your system. If it is not possible for you to establish the 1:1 relationship between the number of partitions and the number of processors, specify the number of partitions as a multiple factor of the number of processors.

▶ Think about partitioning a table if it is a huge one, i.e., if it contains at least several hundred thousands of rows.

▶ Do not partition the data of a table by a column that changes frequently. If the partitioning is done by a column that changes often, any update operation of that column can force the system to move the modified rows from one partition to another, and this could be very time consuming.

▶ For optimal performance in data warehouse systems, partition the tables to increase parallelism, but do not partition their indices. Place the indices in a separate filegroup. (For the detailed discussion of data warehouse systems, see Chapters 25 and 26.)

Conclusion

SQL Server 2005 supports range partitioning of data and indices, which is entirely transparent to the application. Range partitioning partitions rows based on the value of the partition key. In other words, the data is divided using the values of the partition key.

If you want to partition your data, you must complete the following steps:

▶ Create a filegroup for each partition

▶ Create partition function and partition scheme

▶ Create partitioned indices (if necessary)

Using different filegroups to separate table data, you achieve better performance, higher data availability, and easier maintenance.

The partition function is used to map the rows of a table or index into partitions based on the values of a specified column. To create a partition function, use the CREATE PARTITION FUNCTION statement. To associate a partition function with specific filegroups, use partition scheme.

When you partition table data, the indices that are associated with that table can be partitioned, too. You can partition table indices using the existing partition schema for that table or a different one.

The next chapter discusses the capability of the SQL Server system to copy data from a source database to one or more target databases using data replication.

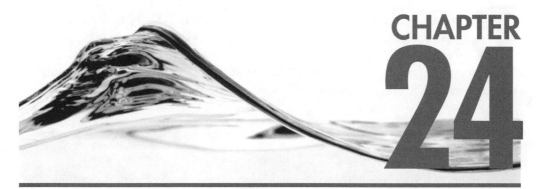

CHAPTER

24

Data Replication

IN THIS CHAPTER

Distributed Data

SQL Server Replication—An Overview

Managing Replication

B esides distributed transactions, data replication is the way to achieve a distributed data environment. A general discussion of these two methods is given in the introductory part of this chapter. After that, SQL Server replication elements are introduced, and the existing replication types are shown. The last part of the chapter covers various aspects of managing replication.

Distributed Data

Today, market forces require most companies to set up their computers (and the applications running on them) so they focus on business and on customers. As a result, data used by these applications must be available ad hoc on different locations and at different times. Such a data environment is provided by several distributed databases that include multiple copies of the same information.

The traveling salesperson provides a good example of the use of a distributed data environment. During the day, the salesperson usually uses a laptop to query all necessary information from the database (prices and availability of products, for example) in order to inform customers on the spot. Afterwards, in the hotel room, he or she again uses the laptop—this time to transmit data (about the sold products) to headquarters.

From this scenario, you can see that a distributed data environment has several benefits compared to centralized computing:

▶ It is directly available to the people who need it, when they need it.

▶ It allows local users to operate autonomously.

▶ It reduces network traffic.

▶ It makes nonstop processing cheaper.

On the other hand, a distributed data environment is much more complex than the corresponding centralized model and therefore requires much more planning and administration.

Methods for Distributing Data

There are two general methods for distributing data on multiple database servers:

▶ Distributed transactions

▶ Data replication

A distributed transaction is a transaction where all updates to all locations (where the distributed data is stored) are gathered together and executed synchronously. Distributed database systems use a method called *two-phase commit* to implement distributed transactions.

Each database involved in a distributed transaction has its own recovery technique, which is used in case of error. (Remember that all statements inside a transaction are executed in their entirety or are cancelled.) A global recovery manager (called a coordinator) coordinates the two phases of distributed processing.

In the first phase of this process, the coordinator checks whether all participating sites are ready to execute their part of the distributed transaction. The second phase consists of the actual execution of the transaction at all participating sites. During this process, any error at any site causes the coordinator to stop the transaction. In this case, it sends a message to each local recovery manager to undo the part of the transaction that is already executed at that site.

NOTE

The Microsoft Distributed Transaction Coordinator (DTC) supports distributed transactions using two-phase commit.

During the data replication process, copies of the data are distributed from a source database to one or more target databases located on separate computers. Because of this, data replication differs from distributed transactions in two ways: timing and delay in time.

In contrast to the distributed transaction method, in which all data is the same on all participating sites at the same time, data replication allows sites to have different data at the same time. Additionally, data replication is an asynchronous process. This means there is a certain delay during which all copies of data are matched on all participating sites. (This delay can last from a couple of seconds to several days or weeks.)

Data replication is, in most cases, a better solution than distributed transactions because it is more reliable and cheaper. Experience with two-phase commit has shown that administration becomes very difficult if the number of participating sites increases. Also, the increased number of participating sites decreases the reliability, because the probability that a local part of a distributed transaction will fail increases with the increased number of nodes. (If one local part fails, the entire distributed transaction will fail, too.)

Another reason to use data replication instead of centralized data is performance: clients at the site where the data is replicated experience improved performance because they can access data locally rather than using a network to connect to a central database server.

SQL Server Replication—An Overview

Generally, data replication is based on two different concepts:

▶ Using transaction logs

▶ Using triggers

As already stated in Chapter 20, the database server keeps all values of modified rows ("before" as well as "after" values) in system files called transaction logs. If selected rows need to be replicated, the system starts a new process that reads the data from the transaction log and sends it to one or more target databases.

The other method is based upon triggers. The modification of a table that contains data to be replicated fires the corresponding trigger, which in turn creates a new table with the data and starts a replication process.

Both concepts have their benefits and disadvantages. The log-based replication is characterized by improved performance, because the process that reads data from the transaction log runs asynchronously and has little effect on the performance of the overall system. On the other hand, the implementation of log-based replication is very complex for database companies, because the database system not only has to manage additional processes and buffers but also has to solve the concurrency problems between system and replication processes that access the transaction log.

NOTE

The SQL Server system uses both concepts: the transaction log method for transactional replication processing and triggers for merge replication processing. (Transactional and merge replication processing are described in detail later in this chapter.)

Publishers, Distributors, and Subscribers

SQL Server replication is based on the so-called publisher–subscriber metaphor. This metaphor describes the different roles servers can play in a replication process. One or more servers publish data that other servers can subscribe to. In between there exists a distributor that stores the changes and forwards them further (to the subscribers). Hence, a node can have three roles in a replication scenario:

▶ Publisher

▶ Distributor

▶ Subscriber

A publisher (or publishing server) maintains its source databases, makes data available for replication, and sends the modified data to the distributor. A distributor (or distribution server) receives all changes to the replicated data from the publisher and stores and forwards them to the appropriate subscribers. A subscriber (or subscribing server) receives and maintains published data.

A SQL Server system can play many roles in a replication process. For example, a server can act as the publisher and the distributor at the same time. This scenario is appropriate for a process with few replications and few subscribers. If there are a lot of subscribers for the publishing information, the distributor can be located on its own server. Figure 24-1 shows a complex scenario in which there are multiple publishers and multiple subscribers. (See also the section "Replication Models" later in this chapter.)

NOTE

You can replicate only user-defined databases.

Publications and Articles

The unit of data to be published is called a publication. An article contains data from a table and/or one or more stored procedures. A table article can be a single table or a subset of data in a table. A stored procedure article can contain one or more stored procedures that exist at the publication time in the database.

A publication contains one or more articles. Each publication can contain data only from one database.

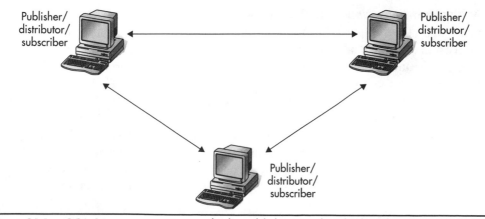

Figure 24-1   *SQL Server can act as multiple publishers and multiple subscribers.*

NOTE

A publication is the basis of a subscription. This means you cannot subscribe directly to an article, because an article is always part of a publication.

A *filter* is the process that restricts information, producing a subset (of a table). Therefore, a publication contains one or more of the following items that specify types of table articles:

▶ Table

▶ Vertical filter

▶ Horizontal filter

▶ A combination of vertical and horizontal filters

NOTE

There are certain restrictions on filtering data regarding merge replication.

A vertical filter contains a subset of the columns in a table. A horizontal filter contains a subset of rows in a table.

A subscription can be initiated in two different ways:

▶ Using a push subscription

▶ Using a pull subscription

With a *push subscription*, all the administration of setting up subscriptions is performed on the publisher during the definition of a publication. Push subscriptions simplify and centralize administration, because the usual replication scenario contains one publisher and many subscribers. The benefit of a push subscription is higher security, because the initialization process is managed at one place. On the other hand, the performance of the distributor can suffer because the overall distribution of subscriptions runs at once.

With a *pull subscription*, the subscriber initiates the subscription. The pull subscription is more selective than the push subscription, because the subscriber can select publications to subscribe to. In contrast to the push subscription, the pull subscription should be used for publications with low security and a high number of subscribers.

NOTE

The downloading of data from the Internet is a typical form of pull subscription.

Replication Types

The SQL Server system provides three types of data replication:

▶ Transactional

▶ Snapshot

▶ Merge

All three types of replication can be used within a database, because each publication can have a different type of replication.

Transactional Replication

In transactional replication, the transaction log is used to replicate data. All transactions that contain the data to be replicated are marked for replication. A SQL Server component called Log Reader Agent searches for marked transactions and copies them from the transaction log on the publisher to the **distribution** database (see below). Another component— Distribution Agent—moves transactions to subscribers, where they are applied to the target tables in the subscription databases.

NOTE

All tables published using transactional replication must explicitly contain a primary key. The primary key is required to uniquely identify the rows of the published table, because row is a transfer unit in transactional replication.

Transactional replication can replicate tables (or parts of tables) and one or more stored procedures. The use of stored procedures by transactional replication increases performance, because the amount of data to be sent over a network is usually significantly smaller. Instead of replicated data, only the stored procedure is sent to the subscribers, where it is executed. You can configure the delay of synchronization time between the publisher on one side and subscribers on the other during a transactional replication. (All these changes are propagated by Log Reader Agent and Distribution Agent.)

The **distribution** database is a system database that is installed on the distributor when the replication process is initiated. This database holds all replicated transactions from publications and publishers that need to be forwarded to the subscribers. It is heavily used only by transactional replications.

NOTE

Before transactional replications can begin, a copy of the entire database must be transferred to each subscriber; this is performed by executing a snapshot.

Snapshot Replication

The simplest type of replication, snapshot replication, copies the data to be published from the publisher to all subscribers. (The difference between snapshot replication and transactional replication is that the former sends all the published data and the latter only the changes of data to the subscribers.)

Snapshot replication is executed using the **bcp** utility. A SQL Server component called Snapshot Agent generates the schema and data of the published tables and stores them in files. The table schema is stored in the file with the suffix **.sch**, while the data is stored in the file with the suffix **.bcp**. The schema of a table and the corresponding data file build the synchronization set that represents the snapshot of the table at a particular time.

NOTE
Transactional and snapshot replication are one-way replications, which means the only changes to the replicated data are made at the publishing server. Therefore, the data at all subscription servers is read-only, except for the changes made by replication processes.

In contrast to transactional replication, snapshot replication requires no primary key for tables. The reason is obvious: the unit of transfer in snapshot replication is the entire database and not rows of a table. Another difference between these two replication types concerns a delay in time: the snapshot replication will be replicated periodically, which means the delay is significant because all data (changed and unchanged) are transferred from the publisher to the subscribers.

NOTE
*Snapshot replication does not use the **distribution** database directly. However, the **distribution** database contains status information and other details that are used by snapshot replication.*

Merge Replication

In transactional and snapshot replication, the publisher sends the data, and a subscriber receives it. (There is no possibility that a subscriber sends replicated data to the publisher.) Merge replication allows the publisher as well as subscribers to update data to be replicated. Because of that, conflicts can arise during a replication process.

After the creation of a publication at the publication server, the SQL Server component called Snapshot Agent prepares files containing table schema and data and stores them in the distribution working folder at the distributor site. (During the merge replication, the **distribution** database contains only the status of the replication process.) The synchronization job is then used by another component—Merge Agent—that sends all changed data to the other sites. Before the send process is started, Merge Agent also stores the appropriate information that is used to track updated conflicts.

When you use the merge replication scenario, SQL Server makes three important changes to the schema of the publication database:

▶ It identifies a unique column for each replicated row.

▶ It adds several system tables.

▶ It creates triggers for tables in which data are replicated.

The database server creates or identifies a unique column in the table with the replicated data. If the base table already contains a column with the UNIQUEIDENTIFIER data type and ROWGUIDCOL property, the server uses that column to identify each replicated row. If there is no such column in the table, the server adds the column **rowguid** of the UNIQUEIDENTIFIER data type with the ROWGUIDCOL property.

NOTE

UNIQUEIDENTIFIER columns may contain multiple occurrences of a value. The ROWGUIDCOL property additionally indicates that the values of the column of the UNIQUEIDENTIFIER data type uniquely identify rows in the table. Therefore, a column of the data type UNIQUEIDENTIFIER with the ROWGUIDCOL property contains unique values for each row across all networked computers in the world and thus guarantees the uniqueness of replicated rows across multiple copies of the table on the publisher and subscribers.

The addition of new system tables provides the way to detect and resolve any update conflict. SQL Server stores all changes concerning the replicated data in the merge system tables **msmerge_contents** and **msmerge_tombstone** and joins them (using the **rowguid** property of the existing column with the UNIQUEIDENTIFIER data type) with the table that contains replicated data to resolve the conflict.

SQL Server creates triggers on tables that contain replicated data on all sites to track changes to the data in each replicated row. These triggers determine the changes made to the table, and they record them in the system tables **msmerge_contents** and **msmerge_tombstone**.

A conflict detection is done by Merge Agent using the column lineage of the **msmerge_contents** system table when a conflict is detected. The resolution of it can be either priority based or custom based.

Priority-based resolution means that any conflict between new and old values in the replicated row is resolved automatically based on assigned priorities. (The special case of the priority-based method specifies the "first wins" method, where the timely first change of the replicated row is the winner.) The priority-based method is the default. The *custom-based* method uses customized triggers based on business rules defined by the database administrator to resolve conflicts.

Replication Models

The previous section introduced different replication types that the database server uses to distribute data between different nodes. The replication types (transactional, snapshot, and merge) provide the functionality for maintaining replicated data. *Replication models*, on the other hand, are used by a company to design its own data replication. (Each replication model can be implemented using one or more existing replication types.) Both replication type and replication model are usually determined at the same time.

Depending on requirements, several replication models can be used. Three of the basic ones are as follows:

▶ Central publisher with distributor

▶ Central subscriber with multiple publishers

▶ Multiple publishers and multiple subscribers

Central Publisher with Distributor

In the central publisher with distributor model, there is one publisher and usually one distributor. The publisher creates publications that are distributed by the distributor to several subscribers. (This model is the default model.)

If the amount of publishing data is not very large, the publisher and distributor can reside on one server. Otherwise, using two separate servers is recommended because of performance issues. (If there is a heavy load of data to be published, the distributor is usually the bottleneck.) Figure 24-2 shows the replication model with the central publisher and the separate distributor.

The publications designed by this model and received at a subscriber are usually read-only. Therefore, in most cases, the transactional replication is the preferred replication type for this model, although the snapshot replication can also be used.

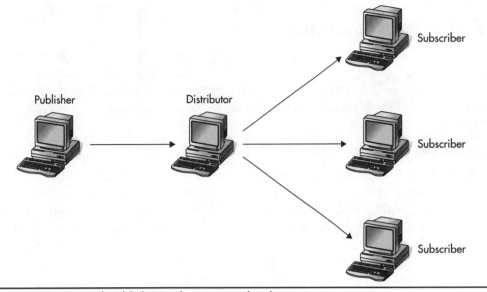

Figure 24-2   *Central publisher with separate distributor*

Central Subscriber with Multiple Publishers

The scenario described at the beginning of this chapter of the travelling salesperson who transmits data to headquarters is a typical example of the central subscriber with multiple publishers. The data are gathered at a centralized subscriber, and several publishers are sending their data.

For this model, you can use either the transactional or the merge replication type, depending on the use of replicated data. If publishers publish (and therefore update) the same data to the subscriber, merge replication should be used. If each publisher has its own data to publish, transactional replication can be used. (In this case, published tables will be filtered horizontally, and each publisher will be the exclusive owner of a particular table fragment.)

Multiple Publishers with Multiple Subscribers

The replication model in which some or all of the servers participating in data replication play the role of the publisher as well as the subscriber is known as multiple publishers with multiple subscribers. In most cases, this model includes several distributors that are usually placed at each publisher (see Figure 24-1).

This model can be implemented using merge replication only, because publications are modified at each publishing server. (The only other way to implement this model is to use the distributed transactions with two-phase commit.)

Managing Replication

All servers that participate in a replication must be registered. (Server registration is described in Chapter 2.) After registering servers, the distribution server, publishing server(s), and subscription server(s) must be set up. The following sections describe configuration of these processes using the corresponding wizards.

Configuring the Distribution and Publication Servers

The distribution server must be installed and the **distribution** database must be configured before publishing databases are installed. A distribution server can be set up using the Configure Distribution wizard. This wizard allows you to configure the distributor and the distribution database and to enable publisher(s). With the wizard you can

- ▶ Specify the local or another server as a distributor
- ▶ Configure the properties of the server as a distributor
- ▶ Create the distribution database and enable publishers
- ▶ Specify the default location of the snapshot files

We will show a scenario for data replication of the sample database using two database systems: **ntb01109** and **ntb01110**. The former will be used as a publisher and distributor, while the latter will be the subscriber. In the first step we will use the Configure Distribution wizard to set up the **ntb01109** server as the distributor, to create the **distribution** database, and to configure the same server as the publisher.

To start the wizard, start SQL Server Management Studio, expand the database server, expand **Replication**, right-click **Local Publications**, and select **Configure Distribution**. The Configure Distribution wizard appears. In the first three steps, choose the distribution server (in our example, this is **ntb01109**), decide how SQL Server Agent will be started (automatically or manually), and select the folder, where snapshots from publisher(s) that use the distribution server will be stored. After that select the name for the distribution database and the locations for its data and transaction log files. In the next step, enable the publisher(s) (in our case, this is again the **ntb01109** server) and choose whether to finish the configuration process immediately or generate the script file to start the distribution configuration later. Figure 24-3 shows the summary of all steps that we have made to configure the **ntb01109** server as the distributor and publisher.

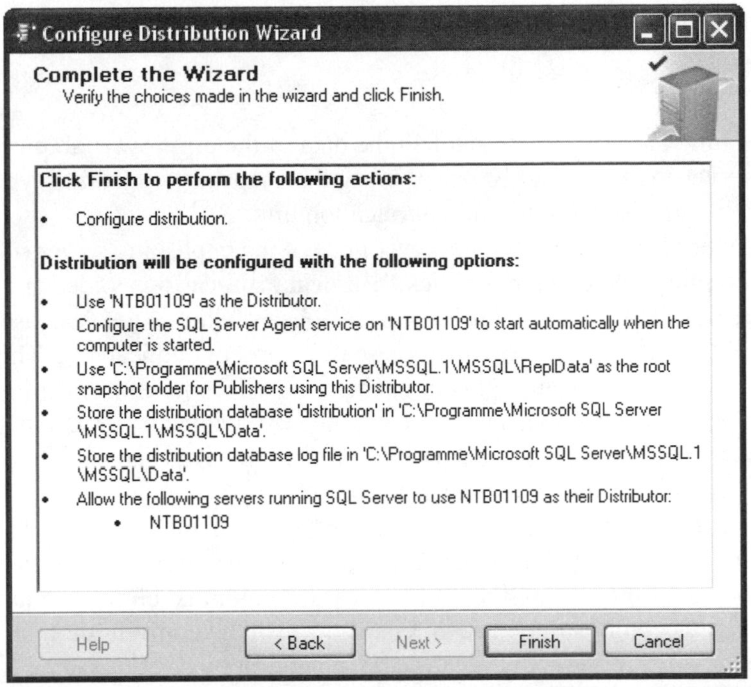

Figure 24-3   *The Complete the Wizard window for the distributor and publisher*

NOTE

*The system procedures **sp_adddistributor** and **sp_adddistributiondb** can also be used to set up the distribution server and the **distribution** database. The system procedure **sp_adddistributor** sets up the distribution server by creating a new row in the **sysservers** system table. The system procedure **sp_adddistributiondb** creates a new distribution database and installs the distribution schema.*

After the distribution and publishing servers are configured, you must set up all issues concerning publishing. This is done with the New Publication wizard, which will be explained in the following section.

Setting Up Publications

You can use the New Publication wizard to specify the following:

► The publication database

► The type of publication to create

► The data and database objects (articles) to include in the publication

▶ Filters for all types of publications

▶ The Snapshot Agent schedule

Let us assume that we want to publish the data of the **employee** table from the **ntb01109** server to the **ntb01110** server using the snapshot replication type. In this case, the entire **employee** table is the publication unit.

To create a publication, expand the server node of the publishing server (**ntb01109**), expand the **Replication** folder, right-click the **Local Publications** folder, and select **New Publication**. The New Publication wizard appears. Choose the database to publish (**sample**) and the publication type (in this case the snapshot publication). Then select at least one object for publication (in our example we select the entire **employee** table). The New Publication wizard also allows you to filter (horizontally or vertically) the data that you want to publish. The snapshot of the selected data can be initialized immediately and/or scheduled to run periodically.

In the next step, specify the security settings for the Snapshot Agent. To do this, click the **Security Settings** button and type the Windows user account under which the Snapshot Agent process will run. (The user account must be written in the form "domain_name\account_name".) Also, you can finish the configuration process immediately or generate the script file to start the publication creation later. Figure 24-4 shows the summary of all steps that we made to set up the **employee** table as a publication unit.

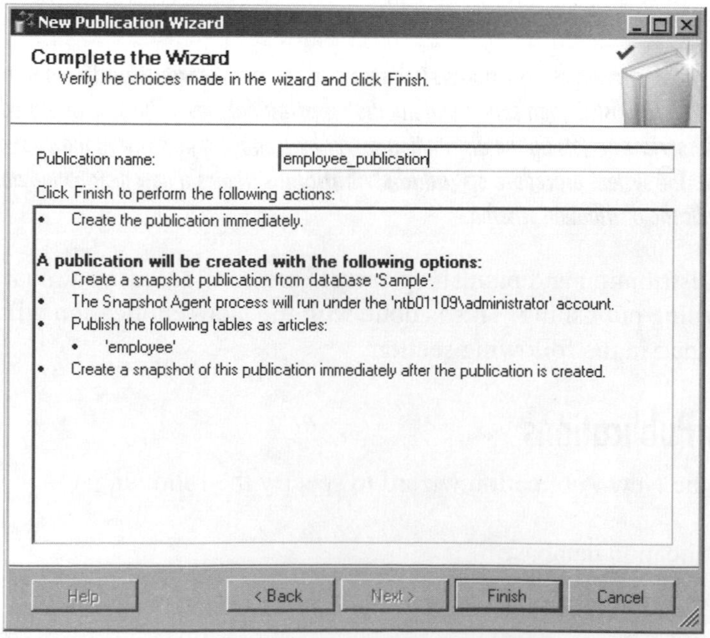

Figure 24-4 *The Complete the Wizard window for the publication unit*

The last step is to configure the subscription servers, which will be discussed in the following section.

Setting Up Subscription Servers

A task that concerns subscribers and must be performed at the publisher is enabling the publisher to subscribe. Use SQL Server Management Studio to enable a subscriber at the publisher. First expand the publishing server, expand **Replication**, right-click **Local Subscriptions**, and select **New Subscriptions**. The New Subscription Wizard appears. In the first step, choose the publication for which you want to create one or more subscriptions. (In our example we chose the **employee_publication** publication, which was already generated with the New Publication wizard.)

In the next step, you must choose between the push and pull subscriptions (see Figure 24-5). A push subscription means that the synchronization of subscriptions is administered centrally. For this replication check **Run all agents at the Distributor** in the **Distribution Agent Location** dialog box. To specify the pull distribution, check **Run each agent at its Subscriber**.

In the next step you must specify all subscription servers. If the subscription servers have not been added, click **Add SQL Server Subscriber** and select all

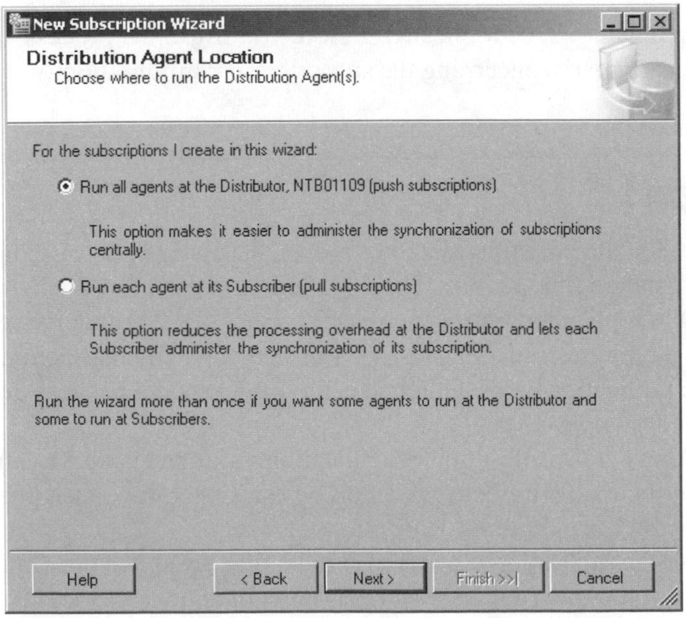

Figure 24-5   *The choice between the push and pull subscriptions*

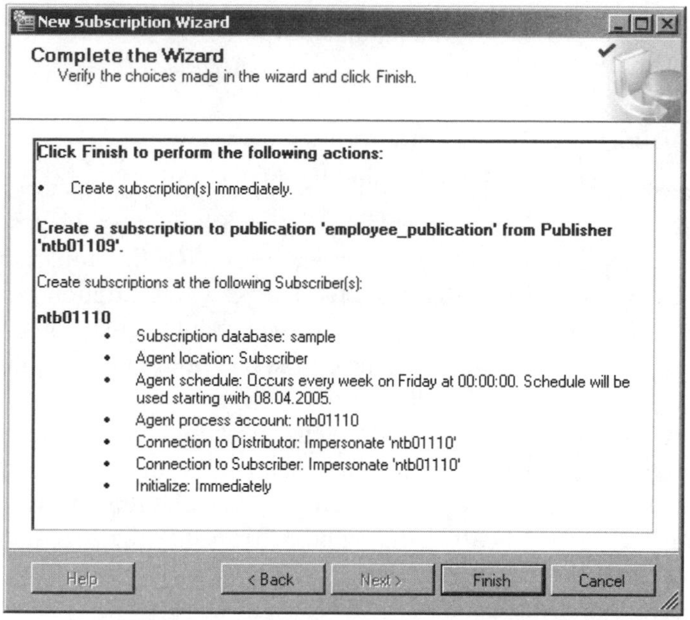

Figure 24-6   *The Complete the Wizard window*

servers to which data will be replicated. Before you finish the process, the wizard shows you the summary concerning the subscription configuration (see Figure 24-6).

Conclusion

Data replication is the preferred method for data distribution, because it is cheaper than using distributed transactions. The SQL Server sytem allows you to choose one of three possible replication types (snapshot, transactional, and merge replication), depending on the physical model you use. Theoretically, any replication model can use any of the replication types, although each (basic) model has a corresponding type that is used in most cases.

A publication is the smallest unit of replication. A single database can have many publications with different replication types. (Otherwise, each publication corresponds to only one database.)

To configure the replication process, you must first set up the distributor server and the distribution system database and configure the publishing server(s). In the next step you must define one or more publications. Finally, the subscription server(s) have to be configured. The SQL Server system supports these steps with three different wizards: the Configure Distribution wizard, New Publication wizard, and New Subscription wizard.

The next chapter begins the Business Intelligence part of the book. It introduces general terms and concepts that you must know about this important topic.

Exercises

E.24.1

Why do you need a primary key for data replication? Which replication type requires a primary key?

E.24.2

How can you limit network traffic and/or database size?

E.24.3

Update conflicts are not recommended. How can you minimize them?

E.24.4

When does the database server use Log Reader Agent, Merge Agent, and Snapshot Agent?

Microsoft Analysis Services

CHAPTER
25

Data Warehousing:
An Introduction

The goal of this chapter is to introduce you to a new (and very important) area of database technology: data warehousing. The first part of the chapter explains the difference between the online transaction processing world on one side and the data warehousing world on the other side. A *data store* for a data warehousing process can be either a data warehouse or a data mart. Both types of data store are discussed, and their differences are listed in the second part of the chapter. The data warehouse design and the need for creation of aggregate tables is explained at the end of the chapter.

Online Transaction Processing vs. Data Warehousing

From the beginning, relational database systems were used almost exclusively to capture primary business data such as orders and invoices using processing based on transactions. This focus on business data has its benefits and its disadvantages. One benefit is that the poor performance of early database systems improved dramatically, so today many database systems can execute thousands of transactions per second (using appropriate hardware). On the other hand, the focus on transaction processing prevented people in the database business from seeing another natural application of database systems: using them to filter and analyze needed information out of all the existing data in an enterprise or department.

Online Transaction Processing

As already stated, performance is one of the main issues for systems that are based upon transaction processing. These systems are called online transaction processing (OLTP) systems. The typical operation for OLTP systems is withdrawing the money from the bank account using a teller machine. OLTP systems have some important properties, such as:

▶   Short transactions—that is, high throughput of data

▶   Many (possibly hundreds or thousands of) users

▶   Continuous read and write operations based on a small number of rows

▶   Data of medium size that is stored in a database

The performance of a database system will increase if transactions in the database application programs are short. The reason is that transactions use locks (see Chapter 14) to prevent possible negative effects of concurrency issues. If transactions are long lasting, the number of locks and their duration increases, decreasing the data availability for other transactions and thus their performance.

Large OLTP systems usually have many users working on the system simultaneously. A typical example is a reservation system for an airline company, which must process thousands of requests for travel arrangements in a single country, or all over the world, almost immediately. In this type of system, most users expect that their response-time requirements will be fulfilled by the system and the system will be available at working hours (or nonstop).

Users of an OLTP system execute their DML statements continuously—that is, they use both read and write operations at the same time and steadily. (Because data is continuously modified, we say that data of an OLTP system is highly dynamic.) All operations (or results of them) on a database usually include only a small amount of data, although it is possible that the database system must access many rows from one or more tables stored in the database.

In recent years, the amount of data stored in an *operational* database (i.e., a database managed by an OLTP system) has increased steadily. Today, there are many databases that store several (or even dozens of) gigabytes of data. As you will see, this amount of data is still relatively small in relation to data warehouses.

Data Warehouse Systems

Data warehousing is the process of integrating enterprise-wide data into a single data store from which end users can run ad hoc queries and reports to analyze the existing data. In other words, the goal of data warehousing is to keep data that can be accessed by users who make their business decisions on the basis of the analysis. These systems are often called *informative* systems, because by accessing data, users get the necessary information for making better business decisions.

The goals of data warehousing systems are different from the goals of OLTP systems. The following is a query that is typical for data warehousing systems: "What is the best-selling product category for each sales region in the third quarter of the year 2005?" Therefore, a data warehousing system has very different properties from those listed above for an OLTP system. The most important properties of a data warehousing system are as follows:

▶   Periodic write operations (load) with queries based on a huge number of rows

▶   Small number of users

▶   Large size of data stored in a database

Besides data load that is executed at regular intervals (usually daily), data warehouse systems are mostly read-only systems. (Therefore, the nature of the data in such a system is static.) As will be explained in detail later in this chapter, data is gathered from different sources, cleaned (made consistent), and loaded into a database called a data warehouse (or data mart). The cleaned data is not modified at all—that is, users query data using SELECT statements to obtain the necessary information.

Because data warehousing systems are used to gain information, the number of users that simultaneously use such a system is relatively small (at most, several dozen). Users of a data warehousing system usually generate reports that display different factors concerning the finances of an enterprise (or department), or they execute complex queries to compare data.

NOTE

Another difference between OLTP and data warehousing systems (that actually affects the user's behavior) is the daily schedule—that is, how those systems are used during a day. An OLTP system can be used nonstop (if it is designed for such a use), while a data warehouse system can be used as soon as data is made consistent and is loaded into the database.

In contrast to databases in OLTP systems that store only current data, data warehousing systems must also track historical data. (Remember that data warehousing systems make comparisons between data gathered in different time periods.) For this reason, the amount of data stored in a data warehouse is very large.

Data Warehouses and Data Marts

A *data warehouse* can be defined as a database that includes all corporate data and that can be uniformly accessed by users. After this concise definition, let's try to explain the notion of a data warehouse more accurately. An enterprise usually has a large amount of data stored at different times and in different databases (or data files) that are managed by distinct DBMSs. These DBMSs need not be relational: some enterprises still have databases managed by hierarchical or network database systems. A special team of software specialists examines source databases (and data files) and converts them into a target store: the data warehouse. Additionally, the converted data in a data warehouse must be consolidated because it holds the information that is the key to the corporation's operational processes. (*Consolidation* of data means that all equivalent queries executed upon a data warehouse at different times provide the same result.) The data consolidation in a data warehouse is provided in several steps:

► Data assembly from different sources (also called extraction)

► Data cleaning (i.e., transformation process)

► Quality assurance of data

Data must be carefully assembled from different sources. In this process, data is extracted from the sources, converted to an intermediate schema, and moved to a temporary work area. For data extraction, you need tools that extract exactly the data that must be stored in the data warehouse.

Data cleaning ensures the integrity of data that has to be stored in the target database. For example, data cleaning must be done on incorrect entries in data fields, such as addresses, or incompatible data types used to define the same data fields in different sources. For this process, the data cleaning team needs special software.

An example will help explain the process of data cleaning more clearly. Suppose there are two data sources that store personal data concerning employees and that both databases have the attribute **Gender**. In the first database, this attribute is defined as CHAR(6), and the data values are "female" and "male." The same attribute in the second database is declared as CHAR(1) with the values "f" and "m." The values of both data sources are correct, but for the target data source you must clean the data— that is, represent the values of the attribute in a uniform way.

The last part of data consolidation—quality assurance of data—involves a data validation process that specifies the data as the end user should view and access it. Because of this, end users should be closely involved in this process. When the process of data consolidation is finished, the data will be loaded in the data warehouse.

NOTE

The whole process of data consolidation is called ETL (extraction, transformation, loading). MS SQL Server provides the component called Integration Services, of which the primary aim is to support users during the ETL process.

By their nature (as a store for the overall data of an enterprise), data warehouses contain huge amounts of data. (Some data warehouses contain terabytes of data.) Also, because they must encompass the enterprise, implementation usually takes two to three years. Because of these disadvantages, many companies start with a smaller solution called a data mart.

Data marts are data stores that include all data at the department level and therefore allow users to access data concerning only a single part of their organization. For example, the marketing department stores all data relevant to marketing in its own data mart, the research department puts the experimental data in the research data mart, and so on. Because of this, a data mart has several advantages over a data warehouse:

▶ Narrower application area

▶ Shorter development time and lower cost

▶ Easier data maintenance

▶ Bottom-up development

As already stated, a data mart includes only the information needed by one part of an organization, usually a department. Therefore, the data that is intended for use by such a small organizational unit can be more easily prepared for the end user's needs.

The development time for a data warehouse averages two years and costs $5 million. On the other hand, costs for a data mart average $200,000, and such a project takes about three to five months. For these reasons, development of a data mart is preferred, especially if it is the first data warehousing project in your organization.

The fact that a data mart contains significantly smaller amounts of data than a data warehouse helps you to reduce and simplify all tasks, such as data extraction, data cleaning, and quality assurance of data. It is also easier to design a solution for a department than for the entire organization. (For more information on data warehousing design and a dimensional model, see the next section of this chapter.)

If you design and develop several data marts in your organization, it is possible to unite them all in one big data warehouse. This bottom-up process has several advantages over designing a data warehouse at once: First, each data mart may contain identical target tables that can be unified in a corresponding data warehouse. Second, some tasks are logically enterprise-wide, such as the gathering of financial information by the accounting department. If the existing data marts will be linked together to build a data warehouse for an enterprise, a global repository (i.e., the data catalog that contains information about all data stored in sources as well as in the target database) is required.

NOTE

Be aware that building a data warehouse by linking data marts can be very troublesome because of possible significant differences in the structure and design of existing data marts. Different parts of an enterprise may use different data models and have different instructions for data representation. For this reason, at the beginning of this bottom-up process it is strongly recommended that you make a single view of all data that will be valid at the enterprise level; do not allow departments to design data separately.

Data Warehouse Design

Only a well-planned and well-designed database will allow you to achieve good performance. Relational databases and data warehouses have a lot of differences that require different design methods. Relational databases are designed using the well-known entity-relationship (ER) model, while the dimensional model is used for the design of data warehouses and data marts. The following section describes the dimensional model.

Dimensional Model

Using relational databases, data redundancy is removed using normal forms (see Chapter 1). The normalization process divides each table of a database that includes redundant data into two separate tables. The process of normalization should be finished when all tables of a database contain only nonredundant data.

The highly normalized tables are advantageous for online transaction processing, because in this case all transactions can be made as simple and short as possible. On the other hand, data warehousing processes are based on queries that operate on a huge amount of data and are neither simple nor short. Therefore, the highly normalized tables do not suit the design of data warehouses, because the goal of data warehouse systems is significantly different: there are few concurrent transactions, and each transaction accesses a very large number of records. (Imagine the huge amount of data belonging to a data warehouse that is stored in hundreds of tables. Most queries will join dozens of large tables to retrieve data. Such queries cannot be performed well, even if you use hardware with parallel processors and a database system with the best performance.)

Data warehouses cannot use the ER model because this model is used to design databases with nonredundant data. The logical model used to design data warehouses is called a *dimensional model*.

NOTE

There is another important reason why the ER model is not suited to the design of data warehouses: the use of data in a data warehouse is unstructured. This means the queries are executed ad hoc, allowing a user to analyze data in totally different ways. (On the other hand, OLTP systems usually have database applications that are hard-coded and therefore contain queries that are not modified often.)

In dimensional modeling, every model is composed of one table that stores measures and several other tables that describe dimensions. The former is called the *fact table*, and the latter are called *dimension tables*. Examples of data that are stored in a fact table include inventory sales and expenditures. Dimensional tables usually include time, account, product, and employee data. Figure 25-1 shows an example of a dimensional model.

Each dimension table usually has a single-part primary key and several other attributes that describe this dimension closely. On the other hand, the primary key of the fact table is the combination of the primary keys of all dimension tables (see Figure 25-1). For this reason, the primary key of the fact table is made up of several foreign keys. (The number of dimensions also specifies the number of foreign keys in the fact table.) As you can see in Figure 25-1, the tables in a dimensional model build a star-like structure. Therefore, this model is often called a *star schema*.

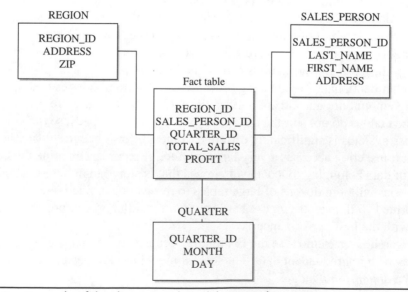

Figure 25-1   *Example of the dimensional model: Star Schema*

Another difference in the nature of data in a fact table and the corresponding dimension tables is that most nonkey columns in a fact table are numeric and additive, because such data can be used to execute necessary calculations. (Remember that a typical query on a data warehouse fetches thousands or even millions of rows at a time, and the only useful operation upon such a huge amount of rows is to apply an aggregate function (sum, maximum, average)). For example, columns like **Units_of_ product_sold, Total_sales, Profit**, or **Dollars_cost** are typical columns in the fact table. (Numerical columns of the fact table that do not build the primary key of the table are called *measures*.)

On the other hand, columns of dimension tables are strings that contain textual descriptions of the dimension. For instance, columns such as **Address, Location**, and **Name** often appear in dimension tables. (These columns are usually used as headers in reports.) Another consequence of the textual nature of columns of dimension tables and their use in queries is that each dimension table contains many more indices than the corresponding fact table. (A fact table usually has only one unique index composed of all columns belonging to the primary key of that table.) Table 25-1 summarizes the differences between fact and dimension tables.

Columns of dimension tables are usually highly *denormalized*, which means that a lot of columns depend on each other. The denormalized structure of dimension tables has one important purpose: all columns of such a table are used as column headers in reports. If the denormalization of data in a dimension table is not desirable (to save disk storage or to improve performance, for example), a dimension table can be decomposed into several subtables. This is usually necessary when columns of a dimension table build hierarchies. (For example, the **Product** dimension could have columns such as **Product_id, Category_id**, and **Subcategory_id** that build three hierarchies, with the primary key, **Product_id**, as the root.) This structure, in which each level of a base entity is represented by its own table, is called a *snowflake schema*. Figure 25-2 shows the snowflake schema of the **Product** dimension.

Fact Table	Dimension Table
(Usually) one in a dimensional model	Usually 10–20
Contains most rows of a data warehouse system	Contains relatively small amount of data
Composite primary key (contains all primary keys of dimension tables)	Usually one column of a table builds the primary key of the table
Columns are numeric and additive	Columns are descriptive and therefore textual

Table 25-1   *The Differences Between Fact and Dimension Tables*

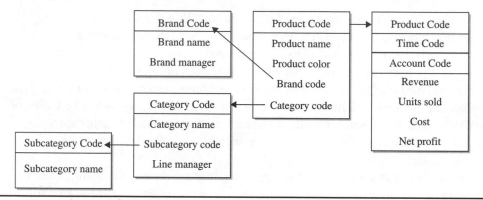

Figure 25-2   *The snowflake schema*

The extension of a star schema into a corresponding snowflake schema has some benefits (reduction of used disk space, for example) and one main disadvantage: the snowflake schema does not allow you to use columns of snowflaked tables as headers—that is, it prevents you from browsing using all columns that are located outside the dimension table. For this reason, the design using the snowflake schema is recommended only in a few very specialized cases.

Cubes and Storage Modes

Data warehousing systems support different types of data storage. Some of these data storage types are based upon a multidimensional database that is also called a cube. A *cube* is a subset of data from the data warehouse that can be organized into multidimensional structures. To define a cube, you first select a fact table from the dimensional schema and identify numerical columns of interest within it. Then you select dimension tables that provide descriptions for the set of data to be analyzed. To demonstrate this, let us show how the cube for car sales analysis might be defined. For example, the fact table may include the columns **Cars_sold, Total_ sales**, and **Costs**; while the tables **Models, Quarters**, and **Region** specify dimension tables. The cube in Figure 25-3 shows all three dimension tables: **Models, Regions**, and **Quarters**.

In each dimension there are discrete values that are called members. For instance, the **Region** dimension may contain the following members: ALL, North America, South America, and Europe. (The ALL member specifies the total of all members in a dimension.)

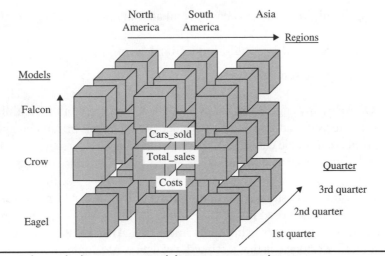

Figure 25-3   *Cube with dimensions Models, Quarters, and Regions*

Additionally, each cube dimension can have a hierarchy of levels that allow users to ask questions at a more detailed level. For example, the **Regions** dimension can include the following level hierarchies: **Country, Province**, and **City**. Similarly, the **Quarters** dimension can include **Month, Week**, and **Day** as level hierarchies.

MOLAP, ROLAP, and HOLAP

MOLAP (Multidimensional Online Analytical Processing) is a type of storage in which the low-level data and their aggregations are stored using a multidimensional cube. On the other hand, ROLAP (relational OLAP) uses the well-known relational databases to store data in a data warehouse. Although the logical content of these two storage types is identical for the same data warehouse, there are some significant differences between them. The advantages of ROLAP storage type are as follows:

▶   Data must not be duplicated.

▶   Materialized (i.e., indexed) views can be used for summaries.

If the data should also be stored in a multidimensional database, a certain amount of data must be duplicated. Therefore, the ROLAP storage type does not need additional storage to copy the low-level data. Also, the calculation of summaries (see the next section) can be executed very quickly with ROLAP if the corresponding summary tables are generated using indexed views.

On the other hand, MOLAP also has several advantages in relation to ROLAP:

▶ Aggregates are stored in a multidimensional form.

▶ Query response is generally faster.

Using MOLAP, many aggregates are precalculated and stored in a multidimensional cube. That way the system does not have to calculate the result of such an aggregate each time it is needed. In the case of MOLAP, the database engine and the database itself are usually optimized to work together, so the query response can be faster than in ROLAP.

HOLAP (hybrid OLAP) storage is a combination of the MOLAP and ROLAP storage types. Aggregation data is stored in MOLAP, while the base data is left in the relational database. (Therefore, for queries using summaries, HOLAP is identical to MOLAP.) The advantage of HOLAP storage is that the low-level data is not duplicated.

Aggregation

Data is stored in the fact table in its most detailed form so that corresponding reports can make use of it. On the other hand (as stated earlier), a typical query on a fact table fetches thousands or even millions of rows at a time, and the only useful operation upon such a huge amount of rows is to apply an aggregate function (sum, maximum, average). This different use of data can reduce performance of ad hoc queries if they are executed on low-level (atomic) data, because time- and resource-intensive calculations will be necessary to perform each aggregate function.

For this reason, low-level data from the fact table should be summarized in advance and stored in intermediate tables. Because of their "aggregated" information, such intermediate tables are called *aggregate tables*, and the whole process is called *aggregation*.

NOTE

An aggregate row from the fact table is always associated with one or more dimension table rows. For example, the dimensional model in Figure 25-1 could contain the following aggregate rows: monthly sales aggregates by salespersons by region; region-level aggregates by salespersons by day.

An example will show why low-level data should be aggregated. An end user may want to start an ad hoc query that displays the total sales of the organization for the last month. This would cause the server to sum all sales for each day in the last month. If there is an average of 500 sales transactions per day in each of 500 stores of the organization, and data is stored at the transaction level, this query would have to read 7,500,000 (500 × 500 × 30 days) rows, and build the sum to return the result. Now let's examine what happens if the data is aggregated in a table that is created using monthly sales by store. In this case, the table will only have 500 rows (the monthly total for each of 500 stores), and the performance gain will be dramatic.

How Much to Aggregate?

Concerning aggregation, there are two extreme solutions: no aggregation at all and exhaustive aggregation for every possible combination of queries that users will need. From the discussion above, it should be clear that no aggregation at all is out of the question because of performance issues. (The data warehouse without any aggregation table probably cannot be used at all as a production data store.) The opposite solution is also not acceptable for several reasons:

▶ Enormous amount of disk space that is needed to store additional data

▶ Overwhelming maintenance of aggregate tables

▶ Initial data load too long

Storing additional data that is aggregated at every possible level consumes an additional amount of disk space that increases the initial disk space by a factor of six or more (depending on the amount of the initial disk space and the number of queries that users will need). The creation of tables to hold the aggregates for all existing combinations is an overwhelming task for the system administrator. Finally, building aggregates at initial data load can have devastating results if this load already lasts for a long time and the additional time is not available.

From this discussion you can see that aggregate tables should be carefully planned and created. During the planning phase, keep these two main considerations in mind when determining what aggregates to create:

▶ Where is the data concentrated?

▶ Which aggregates would most improve performance?

The planning and creation of aggregate tables is dependent on the concentration of data in the columns of the base fact table. In a data warehouse, where there is no activity on a given day, the corresponding row is not stored at all. So if the system loads a large number of rows, as compared to the number of all rows that can be loaded, aggregating by that column of the fact table improves performance enormously. In contrast, if the system loads few rows, as compared to the number of all rows that can be loaded, aggregating by that column is not efficient.

Here is another example to demonstrate the discussion above. For products in the grocery store, only a few of them (say, 15 percent) are actually sold on a given day. If we have a dimensional model with three dimensions **Products, Store**, and **Time**, only 15 percent of the combination of the three corresponding primary keys for the particular day and for the particular store will be occupied. The daily product sales data will thus be *sparse*. In contrast, if all or many products in the grocery store are sold on a given day (because of a special promotion, for example), the daily product sales data will be *dense*.

To find out which dimensions are sparse and which are dense, you have to build rows from all possible combinations of tables and evaluate them. Usually the **Time** dimension is dense, because there are always entries for each day. Given the dimensions **Products, Store**, and **Time**, the combination of the **Store** and **Time** dimensions is dense, because for each day there will certainly be data concerning selling in each store. On the other hand, the combination of the **Store** and **Product** dimensions is sparse. In this case, we can say that the dimension **Product** is generally sparse, because its appearance in combination with other dimensions is sparse.

The choice of aggregates that would most improve performance depends on end users. Therefore, at the beginning of a data warehousing project you should interview end users to collect information on how data will be queried, how many rows will be retrieved by these queries, and other criteria.

Data Access

Data in a data warehouse can be accessed using three general techniques:

- ▶ Reporting
- ▶ Data analysis
- ▶ Data mining

Reporting is the simplest form of data access. A report is just a presentation of a query result in a tabular or matrix form. With OLAP you analyze data interactively;

i.e., it allows you to perform comparisons and calculations along any dimension in a data warehouse.

Data mining is used to explore and analyze large quantities of data in order to discover significant patterns. This discovery is not the only task of data mining: Using this technique you must be able to turn the existing data into information and the information into action. In other words, it is not enough to analyze data; you have to apply the results of data mining meaningfully and take action upon the given results.

With SQL Server 2005, Analysis Services provides a unified and integrated view of all business data as the foundation for these three general techniques.

Conclusion

At the beginning of a data warehouse project, the main question is what to build: a data warehouse or a data mart. Probably the best answer is to start with one or more data marts that can later be united in a data warehouse. Most of the existing tools in the data warehousing market support this alternative.

In contrast to operational databases that use ER models for their design, the design of data warehouses is best done using a dimensional model. These two models show significant differences. If you are already acquainted with the ER model, the best way to learn and use the dimensional model is to forget everything about the ER model and start modeling from scratch.

After this introductory discussion of general considerations about the data warehousing process, the next chapter discusses MS Analysis Services and its components.

Exercises

E.25.1

Discuss the differences between OLTP and data warehousing systems.

E.25.2

Discuss the differences between the ER and dimensional models.

E.25.3

At the beginning of a project with a data warehouse, there is the so-called ETL process (E, extracting; T, transforming; L, loading). Explain these three subprocesses.

E.25.4

Discuss the differences between a fact table and dimension tables.

E.25.5

Discuss the benefits of each of the three storage types (MOLAP, ROLAP, and HOLAP).

E.25.6

Why it is necessary to aggregate data stored in a fact table?

Microsoft Analysis Services

Microsoft Analysis Services are services that are used to manage data that is stored in a data warehouse or data mart. Analysis Services organize data from a data warehouse into multidimensional cubes (see Chapter 25) with aggregates to allow the execution of sophisticated reports and complex queries. The key features of MS Analysis Services are

- ▶ Ease of use
- ▶ Flexible data model
- ▶ Several supported APIs

Analysis Services offer wizards for almost every task that is executed during the design and implementation of a data warehouse. For example, Data Source Wizard allows you to specify one or more data sources, while Cube Wizard is used to create a multidimensional cube where aggregate data are stored.

Ease of use is guaranteed by Business Intelligence Development Studio. You can use this tool to develop databases and other data warehousing objects. This means that Business Intelligence Development Studio offers one interface for developing Analysis Services projects, as well as SQL Server Integration Services and Reporting Services projects. (This tool will be discussed in detail in the next section.)

In contrast to most other data warehouse systems, MS Analysis Services allow you to use the storage mode that is most appropriate for a specific data warehouse system. You can choose between the following storage structures:

- ▶ MOLAP
- ▶ ROLAP
- ▶ HOLAP

In a MOLAP (multidimensional online analytical processing) storage structure, data as well as aggregates are stored in a multidimensional cube. The most important benefit of this structure is that it offers the best performance for data analysis, because Analysis Services use the specialized indexing techniques to improve query performance. On the other hand, this storage structure consumes the most disk space, because data in the cube is duplicated.

ROLAP (relational OLAP) stores the base data and all aggregates in tables of a relational database. (The base data as well as aggregates are stored in the same database.) The benefits of ROLAP are that it does not require extra storage space, and a user can use Transact-SQL for data analysis (see Chapter 27). The disadvantage of this storage structure is its performance: the queries do not execute as quickly as with MOLAP. For this reason, you should use ROLAP for queries that are executed infrequently.

If the base data and all aggregations are separated so that the former is stored in tables of a relational database and the latter in the multidimensional cube, the storage type is called HOLAP (hybrid OLAP). The benefits of storing the base data and aggregations in a HOLAP storage structure are that it consumes less disk space than MOLAP, and it provides fast response for queries on aggregate data.

BI Development Studio

The main component of Analysis Services is Business Intelligence Development Studio. BI Development Studio is a management tool that provides one development platform for Integration Services, Reporting Services, data mining, and Analysis Services. Built on Visual Studio 2005, Development Studio supports an integrated development platform for system developers in the business intelligence area. Debugging, source control, and code development are available for all components of a business intelligence application.

Besides creating and managing cubes, you can use BI Development Studio to design capabilities for SQL Server Integration Services (SSIS) and Reporting Services.

NOTE

The user interface of Business Intelligence Development Studio is very similar to the interface of SQL Server Management Studio. On the other hand, these two tools differ in their deployment: You should use BI Development Studio to develop data warehouses, while SQL Server Management Studio is mainly used to operate and maintain data warehouses and business intelligence database objects.

To start BI Development Studio, click **Start**, select **Programs**, select **Microsoft SQL Server 2005**, and choose **SQL Server Business Intelligence Development Studio**.

The first step in building an analytic application is to create a new project. To build a project click **File**, select **New**, and choose **Project**. In the **New Project** dialog box, click the **Business Intelligence Projects** folder in the **Project Types** pane. In the **Templates** pane, select **Analysis Services Project**. Type the name of the project and its location in the **Name** and **Location** text boxes, respectively (see Figure 26-1). The new project will be created after you click **OK**. (We call the project **Project1**, as you can see from Figure 26-1.)

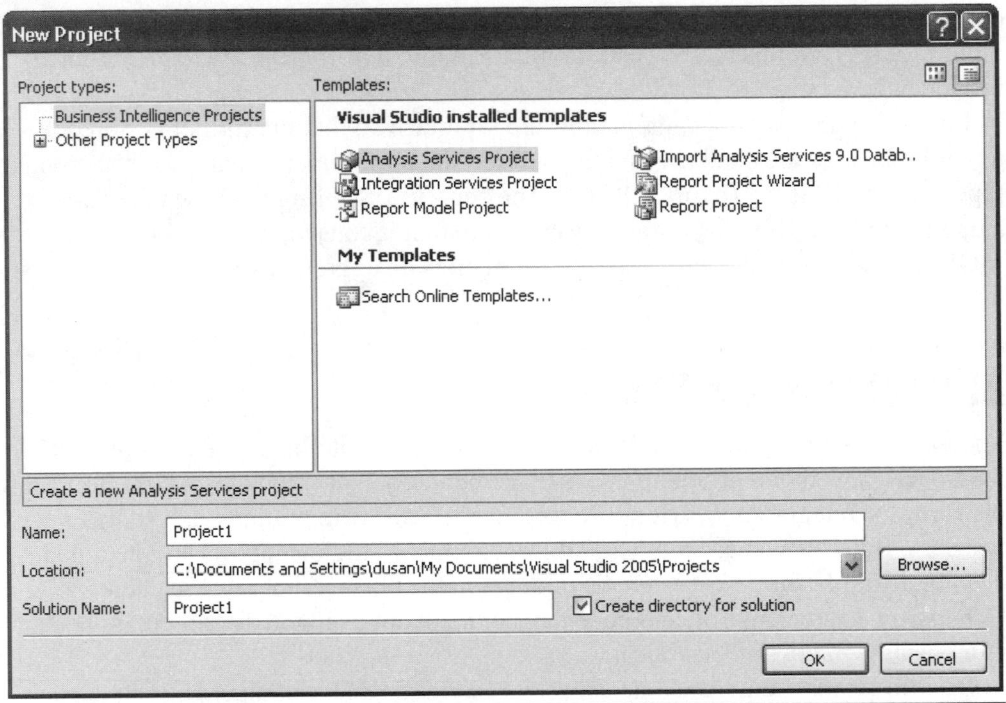

Figure 26-1 *The New Project dialog box*

The new project is always created in a new solution. Hence, the solution is the largest management unit in BI Development Studio, and it always comprises one or more projects. (If the Solution Explorer component, which allows you to view and manage objects in a solution or a project, is not visible, you can view it by clicking **View** in the menu bar and selecting **Solution Explorer**.)

Before we explain how a data source and a data source view can be created, let us take a look at the **Solution Explorer** window with the newly created project. Beneath the project node there are the following folders, among others:

- ▶ Data Sources
- ▶ Data Source Views
- ▶ Cubes
- ▶ Dimensions
- ▶ Mining Structures

The **Data Sources** folder stores the information for connecting to the source database. The **Data Source Views** folder contains information concerning the subset of tables in a source database. The next folder–**Cubes**–comprises all cubes that belong to the project. The **Mining Models** folder allows you to create a data mining model using the Data Mining wizard. These models are based on cube information and view the results as a new dimension or measure.

The **Dimensions** folder contains all dimensions. Analysis Services support two types of dimensions: shared and private. Shared dimensions (also called conformed dimensions) are dimensions that are shared among two or more cubes in the database. Typical shared dimensions are **Time**, **Product**, and **Customer**. Private dimensions are created for an individual cube.

Besides the folders described above, there are several other folders that we will describe later when we discuss the practical use of data warehouse projects.

Once the project is created, you should create a data source. To do this, right-click the **Data Sources** folder in the **Solution Explorer** pane and then select **New Data Source**. The Data Source wizard appears. We will show how the Data Source wizard guides you to create a data source. (In this example we will use the Analysis Services sample database called **AdventureWorksDW** as the data source.)

First, on the **Select how to define the connection** window, make sure the **Create a data source based on an existing or new connection** radio button is chosen and click **New**. In the **Connection Manager** dialog box, select **Native OLE DB/SQL Native Client** and type either **localhost** or the name of your database server as the server name. In the same step choose **Use Windows Authentication** and, from the **Select or enter a database name** drop-down list, choose the **AdventureWorksDW** database. Before clicking **OK**, click the **Test Connection** button to test the connection to the database.

Finally, in the **Completing the Wizard** window, give the name to the new data source and click **Finish**. (In our example we call it **Source1**.) The new data source appears in the **Solution Explorer** pane in the **Data Source** folder (see Figure 26-2).

The next step is to create a view that corresponds to the selected data source. A data source view is used to define the schema information you want to use in your solution. In other words, a data source view contains information concerning the subset of tables from the specified source database. (You should create a data source view when your database comprises hundreds of tables, of which only a few are useful in a business intelligence application.)

To create such a view, right-click the **Data Source Views** folder in the **Solution Explorer** pane and select **New Data Source View**. The Data Source View wizard guides you during all steps that are necessary to create a data source view. (In our example, we create a view called **View1**, which is based upon the **Customer** and **Project** tables as well as their related tables.)

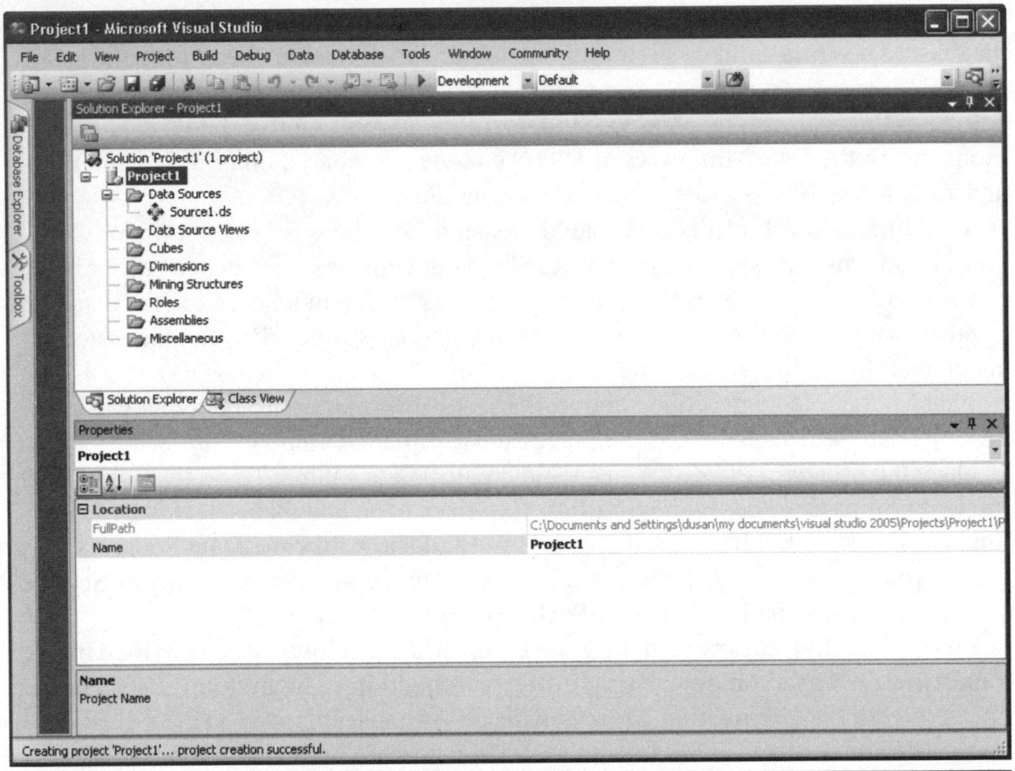

Figure 26-2 *The Solution Explorer pane with new data source*

First, on the **Select a Data Source** page select an existing relational data source (in our example **Source1**) and click **Next**. On the next page—**Select Tables and Views**—you select tables that belong to your cube either as dimension or fact tables. In our example we select the customer and product tables from the **AdventureWorksDW** database. These tables are called **DimCustomer** and **DimProduct**, respectively, and will be used to build cube dimensions. Also, by clicking the **Add Related Tables** button, we instruct the system to find tables that are related to the two selected tables. (To find related tables, the system searches all primary key/foreign key relationships that exist in the database.)

We also add the **DimTime** table, because the time dimension is always a part of a cube. On the **Completing the Wizard** page the system shows the following tables (see Figure 26-3):

▶ DimCustomer

▶ DimProduct

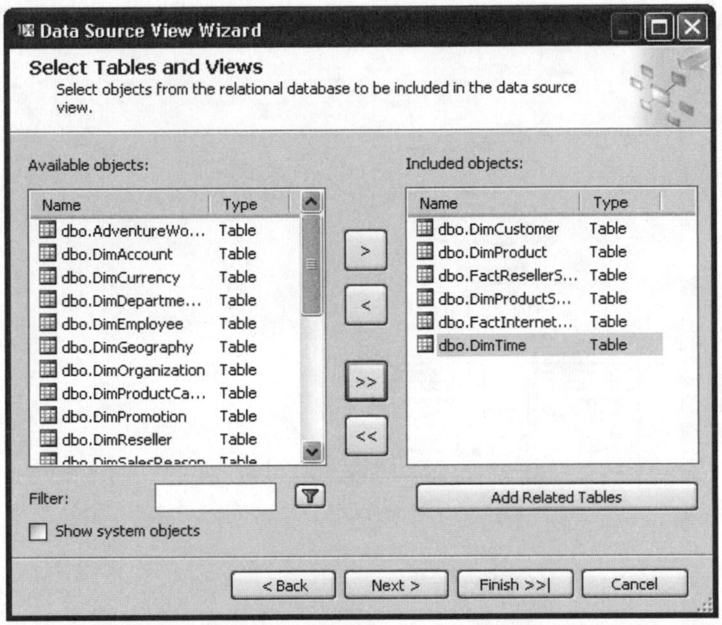

Figure 26-3 *The Select Tables and Views page*

▶ FactResellerSales

▶ DimProductSubCategory

▶ FactInternetSales

▶ DimTime

After the tables are selected, the wizard is completed and Data Source View Designer shows the selected tables (see Figure 26-4). (Data Source View Designer is a tool that is used to show a graphical representation of the data schema you have defined.)

Data Source View Designer offers several useful functions. To inspect the objects you have in your source view, move the mouse to the cross-arrow icon at the bottom-right corner. When the pointer changes to a cross-arrow icon, click the icon. The **Navigation** window appears. Now you can navigate from one part of the diagram to another one. (If you want to find a specific table, use the **Data Source View** function in the menu bar and select **Find Table**.) To view the data in a table, right-click the table and then click **Explore Data**.

You can also create named queries, which are queries that are persistently stored and therefore can be accessed like any table. To create such a query, click the **Data Source View** function in the menu bar and then select **New Named Query**. The **Create Named Query** dialog box allows you to create any query in relation to selected tables.

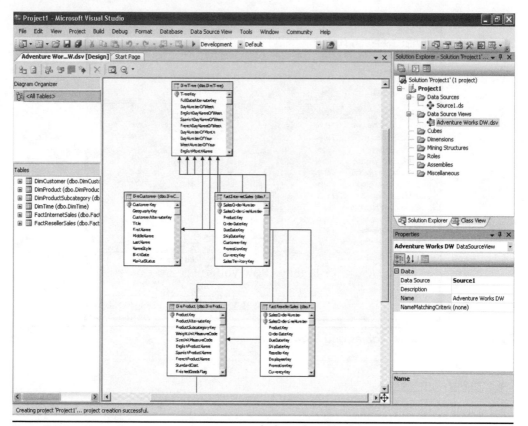

Figure 26-4 *Data Source View Designer with the selected tables*

Analysis Services and Cubes

A cube is a multidimensional structure that contains all or a part of the data from a data warehouse. Each cube contains the following components:

- ▶ Dimensions
- ▶ Members
- ▶ Hierarchies
- ▶ Cells
- ▶ Levels
- ▶ Properties

A dimension is a set of logically related attributes (stored together in a dimensional table) that closely describe measures (stored in the fact table). Although the term "cube" implies three dimensions, a multidimensional cube generally can have many more dimensions. For instance, **Time**, **Product**, and **Customer** are the typical dimensions that are part of many models.

NOTE

*One important dimension of a cube is the **Measures** dimension, which includes all measures defined in the fact table.*

The member specifies each discrete value in a dimension. For instance, the members of a Product dimension could be Computers, Disks, and CPUs. The member can be calculated, meaning that its value is calculated at run time using an expression that is specified during the definition of the member. (Because calculated members are not stored on the disk, they allow you to add new members without increasing the size of a corresponding cube.)

Hierarchies specify groupings of multiple members within each dimension. They are used to refine queries concerning data analysis. Cells are parts of a multidimensional cube that are identified by coordinates (x-, y-, and z-coordinate, if the cube is three-dimensional). This means that a cell is a set containing members from each dimension. For instance, consider a three-dimensional cube in Chapter 25 (see Figure 25-3) that represents car sales for a single region within a quarter. The cells within this cube could be identified with the following coordinates:

► First quarter, South America, Falcon

► Third quarter, Asia, Eagle

When you define hierarchies, you define them in terms of their levels. In other words, levels describe the hierarchy from the highest (most summarized) level to the lowest (most detailed) level of data. The following list displays the possible hierarchy levels for the time dimension:

► Quarter (Q1, Q2, Q3, Q4)

► Month (January, February, ...)

► Day (Day1, Day2, ...)

Creating a Cube

Before creating a cube, you must specify one or more data sources and create a data source view. These two steps are shown in the previous sections. After that, you can use the Cube wizard to create a cube.

To create a cube, right-click the **Cubes** folder of the particular project in the **Solution Explorer** pane and select **New Cube**. The Cube wizard appears. Then, on the **Select Build Method** page, choose **Build the cube using a data source**, check the **Auto build** box, and select **Create attributes and hierarchies**. After you select the data source view, Analysis Services detects the fact and dimension tables (on the **Detecting Fact and Dimension Tables** page) and recommends a schema to you.

The next page, **Identify Fact and Dimension Tables**, allows you to accept the recommended schema or to modify it. (The recommended schema for our example is shown in Figure 26-5.) As you can see from Figure 26-5, the star schema contains two fact tables:

▶ FactInternetSales

▶ FactResellerSales

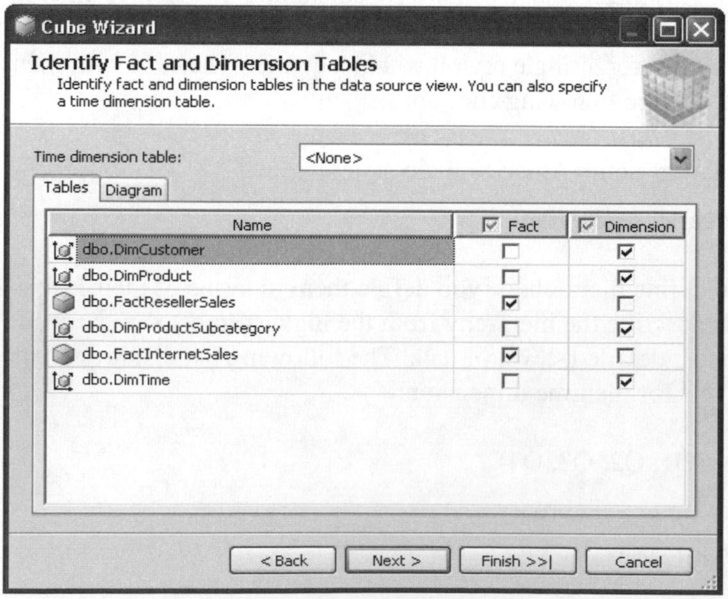

Figure 26-5 *The Identify Fact and Dimension Tables page*

It contains four dimensions:

▶ DimTime

▶ DimProduct

▶ DimProductSubCategory

▶ DimCustomer

On the same page, you can also select the dimension concerning time and choose attributes, which will form the time hierarchy. In our example, the **DimTime** table of the **AdventureWorksDW** database contains data concerning time. For this reason, in the **Time dimension table** drop-down list, we select **DimTime**. The **Select Time Periods** page allows you to choose attributes that form the hierarchy of elements for time dimension. For our example, we select the following hierarchy: **Year ->** **Quarter -> Month -> Date**, and the corresponding columns from the **DimTime** table are **Fiscal Year, Fiscal Quarter, EnglishMonthName**, and **DayNumberOfMonth**, respectively.

In the next step you can use the **Select Measure** page to select measures. The system recommends several measures, which can be accepted or rejected. For our cube the system recommends all measures that are related to both fact tables, **FactInternetSales** and **FactResellerSales**. In our example we choose only the same pair of measures for each fact table: **TotalProductCost** and **SalesAmount**.

In the last step, the Cube wizard automatically detects the hierarchies in the existing dimensions. After this step you can review the created star schema on the **Review New Dimensions** page and finish creating the new cube.

Designing Storage Aggregation and Processing the Cube

As you already know, basic data from the fact table can be summarized in advance and stored in persistent tables. This process is called "aggregation," and it can significantly enhance the response time, because scanning millions of rows to calculate the aggregation on the fly can take a very long time.

There is a tradeoff between storage requirements and the percentage of possible aggregations that are calculated and stored. Calculating all possible aggregations in a cube and their storage on the disk results in the fastest possible response time for all queries, because the response to each query is almost immediate. The disadvantage of this approach is that the storage and processing time required for the aggregations can be substantial.

On the other hand, if no aggregations are calculated and stored, you do not need any additional disk storage, but response time for queries concerning aggregate functions will be slow, because each aggregate has to be calculated on the fly.

MS Analysis Services support the Aggregation Design wizard, which allows you to design aggregations optimally. To start the wizard, click the **Partitions** tab in the Cube Designer. (Figure 26-6 shows the partition view for the **FactInternetSales** fact table.) In the table that appears in the Cube Designer, click the value under the **Aggregations** column. After that click … in the same field. That way you start the Aggregation Design wizard.

In the first step you specify the storage form for your aggregations. To do this, choose the **Standard settings** radio button on the **Specify Storage and Caching Options** page and position the slider bar (see Figure 26-7). The slider bar allows you to select between different storage structures, which are described at the beginning of this chapter. (If you want to store your aggregate in the same storage as your basic data, use MOLAP.)

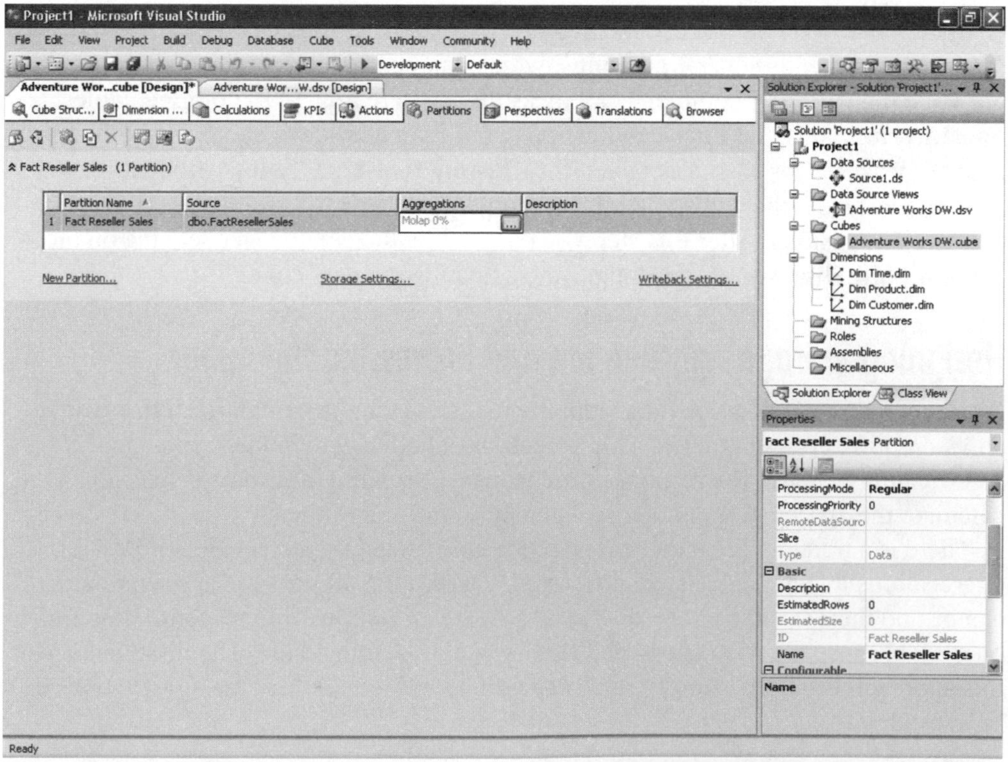

Figure 26-6 *The partition view for the FactInternetSales fact table*

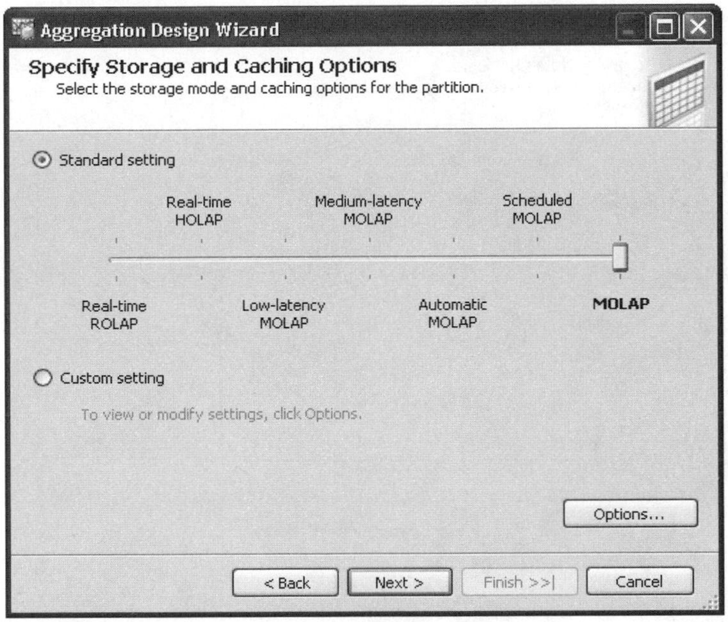

Figure 26-7 *The Specify Storage and Caching Options page*

The next step after selecting the storage structure is to specify the number of members in each attribute. This is done on the **Specify Objects Counts** page. You can either enter object counts in the grid or click the **Count** button to start the wizard, which counts and displays the obtained count number.

In the second to the last step, select aggregation options. You can determine either the maximum amount of disk storage that should be used for precalculated aggregations or the performance gains you want to achieve. (The higher the percentage of precalculated aggregations, the better the performance.) Figure 26-8 shows the **Set Aggregation Options** page that displays after you click **Start**.

On the **Completing the wizard** page, you can choose whether to process aggregate immediately (**Deploy and process now**) or later (**Save the aggregations but do not process them**). The **Process Progress** window shows the deployment progress of processing the cube.

NOTE

A cube must be processed when you first create it and each time you modify it. If a cube has a lot of data and precalculated aggregations, processing the cube can be very time consuming.

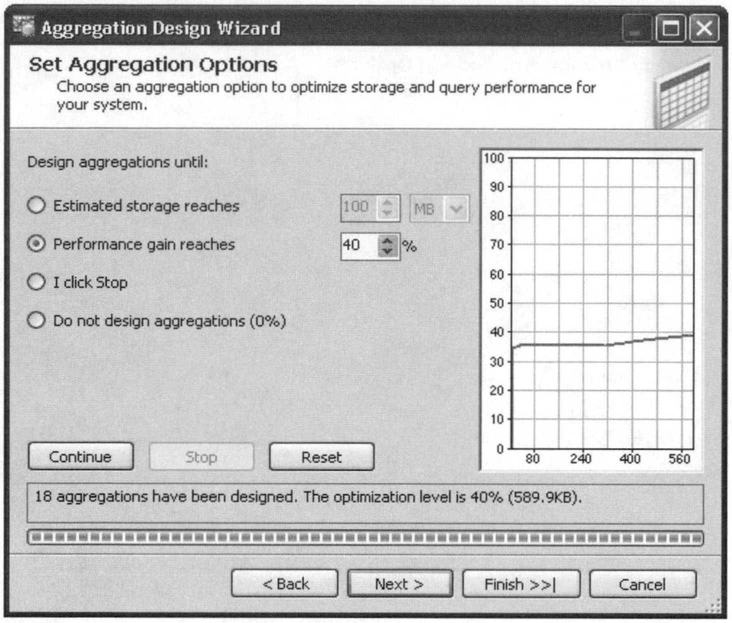

Figure 26-8 *The Set Aggregation Options page*

Browsing a Cube

To browse a cube, right-click the cube name and select **Browse**. The **Browse** view
appears. You can add any of the dimensions to the view, if you right-click the dimension
name in the left pane and select **Add to Column Area**, i.e., **Add to Row Area**. You
can also add a measure from the same pane if you right-click the measure and select
Add to Data Area. Figure 26-9 shows the sales amounts for Internet sales for different
customers and different products. To show these amounts, right-click the **DimProduct**
table and select **Add to Column Area**. Also right-click the **DimCustomer** table and
select **Add to Row Area**. The measure **SalesAmount** from the **FactInternetSales** fact
table will be dropped analogously.

NOTE

*You can use ALT-SHIFT-ENTER to enlarge the **Browse** view of the Cube Designer. The same
keystroke combination reverts back to normal view.*

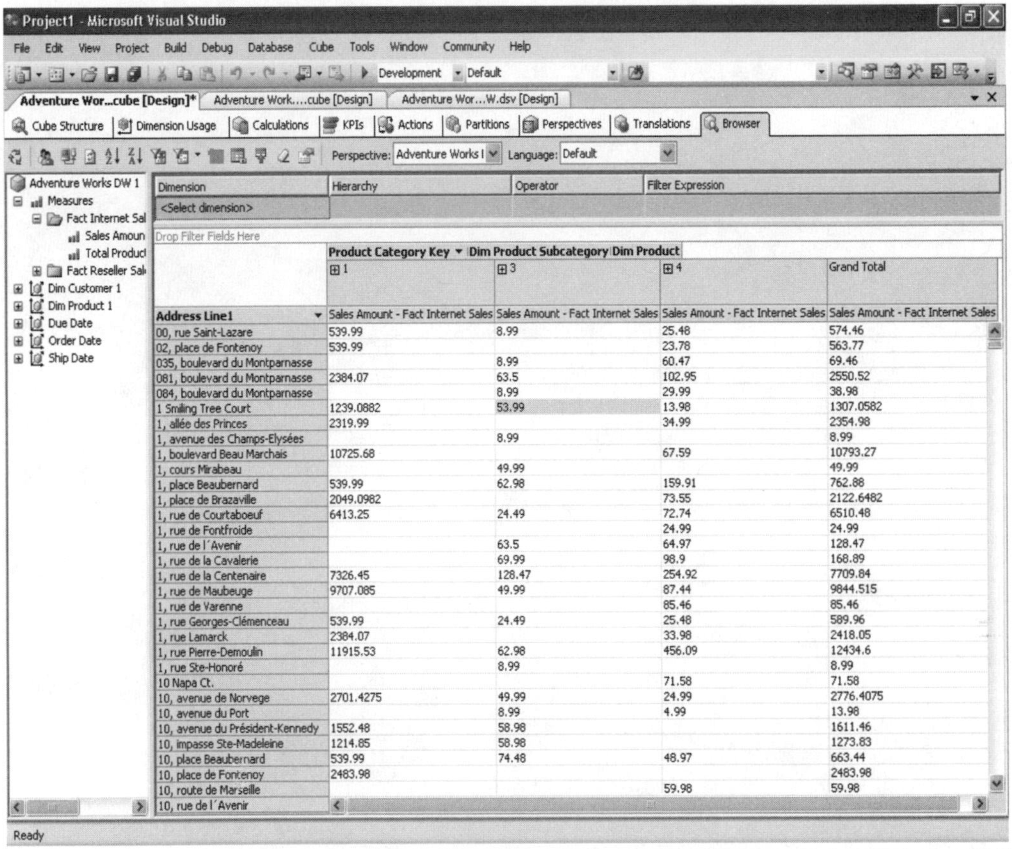

Figure 26-9 Crosstab with sales amounts for Internet sales

Conclusion

With its Analysis Services, Microsoft offers a set of data warehousing services that can be used for entry-level and intermediate-level data analysis. In particular, its ease of use through Business Intelligence Development Studio, which is based upon Visual Studio 2005, will give users an easy way to design and develop data warehouses and/or data marts.

The next chapter describes OLAP extensions in the Transact-SQL language.

Business Intelligence and SQL

IN THIS CHAPTER

OLAP Extensions in Transact-SQL

In Part II of this book we showed a power of Transact-SQL language for managing traditional business data. The language in the earlier versions of SQL Server was not particularly good in complex data analysis. From the beginning, Transact-SQL provided several aggregate functions that could be used to compute simple summary data, such as sum and average. Also, all previous versions support the GROUP BY clause, which offers elementary grouping of data.

The first version of SQL Server, which provided complex data analysis facilities, such as the CUBE operator and the TOP **n** clause, was SQL Server 2000. SQL Server 2005 extends significantly these facilities, introducing ranking functions and several relational operators.

OLAP Extensions in Transact-SQL

SQL:1999 was the first SQL standard that provided solutions for data analysis. This part of the standard is called SQL/OLAP. SQL/OLAP contains among other features the window function, which will be discussed in detail in this section.

SQL Server offers many extensions to the SELECT statement that can be used primarily for decision support operations. Some of these extensions are defined according to the SQL/OLAP standard and some not. SQL extensions that are implemented in SQL Server 2005 for business intelligence can be divided into four groups:

- ▶ CUBE and ROLLUP operators
- ▶ Ranking functions
- ▶ TOP **n** clause
- ▶ PIVOT and UNPIVOT relational operators

The first two operators—CUBE and ROLLUP—are used to add summary rows to the result of a SELECT statement with the GROUP BY clause. Ranking functions generally return a number that specifies the rank of the current row among all rows and that belongs to the specified group. The TOP **n** clause provides the retrieval of the first **n** rows of a query result (usually sorted using some criteria). Finally, the relational operators PIVOT and UNPIVOT can be used to manipulate table-valued expression.

The following sections describe in detail all these Transact-SQL extensions.

CUBE Operator

The GROUP BY clause defines one or more columns as a group such that all rows within any group have the same values for these columns. The CUBE operator introduces additional rows called *summary rows* into the result of a SELECT statement. A GROUP BY summary row is returned for every possible combination of group and subgroup in the result. The following examples show how these operators can be applied.

Example 27.1 creates a table that is used in this chapter to demonstrate Transact-SQL extensions concerning business intelligence.

EXAMPLE 27.1

```
USE sample
create table project_dept
    ( dept_name char( 20 ) not null
    emp_cnt int not null,
    budget float,
    date_month datetime );
insert into project_dept values( 'Research', 5, 50000, '01.01.2002' );
insert into project_dept values( 'Research', 10, 70000, '01.02.2002' );
insert into project_dept values( 'Research', 5, 65000, '01.07.2002' );
insert into project_dept values( 'Accounting', 5, 10000, '01.07.2002' );
insert into project_dept values( 'Accounting', 10, 40000, '01.02.2002' );
insert into project_dept values( 'Accounting', 6, 30000, '01.01.2002' );
insert into project_dept values( 'Accounting', 6, 40000, '01.02.2003' );
insert into project_dept values( 'Marketing', 6, 10000, '01.01.2003' );
insert into project_dept values( 'Marketing', 10, 40000, '01.02.2003' );
insert into project_dept values( 'Marketing', 3, 30000, '01.07.2003' );
insert into project_dept values( 'Marketing', 5, 40000, '01.01.2003' );
```

Example 27.1 creates a new table **project_dept** that contains the number of employees and budget of each project that is controlled by a department. The content of this table is given in Table 27-1.

The following examples will be used to show the difference between the grouping using the GROUP BY clause alone and in combination with the keywords CUBE and ROLLUP. The main difference is that the GROUP BY clause defines one or more columns as a group such that all rows within any group have the same values for those columns. CUBE and ROLLUP provide additional summary rows for grouped data. These summary rows are also called multidimensional summaries.

Example 27.2 uses the GROUP BY clause to group the rows of the **project_dept** table using two criteria: **dept_name** and **emp_cnt**.

dept_name	emp_cnt	budget	date_month
Research	5	50000.0	01.01.2002
Research	10	70000.0	01.02.2002
Research	5	65000.0	01.07.2002
Accounting	5	10000.0	01.07.2002
Accounting	10	40000.0	01.02.2002
Accounting	6	30000.0	01.01.2002
Accounting	6	40000.0	01.02.2003
Marketing	6	100000.0	01.01.2003
Marketing	10	180000.0	01.02.2003
Marketing	3	100000.0	01.07.2003
Marketing	5	120000.0	01.01.2003

Table 27-1   *The Content of the Project_dept table*

EXAMPLE 27.2

```
USE sample
SELECT dept_name, emp_cnt, SUM(budget) sum_of_budgets
    FROM project_dept
    GROUP BY dept_name, emp_cnt
```

The result is

dept_name	emp_cnt	sum_of_budgets
Marketing	3	30000.0
Accounting	5	10000.0
Marketing	5	40000.0
Research	5	115000.0
Accounting	6	70000.0
Marketing	6	10000.0
Accounting	10	40000.0
Marketing	10	40000.0
Research	10	70000.0

The use of the CUBE operator is shown in Example 27.3.

EXAMPLE 27.3

```
USE sample
SELECT dept_name, emp_cnt, SUM(budget) sum_of_budgets
    FROM project_dept
    GROUP BY dept_name, emp_cnt
    WITH CUBE
```

The result is

dept_name	emp_cnt	sum_of_budgets
Accounting	5	10000.0
Accounting	6	70000.0
Accounting	5	10000.0
Accounting	6	70000.0
Accounting	10	40000.0
Accounting	NULL	12000.0
Marketing	3	30000.0
Marketing	5	40000.0
Marketing	6	10000.0
Marketing	10	40000.0
Marketing	NULL	120000.0
Research	5	115000.0
Research	10	70000.0
Research	NULL	185000.0
NULL	NULL	425000.0
NULL	3	30000.0
NULL	5	165000.0
NULL	6	80000.0
NULL	10	150000.0

Besides all rows from the result of Example 27.2, the result of Example 27.3 contains all possible summary rows. A summary row is displayed as NULL in the result, but it is used to indicate all values. For example, the row

    NULL   NULL   425000.0

shows the sum of all budgets of all existing projects in the table, while the row

| NULL | 3 | 30000.0 |

shows the sum of all budgets for all projects that employ exactly three employees.

NOTE

Because the CUBE operator displays every possible combination of groups and summary rows, the number of rows is the same, regardless of the grouping order of columns.

ROLLUP Operator

In contrast to the CUBE operator that returns every possible combination of groups and summary rows, the group hierarchy using the ROLLUP operator is determined by the order in which the grouping columns are specified. Example 27.4 shows the use of the ROLLUP operator.

EXAMPLE 27.4

```
USE sample
SELECT dept_name, emp_cnt, SUM(budget) sum_of_budgets
    FROM project_dept
    GROUP BY dept_name, emp_cnt
    WITH ROLLUP
```

The result is

dept_name	emp_cnt	sum_of_budgets
Accounting	5	10000.0
Accounting	6	70000.0
Accounting	10	40000.0
Accounting	NULL	120000.0
Marketing	3	30000.0
Marketing	5	40000.0
Marketing	6	10000.0
Marketing	10	40000.0
Marketing	NULL	120000.0
Research	5	115000.0

Research	10	70000.0
Research	NULL	185000.0
NULL	NULL	425000.0

As you can see from the result of Example 27.4, the number of retrieved rows in this example is smaller than the number of displayed rows in the previous one. The reason is that the group hierarchy is determined by the order of columns in the GROUP BY clause. For Example 27.4, this means that the summary rows are displayed only for the first column in the GROUP BY clause: **dept_name**.

Example 27.5 shows that changing the order of the grouping columns affects the number of rows produced in the result set.

EXAMPLE 27.5

```
USE sample
SELECT dept_name, emp_cnt, SUM(budget) sum_of_budgets
      FROM project_dept
      GROUP BY emp_cnt, dept_name
      WITH ROLLUP
```

The result is

dept_name	emp_cnt	sum_of_budgets
Marketing	3	30000.0
NULL	3	30000.0
Accounting	5	10000.0
Marketing	5	40000.0
Research	5	115000.0
NULL	5	165000.0
Accounting	6	70000.0
Marketing	6	10000.0
NULL	6	80000.0
Accounting	10	40000.0
Marketing	10	40000.0
Research	10	70000.0
NULL	10	150000.0
NULL	NULL	425000.0

Example 27.5 differs from the previous example in the order of the grouping columns. Because of this, the number of the displayed rows and the content of some of them are different from Example 27.4.

NOTE

As you already know, a summary row is displayed as NULL in the result set. For this reason, the system cannot distinguish the null values that are returned by CUBE and ROLLUP from the "normal" null values. You can use the GROUPING aggregate function to make this distinction.

Ranking Functions

SQL Server 2005 defines several functions that are categorized as ranking functions, i.e., functions that return a ranking value for each row in a partition group. The system supports the following ranking functions:

- ▶ RANK
- ▶ DENSE_RANK
- ▶ ROW_COUNT
- ▶ NTILE

The following example shows the use of the RANK function.

EXAMPLE 27.6

```
USE sample
SELECT RANK() OVER(ORDER BY budget DESC) AS rank_budget,
           dept_name, emp_cnt, budget
    FROM project_dept
    WHERE budget <= 50000;
```

The result is

rank_budget	dept_name	emp_cnt	budget
1	Research	5	50000
2	Accounting	10	40000

2	Accounting	6	40000
2	Marketing	10	40000
2	Marketing	5	40000
6	Marketing	3	30000
6	Accounting	6	30000
8	Accounting	5	10000
8	Marketing	6	10000

Example 27.6 uses the RANK function to return a number (in the first column of the result) that specifies the rank of the row among all rows. The example uses the OVER clause:

OVER (ORDER BY budget DESC)

to sort the result set by the **budget** column in the descending order.

NOTE

The RANK function uses logical aggregation. In other words, if two or more rows in a result set are tied (have a same value in the ordering column), they will have the same rank. The row with the subsequent ordering will have a rank that is one plus the number of ranks that precede the row. For this reason, the RANK function displays "gaps," if two or more rows have the same ranking.

Example 27.7 shows the use of the two other ranking functions: DENSE_RANK and ROW_NUMBER.

EXAMPLE 27.7

```
USE sample
SELECT DENSE_RANK() OVER( ORDER BY budget DESC ) AS rank_budget,
    ROW_NUMBER() OVER( ORDER BY budget DESC ) AS row_number,
    dept_name, emp_cnt, budget
  FROM project_dept
  WHERE budget <= 50000;
```

The result is

rank_budget	row_number	dept_name	emp_cnt	budget
1	1	Research	5	50000
2	2	Accounting	10	40000
2	3	Accounting	6	40000
2	4	Marketing	10	40000
2	5	Marketing	5	40000
3	6	Marketing	3	30000
3	7	Accounting	6	30000
4	8	Accounting	5	10000
4	9	Marketing	6	10000

The first two columns in the result set of Example 27.7 show the values for the DENSE_RANK and ROW_NUMBER functions, respectively. The output of the DENSE_RANK function is similar to the output of the RANK function (see Example 27.6). The only difference is that the DENSE_RANK function returns no "gaps," if two or more ranking values are equal and thus belong to the same ranking.

The use of the ROW_NUMBER function is obvious: It returns the sequential number of a row within a result set, starting at 1 for the first row.

The OVER clause is used in Examples 27.6 and 27.7 to determine the ordering of the result set. This clause is not used only for ordering. Generally, the OVER clause is used to divide the result set produced by the FROM clause into groups (partitions), and then to apply the function to each partition separately.

NOTE

Functions that divide the result set into partitions are called window functions. Window functions can appear only in the SELECT list and in the ORDER BY clause. SQL Server supports two forms of window functions: ranking and aggregate functions.

Example 27.8 shows how the RANK function can be applied to partitions.

EXAMPLE 27.8

```
USE sample
SELECT dept_name, emp_cnt, CAST( budget AS INT ) AS budget, date_month,
    RANK() OVER( PARTITION BY date_month ORDER BY emp_cnt desc ) AS rank
  FROM project_dept;
```

The result is

dept_name	emp_cnt	budget	date_month	rank
Accounting	6	30000	2002-01-01 00:00:00.000	1
Research	5	50000	2002-01-01 00:00:00.000	2
Research	10	70000	2002-02-01 00:00:00.000	1
Accounting	10	40000	2002-02-01 00:00:00.000	1
Research	5	65000	2002-07-01 00:00:00.000	1
Accounting	5	10000	2002-07-01 00:00:00.000	1
Marketing	6	10000	2003-01-01 00:00:00.000	1
Marketing	5	40000	2003-01-01 00:00:00.000	2
Marketing	10	40000	2003-02-01 00:00:00.000	1
Accounting	6	40000	2003-02-01 00:00:00.000	2
Marketing	3	30000	2003-07-01 00:00:00.000	1

In Example 27.8 the result set is divided (partitioned) into eight groups according to the values in the **date_month** column. After that the RANK function is applied to each partition.

NOTE

The main difference between the use of the GROUP BY clause and grouping using the OVER clause is that the OVER clause displays each of the rows from a group (partition) separately, while the GROUP BY clause displays only one row for each group.

As we already stated, window function can be either a ranking function or an aggregate function. Example 27.9 shows the use of aggregate window functions.

EXAMPLE 27.9

```
USE sample
SELECT dept_name,  budget,
 SUM( emp_cnt ) OVER( PARTITION BY dept_name ) AS emp_cnt_sum,
 AVG( budget ) OVER( PARTITION BY dept_name )  AS budget_avg,
 COUNT( dept_name ) OVER( PARTITION BY dept_name ) AS dept_cnt
 FROM project_dept;
```

The result is

dept_name	budget	emp_cnt_sum	budget_avg	dept_cnt
Accounting	10000	27	30000	4
Accounting	40000	27	30000	4
Accounting	30000	27	30000	4
Accounting	40000	27	30000	4
Marketing	10000	24	30000	4
Marketing	40000	24	30000	4
Marketing	30000	24	30000	4
Marketing	40000	24	30000	4
Research	50000	20	61666.6666666667	3
Research	70000	20	61666.6666666667	3
Research	65000	20	61666.6666666667	3

The result set in Example 27.9 is partitioned into three groups using the department names. After that, the aggregate function SUM() is used to calculate the number of employees in each partition. Similarly, the aggregate functions AVG() and COUNT() are used to calculate the average value of budgets and to count the number of employees for every partition, respectively.

Example 27.10 calculates the percentage of the budget for each department in relation to the total budget of the corresponding partition.

EXAMPLE 27.10

```
USE sample
SELECT dept_name, budget, SUM( budget ) OVER( PARTITION BY dept_name ) as
 budget_sum,
 budget/SUM( budget ) OVER( PARTITION BY dept_name ) * 100 AS percentage
 FROM project_dept;
```

The result is

dept_name	budget	budget_sum	percentage
Accounting	10000	120000	8.33333333333333
Accounting	40000	120000	33.3333333333333
Accounting	30000	120000	25
Accounting	40000	120000	33.3333333333333

Marketing	10000	120000	8.33333333333333
Marketing	40000	120000	33.3333333333333
Marketing	30000	120000	25
Marketing	40000	120000	33.3333333333333
Research	50000	185000	27.027027027027
Research	70000	185000	37.8378378378378
Research	65000	185000	35.1351351351351

The query in Example 27.10 calculates the sum of all budgets for each partition. (The partitions are grouped according to the department names.) The total budget of each partition is then used to determine the percentage of the budget of each department in relation to the total budget of all departments in that partition.

You can use several columns from a table to build different partitioning schemas in a query. Example 27.11 shows this.

EXAMPLE 27.11

```
USE sample
SELECT dept_name, CAST( budget AS INT ) AS budget,
 SUM( emp_cnt ) OVER( PARTITION BY budget ) AS emp_cnt_sum,
 AVG( budget ) OVER( PARTITION BY dept_name )  AS budget_avg
 FROM project_dept;
```

The result is

dept_name	budget	emp_cnt_sum	budget_avg
Accounting	10000	11	30000
Accounting	30000	9	30000
Accounting	40000	31	30000
Accounting	40000	31	30000
Marketing	40000	31	30000
Marketing	30000	9	30000
Marketing	40000	31	30000
Marketing	10000	11	30000
Research	50000	5	61666.6666666667
Research	65000	5	61666.6666666667
Research	70000	10	61666.6666666667

The query in Example 27.11 has two different partitioning schemas: one over the values of the **dept_name** column and one over the values of the **budget** column. The former is used to calculate the number of employees in relation to the departments with the same budget. The latter is used to calculate the average value of budgets of departments grouped by their names.

TOP n Clause

The TOP **n** clause specifies the first **n** rows of the query result that are to be retrieved. Example 27.12 shows the use of this clause.

EXAMPLE 27.12

Retrieve eight projects with the highest budgets.

```
USE sample
SELECT TOP 8  dept_name, budget
   FROM project_dept
   ORDER BY budget DESC
```

The result is

dept_name	budget
Research	70000.0
Research	65000.0
Research	50000.0
Accounting	40000.0
Marketing	40000.0
Accounting	40000.0
Marketing	40000.0
Accounting	30000.0

As you can see from Example 27.12, the TOP **n** clause is part of the SELECT list and is written in front of all column names in the list.

The TOP **n** clause can also be used with the additional PERCENT option. In that case, the first **n** percent of the rows are retrieved from the result set. The additional option—WITH TIES—specifies that additional rows will be retrieved from the query result if they have the same value in the ORDER BY column(s) as the last row that belongs to the displayed set. (This option can be used only with the ORDER BY clause.) Example 27.13 shows the use of the WITH TIES option.

EXAMPLE 27.13

Retrieve six projects with the smallest number of employees.

```
USE sample
SELECT TOP 6 WITH TIES  dept_name, emp_cnt, budget
   FROM project_dept
ORDER BY emp_cnt
```

The result is

dept_name	emp_cnt	budget
Marketing	3	30000.0
Marketing	5	40000.0
Research	5	50000.0
Research	5	65000.0
Accounting	5	10000.0
Accounting	6	30000.0
Accounting	6	40000.0
Marketing	6	10000.0

The result of Example 27.13 contains eight rows, because there are three projects with six employees.

SQL Server 2005 allows you to use the TOP **n** clause with UPDATE, DELETE, and INSERT statements.

The following example shows the use of this clause with the UPDATE statement.

EXAMPLE 27.14

```
USE sample
update top (3) project_dept
SET budget = budget * 0.9
 where budget in (select TOP 3 budget
    from project_dept
    order by budget desc) ;
```

In Example 27.14 the UPDATE statement reduces the budget for the three projects with the highest budget.

The following example shows the use of the TOP **n** clause with the DELETE statement.

EXAMPLE 27.15

```
USE sample
DELETE TOP (4)
 FROM project_dept
 WHERE budget IN
  (select TOP 4 budget from project_dept
     order by budget asc)
```

In Example 27.15 the DELETE statement is used to delete four projects with the smallest budget amounts.

PIVOT and UNPIVOT Operators

PIVOT and UNPIVOT are new relational operators that are supported by SQL Server 2005. You can use them to manipulate a table-valued expression into another table. PIVOT transforms such an expression by turning the unique values from one column in the expression into multiple columns in the output, and it performs aggregations on any remaining column values that are desired in the final output.

Example 27.16 shows how PIVOT works.

EXAMPLE 27.16

```
USE sample
select *, month(date_month) as month, year(date_month) as year
 into project_dept_pivot
from project_dept
go
SELECT year, [1] as January, [2] as February, [7] July FROM
( select budget, year, month from project_dept_pivot) p2
PIVOT
(SUM(budget)
FOR month
IN ([1],[2],[7]))
AS P
```

The result is

Year	January	February	July
2002	265000	NULL	NULL
2003	160000	NULL	NULL

The first part of Example 27.16 creates a new table, **project_dept_pivot**, which will be used to demonstrate how the PIVOT operator works. This table is identical to the table **project_dept** (see Example 27.1), except for two new columns: **month** and **year**. The **year** column of the **project_dept_pivot** table contains the years 2002 and 2003, which appear in the **date_month** column of the **project_dept** table. Also, the **month** columns of the **project_dept_pivot** table (January, February, and July) contain the summaries of budgets corresponding to these months in the **project_dept** table.

The second SELECT statement contains an inner query, which is embedded in the FROM clause of the outer query. The PIVOT clause is part of the inner query. It starts with the specification of the aggregation function (in Example 27.16, sum of budgets). The second part specifies the pivot column (**month**) and the values from that column to be used as column headings (in Example 27.16, the first, second, and seventh months of the year). The value for a particular column in a row is calculated using the specified aggregate function over the rows that match the column heading.

NOTE

As you can see from Example 27.15, using all possible values of the pivot column is not required.

The UNPIVOT operator performs the reverse operation of PIVOT, by rotating columns into rows. (Note that UNPIVOT is not the exact reverse of PIVOT, because any null values in the table being transformed cannot be used as column values in the output.)

Conclusion

This chapter introduces SQL/OLAP extensions in Transact-SQL. These extensions support data analysis facilities. SQL Server 2005 supports four different groups of extensions:

- ▶ CUBE and ROLLUP operators
- ▶ Ranking functions
- ▶ TOP **n** clause
- ▶ PIVOT and UNPIVOT relational operators

CUBE and ROLLUP operators are part of the SQL:1999 standard, but their standardized syntax is slightly different from the syntax of the same operators in Transact-SQL. The syntax of the SQL Server 2005 ranking functions RANK, DENSE_RANK, and ROW_NUMBER corresponds exactly to the syntax of the SQL/OLAP standard.

The TOP **n** clause, as well as PIVOT and UNPIVOT operators, are specific Microsoft business intelligence extensions in Transact-SQL.

The next chapter describes Reporting Services, a reporting component of MS Analysis Services.

Microsoft Reporting Services

his chapter describes the SQL Server enterprise reporting solution called Reporting Services. The first part of the chapter explains the main components of this product. Also discussed is the development environment that is used to design and create reports. There are two ways to create a report: by using the Report wizard and by using Report Project. After a report is created, you can deploy it to a Web server. This will be explained in the next section of the chapter. Finally, we show you different ways to deliver a designed and deployed report.

Introduction

In 2003, Microsoft implemented a new component called SQL Server Reporting Services. At first the company intended to deliver the product as part of SQL Server 2005. Instead they released it almost immediately, because the feedback of users who tested the product's beta version was overwhelming.

Another reason for the early release of this product was that Microsoft developed a set of services called Analysis Services as a part of SQL Server 2000. These services are used to manage data stored in a data warehouse, but they didn't comprise reporting, which is one of the three general techniques for accessing data. For this reason, the only way to deliver business information (over the Internet, for example) was to use a third-party reporting tool.

Reporting Services include three main components, which represent an application layer, a server layer, and a data layer, respectively:

- ► Report Manager
- ► Report Server
- ► Report Server database

The following sections describe these components.

Report Manager

Report Manager is a Web-based report access and management tool that runs using Internet Explorer. You can use this tool to create, secure, and maintain the hierarchy of items of a single report server instance. As a report server administrator, you use Report Manager to configure site properties and defaults and to create shared schedules and shared data sources, which make schedules and data source connections more manageable. You can also use Report Manager to configure role-based security.

Report Server

Report Server is the main component of SQL Server 2005 Reporting Services. It is implemented as a Web service as well as a Windows service. The Web service comprises a set of interfaces that client applications can use to access reports over a Web server. The Windows service provides scheduling and delivery services. Both services work together and constitute a single report server instance.

Report Server includes two components:

► Processors

► Extensions

Processors support the integrity of the reporting system, while extensions perform specific functions. There are several default groups for every type of extension that is supported. (Third-party developers can create additional extensions to replace or extend the processing capability of Report Server.)

Through its subcomponents, Report Server processes report requests and retrieves report properties and data. Report Server also processes report models and enforces security by checking on whether the user has the right to access specific database objects.

Report Server Database

The Report Server database is a database managed by the SQL Server system. This database stores the information used by Report Server. The stored information includes report names, descriptions, data source connection information, credential information, parameters, and execution properties. The database also stores security settings and information concerning scheduling and delivering data.

Reporting Services uses two databases to separate persistent data storage from temporary storage requirements. The databases are created together and bound by name. By default, the database names are **reportserver** and **reportservertempdb**. The temporary database is used to store session data, cached reports, and work tables that are generated by the report.

In the following sections we will describe how you can design, deploy, and deliver reports.

Creating Reports

Use Business Intelligence Development Studio to create a report. BI Development Studio is the integrated development environment built on Visual Studio 2005 and designed for the business intelligence system developer. To start BI Development Studio, click **Start**, select **Programs**, select **Microsoft SQL Server 2005**, and choose **SQL Server Business Intelligence Development Studio**.

The first step in building a report is to create a new project to which the report should belong. To build a project, click **File**, select **New**, and choose **Project**. In the **New Project** dialog box, select the **Business Intelligence Projects** folder in the **Project Types** pane. In the **Templates** pane, select **Report Project**. Type the name of the project and its location in the **Name** and **Location** text boxes, respectively (see Figure 28-1). The new project will be created after you click **OK**. The project in our example is called **Report1**, as you can see from Figure 28-1.

NOTE

*The new project is shown in the Solution Explorer pane as a new folder. If the Solution Explorer pane is not visible, click **View** and then select **Solution Explorer**.*

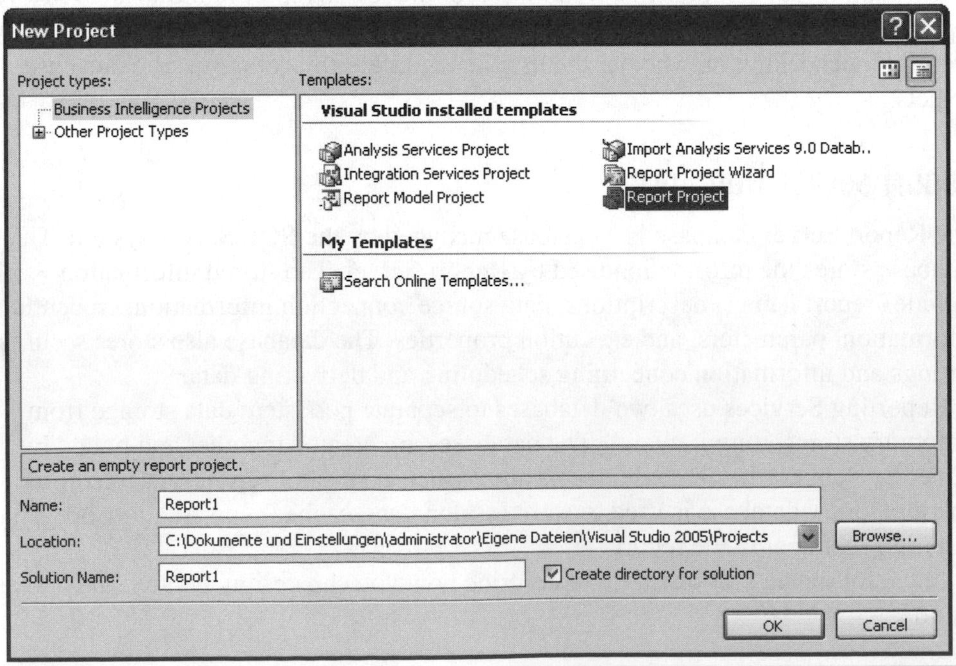

New Project

Project types:
- Business Intelligence Projects
- Other Project Types

Templates:

Visual Studio installed templates

- Analysis Services Project
- Integration Services Project
- Report Model Project
- Import Analysis Services 9.0 Datab..
- Report Project Wizard
- Report Project

My Templates

- Search Online Templates...

Create an empty report project.

Name: Report1

Location: C:\Dokumente und Einstellungen\administrator\Eigene Dateien\Visual Studio 2005\Projects   Browse...

Solution Name: Report1   ☑ Create directory for solution

OK   Cancel

Figure 28-1 *The Report1 dialog box*

A new report can be designed using the following:

▶ Report Designer

▶ Report wizard

NOTE

Report Designer lets you build a report from scratch. For this reason, we will only use the Report wizard to explain how reports can be designed.

Report Wizard

To create a report, expand the project folder, right-click **Reports**, and select **Add New Report**. The welcome page of the Report wizard appears. The wizard allows you to create a report using the following steps:

▶ Select the data source

▶ Specify the query

▶ Select the report type

▶ Specify the report layout

▶ Preview the result set

Select the Data Source

The data source contains information concerning the connection to the source database. At the beginning, type the name of the new data source in the **Select the Data Source** dialog box and click **Edit**. (In our first example we will use the sample database as the data source, which will be called **Source1**.)

NOTE

*Reporting Services can create reports from different relational (SQL Server, Oracle) or multidimensional (Analysis Services) databases. OLE DB and ODBC data sources can be used, too. The **Type** dropdown in the **Select Data Source** dialog box allows you to choose one of different data source types.*

In the **Connection Properties** dialog box, type either **local** or the name of your database server as the server name. In the same step choose either **Use Windows Authentication** or **Use SQL Server Authentication** and, from the **Select or enter**

a database name drop-down list, choose one of the databases as the data source (see Figure 28-2). Before clicking **OK**, click the **Test Connection** button to test the connection to the database. Then click **Next**.

Specify the Query

The next step is to design a query, which should be executed against the selected data source. In the **Design the Query** dialog box you can either type (or paste) an existing query or use the Query Builder component to create a query from scratch.

NOTE

Query Builder corresponds to the similar Access component, which you can use to design queries without knowledge of the SQL language. This component is generally known as QBE (query by example).

Figure 28-2   *The Connection Properties dialog box*

For our first report, we will use the query given in the following example.

EXAMPLE 28.1

```
SELECT dept_name, emp_lname, emp_fname, job, enter_date
    FROM department d JOIN employee e ON d.dept_no = e.dept_no
            JOIN works_on w ON w.emp_no = e.emp_no
    WHERE YEAR(enter_date) = 1998
    ORDER BY dept_name
```

The query in Example 28.1 selects data concerning employees who entered their job in the year 1998. The result set of the query is then sorted by department names.

NOTE

SQL Server checks the names of the tables and columns listed in the query. If the system finds any syntax or semantic errors, it displays the corresponding message in the lower part of the window (see Figure 28-3).

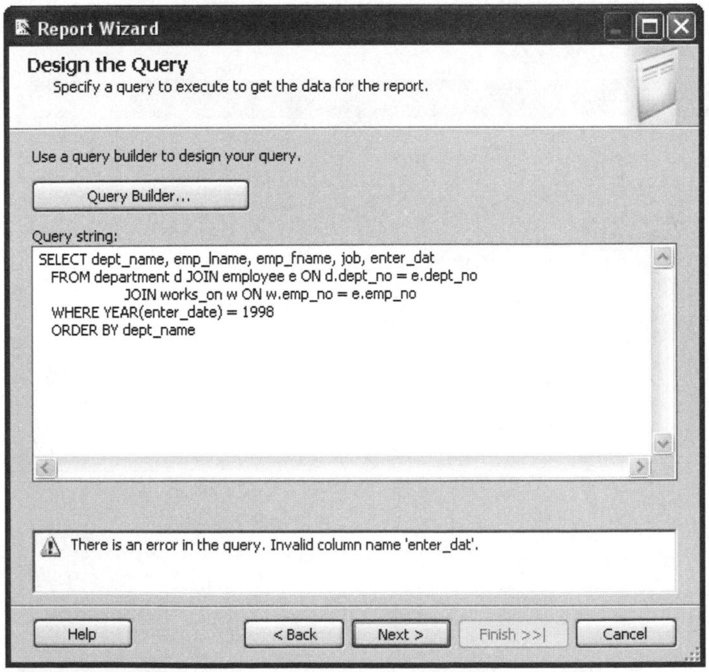

Figure 28-3   *The Design the Query window with the error message*

Select the Report Type

The next step in creating a report is to select the report type. You can choose between a tabular and matrix report type.

The tabular report type creates a report in the tabular form. Columns of the table correspond to the columns from the SELECT list, while the number of rows in the table depends on the result set of the query.

The matrix report type creates a report in the matrix form, which is similar to a table, but provides functionality similar to crosstabs. Unlike a table, which has a static set of columns, matrix columns can be dynamic.

NOTE

You should use the matrix report type whenever you want to create queries for a data warehouse. This means that for matrix report type your query should contain aggregate functions, such as AVG and/or SUM.

The query in Example 28.1 does not contain any aggregate functions. For this reason we chose tabular as the report type. After the report type is selected, the **Design the Table** page appears (see Figure 28-4). This page allows you to decide where all selected columns will be placed in your report.

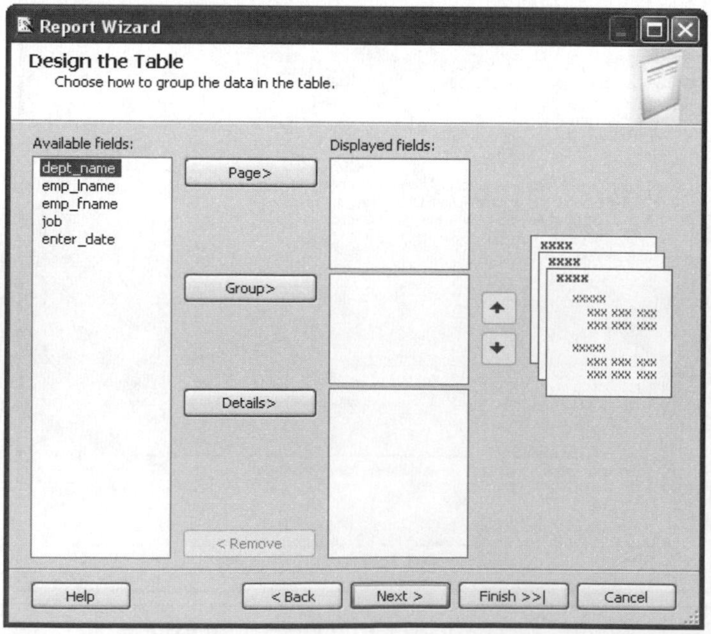

Figure 28-4 *The Design the Table page*

The **Design the Table** page contains two groups of fields:

▶ Available fields

▶ Displayed fields

And it has three "views":

▶ Page

▶ Group

▶ Details

Available fields are the columns from the SELECT list of your query. Each column can be moved to one of the views (**Page**, **Group**, or **Details**). To move a field to **Page**, **Group**, or **Details**, select the field and then click the **Page**, **Group**, or **Details** button, respectively. A displayed field is an available field that is assigned to one of the existing views.

Page lists all columns that appear at the page level, and **Group** lists columns that are used to group the resulting set of the query. The **Details** field is used to display column values that appear in the detail section of the table. Figure 28-5 shows the design of the tabular representation for our resulting set. In our example, the **dept_ name** column will appear at the page level, while the **job** column will be used to group the selected rows. All other columns will be placed in the **Details** field.

NOTE

*The order of the columns can be important, especially for the **Group** view. To change the order of the columns, select a column and click the up or the down button.*

Specify the Report Layout

When you click **Next**, you will specify the layout of your report. You use the **Choose the Table Layout** page to do this. There are several options on this page:

▶ Stepped

▶ Block

▶ Include subtotals

▶ Enable drilldown

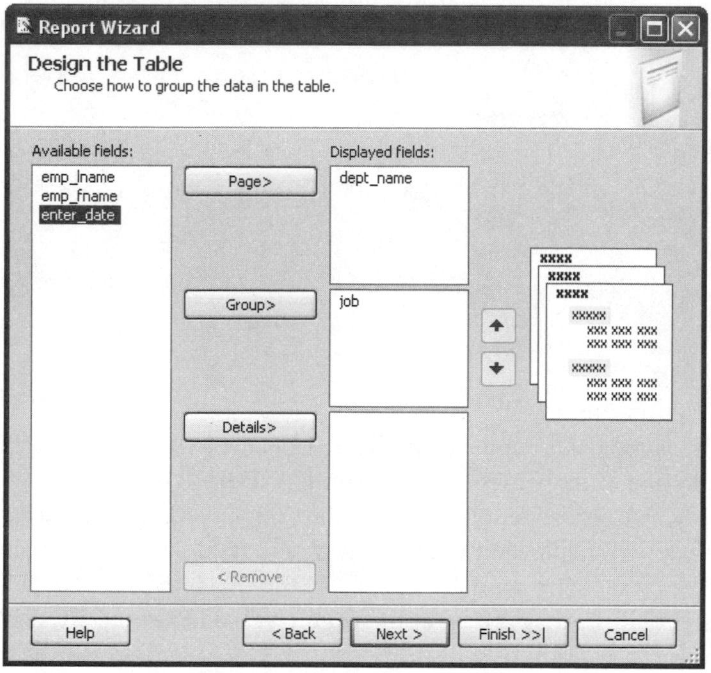

Figure 28-5   *Table representation of the resulting set in Example 28.1*

If you choose **Stepped**, the report will contain one column for each field, with grouping fields appearing in headers to the left of columns from the detail field. In this case, the group footer will not be created. If you include subtotals with this layout type, the subtotal is placed in the group header rows. (We chose this option for our example.)

The **Block** option creates a report that contains one column for each field, with group fields appearing in the first detail row for each group. This layout type has group footers only if the **Include subtotals** option is activated.

The **Enable drilldown** option hides the inner groups of the report and enables a visibility toggle. (You can enable drilldown only if you select the **Stepped** option.)

The last step is to choose a style for your report. You can select a template to apply styles such as font, color, and border style to the report. There are several style templates, such as Bold, Corporate, and Forest.

When using Report Designer instead of the wizard, you will be able to design the whole layout of your report from scratch. It is also possible to use the wizard at the beginning and to change the final layout manually, before deployment of the report.

NOTE

After choosing a report style, there is still one intermediate step if you create a report for the first time. In this step you must choose the URL of the virtual directory of the report server and the deployment folder for your reports.

In the last step you complete the wizard's work by providing a name for the report. Also, you can take a look at the report summary, where all your previous steps during the creation of the report are documented. Click **Finish** to finish the wizard.

Preview the Result Set

When you finish the Report wizard, there are three tabs in the **Report Designer** pane, which you can use to view the created report in different forms. (To open the Report Designer, click **View** and select **Designer**.) The tabs correspond to the following views:

- ▶ Layout
- ▶ Data
- ▶ Preview

The **Layout** tab allows you to view and modify the layout of your report. The **Layout** view consists of the following sections: body, page, header, and page footer. You can use the **Toolbox** and **Properties** windows to manipulate items in the report. To view these windows, select **Toolbox** in the **View** menu. Use the **Toolbox** to select items to place them in one of the sections. Each item on the report design surface contains properties that can be managed using the **Properties** window.

Select the **Data** tab to view the query. You can use this view to display the query in two different forms: using the generic query designer or the graphical query designer. The generic query designer consists of a toolbar and two panes: the **Query** pane and the **Result** pane. The former shows the query you use to create the report, while the latter shows the result set of the query.

The graphical query designer consists of a toolbar and four panes: the **Diagram** pane, the **Grid** pane, the **SQL** pane, and the **Result** pane. The **Diagram** pane shows the ER diagram of all tables that are used in the query, with corresponding referential constraints. The **Grid** pane uses the query-by-example component to display the query in the table form. The **SQL** pane displays the SELECT statement, while the **Result** pane shows the result set of the statement.

To preview the report, click the **Preview** tab. The report runs automatically, using the default parameters that were defined in previous steps.

Parameterized Reports

A parameterized report is one that uses input parameters to complete report processing. The parameters are then used to execute a query that selects specific data for the report. If you design or deploy a parameterized report, you need to understand how parameter selections affect the report.

Parameters in Reporting Services are usually used to filter data. They are specified using the known syntax (**@year**, for instance). If a parameter is specified in a query, a value must be provided to complete the SELECT statement or stored procedure that retrieves data for a report.

You can define a default value for a parameter. If all parameters have default values, the report will immediately display data when the report is executed. If at least one parameter does not have a default value, the report will display data after the user enters all parameter values.

When the report is run in a browser, the parameter is displayed in a box at the top of the report. When the report is run in the **Preview** mode, the value of the parameter will be typed in the corresponding box.

We will use an example to show how you design and deploy a parameterized report. In this example we will describe only those steps that are different from the steps already discussed in Example 28.1.

A query that will be used in the following example selects data from the **AdventureWorksDW** database. For this reason, you have to select and define a new data source. The specification of the new source is identical to the specification of the source called **Source1**, except that you choose the **AdventureWorksDW** database instead of the sample database.

Example 28.2 shows the query.

EXAMPLE 28.2

```
USE AdventureWorksDW
SELECT t.MonthNumberOfYear AS month,
     t.CalendarYear     AS year,
     p.ProductKey       AS product_id,
     SUM(f.UnitPrice)   AS sum_of_sales,
     COUNT(f.UnitPrice) AS total_sales
FROM DimTime t, DimProduct p, FactInternetSales f
WHERE t.TimeKey    = f.OrderDateKey AND
     p.ProductKey = f.ProductKey
     AND CalendarYear = @year
GROUP BY t.CalendarYear, t.MonthNumberOfYear, p.ProductKey
ORDER BY 1
```

The query in Example 28.2 calculates the number and the sum of unit product prices. It also groups the rows according to the list of column names in the GROUP BY clause. The expression

   CalendarYear = @year

in the WHERE clause of the example specifies that the input parameter **@year** in this query is related to the calendar year for which we want to query data.

We choose matrix type for the report. Values of the **CalendarYear** column will be assigned to the **Page** view, values of the **MonthNumberOfYear** columns to the **Columns** view, and the **ProductKey** values to the **Rows** view. The **Detail** view displays the aggregate values sum of sales and total sales (see Figure 28-6).

To start the report in the **Preview** mode, type the value of the **CalendarYear** parameter (2003, for instance) and click **ViewReport**.

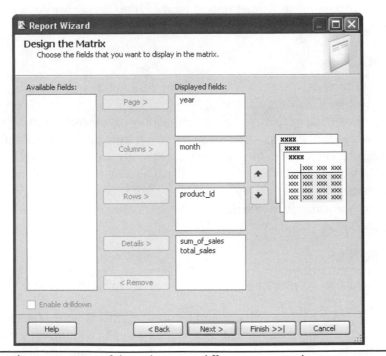

Figure 28-6 *The assignment of the columns to different views in the matrix type*

Processing and Managing Reports

Before we discuss report management, we will explain how reports are processed. Report processing begins with a published report definition, which includes a query, layout information, and code. Report and data processing together create a dataset with layout information, which is stored as an intermediate format. After processing is complete, reports are compiled as a CLR assembly and executed on the report server.

NOTE

For report definition, Microsoft uses the Report Definition Language (RDL). RDL is XML-based language, which is an open schema. This means that developers can extend RDL with additional attributes and elements. When a report is delivered to a user, Reporting Services processes the report definition and transforms the fully processed report into one of the standard formats, such as HTML or PDF.

The intermediate report format is used by the report server for the following report forms:

▶ Cached report

▶ Report snapshot

Caching means that a report will be generated only for the first user who opens it. All other users who work with the same report retrieve it from the cache. As you probably guessed, caching shortens the time to retrieve frequently accessed reports.

A report snapshot is one that contains data captured at a specific point in time. The main difference between a snapshot report and other reports is that reports generally contain query information, while the snapshot record contains the result set of the executed query.

NOTE

A report snapshot is generally used if a report is based on a long-running query.

Generally, you use Report Manager to manage reports. Report Manager is a Web-based report access and management tool that runs in Microsoft Internet Explorer or another browser. The following management functions, among others, can be performed using Report Manager:

▶ View or replace report definition

▶ Manage data source connections

▶ View and configure report history

The description of all management functions provided by Report Manager can be found in Books Online.

Accessing and Delivering Reports

Before you can use or distribute a report, you have to deploy it. This can be done by right-clicking the created report and selecting **Deploy**. The deployment process contains several steps, which are shown in the **Output** pane:

```
------ Build started: Project: R1, Configuration: Debug ------
Build complete -- 0 errors, 0 warnings
------ Deploy started: Project: R1, Configuration: Debug ------
Deploying to http://localhost/ReportServer
Deploying data source '/R1/sample'.
Deploying report '/R1/Report1'.
Deploy complete -- 0 errors, 0 warnings
========== Build: 1 succeeded or up-to-date, 0 failed, 0 skipped ==========
========== Deploy: 1 succeeded, 0 failed, 0 skipped ==========
```

Reports can be accessed and delivered using two methods:

► On-demand

► Subscription-based

The following sections describe these two methods.

On-Demand Reports

On-demand access allows users to select the reports from a report-viewing tool. You can use Report Manager or a browser to view a report. We will explain how you can view on-demand reports using a browser.

SQL Server Reporting Services is a Web application. For this reason, all reports are organized in a hierarchical namespace and accessed through virtual directories in Report Server. Hence, within the browser, navigate to the home page for SQL Server Reporting Services (http://localhost/reportserver), which is the default virtual directory for Report Server (see Figure 28-7). The default virtual directory for Report Manager is **http://localhost/Reports/**. (Both default values can be modified.)

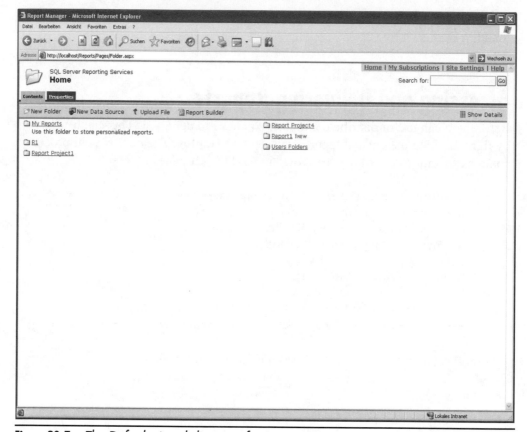

Figure 28-7 *The Default virtual directory for Report Server*

To view a report on demand, select the report from the corresponding folder hierarchy. In this case Report Server creates a temporary snapshot for the purpose of delivering the report. The snapshot is discarded after delivery.

There are several possibilities for running reports on demand. The first one is to specify that a report queries a corresponding data source each time a user runs the report. In this case a new instance of the report is generated each time a new user executes the report.

If you want to enhance performance, cached reports should be your choice. As we already stated, the system creates a cached copy of the report for the first user who opens it. All other users who work with the same report retrieve it from the cache.

Report Subscription

On-demand reporting requires report selection each time you want to view its result. On the other hand, subscription-based access automatically generates and delivers reports to a destination.

Reporting Services supports two kinds of subscriptions:

▶ Personal (standard) subscriptions

▶ Data-driven subscriptions

Personal Subscriptions

A personal subscription usually consists of specific parameters for parameterized reports as well as report presentation options and delivery options.

You can use different tools to make personal subscriptions. We will show how you can use SQL Server Management Studio to create a file share subscription. In Object Explorer, expand the report to which you want to subscribe. (To do this expand **Connect**, select **Reporting Services**, expand the corresponding instance, the folder, where the report is stored, and expand the report.) Right-click the **Subscriptions** folder and click **New Subscription**. Select **Report Server File Share** from the **Notify by** list box. Type a file name for the report in the text box after **File name**. In the **Path** text box, type the path of the folder that contains the report. Select a format and a mode from the **Render format** and **Write mode** list boxes, respectively. Finally, type a user name and password in the corresponding text boxes.

NOTE

*The creation of an e-mail subscription with SQL Server Management Studio is similar, except for the following steps: From the **Notify by** list box, select **Report Server E-Mail**, and in the **To** text box type the e-mail address.*

Data-Driven Subscriptions

A data-driven subscription delivers reports to a list of recipients determined at run time. This type of subscription differs from a personal subscription in the way it gets subscription information: Some settings from a data source are provided at run time, and other settings are provided from the subscription definition. Static aspects of a data-driven subscription include the report that is delivered, the delivery extension, connection information to an external data source that contains subscriber data, and a query. Dynamic settings of the subscription are obtained from the row set produced by the query, including a subscriber list and user-specific delivery extension preferences or parameter values.

Conclusion

Reporting Services are the SQL Server-based enterprise reporting solution. To create a report, use either the Report wizard or Report Designer. The definition of a report, which comprises the corresponding query, layout information, and code, is stored using XML-based Report Definition Language (RDL). Reporting Services process the report definition into one of the standard formats, such as HTML or PDF.

Reports can be accessed on demand or delivered based on a subscription. When you execute a report on demand, a new instance of the report usually will be generated each time you run the report.

Subscription-based reports can be either standard (personal) or data-driven. Reports, which are based on a personal subscription, usually consist of specific parameters as well as report presentation options and delivery options. A data-driven subscription delivers reports to a list of recipients determined at run time.

The next chapter starts the last part of the book. It describes the XML language and the relationship between the language and Transact-SQL.

Exercises

E.28.1

Get the employee numbers and names for all clerks. Create a report in the matrix report type using this query. Use Report Manager to view a report.

E.28.2

Use the sample database and get the budgets of projects and project names being worked on by employees in the Research department that have an employee number < 25000. Create a report in the table report type using this query. Use a browser to view the report.

PART

V

XML Support

CHAPTER
29

Overview of XML

This chapter introduces Extended Markup Language (XML), which has become more and more important as a data storage format. The first part of the chapter describes the World Wide Web, the existing markup languages, and the position of XML as a markup language. The chapter also explains the basic concepts of XML, such as elements, attributes, and namespaces. At the end of the chapter we discuss document type definition (DTD) and schema specification for XML documents.

World Wide Web

The World Wide Web has been gaining enormous importance as a medium, because it is used for many activities. The Web comprises all other Internet services (under the same user interface) and is therefore the most powerful Internet service of all. Generally, the Web has four parts:

- ▶ Web server
- ▶ Web browser
- ▶ HTML (Hypertext Markup Language)
- ▶ HTTP (Hypertext Transfer Protocol)

The web server sends pages (usually HTML pages) to the network. A web browser receives the pages and displays them on screen. (Microsoft Internet Explorer is an example of a web browser.)

You use HTML to create documents for the Web. This language allows you to format data that is shown using a web browser. The simplicity of HTML was one of the reasons that the Web has gained such importance. However, HTML has one main disadvantage: It can tell you only how the data should look. In other words, the language does not allow you to gain any meaning out of the data.

HTML documents are text files that contain tags, and each tag is written in angle brackets. The most important tags are hyperlinks. You use hyperlinks to reference documents that are managed by a web server. Those references build the network that spans the whole Internet. For this reason, it is called the "World Wide Web."

HTTP is a protocol that "connects" a web browser with a web server and sends the available pages from the former to the latter. If the pages contain another hyperlink, the protocol is used to connect to that web server, using the given address.

XML and Related Languages

XML is a language that is used for the digital representation of documents. This language is related to two other languages:

- ▶   SGML
- ▶   HTML

Standard General Markup Language (SGML) is a very powerful markup language that is used for the interchange of large and/or complex documents. (A markup specifies special signs that are used either for formatting documents or to represent the logical structure of documents. LaTEX is an example of a (formatting) markup language.) SGML is used in many areas where there is a necessity for complex documents, such as airplane maintenance. As you will see in just a moment, XML is SGML light—that is, it is a simplified subset of SGML that is primarily used in the Web's world.

HTML is the most important markup language used for the Web. Each HTML document is an SGML document with a fixed document type description. (For the description of fixed document types, see the next section.) Therefore, HTML is just an instance of SGML.

HTML has two important features:

- ▶   It is used only to format a document
- ▶   It is not an extensible language

HTML is a markup language that you can use to describe how the data should look. (On the other hand, this language offers more than a simple formatted language such as LaTEX, because its elements are generalized and descriptive.)

HTML only uses a fixed number of elements. For this reason, you cannot use HTML suitably for particular document types.

XML—Basic Concepts

XML is an HTML-like language that is used for data exchange. In contrast to HTML, which has a fixed number of tags and where each tag has its own meaning, the repertoire of tags in XML is not set in advance, and semantic is not set for any XML tag.

The following example clarifies these and other properties of XML.

EXAMPLE 29.1

```
<?xml version="1.0"?>
<EmployeeList Type="Employee">
    <Title Value="Employee List"></Title>
    <Contents>
        <Employee>
            <Name>
                <Fname>Ann</Fname>
                <Lname>Jones</Lname>
            </Name>
            <No>10102</No>
            <Deptno>d3</Deptno>
            <Address>
                <City>Dallas</City>
                <Street>Main St</Street>
            </Address>
        </Employee>
        <Employee>
            <Name>
                <Fname>John </Fname>
                <Lname>Barrimore</Lname>
            </Name>
            <No>18316</No>
            <Deptno>d1</Deptno>
            <Address>
                <City>Seattle</City>
                <Street>Abbey Rd</Street>
            </Address>
        </Employee>
    </Contents>
</EmployeeList>
```

The structure of XML is very simple. An XML document contains three parts:

▶ An optional first line that tells the program that receives the document the version of XML it is dealing with (see the first line of Example 29.1)

▶ An optional schema (usually written using DTD or XSD; see the section "Document Type Definition" later in this chapter)

▶ A root element, i.e., the element that contains all other elements

You use XML to digitally represent documents. To represent a document, you have to know its structure. For instance, if you consider a book as a document, it can first be broken into chapters (with titles). Each chapter comprises several sections (with their titles and corresponding figures), and each section has one or more paragraphs.

All parts of an XML document that belong to its logical structure are called *elements*. Therefore, in XML, each element represents a component of a document. In Example 29.1, **EmployeeList**, **Title**, and **Contents** are XML elements. Also, each element can contain other elements. (The parts of an element that do not belong to the logical structure of a document are called character data. For instance, words or sentences in a book can be treated as character data.)

All elements of a document build a hierarchy of elements that is called the tree structure of the document. Each structure has an element on the top level that contains all other elements. This element is called the root element. Also, all elements that do not contain any subelements are called leaves.

NOTE

In contrast to HTML, where valid tags are determined by the language specification, tag names in XML are chosen by the programmer.

The XML elements directly nested within other elements are called children. For instance, in Example 29.1, **Name, No**, and **Address** are children of **Employee**, which is a child of **Contents**, which is again a child of the root element **EmployeeList**. (The relationships **ancestor** and **descendant** are also defined in the XML language.)

Each element can have extra information that is attached to it. Such information is called an *attribute*, and it describes the element's properties. Attributes are used together with elements to represent objects (i.e., document types). In the tag

<EmployeeList Type="Employee">

in Example 29.1, **Type** is the name of an attribute that belongs to the element **EmployeeList**, and **Employee** is the attribute value. The following section describes attributes in detail.

XML Attributes

Attributes are used to represent data. On the other hand, elements can also be used for the same purpose. For this reason, it is plausible to ask whether we need attributes at all, because almost everything you can do using attributes is possible to do with (sub)elements.

The following tasks can be accomplished only with attributes:

▶ Attributes can be used to define a unique value

▶ Attributes can be used to enforce a limited kind of referential constraints

NOTE

There is no general rule for the decision of how you should define data. The best rule of thumb is to use an attribute, when a property of an element is general, and to use subelements for a specific property of an element.

An attribute can be specified to be an ID type attribute. The value of the ID attribute must be unique within the XML document. Therefore, the ID attribute is always used to define a unique value.

An attribute of type IDREF must refer to a valid ID declared in the same document. In other words, the value of the IDREF attribute must occur in the document as a value of the corresponding ID attribute.

An attribute of type IDREFS specifies a list of strings, separated by blanks that are references to the values of the ID attribute. For instance, the following line shows the XML fragment of an IDREFS attribute:

<Department Members="10102 18316"/>

(We suppose that the attribute **No** of the **Employee** element is the ID attribute, while the attribute **Members** of the **Department** element is of the type IDREFS.)

The pairs ID/IDREF and ID/IDREFS correspond to primary key/foreign key relationships in the database, with a few differences. In the XML document, the values of different ID type attributes must be distinct. For instance, if you have **CustomerID** and **SalesOrderID** attributes in an XML document, these values must be distinct.

NOTE

The types mentioned above (ID, IDREF, and IDREFS) are part of the document type definition (DTD), which will be discussed later in this chapter.

XML Namespaces

When using XML, you build a vocabulary of terms that are appropriate for the domain in which you model your data. In this situation, different vocabularies can cause naming conflicts when you want to mix them together in an XML document. (This is usually the case when you want to integrate information obtained from different domains.)

This problem can be solved using XML namespaces. Generally, the name of every XML tag must be written in the form **namespace:name**, where **namespace** specifies an XML namespace and **name** is an XML tag.

A namespace is always represented by a worldwide unique URI (*uniform resource identifier*), which is usually a URL but can be an abstract identifier, too.

Example 29.2 shows the use of two namespaces.

EXAMPLE 29.2

```
<Faculty xmlns="http://www.fh-rosenheim.de/informatik"
         xmlns:lib="http:// www.fh-rosenheim.de/bibliothek">
    <Name>Book</Name>
    <Feature>
    <lib:Title>Introduction to Database Systems</lib:Title>
    <lib:Author>A. Finkelstein</lib:Author>
    </Feature>
</Faculty>
```

Namespaces are defined using the **xmlns** attribute. In Example 29.2 we specify two namespaces. The first one is the *default namespace*, because it is specified only with the **xmlns** keyword. This namespace is the shorthand for the namespace http://www.fh-rosenheim.de/informatik. The second namespace is specified in the form **xmlns:lib**. The prefix **lib** serves as the shorthand for http:// www.fh-rosenheim. de/bibliothek.

Tags belonging to the latter namespace should be prefixed with **lib**:. Tags without any prefix belong to the default namespace. (In Example 29.2, there are two tags, belonging to the second namespace: **Title** and **Author**.)

Document Type Definitions

In contrast to HTML, which contains a set of fixed rules that have to be followed when you create a HTML document, XML does not have such rules, because this language is intended for many different application areas. Hence, XML includes languages that are used to specify the document structure.

A set of rules for structuring an XML document is called a document type definition (DTD). A DTD can be specified as part of the XML document, or the XML document contains a uniform resource locator (URL) where the DTD is stored. A document that conforms to the associated DTD is called a valid document.

NOTE

XML does not require that documents have corresponding DTDs, but it requires that documents must be well-formed. (The definition of well-formed documents is given in Chapter 30.)

Example 29.3 shows the DTD for the XML document in Example 29.1.

EXAMPLE 29.3

```
<!DOCTYPE EmployeeList [
<!ELEMENT EmployeeList (Title, Contents)>
<!ELEMENT Title EMPTY>
<!ELEMENT Contents (Employee*)>
<!ELEMENT Employee (Name, No, Deptno, Address)>
<!ELEMENT Name(Fname, Lname)>
<!ELEMENT Fname (#PCDATA)>
<!ELEMENT Lname (#PCDATA)>
<!ELEMENT No (#PCDATA)>
<!ELEMENT Deptno (#PCDATA)>
<!ELEMENT Address (City, Street) >
 <!ELEMENT City (#PCDATA)>
<!ELEMENT Street (#PCDATA)>
<!ATTLIST EmployeeList  Type CDATA #IMPLIED
                Date CDATA #IMPLIED>
  <!ATTLIST Title Value CDATA  #REQUIRED>
]
```

Example 29.3 shows a DTD for the XML document that was shown in Example 29.1. There are several common DTD components: a name (**EmployeeList**, in the example) and a set of ELEMENT and ATTLIST statements. The name of a DTD must conform with the tag name of the root element of the XML document (see Example 29.1) that uses the DTD for validation.

Element type declarations must start with the ELEMENT statement followed by the name of the element type being defined. (Every element in a valid XML document must conform to an element type declared in the DTD.) In Example 29.3, the first ELEMENT statement specifies that the element **EmployeeList** consists of a **Title** and **Contents** elements, in that order. The **Title** element does not contain any subelements.

The sign "*" in the definition of the **Contents** element indicates that there are zero or more elements of the **Employee** type. The elements **Fname, Lname, No, Deptno, City**, and **Street** are declared to be alphanumerical, i.e., of type #PCDATA.

NOTE

*Elements can hold simple or complex types. In Example 29.3, **Address** represents a complex type and **City** a simple type.*

Attributes are declared for specific element types using the ATTLIST statement. This means that each attribute declaration starts with the string <!ATTLIST. Immediately after that comes the attribute's name and its data type. In our example, the **EmployeeList** element is allowed to have the attributes **Type** and **Date**, while the **Title** element can only have the **Value** attribute. (All other elements do not have attributes.)

The #IMPLIED keyword specifies that the corresponding attribute is optional, while the #REQUIRED keyword determines the mandatory form of the attribute.

NOTE

Attributes can hold only simple data types.

Besides the definition of a document's structure, formatting a document can be an important issue for those of you who do not want the web browser, such as Microsoft Internet Explorer, to control the form of the document. For this task, XML supports another language called Extensible Stylesheet Language (XSL), which allows you to describe how the data of your document should be formatted or displayed.

NOTE

The style of a document is described as a separate entity. For this reason, each document without this part will use the default formatting of the web browser.

XML Schema

NOTE

Because of the complexity of XML Schema, we will briefly discuss this topic in the book. (See also Chapter 30 for the discussion of the XML Schema support in SQL Server.)

XML Schema or XML Schema Definition language (XSD) is a DDL for XML documents. It defines a standard set of base types that are supported as types in XML. XML Schema contains many advanced features and is therefore significantly more complex than the DTDs.

The main features of XML Schema are the following:

▶ It uses the same syntax as that used for XML documents. (For this reason, schemas are themselves well-formed XML documents.)

▶ It is integrated with the namespace mechanism. (Although there can be more than one schema definition document for a namespace, a schema definition document defines types in only one namespace.)

▶ It provides a set of base types, the same way SQL provides CHAR, INTEGER, and other standard data types.

▶ It supports primary/foreign key integrity constraints.

Conclusion

XML is a data representation format based on SGML, and it is used more and more as a data storage format. An XML document contains several tags that are chosen by the person who implements the document. All parts of an XML document that belong to its logical structure are called elements. Elements can hold simple or complex data types.

Each element can have extra information that is attached to it. Such information is called an attribute. Attributes can hold only simple data types.

A set of rules that structures an XML document is called a document type definition (DTD). An XML document that conforms to the associated DTD is called a valid document. Instead of DTDs, you can use XML Schema Definition language (XSD) to validate an XML document. XSD comprises data definition statements for XML, the same way DDL (see Chapter 1) contains data definition statements for SQL.

The most important disadvantage of XML is that there is *no common set of schemas*, which could be useful for most XML users to validate their documents.

The next chapter, which is the last chapter of the book, continues to discuss XML, this time in relation to the SQL Server system.

SQL Server 2005 and XML

This chapter discusses the use of Extended Markup Language (XML) in the SQL Server database system. In contrast to the previous chapter, where we introduced general properties of this language, this chapter covers all aspects of the relationship between Extended Markup Language and Transact-SQL. In the first part of the chapter we explain different ways in which XML documents can be stored in relational databases. After that the XML data type is introduced. This base data type is used to store XML documents and fragments in their native form. We also discuss the different ways how XML documents can be displayed using the extended form of the SELECT statement. At the end of the chapter we briefly explain how stored XML documents can be queried using the XQuery language.

NOTE

In this chapter the notion of "XML" is twofold. First, I use this term to specify the language (Extended Markup Language). Second, the same term is used to specify the new data type in SQL Server. During the chapter the term "XML" is used to specify the language, while the phrase "XML data type" specifies the new data type. (Also, "XML column" means a column of XML data type.)

Storing XML in Relational Databases

There are three general ways how XML documents can be stored in relational databases:

- ▶ As large objects (LOBs)
- ▶ Decomposed into columns
- ▶ "Native"

If you store an XML document as an LOB, an exact copy of the data is stored. In this case, XML documents are stored "raw," i.e., in their character string form. The raw form allows you to insert documents very easily. The retrieval of such a document is very efficient, if you retrieve the entire document.

NOTE

Storing XML documents in their character string form was the only way that you could store them with SQL Server 2000. SQL Server 2000 stores XML documents using the text/image data types. In SQL Server 2005, you can use the new data type VARCHAR(MAX) to store XML documents as raw documents.

To decompose an XML document into separate columns of one or more tables, you can use annotated XSD. (The XML Schema Definition language defines a set of standard data types that are supported in XML documents.) In this case, the hierarchical structure of the document is preserved, while order among elements is ignored. (As you already know, the relational model does not support ordering of columns in a table.) Storing XML documents in decomposed form makes it much easier to index an element, if it is placed in its own column.

NOTE

Decomposition of an XML document is also known as "shredding." SQL Server supports the system-defined function OpenXML that is used for decomposition of an XML document.

"Native storage" means that XML documents are stored in their parsed form. In other words, the document is stored in an internal representation (Infoset, for instance) that preserves the XML content of the data. (Infoset is a www.w3.org specification, which provides a set for use in other specifications that need to refer to the information in an XML document.)

The native storage makes it easy to query information based on the structure of the XML document. On the other hand, reconstructing the original form of the XML document is difficult, because the Infoset content may not be an exact copy of the document. (The detailed information about the significant white spaces, order of attributes, and namespace prefixes in XML documents is generally not retained.)

NOTE

SQL Server 2005 supports the native storage of XML documents with the new data type called XML, which will be discussed in detail in the following section.

The XML Data Type

The XML data type enables you to store XML documents in a SQL Server 2005 database. (Such database systems, which store XML documents in a completely parsed form, are called native XML database systems.)

NOTE

In this book we will describe only the native XML storage, because it is the most important storage form for XML documents.

The XML data type is base data type in Transact-SQL; i.e., you can use XML in the same way you use the standard data types, such as INTEGER or CHAR. On the other hand, the XML data type has some limitations:

► An XML column cannot be declared using the UNIQUE clause

► An XML column cannot be declared using the PRIMARY KEY clause

► An XML column cannot be declared using the FOREIGN KEY clause

Generally, you can use the XML data type to declare the following:

► Table columns

► Variables

► Input or output parameters (in stored procedures and user-defined functions)

The following example shows the use of the XML data type to declare a column of a table.

EXAMPLE 30.1

```
USE sample
CREATE TABLE xmltab (id INTEGER NOT NULL PRIMARY KEY,
                     xml_column XML)
```

The CREATE TABLE statement in Example 30.1 creates a table with two columns: **id** and **xml_column**. The **id** column is used to identify uniquely each row of the table. The column called **xml_column** is an XML column, which will be used in the following examples to show how XML documents and fragments can be stored, indexed, and retrieved.

As we already stated, XML documents can be stored in a column of the XML data type. Example 30.2 shows the use of the INSERT statement to store such a document.

EXAMPLE 30.2

```
USE sample
insert into xmltab values (1,
'<?xml version="1.0"?>
<EmployeeList Type="Employee">
    <Title> Value="Employee List"></Title>
    <Contents>
        <Employee>
```

```
            <Name>
                <Fname>Ann </Fname>
                <Lname>Jones</Lname>
            </Name>
            <No>10102</No>
             <Deptno>d3</Deptno>
             <Address>
                    <City>Dallas</City>
                    <Street>Main St</Street>
             </Address>
        </Employee>
        <Employee>
            <Name>
                <Fname>John </Fname>
                <Lname>Barrimore</Lname>
            </Name>
            <No>18316</No>
             <Deptno>d1</Deptno>
             <Address>
                    <City>Seattle</City>
                    <Street>Abbey Rd</Street>
             </Address>
        </Employee>
    </Contents>
</EmployeeList>')
```

The INSERT statement in Example 30.2 inserts two values: the value of the identifier and an XML document. (The inserted XML document is the same document that we used in the previous chapter; see Example 29.1). The SQL Server system will store the XML document shown in Example 30.2 as a binary large object (BLOB). Also, the XML parser checks the syntax of the inserted instance before it is stored. Actually, the parser checks whether the XML document is well-formed or not.

For instance, if you omit the last row of the XML document (</EmployeeList>), the XML parser displays the following error message:

```
Msg 9400, Level 16, State 1, Line 3
XML parsing: line 24, character 0, unexpected end of input
```

If you use the SELECT statement to see the content of the **xmltab** table, SQL Server Management Studio uses XML Editor to display XML documents. (To display the document in the editor, click the corresponding value in the result set.)

Indexing an XML Column

As we already stated, XML instances (values) are stored as BLOBs. Without an index, these BLOBs are decomposed at run time to evaluate a query that can be time-consuming. Therefore, the reason for indexing XML columns is to improve query performance.

> **NOTE**
> *If you want to create any kind of XML indices, the corresponding table must include the explicit definition of the primary key.*

SQL Server supports a primary XML index and three types of secondary XML indices. The primary one indexes all tags, values, and paths within the XML instances in an XML column. Queries use the primary XML index to return scalar values or XML subtrees.

Example 30.3 creates a primary XML index.

EXAMPLE 30.3

```
USE sample
GO
CREATE PRIMARY XML INDEX i_xmlcolumn ON xmltab(xml_column)
```

As you can see from Example 30.3, the creation of a primary XML index is similar to the creation of a "normal" index. A primary XML index uses an XML instance to generate the corresponding relational internal form out of it. That way the repeated runtime generation of the internal form for queries and updates is omitted.

To further improve search performance, you can create secondary XML indices. A primary XML index must exist before secondary indices can be built. You can create three types of XML secondary indices using different keywords:

- ▶ FOR PATH
- ▶ FOR PROPERTY
- ▶ FOR VALUE

If you use the FOR PATH keyword, an XML index will be created over the document structure. (For large XML instances, searching the primary XML index may prove to be slow. In this case, having a secondary index built on the paths and node values as the key fields can significantly speed up index search.)

If you use the FOR VALUE keyword, an XML index will be created over the element and attribute values of the XML column. (This index type can help in content search.)

The FOR PROPERTY keyword creates a secondary index that searches for a property. The following example shows the use of the FOR PATH keyword. (The syntax for creating all other secondary indices is analogous.)

EXAMPLE 30.4

```
USE sample
CREATE  XML INDEX i_xmlcolumn_path ON xmltab(xml_column)
   USING XML INDEX i_xmlcolumn FOR PATH
```

Example 30.4 shows the creation of the secondary XML index with the FOR PATH keyword. The USING clause must be specified, if you want to define any secondary XML index.

XML indices have some limitations in relation to "normal" indices:

▶ XML indices cannot be composite indices

▶ There are no clustered XML indices

NOTE

The reason for creating XML indices is significantly different from the reason for creating "normal" indices. XML indices enhance the performance of XQuery queries, while the performance of SQL queries benefits from "normal" indices.

The ALTER INDEX and DROP INDEX statements are used to alter the structure and drop an XML index, respectively.

Typed vs. Untyped XML

An XML document can be validated and/or well-formed. As you already know from Chapter 29, the well-formed XML document must fulfill the following conditions:

▶ It has a root element

▶ Every opening tag is followed by a matching closing tag

▶ The elements of the document are properly nested

▶ An attribute must have a value, which is quoted

An XML document that conforms to one or more given schema is said to be *schema valid* and is called an *instance* document of the schemas. The XML schemas are used to perform more precise type checks during compilation of queries.

XML data type columns, variables, and parameters may be typed or untyped, i.e., they may conform to a set of schemas or not. In other words, whenever a typed XML instance is assigned to an XML column data type, variable, or parameter, SQL Server validates the instance.

Before we discuss typed XML instances, we will explain the use of XML schemas in SQL Server.

XML Schemas and SQL Server

An XML schema specifies a set of data types that exist in a particular namespace. XML Schema (or XML Schema Definition Language) is a data definition language for XML documents.

SQL Server uses the CREATE XML SCHEMA COLLECTION statement to import the schema components into the database. The following example shows the use of this statement.

EXAMPLE 30.5

```
USE sample
CREATE XML SCHEMA COLLECTION EmployeeSchema AS
   N'<?xml version="1.0" encoding="UTF-16"?>
   <xsd:schema elementFormDefault="unqualified"
     attributeFormDefault="unqualified"
     xmlns:xsd="http://www.w3.org/2001/XMLSchema" >
    <xsd:element name="employees">
      <xsd:complexType mixed="false">
       <xsd:sequence>
         <xsd:element name="fname" type="xsd:string"/>
         <xsd:element name="lname" type="xsd:string"/>
         <xsd:element name="department" type="xsd:string"/>
         <xsd:element name="salary" type="xsd:integer"/>
         <xsd:element name="comments" type="xsd:string"/>
       </xsd:sequence>
      </xsd:complexType>
    </xsd:element>
   </xsd:schema>';
```

Example 30.5 shows how the CREATE XML SCHEMA COLLECTION statement can be used to catalog the **EmployeeSchema** schema as a database object. The XML schema for our example includes attributes (elements) for employees, such as family name, last name, and salary. (A detailed discussion of XML schemas is outside the scope of this introductory book.)

Generally, an XML schema collection has a name, which can be qualified using the relational schema name (**dbo.EmployeeSchema**, for instance). The schema collection consists of one or more schemas that define the types in one or more XML namespaces. If the **targetNamespace** attribute is omitted from an XML schema, that schema does not have an associated namespace. (There is a maximum of one such schema inside an XML schema collection.)

SQL Server 2005 also supports the corresponding ALTER and DROP statements. The ALTER XML SCHEMA COLLECTION statement allows you to add new schemas to an existing XML schema collection, while the DROP XML SCHEMA COLLECTION statement deletes an entire schema collection.

Typed XML Columns, Variables, and Parameters

Each typed XML column, variable, or parameter must be specified with associated schemas. To do this, the name of the schema collection, which is created using the CREATE XML SCHEMA COLLECTION statement, must be written inside the pair of parentheses, after the instance name. Example 30.6 shows this.

EXAMPLE 30.6

```
USE sample
CREATE TABLE xml_persontab
 (id INTEGER,
  xml_person XML(EmployeeSchema))
```

The **xml_person** column in Example 30.6 is associated with the XML schema collection from Example 30.5. This means that all specifications from defined schemas are used to check whether the content of the **xml_person** column is valid. In other words, when you insert a new value in the typed XML column (or modify an existing value), all integrity constraints specified in the schemas are checked.

The specification of an XML schema collection for the typed XML instance can be extended with two keywords:

▶ DOCUMENT

▶ CONTENT

The DOCUMENT keyword specifies that the XML column can only contain XML documents, while the CONTENT keyword is the default value, and it specifies that the XML column can contain either documents or fragments. (Remember, an XML document must have a single root element.)

The following example shows the use of the DOCUMENT keyword.

EXAMPLE 30.7

```
USE sample
CREATE TABLE xml_persontab_doc
 (id INTEGER,
   xml_person XML(DOCUMENT EmployeeSchema))
```

Constructing XML Documents Using the FOR XML Clause

As you already know from Chapter 5, a SELECT statement queries one or more relational tables and displays the corresponding result set. The result set is displayed by default as a table. If you want to retrieve the result set of a query as an XML document or fragment, you can use the FOR XML clause in your SELECT statement. With this clause, you can specify one of the four following modes:

- ▶ RAW
- ▶ AUTO
- ▶ EXPLICIT
- ▶ PATH

NOTE

The FOR XML clause must be specified at the end of the SELECT statement.

The following sections describe each of these modes.

RAW Mode

The FOR XML RAW option transforms each row of the result set into an XML element with the identifier <row>. Each column value is mapped to an attribute of the XML element, in which the attribute name is the same as the column name. (This is true only for the non-null columns.)

Example 30.8 shows the use of the FOR XML RAW option that is specified for the join of the **employee** and **works_on** tables from the sample database.

EXAMPLE 30.8

```
USE sample
SELECT  employee.emp_no, emp_lname, works_on.job
FROM employee, works_on
WHERE employee.emp_no <= 10000
AND employee.emp_no = works_on.emp_no
FOR XML RAW
```

Example 30.8 displays the following XML document fragment:

```
<row emp_no="2581" emp_lname="Hansel      " job="Analyst    " />
<row emp_no="9031" emp_lname="Bertoni     " job="Manager    " />
<row emp_no="9031" emp_lname="Bertoni     " job="Clerk      " />
```

Without the FOR XML RAW option the SELECT statement in Example 30.8 would retrieve the following rows:

emp_no	emp_lname	job
2581	Hansel	Analyst
9031	Bertoni	Manager
9031	Bertoni	Clerk

As you can see from both results, the first output produces one XML element for each row in the result set, while the second result displays the same content as **table**.

AUTO Mode

AUTO mode returns the result set of a query as a simple, nested XML tree. Each table in the FROM clause, from which at least one column appears in the SELECT list, is represented as an XML element. The columns in the SELECT list are mapped to the appropriate element's attributes.

Example 30.9 shows the use of the FOR XML AUTO option.

EXAMPLE 30.9

```
USE sample
SELECT  employee.emp_no, emp_lname, works_on.job
FROM employee, works_on
WHERE employee.emp_no <= 10000
AND employee.emp_no = works_on.emp_no
FOR XML AUTO
```

The result is

```
<employee emp_no="2581" emp_lname="Hansel          ">
  <works_on job="Analyst       " />
</employee>
<employee emp_no="9031" emp_lname="Bertoni          ">
  <works_on job="Manager       " />
  <works_on job="Clerk        " />
</employee>
```

The result in Example 30.9 is significantly different from the result in the previous example, although the SELECT statement for both examples is equivalent (except for the specification of the AUTO keyword instead of RAW). As you can see from Example 30.9, the result set is displayed as the hierarchy of the tables **employee** and **works_on**. This hierarchy is based on the primary-key/foreign-key relationship of both tables. For this reason, the data from the **employee** table is displayed first, and the corresponding data from the **works_on** table is displayed after that, at the lower hierarchy level.

The nesting of the elements in the resulting XML document or fragment is based on the order of tables identified by the columns specified in the SELECT clause; therefore, the order in which column names are specified in the SELECT clause is significant. For this reason, in Example 30.9 the values of the **emp_no** column of the **employee** table form the top element in the resulting XML fragment. The values of the **job** column of the **works_on** table form a subelement within the top element.

EXPLICIT Mode

As you can see from Example 30.9, the result set in the AUTO mode is displayed as a simple, nested XML tree. The queries in AUTO mode are good if you want to generate simple hierarchies, because this mode provides little control over the shape of the XML generated from a query result.

If you want to specify the extended form of the result set, you can use the FOR XML EXPLICIT option. With this option, the result set is displayed as a universal table, which has all the information about the resulting XML tree. The data in the table is vertically partitioned into groups. Each group then becomes an XML element in the result set.

 NOTE

When you use the EXPLICIT mode, you must write a query in a specific way so that the additional information about the desired nesting is explicitly defined.

Example 30.10 shows the use of the FOR XML EXPLICIT option.

EXAMPLE 30.10

```
USE sample
SELECT 1 AS tag, NULL as parent,
    emp_lname AS [employee!1!emp_lname],
    NULL AS [works_on!2!job]
FROM employee
UNION
SELECT  2, 1, emp_lname, works_on.job
FROM employee, works_on
WHERE employee.emp_no <= 10000
    AND employee.emp_no = works_on.emp_no
ORDER BY [employee!1!emp_lname]
FOR XML EXPLICIT
```

The result is

```
<employee emp_lname="Barrimore          " />
<employee emp_lname="Bertoni          ">
  <works_on job="Clerk          " />
  <works_on job="Manager          " />
</employee>
<employee emp_lname="Hansel          ">
  <works_on job="Analyst          " />
</employee>
<employee emp_lname="James          " />
<employee emp_lname="Jones          " />
<employee emp_lname="Moser          " />
<employee emp_lname="Smith          " />
```

As you can see from the SELECT statement in Example 30.10, the FOR XML EXPLICIT option requires two additional metadata columns: **tag** and **parent**. (These two columns are used to determine the primary-key/foreign-key relationship in the XML tree.) The **tag** column stores the tag number of the current element, while the **parent** column stores the tag number of the parent element. (The parent table is the table with the primary key.) If the parent tag is NULL, the row is placed directly under the root element.

PATH Mode

All of the three FOR XML options described above have different disadvantages and restrictions. The FOR XML RAW option supports only one level nesting, while the FOR XML AUTO option requires that all columns selected from the same table occur at the same level. Also, both options do not allow mixing of elements and attributes in the same XML document. On the other hand, the FOR XML EXPLICIT option allows mixing of elements and attributes, but the syntax of this option is cumbersome, as you can see from the previous example.

SQL Server 2005 introduces the new mode, PATH, which allows you to implement almost all queries that require the EXPLICIT mode in a very easy way. In the PATH mode, column names or column aliases are treated as XPath expressions, which indicate how the values are being mapped to XML. (An XPath expression consists of a sequence of nodes, possibly separated by "/". For each slash, the system creates another level of hierarchy in the resulting document.)

Example 30.11 shows the use of the FOR XML PATH option.

EXAMPLE 30.11

```
USE sample
SELECT d.dept_name "@Department",
    emp_fname "EmpName/First",
    emp_lname "EmpName/Last"
FROM   Employee e, department d
WHERE  e.dept_no = d.dept_no
AND    d.dept_no = 'd1'
FOR XML PATH
```

The result is

```
<row Department="Research          ">
  <EmpName>
    <First>John          </First>
```

```
      <Last>Barrimore        </Last>
    </EmpName>
  </row>
  <row Department="Research           ">
    <EmpName>
      <First>Sybill        </First>
      <Last>Moser         </Last>
    </EmpName>
  </row>
```

In the PATH mode, the column names are used as the path in constructing an XML document. The column containing department names starts with '@'. This means that the **Department** attribute is added to the <row> element. All other columns include a '/' in the column name indicating hierarchy. For this reason, the resulting XML document will have the <EmpName> child under the <row> element and <First> and <Last> elements at the next sublevel.

Specifying Directives with Different Modes

SQL Server 2005 supports several different directives, which allow you to produce different results when you want to display XML documents and fragments. The following list shows some of these directives:

▶ TYPE

▶ ELEMENTS (with XSINIL)

▶ ROOT

The following subsections describe these directives.

The TYPE Directive

In SQL Server 2000, if the result of a query is an XML document or fragment, it is returned as a value of text/image data type. SQL Server 2005 supports the XML data type, so you can now store the result of such a query as XML data type by specifying the TYPE directive.

When the TYPE directive is specified, a FOR XML query returns a one-row, one-column result set. (This directive is a common directive, i.e., you can use it in all four modes.) The following example shows the use of the TYPE directive in the AUTO mode.

EXAMPLE 30.12

```
USE sample
DECLARE @x xml
SET @x = (SELECT * FROM department
                FOR XML AUTO, TYPE)
SELECT @x
```

The result is

```
<department dept_no="d1 " dept_name="Research    " location="Dallas " />
<department dept_no="d2 " dept_name="Accounting   " location="Seattle " />
<department dept_no="d3 " dept_name="Marketing    " location="Dallas " />
```

In Example 30.12 we first declare the variable **x** as an XML variable and assign the result of the FOR XML query to it. The last SELECT statement in the batch displays the content of the variable.

NULL Values

As we already know from Chapter 2, SQL Server supports NULL values to specify unknown (or missing) values. In contrast to the relational model, XML does not support NULL values, and those values are omitted in the result sets of FOR XML queries.

SQL Server 2005 allows you to display the missing values in an XML document using the ELEMENTS directive with the XSINIL option. Generally, the ELEMENTS directive constructs the corresponding XML document so that each column value maps to an element. If the column value is NULL, no element is added by default. Specifying the additional XSINIL option, you can request that an element be created for the NULL value as well. In this case, an element with the **xsi:nil** attribute set to true is returned for each NULL value in the column.

The ROOT Directive

Generally, FOR XML queries produce XML fragments, i.e., XML without a corresponding root element. This can be a problem if an API accepts only XML documents as input. SQL Server allows you to add the root element using the ROOT directive. By specifying the ROOT directive in the FOR XML query, you can request a single, top-level element for the resulting XML. (The argument specified for the directive provides the root element.)

The following example shows the use of the ROOT directive.

EXAMPLE 30.13

```
USE sample
SELECT * FROM department
FOR XML AUTO, ROOT ('AllDepartments')
```

The result is

```
<AllDepartments>
 <department dept_no="d1 " dept_name="Research  " location="Dallas  " />
 <department dept_no="d2 " dept_name="Accounting " location="Seattle " />
 <department dept_no="d3 " dept_name="Marketing " location="Dallas  " />
</AllDepartments>
```

The FOR XML query in Example 30.13 displays the XML fragment with all rows from the **department** table. The ROOT directive adds the root specification in the result set with the **AllDepartments** parameter as the root name.

XML Query Languages

 NOTE

In this section we will briefly describe the existing XML query languages. The detailed description of XPath and especially XQuery can be found in Books Online.

There are two query languages for XML:

▶ XPath

▶ XQuery

XPath is the original query language for XML documents. Queries in XPath are based upon the hierarchical structure of XML; that is, nodes are selected using a series of forward slashes. (This syntax is already well known and is used in the UNIX operating system to specify files.)

XQuery is the new query language for XML. This language is much more complex than XPath. (For example, using XQuery you can query multiple documents and the system can optimize a given query.)

SQL Server 2005 supports four functions that can be used to query XML documents with XQuery:

- ▶ xml.value
- ▶ xml.query
- ▶ xml.exist
- ▶ xml.modify

The **xml.value** function accepts an XQuery query as input and returns a single scalar value. The **xml.query** function takes the same input but returns an XML data type as a result. The **xml.exist** function accepts an XQuery query as input and returns 0, 1, or NULL, depending on the query result. If the query result is an empty sequence, the return value is 0. A sequence with at least one item returns 1, and NULL is returned if the value of the column is NULL.

In contrast to the standardized version of XQuery, which at this moment does not have the specifications for update statements, SQL Server also supports the insertion, modification, and deletion of XML documents using the **xml.modify** function.

Conclusion

In contrast to SQL Server 2000, SQL Server 2005 has the full support for XML. The most important feature in this database system is the support for XML data type. The XML data type allows the database system to store XML documents as first class objects.

The values of the XML data type can be schema validated, if one or more schemas are associated with this type. You can determine the exact data types of elements and attributes, only if the corresponding XML document contains types specified by XML schemas. Schema definitions are specified using the CREATE XML SCHEMA COLLECTION statement.

XML also has its own query language(s). The most important query language for XML is XQuery. SQL Server supports most standardized features for the language, as well as some extensions. The most important extension is support for modification of XML documents.

Index